Sources for
America's History

Volume 1: To 1877

Kevin B. Sheets
State University of New York, College at Cortland

BEDFORD/ST. MARTIN'S   Boston ◆ New York

For Bedford/St. Martin's

Publisher for History: Mary V. Dougherty
Senior Executive Editor for History and Technology: William J. Lombardo
Director of Development for History: Jane Knetzger
Developmental Editor: Robin W. Soule
Publishing Services Manager: Andrea Cava
Production Supervisor: Steven Dowling
Executive Marketing Manager: Sandra McGuire
Editorial Assistant: Victoria Royal
Project Management: Books By Design, Inc.
Text Design: Lily Yamamoto, LMY Studios
Cover Design: Marine Miller
Cover Photo: Emigrants Moving with Covered Wagon © Bettmann/Corbis
Composition: Jouve
Printing and Binding: RR Donnelley and Sons

President, Bedford/St. Martin's: Denise B. Wydra
Director of Marketing: Karen R. Soeltz
Production Director: Susan W. Brown
Director of Rights and Permissions: Hilary Newman

Manufactured in the United States of America.

8 7 6 5
f e d c

For information, write: Bedford/St. Martin's, 75 Arlington Street, Boston, MA 02116
    (617-399-4000)

ISBN 978-1-4576-2890-0

PREFACE

Historians are fond of quoting L. P. Hartley's famous line: "The past is a foreign country; they do things differently there." It is a helpful image that emphasizes the distance, remoteness, and inscrutability of the past. Visiting a country whose language you do not speak can be disorienting until you start deciphering the gestures, unlocking the meaning behind facial expressions, and picking apart the cultural practices natives take for granted. For many students, the past is equally disorienting, and to seek safe harbor they ignore differences to emphasize commonalities. "Those people in the past are just like me, except they wear funny clothes." Stripped down, they do resemble us, but more often they encountered their world in radically different ways. Understanding these differences is what makes the study of history so compelling.

My goal in compiling *Sources for America's History* is to help students encounter this different past in its most raw and visceral form. Designed to accompany *America's History*, *America: A Concise History*, and the Value Edition of *America's History*, the sources collected here put students in unmediated contact with those whose experiences shaped our past. Each chapter includes a variety of both obscure and well-known voices, whose testimony highlights key themes of the period. The sources in each chapter give competing perspectives on leading events and ideas. This purposeful tension between sources is not intended to frustrate the reader. Instead, the differing viewpoints introduce students to the challenge that historians face in sifting through the evidence left to us. How do we make sense of the large body of primary sources that we have related to America's half millennium of lived experience?

Textbook authors present an argument about the past, something historians refer to as a "narrative." Those arguments, of course, are based on historians' interpretation and assessment of primary sources. This document collection makes its own argument based on the specific sources selected for inclusion, but invites debate by encouraging the reader to interpret sources in different ways. *Sources for America's History* is designed to encourage a productive intellectual give-and-take, enabling students of history to offer their own perspective on the past. In this way, students join the ongoing discussion among the community of scholars seeking to understand the long and complex history of what became the United States.

To facilitate this effort, *Sources for America's History* includes a number of key features. Each chapter in the collection includes five or six documents that support the periodization and themes of the corresponding parent text chapter. Every chapter begins with an introduction that situates the documents within their wider historical context. Individual documents follow, each accompanied by its own headnote and a set of Reading and Discussion Questions designed to help students practice historical thinking skills. The variety of readings, ranging from speeches and political cartoons by celebrated historical figures to personal letters and diary entries by ordinary people, offers students the opportunity to compare and contrast different types of documents. Each chapter concludes with Comparative Questions designed to encourage students to recognize connections between documents and relate the sources to larger historical themes. To further support the structure of the parent text, unique Part Document Sets at the end of every part section present five or six sources chosen specifically to illustrate the major themes and developments covered in each of the parent text's nine thematic parts, allowing students to make even broader comparisons and connections across time and place.

Acknowledgments

As with any big undertaking, many hands helped craft the book you are holding. Thanks go to Rebecca Edwards from Vassar College, one of the lead authors of *America's History*, for her confidence in me. Several instructors at the college, community college, and high school levels offered insightful suggestions based on their teaching experiences. They will see here many of the suggestions they recommended, though I could not accommodate all of the excellent ideas they shared. Particular thanks go to Matthew Babcock, University of North Texas at Dallas; Edwin Benson, North Harford High School; Christine Bond-Curtright, Edmond Memorial High School; Kyle T. Bulthuis, Utah State University; Jennifer Castillo, Denver School of the Arts; William Decker, Anderson Preparatory Academy; Angela Dormiani, ASTEC Charter High School; Donald W. Maxwell, Indiana State University; Neil Prendergast, University of Washington–Stevens Point; Erica Ryan, Rider University; Paul Rykken, Black River Falls High School; Sheila L. Skemp, University of Mississippi; Michael Smith, San Gorgonio High School; Geoffrey Stewart, University of Western Ontario; John Struck, Floyd Central High School; and Felicia Viator, San Francisco State University.

My editor, Robin Soule, kept me focused while tutoring me through my first experience of textbook publishing. Her improvements on the text make me sound smarter than I really am. The following colleagues at Bedford/St. Martin's helped in innumerable ways, most of which occurred silently and behind the scenes: Bill Lombardo, Sandi McGuire, Laura Arcari, Jen Jovin, and Victoria Royal. Thanks also to Andrea Cava, and especially to Nancy Benjamin, who oversaw the copyediting and saved countless embarrassments. Her contribution reminds me to practice a bit of humility next time I am grading my own students' papers.

My colleagues in the history department at the State University of New York, College at Cortland, have always provided an intellectually enriching environment in which to work and live. Special thanks go to my wife, Laura Gathagan, a medieval historian who resisted the temptation to smirk at the efforts of a nineteenth-century U.S. historian to write intelligibly about the fifteenth and sixteenth centuries. In the middle of this long process, she began calling herself the "Bedford widow" for the many evenings she spent alone while I toiled away. Finally, to my boys, William and Alexander: Daddy's done. Let's go play ball.

INTRODUCTION FOR STUDENTS

I was this close to wearing Eisenhower's pajamas. During my junior year in college, I interned at the Smithsonian's National Museum of American History in Washington, D.C. Every now and again, when I had a few minutes of free time, I poked around the collection of artifacts in storage. There was Lincoln's top hat. On a high shelf was the table where Lee surrendered to Grant. A pullout metal rack filled with paintings also housed a disturbing framed collection of hair from the first sixteen presidents. One day I spied a box containing President Dwight D. Eisenhower's pajamas. These were the PJs Ike wore while recovering in Denver from his 1955 heart attack. Oh, the temptation to slip them on, but reason and self-preservation prevailed. Back on the shelf they went.

Those whom the past enchants were often first beguiled by the stuff of history. Touching those objects helps collapse time, putting us in the immediate presence of someone else at some other time. I once held John Brown's gun and while peering down the long barrel wondered who or what he was aiming at. His trigger finger and mine overlapped and briefly spirited me back to 1850s Pottawatomie, Kansas, where Brown waged his own civil war against slavery. The past is contained in those leavings, the letters and diaries, the political cartoons and music, the paintings and the guns and pajamas. Primary sources bring alive the past and help us to understand its significance and meaning.

This collection of primary sources aims to engage you in a conversation with the past. There will be times when you burst out laughing. Some sources will make you so mad you'll want to throw the book across the room. (Please don't. I spent a lot of time writing it, but I share your frustration.) Other times, you'll shake your head in disbelief. (Yes, they really thought that back then!) You are about to enter an amazing world of difference populated with people some of whom you will admire, many of whom you won't like, and others whom you will despair of ever really knowing or understanding. Good. I hope you laugh. I hope you get mad. I even hope you get confused at times and scratch your head wondering what on earth these people were talking about. Out of your responses to these texts comes insight.

My advice? Read these texts with a fist full of questions. Historians do something called "sourcing" when they first encounter a primary text, and it is a good practice for you, too. Start with the author. *Who wrote or created the source?* What do you know about this person? Was he rich, poor, or middling? Was she educated? Where was he or she born and to what sort of family? You might know the answers to some of these questions, but even if you do not, keeping the questions in mind might help you understand where the author is coming from. *When was this source created?* While it is important to know the date, it can also be revealing to know when in the person's life he or she created the source. Was she a young girl or an older woman raising children? Was he at the beginning of his career or already famous? *What was happening when the source was created?* We call this "context," and it is an important element in making sense of the source you are reading. (You will encounter the word *context* often in the Reading and Discussion Questions and Comparative Questions following the sources and at the end of each chapter.) In addition to author and context, consider audience and purpose. *Who was this source for, and why was it created?* Was the source intended for a public or private audience? Was the source created to persuade or to inform? Was the author talking to allies or foes? What did he or she assume about their audience? A final and related point touches upon the format of the source. *What type of source is it?* Historians think about and interpret sources differently. You might be more honest in a private letter to your spouse than you would be in a letter to a political opponent, for example. Similarly, a campaign poster for a particular candidate has a different purpose than a portrait of a politician commissioned for a private residence. As these examples show, the format of a source is often linked to audience and purpose.

What a source tells a historian is not always self-evident. Very few of the sources that historians use were created *for* historians. (No one writes letters that begin: "Dear Historian of a hundred years from now, here is what I am thinking about the Obama presidency.") Historians need to "read between the lines" to derive meaning. As you read the documents in this book, you can unearth the meaning in these sources by asking questions, thinking about context, paying attention to vocabulary and cultural references, and comparing them to other sources related to the same topic or event.

This form of active reading takes a bit more time than it would if you were to simply read starting at the first word and running through to the end. To truly think like a historian, be an active reader. Engage the texts. Ask them questions. Write in the book. Draw circles around important words or phrases. Write "key point" in the margins where you think the author is hitting his mark. Don't be afraid to throw in a few question marks where you get confused. If you have a furrowed brow, chances are someone else in class is confused, too. Bring it up in discussion and you'll be the class superhero. Take advantage of the questions I pose at the end of each source and chapter. I wrote them to inspire you to go back to the texts and think about what you read. The end-of-chapter Comparative Questions encourage you to see connections between and among multiple texts.

Remember, the past is about having a conversation. These texts speak to one another. It is OK to eavesdrop on their discussions. In fact (here's me being bold), I think you have an obligation to listen in on their chatter. Many of the issues these sources address, though sometimes distant to us in time, remain relevant: What is just? What kind of society do we want to live in? How should we treat each other? How do we balance rights and responsibilities? These enduring questions are not solved by the authors included in this book. But they all have a perspective that helps to clarify our own responses.

My hope is that you will engage these texts to understand how different people, in different places and different times, constructed the specific world they inhabited. I hope, too, that you find your voice and come to know that you have an opportunity and a responsibility to engage in the conversation. The thrill of history is to know that you are part of a very long conversation about meaning. So, the next time you are wearing Ike's PJs while shouldering John Brown's gun, think about the contribution to that conversation you want others to remember you by. What will you say?

CONTENTS

PART 2	BRITISH NORTH AMERICA AND THE ATLANTIC WORLD (1660–1763)	59

CHAPTER 8   Creating a Republican Culture
1790–1820

Sources for
America's History

Volume 1: To 1877

1

Colliding Worlds
1450–1600

In the fifteenth and sixteenth centuries, it was common to refer to the Americas as a "new world" or "virgin soil." Such terms captured the wonder and enthusiasm of European explorers, to whom everything on the continent appeared new and untouched. Those terms also reveal the confidence, or even arrogance, animating many of those explorers, who viewed the continent as a blank slate waiting for them to write the next chapter of Europe's great unfolding destiny. Their visions of gold and glory ultimately came into conflict with the many thousands of indigenous inhabitants who had for centuries developed thriving societies and sophisticated cultures in the Americas. As European worldviews bumped up against indigenous American cultures and beliefs, another group of unwilling participants added to the collision of civilizations, when Africans captured and sold into slavery began populating American shores in the sixteenth century. In this chapter, we illuminate how the interaction of these three worlds transformed North America and forged the modern world.

1-1 | An Englishman Describes the Algonquin People

THOMAS HARIOT, *A Briefe and True Report of the New Found Land of Virginia* (1588)

Much of what Europeans would understand about the indigenous peoples of Virginia came from the evocative descriptions Thomas Hariot provided in his firsthand observations. In 1585, Hariot (c. 1560–1621) accompanied Sir Walter Raleigh on his voyage to establish an English colony on Roanoke Island. While there, he learned the Algonquian language and explored the Chesapeake, producing one of the earliest accurate maps of the North Atlantic coast. After his return to England, Hariot published *A Briefe and True Report of the New Found Land of Virginia*, which made the case for English colonization. In the excerpt included here, Hariot provides the English with a description of the Algonquin Indians' religious beliefs.

It resteth I speake a word or two of the naturall inhabitants, their natures and maners, leaving large discourse thereof untill time more convenient hereafter: now onely so farre foorth, as that you may know, how that they in respect of troubling our inhabiting and planting, are not to be feared; but that they shall have cause both to feare and love us, that shall inhabite with them.

They are a people clothed with loose mantles made of Deere skins, and aprons of the same rounde about their middles; all els naked; of such a difference of statures only as wee in England; having no edge tooles or weapons of yron or steele to offend us withall, neither know they how to make any: those weapons they have, are onlie bowes made of Witch hazle, & arrowes of reeds; flat edged truncheons also of wood about a yard long, neither have they any thing to defend themselves but targets made of barks; and some armours made of stickes wickered together with thread.

Their townes are but small, and neere the sea coast but few, some containing but 10. or 12. houses: some 20. the greatest that we have seene have bene but of 30. houses: if they be walled it is only done with barks of trees made fast to stakes, or els with poles onely fixed upright and close one by another.

Their houses are made of small poles made fast at the tops in rounde forme after the maner as is used in many arbories in our gardens of England, in most townes covered with barkes, and in some with artificiall mattes made of long rushes; from the tops of the houses downe to the ground. The length of them is commonly double to the breadth, in some places they are but 12. and 16. yardes long, and in other some wee have seene of foure and twentie.

In some places of the countrey one onely towne belongeth to the government of a Wiróans or chiefe Lorde; in other some two or three, in some sixe, eight, and more; the greatest Wiróans that yet we had dealing with had but eighteene townes in his government, and able to make not above seven or eight hundred fighting men at the most: The language of every government is different from any other, and the farther they are distant the greater is the difference.

Thomas Hariot, *A Briefe and True Report of the New Found Land of Virginia* (London, 1588).

Their maner of warres amongst themselves is either by sudden surprising one an other most commonly about the dawning of the day, or moone light; or els by ambushes, or some suttle devises: Set battels are very rare, except it fall out where there are many trees, where eyther part may have some hope of defence, after the deliverie of every arrow, in leaping behind some or other.

If there fall out any warres between us & them, what their fight is likely to bee, we having advantages against them so many maner of waies, as by our discipline, our strange weapons and devises els; especially by ordinance great and small, it may be easily imagined; by the experience we have had in some places, the turning up of their heeles against us in running away was their best defence.

In respect of us they are a people poore, and for want of skill and judgement in the knowledge and use of our things, doe esteeme our trifles before thinges of greater value: Notwithstanding in their proper manner considering the want of such meanes as we have, they seeme very ingenious; For although they have no such tooles, nor any such craftes, sciences and artes as wee; yet in those thinges they doe, they shewe excellencie of wit. And by howe much they upon due consideration shall finde our manner of knowledges and craftes to exceede theirs in perfection, and speed for doing or execution, by so much the more is it probable that they shoulde desire our friendships and love, and have the greater respect for pleasing and obeying us. Whereby may bee hoped if meanes of good government bee used, that they may in short time be brought to civilitie, and the embracing of true religion.

Some religion they have alreadie, which although it be farre from the truth, yet being as it is, there is hope it may bee the easier and sooner reformed.

They beleeve that there are many Gods which they call Montóac, but of different sortes and degrees; one onely chiefe and great God, which hath bene from all eternitie. Who as they affirme when hee purposed to make the worlde, made first other goddes of a principall order to bee as meanes and instruments to bee used in the creation and government to follow; and after the Sunne, Moone, and Starres, as pettie goddess and the instruments of the other order more principall. First they say were made waters, out of which by the gods was made all diversitie of creatures that are visible or invisible.

For mankind they say a woman was made first, which by the woorking of one of the goddes, conceived and brought foorth children: And in such sort they say they had their beginning.

But how manie yeeres or ages have passed since, they say they can make no relation, having no letters nor other such meanes as we to keepe recordes of the particularities of times past, but onelie tradition from father to sonne.

They thinke that all the gods are of humane shape, and therfore they represent them by images in the forms of men, which they call Kewasówok one alone is called Kewás; Them they place in houses appropriate or temples which they call Machicómuck; Where they woorship, praie, sing, and make manie times offerings unto them. In some Machicómuck we have seene but one Kewas, in some two, and in other some three; The common sort thinke them to be also gods.

They beleeve also the immortalitie of the soule, that after this life as soone as the soule is departed from the bodie according to the workes it hath done, it is eyther carried to heaven the habitacle of gods, there to enjoy perpetuall blisse and happinesse, or els to a great pitte or hole, which they thinke to bee in the furthest partes of their part of the worlde towarde the sunne set, there to burne continually: the place they call Popogusso.

For the confirmation of this opinion, they tolde mee two stories of two men that had been lately dead and revived againe, the one happened but few yeres before our comming into the countrey of a wicked man which having beene dead and buried, the next day the earth of the grave beeing seene to move, was taken up againe; Who made declaration where his soule had beene, that is to saie very neere entring into Popogusso, had not one of the gods saved him & gave him leave to returne againe, and teach his friends what they should doe to avoid that terrible place of torment.

The other happened in the same yeere wee were there, but in a towne that was threescore miles from us, and it was tolde mee for straunge newes that one being dead, buried and taken up againe as the first, shewed that although his bodie had lien dead in the grave, yet his soule was alive, and had travailed farre in a long broade waie, on both sides whereof grewe most delicate and pleasaunt trees, bearing more rare and excellent fruites then ever hee had seene before or was able to expresse, and at length came to most brave and faire houses, neere which hee met his father, that had beene dead before, who gave him great charge to goe backe againe and shew his friendes what good they were to doe to enioy the pleasures of that place, which when he had done he should after come againe.

What subtilty soever be in the Wiroances and Priestes, this opinion worketh so much in manie of the common and simple sort of people that it maketh them have great respect to their Governours, and also great care what they do, to avoid torment after death, and to enioy blisse; although notwithstanding there is punishment ordained for malefactours, as stealers, whoremoongers, and other sortes of wicked doers; some punished with death, some with forfeitures, some with beating, according to the greatnes of the factes.

And this is the summe of their religion, which I learned by having special familiarity with some of their priestes. Wherein they were not so sure grounded, nor gave such credite to their traditions and stories but through conversing with us they were brought into great doubts of their owne, and no small admiration of ours, with earnest desire in many, to learne more than we had meanes for want of perfect utterance in their language to expresse.

READING AND DISCUSSION QUESTIONS

1. What attitude does Hariot seem to have toward the religion of the Algonquin Indians he encountered?

2. What effect do you imagine Hariot's account of the Algonquins had on his English readers?

1-2 | Peasants Working a Lord's Estate

LIMBOURG BROTHERS, *March: Peasants at Work from the "Très Riches Heures du Duc de Berry"* (15th Century)

The world Hariot described (Document 1-1) probably seemed exotic to Europeans who would have been more familiar with the scene of peasant life depicted in this image from an early-fifteenth-century Book of Hours. Here we see peasants farming a manor, employing ploughs and domesticated animals. In this more cultivated and subdued way of life, peasants worked a lord's land in exchange for the right to use his mill to grind wheat and his oven to bake bread. In turn, the lord offered protection from famine and military conflict. A Book of Hours was a book of prayers meant to be recited at appointed hours during the day. The page reproduced here is for the month of March. The arch above the miniature illustration includes zodiacal references, including Pisces and Aries.

Ms 65/1284 f.3v March: peasants at work on a feudal estate, from the "Très Riches Heures du Duc de Berry" (vellum) (for facsimile copy see 65835), Limbourg Brothers (fl. 1400–1416) / Musée Condé, Chantilly, France / Giraudon / The Bridgeman Art Library.

READING AND DISCUSSION QUESTIONS

1. A French prince, the Duc de Berry, commissioned this illuminated manuscript, depicting scenes important to him. What might this scene tell us about the world de Berry inhabited? What assumptions about society do you think de Berry made?

2. What evidence of a religious worldview does this illuminated book of prayers, complete with Zodiac signs, provide?

3. How would you compare the world shown here with the natural world described by Hariot in Document 1-1?

1-3 | Columbus Encounters Native Peoples
CHRISTOPHER COLUMBUS, *Journal of the First Voyage* (1492)

Christopher Columbus (1451–1506), in the pay of the Spanish court, sailed west from Europe crossing the Atlantic in 1492 en route to India and the legendary hoards of gold and spices rumored to be found in the East. As we know, Columbus failed to reach India, but the world he encountered opened Europe to riches of a different sort. In the journal of Columbus's first voyage, he describes the native peoples he encountered, including comments on their appearance, dress, and behavior toward him. While his comments provide a peek into the native culture, they also reveal Columbus's attitudes and worldview.

Friday, 12th of October

What follows is in the actual words of the Admiral[1] in his book of the first navigation and discovery of the Indies. "I," he says, "that we might form great friendship, for I knew that they were a people who could be more easily freed and converted to our holy faith by love than by force, gave to some of them red caps, and glass beads to put round their necks, and many other things of little value, which gave them great pleasure, and made them so much our friends that it was a marvel to see. They afterwards came to the ship's boats where we were, swimming and bringing us parrots, cotton threads in skeins, darts, and many other things; and we exchanged them for other things that we gave them, such as glass beads and small bells. In fine, they took all, and gave what they had with good will. It appeared to me to be a race of people very poor in everything. They go as naked as when their mothers bore them, and so do the women, although I did not see more than one young girl. All I saw were youths, none more than thirty

---

The Voyages of Columbus and of John Cabot, ed. Edward Gaylord Bourne (New York: Charles Scribner's Sons, 1906), 110–114.

[1]Columbus's journal was lost but not before Bartolome de Las Casas (c. 1484–1566) had summarized the original when preparing his *Historia General de las Indias* (1522). The text we have of Columbus's journal is based on Las Casas's summary. When Las Casas mentions the "Admiral," he is referring to Columbus.

years of age. They are very well made with very handsome bodies, and very good countenances. Their hair is short and coarse, almost like the hairs of a horsetail. They wear the hairs brought down to the eyebrows except a few locks behind, which they wear long and never cut. They paint themselves black, and they are the color of the Canarians, neither black nor white. Some paint themselves white, others red, and others of what color they find. Some paint their faces, others the whole body, some only round the eyes, others only on the nose. They neither care nor know anything of arms, for I showed them swords, and they took them by the blade and cut themselves through ignorance. They have no iron, their darts being wands without iron, some of them having a fish's tooth at the end, and others being pointed in various ways. They are all of fair stature and size, with good faces, and well made. I saw some with marks of wounds on their bodies, and I made signs to ask what it was, and they gave me to understand that people from other adjacent islands came with the intention of seeing them, and that they defended themselves. I believed, and still believe, that they come here from the mainland to take them prisoners. They should be good servants and intelligent, for I observed that they quickly took in what was said to them, and I believe that they would easily be made Christians, as it appeared to me that they had no religion. I, our Lord being pleased, will take hence, at the time of my departure, six natives for your Highnesses, that they may learn to speak. I saw no beast of any kind except parrots, on this island." The above is in the words of the Admiral.

Saturday, 13th of October

"As soon as dawn broke many of these people came to the beach, all youths, as I have said, and all of good stature, a very handsome people. Their hair is not curly, but loose and coarse, like horse hair. In all the forehead is broad, more so than in any other people I have hitherto seen. Their eyes are very beautiful and not small, and themselves far from black, but the color of the Canarians. Nor should anything else be expected, as this island is in a line east and west from the island of Hierro in the Canaries. Their legs are very straight, all in one line, and no belly, but very well formed. They came to the ship in small canoes, made out of the trunk of a tree like a long boat, and all of one piece, and wonderfully worked, considering the country. They are large, some of them holding 40 to 45 men, others smaller, and some only large enough to hold one man. They are propelled with a paddle like a baker's shovel, and go at a marvelous rate. If the canoe capsizes, they all promptly begin to swim, and to bale it out with calabashes that they take with them. They brought skeins of cotton thread, parrots, darts, and other small things which it would be tedious to recount, and they give all in exchange for anything that may be given to them. I was attentive, and took trouble to ascertain if there was gold. I saw that some of them had a small piece fastened in a hole they have in the nose, and by signs I was able to make out that to the south, or going from the island to the south, there was a king who had great cups full, and who possessed a great quantity. I tried to get them to go there, but afterwards I saw that they had no inclination. I resolved to wait until to-morrow in the afternoon and then to depart, shaping a course to the S.W., for, according to what many of them told me, there was land to the S., to the S.W., and N.W., and that the natives from the N.W. often came to attack them, and went on to the S.W. in search of gold and precious stones.

"This island is rather large and very flat, with bright green trees, much water, and a very large lake in the centre, without any mountain, and the whole land so green that it is a pleasure to look on it. The people are very docile, and for the longing to possess our things, and not having anything to give in return, they take what they can get, and presently swim away. Still, they give away all they have got, for whatever may be given to them, down to broken bits of crockery and glass. I saw one give 16 skeins of cotton for three *ceotis* of Portugal, equal to one *blanca* of Spain, the skeins being as much as an *arroba* of cotton thread. I shall keep it, and shall allow no one to take it, preserving it all for your Highnesses, for it may be obtained in abundance. It is grown in this island, though the short time did not admit of my ascertaining this for a certainty. Here also is found the gold they wear fastened in their noses. But, in order not to lose time, I intend to go and see if I can find the island of Cipango. Now, as it is night, all the natives have gone on shore with their canoes."

Sunday, 14th of October

"At dawn I ordered the ship's boat and the boats of the caravels to begot ready, and I went along the coast of the island to the N.N.E., to see the other side, which was on the other side to the east, and also to see the villages. Presently I saw two or three, and the people all came to the shore, calling out and giving thanks to God. Some of them brought us water, others came with food, and when they saw that I did not want to land, they got into the sea, and came swimming to us. We understood that they asked us if we had come from heaven. One old man came into the boat, and others cried out, in loud voices, to all the men and women, to come and see the men who had come from heaven, and to bring them to eat and drink. Many came, including women, each bringing something, giving thanks to God, throwing themselves on the ground and shouting to us to come on shore. But I was afraid to land, seeing an extensive reef of rocks which surrounded the island, with deep water between it and the shore forming a port large enough for as many ships as there are in Christendom, but with a very narrow entrance. It is true that within this reef there are some sunken rocks, but the sea has no more motion than the water in a well. In order to see all this I went this morning, that I might be able to give a full account to your Highnesses, and also where a fortress might be established. I saw a piece of land which appeared like an island, although it is not one, and on it there were six houses. It might be converted into an island in two days, though I do not see that it would be necessary, for these people are very simple as regards the use of arms, as your Highnesses will see from the seven that I caused to be taken, to bring home and learn our language and return; unless your Highnesses should order them all to be brought to

Castile, or to be kept as captives on the same island; for with fifty men they can all be subjugated and made to do what is required of them. Close to the above peninsula there are gardens of the most beautiful trees I ever saw, and with leaves as green as those of Castile in the month[s] of April and May, and much water. I examined all that port, and afterwards I returned to the ship and made sail. I saw so many islands that I hardly knew how to determine to which I should go first. Those natives I had with me said, by signs, that there were so many that they could not be numbered, and they gave the names of more than a hundred. At last I looked out for the largest, and resolved to shape a course for it, and so I did. It will be distant five leagues from this of San Salvador, and the others some more, some less. All are very flat, and all are inhabited. The natives make war on each other, although these are very simple-minded and handsomely-formed people."

READING AND DISCUSSION QUESTIONS

1. Why do you think Columbus focused on these details about the natives he encountered?

2. Besides riches, what motivation for exploration can you see in Columbus's account of his meeting with the natives?

1-4 | Las Casas Describes European Atrocities

BARTOLOME DE LAS CASAS, *A Brief Account of the Destruction of the Indies* (1552)

Bartolome de Las Casas (c. 1484–1566), born in Seville, migrated to Hispaniola early in the sixteenth century and participated in the colonial economy, owning slaves and waging military attacks against the indigenous population. Unlike other Spanish conquerors, however, Las Casas gradually renounced slavery and its cruelties and, by 1514, he was urging others to do the same. His graphic portrayal of Spanish atrocities, published in 1552 as *A Brief Account of the Destruction of the Indies*, describes the tortures inflicted on the indigenous peoples of the West Indies.

America was discovered and found out *Ann. Dom.* 1492, and the Year insuing inhabited by the Spaniards, and afterward a multitude of them travelled thither from Spain for the space of Nine and Forty Years. Their first attempt was on the Spanish Island, which indeed is a most fertile soil, and at present in great reputation for its Spaciousness and Length, containing in Circumference Six Hundred Miles: Nay it is on all sides surrounded with an almost innumerable number of Islands, which we found so well peopled with Natives and Forreigners, that there is scarce any Region in the Universe fortified with so many Inhabitants: But

Bartolome de Las Casas, *A Brief Account of the Destruction of the Indies* (London: R. Hewson, 1689).

the main Land or Continent, distant from this Island Two Hundred and Fifty Miles and upwards, extends it self above Ten Thousand Miles in Length near the sea-shore, which Lands are some of them already discover'd, and more may be found out in process of time: And such a multitude of People inhabits these Countries, that it seems as if the Omnipotent God has Assembled and Convocated the major part of Mankind in this part of the World.

Now this infinite multitude of Men are by the Creation of God innocently simple, altogether void of and averse to all manner of Craft, Subtlety and Malice, and most Obedient and Loyal Subjects to their Native Sovereigns; and behave themselves very patiently, su[b]missively and quietly towards the Spaniards, to whom they are subservient and subject; so that finally they live without the least thirst after revenge, laying aside all litigiousness, Commotion and hatred.

This is a most tender and effeminate people, and [of] so imbecile and unequal-balanced temper, that they are altogether incapable of hard labour, and in few years, by one Distemper or other soon expire, so that the very issue of Lords and Princes, who among us live with great affluence, and fard deliciously, are not more eff[e]minate and tender than the Children of their Husbandmen or Labourers: This Nation is very Necessitous and Indigent, Masters of very slender Possessions, and consequently, neither Haughty, nor Ambitious. They are parsimonious in their Diet, as the Holy Fathers were in their frugal life in the Desert, known by the name of Eremites. They go naked, having no other Covering but what conceals their Pudends from publick sight. An hairy Plad, or loose Coat, about an Ell, or a coarse woven Cloth at most Two Ells long serves them for the warmest Winter Garment. They lye on a coarse Rug or Matt, and those that have the most plentiful Estate or Fortunes, the better sort, use Net-work, knotted at the four corners in lieu of Beds, which the Inhabitants of the Island of Hispaniola, in their own proper Idiom, term *Hammacks*. The Men are pregnant and docible. The natives tractable, and capable of Morality or Goodness, very apt to receive the instill'd principles of Catholick Religion; nor are they averse to Civility and good Manners, being not so much discompos'd by variety of Obstructions, as the rest of Mankind; insomuch, that having suckt in (if I may so express my self) the very first Rudiments of the Christian Faith, they are so transported with Zeal and Furvor in the exercise of Ecclesiastical Sacraments, and Divine Service, that the very Religioso's themselves, stand in need of the greatest and most signal patience to undergo such extream Transports. And to conclude, I my self have heard the Spaniards themselves (who dare not assume the Confidence to deny the good Nature praedominant in them) declare, that there was nothing wanting in them for the acquisition of Eternal Beatitude, but the sole Knowledge and Understanding of the Deity.

The Spaniards first assaulted the innocent Sheep, so qualified by the Almighty, as is premention'd, like most cruel Tygers, Wolves and Lions hunger-starv'd, studying nothing, for the space of Forty Years, after their first landing, but the Massacre of these Wretches, whom they have so inhumanely and barbarously butcher'd and harass'd with several kinds of Torments, never before known, or heard (of which you shall have some account in the following

Discourse) that of Three Millions of Persons, which lived in Hispaniola itself, there is at present but the inconsiderable remnant of scarce Three Hundred. Nay the Isle of Cuba, which extends as far, as Valledolid in Spain is distant from Rome, lies now uncultivated, like a Desert, and intomb'd in its own Ruins. You may also find the Isles of St. John, and Jamaica, both large and fruitful places, unpeopled and desolate. The Lucayan Islands on the North Side, adjacent to Hispaniola and Cuba, which are Sixty in number, or thereabout, together with those, vulgarly known by the name of the Gigantic Isles, and others, the most infertile whereof, exceeds the Royal Garden of Sevil in fruitfulness, a most Healthful and pleasant Climat, is now laid waste and uninhabited; and whereas, when the Spaniards first arriv'd here, about Five Hundred Thousand Men dwelt in it, they are now cut off, some by slaughter, and others ravished away by Force and Violence, to work in the Mines of Hispanioloa [*sic*], which was destitute of Native Inhabitants: For a certain Vessel, sailing to this Isle, to the end, that the Harvest being over (some good Christian, moved with Piety and Pity, undertook this dangerous Voyage, to convert Souls to Christianity) the remaining gleanings might be gathered up, there were only found Eleven Persons, which I saw with my own Eyes. There are other Islands Thirty in number, and upward bordering upon the Isle of St. John, totally unpeopled; all which are above Two Thousand miles in Lenght, and yet remain without Inhabitants, Native, or People.

As to the firm land, we are certainly satisfied, and assur'd, that the Spaniards by their barbarous and execrable Actions have absolutely depopulated Ten Kingdoms, of greater extent than all Spain, together with the Kingdoms of Arragon and Portugal, that is to say, above One Thousand Miles, which now lye wast[e] and desolate, and are absolutely ruined, when as formerly no other Country whatsoever was more populous. Nay we dare boldly affirm, that during the Forty Years space, wherein they exercised their sanguinary and detestable Tyranny in these Regions, above Twelve Millions (computing Men, Women, and Children) have undeservedly perished; nor do I conceive that I should deviate from the Truth by saying that above Fifty Millions in all paid their last Debt to Nature.

Those that arriv'd at these Islands from the remotest parts *of Spain, and* who pride themselves in the Name of Christians, steer'd Two courses principally, in order to the Extirpation, and Exterminating of this People from the face of the Earth. The first whereof was raising an unjust, sanguinolent, cruel War. The other, by putting them to death, who hitherto, thirsted after their Liberty, or design'd (which the most Potent, Strenuous and Magnanimous Spirits intended) to recover their pristin Freedom, and shake off the Shackles of so injurious a Captivity: For they being taken off in War, none but Women and Children were permitted to enjoy the benefit of that Country-Air, in whom they did in succeeding times lay such a heavy Yoak, that the very Brutes were more happy than they: To which Two Species of Tyranny as subalternate things to the Genus, the other innumerable Courses they took to extirpate and make this a desolate People, may be reduced and referr'd.

Now the ultimate end and scope that incited the Spaniards to endeavor the Extirpation and Desolation of this People, was Gold only; that thereby growing opulent in a short time, they might arrive at once at such Degrees and Dignities, as were no wayes consistent with their Persons.

Finally, in one word, their Ambition and Avarice, than which the heart of Man never entertained greater, and the vast Wealth of those Regions; the Humility and Patience of the Inhabitants (which made their approach to these Lands more facil and easie) did much [to] promote the business: Whom they so despicably contemned, that they treated them (I speak of things which I was an Eye Witness of, without the least fallacy) not as Beasts, which I cordially wished they would, but as the most abject dung and filth of the Earth; and so sollicitous they were of their Life and Soul, that the above-mentioned number of People died without understanding the true Faith or Sacraments. And this also is as really true as the praecendent Narration (which the very Tyrants and cruel Murderers cannot deny without the stigma of a lye) that the Spaniards never received any injury from the Indians, but that they rather reverenced them as Persons descended from Heaven, until that they were compelled to take up Arms, provoked thereunto by repeated Injuries, violent Torments, and injust Butcheries.

READING AND DISCUSSION QUESTIONS

1. How does Las Casas characterize the native peoples he writes about? How does his description compare to those provided by Hariot (Document 1-1) and Columbus (Document 1-3)?

2. By the time Las Casas wrote his *Brief Account,* he had been a Dominican friar for nearly thirty years. What role did religion play in shaping his interpretation of Spain's treatment of natives?

1-5 | Huejotzingo Petitions the Spanish King for Relief

COUNCIL OF HUEJOTZINGO, *Letter to the King of Spain* (1560)

Huejotzingo, located in central Mexico, suffered under Aztec domination in the fifteenth century. When Hernán Cortés, the Spanish conquistador, began his campaign against the Aztecs in 1519, the indigenous people of Huejotzingo allied themselves with him. They sided with the victor, for Cortés crushed the Aztecs by 1521, claiming the empire for Spain. In time, the inhabitants of Huejotzingo came to understand the price of empire. In this petition, drafted by the city's council, Huejotzingo's leaders asked the Spanish king for relief from the massive tribute now being demanded of them. Their appeal was ultimately unsuccessful.

Our lord sovereign, king don Felipe our lord, with our words we appear and stand before you, we of Huejotzingo who guard for you your city — we citizens, I

Beyond the Codices, trans. and ed. Arthur J. O. Anderson, Frances Berdan, and James Lockhart (Berkeley: University of California Press, 1976), 179, 181, 183, 185, 187, 189. Copyright © 1976 by The Regents of the University of California. Used by permission of the University of California Press.

the governor and we the alcaldes and councilmen and we the lords and nobles, your men and your servants. Very humbly we implore you: Oh unfortunate are we, very great and heavy sadness and affliction lie upon us, nowhere do your pity and compassion extend over us and reach us, we do not deserve, we do not attain your rulership. And all the while since your subjects the Spaniards arrived among us, all the while we have been looking toward you, we have been confidently expecting that sometime your pity would reach us, as we also had confidence in and were awaiting the mercy of your very revered dear father the ruler of the world, don Carlos the late emperor. Therefore now, our lord sovereign, we bow humbly before you; may we deserve your pity, may the very greatly compassionate and merciful God enlighten you so that your pity is exercised on us, for we hear, and so it is said to us, that you are very merciful and humane towards all your vassals; and as to the time when you pity someone, when before you appears a vassal of yours in poverty, so it is said, then you have pity on him with your very revered majesty, and by the grace of omnipotent God you do it for him. May we now also deserve and attain the same, for every day such poverty and affliction reaches us and is visited on us that we weep and mourn. Oh unfortunate are we, what will happen to us, we your poor vassals of Huejotzingo, we who live in your city? If you were not so far away, many times we would appear before you. Though we greatly wish and desire to reach you and appear before you, we are unable, because we are very poor and do not have what is needed for the journey on the boat nor things to eat nor anything to pay people in order to be able to reach you. Therefore now we appear before you only in our words; we set before you our poor prayer. May you only in your very great Christianity and very revered high majesty attend well to this our prayer.

Our lord sovereign, before anyone told us of or made us acquainted with your fame and your story, most high and feared universal king who rules all, and before we were told or taught the glory and name of our Lord God, before the faith reached us, and before we were Christians, when your servants the Spaniards reached us and your captain general don Hernando Cortés arrived, although we were not yet acquainted with the omnipotent, very compassionate holy Trinity, our Lord God the ruler of heaven and possessor of earth caused us to deserve that in his mercy he enlightened us so that we took you as our king to belong to you and become your people and your subjects; not a single town surpassed us here in New Spain in that first and earliest we threw ourselves toward you, we gave ourselves to you, and furthermore no one intimidated us, no one forced us into it, but truly God caused us to deserve that voluntarily we adhered to you so that we gladly received the newly arrived Spaniards who reached us here in New Spain, for we left our homes behind to go a great distance to meet them; we went twenty leagues to greet captain general don Hernando Cortés and the others whom he led. We received them very gladly, we embraced them, we saluted them with many tears, though we were not acquainted with them, and our fathers and grandfathers also did not know them; but by the mercy of our Lord God we truly came to know them. Since they are our neighbors, therefore we loved them; nowhere did we attack them. Truly we fed them and served them; some arrived sick, so that we carried them in our arms and on our backs, and we served them in many other ways which we are not able to say here. Although the people who are called and named Tlaxcalans indeed helped, yet we strongly pressed them to give aid, and we admonished them not to make war; but though we so admonished them, they made war and fought for fifteen days. But we, when a Spaniard was afflicted, without fail at once we managed to reach him; [there was no one else]. We do not lie in this, for all the conquerers know it well, those who have died and some now living.

And when they began their conquest and war-making, then also we well prepared ourselves to aid them, for out came all of our war gear, our arms and provisions and all our equipment, and we not merely named someone, we went in person, we who rule, and we brought all our nobles and all of our vassals to aid the Spaniards. We helped not only in warfare, but also we gave them everything they needed; we fed and clothed them, and we would carry in our arms and on our backs those whom they wounded in war or who were very ill, and we did all the tasks in preparing for war. And so that they could fight the Mexica with boats, we worked hard; we gave them the wood and pitch with which the Spaniards made the boats. And when they conquered the Mexica and all belonging to them, we never abandoned them or left them behind in it. And when they went to conquer Michoacan, Jalisco, and Colhuacan, and there at Pánuco and there at Oaxaca and Tehuantepec and Guatemala, (we were) the only ones who went along while they conquered and made war here in New Spain until they finished the conquest; we never abandoned them, in no way did we prejudice their war-making, though some of us were destroyed in it [nor was there a single one of our subjects left?], for we did our duty very well. But as to those Tlaxcalans, several of their nobles were hanged for making war poorly; in many places they ran away, and often did badly in the war. In this we do not lie, for the conquerors know it well.

Our lord sovereign, we also say and declare before you that your fathers the twelve sons of St. Francis reached us, whom the very high priestly ruler the Holy Father sent and whom you sent, both taking pity on us so that they came to teach us the gospel, to teach us the holy Catholic faith and belief, to make us acquainted with the single deity God our Lord, and likewise God favored us and enlightened us, us of Huejotzingo, who dwell in your city, so that we gladly received them. When they entered the city of Huejotzingo, of our own free will we honored them and showed them esteem. When they embraced us so that we would abandon the wicked belief in many gods, we forthwith voluntarily left it; likewise they did us the good deed (of telling us) to destroy and burn the stones and wood that we worshipped as gods, and we did it; very willingly we destroyed, demolished, and burned the temples. Also when they gave us the holy gospel, the holy Catholic faith, with very good will and desire we received and grasped it; no one frightened us into it, no one forced us, but very willingly we seized it, and they gave us all the sacraments. Quietly and peacefully we arranged and ordered it among ourselves; no one, neither nobleman nor commoner, was ever tortured or burned for this, as was done on every hand here in New Spain. (The people of) many towns were forced and tortured, were hanged or burned because they did not want to leave idolatry, and unwillingly they received the gospel and faith. Especially those Tlaxcalans pushed out and rejected the fathers, and would not receive the faith, for many of the high nobles were burned, and some hanged, for combating the advocacy and service of our Lord God. But we of Huejotzingo, we your poor vassals, we never did anything in your harm, always we served you in every command you sent or what at your command we were ordered. Very quietly, peacefully we take and grasp it all, though only through the mercy of God do we do it, since it is not within our personal power. Therefore now, in and through God, may you hear these our words, all that we say and declare before you, so that you will take pity on us, so that you will exercise on us your rulership to console us and aid us in (this trouble) with which daily we weep and are sad. We are afflicted and sore pressed, and your town and city of Huejotzingo is as if it is about to disappear and be destroyed. Here is what is being done to us: now your stewards the royal officials and the prosecuting attorney Dr. Maldonado are assessing us a very great tribute to belong to you. The tribute we are to give is 14,800 pesos in money, and also all the bushels of maize.

Our lord sovereign, never has such happened to us in all the time since your servants and vassals the Spaniards came to us, for your servant don Hernando Cortés, late captain general, the Marqués del Valle, in all the time he lived here with us, always greatly cherished us and kept us happy; he never disturbed nor agitated us. Although we gave him tribute, he assigned it to us only with moderation; even though we gave him gold, it was only very little; no matter how much, no matter in what way, or if not very pure, he just received it gladly. He never reprimanded us or afflicted us, because it was evident to him and he understood well how very greatly we served and aided him. Also he told us many times that he would speak in our favor before you, that he would help us and inform you of all the ways in which we have aided and served you. And when he went before you, then you confirmed him and were merciful to him, you honored and rewarded him for the way he had served you here in New Spain. But perhaps before you he forgot us. How then shall we speak? We did not reach you, we were not given audience before you. Who then will speak for us? Unfortunate are we. Therefore now we place ourselves before you, our sovereign lord. And when you sent your representatives, the Presidente and Bishop don Sebastián Ramírez, and the judges, Licentiate Salmerón, Licentiates Ceinos, Quiroga, and Maldonado, they well affirmed and sustained the orders you gave for us people here, us who live in New Spain. In many things they aided us and lightened the very great tribute we had, and from many things that were our tasks they always delivered us, they pardoned us all of it. And we your poor vassals, we of Huejotzingo who dwell in your city, when Licentiate Salmerón came to us and entered the city of Huejotzingo, then he saw how troubled the town was with our tribute in gold, sixty pieces that we gave each year, and that it troubled us because gold does not appear here, and is not to be found in our province, though we searched for it everywhere; then at once Licentiate Salmerón pardoned it on your behalf, so that he made a replacement and substitution of the money. He set our tribute in money at 2,050 pesos. And in all the time he thus assessed us, all the time we kept doing it, we hastened to give it to you, since we are your subjects and belong to you; we never neglected it, we never did poorly, we made it all up. But now we are taken aback and very afraid and we ask, have we done something wrong, have we somehow behaved badly and ill toward you, our lord sovereign, or have we committed some sin against almighty God? Perhaps you have heard something of our wickedness and for that reason now this very great tribute has fallen upon us, seven times exceeding all we had paid before, the 2,000 pesos. And we declare to you that it will not be long before your city of Huejotzingo completely disappears and perishes, because our fathers, grandfathers, and ancestors knew no tribute and gave tribute to no one, but were independent, and we nobles who guard your subjects are now truly very poor. Nobility is seen among us no longer; now we resemble the commoners. As they eat and dress, so do we; we have been very greatly afflicted, and our poverty has reached its culmination. Of the way in which our fathers and grandfathers and forebears were rich and honored, there is no longer the slightest trace among us.

O our lord sovereign king, we rely on you as on God the one deity who dwells in heaven, we trust in you as our father. Take pity on us, have compassion with us. May you especially remember those who live and subsist in the wilds, those who move us to tears and pity; we truly live with them in just such poverty as theirs, wherefore we speak out before you so that afterwards you will not become angry with us when your subjects have disappeared or perished. There ends this our prayer.

READING AND DISCUSSION QUESTIONS

1. What arguments does the Council believe would be convincing to the Spanish king?

2. What does this petition reveal about the extent to which European colonization and domination had affected indigenous culture?

1-6 | Debating the Morality of Slavery

BROTHER LUIS BRANDAON, *Letter to Father Sandoval* (1610)

In the early modern period, colonization and its effects on native populations increasingly became a topic of discussion and debate. In addition to atrocities perpetrated against native populations such as those described by Las Casas (Document 1-4), the growing trade in African slaves raised moral concerns for some. In this March 12, 1610, letter, Brother Luis Brandaon, a Jesuit in Angola, addresses the concerns of Father Sandoval, a Catholic priest serving in Brazil. Angola, on the west coast of Africa, was a Portuguese colony that supplied Africans for the slave trade.

Documents Illustrative of the History of the Slave Trade to America, ed. Elizabeth Donnan (Washington, DC: Carnegie Institution of Washington, 1930), 123–124.

[March 12, 1610.]

Your Reverence writes me that you would like to know whether the negroes who are sent to your parts have been legally captured. To this I reply that I think your Reverence should have no scruples on this point, because this is a matter which has been questioned by the Board of Conscience in Lisbon, and all its members are learned and conscientious men. Nor did the bishops who were in São Thomé, Cape Verde, and here in Loando—all learned and virtuous men—find fault with it. We have been here ourselves for forty years and there have been [among us] very learned Fathers; in the Province of Brazil as well, where there have always been Fathers of our order eminent in letters, never did they consider this trade as illicit. Therefore we and the fathers of Brazil buy these slaves for our service without any scruple. Furthermore, I declare that if any one could be excused from having scruples it is the inhabitants of those regions, for since the traders who bring those negroes bring them in good faith, those inhabitants can very well buy from such traders without any scruple, and the latter on their part can sell them, for it is a generally accepted opinion that the owner who owns anything in good faith can sell it and that it can be bought. Padre Sánchez thus expresses this point in his Book of Marriage, thus solving this doubt of your Reverence. Therefore, we here are the ones who could have greater scruple, for we buy these negroes from other negroes and from people who perhaps have stolen them; but the traders who take them away from here do not know of this fact, and so buy those negroes with a clear conscience and sell them out there with a clear conscience. Besides I found it true indeed that no negro will ever say he has been captured legally. Therefore your Reverence should not ask them whether they have been legally captured or not, because they will always say that they were stolen and captured illegally, in the hope that they will be given their liberty. I declare, moreover, that in the fairs where these negroes are bought there are always a few who have been captured illegally because they were stolen or because the rulers of the land order them to be sold for offenses so slight that they do not deserve captivity, but these are few in number and to seek among ten or twelve thousand who leave this port every year for a few who have been illegally captured is an impossibility, however careful investigation may be made. And to lose so many souls as sail from here—out of whom many are saved—because some, impossible to recognize, have been captured illegally does not seem to be doing much service to God, for these are few and those who find salvation are many and legally captured.

READING AND DISCUSSION QUESTIONS

1. How does Brandaon attempt to calm Sandoval's anxiety about the slave trade?

2. What does this letter tell you about the extent of the slave trade by the early seventeenth century?

3. What evidence of the Church's role in debates over slavery does this document provide?

▪ COMPARATIVE QUESTIONS ▪

1. How do these sources illustrate the extent to which European culture had an impact on native peoples?

2. In what ways did Hariot, Columbus, and Las Casas apply a European "lens" to their views of indigenous peoples?

3. What similarities between European and American society and culture can be glimpsed through the windows opened by these sources?

4. How might the authors of these various texts have assessed the advantages and costs of colonization?

2

American Experiments
1521–1700

The "age of exploration" resulted in the establishment of many different colonies in the Americas. As no single model prevailed, the sixteenth and seventeenth centuries are best understood as a period of colonial experimentation. European colonists projected onto their communities the intellectual and cultural hallmarks of the world they left behind, but the unique challenges they faced also demanded change and innovation. The new world was not "discovered" so much as it was forged through crisis and adaptation by the Europeans, Native Americans, and imported Africans who found themselves occupying common ground.

This chapter focuses on the forces that shaped colonial society and the ways that colonists interacted with their new surroundings. In the Spanish tribute colonies, Europeans extracted resources from indigenous peoples, but their efforts were met with native resistance. In New England, John Winthrop viewed the planting of a colony as a leap of faith, but even the Puritans' godly commonwealth faced conflict as the religious debates that wracked Europe spread to the colonies. As plantations were established, changing systems of trade and a growing dependence on race-based slavery came to define enduring racial and economic patterns. Finally, as colonists were not settling an empty continent, in many ways their experiences were shaped by conflicts and encounters with indigenous peoples.

2-1 | Indians Resist Spanish Conquest
Testimony of Acoma Indians (1599)

The colonies that Spain established in the Americas rewarded their conquistadors with rich land from which they extracted labor and tribute from conquered indigenous peoples. Spain's process of imposing Catholicism and its cultural and political interests onto its colonies, while

---

From *Don Juan de Oñate: Colonizer of New Mexico, 1595–1628*, trans. and ed. George P. Hammond and Agapito Rey, vol. 5 (Albuquerque: University of New Mexico Press, 1953), 464–468.

largely successful, was sometimes met with resistance from the Indian majority. In the pueblo of Acoma in 1598, Indians attacked and killed several Spanish officials. The source included here is the official Spanish report of the incident, including the testimony from several Indians.

Statement of Indian Caoma

On this same day, February 9, the governor ordered testimony taken from an Indian through Don Tomás, a Christian Indian interpreter, who swore by God and a cross in due legal manner to declare faithfully all that might be said by this and the other Indians in their testimony. He said: "I so swear, amen."

The interpreter said that this Indian was named Caoma, a native of the pueblo of Acoma, and the captain of one of the wards of this pueblo. Not being a Christian he was not asked to take an oath. He explained through the interpreter that he was not present at Acoma when they killed the maese de campo and the others, as he had gone to the country. When he returned on the night of the day they were killed, the Indians at the pueblo told him how the maese de campo and his men came to the pueblo and asked the natives to furnish them with the maize and flour which they needed, and because they asked for such large amounts they killed them. He was very sorry for what the Indians had done and denounced them for it. Then the governor asked him to explain why it was that when the sargento mayor and the soldiers went to his pueblo to summon them to peace, the Indians, instead of submitting, attacked with arrows, stones, and clubs. He replied that they refused to come down peacefully and to be friends because they had already killed the Spaniards, but he urged the Indians, both men and women, all of whom hurled stones, to submit peacefully, but they refused.

This witness was asked to tell who dug up the two small field pieces, the horseshoes, and other iron goods that the Spaniards had buried near Acoma when they were unable to carry it further. He answered that Indians of the pueblo dug it up, carried it away, and divided it among themselves, each one taking his share. This is the truth and what he knows. He gave this testimony in the presence of Captain Alonso Gómez, his defense attorney, who signed it, together with the governor. Don Juan de Oñate. Alonso Gómez Montesinos. Before me, Juan Gutiérrez Bocanegra, secretary.

Statement of Cat-ticati

Immediately thereafter, on this same day, the governor called before him an Indian named Cat-ticati, a native of the pueblo of Acoma, who testified through the interpreter that he did not know how old he was, but perhaps about thirty-five years. He declared that he was not present when the maese de campo and the other soldiers were killed, but that he learned about it at the pueblo when he returned. They had killed them because they asked for maize, flour, and blankets.

Asked why the Indians refused to accept peace and to come down from the pueblo when the sargento mayor summoned them, he replied that they declined to submit and accept peace since they had already killed the Spaniards.

Asked why, when the sargento mayor offered them peace, they not only rejected it but shot arrows and hurled rocks and insulting words, he replied that some shot arrows and threw stones but there were some who did not want to fight. To other questions he replied that he was telling the truth. All of this took place in the presence of his defense attorney, who signed his testimony, together with the governor. Don Juan de Oñate. Alonso Gómez Montesinos. Before me, Juan Gutiérrez Bocanegra, secretary.

Testimony of Indian Taxio

This same day the governor called before him an Indian named Taxio, a native of the pueblo of Acoma, who did not know how old he was, but who seemed to be about twenty-three years.

Asked why he and the other Indians of Acoma killed the maese de campo and ten other soldiers and two servants, he said that when they began to kill them, he was at home, but when he heard the shouting that they were killing the Spaniards, he went up to the roof and stayed there and saw a dead Spaniard and that the others whom they had killed had been thrown down the rocks.

Asked why, when the sargento mayor offered the Indians peace, he and the others did not come down to accept but shot many arrows and threw rocks and cried for the Spaniards to come on and fight, he said that the old people and other leading Indians did not want peace, and for this reason they attacked with arrows and stones.

Asked why the Indian women threw rocks and helped in the fight, he said it was because they were together with the men and therefore they took part in the demonstrations and the fighting. He made this statement in the presence of the defender, who signed it. To other questions he said that he had spoken the truth, and he ratified his testimony, after it was explained to him. The interpreter did not sign this statement or the others, because he did not know how. Don Juan de Oñate. Alonso Gómez Montesinos. Before me, Juan Gutiérrez Bocanegra, secretary.

Statement of Indian Xunusta

This same day the governor called before him an Indian who, according to the interpreter, was named Xunusta, a native of the pueblo of Acoma. He did not know how old he was, but seemed to be about twenty-two years.

Asked why he and the other Indians of the pueblo had killed the maese de campo and his men, he said that the Spaniards first killed an Indian, and then all the Indians became very angry and killed them.

Asked why it was that when the sargento mayor asked them to accept peace they did not come down from the pueblo but shot many arrows and threw rocks and clubs, both men and women taking part in the fray, he said that some of the Indians wanted to make peace but others did not, and because they could not agree, they would not submit. This statement was given in the presence of their defender, who signed it, but the interpreter did not because he did not know how to write, though he ratified the testimony when it was read to him. Don Juan de Oñate. Alonso Gómez Montesinos. Before me, Juan Gutiérrez Bocanegra, secretary.

Statement of Indian Excasi

Immediately thereafter, on this same day, the governor called before him an Indian who, according to the interpreter, was named Excasi, a native of the pueblo of Acoma. He did not know his age, but seemed to be about twenty-five years.

Asked why he and the other Indians of the pueblo killed the maese de campo, two captains, eight soldiers, and two servants, he said that he did not see them killed but that he saw his people throw the bodies down the rocks. He had heard it said that they killed the Spaniards because a soldier either asked for or took a turkey.

Asked why the Indians did not accept peace when the sargento mayor appealed to them and asked them to come down and be friends, which he did many times, the Indian said that he did not want to fight, but others did, and therefore they did not submit.

Asked why they shot arrows and threw stones from the pueblo when they had been summoned to peace, he repeated what he had already said. This is the truth, and he ratified it. Done in the presence of the defender, who signed. Don Juan de Oñate. Alonso Gómez de Montesinos. Before me, Juan Gutiérrez Bocanegra, secretary.

Statement of Indian Caucachi

Immediately thereafter, on this same day, the governor called before him an Indian who, according to the interpreter, was called Caucachi, a native of the pueblo of Acoma. He did not know how old he was, but appeared to be about fifty.

Asked why he and the other Indians of the pueblo had killed the maese de campo and the other ten Spaniards and two servants, he said that the Spaniards had wounded an Acoma Indian and for this reason his people became angry and killed them.

Asked why it was that when the sargento mayor asked them to accept peace, they not only refused his offer but cried out that they wanted to fight and shot arrows and hurled stones, he said that since some of the Acomas did not wish to make friends, they began to fight. He was asked other questions, but replied that what he had said was the truth. He ratified his testimony in the presence of his defender, who signed. Don Juan de Oñate. Alonso Gómez Montesinos. Before me, Juan Gutiérrez Bocanegra, secretary.

READING AND DISCUSSION QUESTIONS

1. Whose point of view does this source express? How does that perspective shape your understanding of the event it describes?

2. What inferences can you draw about the daily relationships between the Spanish rulers and the Indians in the pueblo of Acoma?

3. Compare the testimony of these Indians. How do you explain any contradictions you find? What limitations does this source present to the historian trying to reconstruct the events it claims to describe?

2-2 | "City Upon a Hill" Sermon

JOHN WINTHROP, *A Model of Christian Charity* (1630)

John Winthrop (1588–1649) was a Puritan lawyer who, like others of his faith, feared God's punishment for what he regarded as England's corruption and moral depravity. Hoping to escape the wrath to come and to establish a colony where they would be free from the king's anti-Puritan policies, Winthrop led some seven hundred migrants to Massachusetts Bay to settle the colony in 1630. Winthrop's vision for Massachusetts Bay is beautifully expressed in his oft-quoted sermon, *A Model of Christian Charity*, which he wrote on board the ship *Arbella*.

Christian Charitie

A Modell Hereof

God Almighty in his most holy and wise providence, hath soe disposed of the condition of mankind, as in all times some must be rich, some poore, some high and eminent in power and dignitie; others mean and in submission.

The Reason Hereof

1 Reas. First to hold conformity with the rest of his world, being delighted to show forth the glory of his wisdom in the variety and difference of the creatures, and the glory of his power in ordering all these differences for the preservation and good of the whole; and the glory of his greatness, that as it is the glory of princes to have many officers, soe this great king will have many stewards, Counting himself more honoured in dispensing his gifts to man by man, than if he did it by his owne immediate hands.

2 Reas. Secondly that he might have the more occasion to manifest the work of his Spirit: first upon the wicked in moderating and restraining them: soe that the riche and mighty should not eate upp the poore nor the poore and dispised rise upp against and shake off theire yoake. Secondly In the regenerate, in exerciseing his graces in them, as in the grate ones, theire love, mercy, gentleness, temperance &c., in the poore and inferior sorte, theire faithe, patience, obedience etc.

John Winthrop, *A Modell of Christian Charity* 3rd Series, vol. 7 (Boston: Collections of the Massachusetts Historical Society, 1838), 33–35, 39–48.

3 Reas. Thirdly, that every man might have need of others, and from hence they might be all knitt more nearly together in the Bonds of brotherly affection. From hence it appears plainly that noe man is made more honourable than another or more wealthy etc., out of any particular and singular respect to himselfe, but for the glory of his creator and the common good of the creature, man. . . . All men being thus (by divine providence) ranked into two sorts, riche and poore; under the first are comprehended all such as are able to live comfortably by their own meanes duely improved; and all others are poore according to the former distribution. There are two rules whereby we are to walk one towards another: Justice and Mercy. . . . There is likewise a double Lawe by which wee are regulated in our conversation towardes another; in both the former respects, the lawe of nature and the lawe of grace, or the morrall lawe or the lawe of the gospel. . . . By the first of these lawes man as he was enabled soe withall is commanded to love his neighbour as himself. Upon this ground stands all the precepts of the morrall lawe, which concernes our dealings with men. To apply this to the works of mercy; this lawe requires two things. First that every man afford his help to another in every want or distresse. Secondly, that hee performe this out of the same affection which makes him carefull of his owne goods, according to that of our Savior, (Math.) Whatsoever ye would that men should do to you. . . .

This lawe of the Gospell propounds likewise a difference of seasons and occasions. There is a time when a christian must sell all and give to the poor, as they did in the Apostles times. There is a time allsoe when christians (though they give not all yet) must give beyond their abillity, as they of Macedonia, Cor. 2, 6. Likewise community of perills calls for extraordinary liberality, and soe doth community in some speciall service for the churche. Lastly, when there is no other means whereby our christian brother may be relieved in his distress, we must help him beyond our ability rather than tempt God in putting him upon help by miraculous or extraordinary meanes. . . .

[Concerning] the affection from which [the] exercise of mercy must arise, the Apostle tells us that this love is the fullfilling of the lawe . . . the way to drawe men to the workes of mercy, is not by force of Argument from the goodness or necessity of the worke; for though this cause may enforce, a rationall minde to some present act of mercy, as is frequent in experience, yet it cannot worke such a habit in a soule, as shall make it prompt upon all occasions to produce the same effect, but by frameing these affections of love in the hearte which will as naturally bring forthe the other, as any cause doth produce the effect.

The deffinition which the Scripture gives us of love is this. Love is the bond of perfection, first it is a bond or ligament. Secondly it makes the worke perfect. There is noe body but consists of partes and that which knitts these partes together, gives the body its perfection, because it makes eache parte soe contiguous to others as thereby they doe mutually participate with each other, both in strengthe and infirmity, in pleasure and paine. To instance in the most perfect of all bodies; Christ and his Church make one body; the severall partes of this body considered a parte before they were united, were as disproportionate and as much disordering as soe many contrary quallities or elements, but when Christ comes, and by his spirit and love knitts all these partes to himselfe and each to other, it is become the most perfect and best proportioned body in the world. . . .

From hence we may frame these conclusions. First of all, true Christians are of one body in Christ. . . . Ye are the body of Christ and members of their parte. All the partes of this body being thus united are made soe contiguous in a speciall relation as they must needes partake of each other's strength and infirmity; joy and sorrowe, weale and woe. . . . If one member suffers, all suffer with it, if one be in honor, all rejoyce with it. Secondly. The ligaments of this body which knitt together are love. Thirdly. Noe body can be perfect which wants its proper ligament. . . . This sensibleness and sympathy of each other's conditions will necessarily infuse into each parte a native desire and endeavour, to strengthen, defend, preserve and comfort the other. . . .

The next consideration is how this love comes to be wrought. Adam in his first estate was a perfect modell of mankinde in all their generations, and in him this love was perfected in regard of the habit. But Adam, rent himselfe from his Creator, rent all his posterity allsoe one from another; whence it comes that every man is borne with this principle in him to love and seeke himselfe onely, and thus a man continueth till Christ comes and takes possession of the soule and infuseth another principle, love to God and our brother, and this latter haveing continuall supply from Christ, as the head and roote by which he is united, gets the predomining in the soule, soe by little and little expells the former. . . . Now when this quallity is thus formed in the soules of men, it workes like the Spirit upon the drie bones. . . . It gathers together the scattered bones, or perfect old man Adam, and knitts them into one body againe in Christ, whereby a man is become againe a living soule.

The third consideration is concerning the exercise of this love. . . . wee must take in our way that maxime of philosophy. Simile simili gaudet, or like will to like. . . . This is the cause why the Lord loves the creature, soe farre as it hathe any of his Image in it; he loves his elect because they are like himselfe, he beholds them in his beloved sonne. So a mother loves her childe, because shee throughly conceives a resemblance of herselfe in it. Thus it is betweene the members of Christ; eache discernes, by the worke of the Spirit, his oune Image and resemblance in another, and therefore cannot but love him as he loves himself. . . .

2nly. In regard of the pleasure and content that the exercise of loue carries with it, as wee may see in the naturall body. . . . Soe is it in all the labour of love among Christians. The partie loving, reapes love again . . . which the soule covetts more then all the wealthe in the world. . . . Nothing yeildes more pleasure and content to the soule then when it findes that which it may love fervently; for to love and live beloved is the soule's paradise both here and in heaven. In the State of wedlock there be many comforts to learne out of the troubles of that Condition; but let such as have tryed the most, say if there be any sweetness in that Condition comparable to the exercise of mutuall love. . . .

It rests now to make some application of this discourse. . . . Herein are [four] things to be propounded; first the persons, secondly the worke, thirdly the end, fourthly the meanes.

First. For the persons. Wee are a company professing ourselves fellow members of Christ, in which respect onely though wee were absent from each other many miles, and had our imployments as farre distant, yet wee ought to account ourselves knitt together by this bond of love, and, live in the exercise of it, if wee would have comforte of our being in Christ. . . . Secondly for the worke wee have in hand. It is by a mutuall consent, through a speciall overvaluing providence and a more than an ordinary approbation of the Churches of Christ, to seeke out a place of cohabitation and Consorteshipp under a due forme of Government both civill and ecclesiasticall. In such cases as this, the care of the publique must oversway all private respects, by which, not only conscience, but meare civill pollicy, dothe binde us. For it is a true rule that particular Estates cannot subsist in the ruin of the publique. Thirdly the end is to improve our lives to doe more service to the Lord; the comforte and encrease of the body of Christe, whereof we are members; that ourselves and posterity may be the better preserved from the common corruptions of this evill world, to serve the Lord and worke out our Salvation under the power and purity of his holy ordinances. Fourthly for the meanes whereby this must be effected. They are twofold, a conformity with the worke and end wee aime at. These wee see are extraordinary, therefore wee must not content ourselves with usuall ordinary meanes. Whatsoever wee did, or ought to have, done, when wee lived in England, the same must wee doe, and more allsoe, where wee goe. That which the most in theire churches mainetaine as truthe in profession onely, wee must bring into familiar and constant practise; as in this duty of love, wee must love brotherly without dissimulation, wee must love one another with a pure hearte fervently. Wee must beare one anothers burthens. We must not looke onely on our owne things, but allsoe on the things of our brethren. Neither must wee thinke that the Lord will beare with such faileings at our hands as he dothe from those among whome wee have lived; and that for these 3 Reasons; 1. In regard of the more neare bond of mariage between him and us, wherein hee hath taken us to be his, after a most strickt and peculiar manner, which will make them the more jealous of our love and obedience. Soe he tells the people of Israell, you onely have I knowne of all the families of the Earthe, therefore will I punishe you for your Transgressions. Secondly, because the Lord will be sanctified in them that come neare him. We know that there were many that corrupted the service of the Lord; some setting upp altars before his owne; others offering both strange fire and strange sacrifices allsoe. . . . Thirdly when God gives a speciall commission he lookes to have it strictly observed in every article. . . . Thus stands the cause betweene God and us. We are entered into Covenant with Him for this worke. Wee have taken out a commission. The Lord hath given us leave to drawe our own articles. Wee have professed to enterprise these and those accounts, upon these and those ends. Wee have hereupon besought Him of favour and blessing. Now if the Lord shall please to heare us, and bring us in peace to the place we desire, then hath hee ratified this covenant and sealed our Commission, and will expect a strict performance of the articles contained in it; but if wee shall neglect the observation of these articles which are the ends wee have propounded, and, dissembling with our God, shall fail to embrace this present world and prosecute our carnall intentions, seeking greate things for ourselves and our posterity, the Lord will surely breake out in wrathe against us; be revenged of such a [sinful] people and make us knowe the price of the breache of such a covenant.

Now the onely way to avoyde this shipwracke, and to provide for our posterity, is to followe the counsell of Micah, to doe justly, to love mercy, to walk humbly with our God. For this end, wee must be knitt together, in this worke, as one man. Wee must entertaine each other in brotherly affection. Wee must be willing to abridge ourselves of our superfluities, for the supply of other's necessities. Wee must uphold a familiar commerce together in all meekeness, gentlenes[s], patience and liberality. Wee must delight in eache other; make other's conditions our oune; rejoice together, mourne together, labour and suffer together, allwayes haveing before our eyes our commission and community in the worke, as members of the same body. Soe shall wee keepe the unitie of the spirit in the bond of peace. The Lord will be our God, and delight to dwell among us, as his oune people, and will command a blessing upon us in all our wayes. Soe that wee shall see much more of his wisdome, power, goodness and truthe, than formerly wee have been acquainted with. Wee shall finde that the God of Israell is among us, when ten of us shall be able to resist a thousand of our enemies; when hee shall make us a prayse and glory that men shall say of succeeding plantations, "the Lord make it likely that of New England." For wee must consider that wee shall be as a citty upon a hill. The eies of all people are uppon us. Soe that if wee shall deale falsely with our God in this worke wee have undertaken, and soe cause him to withdrawe his present help from us, wee shall be made a story and a by-word through the world. Wee shall open the mouthes of enemies to speake evill of the wayes of God, and all professors for God's sake. Wee shall shame the faces of many of God's worthy servants, and cause theire prayers to be turned into curses upon us till wee be consumed out of the good land whither wee are a goeing.

I shall shutt upp this discourse with that exhortation of Moses, that faithfull servant of the Lord, in his last farewell to Israell, Deut. 30. Beloved there is now sett before us life and good, Death and evill, in that wee are commanded this day to love the Lord our God, and to love one another, to walke in his wayes and to keepe his Commandements and his Ordinance and his lawes, and the articles of our Covenant with him, that wee may live and be multiplied, and that the Lord our God may blesse us in the land whither wee goe to possesse it. But if our heartes shall turne away, soe that wee will not obey, but shall be seduced, and worshipp and serve other Gods, our pleasure and proffitts, and serve them; it is propounded unto us this day, wee shall surely perishe out of the good land whither wee passe over this vast sea to possesse it;

> Therefore lett us choose life,
> that wee, and our seede,
> may live, by obeyeing His
> voice, and cleaveing to Him,
> for Hee is our life and
> our prosperity.

READING AND DISCUSSION QUESTIONS

1. Winthrop uses the metaphor of a "body" to describe the Puritan community he envisions for Massachusetts Bay. What was his vision for this "body"?

2. Compare the values expressed here with your own. What value do you think Winthrop might have placed on such contemporary "American" values as individualism and privacy?

2-3 | The Limits of the Puritan Community
The Trial of Anne Hutchinson (1637)

The Christian charity that John Winthrop (Document 2-2) extolled did not extend to all members of the new colonial society. Anne Hutchinson (1591–1643) arrived in the Massachusetts Bay Colony in 1634 and within a few years was embroiled in a religious and political crisis. Like all Calvinists, Hutchinson believed that God's grace alone could save one's soul and that individuals could not earn their way to heaven through good deeds. While some ministers had accepted outward signs of grace as evidence of salvation, assuming that only the elect could lead saintly lives, Hutchinson rejected this. When she began holding prayer meetings and questioning the doctrines of some Bay Colony ministers, Hutchinson was put on trial and eventually banished. This selection comes from the transcript of Hutchinson's trial. The governor who leads the questioning is Winthrop.

Mr. Winthrop, governor. Mrs Hutchinson, you are called here as one of those that have troubled the peace of the commonwealth and the churches here; you are known to be a woman that hath had a great share in the promoting and divulging of those opinions that are the cause of this trouble . . . you have maintained a meeting and an assembly in your house that hath been condemned by the general assembly as a thing not tolerable nor comely in the sight of God nor fitting for your sex, and notwithstanding that was cried down you have continued the same. Therefore we have thought good to send for you to understand how things are, that if you be in an erroneous way we may reduce you that so you may become a profitable member here among us, otherwise if you be obstinate in your course that then the court may take such course that you may trouble us no further. Therefore I would intreat you to express whether you do not hold and assent in practice to those opinions and factions that have been handled in court already, that is to say, whether you do not justify Mr. Wheelwright's sermon and the petition.

Mrs. Hutchinson. I am called here to answer before you but I hear no things laid to my charge.

Gov. I have told you some already and more I can tell you.

Mrs. H. Name one, Sir.

Thomas Hutchinson, *The History of the Province of Massachusets-Bay* (Boston: Thomas and John Fleet, 1767), 482–483, 507–509, 515, 519–520.

Gov. Have I not named some already?

Mrs. H. What have I said or done?

Gov. Why for your doings, this you did harbor and countenance those that are parties in this faction that you have heard of.

Mrs. H. That's matter of conscience, Sir.

Gov. Your conscience you must keep, or it must be kept for you. . . .

Mrs. H. If you please to give me leave I shall give you the ground of what I know to be true. Being much troubled to see the falseness of the constitution of the Church of England, I had like to have turned Separatist. Whereupon I kept a day of solemn humiliation and pondering of the thing; this scripture was brought unto me—he that denies Jesus Christ to be come in the flesh is antichrist. This I considered of and in considering found that the papists did not deny him to be come in the flesh, nor we did not deny him—who then was antichrist? Was the Turk antichrist only? The Lord knows that I could not open scripture; he must by his prophetical office open it unto me. . . . I bless the Lord, he hath let me see which was the clear ministry and which the wrong. Since that time I confess I have been more choice and he hath left me to distinguish between the voice of my beloved and the voice of Moses, the voice of John the Baptist and the voice of antichrist, for all those voices are spoken of in scripture. Now if you do condemn me for speaking what in my conscience I know to be truth I must commit myself unto the Lord.

Mr. Nowel [assistant to the Court]. How do you know that was the spirit?

Mrs. H. How did Abraham know that it was God that bid him offer his son, being a breach of the sixth commandment?

Dep. Gov. By an immediate voice.

Mrs. H. So to me by an immediate revelation.

Dep. Gov. How! an immediate revelation.

Mrs. H. By the voice of his own spirit to my soul. I will give you another scripture, Jer[emiah] 46: 27-28—out of which the Lord showed me what he would do for me and the rest of his servants. But after he was pleased to reveal himself to me I did presently, like Abraham, run to Hagar. And after that he did let me see the atheism of my own heart, for which I begged of the Lord that it might not remain in my heart, and being thus, he did show me this (a twelvemonth after) which I told you of before. . . . Therefore, I desire you to look to it, for you see this scripture fulfilled this day and therefore I desire you as you tender the Lord and the church and commonwealth to consider and look what you do. You have power over my body but the Lord Jesus hath power over my body and soul; and assure yourselves thus much, you do as much as in you lies to put the Lord Jesus Christ from you, and if you go on in this course you begin, you will bring a curse upon you and your posterity, and the mouth of the Lord hath spoken it. . . .

Gov. Daniel was delivered by miracle; do you think to be deliver'd so too?

Mrs. H. I do here speak it before the court. I look that the Lord should deliver me by his providence. . . .

Gov. I am persuaded that the revelation she brings forth is delusion. . . .

Gov. The court hath already declared themselves satisfied concerning the things you hear, and concerning the troublesomeness of her spirit and the danger of her course amongst us, which is not to be suffered. Therefore if it be the mind of the court that Mrs. Hutchinson for these things that appear before us is unfit for our society, and if it be the mind of the court that she shall be banished out of our liberties and imprisoned till she be sent away, let them hold up their hands.

[All but three did so.]

Gov. Mrs. Hutchinson, the sentence of the court you hear is that you are banished from out of our jurisdiction as being a woman not fit for our society, and are to be imprisoned till the court shall send you away.

Mrs. H. I desire to know wherefore I am banished?

Gov. Say no more. The court knows wherefore and is satisfied.

READING AND DISCUSSION QUESTIONS

1. According to the transcript, why did Hutchinson run afoul of the colony's leaders? What is the charge against her?

2. Why do the colony's leaders react so strongly when Hutchinson claimed a divine revelation?

3. To what extent were Hutchinson's problems a result of her being female? What does her case reveal about the extent (or absence) of gender equality in Puritan society?

2-4 | Maryland Protects Religious Belief
Maryland Act of Religious Toleration (1649)

Only a dozen years after Anne Hutchinson was banished from Massachusetts Bay, the Maryland Assembly passed the 1649 Toleration Act, which guaranteed religious freedom to all Christians in the colony. This was important to the colony's many Catholics, who feared persecution from the growing presence of Protestants. Protestants had recently threatened the power of the Catholic proprietor Cecilius Calvert, Lord Baltimore, and Calvert urged passage of the Toleration Act just months after the Catholic-sympathizing Charles I of England was beheaded.

Forasmuch as in a well governed and [Christian] Com[m]on Wea[l]th matters concerning Religion and the honor of God ought in the first place to bee taken, into serious consideracon and endeavoured to bee settled. Be it therefore ordered and enacted by the Right [Honorable] Cecilius Lord Baron of Baltemore absolute Lord and Proprietary of this Province with the advise and consent of this Generall

Proceedings and Acts of the General Assembly of Maryland, ed. William Hand Browne (Baltimore: Maryland Historical Society, 1883), 244–247.

Assembly. That whatsoever p[er]son or p[er]sons within this Province and the Islands thereunto belonging shall from henceforth blaspheme God, that is Curse him, or deny our Saviour Jesus Christ to bee the sonne of God, or shall deny the holy Trinity the father sonne and holy Ghost, or the Godhead of any of the said Three p[er]sons of the Trinity or the Unity of the Godhead, or shall use or utter any reproachfull Speeches, words or language concerning the said Holy Trinity, or any of the said three p[er]sons thereof, shalbe punished with death and confiscaton or forfeiture of all his or her lands and goods to the Lord Proprietary and his heires, And bee it also Enacted by the Authority and with the advise and assent aforesaid. That whatsoever p[er]son or p[er]sons shall from henceforth use or utter any reproachfull words or Speeches concerning the blessed Virgin Mary the Mother of our Saviour or the holy Apostles or Evangelists or any of them shall in such case for the first offence forfeit to the said Lord Proprietary and his heirs Lords and Proprietaries of this Province the sume of five pound Sterling or the value thereof to be Levyed on the goods and chattells of every such p[er]son soe offending, but in case such Offender or Offenders, shall not then have goods and chattells sufficient for the satisfyeing of such forfeiture, or that the same bee not otherwise speedily satisfyed that then such Offender or Offenders shalbe publiquely whipt and bee ymprisoned during the pleasure of the Lord Proprietary or the [Lieutenant] or cheife Governor of this Province for the time being. And that every such Offender or Offenders for every second offence shall forfeit tenne pound sterling or the value thereof to bee levyed as aforesaid, or in case such offender or Offenders shall not then have goods and chattells within this Province sufficient for that purpose then to bee publiquely and severely whipt and imprisoned as before is expressed. And that every p[er]-son or p[er]sons before mentioned offending herein the third time, shall for such third Offence forfeit all his lands and Goods and bee for ever banished and expelled out of this Province. And be it also further Enacted by the same authority advise and assent that whatsoever p[er]son or p[er]sons shall from henceforth uppon any occasion of Offence or otherwise in a reproachful manner or Way declare call or denominate any p[er]son or p[er]sons whatsoever inhabiting residing traffiqueing trading or comerceing within this Province or within any the Ports, Harbors, Creeks or Havens to the same belonging an heritick, Scismatick, Idolator, puritan, Independant, Prespiterian popish prest, Jesuite, Jesuited papist, Lutheran, Calvenist, Anabaptist, Brownist, Antinomian, Barrowist, Roundhead, Sep[ar]atist, or any other name or terme in a reproachfull manner relating to matter of Religion shall for every such Offence forfeit and loose the some [of] tenne shillings sterling or the value thereof to bee levyed on the goods and chattells of every such Offender and Offenders, the one half thereof to be forfeited and paid unto the person and persons of whom such reproachfull words are or shalbe spoken or uttered, and the other half thereof to the Lord Proprietary and his heires Lords and Proprietaries of this Province, But if such p[er]son or p[er]sons who shall at any time utter or speake any such reproachfull words or Language shall not have Goods or Chattells sufficient and overt within this Province to bee taken to satisfie the penalty aforesaid or that the same bee not otherwise speedily satisfyed, that then the p[er]son or p[er]sons soe offending shalbe publickly whipt, and shall suffer imprisonmt without baile or maineprise untill he shee or they respectively shall satisfy the party soe offended or greived by such reproachfull Language by asking him or her respectively forgivenes publiquely for such his Offence before the Magistrate or cheife Officer or Officers of the Towne or place where such Offence shalbe given. And be it further likewise Enacted by the Authority and consent aforesaid That every person and persons within this Province that shall at any time hereafter p[ro]phane the Sabbath or Lords day called Sunday by frequent swearing, drunkennes or by any uncivill or disorderly recreacon, or by working on that day when absolute necessity doth not require it shall for every such first offence forfeit 2s. 6d sterling or the value thereof, and for the second offence 5s sterling or the value thereof, and for the third offence and soe for every time he shall offend in like manner afterwards 10s sterling or the value thereof. And in case such offender and offenders shall not have sufficient goods or chattells within this Province to satisfy any of the said Penalties respectively hereby imposed for prophaning the Sabbath or Lords day called Sunday as aforesaid, That in Every such case the [party] soe offending shall for the first and second offence in that kinde be imprisoned till hee or shee shall publickly in open Court before the cheife Commander Judge or Magistrate, of that County Towne or precinct where such offence shalbe committed acknowledg the Scandall and offence he hath in that respect given against God and the good and civill Governemt. of this Province And for the third offence and for every time after shall also bee publickly whipt. And whereas the inforceing of the conscience in matters of Religion hath frequently fallen out to be of dangerous Consequence in those commonwealthes where it hath been practised, And for the more quiett and peaceable governemt. of this Province, and the better to [preserve] mutuall Love and amity amongst the Inhabitants thereof. Be it Therefore also by the Lo: Proprietary with the advise and consent of this Assembly Ordeyned & enacted (except as in this [present] Act is before Declared and sett forth) that noe person or p[er]sons whatsoever within this Province, or the Islands, Ports, Harbors, Creekes, or havens thereunto belonging professing to beleive in Jesus Christ, shall from henceforth bee any waies troubled, Molested or discountenanced for or in respect of his or her religion nor in the free exercise thereof within this Province or the Islands thereunto belonging nor any way compelled to the beleife or exercise of any other Religion against his or her consent, soe as they be not unfaithfull to the Lord Proprietary, or molest or conspire against the civill Governemt. established or to bee established in this Province under him or his heires. And that all & every p[er]son and p[er]sons that shall presume Contrary to this Act and the true intent and meaning thereof directly or indirectly either in person or estate willfully to wrong disturbe trouble or molest any person whatsoever within this Province professing to beleive in Jesus Christ for or in respect of his or her religion or the free exercise thereof within this Province other than is provided for in this Act that such p[er]son or p[er]sons soe offending, shalbe compelled to pay trebble damages to the party soe wronged or molested, and for every such offence shall also forfeit 20s sterling in money or the value thereof, half thereof for the use of the Lo: Proprietary, and his heires Lords and Proprietaries of this Province, and the other half for the use of the party soe wronged or molested as aforesaid, Or if the p[ar]tie soe offending as aforesaid shall refuse or bee unable to recompense the party soe wronged, or to satisfy such fyne or forfeiture, then such Offender shalbe severely punished by publick whipping & imprisonmt during the pleasure of the Lord Proprietary, or his [Lieutenant] or cheife Governor of this Province for the tyme being without baile or maineprise And bee it further alsoe Enacted by the authority and consent aforesaid That the Sheriff or other Officer or Officers from time to time to bee appointed & authorized for that purpose, of the County Towne or precinct where every particular offence in this p[re]sent Act conteyned shall happen at any time to bee comitted and whereuppon there is hereby a forfeiture fyne or penalty imposed shall from time to time distraine and seise the goods and estate of every such p[er]son soe offending as aforesaid against this p[re]sent Act or any p[ar]t thereof, and sell the same or any part thereof for the full satisfaccon of such forfeiture, fine, or penalty as aforesaid, Restoring unto the p[ar]tie soe offending the Remainder or overplus of the said goods or estate after such satisfaccon soe made as aforesaid

The freemen have assented.

READING AND DISCUSSION QUESTIONS

1. What might Lord Baltimore and the Maryland Assembly have been trying to accomplish with their passage of the Toleration Act?

2. What might the Toleration Act reveal to us about the state of affairs in the colony at the time?

3. How did the events taking place in England at that time affect the decisions being made in the colonies?

2-5 | Slave Labor on the Rise
EDMUND WHITE, *Letter to Joseph Morton* (1687)

The colonies participated in a transatlantic economy regulated by a series of Navigation Acts passed by the English Parliament in the seventeenth century. In addition to the sugar, rice, and tobacco exported to England, African slaves were imported to England's North American colonies in increasing numbers by the end of the century. Colonists experimented with different forms of labor, including using white indentured servants, before embracing a race-based slave-labor agricultural system in the Americas. In the letter reproduced here, Edmund White writes from London to South Carolina governor Joseph Morton in February 1687 expressing the advantages of "negroes" over white servants.

The South Carolina Historical and Genealogical Magazine, vol. XXX (January 1929): 2–4.

Sir. . . .

If anything be recoverable there my Lord Cardross told me negroes were more desirable tha[n] English servants [and] such you may have enough of from Barbadoes: or if you desire to be concerned in a small vessel from hence to Ginny [and] your port the Royall Comp[any] now gives leave uppon the allowance of 20 pr. cent? or thereabouts for any vessell to trade to any of their ports [and] they furnish the cargo cheaper than others can buy [and] so the East India Comp[any] permitts ships to trade to this coast: allowing the Comp[any] such a certain profit. Now if you [and] Mr. Grimball or any other would joyne in ordering their corresponds here to fitt out a small vessell to the byte or other port on the Coast of Ginny I understand how to manage it to the best advantage. I have twice lett ships to the Royall Comp[any] but their termes are so hard that they make the owner tak out their freight [1/3] in money [and 2/3rds] in negroes at 15 lb pr head if to Barbadoes; [and] 16 lb pr. head for other ports. Now at Barbadoes I sold the negroes but for 11 lb a head bills of exc. [and] at Nevis for 3000 lb sugr a head but the accompt is not yet cleared [and] it was A . . . er they arrived: so that losing 4 lb a head by the freight negroes there was loss by the ship [and] I gave over those voyages: If you approve not of this way or can have none to joyne [with] you, then write to Coll John Johnson at Barbados that was Major Johnson (for I understand by his son in law Capt Mercer that resides here, that he is much at the bridge though he hath a plantation) that he would do you the kindness, when any bargaine of negroes is to be had, he would buy them for you and keep them upon his plantation till he can send them you [and] this he can doe with much care [and] the negroes will be the better after they have been ashore for sometime an their work will be worth their keeping [and] he may draw upon me [and] I doubt not but he will buy of masters of ships for bills of exchange at 11 or 12 lb a head [and] that will certainly be the most profitable for you [and] you need not trouble your friends for servants from hence: you still fill up yr letters with the bad conditions of the Milkmayd I sent. I shall endeavor the next ship to gett another having lately heard of one that was willing to goe upon wages, and the same party I hope will supply me when I want one. But as to all other serv[ants] let [your] negroes be taught to be smiths shoemakers [and] carpenters [and] bricklayers: they are capable of learning anything [and] I find when they are kindly used [and] have their belly full of victualls and clothes, they are the truest servants: one Coll. Bach that came lately from Jamaica had 100 slaves upon his plantation that prayed God to bless him when he came away [and] prayed him not to dispose of the plantation for they would rather dye than serve another M[aste]r: [and] there was an instance of negroes that did hang themselves on a tree as soon as they heard the plantation was sold: so my friend promised he would not sell [and] since he is dead his widow keeps it during her lyfe; such a love this was between Mr and Mrs [and] slaves: [and] I have often thought: If they could be brought to the knowledge of Christ what a happiness it would be that they came out of their owne country.

READING AND DISCUSSION QUESTIONS

1. What does this letter reveal about the extent of the slave trade by the end of the seventeenth century?

2. What role did Barbados play in the American slave trade?

3. What can you infer from the letter about the author's attitude toward Africans? How is his point of view shaped by his assumptions about race?

2-6 | Spreading the Gospel Among the Iroquois

REV. FATHER LOUIS CELLOT, *Letter to Father François Le Mercier* (1656)

The French Jesuit mission to the Hurons and Iroquois in "New France," the region of Quebec between the Great Lakes and the St. Lawrence River, provides another example of cultural conflict and adaptation. By the mid-seventeenth century, the Jesuits had achieved some success and some fatal failures in their efforts to spread God's word among North American tribes. While spreading their Christian beliefs, they also developed an understanding and appreciation for native cultures. Jesuits sent letters, like this one from 1656, to report the wonder working of God among the "Savages," but they also show the extent to which native and European cultures responded to each other.

[M]Y REVEREND FATHER,
Pax Christi.
After addressing all our vows to Heaven to implore its aid we have recourse to your Reverence to ask your holy blessing, before embarking on the most dangerous and likewise the most glorious enterprise that can be undertaken in this country. We are on the eve of our departure to go and collect what remains of the blood of the Son of God among those peoples, where we have had the happiness of shedding our own and of carrying the light of the Faith to them, although their sole design hitherto has been to extinguish it; that is, we go to establish ourselves among the Iroquois. I think that, in mentioning those Barbarians, I say all that can be said; for their name alone shows the risk which we run and the glory which will accrue to God from the execution of that design.

We are not ignorant of the fact that these Savages have eaten us with relish and have drunk with pleasure the blood of the Fathers of our Society; that their hands and their lips are still wet with it, and that the fires in which they roasted their limbs are not yet quite extinguished. We have not forgotten the conflagrations that they have kindled to consume our houses, and the cruelty that they have practiced on our bodies, which still bear its marks. We know that their

The Jesuit Relations and Allied Documents: Travels and Explorations of the Jesuit Missionaries in New France, 1610–1791, ed. Reuben Gold Thwaites (Cleveland: The Burrows Brothers, 1898), 52–65.

whole policy consists in knowing well how to plot treachery, and to conceal all their plans for it; that no Nero or Diocletian ever declared himself so strongly against the Christians as these bloodthirsty Savages have done against us; and that the Faith would at the present moment be received among many Infidel Nations, had they not surpassed in rage and fury the greatest persecutors of Jesus Christ. We have not yet been able to dry the tears in which, for six years, our eyes have been bathed when we cast them upon the flourishing condition of the Huron Church before those Oppressors had sapped its foundations, making Martyrs of its Pastors, and Saints of most of its members; and leaving but a very pitiful remnant, who have sought refuge under the wing of the French, the only asylum left them in their misfortune. We see that, ever since that first havoc, they have always pushed on their conquests, and have made themselves so redoubtable in this country that everything gives way before their arms. They still have strength in their hands, and perhaps treachery in their hearts; and our allies are so weakened and so reduced in numbers, that barely enough remain to preserve the names of many very populous and very important nations. Notwithstanding all that, we consider ourselves so convinced of the will of God—who, of old, turned his greatest persecutors into his most illustrious Apostles—that we have no doubt that, at the present time, he opens the door to his Preachers, that they might go and plant the faith in the very heart of his enemies, triumph over their barbarity, change those Wolves and Tigers into Lambs, and bring them into the fold of Jesus Christ.

It is not without reason that we conceive such bright hopes. The manifestations of Divine providence and the means employed by its guidance, which has so well directed matters to the point at which they have now arrived, compel us to admit that we cannot, without extreme cowardice, disappoint the expectations that God has caused to arise for us where we least expected them. Had we not observed the finger of God at the outset and in the course of this undertaking, we would have mistrusted our own zeal, and have feared that we were acting with more fervor than prudence; for all human appearances seem to contend against our resolution. But God acts so manifestly, in the whole of this matter, that no one can doubt that it is a work of his hand, the execution and the glory whereof belong solely to him. For what power other than his could force these peoples, inflated with pride on account of their victories, not only to come and seek a peace with us of which they seemed to have no need, but also to place themselves unarmed in our hands, and throw themselves at our feet, begging us to accept them as our friends, when we were so weak that we could no longer withstand them as enemies? They had but to continue, to massacre the remainder of the French Colony, for they met with hardly any resistance either from the French or from the savages, our Confederates; and, nevertheless, for over three years, they incessantly sent presents and embassies to ingratiate themselves with us, and to solicit us to make peace. Old and young, women and children, place themselves at our mercy; they enter our forts; they act confidently with us, and spare no effort to open their hearts to us, and to make us read therein that all their solicitations are as sincere as they are pressing.

They are not content with coming to us, but for a long time they invite us to go to them, and offer us the finest land that they have, and that is to be found in this New world. Neither the necessities of trade nor the hopes of our protection induce them to do all that; for they have hitherto had and still enjoy both those things with the Dutch, much more advantageously than they can ever hope to do with the French. But it is the act of God; he has, doubtless, lent an ear to the blood of the Martyrs, which is the seed of Christians, and which now causes them to spring up in this land that was watered by it. For, not only have those greatest enemies of the Faith given presents to declare that they wish to embrace it; not only have they asked for Preachers to instruct them, and publicly professed in open Council that they were Believers; but the Fathers of our Society who have passed the last winter with them have also observed so many good dispositions for the planting of a new Church among them, not only from the miraculous things that have happened there, as Your Reverence will see in the Journal, but also from the numerous first-fruits already consecrated to heaven, that we depart, with all confidence, to cause the name of Jesus Christ to resound in those lands where the Devil has always been master from the beginning of the world.

If those peoples are so anxious to have us in their country, we feel no less eagerness to leave ours, and to go among them. And this is another proof of the will of God, who disposes all things so opportunely that I find myself equally and agreeably importuned from two very different directions, on one side, by the Iroquois, who urge us; on the other, by our Fathers and Brethren, who eagerly ask to be allowed to join the party. The desire of the former and the zeal of the latter compel me to satisfy them all; and, although the former have hitherto manifested nothing but cruelty, the latter feel only an affection for them, which makes them hold life cheap, and lavish it generously, for the salvation of those who have so often sought to put them to death. I have no doubt that God—who himself governs his work, and who inspires that fervor in the Fathers of our Society who are in these countries—will do likewise in our Houses in France; and will induce many to come and have a share in Conquests so brilliant, although accompanied by incredible labors and very great dangers—or rather, by lofty hopes of dying on the field of battle. I can readily imagine that they Will cast themselves at the feet of Your Reverence, as I see them here embracing mine, in order to obtain the greatest favor that a member of the society of Jesus can expect to obtain; for he can never hope for a greater honor than that of sacrificing himself to carry into barbarism the name of his leader, and to cause him to be adored by the Iroquois.

Divine providence also manifests itself by giving us at this moment a goodly number of our Fathers, who not only have the courage to expose themselves to everything, but also possess the capacity of teaching those Barbarians, whose language, as well as that of many other Nations still more remote, is not very different from that of the Hurons. It is this that revives their fervor and gives to old men, broken down after glorious labors, the courage to desire to go among those peoples, and to spend the remainder of their lives, with the same zeal that they manifested fifteen or twenty years ago when they labored in the Huron Missions. Even those who do not belong to our body feel in their hearts some sparks of the same ardor, and offer to lend a hand to so grand a work. Were one to believe them, either New France would be almost entirely Iroquois, or we would no longer have any French except among the Iroquois, so greatly are they convinced of the sincerity of those nations. That is why, after having well implored the assistance of the Holy Ghost and deliberated upon all the circumstances of that peace, there is not a single person who can reasonably doubt that they are earnest in so persistently seeking to obtain it. . . .

Such is the state of affairs; and such are the effects of so many prayers, mortifications, fasts, alms, and good works, which have been performed in both Frances, and have caused so great a design to be conceived. But, as the undertaking is arduous and difficult of execution, we beg those pious Souls to continue their fervor, so that God may continue to pour his blessings on this country. And, for my part, I beg Your Reverence and all our Fathers and Brethren of your Province to lift your hands to heaven, while we go to declare war against Infidelity, and to fight the devil in the very heart of his country, I am, with all possible respect and submission,

Your Reverence's
Very humble and very obedient servant in Our Lord,
From Montréal, this FRANÇOIS LE MERCIER,
6th of June, 1656

READING AND DISCUSSION QUESTIONS

1. What was the author of this letter trying to accomplish?

2. How does the language of the letter reveal cultural assumptions Jesuit missionaries made about native peoples and culture?

3. What evidence does this letter provide about Jesuit success among the Iroquois?

■ COMPARATIVE QUESTIONS ■

1. What similarities and differences in religious practice do you see in the North American colonies?

2. What do the sources reveal about Europeans' treatment of their non-European neighbors in North America?

3. According to these sources, what were the major challenges facing Europeans settling the North American colonies?

4. To what extent did affairs in Europe affect daily life in the colonies?

DOCUMENT SET

Developing Patterns of Atlantic World Exchange
1450–1700

Imagine the sensation coursing through an Iroquois's body as he spied a European for the first time. What thrill of excitement, wonder, or terror must have seized him, transfixed by a foreboding of change and conflict? The early history of America is very much the story of such encounters. In the Atlantic world during the era of colonization, three richly diverse civilizations (Europeans, Native Americans, and Africans) met and engaged in a lively exchange of goods, peoples, diseases, and ideas that would transform the lives of all involved and shape the formation of North American colonial societies.

The patterns of exchange that emerged resulted in a cultural cross-fertilization as the three groups influenced and were influenced by contact with each other. Europeans and Native Americans traded foods, goods, and cultural assumptions that impacted the diets, trade networks, and worldviews of each. Enslaved Africans brought to the Americas against their will adapted their complex cultural traditions to New World experiences, in turn influencing both Europeans and Native Americans. This exchange left none unaffected, but the benefits were unequally felt, as enslaved Africans knew immediately and as Native Americans discovered when imported European germs decimated their numbers. The colonial societies that emerged on the North American continent were forged by this dynamic exchange.

P1-1 | The Aztec God Tlaloc with Maize

Meal of Maize and Beans, the Sixth Month of the Aztec Solar Calendar (c. 1585)

Much of what we know about the native peoples of the Americas comes filtered through European eyes. Such is the case with this source, a sixteenth-century image from a Jesuit codex (or book) that describes the history and culture of the Aztecs. In this image, Tlaloc, an Aztec god, is shown holding a stalk of corn (or maize), an important indigenous American crop previously unknown to Europeans. This commodity became part of the cross-Atlantic "Columbian Exchange" of foods, goods, and ideas.

Courtesy of the John Carter Brown Library at Brown University.

READING AND DISCUSSION QUESTIONS

1. What does the composition of the image suggest about the importance of maize in Aztec society? What might be the significance of the pictorial elements in this illustration?

2. In what way does this image reveal the extent of the cultural contact between native Aztecs and European colonists?

3. How might a historian use this image to discuss the European interest in Native American culture and the trade in American commodities?

P1-2 | Florida Natives Welcome the Returning French

THEODORE DE BRY, *The Natives of Florida Worship the Column Erected by Commander on His First Voyage* (1591)

As with the Aztec image in the preceding source, this engraving is of European origin, from the pen of Theodore de Bry, so the story it tells privileges the European perspective. Here we see the Timucua, a Native American people in what is now north Florida, welcoming the return of a group of French explorers. An earlier French explorer had erected the column as a monument to the French king, but the native people are shown worshipping it as if it were a god. The column has been wreathed with native garlands, and the foreground showcases North American foodstuffs offered to the visiting Europeans.

READING AND DISCUSSION QUESTIONS

1. What evidence of cultural exchange between Native Americans and Europeans can you see in this illustration? What can you discern about how the artist may have valued that exchange?

2. Who do you think was the audience for this image, and what effect do you imagine the artist hoped to have on those viewing it?

P1-3 | A European Encounters the Algonquin Indians

THOMAS MORTON, *Manners and Customs of the Indians (of New England)* (1637)

While many colonists disparaged Native Americans, Thomas Morton stands out for the esteem with which he held the Algonquin people. Morton migrated to New England in 1622 and established trade with local native populations, a move that angered Puritans who assumed his relationships were tinged with immorality and godlessness. In *New English Canaan* (1637), Morton describes the exchange of native and European commodities and speculates on the advantages this trade might bring.

Of Their Traffic and Trade With One Another: Although these people have not the use of navigation, whereby they may traffic as other nations, that are civilized, use to do, yet do they barter for such commodities as they have, and have a kind of beads instead of money, to buy withal such things as they want, which they call Wampampeak; and it is of two sorts, the one is white, the other is of a violet color. These are made of the shells of fish. The white with them is as silver with us; the other as our gold; and for these beads they buy and sell, not only amongst themselves, but even with us. We have used to sell any of our commodities for this Wampampeak, because we know we can have beaver again of them for it: and these beads are current in all the parts of New England, from one end of the coast to the other.

And although some have endeavored by example to have the like made of the same kind of shells, yet none have ever, as yet, attained to any perfection in the composure of them, but that the savages have found a great difference to be in the one and the other; and have known the counterfeit beads from those of their own making; and have, and do slight them. The skins of beasts are sold and bartered, to such people as have none of the same kind in the parts where they live. Likewise they have earthen pots of divers sizes, from a quart to a gallon, two or three to boil their victuals in; very strong, though they be thin like our iron pots. They have dainty wooden bowls of maple, of high price amongst them; and these are dispersed by bartering one with the other, and are but in certain parts of

The Library of Original Sources, vol. 5, ed. Oliver J. Thatcher (Milwaukee: University Research Extension Co., 1907), 360–377.

the country made, where the several trades are appropriated to the inhabitants of those parts only. So, likewise (at the season of the year), the savages that live by the seaside for trade with the inlanders for fresh water, reles curious silver reles which are bought up of such as have them not frequent in other places: chestnuts, and such like useful things as one place affords, are sold to the inhabitants of another, where they are a novelty accounted amongst the natives of the land. And there is no such thing to barter withal, as is their Wampampeak.

Of Their Magazines or Store Houses: These people are not without providence, though they be uncivilized, but are careful to preserve food in store against winter; which is the corn that they labor and dress in the summer. And, although they eat freely of it, while it is growing, yet have they a care to keep a convenient portion thereof to relieve them in the dead of winter (like to the ant and the bee), which they put under ground. Their barns are holes made in the earth, that will hold a hogshead of corn a piece in them. In these (when their corn is out of the husk and well dried) they lay their store in great baskets (which they make of bark) with mats under, about the sides, and on the top; and putting it into the place made for it, they cover it with earth; and in this manner it is preserved from destruction or putrefaction; to be used in case of necessity, and not else.

And I am persuaded, that if they knew the benefit of salt (as they may in time), and the means to make salt meat fresh again, they would endeavor to preserve fish for winter, as well as corn; and that if anything bring them to civility, it will be the use of salt, to have food in store, which is a chief benefit in a civilized commonwealth. These people have begun already to incline to the use of salt. Many of them would beg salt of me to carry home with them, that had frequented our homes and had been acquainted with our salt meats; and salt I willingly gave them, although I sold them all things else, only because they should be delighted with the use thereof, and think it a commodity of no value in itself, although the benefit was great that might be had by the use of it. . . .

Of a Great Mortality That Happened Amongst the Natives of New England About the Time That the English Came There to Plant: It fortuned some few years before the English came to inhabit at New Plymouth, in New England, that upon some distaste given in the Massachusetts bay by the Frenchmen, then trading there with the natives for beaver, they set upon the men at such advantage that they killed many of them, burned their ship, then riding at anchor by an island there, now called Peddocks island, in memory of Leonard Peddock that landed there (where many wild anckies[1] haunted that time, which he thought had been tame), distributing them unto five sachems, which were lords of the several territories adjoining: they did keep them so long as they lived, only to sport themselves at them, and made these five Frenchmen fetch them wood and water, which is the general work that they require of a servant. One of these five men, outliving the rest, had learned so much of their language as to rebuke them

---

[1]**anckies:** A reference to a now extinct flightless bird once common to North America.

for their bloody deed, saying that God would be angry with them for it, and that he would in his displeasure destroy them; but the savages (it seems boasting of their strength), replied and said, that they were so many that God could not kill them.

But contrary-wise, in short time after the hand of God fell heavily upon them, with such a mortal stroke that they died on heaps as they lay in their houses; and the living, that were able to shift for themselves, would run away and let them die, and let their carcasses lie above the ground without burial. For in a place where many inhabited, there had been but one left to live to tell what became of the rest; the living being (as it seems) not able to bury the dead, they were left for crows, kites and vermin to prey upon. And the bones and skulls upon the several places of their habitations made such a spectacle after my coming into those parts, that, as I travelled in that forest near the Massachusetts, it seemed to me a new found Golgatha. . . .

Of their Acknowledgement of the Creation, and Immortality of the Soul: Although these savages are to be found without religion, law and king (as Sir William Alexander has well observed), yet are they not altogether without the knowledge of God (historically); for they have it amongst them by tradition that God made one man and one woman, bade them live together and get children, kill deer, beasts, birds, fish and fowl, and what they would at their pleasure; and that their posterity was full of evil, and made God so angry that he let in the sea upon them, and drowned the greatest part of them, that were naughty men (the Lord destroyed so); and they went to Sanaconquam, who feeds upon them (pointing to the center of the earth, where they imagine is the habitation of the devil); the other (which were not destroyed) increased the world, and when they died (because they were good) went to the house of Kytan, pointing to the setting of the sun; where they eat all manner of dainties, and never take pains (as now) to provide it. Kytan makes provision (they say) and saves them labor; and there they shall live with him forever, void of care. And they are persuaded that Kytan is he that makes corn grow, trees grow, and all manner of fruits.

And that we that use the book of common prayer do it to declare to them, that cannot read, what Kytan has commanded us, and that we do pray to him with the help of that book; and do make so much account of it, that a savage (who had lived in my house before he had taken a wife, by whom he had children) made this request to me (knowing that I always used him with much more respect than others), that I would let his son be brought up in my house, that he might be taught to read in that book; which request of his I granted; and he was a very joyful man to think that his son should thereby (as he said) become an Englishman; and then he would be a good man. I asked him who was a good man; his answer was, he that would not lie, nor steal.

READING AND DISCUSSION QUESTIONS

1. What conclusion can you draw from Morton's account about the importance of trade for both Native Americans and European colonists? What positive and negative effects does he describe?

2. What can you infer from the document about Morton's view of the long-term relationship between Algonquins and their European-colonist neighbors and the importance of trade to that relationship? How do you think Morton would interpret New England's subsequent history with Native Americans?

3. Can you identify any evidence of remaining "cultural superiority" in Morton's account of Algonquin culture?

P1-4 | The Trade in Goods and Slaves

THOMAS PHILLIPS, *A Journal of a Voyage Made in the Hannibal* (1693–1694)

This firsthand account of the African slave trade reveals the highly developed cross-Atlantic network in commodity exchange that had developed by the end of the seventeenth century. Thomas Phillips, who was the *Hannibal*'s commander, brought European-made products to trade with African kings and chiefs in exchange for slaves whom he then transported to St. Thomas and Barbados for sale primarily to plantation owners cultivating sugar, then a prized commodity in Europe.

[*Feb. 27.*] The castle of Cabo Corce is the chief of all those our African company have upon this coast, and where their agents or chief factors always reside, to which all the other factories are subordinate. This castle has a handsome prospect from the sea, and is a very regular and well contriv'd fortification, and as strong as it can be well made, considering its situation, being encompass'd with a strong and high brick wall, thro' which you enter by a well-secur'd and large gate facing the town, and come into a fine and spacious square wherein 4 or 500 men may very conveniently be drawn up and exercis'd. It has four flankers which have a cover'd communication with each other, and are mounted with good guns. . . .

In this castle the agents and factors have genteel convenient lodgings; and as to the soldiers, I believe there are not better barracks anywhere than here, each two having a handsome room allow'd them, and receive their pay duly and justly in gold dust once a week for their subsistence. The castle has in all about forty guns mounted, some of them brass, and commonly 100 white men in garrison, with a military land officer to discipline and command them under the agents. . . .

Documents Illustrative of the History of the Slave Trade to America, ed. Elizabeth Donnan (Buffalo: William S. Hein & Co., 2002), 395–403, 408–410.

I also carried there on account of the African company, muskets, niconees, tapseals, baysadoes, brass kettles, English carpets, Welsh plains, lead bars, firkins of tallow, powder, etc. None of which did answer expectation, being forc'd to bring back to England a great part of them; and those we sold were at a very low rate. . . .

At Cabo Corce we took in part of the Indian corn order'd us for the provision of our negroes to Barbadoes, the allowance being a chest which contains about four bushels for every negro. It is charg'd the company at two achies per chest, and bare measure; but we could buy better of the blacks at an achy and ½, and heap'd measure. Here is some palm oil, but it is cheaper at Whidaw, tho' the island of St. Thomas is the cheapest place, and where there is most plenty of it. . . .

[*Apr. 26.*] . . . and after dinner I went ashore to Mr. Searle the factor here, to know where and when we should send for the corn assign'd us here by the chief merchants at cape Corce, there being not enough to supply us there, and therefore were to call for the rest at this place, and Acna [Accra?], to compleat our quantity of 700 chests each. Mr. Searle immediately order'd what quantity he had to be delivered us whenever our boats came for it, and entertain'd us very lovingly till night when Capt. Shurley and I went on board. Animabo lies in the Kingdom of Fantine, is a pretty large town; the negro inhabitants are accounted very bold and stout fellows, but the most desperate treacherous villains, and greatest cheats upon the whole coast, for the gold here is accounted the worst, and the most mix'd with brass, of any in Guiney; it lies about 4 leagues to the East of Cabo Corce. Our castle is pretty strong, of about 18 guns, where we were very kindly entertained by Mr. Searle some days, and by Mr. Cooper at Aga on other days. Aga is a small thatch'd house, about half a mile to the east from Animabo, on the sea-shore, having little or no defence except a few muskets. . . .

May the 12th. . . . Here [Accra] Mr. John Bloome the factor order'd us the remainder of our corn, to compleat 700 chests apiece, which we got aboard, fill'd some water, and had pretty good trade. . . .

May the 19th. Steering along shore within three leagues, with fine easy gale, we spy'd a canoe making off towards us, whereupon we lay by and staid for her; when she came aboard the master of her brought in three women and four children to sell, but they ask'd very dear for them, and they were almost dead for want of victuals, looking like meer skeletons, and so weak that they could not stand, so that they were not worth buying; he promis'd to procure us 2 or 300 slaves if we would anchor, come ashore, and stay three or four days, but judging what the others might be, by the sample he brought us, and being loth to venture ashore upon his bare word, where we did not use to trade, and had no factory, we sent him away, and pursu'd our voyage; besides that we were upon the Alampo coast, which negroes are esteem'd the worst and most washy of any that are brought to the West-Indies, and yield the least price; why I know not, for they seem as well limb'd and lusty as any other negroes, and the only difference I perceiv'd in them, was, that they are not so black as the others, and are all circumcis'd, which no negroes else upon the whole coast (as I observ'd) are: The negroes most in demand at Barbadoes, are the gold coast, or, as they call them,

Cormantines,[1] which will yield 3 or 4 *l.* a head more then the Whidaws, or, as they call them, Papa negroes; but these are preferr'd before the Angola, as they are before the Alampo, which are accounted the worst of all. . . .

May the 21st. This morning I went ashore at Whidaw, accompany'd by my doctor and purser, Mr. Clay, the present Capt. of the East-India Merchant, his doctor and purser, and about a dozen of our seamen for our guard, arm'd, in order here to reside till we could purchase 1300 negro slaves, which was the number we both wanted, to compleat 700 for the Hannibal, and 650 for the East-India Merchant, according to our agreement in our charter-parties with the royal African company; in procuring which quantity of slaves we spent about nine weeks. . . .

Our factory [at Whydah] lies about three miles from the sea-side, where we were carry'd in hamocks, which the factor Mr. Joseph Peirson, sent to attend our landing, with several arm'd blacks that belong'd to him for our guard; we were soon truss'd in a bag, toss'd upon negroes heads, and convey'd to our factory. . . .

Our factory built by Capt. Wiburne, Sir John Wiburne's brother, stands low near the marshes, which renders it a very unhealthy place to live in; the white men the African company send there, seldom returning to tell their tale: 'tis compass'd round with a mud-wall, about six foot high, and on the south-side is the gate; within is a large yard, a mud thatch'd house, where the factor lives, with the white men; also a store-house, a trunk for slaves, and a place where they bury their dead white men, call'd, very improperly, the hog-yard; there is also a good forge, and some other small houses. . . . And here I must observe that the rainy season begins about the middle of May, and ends the beginning of August, in which space it was my misfortune to be there, which created sicknesses among my negroes aboard, it being noted for the most malignant season by the blacks themselves, who while the rain lasts will hardly be prevail'd upon to stir out of their huts. . . .

The factory prov'd beneficial to us in another kind; for after we had procured a parcel of slaves, and sent them down to the sea-side to be carry'd off, it sometimes proved bad weather, and so great a sea, that the canoes could not come ashore to fetch them, so that they returned to the factory, where they were secured and provided for till good weather presented, and then were near to embrace the opportunity, we sometimes shipping off a hundred of both sexes at a time.

The factor, Mr. Peirson, was a brisk man, and had good interest with the king, and credit with the subjects, who knowing their tempers, which is very dastard, had good skill in treating them both civil and rough, as occasion requir'd; most of his slaves belonging to the factory, being gold coast negroes, who are very bold, brave, and sensible, ten of which would beat the best forty men the king of Whidaw had in his kingdom; besides their true love, respect and fidelity

---

[1]**Cormantines**: Gold Coast slaves from the West African region now called Ghana.

to their master, for whose interest or person they will most freely expose their own lives. . . .

As soon as the king understood of our landing, he sent two of his cappasheirs, or noblemen, to compliment us at our factory, where we design'd to continue, that night, and pay our devoirs to his majesty next day, which we signify'd to them, and they, by a foot-express, to their monarch; whereupon he sent two more of his grandees to invite us there that night, saying he waited for us, and that all former captains used to attend him the first night: whereupon being unwilling to infringe the custom, or give his majesty any offence, we took our hamocks, and Mr. Peirson, myself, Capt. Clay, our surgeons, pursers, and about 12 men, arm'd for our guard, were carry'd to the king's town, which contains about 50 houses. . . .

We returned him thanks by his interpreter, and assur'd him how great affection our masters, the royal African company of England, bore to him, for his civility and fair and just dealings with their captains; and that notwithstanding there were many other places, more plenty of negro slaves that begg'd their custom, yet they had rejected all the advantageous offers made them out of their good will to him, and therefore had sent us to trade with him, to supply his country with necessaries, and that we hop'd he would endeavour to continue their favour by his kind usage and fair dealing with us in our trade, that we may have our slaves with all expedition, which was the making of our voyage; that he would oblige his cappasheirs to do us justice, and not impose upon us in their prices; all which we should faithfully relate to our masters, the royal African company, when we came to England. He answer'd that the African company was a very good brave man; that he lov'd him; that we should be fairly dealt with, and not impos'd upon; But he did not prove as good as his word; nor indeed (tho' his cappasheirs shew him so much respect) dare he do any thing but what they please . . . so after having examin'd us about our cargoe, what sort of goods we had, and what quantity of slaves we wanted, etc., we took our leaves and return'd to the factory, having promised to come in the morning to make our palavera, or agreement, with him about prices, how much of each of our goods for a slave.

According to promise we attended his majesty with samples of our goods, and made our agreement about the prices, tho' not without much difficulty; he and his cappasheirs exacted very high, but at length we concluded as per the latter end; then we had warehouses, a kitchen, and lodgings assign'd us, but none of our rooms had doors till we made them, and put on locks and keys; next day we paid our customs to the king and cappasheirs, as will appear hereafter; then the bell was order'd to go about to give notice to all people to bring their slaves to the trunk to sell us: this bell is a hollow piece of iron in shape of a sugar loaf, the cavity of which could contain about 50 lb. of cowries: This a man carry'd about and beat with a stick, which made a small dead sound. . . .

Capt. Clay and I had agreed to go to the trunk to buy the slaves by turns, each his day, that we might have no distraction or disagreement in our trade, as often happens when there are here more ships than one, and the commanders can't set their horses together, and go hand in hand in their traffick, whereby they have a check upon the blacks, whereas their disagreements create animosities, underminings, and out-bidding each other, whereby they enhance the prices to their general loss and detriment, the blacks well knowing how to make the best use of such opportunities, and as we found make it their business, and endeavour to create and foment misunderstandings and jealousies between commanders, it turning to their great account in the disposal of their slaves.

When we were at the trunk, the king's slaves, if he had any, were the first offer'd to sale, which the cappasheirs would be very urgent with us to buy, and would in a manner force us to it ere they would shew us any other, saying they were the Reys Cosa, and we must not refuse them, tho' as I observ'd they were generally the worst slaves in the trunk, and we paid more for them than any others, which we could not remedy, it being one of his majesty's prerogatives: then the cappasheirs each brought out his slaves according to his degree and quality, the greatest first, etc. and our surgeon examin'd them well in all kinds, to see that they were sound wind and limb, making them jump, stretch out their arms swiftly, looking in their mouths to judge of their age; for the cappasheirs are so cunning, that they shave them all close before we see them, so that let them be never so old we can see no grey hairs in their heads or beards; and then having liquor'd them well and sleek with palm oil, 'tis no easy matter to know an old one from a middle-age one, but by the teeths decay; but our greatest care of all is to buy none that are pox'd, lest they should infect the rest aboard. . . .

When we had selected from the rest such as we liked, we agreed in what goods to pay for them, the prices being already stated before the king, how much of each sort of merchandize we were to give for a man, woman, and child, which gave us much ease, and saved abundance of disputes and wranglings, and gave the owner a note, signifying our agreement of the sorts of goods; upon delivery of which the next day he receiv'd them; then we mark'd the slaves we had bought in the breast, or shoulder, with a hot iron, having the letter of the ship's name on it, the place being before anointed with a little palm oil, which caus'd but little pain, the mark being usually well in four or five days, appearing very plain and white after.

When we had purchas'd to the number of 50 or 60 we would send them aboard, there being a cappasheir, intitled the captain of the slaves, whose care it was to secure them to the water-side, and see them all off; and if in carrying to the marine any were lost, he was bound to make them good, to us, the captain of the trunk being oblig'd to do the like, if any ran away while under his care, for after we buy them we give him charge of them till the captain of the slaves comes to carry them away: These are two officers appointed by the king for this purpose, to each of which every ship pays the value of a slave in what goods they like best for their trouble, when they have done trading; and indeed they discharg'd their duty to us very faithfully, we not having lost one slave thro' their neglect in 1300 we bought here.

There is likewise a captain of the sand, who is appointed to take care of the merchandize we have come ashore to trade with, that the negroes do not plunder them, we being often forced to leave goods a whole night on the sea shore, for want of porters to bring them up; but notwithstanding his care and authority, we often came by the loss, and could have no redress.

When our slaves were come to the seaside, our canoes were ready to carry them off to the longboat, if the sea permitted, and she convey'd them aboard ship, where the men were all put in irons, two and two shackled together, to prevent their mutiny, or swimming ashore.

The negroes are so wilful and loth to leave their own country, that they have often leap'd out of the canoes, boat and ship, into the sea, and kept under water till they were drowned, to avoid being taken up and saved by our boats, which pursued them; they having a more dreadful apprehension of Barbadoes than we can have of hell, tho' in reality they live much better there than in their own country; but home is home, etc: we have likewise seen divers of them eaten by the sharks, of which a prodigious number kept about the ships in this place, and I have been told will follow her hence to Barbadoes, for the dead negroes that are thrown over-board in the passage. I am certain in our voyage there we did not want the sight of some every day, but that they were the same I can't affirm.

We had about 12 negroes did wilfully drown themselves, and others starv'd themselves to death; for 'tis their belief that when they die they return home to their own country and friends again.

I have been inform'd that some commanders have cut off the legs and arms of the most wilful, to terrify the rest, for they believe if they lose a member, they cannot return home again: I was advis'd by some of my officers to do the same, but I could not be perswaded to entertain the least thought of it, much less put in practice such barbarity and cruelty to poor creatures, who, excepting their want of christianity and true religion (their misfortune more than fault) are as much the works of God's hands, and no doubt as dear to him as ourselves; nor can I imagine why they should be despis'd for their colour, being what they cannot help, and the effect of the climate it has pleas'd God to appoint them. I can't think there is any intrinsick value in one colour more than another, nor that white is better than black, only we think so because we are so, and are prone to judge favourably in our own case, as well as the blacks, who in odium of the colour, say, the devil is white, and so paint him. . . .

Having bought my compliment of 700 slaves, *viz.* 480 men and 220 women, and finish'd all my business at Whidaw, I took my leave of the old king, and his cappasheirs, and parted, with many affectionate expressions on both sides, being forced to promise him that I would return again the next year, with several things he desired me to bring him from England; and having sign'd bills of lading to Mr. Peirson, for the negroes aboard, I set sail the 27th of July in the morning, accompany'd with the East-India Merchant, who had bought 650 slaves, for the island of St. Thomas, with the wind at W.S.W. . . .

We supply'd ourselves with some Indian corn, figolas, or kidney-beans, plantins, yams, potatoes, cocoa-nuts, limes, oranges, etc., for the use and refreshment of our negroes, at the following rates, *viz.*

Indian corn at two alcars per dollar.

Figolas or kidney beans, at dollars three per chest, which would contain near four bushels.

Plantins at dollars two and a half per thousand, by tale.

Yams, which are great large roots, and eat very sweet, much like potato in taste, at dollars 25 per thousand, by tale.

Cocoa-nuts at dollars 10 per thousand nuts.

Limes, oranges, limons, bananas, etc. for little or nothing. . . .

Having completed all my business ashore in fourteen days that I lay here, yesterday in the afternoon I came off with a resolution to go to sea. Accordingly about six in the evening we got up our anchors, and set sail for Barbadoes, being forc'd to leave the East-India Merchant behind, who could not get ready to sail in nine or ten days; which time I could not afford to stay, in respect to the mortality of my negroes, of which two or three died every day, also the small quantity of provisions I had to serve for my passage to Barbadoes. . . .

We spent in our passage from St. Thomas to Barbadoes two months eleven days, from the 25th of August to the 4th of November following: in which time there happen'd much sickness and mortality among my poor men and negroes, that of the first we buried 14, and of the last 320, which was a great detriment to our voyage, the royal African company losing ten pounds by every slave that died, and the owners of the ship ten pounds ten shillings, being the freight agreed on to be paid them by the charter-party for every negroe deliver'd alive ashore to the African company's agents at Barbadoes; whereby the loss in all amounted to near 6560 pounds sterling. The distemper which my men as well as the blacks mostly die of, was the white flux, which was so violent and inveterate, that no medicine would in the least check it; so that when any of our men were seiz'd with it, we esteem'd him a dead man, as he generally proved. I cannot imagine what should cause it in them so suddenly, they being free from it till about a week after we left the island of St. Thomas. And next to the malignity of the climate, I can attribute it to nothing else but the unpurg'd black sugar, and raw unwholesome rum they bought there, of which they drank in punch to great excess, and which it was not in my power to hinder, having chastis'd several of them, and flung over-board what rum and sugar I could find. . . .

The negroes are so incident to the small-pox, that few ships that carry them escape without it, and sometimes it makes vast havock and destruction among them: but tho' we had 100 at a time sick of it, and that it went thro' the ship, yet we lost not above a dozen by it. All the assistance we gave the diseased was only as much water as they desir'd to drink, and some palm-oil to anoint their sores, and they would generally recover without any other helps but what kind nature gave them.

One thing is very surprizing in this distemper among the blacks, that tho' it immediately infects those of their own colour, yet it will never seize a white man; for I had several white men and boys aboard that had never had that distemper, and were constantly among the blacks that were sick of it, yet none of them in the least catch'd it, tho' it be the very same malady in its effects, as well as symptoms, among the blacks, as among us in England, beginning with the pain in the head, back, shivering, vomiting, fever, etc. But what the small-pox spar'd, the flux swept off, to our great regret, after all our pains and care to give them their messes in due order and season, keeping their lodgings as clean and sweet as possible, and enduring so much misery and stench so long among a parcel of creatures nastier than swine; and after all our expectations to be defeated by their mortality. No gold-finders can endure so much noisome slavery as they do who carry negroes; for those have some respite and satisfaction, but we endure twice the misery; and yet by their mortality our voyages are ruin'd, and we pine and fret our selves to death, to think that we should undergo so much misery, and take so much pains to so little purpose.

I deliver'd alive at Barbadoes to the company's factors 372, which being sold, came out at about nineteen pounds per head one with another. . . .

READING AND DISCUSSION QUESTIONS

1. What evidence does Phillips's account provide to the historian writing a history of the Atlantic world trade during the late seventeenth century?

2. Analyze Phillips's account of his slave-trading activities for any evidence that he shared (or was untroubled by) the concerns that traffic in slaves raised for someone like Father Sandoval, whose queries prompted Brother Luis Brandaon's justification of the trade (Document 1-6).

P1-5 | Making the Case for Colonization
RICHARD HAKLUYT, *A Discourse of Western Planting* (1584)

Richard Hakluyt, like many Europeans, strongly endorsed the colonization of the Americas, pointing to the manifold advantages available to those nations that planted settlements there. In 1584, Hakluyt, a geographer and a leading figure in court politics, addressed Elizabeth I in support of Sir Walter Raleigh's design to establish the Virginia colony. In his *Discourse*, Hakluyt joined religious and political arguments in support of colonization with a vision of English trade in New World goods, providing a market for English manufactures and a source of materials for home consumption.

A [brief] collection of certaine reasons to induce her Majestie and the state to take in hande the westerne voyadge and the plantinge there.

1. The soyle yeldeth, and may be made to yelde, all the severall comodities of Europe, and of all kingdomes, domynions, and territories that England tradeth withe, that by trade of marchandize cometh into this realme.

Richard Hakluyt, *Discourse Concerning Western Planting*, ed. Lenard Woods and Charles Deane (Cambridge, MA: Press of John Wilson and Son, 1877), 152–161.

2. The passage thither and home is neither to longe nor to shorte, but easie, and to be made twise in the yere.

3. The passage cutteth not nere the trade of any prince, nor nere any of their contries or territories, and is a safe passage, and not easie to be annoyed by prince or potentate whatsoever.

4. The passage is to be perfourmed at all times of the yere, and in that respecte passeth our trades in the Levant Seas within the Straites of Juberalter, and the trades in the seas within the Kinge of Denmarkes Straite, and the trades to the portes of Norwey and of Russia, &c.; for as in the south weste Straite there is no passage in somer by lacke of windes, so within the other places there is no passage in winter by yse [ice] and extreme colde.

5. And where England nowe for certen hundreth yeres last passed, by the peculiar comoditie of wolles, and of later yeres by clothinge of the same, hath raised it selfe from meaner state to greater wealthe and moche higher honour, mighte, and power then before, to the equallinge of the princes of the same to the greatest potentates of this parte of the worlde; it cometh nowe so to passe, that by the greate endevour of the increase of the trade of wolles in Spaine and in the West Indies, nowe daily more and more multiplienge, that the wolles of England, and the clothe made of the same, will become base, and every day more base then other; which, prudently weyed, [yet] behoveth this realme, [if] it meane not to returne to former olde meanes and basenes, but to stande in present and late former honour, glorye, and force, and not negligently and sleepingly to slyde into beggery, to foresee and to plante at Norumbega or some like place, were it not for any thing els but for the hope of the vent of our woll indraped, the principall and in effecte the onely enrichinge contynueinge naturall comoditie of this realme. And effectually pursueinge that course, wee shall not onely finde on that tracte of lande, and especially in that firme northwarde (to whome warme clothe shalbe righte wellcome), an ample vente, but also shall, from the north side of that firme, finde oute knowen and unknowen ilandes and domynions replenished with people that may fully vent the aboundaunce of that our comoditie, that els will in fewe yeres waxe of none or of small value by forreine aboundaunce, &c.; so as by this enterprice wee shall shonne the ymmynent mischefe hanginge over our heades, that els muste nedes fall upon the realme, without breache of peace or sworde drawen againste this realme by any forreine state; and not offer our auncient riches to scornefull neighboures at home, nor sell the same in effecte for nothinge, as wee shall shortly, if presently it be not provaided for. The increase of the wolles of Spaine and America is of highe pollicie, with greate desire of our overthrowe, endevoured; and the goodnes of the forren wolles our people will not enter into the consideration of, nor will not beleve aughte, they be so sotted with opinion of their owne; and, yf it be not foresene and some such place of vent provided, farewell the goodd state of all degrees in this realme.

6. This enterprise may staye the Spanishe Kinge from flowinge over all the face of that waste firme of America, yf wee seate and plante there in time. . . . And England possessinge the purposed place of plantinge, her Majestie may, by the benefete of the seate, havinge wonne goodd and royall havens, have plentie of

excellent trees for mastes, of goodly timber to builde shippes and to make greate navies, of pitche, tarr, hempe, and all thinges incident for a navie royall, and that for no price, and withoute money or request. Howe easie a matter may yt be to this realme, swarminge at this day with valiant youthes, rustinge and hurtfull by lacke of employment, and havinge goodd makers of cable and of all sortes of cordage, and the best and moste connynge shipwrights of the worlde, to be lordes of all those sees, and to spoile Phillipps Indian navye, and to deprive him of yerely passage of his treasure into Europe, and consequently to abate the pride of Spaine and of the supporter of the greate Antechriste of Rome, and to pull him downe in equallitie to his neighbour princes, and consequently to cutt of the common mischefes that come to all Europe by the peculiar aboundaunce of his Indian treasure, and thiss withoute difficultie.

7. This voyadge, albeit it may be accomplished by barke or smallest pynnesse for advise or for a necessitie, yet for the distaunce, for burden and gaine in trade, the marchant will not for profitts sake use it but by shippes of greate burden; so as this realme shall have by that meane shippes of greate burden and of greate strengthe for the defence of this realme, and for the defence of that newe seate, as nede shall require, and withall greate increase of perfecte seamen, which greate princes in time of warres wante, and which kinde of men are neither nourished in fewe daies nor in fewe yeres.

8. This newe navie of mightie newe stronge shippes, so in trade to that Norumbega and to the coastes there, shall never be subjecte to arreste of any prince or potentate, as the navie of this realme from time to time hath bene in the portes of thempire, in the portes of the Base Contries, in Spaine, Fraunce, Portingale, &c., in the tymes of Charles the Emperour, Fraunces the Frenche kinge, and others; but shall be alwayes free from that bitter mischeefe, withoute grefe or hazarde to the marchaunte or to the state, and so alwaies readie at the comaundement of the prince with mariners, artillory, armor, and munition, ready to offende and defende as shalbe required.

9. The greate masse of wealthe of the realme imbarqued in the marchantes shippes, caried oute in this newe course, shall not lightly, in so farr distant a course from the coaste of Europe, be driven by windes and tempestes into portes of any forren princes, as the Spanishe shippes of late yeres have bene into our portes of the Weste Contries, &c.; and so our marchantes in respecte of private state, and of the realme in respecte of a generall safetie from venture of losse, are by this voyadge oute of one greate mischefe.

10. No forren commoditie that comes into England comes withoute payment of custome once, twise, or thrise, before it come into the realme, and so all forren comodities become derer to the subjectes of this realme; and by this course to Norumbega forren princes customes are avoided; and the forren comodities cheapely purchased, they become cheape to the subjectes of England, to the common benefite of the people, and to the savinge of greate treasure in the realme; whereas nowe the realme becomethe poore by the purchasinge of forreine comodities in so greate a masse at so excessive prices.

11. At the firste traficque with the people of those partes, the subjectes of this realme for many yeres shall chaunge many cheape comodities of these partes for thinges of highe valor there not estemed; and this to the greate inrichinge of the realme, if common use faile not.

12. By the greate plentie of those regions the marchantes and their factors shall lye there cheape, buye and repaire their shippes cheape, and shall returne at pleasure withoute staye or restrainte of forreine prince; whereas upon staies and restraintes the marchaunte raiseth his chardge in sale over of his ware; and, buyenge his wares cheape, he may mainteine trade with smalle stocke, and withoute takinge upp money upon interest; and so he shalbe riche and not subjecte to many hazardes, but shalbe able to afforde the comodities for cheape prices to all subjectes of the realme.

13. By makinge of shippes and by preparinge of things for the same, by makinge of cables and cordage, by plantinge of vines and olive trees, and by makinge of wyne and oyle, by husbandrie, and by thousandes of thinges there to be done, infinite nombers of the Englishe nation may be set on worke, to the unburdenynge of the realme with many that nowe lyve chardgeable to the state at home.

14. If the sea coste serve for makinge of salte, and the inland for wine, oiles, oranges, lymons, figges, &c., and for makinge of yron, all which with moche more is hoped, withoute sworde drawen, wee shall cutt the combe of the Frenche, of the Spanishe, of the Portingale, and of enemies, and of doubtfull frendes, to the abatinge of their wealthe and force, and to the greater savinge of the wealthe of the realme.

15. The substaunces servinge, wee may oute of those partes receave the masse of wrought wares that now wee receave out of Fraunce, Flaunders, Germanye, &c.; and so wee may daunte the pride of some enemies of this realme, or at the leaste in parte purchase those wares, that nowe wee buye derely of the Frenche and Flemynge, better cheape; and in the ende, for the parte that this realme was wonte to receave, dryve them oute of trade to idlenes for the settinge of our people on worke.

16. Wee shall by plantinge there inlarge the glory of the gospell, and from England plante sincere relligion, and provide a safe and a sure place to receave people from all partes of the worlde that are forced to flee for the truthe of Gods worde.

17. If frontier warres there chaunce to aryse, and if thereupon wee shall fortifie, yt will occasion the trayninge upp of our youthe in the discipline of warr, and make a nomber fitt for the service of the warres and for the defence of our people there and at home.

18. The Spaniardes governe in the Indies with all pride and tyranie; and like as when people of contrarie nature at the sea enter into gallies, where men are tied as slaves, all yell and crye with one voice, *Liberta, liberta,* as desirous of libertie and freedome, so no doubte whensoever the Queene of England, a prince of such clemencie, shall seate upon that firme of America, and shalbe reported

throughe oute all that tracte to use the naturall people there with all humanitie, curtesie, and freedome, they will yelde themselves to her government, and revolte cleane from the Spaniarde, and specially when they shall understande that she hathe a noble navie, and that she aboundeth with a people moste val-iaunte for theyr defence. . . . [H]er Majestie and her subjectes may bothe enjoye the treasure of the mynes of golde and silver, and the whole trade and all the gaine of the trade of marchandize, that nowe passeth thither by the Spaniardes onely hande, of all the comodities of Europe; which trade of marchandize onely were of it selfe suffycient (withoute the benefite of the riche myne) to inriche the subjectes, and by customes to fill her Majesties coffers to the full. And if it be highe pollicie to mayneteyne the poore people of this realme in worke, I dare affirme that if the poore people of England were five times so many as they be, yet all mighte be sett on worke in and by workinge lynnen, and suche other thinges of marchandize as the trade into the Indies dothe require.

19. The present shorte trades causeth the maryner to be cast of, and ofte to be idle, and so by povertie to fall to piracie. But this course to Norumbega beinge longer, and a contynuaunce of themploymente of the maryner, dothe kepe the maryner from ydlenes and from necessitie; and so it cutteth of the principal actions of piracie, and the rather because no riche praye for them to take cometh directly in their course or any thing nere their course.

20. Many men of excellent wittes and of divers singuler giftes, overthrowen by suertishippe, by sea, or by some folly of youthe, that are not able to live in England, may there be raised againe, and doe their contrie goodd service; and many nedefull uses there may (to greate purpose) require the savinge of greate nombers, that for trifles may otherwise be devoured by the gallowes.

21. Many souldiers and servitours, in the ende of the warres, that mighte be hurtfull to this realme, may there be unladen, to the common profite and quiet of this realme, and to our forreine benefite there, as they may be employed.

22. The frye of the wandringe beggars of England, that growe upp ydly, and hurtefull and burdenous to this realme, may there be unladen, better bredd upp, and may people waste contries to the home and forreine benefite, and to their owne more happy state.

23. If Englande crie oute and affirme, that there is so many in all trades that one cannot live for another, as in all places they doe, this Norumbega (if it be thoughte so goodd) offreth the remedie.

READING AND DISCUSSION QUESTIONS

1. What conclusions can you draw about European perceptions of North America's potential from Hakluyt's arguments in support of colonization?

2. To what extent do you think Hakluyt's sixteenth-century vision of colonization was realized during the seventeenth century? What aspects of the cultural exchange between Europeans, North American natives, and Africans did he fail to anticipate?

▪ COMPARATIVE QUESTIONS ▪

1. What do these sources reveal about the challenges facing the various cultures that collided in the early period of American colonial settlement?

2. Compare European assessments of Africans and Native Americans. What differences do you see in how Europeans described these two different groups of people? How, for example, do the attitudes displayed by Columbus (Document 1-3), Thomas Morton (Document P1-3), and Father Louis Cellot (Document 2-6) toward Native Americans differ from those expressed about Africans by Thomas Phillips (Document P1-4) and Edmund White (Document 2-5)?

3. What might you rank as the most historically significant effect of the cultural exchange between Europeans, Native Americans, and Africans during the period from the mid-fifteenth century to the end of the seventeenth century? In answering this question, what definition of "historically significant" helps you to evaluate the evidence?

4. To what extent did the patterns of exchange between Europeans, Africans, and Native Americans shape the development of the North American colonies?

3

The British Atlantic World
1660–1750

In England in 1688, the much-despised King James II was deposed during the Glorious Revolution. From the late seventeenth to the mid-eighteenth century, the British colonies in North America entered into their maturity under the new limited monarchy of William and Mary. Several sources included here hint at the growing self-consciousness of North American colonists who increasingly viewed themselves as British subjects with rights that government was bound to respect.

Political maturity went hand in hand with colonial economic development. As Great Britain developed its Atlantic trade, the colonies became critical partners in the imperial trade networks. One tragic consequence of economic expansion was the increased use and reliance on slave labor, the effects of which are described in two of the sources included here. Great Britain's imperial ambitions also resulted in a series of military conflicts with its European neighbors that spread to the North American colonies. Unable to avoid warfare, some colonists developed strategic alliances with Native Americans. The willingness of Native Americans to ally with the colonists had less to do with friendly feelings toward the Americans and more with their recognition of the colonists' growing power on the continent.

3-1 | Bostonians Welcome the Glorious Revolution

The Declaration of the Gentlemen, Merchants and Inhabitants of Boston, and the Country Adjacent (1689)

Following the 1660 restoration of the Stuart monarchy, relations between Massachusetts Bay and England deteriorated. James II revoked the colony's charter and instituted the Dominion of New England with the wildly unpopular and authoritarian Sir Edmund Andros appointed governor in 1686. When news of James II's overthrow reached the colonies in April 1689, Bostonians immediately drafted a declaration, a portion of which appears below, which detailed their complaints against the Andros regime. As a result of the colonial challenge to his leadership, Andros's government fell and colonists reasserted local representative government.

April 18, 1689.

I. We have seen more than a decad of Years rolled away since the English World had the Discovery of an horrid Popish Plot, wherein the bloody Devotoes of Rome had in their Design and Prospect no less than the Extinction of the Protestant Religion: which mighty Work they called the utter subduing of a Pestilent Heresy; wherein (they said) there never were such Hopes of Success since the Death of Queen Mary, as now in our Days. And we were of all Men the most insensible, if we should apprehend a Countrey so remarkable for the true Profession and pure Exercise of the Protestant Religion as New-England is, wholly unconcerned in the Infamous Plot. To crush and break a Countrey so entirely and signally made up of Reformed Churches, and at length to involve it in the miseries of an utter Extirpation, must needs carry even a Supcrerogation of Merit with it among such as were intoxicated with a Bigotry inspired into them by the great Scarlet Whore.

II. To get us within the reach of the Desolation desired for us, it was no improper thing that we should first have our Charter vacated, and the Hedge which kept us from the wild Beasts of the Field, effectually broken down. The Accomplishment of this was hastned by the unwearied Sollicitations and slanderous Accusations of a Man, for his Malice and Falshood well known unto us all. Our Charter was with a most injurious Pretence (and scarce that) of Law, condemned before it was possible for us to appear at Westminster in the legal Defence of it; and without a fair leave to answer for our selves, concerning the Crimes falsly laid to our Charge, we were put under a President and Council, without any liberty for an Assembly, which the other American Plantations have, by a Commission from his Majesty.

III. The Commission was as Illegal for the Form of it, as the Way of obtaining it was Malicious and Unreasonable: yet we made no Resistance thereunto as we

Narratives of the Insurrections, 1675–1690, ed. Charles M. Andrews (New York: Charles Scribner's Sons, 1915), 175–182.

could easily have done; but chose to give all Mankind a Demonstration of our being a People sufficiently dutiful and loyal to our King: and this with yet more Satisfaction, because we took Pains to make our selves believe as much as ever we could of the Whedle then offer'd unto us; That his Magesty's Desire was no other then the happy Encrease and Advance of these Provinces by their more immediate Dependance on the Crown of England. And we were convinced of it by the Courses immediately taken to damp and spoyl our Trade; whereof Decayes and Complaints presently filled all the Country; while in the mean time neither the Honour nor the Treasure of the King was at all advanced by this new Model of our Affairs, but a considerable Charge added unto the Crown.

IV. In little more than half a Year we saw this Commission superseded by another yet more absolute and Arbitrary, with which Sir Edmond Andross arrived as our Governour: who besides his Power, with the Advice and Consent of his Council, to make Laws and raise Taxes as he pleased, had also Authority by himself to Muster and Imploy all Persons residing in the Territory as occasion shall serve; and to transfer such Forces to any English Plantation in America, as occasion shall require. And several Companies of Souldiers were now brought from Europe, to support what was to be imposed upon us, not without repeated Menaces that some hundreds more were intended for us.

V. The Government was no sooner in these Hands, but Care was taken to load Preferments principally upon such Men as were Strangers to and Haters of the People: and every ones Observation hath noted, what Qualifications recommended a Man to publick Offices and Employments, only here and there a good Man was used, where others could not easily be had; the Governour himself, with Assertions now and then falling from him, made us jealous that it would be thought for his Majesties Interest, if this People were removed and another succeeded in their room: And his far-fetch'd Instruments that were growing rich among us, would gravely inform us, that it was not for his Majesties Interest that we should thrive. But of all our Oppressors we were chiefly squeez'd by a Crew of abject Persons fetched from New York, to be the Tools of the Adversary, standing at our right Hand; by these were extraordinary and intollerable Fees extorted from every one upon all Occasions, without any Rules but those of their own insatiable Avarice and Beggary; and even the probate of a Will must now cost as many Pounds perhaps as it did Shillings heretofore; nor could a small Volume contain the other Illegalities done by these Horse-leeches in the two or three Years that they have been sucking of us; and what Laws they made it was as impossible for us to know, as dangerous for us to break; but we shall leave the Men of Ipswich or Plimouth (among others) to tell the Story of the Kindness which has been shown them upon this Account. Doubtless a Land so ruled as once New-England was, has not without many Fears and Sighs beheld the wicked walking on every Side, and the vilest Men exalted.

VI. It was now plainly affirmed, both by some in open Council, and by the same in private Converse, that the People in New-England were all Slaves, and the only difference between them and Slaves is their not being bought and sold;

and it was a Maxim delivered in open Court unto us by one of the Council, that we must not think the Priviledges of English men would follow us to the End of the World: Accordingly we have been treated with multiplied Contradictions to Magna Charta, the Rights of which we laid claim unto. Persons who did but peaceably object against the raising of Taxes without an Assembly, have been for it fined, some twenty, some thirty, and others fifty Pounds. Packt and pickt Juries have been very common things among us, when, under a pretended Form of Law, the Trouble of some honest and worthy Men has been aimed at: but when some of this Gang have been brought upon the Stage, for the most detestable Enormities that ever the Sun beheld, all Men have with Admiration seen what Methods have been taken that they might not be treated according to their Crimes. Without a Verdict, yea, without a Jury sometimes have People been fined most unrighteously; and some not of the meanest Quality have been kept in long and close Imprisonment without any the least Information appearing against them, or an Habeas Corpus allowed unto them. In short, when our Oppressors have been a little out of Mony, 'twas but pretending some Offence to be enquired into, and the most innocent of Men were continually put into no small Expence to answer the Demands of the Officers, who must have Mony of them, or a Prison for them, tho none could accuse them of any Misdemeanour.

VII. To plunge the poor People every where into deeper Incapacities, there was one very comprehensive Abuse given to us; Multitudes of pious and sober Men through the Land scrupled the Mode of Swearing on the Book, desiring that they might Swear with an uplifted Hand, agreeable to the ancient Custom of the Colony; and though we think we can prove that the Common Law amongst us (as well as in some other places under the English Crown) not only indulges, but even commands and enjoins the Rite of lifting the Hand in Swearing; yet they that had this Doubt, were still put by from serving upon any Juries; and many of them were most unaccountably Fined and Imprisoned. Thus one Grievance is a Trojan Horse, in the Belly of which it is not easy to recount how many insufferable Vexations have been contained.

VIII. Because these Things could not make us miserable fast enough, there was a notable Discovery made of we know not what flaw in all our Titles to our Lands; and tho, besides our purchase of them from the Natives, and besides our actual peaceable unquestioned Possession of them for near threescore Years, and besides the Promise of K. Charles II. in his Proclamation sent over to us in the Year 1683, That no Man here shall receive any Prejudice in his Free-hold or Estate, We had the Grant of our Lands, under the Seal of the Council of Plimouth: which Grant was Renewed and Confirmed unto us by King Charles I. under the Great Seal of England; and the General Court which consisted of the Patentees and their Associates, had made particular Grants hereof to the several Towns (though 'twas now deny'd by the Governour, that there was any such Thing as a Town) among us; to all which Grants the General Court annexed for the further securing of them, A General Act, published under the Seal of the Colony, in the Year 1684. Yet we were every day told, That no Man was owner of a Foot of Land in all the Colony. Accordingly, Writs of Intrusion began every where to be served on

People, that after all their Sweat and their Cost upon their formerly purchased Lands, thought themselves Freeholders of what they had. And the Governor caused the Lands pertaining to these and those particular Men, to be measured out for his Creatures to take possession of; and the Right Owners, for pulling up the Stakes, have passed through Molestations enough to tire all the Patience in the World. They are more than a few, that were by Terrors driven to take Patents for their Lands at excessive rates, to save them from the next that might petition for them: and we fear that the forcing of the People at the Eastward hereunto, gave too much Rise to the late unhappy Invasion made by the Indians on them. Blanck Patents were got ready for the rest of us, to be sold at a Price, that all the Mony and Moveables in the Territory could scarce have paid. And several Towns in the Country had their Commons begg'd by Persons (even by some of the Council themselves) who have been privately encouraged thereunto, by those that sought for Occasions to impoverish a Land already Peeled, Meeted out and Trodden down.

IX. All the Council were not ingaged in these ill Actions, but those of them which were true Lovers of their Country were seldom admitted to, and seldomer consulted at the Debates which produced these unrighteous Things: Care was taken to keep them under Disadvantages; and the Governor, with five or six more, did what they would. We bore all these, and many more such Things, without making any attempt for any Relief; only Mr. Mather,[1] purely out of respect unto the Good of his Afflicted Country, undertook a Voyage into England; which when these Men suspected him to be preparing for, they used all manner of Craft and Rage, not only to interrupt his Voyage, but to ruin his Person too. God having through many Difficulties given him to arrive at White-hall, the King, more than once or twice, promised him a certain Magna Charta for a speedy Redress of many Things which we were groaning under: and in the mean time said, That our Governor should be written unto, to forbear the Measures that he was upon. However, after this, we were injured in those very Things which were complained of; and besides what Wrong hath been done in our Civil Concerns, we suppose the Ministers and the Churches every where have seen our Sacred Concerns apace going after them: How they have been Discountenanced, has had a room in the Reflection of every Man, that is not a Stranger in our Israel.

X. And yet that our Calamity might not be terminated here, we are again Briar'd in the Perplexities of another Indian War; how, or why, is a mystery too deep for us to unfold. And tho' 'tis judged that our Indian Enemies are not above 100 in Number, yet an Army of One thousand English hath been raised for the Conquering of them; which Army of our poor Friends and Brethren now under Popish Commanders (for in the Army as well as in the Council, Papists are in Commission) has been under such a Conduct, that not one Indian hath been

---

[1]**Mather:** The Reverend Increase Mather, a leading Puritan minister, who lobbied on behalf of the colony in England.

kill'd, but more English are supposed to have died through sickness and hardship, than we have Adversaries there alive; and the whole War hath been so managed, that we cannot but suspect in it a Branch of the Plot to bring us low; which we leave to be further enquir'd into in due time.

XI. We did nothing against these Proceedings, but only cry to our God; they have caused the cry of the Poor to come unto him, and he hears the cry of the Afflicted. We have been quiet hitherto, and so still we should have been, had not the Great God at this time laid us under a double engagement to do something for our Security: besides what we have in the strangely unanimous Inclination which our Countrymen by extreamest necessities are driven unto. For first, we are informed that the rest of the English America is alarmed with just and great Fears, that they may be attaqu'd by the French, who have lately ('tis said) already treated many of the English with worse then Turkish Cruelties; and while we are in equal Danger of being surprised by them, it is high time we should be better guarded, than we are like to be while the Government remains in the hands by which it hath been held of late. Moreover, we have understood, (though the Governour has taken all imaginable care to keep us all ignorant thereof) that the Almighty God hath been pleased to prosper the noble Undertaking of the Prince of Orange,[2] to preserve the three Kingdoms from the horrible brinks of Popery and Slavery, and to bring to a condign Punishment those worst of Men, by whom English Liberties have been destroy'd; in compliance with which glorious Action we ought surely to follow the Patterns which the Nobility, Gentry and Commonalty in several parts of those Kingdoms have set before us, though they therein chiefly proposed to prevent what we already endure.

XII. We do therefore seize upon the Persons of those few ill Men which have been (next to our Sins) the grand Authors of our Miseries; resolving to secure them, for what Justice, Orders from his Highness with the English Parliament shall direct, lest, ere we are aware, we find (what we may fear, being on all sides in Danger) our selves to be by them given away to a Forreign Power, before such Orders can reach unto us; for which Orders we now humbly wait. In the mean time firmly believing, that we have endeavoured nothing but what meer Duty to God and our Country calls for at our Hands: We commit our Enterprise unto the Blessing of Him, who hears the cry of the Oppressed, and advise all our Neighbours, for whom we have thus ventured our selves, to joyn with us in Prayers and all just Actions, for the Defence of the Land.

READING AND DISCUSSION QUESTIONS

1. What charges do the inhabitants of Boston make against the Andros regime?
2. What rights do Bostonians claim? Upon what do they base their claims?

---

[2]**Prince of Orange**: William of Orange, who became William III, reigning as king of England, Ireland, and Scotland.

3. To what extent does this document suggest an important turning point within the long period between 1607 and 1750 covered by this chapter?

3-2 | The Onondaga Pledge Support to Colonies

CANASSATEGO, *Papers Relating to an Act of the Assembly of the Province of New York* (1742)

As the colonies developed, settlers in search of land began moving farther west away from the eastern seaboard. Frequently, this movement put them in contact with Native Americans upon whose lands they encroached. Treaties had attempted to settle land disputes, but conflict often persisted. In this source, Canassatego (c. 1684–1750), an Onondaga leader and representative of the Iroquois Confederacy, speaks to Brother Onas (the governor of Pennsylvania, George Thomas). The two leaders met in July 1744 to negotiate the Treaty of Lancaster between Virginia, Maryland, and the Iroquois. References to the French threat remind us of the persisting tensions between the two European rivals.

Brother Onas,

Yesterday you expressed your Satisfaction in having been instrumental to our meeting with our Brethren of Virginia and Maryland, we, in return, assure you, that we have great Pleasure in this Meeting, and thank you for the Part you have had in bringing us together, in order to create a good Understanding, and to clear the Road; and, in Token of our Gratitude, we present you with this String of Wampum.

Which was received with the usual Ceremony.

Brother Onas,

You was pleased Yesterday to inform us, "That War had been declared between the great King of England and the French King; that two great Battles had been fought, one by Land, and the other at Sea; with many other Particulars." We are glad to hear the Arms of the King of England were successful, and take part with you in your Joy on this Occasion. You then came nearer Home, and told us, "You had left your House, and were come thus far on Behalf of the whole People of Pensylvania to see us; to renew your Treaties, to brighten the Covenant-Chain, and to confirm your Friendship with us." We approve this Proposition, we thank you for it. We own, with Pleasure, that the Covenant-Chain between us and Pensylvania is of old Standing, and has never contracted any Rust; we wish it may always continue as bright as it has done hitherto; and, in Token of the Sincerity of our Wishes, we present you with this Belt of Wampum.

Which was received with the Yo-hah.

The History of the Five Indian Nations of Canada (London: T. Osborne, 1747), 143–145.

Brother Onas,

You was pleased Yesterday to remind us of our mutual Obligation to assist each other in case of a War with the French, and to repeat the Substance of what we ought to do by our Treaties with you; and that as a War had been already entered into with the French, you called upon us to assist you, and not to suffer the French to march through our Country to disturb any of your Settlements.

In answer, we assure you we have all these Particulars in our Hearts, they are fresh in our Memory. We shall never forget that you and we have but one Heart, one Head, one Eye, one Ear, and one Hand. We shall have all your Country under our Eye, and take all the Care we can to prevent any Enemy from coming into it; and, in proof of our Care, we must inform you, that before we came here, we told Onandio, our Father, as he is called, that neither he, nor any of his People, should come through our Country, to hurt our Brethren the English, or any of the Settlements belonging to them; there was Room enough at Sea to fight, there he might do what he pleased, but he should not come upon our Land to do any Damage to our Brethren. And you may depend upon our using our utmost Care to see this effectually done; and, in Token of our Sincerity, we present you with this Belt of Wampum.

Which was received with the usual Ceremony.

After some little Time the Interpreter said, Canassatego had forgot something material, and desired to mend his Speech, and to do so as often as he should omit any thing of Moment, and thereupon he added:

The Six Nations have a great Authority and Influence over sundry Tribes of Indians in Alliance with the French, and particularly over the Praying Indians, formerly a Part with ourselves, who stand in the very Gates of the French; and, to shew our further Care, we have engaged these very Indians, and other Indian Allies of the French for you. They will not join the French against you. They have have [*sic*] agreed with us before we set out. We have put the Spirit of Antipathy against the French in those People. Our Interest is very considerable with them, and many other Nations, and as far as ever it extends, we shall use it for your Service.

READING AND DISCUSSION QUESTIONS

1. What does Canassatego's speech reveal about the role Native Americans played in the disputes between British colonists and their French rivals?
2. What is Canassatego trying to accomplish with his speech?

3-3 | Virginia Tightens Slave Codes

THE GENERAL ASSEMBLY OF VIRGINIA, *An Act for Suppressing Outlying Slaves* (1691)

By the end of the seventeenth century, the British colonies in North America had transitioned from indentured servants to African slaves as their primary source of labor. In Virginia, this transition was hastened by Bacon's Rebellion, which demonstrated to colonial leaders the value of creating a permanent underclass defined by race. As Virginians struggled to make sense of slavery's social implications, the growing number of African slaves in the colony presented new challenges. The Virginia legislature attempted to address some of those issues with this 1691 act.

Whereas many times negroes, mulattoes, and other slaves unlawfully absent themselves from their masters and mistresses service, and lie hid and lurk in obscure places killing hoggs and committing other injuries to the inhabitants of this dominion, for remedy whereof for the future, *Be it enacted by their majesties lieutenant governour, councell and burgesses of this present generall assembly, and the authoritie thereof, and it is hereby enacted*, that in all such cases upon intelligence of any such negroes, mulattoes, or other slaves lying out, two of their majesties justices of the peace of that county, whereof one to be of the quorum, where such negroes, mulattoes or other slave shall be, shall be impowered and commanded, and are hereby impowered and commanded to issue out their warrants directed to the sherrife of the same county to apprehend such negroes, mulattoes, and other slaves, which said sherriffe is hereby likewise required upon all such occasions to raise such and soe many forces from time to time as he shall think convenient and necessary for the effectual apprehending such negroes, mulattoes and other slaves, and in case any negroes, mulattoes or other slave or slaves lying out as aforesaid shall resist, runaway, or refuse to deliver and surrender him or themselves to any person or persons that shall be by lawfull authority employed to apprehend and take such negroes, mulattoes or other slaves that in such cases it shall and may be lawfull for such person and persons to kill and distroy such negroes, mulattoes, and other slave or slaves by gunn or any otherwaise whatsoever.

Provided that where any negroe or mulattoe slave or slaves shall be killed in pursuance of this act, the owner or owners of such negro or mulatto slave shall be paid for such negro or mulatto slave four thousand pounds of tobacco by the publique. And for prevention of that abominable mixture and spurious issue which hereafter may encrease in this dominion, as well by negroes, mulattoes, and Indians intermarrying with English, or other white women, as by their

The Statutes at Large; Being a Collection of All the Laws of Virginia, From the First Session of the Legislature in the Year 1619, ed. William Waller Hening (Philadelphia: Thomas DeSilver, 1823), 86–88.

unlawfull accompanying with one another, *Be it enacted by the authoritie aforesaid, and it is hereby enacted,* that for the time to come, whatsoever English or other white man or woman being free shall intermarry with a negroe, mulatto, or Indian man or woman bond or free shall within three months after such marriage be banished and removed from this dominion forever, and that the justices of each respective countie within this dominion make it their perticular care, that this act be put in effectuall execution. *And be it further enacted by the authoritie aforesaid, and it is hereby enacted,* That if any English woman being free shall have a bastard child by any negro or mulatto, she pay the sume of fifteen pounds sterling, within one moneth after such bastard child shall be born, to the Church wardens of the parish where she shall be delivered of such child, and in default of such payment she shall be taken into the possession of the said Church wardens and disposed of for five yeares, and the said fine of fifteen pounds, or whatever the woman shall be disposed of for, shall be paid, one third part to their majesties for and towards the support of the government and the contingent charges thereof, and one other third part to the use of the parish where the offence is committed, and the other third part to the informer, and that such bastard child be bound out as a servant by the said Church wardens untill he or she shall attaine the age of thirty yeares, and in case such English woman that shall have such bastard child be a servant, she shall be sold by the said church wardens, (after her time is expired that she ought by law to serve her master) for five yeares, and the money she shall be sold for divided as is before appointed, and the child to serve as aforesaid.

And forasmuch as great inconveniences may happen to this country by the setting of negroes and mulattoes free, by their either entertaining negro slaves from their masters service, or receiveing stolen goods, or being grown old bringing a charge upon the country; for prevention thereof, *Be it enacted by the authority aforesaid, and it is hereby enacted,* That no negro or mulatto be after the end of this present session of assembly set free by any person or persons whatsoever, unless such person or persons, their heires, executors or administrators pay for the transportation of such negro or negroes out of the countrey within six moneths after such setting them free, upon penalty of paying of tenn pounds sterling to the Church wardens of the parish where such person shall dwell with, which money, or so much thereof as shall be necessary, the said Church wardens are to cause the said negro or mulatto to be transported out of the countrey, and the remainder of the said money to imploy to the use of the poor of the parish.

READING AND DISCUSSION QUESTIONS

1. What specific concerns are Virginians attempting to address with this legislation?
2. What does this document suggest about the Virginia colonists' notions about race, identity, and sexual relations between different racial groups?

3-4 | Gentility and the Planter Elite

WILLIAM BYRD II, *Diary Entries* (1709–1712)

Though Virginia planters like William Byrd II lived on the periphery of the British Empire, they emulated the manners and interests of Britain's aristocratic class. Byrd was born in Virginia in 1674, but educated in London. When his father died, he returned to Virginia to manage the family lands that he inherited. Byrd's diary reveals his efforts to cultivate gentility through the books he read, the behavior he exhibited, and the relations he nurtured with peers and subordinates. Byrd's life demonstrates a growing self-consciousness among southern elites eager to fashion identities at the intersection of British and colonial cultures.

June 1709

15. I rose at 5 o'clock and read two chapters in Hebrew and some Greek in Josephus. I said my prayers and ate milk for breakfast. Captain C-l-t brought me some letters from England and offered me freight in his ship. He brought a parson with him, Mr. Goodwin. He ate his breakfast here and went away about 9 o'clock. I ate dry beef for dinner, and chicken. While we were at dinner Captain M-r-n came with some more letters. He brought me a coaler recommended by Colonel Blakiston. He brought me also some goods for my wife, to an extravagant value. My letters gave me a sad prospect of the tobacco trade in England. My wife continued very ill. I sent Tommy to Williamsburg to inquire for my letters. I took a walk about the plantation. I said my prayers and had good thoughts, good humor and good health, thanks be to God Almighty, only I feared I was going to have the piles.

16. I rose at 5 o'clock and read a chapter in Hebrew and a little Greek. I neglected to say my prayers and ate milk for breakfast. Mr. Bland's boy brought me abundance of letters from Williamsburg, out of the men-of-war. I spent all the morning in reading them. My orders for being of the Council arrived among the rest. By these letters I learned that tobacco was good for nothing, that protested bills would ruin the country, that our trade with the Carolina Indians was adjusted in England, that my sister Braynes was in [prison by the cruelty of C-r-l-y], that my salary was in a fair way of being increased, that the College was like to be rebuilt by the Queen's bounty, that there was a probability of a peace next winter. I ate mutton for dinner. While we were at dinner, Colonel Harrison, Mr. Commissary, and Mr. Wormeley came to see us, but would not eat with us. They likewise brought me some letters. Captain Wilcox dined with us. His people brought me a box of [. . .] from P-r-c-r. I walked about the plantation. Mr. Wormeley and I played at billiards and I won half a crown. I said my prayers. All the company went away. I had good health, good thoughts, and good humor, thank God Almighty.

William Byrd, *The Secret Diary of William Byrd of Westover 1709–1712*, ed. Louis B. Wright and Marion Tinling (Richmond, VA: The Dietz Press, 1941).

17. I rose at 5 o'clock and read some Greek in Josephus and perused some of my new books. I said my prayers, and ate milk for breakfast. I settled my accounts. We expected some company but they disappointed us. I ate roast mutton for dinner. In the afternoon we rode to my neighbor Harrison's where we stayed till the evening with Mr. [Gee]. Here I ate some apple pie. Mr. Harrison had the same bad account of tobacco in England and advised me to ship none by this ship. I promised to give no more than £12 per ton. He told me that several gentlemen were extremely in debt with Mr. Perry. In the evening we returned home, where we found all very well, thanks be to God Almighty. I said my prayers and had good health, good thoughts, and good humor, thanks be to God Almighty. . . .

25. I rose at 6 o'clock this morning and read two chapters in Hebrew and some Greek in Josephus. I said my prayers and ate milk for breakfast. I danced my dance. Tom S-d-s-n came from Falling Creek and told me the stone cutter was dead [w-l m-l-r]. I read some Latin and some news. I ate some bacon fraise for dinner. In the afternoon Mr. Bland's sloop brought my things from aboard Captain M-r-n's ship, which had received no damage. My man John got drunk, for which I reprimanded him severely. I walked about the plantation in the evening. I said my prayers and had good thoughts, good health, and good humor, thanks be to God Almighty. . . .

27. I rose at 5 o'clock and read two chapters in Hebrew and some Greek in Josephus. I said my prayers and ate milk for breakfast. I danced my dance. I made an invoice of the things that my wife could spare to be sold. I settled the accounts of protested bills. I ate mutton for dinner. My wife was in tears about her [cargo] but I gave her some comfort after dinner. Mr. Bland came with Henry Randolph to see me and soon after Mr. Harrison and his wife and daughter. They stayed till 7 o'clock and then went away. In the evening we took a walk [about] the plantation. I recommended myself to God in a short prayer. I had good health, good thoughts, and good humor, thanks be to God Almighty. Tom was whipped for not telling me that he was sick.

28. I rose at 5 o'clock and read two chapters in Hebrew and some Greek in Josephus. I said my prayers and ate milk for breakfast. The sloop came up with my things from Captain Browne with my goods which were not so much damaged as I expected. I was angry with the people for staying so long. They sailed away this morning with George the coaler to Falling Creek. I ate cold mutton and sallet for dinner. In the afternoon I read some news and some Latin and also some Greek in Homer. In the evening I took a walk about the plantation. I said my prayers. I had good health, good thoughts, and good humor, thanks be to God Almighty.

29. I rose at 5 o'clock and read only some Greek in Josephus, because I was hindered by Daniel who came last night from Williamsburg where the sea sloop is safe arrived, thanks be to God Almighty. Two of her men were pressed by the men-of-war, notwithstanding the proclamation. Wheat sold for about six shillings a bushel in Madeira and wine for £8 a pipe with the exchange. Captain Browne and Captain Collins came to see me. I said my prayers and ate milk for

breakfast. I began to reap my wheat. I ate bacon and pork for dinner. In the afternoon Mr. Bland came to counsel the proper measures to be taken with the sloop and it was agreed he should go down to take care of the cargo and he went accordingly and was caught in a great shower of rain. Daniel behaved himself very foolishly. In the evening the rain hindered my walking and lasted above an hour. I said my prayers. I had good health, good thoughts, and good humor, thanks be to God Almighty. . . .

February 1711

5. I rose about 8 o'clock and found my cold still worse. I said my prayers and ate milk and potatoes for breakfast. My wife and I quarreled about her pulling her brows. She threatened she would not go to Williamsburg if she might not pull them; I refused, however, and got the better of her, and maintained my authority. About 10 o'clock we went over the river and got to Colonel Duke's about 11. There I ate some toast and canary. Then we proceeded to Queen's Creek, where we found all well, thank God. We ate roast goose for supper. The women prepared to go to the Governor's the next day and my brother and I talked of old stories. My cold grew exceedingly bad so that I thought I should be sick. M. _____ gave me some sage tea and leaves of [s-m-n-k] which made me mad all night so that I could not sleep but was much disordered by it. I neglected to say my prayers in form but had good thoughts, good humor, and indifferent health, thank God Almighty.

6. I rose about 9 o'clock but was so bad I thought I should not have been in condition to go to Williamsburg, and my wife was so kind to [say] she would stay with me, but rather than keep her from going I resolved to go if possible. I was shaved with a very dull razor, and ate some boiled milk for breakfast but neglected to say my prayers. About 10 o'clock I went to Williamsburg without the ladies. As soon as I got there it began to rain, which hindered about [*sic*] the company from coming. I went to the President's where I drank tea and went with him to the Governor's and found him at home. Several gentlemen were there and about 12 o'clock several ladies came. My wife and her sister came about 2. We had a short Council but more for form than for business. There was no other appointed in the room of Colonel Digges. My cold was a little better so that I ventured among the ladies, and Colonel Carter's wife and daughter were among them. It was night before we went to supper, which was very fine and in good order. It rained so that several did not come that were expected. About 7 o'clock the company went in coaches from the Governor's house to the capitol where the Governor opened the ball with a French dance with my wife. Then I danced with Mrs. Russell and then several others and among them the rest Colonel Smith's son, who made a sad freak. Then we danced country dances for an hour and the company was carried into another room where was a very fine collation of sweetmeats. The Governor was very gallant to the ladies and very courteous to the gentlemen. About 2 o'clock the company returned in the coaches and because the drive was dirty the Governor carried the ladies into their coaches. My wife

and I lay at my lodgings. Colonel Carter's family and Mr. Blair were stopped by the unruliness of the horses and Daniel Wilkinson was so gallant as to lead the horses himself through all the dirt and rain to Mr. Blair's house. My cold continued bad. I neglected to say my prayers and had good thoughts, good humor, but indifferent health, thank God Almighty. It rained all day and all night. The President had the worst clothes of anybody there.

7. I rose at 8 o'clock and found my cold continued. I said my prayers and ate boiled milk for breakfast. I went to see Mr. Clayton who lay sick of the gout. About 11 o'clock my wife and I went to wait on the Governor in the President's coach. We went there to take our leave but were forced to stay all day. The Governor had made a bargain with his servants that if they would forbear to drink upon the Queen's birthday, they might be drunk this day. They observed their contract and did their business very well and got very drunk today, in such a manner that Mrs. Russell's maid was forced to lay the cloth, but the cook in that condition made a shift to send in a pretty little dinner. I ate some mutton cutlets. In the afternoon I persuaded my wife to stay all night in town and so it was resolved to spend the evening in cards. My cold was very bad and I lost my money. About 10 o'clock the Governor's coach carried us home to our lodgings where my wife was out of humor and I out of order. I said a short prayer and had good thoughts and good humor, thank God Almighty. . . .

May 1712

22. I rose about 6 o'clock and read two chapters in Hebrew and some in Greek in Lucian. I said my prayers and ate boiled milk for breakfast. I danced my dance. It rained a little this morning. My wife caused Prue to be whipped violently notwithstanding I desired not, which provoked me to have Anaka whipped likewise who had deserved it much more, on which my wife flew into such a passion that she hoped she would be revenged of me. I was moved very much at this but only thanked her for the present lest I should say things foolish in my passion. I wrote more accounts to go to England. My wife was sorry for what she had said and came to ask my pardon and I forgave her in my heart but she seemed to resent, that she might be the more sorry for her folly. She ate no dinner nor appeared the whole day. I ate some bacon for dinner. In the afternoon I wrote two more accounts till the evening and then took a walk in the garden. I said my prayers and was reconciled to my wife and gave her a flourish in token of it. I had good health, good thoughts, but was a little out of humor, for which God forgive me.

READING AND DISCUSSION QUESTIONS

1. To what extent does the diary provide evidence for Byrd's self-fashioning as both a colonial American elite and a British subject?

2. From the excerpt, what can you infer about the role Byrd saw himself playing in colonial American society? What roles do you see him playing within his household, colony, and empire?

3. Why might Byrd have written and kept a diary? Do you think he expected others to read it? Evaluate the diary as a source for historians interested in understanding early-eighteenth-century Virginia society. What are its advantages and limitations?

3-5 | Trade Creates Dynamic Commercial Economy

JOHN BARNARD, *The Autobiography of the Rev. John Barnard* (1766)

The local impact of the Atlantic trade is clearly evident in this reminiscence by the Reverend John Barnard (1681–1770) of Marblehead, Massachusetts. Barnard was a graduate of Harvard and studied for the ministry under the famous Puritan leaders Increase and Cotton Mather. Barnard delivered more than six thousand sermons during his long life. In his autobiography, a portion of which is included here, he describes some of the changes he witnessed as Marblehead became ever more connected to British trade networks.

When I first came, [in 1714] there were two companies of poor, smoke-dried, rude, ill-clothed men, trained to no military discipline but that of *"whipping the snake,"* as they called it; whereas now, [in 1766] and for years past, we are a distinct regiment, consisting of seven full companies, well clad, of bright countenances, vigorous and active men, so well trained in the use of their arms, and the various motions and marches, that I have heard some Colonels of other regiments, and a Brigadier General say, they never saw throughout the country, not in their own regiment, no, nor in Boston, so goodly an appearance of spirited men, and so well exercised a regiment. When I came, there was not so much as one proper carpenter, nor mason, nor tailor, nor butcher in the town, nor any thing of a market worth naming; but they had their houses built by country workmen, and their clothes made out of town, and supplied themselves with beef and pork from Boston, which drained the town of its money. But now we abound in artificers, and some of the best, and our markets large, even to a full supply. And, what above all I would remark, there was not so much as one foreign trading vessel belonging to the town, nor for several years after I came into it; though no town had really greater advantages in their hands. The people contented themselves to be the slaves that digged in the mines, and left the merchants of Boston, Salem, and Europe, to carry away the gains; by which means the town was always in dismally poor circumstauces, involved in debt to the merchants more than they were worth; nor could I find twenty families in it that, upon the best examination, could stand upon their own legs; and they were generally as rude, swearing, drunken, and fighting a crew, as they were poor. Whereas, not only are the public ways vastly mended, but the manners of the people greatly cultivated; and we have many gentleman-like and polite families, and the very fishermen generally scorn the rudenesses of the former generation.

I soon saw that the town had a price in its hands, and it was a pity they had not a heart to improve it. I therefore laid myself out to get acquaintance with the English masters of vessels, that I might by them be let into the mystery of the fish trade, and in a little time I gained a pretty thorough understanding in it. When I saw the advantages of it, I thought it my duty to stir up my people, such as I thought would hearken to me, and were capable of practising upon the advice, to send the fish to market themselves, that they might reap the benefit of it, to the enriching themselves, and serving the town. But, alas! I could inspire no man with courage and resolution enough to engage in it, till I met with Mr. Joseph Swett, a young man of strict justice, great industry, enterprising genius, quick apprehension, and firm resolution, but of small fortune. To him I opened myself fully, laid the scheme clearly before him, and he hearkened unto me, and was wise enough to put it in practice. He first sent a small cargo to Barbadoes. He soon found he increased his stock, built vessels, and sent the fish to Europe, and prospered in the trade, to the enriching of himself; and some of his family, by carrying on the trade, have arrived at large estates. The more promising young men of the town soon followed his example; that now we have between thirty and forty ships, brigs, snows, and topsail schooners engaged in foreign trade. From so small a beginning the town has risen into its present flourishing circumstances, and we need no foreigner to transport our fish, but are able ourselves to send it all to the market. Let God have the praise, who has redeemed the town from a state of bondage into a state of liberty and freedom.

READING AND DISCUSSION QUESTIONS

1. How does Barnard measure progress? What kinds of changes over time does he identify as evidence of Marblehead's development?

2. What factors does he identify as key to the colony's rapid advance?

3. What do you think Barnard meant when he thanked God for redeeming the colony from a "state of bondage into a state of liberty and freedom"?

3-6 | Colonists Assert Their Rights
LORD CORNBURY, *Letter to the Lords of Trade* (1704)

One measure of the colonists' growing independence can be seen in the letter Lord Cornbury sent to the Lords of Trade. Cornbury was Edward Hyde, the 3rd Earl of Clarendon (1661–1723), who served as the colonial governor of New York and New Jersey from 1701 to 1708.

Documents Relative to the Colonial History of the State of New York, ed. E. B. O'Callaghan (Albany, NY: Weed, Parsons and Company, Printers, 1854), 1120–1123.

Queen Anne removed him from office after complaints of misconduct mounted against him. (His political opponents also spread scurrilous rumors that he dressed in women's clothing.) In this letter, Cornbury discusses relations with Native Americans and exposes what he described as the colonial assembly's "sawcy" behavior. New Yorkers were acting in ways that he believed challenged the royal prerogative.

My Lords.

In my letter of the 30th of June last I gave Your Lord[ships] an account of the reasons why no more of my letters came safe to Your hands, occasioned by the taking of our homeward bound ships and the want of intelligence here from other parts of the Continent. I did acquaint Your Lord[ships] that I hoped to propose a remedy for the latter, at my meeting with Coll. Nicholson and Coll Seymour at which time I likewise hoped we should have seen Coll. Dudley, he having writ me word, that he would meet them here; I did intend to have proposed to them, the laying a Tax in each province by Act of Assembly, for the settling and defraying the charges of the post, which then might have gone from Boston to North Carolina; but this meeting was hindered by several accidents; first, Coll. Dudley was busy about his expedition to the Eastward, Coll. Nicholson was hindered by the sitting of the Assembly of Virginia, and as soon as the Assembly of New Yorke was over, and I thought to go into New Jersey, to the Assembly which was to sit at Burlington, I was forced to adjourn them, in order to go up to Albany where there was an alarum that the French were marching towards that place with a thousand French and Indians. I went, and when I arrived there I found the people in a very great consternation, but that was over in a few days, by the arrival of some Indians, I had sent out, to see if they could discover any number of men marching our way; at their return, they informed me they had been as far as the Lake without seeing any body, but that upon the Lake they had met some Ottawawa Indians who had informed them that three hundred French and Indians were marched with a design to attempt Northampton in New England, but that they could not find, there were any marching our way. However, by this accident, I had an opportunity to see how far we may depend upon our own people, and the Indians too in case of need, and I must say the Militia of the County of Albany were very ready if the Ennemy had been coming; I could in eight and forty hours time have drawn together upwards of seven hundred men, reckoning the Garrison, the Militia of Albany, and that of Ulster Counties; and the Indians of the Five Nations were so ready that they all left their Castles and were coming towards Albany before I could send them any orders; at the same time that I was at Albany where I stayed but ten days, there was an Alarum at New Yorke occasioned by a Gentleman who coming from Long Island informed the Council, that ten French Men-of-war were come within Sandy hook, upon this the Gentlemen of the Council sent an express to me to desire me to make what haste I could down to New Yorke, and at the same time sent to the Collonels of the Militia in the several Counties about New Yorke to get their men ready to oppose the Ennemy. I did make all the haste I could, but before I could get to York, their fears were over, for the ten Men of Warr were dwindled away to one French privateer of fourteen Gunns who took just without Sandy hook a ship commanded by one Sinclair who was bound to this Port from England, on board of whom were all the packetts your Lord[ships] were pleased to send me, they were given into the charge of one Glenerosse a Merchant of this place who left them on Board by which means, they are fallen into the hands of the Ennemy. I can not say that the Militia of this City did their duty, for very many of the Dutchmen run away into the woods, but the Militia of Long Island deserve to be commended; Coll. Willet who commands the Militia of Queen's County, in ten hours time brought a thousand men within an hour's march of New York, the Militia of King's County was likewise in good readiness, but their being no occasion for them they were sent home. By this account Your Lord[ships] will perceive, how necessary it is to have a standing Force in this Province, where we are exposed to the invasions of the Enemy by sea in the Southern parts of it, and to the attacks of the French and Indians by land in the Northern parts of it. If the proposal I made to your Lord[ships] formerly had been approved of, I make no doubt but it might have been effected with much less charge than the business of Guardaloupe has cost, and I conceive would have been a much greater advantage to the Crown of England, than the taking of that Island could have been. The more I inquire into that matter the more feasible I find it, but not with a less force than I proposed to your Lord[ships]. I have seen a copy of a memorial Mr Livingston laid before Your Board, in which he seems to be of opinion that a Regiment of well disciplined men with some Officers to head the men that might be raised here would be sufficient, and perhaps it might have been so when Sir William Phipps attempted the taking of it, but the case is much altered since that time, for that attempt though very ill contrived and worse executed, did so fully convince them, how easy it was to take Quebeck, that they have made it much stronger than it ever was, and have erected very good Batteries along the Water-side which will make that undertaking more difficult than it was then, and the reason, that made me propose so much a greater force than Mr Livingston has mentioned, is because I should be very sorry to propose any thing less than will effect the thing proposed, and if I have proposed a greater Force than is of absolute necessity, I hope I shall not be blamed for that; I did it because I was not willing so good a thing should miscarry for want of sufficient Force, and the same reason still remaining I can not help being of the same mind still.—When the Eagle Galley sailed it was so soon after the Assembly was adjourned, that the Clerk could not get a copy of their proceedings ready to send by that ship, therefore I now send it to your Lord[ships] by which you will perceive that the Assembly here is going into the same methods, that the Assembly's of some other Provinces upon this Continent have fallen into, who think themselves equal to the House of Commons of England, and that they are intituled to all the same powers and priviledges, that a House of Commons in England enjoys; how dangerous it may be to suffer them to enjoy and exercise such powers, I need not tell your Lord[ships], only I shall observe that the holding of General Assembly in these parts of the world, has been settled neither by Act of Parliament in England, nor by Act of Assembly here, so that the holding General Assemblies here is purely by the grace and favour of the Crown. This I have told them often, but notwithstanding that, they will pass no Bill for the service of the Queen, nor even for their own defence, unless they can have such Clauses in, as manifestly incroach upon the prerogative of the Crown or in some measure destroy the power of the Governour (which will pretty well appear by a Bill prepared by them this Sessions, a copy of which I herewith send to Your Lord[ships]). I did not think proper to suffer either, so I adjourned the Assembly to the 2nd day of October. I did once intend to have dissolved them, but upon the account I had, that some persons here, had put them upon those methods, in hopes to provoke me to dissolve them, and the assurances I had from several of the members, that they would take better measures if they might have another sessions, I adjourned them to the second day of October, at which time they met, but instead of taking better measures, they have gone on in the same, where they dont only incroach upon my right (for that I should not have minded) but they take it upon them to appoint at what rates the money shall pass here, which I take to be the undoubted right of the Queen — Your Lord[ships] will perceive by the copy's I send herewith that the Gentlemen of the Council made proper Amendments to the Bill, but these Gentlemen have thought fit to declare, in their messague to the Council on the 4th of this month (that it is inconvenient for that house to admit of any amendment made by the Council to a Mony Bill) by which Your Lord[ships] will easily see, that they intend to make the Council as inconsiderable as they can, it is a thing was never attempted by any of their predecessors, but as the Country increases, they grow sawcy, and no doubt but if they are allowed to go on, they will improve upon it, how far that may be of service to the Queen I leave Your Lord[ships] to Judge. I have lately perused the grant made by King Charles the 2nd to His Royal Highness the Duke of York of all the lands from a place called St Croix to the Eastward of New England to the Eastern shore of Delawarre River, by which it appears that, that grant impowered the Duke of York to correct, punish, pardon, Govern and Rule all such the subjects ettc., as shall from time to time adventure themselves into any of the parts or places aforesaid, or that shall or do at any time hereafter inhabit within the same, according to such Laws, Orders, Ordinances, Directions and Instruments, as by the said Duke of York, or his assigns should be established, and in defect thereof in cases of necessity according to the good discretions of his Deputies, Commissioners, Officers or Assigns, respectively, as well in all causes and matters capital and Criminal or Civil, both marine and others ettc. as will more plainly appear to Your Lord[ships] by the Copy I herewith send of the said grant, and it is certain that in the time that Mylord Limerick was Governour of this Province for His Royal Highness the Duke of York, he Governed without Assemblies, and even after King James came to the Throne, the same Lord continued the same method; and certainly if the late King Charles the Second could grant that power to the Duke of York at that time Her Majesty may exert the same power if she pleases. I intreat Your Lord[ships] to believe that I am not pleading for the laying aside of Assembly's, it is far from my thoughts, but I think it my duty to acquaint you with what I take to be the Queen's right, especially when Assembly's begin to be refractory; when I have done that, I have done my duty, and shall wait Your Lord[ships'] declarations, which I shall always punctually observe—In the mean time, I have this day dissolved the Assembly and intend to issue writts for the calling of another in March next, which I hope will behave themselves better than the last, however I am sure they can't be worse;—I am going to morrow to New Jersey to the Assembly there. I take the liberty to beg your Lord[ships] that I may have all manner of stores sent over, I have not a hundred and twenty barrells of powder left, and several of them are spoiled, I have no small arms at all, no Cartouch boxes nor paper, not one bed for the men to lye upon, but what has been peiced over and over again, not a sword in the Garrison, nor a dagger if the Enemy should attempt any thing upon our frontiers this winter, we shall not have powder enough left for salutes. I intreat Your Lord[ships] to intercede with the Queen that some presents may be sent over for the Indians, for if we must buy them here they will cost three times the price they will cost in England and sometimes the goods proper for the Indians, are not to be got here for money, such as light guns, Duffles, Strowds, Kettles, Hatchets, Stockings, Blankets and powder; and till Canada is reduced, we shall never be able to keep the Indians steady without presents. I must further intreat Your Lord[ships] to intercede with Mylord High Admiral, that a Man of War may be appointed for this province, if there is not one appointed—The French privateers will intirely distroy our Trade to the West Indies, which will soon distroy our Trade of this place which consists chiefly in flour and provisions, and if I may propose, a ship of 40 gunns will be the fittest for this place. Thus I have given Your Lord[ships] an account of our present condition. I intreat you to represent our condition to Her Majesty that we may be supplyed early in the spring, else we shall be in a very poor condition even to defend ourselves if we should be attacked; however I intreat Your Lord[ships] to believe that nothing shall be wanting on my part for the Queen's service, as long as Her Majesty shall please to command me to serve her here—I am—My Lords,

Your Lord[ships'] most faithful

New Yorke   humble servant
Nov 6th 1704.   CORNBURY

READING AND DISCUSSION QUESTIONS

1. What conclusion about the eighteenth-century circulation of news and information can you draw by analyzing Cornbury's letter?

2. How did the tensions between England and France manifest themselves locally, according to Cornbury's letter?

3. What is the nature of the complaint Cornbury makes against the assembly of New York? To what extent was the New York Assembly exercising its "independence"?

■ COMPARATIVE QUESTIONS ■

1. Evaluate and synthesize the evidence from this chapter to support or challenge the argument that eighteenth-century colonists developed a growing awareness of their rights.

2. What do the sources included in this chapter reveal about the role of economics as a cause in colonial political development during the eighteenth century?

3. Compare the ways "Indians" are discussed in these documents. What might account for the differences you see?

4. How do you assess the political, social, and economic impact of slavery in this period? What may have been some of the short- or long-term effects of the growth of this system during the period?

4

Growth, Diversity, and Conflict

1720–1763

"Plenty of good land, and liberty to manage their own affairs their own way, seem to be the two great causes of the prosperity of all new colonies," argued Adam Smith in *The Wealth of Nations*. In the middle decades of the eighteenth century, the American colonies enjoyed just these favorable conditions. Parliament took a laissez-faire approach to colonial government, and the colonies grew in size, population, and demographic complexity. As settlers pushed in from the coast to establish new farms, the growing standard of living enticed Europeans to try their luck, increasing immigration and adding to the ethnic and cultural mix.

As the colonial population grew, trade between the colonies and England soared. Raw materials crossed the Atlantic in ships that returned full of the finished goods pumping out of British factories. The colonial gentry displayed their refinement through consumption, but of course not everyone had the means to do so. In areas like the impoverished region of the colonial backcountry that Anglican minister Charles Woodmason encountered, religious revivalism spread widely. The Great Awakening induced religious enthusiasm and challenged conventional sources of spiritual and social authority. Political authority, too, became contested as the French and Indian War reminded colonists that they were still a dependent part of the British Empire.

4-1 | A Revivalist Warns Against Old Light Ministers

GILBERT TENNENT, *Dangers of an Unconverted Ministry* (1740)

Beginning in the late 1730s, a series of religious revivals swept the colonies. Though not part of a single or unified movement, revival ministers embraced a similar emotionally charged style designed to affect parishioners' conscience and drive them to intense introspection. Many in the pews who heard these exhorting sermons manifested religious "enthusiasm," behavior that was repudiated by more conservative and traditional church leaders. A divide emerged in many churches between revivalists (sometimes called New Light ministers) and their more settled counterparts (Old Lights). Prominent among the New Lights was Gilbert Tennent (1703–1764), whose famous sermon is excerpted here. Sermons like this one emboldened parishioners to challenge ministerial authority and in some cases led to church schisms and a more egalitarian religious experience.

Mark VI. 34

And Jesus, when he came out, saw much People and was moved with Compassion towards them, and because they were as Sheep not having a Shepherd.

As a faithful Ministry is a great Ornament, Blessing and Comfort, to the Church of GOD; even the Feet of such Messengers are beautiful: So on the contrary, an ungodly Ministry is a great Curse and Judgment: These Caterpillars labour to devour every green Thing.

There is nothing that may more justly call forth our saddest Sorrows, and make all our Powers and Passions mourn, in the most doleful Accents, the most incessant, insatiable, and deploring Agonies; than the melancholly Case of such, who have no faithful Ministry! This Truth is set before our Minds in a strong Light, in the Words that I have chosen now to insist upon! in which we have an Account of our LORD's Grief with the Causes of it.

We are informed, That our dear Redeemer was moved with Compassion towards them. The Original Word signifies the strongest and most vehement Pity, issuing from the innermost Bowels.

But what was the Cause of this great and compassionate Commotion in the Heart of Christ? It was because he saw much People as Sheep, having no Shepherd. Why, had the People then no Teachers? O yes! they had Heaps of Pharisee-Teachers, that came out, no doubt after they had been at the Feet of *Gamaliel* the usual Time, and according to the Acts, Cannons, and Traditions of the Jewish Church. But notwithstanding of the great Crowds of these Orthodox, Letter-learned and regular Pharisees, our Lord laments the unhappy Case of that great Number of People, who, in the Days of his Flesh, had no better Guides: Because that those were as good as none (in many Respects) in our Saviour's Judgment. For all them, the People were as Sheep without a Shepherd. . . .

The Great Awakening: Documents on the Revival of Religion, 1740–1745, ed. Richard L. Bushman (New York: Atheneum, 1970), 87–93.

The old Pharisees, for all their long Prayers and other pious Pretences, had their Eyes, with *Judas*, fixed upon the Bag. Why, they came into the Priest's Office for a Piece of Bread; they took it up as a Trade, and therefore endeavoured to make the best Market of it they could. O Shame! . . .

Natural Men have no Call of GOD to the Ministerial Work under the Gospel-Dispensation.

Isn't it a principal Part of the ordinary Call of GOD to the Ministerial Work, to aim at the Glory of GOD, and, in Subordination thereto, the Good of Souls, as their chief Marks in their Undertaking that Work? And can any natural Man on Earth do this? No! no! Every Skin of them has an evil Eye; for no Cause can produce Effects above its own Power. Are not wicked Men forbid to meddle in Things sacred? . . .

Natural Men, not having true Love to Christ and the Souls of their Fellow-Creatures, hence their Discourses are cold and sapless, and as it were freeze between their Lips. And not being sent of GOD, they want that divine Authority, with which the faithful Ambassadors of CHRIST are clothed, who herein resemble their blessed Master, of whom it is said, That *He taught as one having Authority, and not as the Scribes.* Matth. 7. 29.

And Pharisee-Teachers, having no Experience of a special Work of the Holy Ghost, upon their own Souls, are therefore neither inclined to, nor fitted for, Discoursing, frequently, clearly, and pathetically, upon such important Subjects. The Application of their Discourses, is either short, or indistinct and general. They difference not the Precious from the Vile, and divide not to every Man his Portion, according to the Apostolical Direction to *Timothy.* No! they carelessly offer a common Mess to their People, and leave it to them, to divide it among themselves, as they see fit. This is indeed their general Practice, which is bad enough: But sometimes they do worse, by misapplying the Word, through Ignorance, or Anger. They often strengthen the Hands of the Wicked, by promising him Life. They comfort People, before they convince them; sow before they plow; and are busy in raising a Fabrick, before they lay a Foundation. These fooling Builders do but strengthen Men's carnal Security, by their soft, selfish, cowardly Discourses. They have not the Courage, or Honesty, to thrust the Nail of Terror into sleeping Souls. . . .

Their Prayers are also cold; little child-like Love to God or Pity to poor perishing Souls, runs thro' their Veins. Their Conversation hath nothing of the Savour of Christ, neither is it perfum'd with the Spices of Heaven. . . . Poor Christians are stunted and starv'd, who are put to feed on such bare Pastures, and such dry Nurses. . . . O! it is ready to break their very Hearts with Grief, to see how lukewarm those Pharisee-Teachers are in their publick Discourses, while Sinners are sinking into Damnation, in Multitudes! . . . Is a blind Man fit to be a Guide in a very dangerous Way? Is a dead Man fit to bring others to Life? a mad Man fit to give Counsel in a Matter of Life and Death? Is a possessed Man fit to cast out Devils? a Rebel, an Enemy to GOD, fit to be sent on an Embassy of Peace, to bring Rebels into a State of Friendship with GOD? a Captive bound in the Massy Chains of Darkness and Guilt, a proper Person to set others at Liberty? a

Leper, or one that has Plague-sores upon him, fit to be a good Physician? Is an ignorant Rustick, that has never been at Sea in his Life, fit to be a Pilot, to keep Vessels from being dashed to Pieces upon Rocks and Sand-banks? *'Is'nt an unconverted Minister like a Man who would learn others to swim, before he has learn'd it himself, and so is drowned in the Act, and dies like a Fool?'* I may add, That sad Experience verifies what has been now observed, concerning the Unprofitableness of the Ministry of unconverted Men. Look! into the Congregations of unconverted Ministers, and see what a sad Security reigns there; not a Soul convinced that can be heard of, for many Years together; and yet the Ministers are easy: for they say they do their Duty! . . .

My *Brethren*, We should mourn over those, that are destitute of faithful Ministers, and sympathize with them. Our Bowels should be moved with the most compassionate Tenderness, over those dear fainting Souls, that are as *Sheep having no Shepherd*; and that after the Example of our blessed LORD.

Dear Sirs! we should also most *earnestly pray* for them, that the compassionate Saviour may preserve them, by his *mighty* Power, thro' Faith unto Salvation; support their sinking Spirits, under the *melancholy Uneasinesses of a dead Ministry*; sanctify and sweeten to them the *dry* Morsels they get under such blind Men, when they have none better to repair to.

And more especially, *my Brethren*, we should pray to the LORD of the Harvest, to send forth faithful Labourers into his Harvest; seeing that the Harvest truly is plenteous, but the Labourers are few. And O Sirs! how humble, believing, and importunate should we be in this Petition! O! let us follow the LORD, Day and Night, with Cries, Tears, Pleadings and Groanings upon this Account! For GOD knows there is great *Necessity* of it. *O! thou Fountain of Mercy, and Father of Pity, pour forth upon thy poor Children a Spirit of Prayer, for the Obtaining this important Mercy! Help, help, O Eternal GOD and Father, for Christ's sake!*

And indeed, *my Brethren*, we should join our Endeavours to our *Prayers*. The most likely Method to stock the Church with a faithful *Ministry*, in the present Situation of Things, the publick Academies being so much corrupted and abused generally, is, To encourage private Schools, or Seminaries of Learning, which are under the Care of skilful and experienced Christians; in which those only should be admitted, who upon strict Examination, have in the Judgment of a reasonable *Charity*, the plain Evidences of experimental Religion. Pious and experienced Youths, who have a good natural Capacity, and great Desires after the Ministerial Work, from good Motives, might be sought for, and found up and down in the *Country*, and put to Private Schools of the Prophets; especially in such Places, where the Publick ones are not. This Method, in my Opinion, has a *noble Tendency*, to build up the Church of God. And those who have any Love to Christ, or Desire after the Coming of his Kingdom, should be *ready*, according to their Ability, to give somewhat, from time to time, for the Support of such poor Youths, who have nothing of their own. And truly, Brethren, this *Charity* to the Souls of Men, is the most noble kind of *Charity*—O! if the Love of God be in you, it will constrain you to do something, to promote so noble and necessary a Work. It looks Hypocrite-like to go no further, when other Things are required, than *cheap*

Prayer. Don't think it much, if the Pharisees should be offended at such a Proposal; these subtle selfish Hypocrites are wont to be scar'd about their Credit, and their Kingdom; and truly they are both little worth, for all the Bustle they make about them. If they could help it, they wo'dn't let one faithful Man come into the Ministry; and therefore their Opposition is an encouraging Sign. Let all the Followers of the Lamb stand up and act for GOD against all Opposers: Who is upon GOD's Side? who?

The Improvement of this Subject remains. And

1. If it be so, That the Case of those, who have no other, or no better than Pharisee-Teachers, is to be pitied: Then what a Scrole and Scene of Mourning, and Lamentation, and Wo, is opened! because of the Swarms of Locusts, the Crowds of Pharisees, that have as *covetously* as *cruelly*, crept into the Ministry, in this adulterous Generation! who as nearly resemble the Character given of the old Pharisees, in the Doctrinal Part of this Discourse, as one Crow's Egg does another. It is true some of the modern Pharisees have learned to prate a little more *orthodoxly* about the New Birth, than their Predecessor *Nicodemus*, who are, in the mean Time, as great Strangers to the feeling Experience of it, as he. They are blind who see not this to be the Case of the Body of the Clergy, of this Generation. And O! that our Heads were Waters, and our Eyes a Fountain of Tears, that we could *Day* and *Night* lament, with the utmost Bitterness, the doleful Case of the poor Church of God, upon this account.

2. From what has been said, we may learn, That such who are contented under a *dead Ministry*, have not in them the Temper of that Saviour they profess. It's an awful Sign, that they are as blind as Moles, and as dead as Stones, without any spiritual Taste and Relish. And alas! isn't this the Case of Multitudes? If they can get one, that has the Name of a Minister, with a Band, and a black Coat or Gown to carry on a *Sabbath-days* among them, although never so coldly, and *insuccessfully*; if he is free from gross Crimes in Practice, and takes good Care to keep at a due Distance from their Consciences, and is never troubled about his Insuccessfulness; O! think the poor Fools, that is a fine Man indeed; our Minister is a prudent charitable Man, he is not always harping upon Terror, and sounding Damnation in our Ears, like some rash-headed Preachers, who by their uncharitable Methods, are ready to put poor People out of their Wits, or to run them into Despair; O! how terrible a Thing is that Dispair! Ay, our Minister, honest Man, gives us good Caution against it. Poor silly Souls! consider *seriously* these Passages, of the Prophet, *Jeremiah* 5. 30,31.

3. We may learn, the Mercy and Duty of those that enjoy a *faithful Ministry.* Let such *glorify* GOD, for so distinguishing a Privilege, and labour to walk worthy of it, to all Well-pleasing; lest for their Abuse thereof, they be exposed to a greater Damnation.

4. If the Ministry of natural Men be as it has been represented; Then it is both lawful and expedient to go from them to hear Godly Persons; yea, it's so far from being sinful to do this, that one who lives under a pious Minister of lesser Gifts, after having honestly endeavour'd to get Benefit by his Ministry, and yet gets little or none, but doth find real Benefit and more Benefit elsewhere; I say, he may

lawfully go, and that *frequently*, where he gets most Good to his precious Soul, after regular Application to the Pastor where he lives, for his Consent, and proposing the Reasons thereof; when this is done in the Spirit of Love and Meekness, without Contempt of any, as also without rash *Anger* or vain *Curiosity*.

READING AND DISCUSSION QUESTIONS

1. What does Tennent argue is the danger of an unconverted ministry?
2. What effect might Tennent have expected his sermon to have on those who heard it?
3. From Tennent's description, what differences do you think he saw between New Light and Old Light ministers?

4-2 | Sarah Osborn on Her Experiences During the Religious Revivals

SARAH OSBORN, *Memoirs of the Life of Mrs. Sarah Osborn* (1814)

Sarah Osborn's (1714–1797) memoir movingly illustrates the anguish of a woman caught in the grip of religious doubt. Born in London, Osborn emigrated to America when still a child, living in Boston, then Newport, Rhode Island, where she spent most of her life. Her husband died at sea, leaving her a widow with a small child. Despite these hardships, she persevered but experienced repeated crises of faith. In the section of her memoir excerpted here, Osborn recounts the moment of her spiritual "awakening." Osborn's account reminds us that the religious revivals appealed to women whose experience of grace empowered them in a culture where women had few if any means of formal power or authority.

Thus I continued from day to day, in such ecstacies of joy, thirsting for full sanctification, and more intimate communion with God; daily asking what I should render to him for all his benefits to such an hell deserving sinner; earnestly begging that God would find out some way for me, that I might be made instrumental in advancing his kingdom and interest in the world. O, how I dreaded being an unprofitable servant. The employment I still followed seemed to encourage me to hope God intended to make use of me for the instruction of little ones; which caused me often to bless God for placing me in that calling. And though I know that in every thing I offend, and in all come short of God's glory; so that every performance has need of washing in the blood of Christ; yet it is a comfort to me, to this day, that I was enabled by grace to labour with the little souls, then committed to my charge; but desire to be humbled that I did no more. O, that I had been more faithful! Surely I longed that all the world, but especially those

Memoirs of the Life of Mrs. Sarah Osborn, ed. Samuel Hopkins (Catskill, NY: N. Elliot, 1814), 33–37.

dear to me by the bonds of nature or friendship, might be convinced of sin, and come to a glorious Christ. I thought I could even spend and be spent for them. I thought I could travail in birth till Christ was formed in them. And when I saw any giving themselves a liberty to sin, I could not, at some times, refrain from reproving them. Some would tell me I was turned fool, and distracted, when I said I had been a vile sinner, for every body knew I had been a sober woman all my days; and yet I used to do such things too, as well as they: And what was the matter *now*? Sometimes they would say, "This fit will be over quickly." But all such answers as these, of which I had a great many, would serve to humble me yet more, and put me upon pleading for persevering grace, that I might never bring dishonor upon the name of God. And indeed, all the trials I met with, which were various, had, through the abounding goodness of God, this effect, *to quicken me yet more*.

But Satan had still a desire to sift me as wheat. He assaulted me daily; but those words of the blessed Jesus were frequently applied for my support, "I have prayed for thee, that thy faith fail not." One night in particular, when watching with a dear friend, who was sick, Satan assaulted me in as furious a manner, seemingly, as though he had appeared in bodily shape, though with my bodily eyes I saw nothing. I believe the combat lasted, at least, two hours, as fierce as though I had talked with him face to face. He again ranked all my sins before my eyes, telling me it was impossible, notwithstanding my great hopes, for me ever to be saved. He was still sure of me, and would not let me go. I should surely turn back again, and worse than ever. It is impossible to relate the tenth part of the fiery darts he flung at me. But I was composed, not in the least daunted; but could prove him a liar in every thing he suggested, by scripture, which flowed into my mind, as though I had learned it all by heart. Never had I such a variety of scripture texts at my command in all my life, either before, or since. There was nothing he could allege against me, but if I knew it was true, I immediately subscribed to it; and then flew to the particular properties of the blood of Christ, which I found sufficient for me. Thus I overcame him by the blood of the Lamb; and was left, in the issue, filled with the consolations of the blessed Spirit; triumphing over Satan; blessing and praising God for delivering me out of the hand of this cruel tyrant; adoring the lovely Jesus. And thus I spent the remainder of that night. O, how sweet it was to me! I longed for more strength to praise and love; and even to be dissolved, and to be with Christ.

Thus I continued for some time, rejoicing and resolving, by assisting grace, to press forward, and by all means to make my calling and election sure. Then I wrote my experience to be communicated to the Church; and I was admitted, February 6, 1737, to partake of that holy ordinance of the Lord's Supper. But it is impossible for me to express the ecstacy of joy I was in, when I saw myself there, who was by nature a child of wrath, an heir of hell, and by practice a rebel against God, a resister of his grace, a piercer of the lovely Jesus, unworthy of the crumbs that fall; yet, through free grace, compelled to come in, and partake of children's bread. It was indeed sweet to me to feed by faith on the broken body of my dearest Lord. Surely it did humble me to the dust, and filled me with self abhorrence, as I meditated on his sufferings and death, and knew my sins to be the procuring cause. But when I came to take the cup, and by faith to apply the precious properties of the blood of Christ to my soul, the veil of unbelief seemed to drop off, and I was forced to cry out, "My Lord, and my God," when I beheld the hole in his side, and the prints of the nails. And I could not but, in the words of Peter, appeal to him, ["]Lord, thou knowest all things, thou knowest that I love thee." O then I was admitted, with the beloved disciple, to lean on his breast! O, astonishing grace, and unspeakable joy, to see God reconciled to me, in and through him; and he bidding me welcome to his table! The Holy Spirit, by his powerful influences, applied all this for my strong consolation. O, what a feast is this, when intimate communion with the glorious God is thus obtained! When strong covenant engagements with him are renewed; I being assured that he was my God, and giving myself, body and soul, to him forever, and rejoicing in him as my only portion forever more. Surely, I thought, I could never enough adore the lovely Jesus for appointing such an ordinance as this.

READING AND DISCUSSION QUESTIONS

1. How does Osborn describe the conversion experience?

2. What evidence can you see here of the reaction from others who witnessed her religious awakening?

3. Why does Osborn choose to devote so much of her memoir to her spiritual struggles? What audience was she writing for?

4-3 | Anglican Minister on the Manners and Religion of the Carolina Backcountry

CHARLES WOODMASON, *Journal* (1766–1768)

Charles Woodmason's (1720–1789) experiences in the South highlight key themes of this period, not least of which is the cultural diversity of the colonies. As an Anglican minister, Woodmason served at different times two divergent groups: the planter class in Charleston, and then later the religiously diverse and scattered settlements of the South Carolina backcountry. The Church of England (Anglicanism) was the established church in South Carolina, but that hardly mattered to the frontier Presbyterians and Baptists, many of whom resented the well-heeled Anglicans who controlled power and purse. In this excerpt, Woodmason describes his work on the Carolina frontier.

Saturday September 3) Rode down the Country on the West Side the Wateree River into the Fork between that and the Congaree River—This is out of my Bounds—But their having no Minister, and their falling (therefrom) continually

The Carolina Backcountry on the Eve of the Revolution, ed. Richard J. Hooker (Chapel Hill: University of North Carolina Press, 1953), 60–63.

from the Church to Anabaptism, inclin'd me to it—The People received me gladly and very kindly. Had on Sunday 4—a Company of about 150—Most of them of the Low Class—the principal Planters living on the Margin of these Rivers.

Baptiz'd 1 Negroe Man—2 Negroe Children—and 9 White Infants and married 1 Couple—The People thanked me in the most kind Manner for my Services—I had very pleasant Riding but my Horse suffered Greatly. The Mornings and Evenings now begin to be somewhat Cool, but the Mid day heat is almost intolerable—Many of these People walk 10 or 12 Miles with their Children in the burning Sun—Ought such to be without the Word of God, when so earnest, so desirous of hearing it and becoming Good Christians, and good Subjects! How lamentable to think, that the Legislature of this Province will make no Provision—so rich, so luxurious, polite a People! Yet they are deaf to all Solicitations, and look on the poor White People in a Meaner Light than their Black Slaves, and care less for them. Withal there is such a Republican Spirit still left, so much of the Old Leaven of Lord Shaftsbury and other the 1st principal Settlers still remains, that they seem not at all disposed to promote the Interest of the Church of England—Hence it is that above 30,000£ Sterling have lately been expended to bring over 5 or 6000 Ignorant, mean, worthless, beggarly Irish Presbyterians, the Scum of the Earth, and Refuse of Mankind, and this, solely to ballance the Emigrations of People from Virginia, who are all of the Established Church.——50 [miles]; [total] Miles 2846

It will require much Time and Pains to New Model and form the Carriage and Manners, as well as Morals of these wild Peoples—Among this Congregation not one had a Bible or Common Prayer—or could join a Person or hardly repeat the Creed or Lords Prayer—Yet all of 'em had been educated in the Principles of our Church. So that I am obliged to read the Whole Service, omitting such Parts, as are Repetitious, and retaining those that will make the different Services somewhat Uniform—Hence it is, that I can but seldom use the Litany, because they know not the Responses.

It would be (as I once observ'd before) a Great Novelty to a Londoner to see one of these Congregations—The Men with only a thin Shirt and pair of Breeches or Trousers on—barelegged and barefooted—The Women bareheaded, barelegged and barefoot with only a thin Shift and under Petticoat—Yet I cannot break [them?] of this—for the heat of the Weather admits not of any [but] thin Cloathing—I can hardly bear the Weight of my Whig and Gown, during Service. The Young Women have a most uncommon Practise, which I cannot break them off. They draw their Shift as tight as possible to the Body, and pin it close, to shew the roundness of their Breasts, and slender Waists (for they are generally finely shaped) and draw their Petticoat close to their Hips to shew the fineness of their Limbs—so that they might as well be in Puri Naturalibus[1]—Indeed Nakedness is not censurable or indecent here, and they expose themselves often quite

---

[1]**Puri Naturalibus**: puris naturalibus, or naked.

Naked, without Ceremony—Rubbing themselves and their Hair with Bears Oil and tying it up behind in a bunch like the Indians—being hardly one degree removed from them—In few Years, I hope to bring about a Reformation, as I already have done in several Parts of the Country. . . .

I would not wish my worst Enemy to come to this Country (at least to this) Part of it to combat perpetually with Papists, Sectaries, Atheists and Infidels— who would rather see the Poor People remain Heathens and Ignorants, than to be brought over to the Church. Such Enemies to Christ and his Cross, are these vile Presbyterians. . . .

Thus You have a Journal of two Years—In which have rode near Six thousand Miles, almost on one Horse. Wore my Self to a Skeleton and endured all the Extremities of Hunger, Thirst, Cold, and Heat. Have baptized near 1200 Children—Given 200 or more Discourses—Rais'd almost 30 Congregations—Set on foot the building of sundry Chapels Distributed Books, Medicines, Garden Seed, Turnip, Clover, Timothy Burnet, and other Grass Seeds—with Fish Hooks—Small working Tools and variety of Implements to set the Poor at Work, and promote Industry to the amount of at least One hundred Pounds Sterling: Roads are making—Boats building—Bridges framing, and other useful Works begun thro' my Means, as will not only be of public Utility, but make the Country side wear a New face, and the People become New Creatures. And I will venture to attest that these small, weak Endeavours of mine to serve the Community, has (or will) be of more Service to the Colony, than ever Mr. Whitfield's[2] Orphan House was, or will be. On which he has [Ms. torn, one word missing] Twelve Thousand Pounds Sterling (by [Ms. torn]) from which Mankind has not been twelve pence benefitted.

READING AND DISCUSSION QUESTIONS

1. How does Woodmason's Anglicanism shape his observations of non-Anglicans he encountered on the western frontier of South Carolina?

2. Based on Woodmason's comments, why might backcountry Carolinians have resented his efforts to minister to them?

3. What can Woodmason's journal teach us about the cultural, religious, and class diversity of mid-eighteenth-century colonial society?

---

[2]"Mr. Whitfield" is the Reverend George Whitefield, the most popular Great Awakening minister in the colonies. Wherever he preached, Whitefield took up a collection for an orphanage he founded in Georgia.

4-4 | Franklin Calls for Colonial Unity

BENJAMIN FRANKLIN, *Albany Plan of Union* (1754)

The tension that Charles Woodmason (Document 4-3) witnessed between the established religious authority in South Carolina and those who resisted its control was just one of the many complex divisions that existed within and among Britain's North American colonies. Over the course of the eighteenth century, colonists' attachment to local rule and self-government presented a challenge to British efforts to maintain control and colonial unity, especially in the 1750s when Britain was again at war with France. In 1754, Benjamin Franklin drafted the Albany Plan of Union urging the disparate colonies to ally together for common cause. Though Franklin's plan failed to materialize, it introduced key concepts that would later influence the American constitutional government.

It is proposed that humble application be made for an act of Parliament of Great Britain, by virtue of which one general government may be formed in America, including all the said colonies, within and under which government each colony may retain its present constitution, except in the particulars wherein a change may be directed by the said act, as hereafter follows.

1. That the said general government be administered by a President-General, to be appointed and supported by the crown; and a Grand Council, to be chosen by the representatives of the people of the several Colonies met in their respective assemblies.

2. That within—months after the passing such act, the House of Representatives that happen to be sitting within that time, or that shall [be] especially for that purpose convened, may and shall choose members for the Grand Council, in the following proportion, that is to say,

Massachusetts Bay	7
New Hampshire	2
Connecticut	5
Rhode Island	2
New York	4
New Jersey	3
Pennsylvania	6
Maryland	4
Virginia	7
North Carolina	4
South Carolina	4
	48

3. —who shall meet for the first time at the city of Philadelphia, being called by the President-General as soon as conveniently may be after his appointment.

Documents Illustrative of the Formation of the Union of the American States (Washington, DC: Government Printing Office, 1927).

4. That there shall be a new election of the members of the Grand Council every three years; and, on the death or resignation of any member, his place should be supplied by a new choice at the next sitting of the Assembly of the Colony he represented.

5. That after the first three years, when the proportion of money arising out of each Colony to the general treasury can be known, the number of members to be chosen for each Colony shall, from time to time, in all ensuing elections, be regulated by that proportion, yet so as that the number to be chosen by any one Province be not more than seven, nor less than two.

6. That the Grand Council shall meet once in every year, and oftener if occasion require, at such time and place as they shall adjourn to at the last preceding meeting, or as they shall be called to meet at by the President-General on any emergency; he having first obtained in writing the consent of seven of the members to such call, and sent duly and timely notice to the whole.

7. That the Grand Council have power to choose their speaker; and shall neither be dissolved, prorogued, nor continued sitting longer than six weeks at one time, without their own consent or the special command of the crown.

8. That the members of the Grand Council shall be allowed for their service ten shillings sterling per diem, during their session and journey to and from the place of meeting; twenty miles to be reckoned a day's journey.

9. That the assent of the President-General be requisite to all acts of the Grand Council, and that it be his office and duty to cause them to be carried into execution.

10. That the President-General, with the advice of the Grand Council, hold or direct all Indian treaties, in which the general interest of the Colonies may be concerned; and make peace or declare war with Indian nations.

11. That they make such laws as they judge necessary for regulating all Indian trade.

12. That they make all purchases from Indians, for the crown, of lands not now within the bounds of particular Colonies, or that shall not be within their bounds when some of them are reduced to more convenient dimensions.

13. That they make new settlements on such purchases, by granting lands in the King's name, reserving a quitrent to the crown for the use of the general treasury.

14. That they make laws for regulating and governing such new settlements, till the crown shall think fit to form them into particular governments.

15. That they raise and pay soldiers and build forts for the defence of any of the Colonies, and equip vessels of force to guard the coasts and protect the trade on the ocean, lakes, or great rivers; but they shall not impress men in any Colony, without the consent of the Legislature.

16. That for these purposes they have power to make laws, and lay and levy such general duties, imposts, or taxes, as to them shall appear most equal and just (considering the ability and other circumstances of the inhabitants in the several Colonies), and such as may be collected with the least inconvenience to the

people; rather discouraging luxury, than loading industry with unnecessary burdens.

17. That they may appoint a General Treasurer and Particular Treasurer in each government when necessary; and, from time to time, may order the sums in the treasuries of each government into the general treasury; or draw on them for special payments, as they find most convenient.

18. Yet no money to issue but by joint orders of the President-General and Grand Council; except where sums have been appropriated to particular purposes, and the President-General is previously empowered by an act to draw such sums.

19. That the general accounts shall be yearly settled and reported to the several Assemblies.

20. That a quorum of the Grand Council, empowered to act with the President-General, do consist of twenty-five members; among whom there shall be one or more from a majority of the Colonies.

21. That the laws made by them for the purposes aforesaid shall not be repugnant, but, as near as may be, agreeable to the laws of England, and shall be transmitted to the King in Council for approbation, as soon as may be after their passing; and if not disapproved within three years after presentation, to remain in force.

22. That, in case of the death of the President-General, the Speaker of the Grand Council for the time being shall succeed, and be vested with the same powers and authorities, to continue till the King's pleasure be known.

23. That all military commission officers, whether for land or sea service, to act under this general constitution, shall be nominated by the President-General; but the approbation of the Grand Council is to be obtained, before they receive their commissions. And all civil officers are to be nominated by the Grand Council, and to receive the President-General's approbation before they officiate.

24. But, in case of vacancy by death or removal of any officer, civil or military, under this constitution, the Governor of the Province in which such vacancy happens may appoint, till the pleasure of the President-General and Grand Council can be known.

25. That the particular military as well as civil establishments in each Colony remain in their present state, the general constitution notwithstanding; and that on sudden emergencies any Colony may defend itself, and lay the accounts of expense thence arising before the President-General and General Council, who may allow and order payment of the same, as far as they judge such accounts just and reasonable.

READING AND DISCUSSION QUESTIONS

1. What are the key elements in Franklin's plan of union? How does he envision the colonies working together?

2. What need was the plan of union designed to meet?

3. Why do you think the plan failed to garner enough support to bring it into effect?

4-5 | Colonists Argue for an Alliance with Indians Against the French

State of the British and French Colonies in North America (1755)

As we saw in Chapter 3, relations between British colonists and Native Americans were strained throughout the eighteenth century. Native American peoples resented colonial encroachment, but many also realized the futility of prolonged resistance and forged alliances when doing so suited their interests. For their part, the American colonists quickly recognized the key role that native peoples could play in defending themselves from French assaults as the French and Indian War began in 1756. In this source, published just before hostilities with France were formalized, an anonymous author argues for the necessity of befriending native peoples.

The Necessity of Using Indians in War, and of Gaining Their Friendship

The next preliminary point to be effected, is to secure the Indians in our interest; on account, as well of recovering and extending our trade, as of securing our colonies against the attack either of French or Indians.

Their way of making war and fighting is quite different from the European. They do not draw into the open field but shoot from behind trees; and are exceeding dextrous both at hitting their mark and sheltering themselves from the enemies fire or pursuit: for, there is no room for horse in countries overgrown with woods, which gave occasion to this way of fighting; and there is no overtaking them on foot they run so swiftly.

Therefore, in case of any war, either with Indians alone, or where they are auxiliaries, we must have Indians to oppose Indians. They must be fought with their own way. Regular forces being wholly unacquainted with their way of making war can be of no service against them: they are only of use to defend a fort, or to support Indian forces against regular troops. Besides, being used to fire from walls, they scorn to shoot from behind trees; and would rather die than go out of their own road to practise such a low kind of military art. Not considering that the nature of the country, which is, as it were, one continued wood, requires that way of going to war, and that of all the methods of fighting that is best which is safest.

The French of Canada know the importance of Indians on this account, and therefore never undertake any expedition without them. A memorable deliverance taught them this caution. In 1687 the marquis de Nonville, governor of Quebek, having landed 2100 men at Tierondoquot, 300 of them Indians, with design to surprize the chief village of the Sennekas, whom he intended to destroy; was surprized himself in the woods, within a mile of the place, by 500 of that nation: who starting suddenly from the ground where they had lain flat, raised the war shout, and discharged their musquets. This put his troops into such a consternation, that they began to run on every side; and in the confusion fired on

State of the British and French Colonies in North America (London: A. Millar, 1755), 69–75.

one another, while the Sennekas fell on pell-mell. So that had not the French Indians, acquainted with their way of fighting, come up, all must have been destroyed; and the French, very likely, driven out of Canada, for the whole force of it was employed in this expedition.

The French, since that time, make use of Indians more than ever: and since they make use of them, there is still the more reason why we should; unless we had men enough of our own trained to their manner of making war.

Besides; the advantage of having the Indians our friends, may be inferred from the mischiefs they have done ourselves as well as the French; and the danger they have put the colonies in, both from within and without, when our enemies. Altho' the English, by dint of numbers, were able to support the wrongs which they did the Indians, and either destroyed or subdued them within the colonies; yet it cost them much blood and labour before they effected it; particularly in Virginia and New England; especially this last colony: where made such vigorous efforts at several times, and continued the war with so much obstinacy, even tho' much reduced by them; that the English, notwithstanding their great superiority in numbers, were scarce able to withstand them, and but for certain lucky incidents, might have been driven out of all their settlements. Those who left the country, preserve to this day their ancient animosities; and being joined by the other eastern tribes, continue to harrass the borders of the English, and do them all the mischief they can. They are now the more able to take revenge with more safety to themselves; as, having a large country to retreat in, they cannot be so easily surrounded by the English, and oppressed by numbers as they were when inclosed within the colonies, where it would have been better to have kept them by good usage. . . .

In 1687, the English Indians, to revenge some ill usage, by the instigation of the French, invaded the frontiers of New England, and commenced a war, which all the powers of the country could not extinguish in ten years.

I shall produce but one instance more to shew what mischief the Indians may be able to do us, when our enemies. In the war, carried on about 1718, by the Spanish Indians against Carolina (the two provinces then being in one) this colony unable to defend itself against them, either by their own force, or that of the other colonies joined with them, were obliged at last to crave assistance from England, before they could do any good against them, as hath been mentioned before. Does not this confirm what has been already suggested of the danger the colonies would be in for want of Indians, should the French at any time invade them with their confederate Indian nations? In short, an Indian war has always been dreaded, as it has always been fatal to the colonies.

All the colony writers recommend the gaining the Indian friendship, as a matter of great importance to them. One of Carolina says, that the province is much strengthened by them; and that if trained to fire arms they would be very useful to that province, not only in case of an invasion to repel the enemy, but also by drawing other Indians to the English interest, or else destroying those who were not to be gained.

It must be confessed, that they are of great use, in either defending or invading a country. They are extremely skilful in the art of surprizing, and watching the motions of an enemy: they always know where to find you; but you never know where to find them: they disperse themselves thro' a country singly, or in very small parties, and lie on the lurch, to pick up stragglers, or procure intelligence: in which they act with an astonishing patience and indefatigableness, beyond any thing which an European could undergo; remaining in one place, and often in one posture, for whole days and weeks together, till they find an opportunity to strike their stroke, or compass their design, whatever it may be.

"Every Indian," says Mr. Kennedy,[1] "is a hunter; and as their manner of making war, by skulking, surprizing, and killing particular persons and families, is just the same as their hunting, only changing the object, every Indian is a disciplined soldier. Soldiers of this kind are always wanted in the colonies in an Indian war [or when Indians are employed] for the European military discipline is of little use in these woods." There is, therefore, an indispensible necessity of making use of Indians in our wars, unless we had men enough of our own trained in that fort of military exercise.

The French, indeed, have a great number of such people called Courieurs de Bois, as expert in the Indian way of fighting as the Indians themselves, as hath been taken notice of before; and therefore might be able to do without Indians, altho' they make use of them. But this is an advantage which the colonies have not; for, altho' in the southern provinces there may be a good many men, as expert in the Indian way of fighting, as the French Courieurs de Bois, yet they are under no kind of discipline or command, except those of the considerable Indian traders, their masters; and therefore cannot properly be considered as any publick force or real strength. In the northern colonies New England being surrounded with hostile Indians, and having still some within itself of the same race, necessity has produced rangers among the inhabitants, without whom there could be no dealing with such enemies. But New York depending on the neighbourhood of the five nations for its security, and making the French their factors with the Indians, by selling their goods to them, had few or no rangers at all before that illicit traffic at Albany was prohibited, and the trade laid open in 1720; since which time the young men being encouraged to go among the Indians, the only way of breeding rangers, that province begins to be furnished with them. Altho' rangers are so numerous among the French, that they might do without the Indians, yet they not only cherish those who live in the country inhabited by themselves, but seek the friendship of all the nations round about them, far and near. On the contrary, the English do neither, especially in the northern colonies: for they have not only exterminated all Indian nations who formerly dwelt in the countries now possessed by them, but instead of making friends of those who

---

[1]**Mr. Kennedy**: Archibald Kennedy, the author of *The Importance of Gaining and Preserving the Friendship of Indians to the British Interest Considered* (1752).

live in the neighbourhood of the colonies, are at variance with them all, excepting the six nations and their allies, whom yet they seem industrious rather to disoblige than keep in their interest; altho' they have been all along the chief, and to New York the only defence against the French, and their numerous tribes of Indians.

READING AND DISCUSSION QUESTIONS

1. What advantage does the author suggest the native peoples bring to the colonial cause?

2. What difference in war-making does the author see between European and Native American warriors?

3. What does this source suggest about the changing relationship between colonial Americans and the native peoples they encountered?

4-6 | The North Carolina Regulators Protest British Control
Petition from the Inhabitants of Orange County, North Carolina (1770)

New tensions arose in the years immediately following the British and American victory during the French and Indian War (1754–1763). To pay their large war debt, the British Parliament began imposing more taxes and regulations on the colonies, inciting colonial resistance. At the same time, in the western regions of colonies such as North and South Carolina, debt-laden farmers protested political, judicial, and economic policies disadvantageous to their interests. Disciplined mobs formed in these western regions to protest the use of British forces to defeat them and the prejudicial court actions that, in many cases, deprived them of their farms. This Regulator movement, though ultimately unsuccessful, revealed the class conflicts that divided colonists and pitted British subjects in America against royal representatives and their colonial dependents. While Regulators destroyed property, refused to pay taxes, and disrupted government, they also issued petitions and drew on the language of rights to plead their case.

The Humble Petition of the Inhabitants of Orange County humbly sheweth,

That as it is a Maxim in our Laws that no Law Statute or Custom which are against Gods Law or principalls of nature can be of any validity but are all null.

If therefore Laws themselves when against Reason and Justice are null and void much more the practice used by men in the Law which is contrary to the Law as well as Reason Justice and Equity ought to be condemned and surely it is against Justice Reason and Equity to exact Taxes and extort Fees that are unlawful from the poor industrious Farmers — Yet these are but a few of a great many more evils of that nature which has been of a long time our sad case and

The Colonial Records of North Carolina, Vol. VIII, 1769 to 1771, ed. William L. Saunders (Raleigh, NC: Josephus Daniels, Printer to the State, 1890), 231–234.

condition and to such a degree general among so many of the men of the Law that we quite despaired of any redress being to be had that way. But as you the Governor Kings Attorney Generall and other Gentlemen of the Law pledged to us your words your honours your oaths that we could and should be redressed by the Law it would be tedious as well as unnecessary to recite the world of fatigue expence and Trouble that we have been at to obtain redress in that way but in vain — for though so many of the Officers as has been convicted yet we can obtain none of our money back — but instead of refunding they still continue to take the same Fees James Watson and John Butler excepted — And notwithstanding the wheels in this work run so heavy we have so many of the Court Party against us yet we might nevertheless [have gained] our point could we have obtained Jurors of unprejudiced Men — for though the Law impowers the Justices of the Inferior Courts to appoint the Jurys yet it was to the end they might be chosen of unprejudiced Men, this was the spirit end and design of the Law — But it has so happened that too many of our Justices are partys concerned some of them being insolvent high Sheriffs themselves and others insolvent Sheriffs securities, yet under all this disadvantage as we labored against this very unfair dealing the goodness of our course and the uprightness of our Intentions gained ground with such Justices as was not parties concerned and for some Courts past a few of the Jurors was unprejudiced Men, but at our last Inferior Court Tyree Harris and Thomas Lloyd took a most notorious and bare faced advantage of choosing the Judges [juries] on the first day of the Court contrary to the known and usual custom and have made up the Jury mostly of Men well known to be prejudiced in favor of extortionate Officers and of such Officers themselves. Tyree Harris at whose instance we suppose it was done was high Sheriff for the years 1766 & 1767, whose accounts are yet unsettled, and likely we may be sued by the Treasurer as well as the Vestry to the Court besides almost may we believe every under Sheriff he had is inditable for their Extortions and exactions of Tax[es] and most of them have already been found guilty and though they attempt to make you believe the charge against them for exacting 4d 0d & a shilling extraordinary from ignorant Men Women and in remote neighbourhoods to be a false charge yet it is not only notoriously known to be the truth by hundreds of people from whom and among whom they exacted it, but at the same time they exacted 4d more from every man in the County in the very same Tax and though this was what we had some Item of from the very beginning yet we could never come at the certainty thereof till now, we think it can be proved beyond all doubt and this is a very particular matter of great weight and moment as it was one immediate cause of the rise of the mob and for which reason we suppose the most strenuous methods has been used to hinder it from coming to light. In the next place Thomas Lloyd may also be said to be a party concerned as he is one of the insolvent Sheriffs Securities and likewise the Justice who committed H. Husband without a Warrant proof of any crime and without a Mittimus, besides all this he has been Vestry Man and Church Warden frequently these Ten years past and more during which time the Vestry accounts are unsettled and irregularly kept and large Ballances behind. Thomas Hart being the only Sheriff that ever settled which was for 1762, the particulars of whose accounts is also kept from the eyes of the public, all which is contrary to Law and for which neglect the Church Wardens and Clerks are indictable.

Mr Chief Justice you at our last Court seemed to be somewhat prejudiced against us in a speech that you made in which you signified your Jealosie that we acted through Malice, Ambition &c: But concluding if what we did was from motives to promote Justice detect Extortion &c: for the publick good that you wished us all the success imaginable and heartily concurred with us in our undertaking. Oh that you might be sincere and could but a known our hearts. However be that as it will your Speech could not but afford us consolation and encouragement to persevere for we could lay our hands on our hearts and call God to witness in ourselves that this was our whole sole end and purpose and that too out of pure necessity to keep ourselves and innocent helpless Neighbors from utter ruin our whole properties having become quite insecure as well as our characters — As the two persons who was indicted last Court for perjury by reason they had indicted and witnessed against Extortions are two honest innocent men — Yea we need say no more but that we know these two men are honest men of good characters and innocent of that charge, whereas on the contrary to pick the whole country there cannot be found men of much worse characters than many or most of those who have sworn against them. As for the objection that some pretend to make (to wit) that it is hard to find Jurymen but what is prejudiced to one side or t' other this objection has not the least foundation in Truth or Reason Absolutely no more than if a gang of horse thieves had been numerous and formidable enough to have engaged the same attention and concern of the publick — for those Extortioners and Exactors of Tax are certainly more dangerous than those Thieves and in the next place they and all who espouse their cause knowingly are as to numbers inconsiderably small, only that they have the handling the Law chiefly in their own hands — our late Elections help to prove this Diversion; we carried our Elections for Vestrymen twenty five to one — The consequence of not trying these men subject to Law is wooden shoes and uncombed hair — What sense or reason is there in saying any are prejudiced to our side for what is it we have done — we have labored honestly for our Bread and studied to defraud no man nor live on the spoils of other mens labors nor snatched the Bread out of other mens hands. Our only crime with which they can charge us is vertue in the very highest degree namely to risque our all to save our Country from Rapine and Slavery in our detecting of practices which the Law itself allows to be worse than open Robbery — It is not one in a hundred or a thousand of us who have broke one Law in this our struggle for only common Justice which it is even a shame for any Government or any set of Men in the Law once to have denyed us off — Whereas them as has acted the most legally are the most torn to pieces by the Law through malicious prosecutions carried against them.

To sum up the whole matter of our Petition in a few words it is namely these that we may obtain unprejudiced Jurys, That all extortionate Officers Lawyers and Clerks may be brought to fair Tryals — That the Collectors of publick money may be called to proper settlements of their accounts, namely the Sheriffs for the years 1764, 1765, 1766 & 1767 to which time the taxes was generally collected (a small part of the last year excepted) the refusing to settle for which or give us any satisfaction occasioned the past disturbances — If We cannot obtain this that we may have some security for our properties more than the bare humour of officers, we can see plainly that we shall not be able to live under such oppressions and to what extremities this must drive us you can as well judge of as we can ourselves, we having no other determination but to be redressed and that to be in a legal and lawful way — As we are serious and in good earnest and the Cause respects the whole Body of the people it would be loss of time to enter into arguments on particular points for though there is a few men who have the gift or art of reasoning yet every man has a feeling and knows when he has justice done him as well as the most learned.

Therefore that Justice which every man will be ashamed to own that ever he denied us of when in his power to grant is the prayer of our Petition and your Petitioners as in duty bound shall ever pray.

Signed by 174 Subscribers.

READING AND DISCUSSION QUESTIONS

1. Identify the specific grievances that Regulators in Orange County have against the royal government of North Carolina.

2. How do the Regulators frame their argument in this petition? Who was the audience for the petition?

3. What does the Regulator movement reveal about colonial politics on the eve of the Revolution?

■ COMPARATIVE QUESTIONS ■

1. What were the major sources of conflict affecting colonial American society during the middle decades of the eighteenth century?

2. To what extent did religion unite or divide colonial society?

3. Why was colonial unity so difficult to achieve in these years?

4. How and to what extent did considerations of class define or enhance the conflicts of this period?

DOCUMENT SET

The Causes and Consequences of the Peopling of North America
1660–1763

The century following the Stuart Restoration was a period of dynamic growth, witnessing a massive movement of peoples to and within the North American colonies. The resulting demographic diversity in the colonies is attributable to the migration of both Europeans and unwilling Africans who joined the existing Native American populations. This mingling of diverse peoples and their distinctive cultures profoundly shaped each in the process of forming a new British North American world.

The American Indian population felt the effect of these migrations of people most keenly as their communities were impacted by warfare with European colonists and the spread of unfamiliar germs. The spread of disease to native peoples decimated their numbers, leaving them vulnerable to the geographical ambitions of Europeans. The peopling of North America during the seventeenth and eighteenth centuries enriched some, but destroyed others. Through these migrations, no one was left untouched, as the sources in this document set show.

P2-1 | The Horrors of the Middle Passage

OLAUDAH EQUIANO, *The Interesting Narrative of the Life of Olaudah Equiano, or Gustavus Vassa, the African. Written by Himself* (1794)

Few eighteenth-century first-person accounts of slavery's Middle Passage exist, which makes Olaudah Equiano's autobiography especially valuable. Born in Africa, but kidnapped and sold as a child into slavery, Equiano, also known as Gustavus Vassa, describes the harrowing conditions enslaved Africans endured in their forced migration across the Atlantic. Unlike most in his condition, Equiano was ultimately able to purchase his freedom and flee to Europe, where he became a leading abolitionist.

The first object which saluted my eyes when I arrived on the coast was the sea, and a slave ship, which was then riding at anchor, and waiting for its cargo. These filled me with astonishment, which was soon converted into terror, which I am yet at a loss to describe, nor the then feelings of my mind. When I was carried on board I was immediately handled, and tossed up, to see if I were found, by some of the crew; and I was now persuaded that I had got into a world of bad spirits, and that they were going to kill me. Their complexions too differing so much from ours, their long hair, and the language they spoke, which was very different from any I had ever heard, united to confirm me in this belief. Indeed, such were the horrors of my views and fears at the moment, that, if ten thousand worlds had been my own, I would have freely parted with them all to have exchanged my condition with that of the meanest slave in my own country. When I looked round the ship too, and saw a large furnace or copper boiling, and a multitude of black people of every description [chained] together, every one of their countenances expressing dejection and sorrow, I no longer doubted of my fate, and, quite overpowered with horror and anguish, I fell motionless on the deck and fainted. When I recovered a little, I found some black people about me, who I believed were some of those who brought me on board, and had been receiving their pay; they talked to me in order to cheer me, but all in vain. I asked them if we were not to be eaten by those white men with horrible looks, red faces, and long hair? They told me I was not; and one of the crew brought me a small portion of spirituous liquor in a wine glass; but, being afraid of him, I would not take it out of his hand. One of the blacks therefore took it from him and gave it to me, and I took a little down my palate, which, instead of reviving me, as they thought it would, threw me into the greatest consternation at the strange feeling it produced having never tasted any such liquor before. Soon after this, the blacks who brought me on board went off, and left me abandoned to despair. I now saw myself deprived of all chance of returning to my native country, or even the least glimpse of hope of gaining the shore, which I now considered as friendly: and

The Interesting Narrative of the Life of Olaudah Equiano, or Gustavus Vassa, The African. Written by Himself (London: Printed for and Sold by the Author, 1794), 46–57.

even wished for my former slavery, in preference to my present situation, which was filled with horrors of every kind, still heightened by my ignorance of what I was to undergo. I was not long suffered to indulge my grief; I was soon put down under the decks, and there I received such a salutation in my nostrils as I had never experienced in my life; so that with the loathsomeness of the stench, and crying together, I became so sick and low that I was not able to eat, nor had I the least desire to taste any thing. I now wished for the last friend, Death, to relieve me; but soon, to my grief, two of the white men offered me eatables; and, on my refusing to eat, one of them held me fast by the hands, and laid me across, I think, the windlass, and tied my feet, while the other flogged me severely. I had never experienced any thing of this kind before; and although not being used to the water, I naturally feared that element the first time I saw it; yet, nevertheless, could I have got over the nettings, I would have jumped over the side; but I could not; and, besides, the crew used to watch us very closely who were not chained down to the decks, lest we should leap into the water; and I have seen some of these poor African prisoners most severely cut for attempting to do so, and hourly whipped for not eating. This indeed was often the case with myself. In a little time after, amongst the poor chained men, I found some of my own nation, which in a small degree gave ease to my mind. I inquired of them what was to be done with us? They give me to understand we were to be carried to these white people's country to work for them. I then was a little revived, and thought, if it were no worse than working, my situation was not so desperate: but still I feared I should be put to death, the white people looked and acted, as I thought, in so savage a manner; for I had never seen among any people such instances of brutal cruelty; and this not only shewn towards us blacks, but also to some of the whites themselves. One white man in particular I saw, when we were permitted to be on deck, flogged so unmercifully with a large rope near the foremast, that he died in consequence of it; and they tossed him over the side as they would have done a brute. This made me fear these people the more; and I expected nothing less than to be treated in the same manner. I could not help expressing my fears and apprehensions to some of my countrymen: I asked them if these people had no country, but lived in this hollow place the ship? They told me they did not, but came from a distant one. "Then," said I, "how comes it in all our country we never heard of them?" They told me, because they lived so very far off. I then asked, where were their women? Had they any like themselves! I was told they had: "And why," said I, "do we not see them?" [T]hey answered, because they were left behind; I asked how the vessel could go? They told me they could not tell; but that there were cloth put upon the masts by the help of the ropes I saw, and then the vessel went on; and the white men had some spell or magic they put in the water when they liked in order to stop the vessel. I was exceedingly amazed at this account, and really thought they were spirits. I therefore wished much to be from amongst them, for I expected they would sacrifice me: but my wishes were vain; for we were so quartered that it was impossible for any of us to make our escape. While we staid on the coast I was mostly on deck; and one day, to my great astonishment, I saw one of these vessels coming in with the sails up. As soon as the whites saw it, they gave a great shout, at which we were amazed; and the more so as the vessel appeared larger by approaching nearer. At last she came to an anchor in my sight, and when the anchor was let go, I and my countrymen who saw it were lost in astonishment to observe the vessel stop; and were now convinced it was done by magic. Soon after this the other ship got her boats out, and they came on board of us, and the people of both ships seemed very glad to see each other. Several of the strangers also shook hands with us black people, and made motions with their hands, signifying, I suppose, we were to go to their country; but we did not understand them. At last, when the ship we were in had got in all her cargo, they made ready with many fearful noises, and we were all put under deck, so that we could not see how they managed the vessel. But this disappointment was the least of my sorrow. The stench of the hold while we were on the coast was so intolerably loathsome, that it was dangerous to remain there for any time, and some of us had been permitted to stay on the deck for the fresh air; but now that the whole ship's cargo were confined together, it became absolutely pestilential. The closeness of the place, and the heat of the climate, added to the number in the ship, which was so crouded that each had scarcely room to turn himself, almost suffocated us. This produced copious perspirations, so that the air soon became unfit for respiration, from a variety of loathsome smells, and brought on a sickness amongst the slaves, of which many died, thus falling victims to the improvident avarice, as I may call it, of their purchasers. This wretched situation was again aggravated by the galling of the chains, now become insupportable; and the filth of the necessary tubs, into which the children often fell, and were almost suffocated. The shrieks of the women, and the groans of the dying, rendered the whole a scene of horror almost inconceivable. Happily perhaps for myself I was soon reduced so low here that it was thought necessary to keep me almost always on deck; and from my extreme youth I was not put in fetters. In this situation I expected every hour to share the fate of my companions, some of whom were almost daily brought upon deck at the point of death, which I began to hope would soon put an end to my miseries. Often did I think many of the inhabitants of the deep much more happy than myself; I envied them the freedom they enjoyed, and as often wished I could change my condition for theirs. Every circumstance I met with served only to render my state more painful, and heighten my apprehensions and my opinion of the cruelty of the whites. One day they had taken a number of fishes; and when they had killed and satisfied themselves with as many as they thought fit, to our astonishment who were on the deck, rather than give any of them to us to eat, as we expected, they tossed the remaining fish into the sea again, although we begged and prayed for some as well as we could, but in vain; and some of my countrymen, being pressed by hunger, took an opportunity, when they thought no one saw them, of trying to get little privately; but they were discovered, and the attempt procured them some very severe floggings.

One day, when we had a smooth sea, and moderate wind, two of my wearied countrymen, who were chained together (I was near them at the time), preferring death to such a life of misery, somehow made through the nettings, and jumped into the sea; immediately another quite dejected fellow, who, on account of his illness, was suffered to be out of irons, also followed their example; and I believe many more would very soon have done the same, if they had not been prevented by the ship's crew who were instantly alarmed. Those of us that were the most active were, in a moment, put down under the deck; and there was such a noise and confusion amongst the people of the ship as I never heard before, to stop her, and get the boat out to go after the slaves. However, two of the wretches were drowned, but they got the other, and afterwards flogged him unmercifully, for thus attempting to prefer death to slavery. In this manner we continued to undergo more hardships than I can now relate; hardships which are inseparable from this accursed trade. — Many a time we were near suffocation, from the want of fresh air, which we were often without for whole days together. This, and the stench of the necessary tubs, carried off many. . . .

At last, we came in sight of the island of Barbadoes, at which the whites on board gave a great shout, and made many signs of joy to us. We did not know what to think of this; but, as the vessel drew nearer, we plainly saw the harbour, and other ships of different kinds and sizes: and we soon anchored amongst them off Bridge Town. Many merchants and planters now came on board, though it was in the evening. They put us in separate parcels, and examined us attentively. — They also made us jump, and pointed to the land, signifying we were to go there. We thought by this we should be eaten by these ugly men, as they appeared to us; and when, soon after we were all put down under the deck again, there was much dread and trembling among us, and nothing but bitter cries to be heard all the night from these apprehensions, insomuch that at last the white people got some old slaves from the land to pacify us. They told us we were not to be eaten, but to work, and were soon to go on land, where we should see many of our country people. This report eased us much; and sure enough, soon after we landed, there came to us Africans of all languages. We were conducted immediately to the merchant's yard, where we were all pent up together like so many sheep in a fold, without regard to sex or age. As every object was new to me, every thing I saw filled me with surprise. What struck me first was, that the houses were built with bricks, in stories, and in every other respect different from those I have seen in Africa. . . .

We were not many days in the merchant's custody before we were sold after their usual manner, which is this: — On a signal given, (as the beat of a drum), the buyers rush at once into the yard where the slaves are confined, and make choice of that parcel they like best. The noise and clamour with which this is attended, and the eagerness visible in the countenances of the buyers, serve not a little to increase the apprehension of the terrified Africans, who may well be supposed to consider them as the ministers of that destruction to which they think themselves devoted. In this manner, without scruple, are relations and friends separated, most of them never to see each other again. I remember in the vessel in which I was brought over, in the men's apartment, there were several brothers, who, in the sale, were sold in different lots; and it was very moving on this occasion to see and hear their cries at parting. O, ye nominal Christians! Might not an African ask you, learned you this from your God? Who says unto you, Do unto all men as you would men should do unto you. Is it not enough that we are torn from our country and friends to toil for your luxury and lust of gain? Must every tender feeling be likewise sacrificed to your avarice? Are the dearest friends and relations, now rendered more dear by their separation from their kindred, still to be parted from each other, and thus prevented from cheering the gloom of slavery with the small comfort of being together, and mingling their sufferings and sorrows? Why are parents to lose their children, brothers their sisters, or husbands their wives? Surely this is a new refinement in cruelty, which, while it has no advantage to atone for it, thus aggravates distress, and adds fresh horrors even to the wretchedness of slavery.

READING AND DISCUSSION QUESTIONS

1. What does Equiano's account tell us about enslaved Africans' experiences of migration from their homelands to the Americas?
2. While reading Equiano's story, what can you infer about the ways he and others like him adapted to the new social and physical environments both aboard ship and upon arrival in Barbados?

P2-2 | German Immigrant Describes Carolina Opportunities
Letter from Christen Janzen to His Family (1711)

Hundreds of thousands of Europeans crossed the Atlantic during the seventeenth and eighteenth centuries to find better prospects in the Americas. English and non-English migrants, to say nothing of the enslaved Africans, created a religiously and culturally diverse North American population. German immigrants often settled in Pennsylvania, but many others took up farming in North and South Carolina. In this source, Christen Janzen, who emigrated from the Siebentaler, a region in southwestern Germany, writes home to his family to describe his new life in North Carolina.

God greet you most beloved souls, father, mother, related friends, and neighbors, always with our thousandfold greetings and obedient service. I wish you at this time to learn of my health, and to know that I must make my writing as short as I can compose it. I hope that you have the letters that I wrote from Holland and England. The most essential contents are that we came the 10th of June to New Castle in England, but the 6th I became a very sad widower.

In New Castle we lay five weeks. The 17th of July went aboard the ship and lay eight days at anchor. After that we sailed, under the all-powerful protection of God, safely to land in Virginia. Also did not lose a person. A young son was

Christoph Von Graffenried's Account of the Founding of New Bern, ed. Vincent H. Todd (Raleigh, NC: Edwards & Broughton Printing Co., 1920), 316–320.

born on the sea. His father's name is Benedict Kupferschmied. He worked a year for our dear brother, Christian Bürki. After that we went about a hundred hours by water and land, yet always guided and fed, and the people everywhere have done us much kindness and there is in this country no innkeeper. All go from one place to another for nothing and consider it an insult if one should wish to ask the price.

Brought here hale and hearty, the shoemaker Moritz did not die till he was on his farm. He was well on the whole journey. No one else of us Siebentaler people has died, but of the others though, three Palatines. Of the people among whom we live, however, a good many have died.

Regarding the land in general. It is almost wholly forest, with indescribably beautiful cedar wood, poplars, oaks, beech, walnut and chestnut trees. But the walnuts are very hard and full of indentations and the chestnuts very small but good. There is sassafras also, and so many other fragrant trees that I cannot describe the hundredth part. Cedar is red like the most beautiful veined cherry and smells better than the finest juniper. They are, commonly, as well as the other trees, fifty to sixty feet below the limbs.

The land in general is almost everywhere black dirt and rich soil, and everyone can get as much as he will. There are five free years. After that one is to give for an acre, which is much greater than a Juchart with us, two pennies. Otherwise it is entirely free, one's own to use and to leave to his heirs as he wishes. But this place has been entirely uninhabited, for we have not seen any signs nor heard that anything else ever was here except the so-called wild and naked Indians. But they are not wild, for they come to us often and like to get clothes of us. This is done when they pay with wild meat and leather, bacon, beans, corn, which the women plant and the men hunt; and when they, as most frequently happens, guide the Christians through the forest and show new ways. They have huts of cedar bark. Some also can speak English well. They have an idol and hold festivals at certain times. But I am sorry to say, of the true God they do not want to know anything.

With regard to the rearing of cattle. It costs almost nothing for the raising, as the booklet printed at Frankfort says, for all stock pastures in the winter as well as in the summer. And I know of nothing to find fault with in the booklet mentioned regarding these two items, although it writes of South Carolina.

They butcher also no young animals, so one can conclude how quickly the number can increase. The cows give scarcely half so much as with you for the calves suck so long; until they are a year and a half old and in turn have young. We buy a cow with a calf for three pounds sterling or twelve thalers, a hog for one pound, with young or fat; a sheep also for as much. They have but few goats, but I have seen some. Squire Michel told me they wished to bring some here to us. Wild and unplanted tree-fruits are not to be found here so good as Kocherthal[1]

---

[1]**Kocherthal**: Joshua von Kocherthal, Lutheran pastor from southern Germany, published in 1706 a pamphlet recommending South Carolina as a promising land for German settlers. Two years later he led refugees to New York under a grant from England's Queen Anne.

writes of South Carolina. I have seen no cherries yet. There are many grape-vines and many grapes on them, of which some are good to eat; and it can well be believed, if one had many together (they would do well). We are going to try to plant them for everything grows up very quickly and all fruit is of very good taste, but we do not enjoy them much yet.

We lie along a stream called Neuse. There six years ago the first (people), English, until two years ago (when) the Swiss people (came), began the cultivation. They are, as it seems to me, rather rich in cattle, all sorts of crops, the finest tree-fruit, and that, the whole year (except for) two months. From the nature of things we were behind in that regard, so that we do not have it yet; but we hope, through God's blessings to get it. We came shortly before Christmas and we have by God's blessing, Zioria, my son-in-law Peter Reutiger, and I, and others besides, much stronger houses than the English; have also cleared land in addition, and the most have put fences around.

It is to be hoped that now from the ground and the cattle we will get enough, through the grace of God who has always stretched out his hand helpfully and has brought us safely and unhindered through so many enemies, spiritual and worldly, and over the great sea. But one thing lies heavy on us which I cannot write without weeping, namely the lack of a true and zealous pastor. For we have indeed cause to complain with Asaph, our sign we see no more, no prophet preaches to us any more, no teacher teaches us any more. We have, indeed, prayers in our houses every Sunday, but the zeal to cleanse away the canker of our old sins is so small that it is to be feared it will consume everything to the foundation, if the pitying God does not come to our help.

If it had pleased the good God to send some of our brethren and sisters or at least Christian Bürki as an instrument, as a physician of body and soul, I should have had good hopes that the light among us would not become an evil smelling lamp, for I do not believe there is a person here, either English, German, or French who would not have loved him heartily; I believe that his profession is especially good here and that he could have an estate according to his wish without doing work in the fields. For of good liquor and such medicine there is the greatest lack in this country, therefore I have a friendly request to make of you, dear brother; namely, as follows. I have married Christina Christeler, a widow of Sannen. I am her third husband. By the first she has four children. Two died in London. Her husband and one child upon the sea. But the eldest, a boy of thirteen, named Benedict Plösch, is at Mörigen in the baliwick Nidauw, staying with his deceased father's clientage. And he was alive four years ago. Her father was named Peter Christeler. Christen Walcker, who, with his wife died here in this country and left eight children, said to her that she has a rather large inheritance from her late father, left with her brother Moritz Christeler, for he has received a hundred pounds of it. When you go to Sannen to ask about it, I hope Heinrich Perret will be able to help you; for they have been nearest neighbors. And if it is as Walcker says you can take it into your hands.

Because my wife understands brewing so well and has done it for years, and the drink is very scarce here and neither money nor brewing pots are to be obtained here, otherwise I would not think of such a thing for you to do. But the pot must have two pipes but no worm; and if some reliable people should not be coming, would Mr. Ritter still be so good as to get it to me here; also four pounds worth of spice, such as ginger, pepper, safron, nutmegs, galangale,[2] cloves, each according to the proportion of the money? For here there is nothing but laurel. I have seen it on trees in the forest. But if there should be nothing to be got from the inheritance, I would most kindly beg you and my father, if he is still alive, to still help me somewhat from my own, for it is very important to me and especially to the women folks, who are very scarce here.

If only more people should wish to come, I advise that they take women with them if they want to have any, for here some of the very best men find no wives, because they are not here.

The journey is easily to be made if one can supply himself properly with old cheese, dried meat, and dried fruit, vinegar, wine, beer, and casks, butter, biscuits, in fine whatever is good to eat and feasible to transport, also a pan or kettle that is narrow at the top and broad below; for when the sea is violent the ship lies over on one side so that things are spilt. Yet I have never heard that a ship has sunk upon the high sea.

Whoever could provide himself with the things named above and should make an agreement with the ship captain that he give him liberty to cook and a good place to lie the voyage would not be hard. For we had young and old people, all are hale and hearty. Whatever one brings here in the way of wares is worth at least as much again. Linen cloth and glass would be especially needed, and is to be purchased very well in Holland.

Peter Röhtiger and my two daughters greet you, for we live beside each other. Dichtli is still with me, and I am delivering the greeting of us all to our dear and faithful pastor, to the whole number of honored persons, especially Godfather Kilchmeyer Dreuthart, and Andreas Aescher, Christen Jantz.

I would have much to write. I must break off. Have patience with my bad writing, for whoever sees my hand and labor will believe that I have not written and studied much. Greet for us Christien Bürki and I should be glad if he could hear the contents of this letter.

I remain your well affectioned servant, and my parents' obedient son until death.

Greet for us Anna Drus, [also] Speismann's people, and your sister and relatives, also my father's sister, and first of all the school-master.

READING AND DISCUSSION QUESTIONS

1. What do you think Janzen's purpose was in writing this letter home to his family and friends?

---

[2]**galangale**: Galangale, or ganangal, is a ginger-like spice.

2. How does Janzen's letter help you to understand the reasons why Europeans migrated to North America?

3. What are some of the advantages and disadvantages of using Janzen's letter as a source for understanding how eighteenth-century migrants adapted to their new circumstances?

P2-3 | An Indentured Servant Confesses to Murder

The Vain Prodigal Life and Tragical Penitent Death of Thomas Hellier (1680)

Thomas Hellier was a twenty-eight-year-old indentured servant who emigrated from Dorset, England, to Virginia in the late seventeenth century. His tragic story points to the disparity between the expectations that motivated his migration and the reality he faced once he arrived. While many who suffered similar disillusionment adapted to their new environments and survived as best they could, Hellier chose a different, more dreadful path, savagely murdering his masters. In time, colonists shifted from the use of indentured servants, bound for a period of seven years, to a slave-based agricultural economy, whose laborers were bound for life.

Thus had I trifled away and mis-spent my ten pounds and the price of my horse. Next, to supply necessity, I sold my Cloaths for want of money: so walking up Tower-ditch, I going in at the Eagle and Childe, enquired if there were any Ship-Captain quartered there? One replied, There was no Ship-Captain quartered in that house, but that he himself was concern'd about Seafaring matters. I enquired to what parts he was concern'd? He answered, To Virginia: So asked withal, if I were minded for that Country; if I were, I should have Meat, Drink, and Apparel, with other Necessaries provided for me. I replied, I had heard so bad a character of that Country, that I dreaded going thither, in regard I abhorred the Ax and the Haw. He told me, he would promise I should onely be employ'd in Merchants Accompts, and such Employments to which I had been bred, if they were here used.

On August the 10th, 77, I being over-perswaded, went on board the *Young Prince* Captain Robert Morris Commander; on the 5th of September ditto, the *Young Prince* weighed Anchor from the Downs; and on the 25th of October following, she arrived within the Capes of Virginia, and dropt Anchor at Newpersnews.

I was delivered into the custody and dispose of one Lewis Connor of Barmedoe hundred Virginia, who sold me off to one Cutbeard Williamson, living at a Plantation call'd Hard Labour, belonging to Westover-Parish in Charles

A Documentary History of American Industrial Society, vol. 1, ed. John R. Commons, Ulrich B. Phillips, Eugene A. Gilmore, Helen L. Sumner, and John B. Andrews (Cleveland: Arthur H. Clark Company, 1910), 360–365.

City County Virginia: which said Williamson promised me I should be employed in Teaching his Children, and not be set to any laborious work, unless necessity did compel now and then, meerly for a short spurt. But nevertheless, though I wanted not for Cloaths nor Victuals, yet I found their dealings contrary to their fair promises; which much disheartened me. And though my labour at the Howe was very irksome, and I was however resolved to do my utmost endeavour at it; yet that which embittered my life, and made everything I took in hand burdensome to me, was the unworthy ill-usage which I received daily and hourly from my ill-tongued Mistriss; who would not only rail, swear and curse at me within doors, whenever I came into the house casting on me continually biting Taunts and bitter Flouts; but like a live Ghost would impertinently haunt me, when I was quiet in the Ground at work. And although I silently wrought as fast as she rail'd, plying my labour, without so much as muttering at her, or answering any thing good or bad; yet all the silence and observance that I could use, would not charm her vile tongue. These things burning and broyling in my Breast, tempted me to take the trip, and give my master the bag to hold; thereupon I vamped off, and got on board Capt. Larimore's ship, where I remained eleven days, or thereabouts, the Ship then riding at Warwicks-Creek Bay.

I was absent from my Master's business almost three weeks, but at length my Master hunting about, and searching to and fro, had discovered where I was, and so sending a Messenger, fetched me back home again. As I was upon my return homeward, I had a design to have knock the Messenger on the head; for which purpose I took up a great stone and carried it along in my hand a good way, unknown to the man: but my heart failing me, I let drop that design. At length home I came, begg'd pardon of my Master for my fault, and all seemed pretty well again. But my usage proving still worse than before, my Mistress ever taunting me with her odious and inveterate Tongue, do all I would, and strive all the ways whatever I could, she, I found, was no whit pacified toward me. Whereupon I began to cast about and bethink my self, which way to rid me of that Hell upon Earth, yet still seeking if possible to weather it, but all in vain.

At last, Satan taking advantage of my secret inward regret, suggested to my vicious corrupt minde, that by ridding my Master and Mistress out of the way, I might with ease gain my Freedom, after which time I sought all opportunities to effectuate and bring to pass my said horrid contrivance: Concluding, when they were dead, I should be a Freeman. Which said execrable Project I attempted and put in execution May 24, 1678. Thus . . .

Betimes in the Morning before day, I put on my best cloaths, then got my Ax, and attempted two or three times to enter my Master's Lodging-room, still my heart failing me, I stept back again; but however at length in I rushed: A Servant-maid, who lay every night in the same Room, passed along by me the same time with her bed on her shoulder, or under her arm, to whom I offer'd no violence, but let her pass untouched; nor had I meddled with her, had she kept out of my way. From her I passed on to my Masters Bed, and struck at him with the Ax, and gave him several blows, as near as I could guess, upon the Head: I do believe I had so unhappy an aim with my hand, that I mortally wounded him the first blow. My Mistress in the interim got out of Bed, and got hold of a Chair, thinking to defend her self; and when I came toward her, struggled, but I proved to hard for her; She begg'd me to save her Life, and I might take what I would, and go my way. But all in vain, nothing would satisfie but her Life, whom I looked on as my greatest Enemy; so down she went without Mercy. The Wench to whom I intended no hurt, returned, as I suppose to rescue her Mistress; whereupon she suffer'd the same cruel Fate with the other two.

After this Tragedy I broke open a Closet, and took provision for my Journey, and rummaging my Mistress Chest, I took what I thought fit, as much as loaded a good lusty Horse; So taking my Master's Gun in my hand, away I hastened: But while the Horse stood without door, a neighbor came to the house, with an excuse to borrow the said Horse. To whom I frowning, answered very roughly, and threatening him, bid him be gone, he could not have the Horse; who departed, and (I suppose) betrayed to the other Neighbours some jealousie he had conceived, concerning some Mischief I had been doing. A Childe also belonging to the Family was run forth to betray the business. But before any body came, I was gone upon my intended progress with my Master's Horse loaded, and his gun in my hand.

After wandering the unknown Woods a tedious time, to and fro, and finding no path, I struck up towards a Plantation belonging to one Gilly, near Chicka-hommony Swamp, where I had a Ship-mate living; here I found a Path, and following that Path, it led me up to the house, where finding my Ship-mate, I enquir'd the nearest way to the Falls of James River: Who told me, he knew not the way, but said, he would go and enquire; so he called his Master's Son, who asked, if I would not walk into the house, and eat before I went. I said it was too early for me to eat: The said Gilly's Son-in-law came forth also, and very urgent they were to have me walk in and smoke Tobacco, seeing I would not eat. I told them, I would not smoke, but desired them to direct me my way, (still keeping my Gun in my hand, I being as shie of them, as they were watchful over me.) At last they told me, they would shew me the way; one walking before me, and the other following me, who led me to a Passage over a Water: where before I passed over, I had some occasion to lay my Gun out of my hand: Whereupon one laying hold of the Gun, said, This is a compleat Gun, and withal fired it off: Whereupon I discern'd my self surprised.

They told me I was to go no farther: So they seising me, I struggled a while, and had like to have been too hard for one of the men. But Gilly himself hearing the report of the Gun, run down toward the place; so being overpower'd, I was forced to submit to have my hands bound. Upon this seisure I was struck with silence, not having power either to confess or deny the Fact. They forthwith brought me before Mr. John Stith, the next Justice of Peace; This happened May 25, 1678. I had no power to answer the Justice to any thing, only I begg'd that I might have a Minister sent for to me, and then I should relate the whole matter. One Mr. Williams was sent to me the next morning (being Saturday) to whom I acknowledged the whole matter. After conference with the said Minister, I began by degrees to be rendred sensible of the heinousness of my horrid and bloudy

Crime; for which I was Tryed at James-Town, July 26, 1678. And was Sentenced to be Hang'd in Chains the 27, ditto; according to which just Sentence, I am now deservedly to suffer here this instant 5th of August, 1678.

READING AND DISCUSSION QUESTIONS

1. What was Hellier's motivation for traveling to the colonies?

2. What can you infer about the daily life within a small plantation family from Hellier's testimony? What clues can the historian use to re-create the world Hellier entered?

3. Compare the challenges Hellier faces to those faced by other new arrivals in the colonies like Christen Janzen (Document P2-2) or Olaudah Equiano (Document P2-1).

P2-4 | Celebrating an Indian Defeat
A Ballad of Pigwacket (1725)

The endemic warfare of the eighteenth century, which witnessed European empires contesting for power, spilled over into the North American colonies. British colonists fought Native Americans in a long series of frontier skirmishes, like the one commemorated in this 1725 song. Captain John Lovewell (1691–1725) and his New England men attacked and defeated the Abenaki Indians at the Battle of Pequawket (Pigwacket) along the Maine frontier, causing them to retreat north to Canada. Here we see the effect of warfare on Indian peoples and the ideas and beliefs about them that British Americans held.

1. Of worthy Captain Lovewell, I purpose now to sing,
How valiantly he served his country and his King;
He and his valiant soldiers, did range the woods full wide,
And hardships they endured to quell the Indian's pride.

2. 'Twas nigh unto Pigwacket, on the eighth day of May,
They spied a rebel Indian soon after break of day;
He on a bank was walking, upon a neck of land,
Which leads into a pond as we're made to understand.

3. Our men resolv'd to have him, and travell'd two miles round,
Until they met the Indian, who boldly stood his ground;
Then speaks up Captain Lovewell, "take you good heed," says he,
"This rogue is to decoy us, I very plainly see.

American History Told by Contemporaries, Volume II: Building of the Republic, 1689–1783 (New York: The Macmillan Company, 1901), 344–346.

4. "The Indians lie in ambush, in some place nigh at hand,
In order to surround us upon this neck of land;
Therefore we'll march in order, and each man leave his pack,
That we may briskly fight them when they make their attack."

5. They came unto this Indian, who did them thus defy,
As soon as they came nigh him, two guns he did let fly,
Which wounded Captain Lovewell, and likewise one man more,
But when this rogue was running, they laid him in his gore.

6. Then having scalp'd the Indian, they went back to the spot,
Where they had laid their packs down, but there they found them not,
For the Indians having spy'd them, when they them down did lay,
Did seize them for their plunder, and carry them away.

7. These rebels lay in ambush, this very place hard by,
So that an English soldier did one of them espy,
And cried out, "here's an Indian," with that they started out,
As fiercely as old lions, and hideously did shout.

8. With that our valiant English, all gave a loud huzza,
To shew the rebel Indians they fear'd them not a straw:
So now the fight began, and as fiercely as could be,
The Indians ran up to them, but soon were forced to flee.

9. Then spake up Captain Lovewell, when first the fight began,
"Fight on my valiant heroes! you see they fall like rain."
For as we are inform'd, the Indians were so thick,
A man could scarcely fire a gun and not some of them hit.

10. Then did the rebels try their best our soldiers to surround,
But they could not accomplish it, because there was a pond,
To which our men retreated and covered all the rear,
The rogues were forc'd to flee them, altho' they skulked for fear.

11. Two logs there were behind them that close together lay,
Without being discovered, they could not get away;
Therefore our valiant English, they travell'd in a row,
And at a handsome distance as they were wont to go.

12. 'Twas ten o'clock in the morning, when first the fight begun,
And fiercely did continue until the setting sun;
Excepting that the Indians some hours before 'twas night,
Drew off into the bushes and ceas'd a while to fight,

13. But soon again returned, in fierce and furious mood,
Shouting as in the morning, but yet not half so loud;
For as we are informed, so thick and fast they fell,
Scarce twenty of their number, at night did get home well.

14. And that our valiant English, till midnight there did stay,
To see whether the rebels would have another fray;
But they no more returning, they made off towards their home,
And brought away their wounded as far as they could come.

15. Of all our valiant English, there were but thirty-four,
And of the rebel Indians, there were about forescore.
And sixteen of our English did safely home return,
The rest were kill'd and wounded, for which we all must mourn.

16. Our worthy Captain Lovewell among them there did die,
They killed Lieut. Robbins, and wounded good young Frye,
Who was our English Chaplain; he many Indians slew,
And some of them he scalp'd when bullets round him flew.

17. Young Fullam too I'll mention, because he fought so well,
Endeavouring to save a man, a sacrifice he fell;
But yet our valiant Englishmen in fight were ne'er dismay'd,
But still they kept their motion, and Wyman's Captain made,

18. Who shot the old chief Paugus, which did the foe defeat,
Then set his men in order, and brought off the retreat;
And braving many dangers and hardships in the way,
They safe arriv'd at Dunstable, the thirteenth day of May.

READING AND DISCUSSION QUESTIONS

1. What point of view toward the Abenaki Indians does the author of this ballad hold? Who do you think was his or her audience?

2. What does this source suggest about the long-term effect of warfare and the population movements of British Americans on native peoples?

P2-5 | Colonial Settlements Raise Indian Alarms
Journal of James Kenny (1761–1763)

In the early 1760s, James Kenny was in charge of the trading store near Pittsburgh, in western Pennsylvania, an outpost established by the colony's Commissioners of Indian Affairs. Colonial authorities were clearly responding to the movement of white settlers to interior regions while establishing control over frontier land heretofore occupied by American Indians. As Kenny begins his diary, the North American phase of the French and Indian War was winding down. Here, he discusses colonists' encounters with American Indians.

9th.—Frederick Post came here from Tuscorawas & having a meeting with ye Indians there, before they set off (to ye Treaty) at Detroit, he let them know that the good Spirit had sent him amongst them in order to do them good & inform them in ye Christian Principels, to which they answer'd that they were very willing of his living amongst them, but not on them tearms, as they seen no better fruits or works amongst Christians than amongst themselves, but he told them that ye good spirit was with him, when he came to them in ye War time & that they had no reason to repent of his coming amongst them that time, and that now if they did not receive him on ye tearms he mentioned ye Good Spirit ordered him to leave them, and go to some others, having made them as ye head men of that Nation ye first offer & call'd for his Horse to be gone, but they would not consent to let him go, so he is now prepairing materials in order to build a House to live in, & keep School, & instruct them as far as he can or they will receive, but tells them that their hearts are not prepair'd to hear the gosple.

12th.—About this time ye Beaver King & Shingas came here & held a small council wt Geo. Croughan,[1] & ye Beaver told me they would go to Philadelphia next Spring to Confirm their alliance with our Province. . . .

16th.—One Agness Miller, being a Captive amongst ye Shawnes, was delivered up here as also two other little Girls, Daughters of Charles Stuward & James McBride, taken from ye Coves, one of them being taken by Shingus & belon'd to Pisquition. Langdale had orders from Israel Pemberton to advance £20 for redeeming Agness, but she being deliver'd up cost nothing.

23d—Langdale left this place and set off home, after leaving a Protest in Writing with me (as he was just going) being against all Josiah Davenports & my Actings in ye Store since ye Day he left it in order chiefly, as he told me, to clear himself if any thing happen'd in ye Goods which he said was only matter of form, as he never alledg'd any dishonesty to any of us. One Blaine ye officer which Commands at Ligonier came here. I have had no Answer as yet from ye Commiss^s,

---

John W. Jordan, ed., "Journal of James Kenny, 1761–1763," *The Pennsylvania Magazine of History and Biography*, vol. XXXVII (1913): 25–30.

[1]**Geo. Croughan**: George Croughan served as deputy Indian agent in the Ohio frontier. Beaver King (or Tamaqui) and Shingas were both leaders of the Delaware Indians.

which gives Frederick Post some encouragement (if I am set at liberty) to go to see him to Tuscorawas.

11ᵐᵒ 1ˢᵗ. — The Shawana Chiefs came here & Held a Treaty of Peace with Geo. Croghan where none was admitt'd but Croghan's Assistant, (Thomas Hutchins) & himself & Indians I heard they promis'd to keep in friendship with yᵉ English for ever & blam'd yᵉ French for drawing them away from yᵉ English Intrest. . . .

12ᵗʰ. — Many Traders gone with Goods to Trade at yᵉ Indians Towns. One Thomas Cape that was Prisoner amongst yᵉ Shawanas, being taken from Cape Capen in Virginia, being set free, we have taken him to live with us. . . .

19ᵗʰ. — The Fort Banks here is very near raise'd which makes it look much Stronger than it was in times of more danger by accounts, yᵉ front next yᵉ Inhabitants being of Brick and Corners of yᵉ Angles of Hewn Stone, about [?] foot High yᵉ Back part next yᵉ Point where yᵉ two Rivers Meets being of Earth & soded all so that it grows thick of long Grass that was done last year & they have Moov'd yᵉ Bank several times this Summer its four Squair with a Row of Barracks along each Squair three Rows of which are Wooden frame work & yᵉ Row on yᵉ Bank side next yᵉ point is Brick also a large Brick House built this summer in yᵉ South East Corner of yᵉ Roof being now aputing on, having fine Steps at yᵉ Door of Hewn free Stone, a Cellar all under it, at yᵉ Bank Side of yᵉ Barracks opens yᵉ Doors of yᵉ Magazines Vaults & Dungeons lying under yᵉ Great Banks of Earth thrown out of yᵉ Great Trinches all Round in these are kept yᵉ Strores of Amunition &c & Prisoners that are to be tried for their Lives, in these Vaults are no light but as they carry Lanthorns, on yᵉ South East Bastion stands a High Poal like a Mast & top Mast to Hoist yᵉ flag on which is Hoisted on every first Day of yᵉ Week from about Eleven to One o'Clock & on State Days &c there are three Wells of Water wall'd in yᵉ fort, & a Squair of Clear Ground in yᵉ inside of about 2 Acres.

20ᵗʰ. — I have been Inform'd by a Young Man that was order'd by yᵉ Commanding Officer, Collonel Bouquet, (this Sumer) to Number all yᵉ Dwelling Houses without yᵉ Fort marking the number on each Door that there was above one Hundred Houses but yᵉ Highest number I have seen by beter [account] there is 150 Houses, to take notice of I think was Seventy Eight, these being yᵉ Inhabitants of Pittsburgh, where two years ago I have seen all yᵉ Houses that were without yᵉ Little Fort they had then, thrown Down, only One, which stands yet, also two that was within that little fort is now standing being yᵉ Hospital now, all yᵉ rest being Built since, which if yᵉ Place continues to Increase near this manner it must soon be very large, which seems likely to me.

21ˢᵗ. — As to yᵉ Government of yᵉ Place at p[re]sent yᵉ Chief Laws have been Out by yᵉ General's Orders, which are Viz 1ˢᵗ That all Subjects may by applying to yᵉ Chief Enginear Build Houses, but none to Sell or Rent any; that no person shall buy of yᵉ Indians, Horses nor Bells, &c.

11ᵐᵒ 21ˢᵗ. — To Sell no Rum or Strong Liquor nor give to Indians on Pain of having their Houses pull'd Down, & yᵉ Transgressors being banished the place. There was also some time ago, restrections about Selling the Indians Powder & Lead to exceed five pounds for one man at Once of Each & that there must be no dealing in Trade after yᵉ Evening Gun is fired after Sun Down. Some people have had their Houses pull'd Down for ye Brech of some of these Laws & themselves Banish'd.

25^(th). — This Day ye Provincial Soldiers Time expired, but are not discharged, y^e [Colonel] waiting for an answer whether they shall be continued over ye Winter.

27^(th). — Y^e Provincial Soldiers disarts without a Discharge & seems to be as willing to return, many of them as they were to List being kept to Constant Labour here at Building ye Banks of ye fort quarring Stone & Cutting Wood, which they perform'd as expeditiously as any that has work'd here & I heard that the [Colonel] should say they done an emense sight of work for ye time, so that our province has no small Share in raising ye Banks of Fort Pitt.

30^(th). — We have been very Busey in getting Home a Stock of fire-wood being Cut about a Mile up ye Allegheny & 150 Yards from ye River side some we haul'd with a Cart to ye River & some Carried & brought it home with a Battoe.

12^(mo) 1^(st). — Many of ye Inhabitants here have hired a School Master & Subscrib'd above Sixty Pounds for this Year to him, he has about Twenty Schollars, likewise ye Soberer sort of People seemes to Long for some publick way of Worship, so ye School Master Reads ye Littany & Common Prayer on ye first Days to a Congregation of different Principels (he being a Prisbiterant) where they behave very Grave (as I hear), on ye occasion ye Children also are brought to Church as they Call it.

5^(th). — The Provincials are discharged & Marches off with [Colonel] Burd, this Place having but few Soldiers left in it.

Here is about 51 of ye Sennica Nation Wariors, with a Steady big Old Man, their Head, going to War against ye Cherokees. They have made a Speech at their Coming that we should not think hard of them Concerning ye Conspiracy they began this last Sumer, as that matter was Settled & they intend to live in peace with us for ye futor, & being in need of some necessaries they hop'd we would supply them as they were going against ye common Enemy to us as to them. This Nation are Said to be ye most against ye English of any of ye Six Nations. . . .

Sennica Wariors have got ye last provissions allow'd them this Day with orders to go being Supply'd with all they ask'd, they are very troublesome by crowding into ye Houses & thronging our fire Places, but behaves Civell ye Indians in General being so theevish that we are under ye necessity to watch them with ye utmost care & must be loosers after in some things unless we had as many spyes as they have thieves; this makes them fare ye worse amongst us, as we are affraid to let them Sleep in our Houses, or indulge them to tarry any longe time, but many of them are so good natured that they wont be affronted readily.

12^(mo) 8^(th). — The Head Sennica Warior dealt Seven large Bucksins with me, when many of them Croud'd in ye Store being very Theivish (ye Agent being out) ye Warior seem'd not easy pleas'd with his full Pay which he took in Powder, so I gave him a Loaf of Bread which was satisfactory to them; one of them bringing a small Skin want'd Brass Wire for it, but could hardly please himself amongst a variety of sorts, telling me to hand more, which I looked upon it as a Stratagem to keep me bussie that ye others might have oppertunity to Steal something. Several of 'em want'd to get behind ye Counter but I always turn'd em back & all they got was a Handful of salt. One took out a kegg that stood behind ye door, whilst my Brother just step'd out, so I turn'd them all out & ye Hindmost stop'd by ye door & begg'd for a Little Salt, so I gave him a Handfull he being disappoint'd in Stealing of it.

READING AND DISCUSSION QUESTIONS

1. Is there anything in Kenny's account of life in western Pennsylvania that might have caused anxiety among the Native Americans living near the fort? What, for instance, might they have thought about Kenny's description of Fort Banks?

2. What does this source suggest about how the western migration of colonial peoples affected the Native American populations that they encountered?

3. How does Kenny describe the Native Americans who traded with the colonists? How would you use this source as evidence for mid-eighteenth-century Americans' attitudes toward Native Americans?

■ COMPARATIVE QUESTIONS ■

1. What do these sources suggest about the movement of various groups to and within the Americas during the era of colonization?

2. Compare the depiction of Native Americans in the Ballad of Pigwacket and in Kenny's journal. What similarities and differences do you see? What do these sources suggest about how the movement of colonial peoples affected Native American groups?

3. What challenge does the Ballad of Pigwacket present to the historian seeking evidence of the past? Are these sources "trustworthy"? How is this source different from Janzen's letter, for example?

4. How did various groups adapt to their new social and physical environments? Compare the image of Native Americans related in Kenny's journal with Canassatego's speech (Document 3-2).

5

The Problem of Empire
1763–1776

In late 1774, General Thomas Gage, the royally appointed governor of Massachusetts, wrote desperate messages home describing the crumbling state of colonial affairs. "Conciliating, Moderation, Reasoning is over, Nothing can be done but by forceable Means." The impasse Gage found upon taking up his duties had developed over the course of a decade. With the successful conclusion of the French and Indian War (1754–1763), Parliament tightened its administration of the colonies and sought to raise revenue to pay off wartime debts. Colonists who had been lightly governed before, now felt the sting of Parliament's attention, and many resented the stricter colonial administration.

Richard Bland's 1766 essay, which opens this chapter, defended colonial rights and questioned Parliament's authority to legislate for the colonies. Some colonists recognized Parliament's claim of authority as legitimate, blamed excessive "liberty" for the unrest, and decried what they described as mob violence. However, by 1776, many colonists had rejected Parliament's claims of authority to legislate for them and were convinced that Britain had overstepped its rights. All that remained was some kindred loyalty to the king, but Thomas Paine's commonsense attack on monarchy destroyed even that. The ties connecting colony to empire through the person of the king had snapped. The result was revolution.

5-1 | A Virginia Planter Defends the Natural Rights of Colonies

RICHARD BLAND, *Inquiry into the Rights of the British Colonies* (1766)

The American Revolution was an extraordinary war of words. Long before Lexington and Concord, colonists fought verbal battles convincing themselves and others that the British Parliament was acting contrary to the rights of colonists. The colonists were British subjects, and they claimed their rights as such. Richard Bland (1710–1776), a Virginia planter and lawyer who was elected to the First and Second Continental Congresses, defended what he considered to be the colonists' natural rights. This argument, that the rights of colonists were theirs by nature and not the gift of king or Parliament, framed the debate and would eventually figure into Jefferson's bold claim in the Declaration of Independence that each was entitled to his inalienable right to life, liberty, and the pursuit of happiness.

SIR,

I take the Liberty to address you, as the Author of "The Regulations lately made concerning" the Colonies, and the Taxes imposed upon "them considered." It is not to the Man, whoever you are, that I address myself; but it is to the Author of a Pamphlet which, according to the Light I view it in, endeavours to fix Shackles upon the American Colonies: Shackles which, however nicely polished, can by no Means sit easy upon Men who have just Sentiments of their own Rights and Liberties. . . .

I have undertaken to examine, with an honest Plainness and Freedom, whether the Ministry, by imposing Taxes upon the Colonies by Authority of Parliament, have pursued a wise and salutary Plan of Government, or whether they have exerted pernicious and definitive Acts of Power. . . .

The Question is whether the Colonies are represented in the British Parliament or not? You affirm it to be an indubitable Fact: that they are represented, and from thence you infer a Right in the Parliament to impose Taxes of every Kind upon them. You do not insist upon the *Power*, but upon the *Right* of Parliament to impose Taxes upon the Colonies. This is certainly a very proper Distinction, as *Right* and *Power* have very different Meanings, and convey very different Ideas: For had you told us that the Parliament of Great Britain have *Power*, by the Fleets and Armies of the Kingdom, to impose Taxes and to raise Contributions upon the Colonies, I should not have presumed to dispute the Point with you; but as you insist upon the *Right* only, I must beg Leave to differ from you in Opinion, and shall give my Reasons for it.

But I must first recapitulate your Arguments in Support of this Right in the Parliament. You say "the Inhabitants of the Colonies do not indeed choose Members of Parliament, neither are nine Tenths of the People of Britain Electors;

An Inquiry into the Rights of the British Colonies, ed. Earl Gregg Swem (Richmond, VA: Appeals Press, Inc. for the Williams Parks Club, 1922), 3–7, 9–13, 21, 25–28, 30.

for the Right of Election is annexed to certain Species of Property, to peculiar Franchises, and to Inhabitancy in some particular Places. . . ."

"All British Subjects are really in the same [situation]; none are actually, all are virtually, represented in Parliament: For every Member of Parliament fits in the House not as a Representative of his own Constituents, but as one of that august Assembly by which all the Commons of Great Britain are represented. . . ."

Notwithstanding this Way of reasoning, I cannot comprehend how Men who are excluded from voting at the Election of Members of Parliament can be represented in that Assembly, or how those who are elected do not fit in the House as Representatives of their Constituents. These Assertions appear to me not only paradoxical, but contrary to the fundamental Principles of the English Constitution. . . .

It is from the Laws of the Kingdom, founded upon the Principles of the Law of Nature, that we are to show the Obligation every Member of the State is under to pay Obedience to its Institutions. From these Principles I shall endeavour to prove that the Inhabitants of Britain, who have no Vote in the Election of Members of Parliament, are not represented in that Assembly, and yet that they owe Obedience to the Laws of Parliament; which, as to them, are constitutional, and not arbitrary. As to the Colonies, I shall consider them afterwards. . . .

Men in a State of Nature are absolutely free and independent of one another as to sovereign Jurisdiction, but when they enter into a Society, and by their own Consent become Members of it, they must submit to the Laws of the Society according to which they agree to be governed; for it is evident, by the very Act of Association, that each Member subjects himself to the Authority of that Body in whom, by common Consent, the legislative Power of the State is placed: But though they must submit to the Laws, so long as they remain Members of the Society, yet they retain so much of their natural Freedom as to have a Right to retire from the Society, to renounce the Benefits of it, to enter into another Society, and to settle in another Country; for their Engagements to the Society, and their Submission to the publick Authority of the State, do not oblige them to continue in it longer than they find it will conduce to their Happiness, which they have a natural Right to promote. This natural Right remains with every Man, and he cannot justly be deprived of it by any civil Authority. Every Person therefore who is denied his Share in the Legislature of the State to which he had an [original] Right, and every Person who from his particular Circumstances is excluded from this great Privilege, and refuses to exercise his natural Right of quitting the Country, but remains in it, and continues to exercise the Rights of a Citizen in all other Respects, must be subject to the Laws which by these Acts he *implicitly*, or to use your own Phrase, *virtually* consents to: For Men may subject themselves to Laws, by consenting to them *implicity*; that is, by conforming to them, by adhering to the Society, and accepting the Benefits of its Constitution, as well, as *explicitly* and directly, in their own Persons, or by their Representatives substituted in their Room. . . .

It is evident that the Obligation of the Laws of Parliament upon the People of Britain who have no Right to be Electors does not arise from their being *virtually* represented, but from a quite different Principle; a Principle of the Law of Nature, true, certain, and universal, applicable to every Sort of Government, and not contrary to the common Understandings of Mankind.

If what you say is a real Fact, that nine Tenths of the People of Britain are deprived of the high Privilege of being Electors, it shows a great Defect in the present Constitution, which has departed so much from its original Purity; but never can prove that those People are even *virtually* represented in Parliament. . . .

But if those People of Britain who are excluded from being Electors are not represented in Parliament, the Conclusion is much stronger against the People of the Colonies being represented; who are considered by the British Government itself, in every Instance of Parliamentary Legislation, as a distinct People. It has been determined by the Lords of the Privy Council that "Acts of Parliament made in England without naming the foreign Plantations will not bind them." Now what can be the Reason of this Determination, but that the Lords of the Privy Council are of Opinion the Colonies are a distinct People from the Inhabitants of Britain, and are not represented in Parliament. If, as you contend, the Colonies are *exactly in the same Situation* with the Subjects in Britain, the Laws will in every Instance be equally binding upon them, as upon those Subjects, unless you can discover two Species of *virtual* Representation; the one to respect the Subjects in Britain, and always existing in Time of Parliament; the other to respect the Colonies, a mere Non-Entity, if I may be allowed the Term, and never existing but when the Parliament thinks proper to produce it into Being by any particular Act in which the Colonies happen to be named. . . .

I will not dispute the Authority of the Parliament, which is without Doubt supreme within the Body of the Kingdom, and cannot be abridged by any other Power; but may not the King have Prerogatives which he has a Right to exercise without the Consent of Parliament? If he has, perhaps that of granting License to his Subjects to remove into a *new* Country, and to settle therein upon particular Conditions, may be one. If he has no such Prerogative, I cannot discover how the Royal Engagements can be made good, that "the Freedom and other Benefits of the British Constitution" shall be secured to those People who shall settle in a new Country under such Engagements; the Freedom, and other Benefits of the British Constitution, cannot be secured to a People without they are exempted from being taxed by any Authority but that of their Representatives, chosen by themselves. This is an essential Part of British Freedom. . . .

I hope I shall not be charged with Insolence, in delivering the Sentiments of an honest Mind with Freedom: I am speaking of the *Rights* of a People; *Rights* imply *Equality* in the Instances to which they belong, and must be treated without Respect to the Dignity of the Persons concerned in them. If "the British Empire in Europe and in America is the same Power," if the "Subjects in both are the same People, and all equally participate in the Adversity and Prosperity of the Whole," what Distinctions can the Difference of their Situations make, and why is this Distinction made between them? Why is the Trade of the Colonies more circumscribed than the Trade of Britain? And why are Impositions laid upon the one which are not laid upon the other? If the Parliament "have a *Right* to impose Taxes of every Kind upon the Colonies," they ought in Justice, as the same People, to have the same Sources to raise them from: Their Commerce ought to be equally free with the Commerce of Britain, otherwise it will be loading them with [burdens] at the same Time that they are deprived of Strength to sustain them; it will be forcing them to make Bricks without Straw. I acknowledge the Parliament is the sovereign legislative Power of the British Nation, and that by a full Exertion of their Power they can deprive the Colonists of the Freedom and other Benefits of the British Constitution which have been secured to them by our Kings; they can abrogate all their civil Rights and Liberties; but by what *Right* is it that the Parliament can exercise such a Power over the Colonists, who have as natural a Right to the Liberties and Privileges of *Englishmen* as if they were actually resident within the Kingdom? The Colonies are subordinate to the Authority of Parliament; subordinate I mean in Degree, but not absolutely so: For if by a Vote of the British Senate the Colonists were to be delivered up to the Rule of a French or Turkish Tyranny, they may refuse Obedience to such a Vote, and may oppose the Execution of it by Force. Great is the Power of Parliament, but, great as it is, it cannot, constitutionally, deprive the People of their *natural* Rights; nor, in Virtue of the same Principle, can it deprive them of their *civil* Rights, which are founded in Compact, without their own Consent. There is, I confess, a considerable Difference between these two Cases as to the Right of Resistance: In the first, if the Colonists should be dismembered from the Nation by Act of Parliament, and abandoned to another Power, they have a natural Right to defend their Liberties by open Force, and may lawfully resist; and, if they are able, repel the Power to whose Authority they are abandoned. But in the other, if they are deprived of their civil Rights, if great and manifest Oppressions are imposed upon them by the State on which they are dependent, their Remedy is to lay their Complaints at the Foot of the Throne, and to suffer patiently rather than disturb the publick Peace, which nothing but a Denial of Justice can excuse them in breaking. But if this Justice should be denied, if the most humble and dutiful Representations should be rejected, nay not even deigned to be received, what is to be done? To such a Question Thucydides would make the Corinthians reply, that if "a decent and condescending Behaviour is shown on the Part of the Colonies, it would be safe in the Mother State to press too far on such Moderation:" And he would make the *Corcyreans* answer, that "every Colony, whilst used in a proper Manner, ought to pay Honour and Regard to its Mother State; but, when treated with Injury and Violence, is become an Alien. They were not sent out to be the Slaves, but to be the Equals of those that remain behind."

But, according to your Scheme, the Colonies are to be prohibited from uniting in a Representation of their general Grievances to the common Sovereign. This Moment "the British Empire in Europe and in America is the same Power; its Subjects in both are the same People; each is equally important to the other, and mutual Benefits, mutual Necessities, cement their Connexion." The next Moment "the Colonies are unconnected with each other, different in their Manners, opposite in their Principles, and clash in their Interests and in their Views, from Rivalry in Trade, and the Jealousy of Neighbourhood. This happy

Division, which was effected by Accident, is to be continued throughout by Design; and all Bond of Union between them" is excluded from your vast System. *Divide et impera* is your Maxim in Colony Administration, lest "an Alliance should be formed dangerous to the Mother Country." Ungenerous Insinuation! detestable Thought! abhorrent to every Native of the Colonies! who, by an Uniformity of Conduct, have ever demonstrated the deepest Loyalty to their King, as the Father of his People, and an unshaken Attachment to the Interest of Great Britain. But you must entertain a most despicable Opinion of the Understandings of the Colonists to imagine that they will allow Divisions to be fomented between them about inconsiderable Things, when the closest Union becomes necessary to maintain in a constitutional Way their dearest Interests. . . .

I flatter myself, by what has been said, your Position of a *virtual* Representation is sufficiently refuted; and that there is really no such Representation known in the British Constitution, and consequently that the Colonies are not subject to an *internal* Taxation by Authority of Parliament.

READING AND DISCUSSION QUESTIONS

1. In this document, Bland invokes Thucydides, a fifth-century Greek historian and general during the Peloponnesian War, in crafting his argument for colonial rights. How does he use this classical reference to make his point, and why might he have done so? What does his use of a classical reference suggest about the audience he wrote for?

2. How does Bland's argument narrow the authority that Parliament claims over the colonies?

3. Bland accuses Parliament of adopting a policy he describes as *"divide et impera."* What do you think he means in this context? What does he seem to anticipate the colonists' reaction to be?

5-2 | Colonists Protest Parliament's Acts
STAMP ACT CONGRESS, *Declaration of Rights* (1765)

The Stamp Act, passed by Parliament in 1765, attempted to raise revenue by requiring all colonists to pay a tax in the form of stamps affixed to all printed materials, including newspapers and legal documents. Many colonists objected to this measure, which to them seemed to depart from Parliament's traditionally limited exercise of authority. Protests quickly built momentum, resulting in the calling of the first congress, or meeting, of the colonies, which was held in New York on October 7, 1765. This Stamp Act Congress issued a "declaration of rights," which is reproduced below. Parliament, wishing to avoid conflict, repealed the Stamp Act but passed the Declaratory Act, which affirmed Parliament's authority.

Journal of the First Congress of the American Colonies (New York: E. Winchester, 1845), 27–29.

The members of this congress, sincerely devoted, with the warmest sentiments of affection and duty to His Majesty's person and government, inviolably attached to the present happy establishment of the Protestant succession, and with minds deeply impressed by a sense of the present and impending misfortunes of the British colonies on this continent; having considered as maturely as time would permit, the circumstances of said colonies, esteem it our indispensable duty to make the following declarations, of our humble opinions, respecting the most essential rights and liberties of the colonists, and of the grievances under which they labor, by reason of several late acts of Parliament.

1st. That His Majesty's subjects in these colonies owe the same allegiance to the crown of Great Britain that is owing from his subjects born within the realm, and all due subordination to that august body, the Parliament of Great Britain.

2d. That His Majesty's liege subjects in these colonies are entitled to all the inherent rights and privileges of his natural born subjects within the kingdom of Great Britain.

3d. That it is inseparably essential to the freedom of a people, and the undoubted rights of Englishmen, that no taxes should be imposed on them, but with their own consent, given personally, or by their representatives.

4th. That the people of these colonies are not, and from their local circumstances cannot be, represented in the House of Commons in Great Britain.

5th. That the only representatives of the people of these colonies are persons chosen therein, by themselves; and that no taxes ever have been or can be constitutionally imposed on them but by their respective legislatures.

6th. That all supplies to the crown, being free gifts of the people, it is unreasonable and inconsistent with the principles and spirit of the British constitution for the people of Great Britain to grant to His Majesty the property of the colonists.

7th. That trial by jury is the inherent and invaluable right of every British subject in these colonies.

8th. That the late act of Parliament entitled, "An act for granting and applying certain stamp duties, and other duties in the British colonies and plantations in America, etc.," by imposing taxes on the inhabitants of these colonies, and the said act, and several other acts, by extending the jurisdiction of the courts of admiralty beyond its ancient limits, have a manifest tendency to subvert the rights and liberties of the colonists.

9th. That the duties imposed by several late acts of Parliament, from the peculiar circumstances of these colonies, will be extremely burthensome and grievous, and, from the scarcity of specie, the payment of them absolutely impracticable.

10th. That as the profits of the trade of these colonies ultimately center in Great Britain, to pay for the manufactures which they are obliged to take from thence, they eventually contribute very largely to all supplies granted there to the crown.

11th. That the restrictions imposed by several late acts of Parliament on the trade of these colonies will render them unable to purchase the manufactures of Great Britain.

12th. That the increase, prosperity, and happiness of these colonies depend on the full and free enjoyment of their rights and liberties, and an intercourse, with Great Britain, mutually affectionate and advantageous.

13th. That it is the right of the British subjects in these colonies to petition the king or either house of Parliament.

Lastly, That it is the indispensable duty of these colonies to the best of sovereigns, to the mother-country, and to themselves, to endeavor, by a loyal and dutiful address to His Majesty, and humble application to both houses of Parliament, to procure the repeal of the act for granting and applying certain stamp duties, of all clauses of any other acts of Parliament whereby the jurisdiction of the admiralty is extended as aforesaid, and of the other late acts for the restriction of the American commerce.

READING AND DISCUSSION QUESTIONS

1. How does the argument for colonial rights advanced here compare to the argument Bland made in 1766?

2. How would you characterize the tone of this declaration of rights? Why, for instance, do the representatives of the Congress enumerate their points in this order?

3. The declaration discusses the "rights and liberties" of the colonists. What specific rights and liberties were they claiming?

5-3 | A Loyalist Decries the Boston Mob

PETER OLIVER, *Origin and Progress of the American Rebellion* (1781)

The repeal of the Stamp Act only temporarily calmed the storm. Parliament introduced new taxes in 1767, leading to colonial boycotts of British goods. Relations strained over the next few years as self-styled "patriots" focused their anger at Parliament on its local representatives: those "loyalists" in the colonies who supported Britain's policies. Many Loyalists found themselves attacked, intimidated, and physically abused. To Peter Oliver (1713–1779), chief justice of the Massachusetts Superior Court, Patriots were rebels acting with mob vigilantism. In his 1781 book, published after he had fled the colonies for England, he included snippets, reproduced below, from Boston's newspapers detailing scenes of mob violence.

August 1774

A Mob in Berkshire assembled, & forced the Justices of the Court of common Pleas from their Seats on the Bench, and shut up the Court House, preventing any Proceedings at Law. At the same Time driving one of his Majesty's Justices of

Peter Oliver's Origin & Progress of the American Rebellion, ed. Douglass Adair and John A. Schutz (Stanford, CA: Stanford University Press), 152–157.

the Peace from his Dwelling House, so that he was obliged to repair to Boston for Protection by the Kings Troops.

At Taunton also, about 40 Miles from Boston, the Mob attacked the House of Daniel Leonard Esqr., one of his Majesty's Justices of the Peace; & a Barrister at Law. They fired Bullets into the House, & obliged him to fly from it to save his Life.

A Colo. [Colonel] Gilbert, a Man of Distinction & a firm Loyalist, living at Freetown, about 50 Miles from Boston, being absent about 20 Miles from his Home, was attacked by a Mob of above an 100 Men, at Midnight. But being a Man of great Bravery & Strength, he, by his single Arm, beat them all off. And on the same Night, & at the same Place, Brigadier Ruggles, a distinguished Friend of Government, & for many Years a Member of the general Assembly, was attacked by the same Mob; but by his firm Resolution he routed them all. They, in Revenge, cut his Horses Tail off & painted him all over. The Mob found that Paint was cheaper than Tar and Feathers.

September 1774

The Attorny General, Mr. Seawall, living at Cambridge, was obliged to repair to Boston under the Protection of the King's Troops. His House at Cambridge was attacked by a Mob, his Windows broke, & other Damage done; but by the Intrepidity of some young Gentlemen of the Family, the Mob were dispersed.

About the same Time Thomas Oliver Esqr. the Lieut Govr. of Massachusetts Province, was attacked in his House at Cambridge, by a Mob of 4000 Men; & as he had lately been appointed, by his Majesty, one of the new Council, they forced him to resign that Office; but this Resignation did not pacify the Mob; he was soon forced to fly to Boston for Protection. This Mob was not mixed with tag, rag & Bobtail only, Persons of Distinction in the Country were in the Mass, & as the Lieut. Governor was a Man of Distinction, he surely ought to be waited upon by a large Cavalcade & by Persons of Note.

In this Month, also, a Mob of 5000 collected at Worcester, about 50 Miles from Boston, a thousand of whom were armed. It being at the Time when the Court of Common Pleas was about sitting, the Mob made a lane, & compelled ye. Judges, Sheriff, & Gentlemen of the Bar, to pass & repass them, Cap in Hand, in the most ignominious Manner; & read their Disavowall of holding Courts under the new Acts of Parliament, no less than Thirty Times in the Procession.

Brigadier Ruggles's House at Hardwicke, about 70 Miles from Boston, was also plundered of his Guns, & one of his fine Horses poisoned.

Colo. Phips the high Sheriff of Middlesex, was obliged to promise not to serve any Processes of Courts; & retired to Boston for Protection.

A Committee, with a Justice Aikin at their Head, & a large Mob at their Heels, met at Taunton aforesaid, at Term Time, & forbid the Court of Common Pleas to sit.

Peter Oliver Esqr., a Justice of the Peace at Middleborough, was obliged by the Mob to sign an Obligation not to execute his Office under the new Acts. At the same Place, a Mr. Silas Wood, who had signed a Paper to disavow the riotous

Proceedings of the Times, was dragged by a Mob of 2 or 300 Men about a Mile to a River, in Order to drown him; but one of his Children hanging around him with Cries & Tears, he was induced to recant, though, even then, very reluctantly.

The Mob at Concord, about 20 Miles from Boston, abused a Deputy Sheriff of Middlesex, & compelled him, on Pain of Death, not to execute the Precepts for a new Assembly; they making him pass through a Lane of them, sometimes walking backwards, & sometimes forward, Cap in Hand, & they beating him.

Revd. Mr. Peters, of Hebron in Connecticut, an Episcopalian Clergyman, after having his House broke into by a Mob, & being most barbarously treated in it, was stript of his Canonicals, & carried to one of their Liberty Poles, & afterwards drove from his Parish. He had applied to Governor Trumble & to some of the Magistrates, for Redress; but they were as relentless as the Mob; & he was obliged to go to England incognito, having been hunted after, to the Danger of his Life.

William Vassall Esqr., a Man of Fortune, and quite inoffensive in his publick Conduct, tho' a Loyalist, was travelling with his Lady from Boston to his Seat at Bristol, in Rhode Island Government, about 60 Miles from Boston, & were pelted by the Mob in Bristol, to the endangering of their Lives.

All the Plimouth Protestors against Riots, as also all the military Officers, were compelled by a Mob of 2000 Men collected from that County & the County of Barnstable to recant & resign their military Commissions. Although the Justices of the Peace were then sitting in the Town of Plimouth, yet the Mob ransack'd the House of a Mr. Foster, a Justice of the Court of Common Pleas, a Man of 70 Years of Age, which obliged him to fly into the Woods to secrete himself, where he was lost for some Time and was very near to the loosing of his Life. Afterwards, they deprived him of his Business, & would not suffer him to take the Acknowledgment of a Deed.

A Son of one of the East India Companies Agents being at Plimouth collecting Debts, a Mob roused him, in the Night, & he was obliged to fly out of the Town; but ye. Midnight favoured his Escape.

December 1774

A Jesse Dunbar, of Hallifax, in the County of Plimouth, an honest Drover, had bought a fat Ox of one of his Majesty's new Council, & carried it to Plimouth for sale. The Ox was hung up & skinned. He was just upon quartering it, when the Town's Committee came to the Slaughter House, & finding that the Ox was bought of one of the new Councellors, they ordered it into a Cart, & then put Dunbar into the Belly of the Ox and carted him 4 Miles, with a Mob around him, when they made him pay a Dollar after taking three other Cattle & an Horse from him. They then delivered him to another Mob, who carted him 4 Miles further, & forced another Dollar from him. The second Mob delivered him to a third Mob, who abused him by throwing Dirt at him, as also throwing the Offals, in his Face & endeavoring to cover him with it, to the endangering his Life, & after other

Abuses, & carrying him 4 Miles further, made him pay another Sum of Mony. They urged the Councellors Lady, at whose House they stopped, to take the Ox; but she being a Lady of a firm Mind refused; upon which they tipped the Cart up & the Ox down into the Highway, & left it to take Care of itself. And in the Month of February following, this same Dunbar was selling Provisions at Plimouth, when the Mob seized him, tied him to his Horse's Tail, & in that Manner drove him through Dirt & mire out of the Town, & he falling down, his Horse hurt him.

In November 1774, David Dunbar of Hallifax aforesaid, being an Ensign in the Militia, a Mob headed by some of the Select Men of the Town, demand[ed] his Colours of him. He refused, saying, that if his commanding Officer demanded them he should obey, otherwise he would not part with them: upon which they broke into his House by Force & dragged him out. They had prepared a sharp Rail to set him upon; & in resisting them they seized him (by his private parts) & fixed him upon the Rail, & was held on it by his Legs & Arms, & tossed up with Violence & greatly bruised so that he did not recover for some Time. They beat him, & after abusing him about two Hours he was obliged, in Order to save his Life, to give up his Colours.

Quaere — Whether it would not have been as strictly legal to have stolen the Colours from his House, without all this Parade?

The Mob Committee, of the County of York, where Sr. William Pepperells large Estate lay, ordered that no Person should hire any of his Estates of him, nor buy any Wood of him, nor pay any Debts to him that were due to him.

One of the Constables of Hardwick, for refusing to pay the Provincial Collection of Taxes which he had gathered, to the new Receiver General of the rebel Government, was confined & bound for 36 Hours, & not suffered to lie in a Bed, & threatened to be sent to Simsbury Mines in Connecticut. These Mines being converted into a Prison, 50 Feet under Ground, where it is said that many Loyalists have suffered. The Officers Wife being dangerously ill, they suffered him to see her, after he had complied.

The aforementioned Colo. Gilbert was so obnoxious for his Attachment to Government, that the Mobs being sometimes afraid to attack him openly, some of them secretly fired Balls at him in the Woods. And as he was driving a Number of Sheep to his Farm, he was attacked by 30 or 40 of them, who robbed him of part of the Flock, but he beat the Mob off. And this same Colo. Gilbert was, some Time after, travelling on his Business, when he stopped at an Inn to bait his Horse. Whilst he was in the House, some Person lift up the Saddle from his Horse & put a Piece of a broken Glass Bottle under the Saddle; & when the Colo. mounted, the Pressure run the Glass into the Horses back, which made him frantick. The Horse threw his rider, who was so much hurt as not to recover his Senses 'till he was carried & arrived at his own House, at 3 Miles distance.

In September 1774, when the Court of Common Pleas was assembled for the Business of the Term, at Springfield, a large Mob collected, & prevented the sitting of the Court; they would not suffer Bench or Bar to enter the Court House; but obliged Bench, Sheriffs & Bar, with their Hats off, in a most humiliating Manner, to desist.

February 1775

A Number of Ladies, at Plimouth, attempted to divert their selves at the publick Assembly Room; but not being connected with the rebel Faction, the Committee Men met, and the Mob collected who flung Stones & broke the Windows & Shutters of the Room, endangering the Lives of the Company, who were obliged to break up, & were abused to their Homes.

Soon after this, the Ladies diverted their selves by riding out of Town, but were followed & pelted by the Mob, & abused with the most indecent Language.

The Honble. Israel Williams Esqr., who was appointed one of his Majesty's new Council, but had refused the Office by Reason of bodily Infirmities, was taken from his House, by a Mob, in the Night, & carried several Miles; then carried home again, after being forced to sign a Paper which they drafted; & a guard set over him to prevent his going from Home.

A Parish Clerk of an Episcopal Church at East Haddum in Connecticut, a Man of 70 Years of Age, was taken out of his Bed in a Cold Night, & beat against his Hearth by Men who held him by his Arms & Legs. He was then laid across his Horse, without his Cloaths, & drove to a considerable Distance in that naked Condition. His Nephew Dr. Abner Beebe, a Physician, complained of the bad Usage of his Uncle, & spoke very freely in Favor of Government; for which he was assaulted by a Mob, stripped naked, & hot Pitch was poured upon him, which blistered his Skin. He was then carried to an Hog Sty & rubbed over with Hogs Dung. They threw the Hog's Dung in his Face, & rammed some of it down his Throat; & in that Condition exposed to a Company of Women. His House was attacked, his Windows broke, when one of his Children was sick, & a Child of his went into Distraction upon this Treatment. His Gristmill was broke, & Persons prevented from grinding at it, & from having any Connections with him.

All the foregoing Transactions were before the Battle of Lexington, when the Rebels say that the War began.

READING AND DISCUSSION QUESTIONS

1. What propaganda value do you think these reports of violence lent to the Loyalist cause?

2. Describe the differences you see in the way Oliver depicts the Patriots and the way they presented themselves, for example, in the Stamp Act Congress.

3. According to Oliver's evidence, what were the rebels attacking and why?

5-4 | Worcester Loyalists Protest the Committee of Safety
A Protest by the Worcester, Massachusetts, Selectmen (1774)

As tensions in the colonies grew, committees of correspondence rapidly emerged as extra-legal governments, sharing information and news and enforcing Patriot policies such as colonial boycotts of British imports. Many Loyalists worried about the activities of these unelected and unaccountable groups. In 1774, the selectmen in Worcester, Massachusetts, demanded that those connected to the committee submit to a public examination of their papers and actions. This motion was defeated, but a protest by Loyalists, reproduced below, was entered into the public record and subsequently printed in the Boston papers. When Patriots became aware of this, they physically forced the town clerk, with inky fingers, to blot out the Loyalists' protest.

At a meeting of the inhabitants of the Town of Worcester, held there on the 20th day of June, A. D. 1774, pursuant to an application made to the Selectmen by 43 voters and freeholders of the same town, dated the 20th day of May last, therein among other things, declaring their just apprehensions of the fatal consequences that may follow the many riotous and seditious actions that have of late times been done and perpetrated in divers places within this Province; the votes and proceedings of which meeting are by us deemed irregular and arbitrary:

Wherefore we, some of us who were petitioners for the said meeting, and others, inhabitants of the town, hereunto subscribing, thinking it our indispensable duty, in these times of discord and confusion in too many of the towns within this Province, to bear testimony in the most open and unreserved manner against all riotous, disorderly and seditious practices, must therefore now declare, that it is with the deepest concern for public peace and order, that we behold so many whom we used to esteem sober, peaceable men, so far deceived, deluded and led astray, by the artful, crafty and insidious practices of some evil-minded and ill-disposed persons, who, under the disguise of patriotism, and falsely styling themselves the friends of liberty, some of them neglecting their own proper business and occupation, in which they ought to be employed for the support of their families, spending their time in discoursing of matters they do not understand, raising and propagating falsehoods and calumnies of those men they look up to with envy, and on whose fall and ruin they wish to rise, intend to reduce all things to a state of tumult, discord and confusion.

And in pursuance of those evil purposes and practices, they have imposed on the understanding of some, corrupted the principles of others, and distracted the minds of many, who under the influence of this delusion, have been tempted to act a part that may prove, and that has already proved, extremely prejudicial to the Province, and as it may be, fatal to themselves; bringing into real danger,

Worcester Town Records, From 1753 to 1783, ed. Franklin P. Rice (Worcester, MA: The Worcester Society of Antiquity, 1882), 230–232.

and in many instances destroying, that liberty and property we all hold sacred, and which they vainly and impiously boast of defending at the expense of their blood and treasure.

And as it appears to us that many of this town seem to be led aside by strange opinions, and are prevented coming to such prudent votes and resolutions as might be for the general good and the advantage of this town in particular, agreeably to the request of the petitioners for this meeting.

And as the town has refused to dismiss the persons styling themselves the Committee of Correspondence for the town, and has also refused so much as to call on them to render an account of their past dark and pernicious proceedings:

We therefore, whose names are hereunto Subscribed, do each of us declare and protest, it is our firm opinion, that the Committees of Correspondence in the several towns of this Province, being creatures of modern invention, and constituted as they be, are a legal grievance, having no legal foundation, contrived by a junto[1] to serve particular designs and purposes of their own, and that they as they have been and are now managed in this town, are a nuisance. And we fear, it is in a great measure owing to the baneful influence of such committees, that the teas of immense value, lately belonging to the East India Company, were, not long since, scandalously destroyed in Boston, and that many other enormous acts of violence and opression have been perpetrated, whereby the lives of many honest worthy persons have been endangered and their property destroyed.

It is by these committees also, that papers have been lately published, and are now circulating through the Province, inviting and wickedly tempting all persons to join them, fully implying, if not expressly denouncing the destruction of all that refuse to subscribe those unlawful combinations, tending directly to sedition, civil war and rebellion.

These and all such enormities, we detest and abhor, and the authors of them we esteem enemies to our King and country, violators of all law and civil liberty, the malevolent disturbers of the peace of society, subverters of the established constitution, and enemies of mankind.

READING AND DISCUSSION QUESTIONS

1. How do the Loyalists attempt to undermine the Patriot cause in this document? What do the Loyalists suggest is their motivation?

2. What does the manner in which the Loyalist authors describe the committee of correspondence members tell us about the attitudes of Loyalists themselves? What distinctions do they draw between themselves and others?

---

[1]**junto**: A small group, often secret, united for some common cause or purpose.

5-5 | The Danger of Too Much Liberty

THOMAS HUTCHINSON, *Letter to Thomas Whately* (1769)

As all sides attempted to understand the cause of the conflict between crown and colony, different actors diagnosed the problem in different ways. For Patriots, the culprit was Parliament's encroachment on their natural rights and liberties. For Loyalists, such as Governor Thomas Hutchinson of Massachusetts, excessive regard for their liberties encouraged colonists to act in ways contrary to their interests as subjects of the British crown. Hutchinson wrote a series of letters to Thomas Whately, a former member of Parliament and the Board of Trade. In one of those letters, reproduced below, Hutchinson offers his advice on restraining the colonists. These letters were leaked to Benjamin Franklin, then in London, and published in the Boston newspapers in 1773, inflaming the Patriots who already assumed Hutchinson was conspiring against their interests.

Boston, 20th January 1769.

Dear Sir,

You have laid me under very great obligations by the very clear and full account of proceedings in Parliament, which I received from you by Capt. Scott. You have also done much service to the people of the province. For a day or two after the ship arrived, the enemies of government gave out that their friends in Parliament were increasing, and all things would be soon on the old footing; in other words that all acts imposing duties would be repealed, the Commissioners board dissolved, the customs put on the old footing, and illicit trade be carried on with little or no hazard. It was very fortunate that I had it in my power to prevent such a false representation from spreading through the province. I have been very cautious of using your name, but I have been very free in publishing abroad the substance of your letter, and declaring that I had my intelligence from the best authority, and have in a great measure defeated the ill design in raising and attempting to spread so groundless a report. What marks of resentment the Parliament will show, whether they will be upon the province in general or particular persons, is extremely uncertain, but that they will be placed somewhere is most certain, and I add, because I think it ought to be so that those who have been most steady in preserving the constitution and opposing the licentiousness of such as call themselves Sons of Liberty will certainly meet with favor and encouragement.

This is most certainly a crisis. I really wish that there may not have been the least degree of severity beyond what is absolutely necessary to maintain, I think I may say to you the dependance which a colony ought to have upon the parent state; but if no measures shall have been taken to secure this dependance, or nothing more than some declaratory acts or resolves, it is all over with us. The friends of government will be utterly disheartened, and the friends of anarchy will be afraid of nothing be it ever so extravagant.

The Letters of Governor Hutchinson and Lieut. Governor Oliver (London: J. Wilkie, 1774), 15–17.

The last vessel from London had a quick passage. We expect to be in suspense for the three or four next weeks and then to hear our fate. I never think of the measures necessary for the peace and good order of the colonies without pain. There must be an abridgment of what are called English liberties. I relieve myself by considering that in a remove from the state of nature to the most perfect state of government there must be a great restraint of natural liberty. I doubt whether it is possible to project a system of government in which a colony 3000 miles distant from the parent state shall enjoy all the liberty of the parent state. I am certain I have never yet seen the projection. I wish the good of the colony when I wish to see some further restraint of liberty rather than the connexion with the parent state should be broken; for I am sure such a breach must prove the ruin of the colony. Pardon me this excursion, it really proceeds from the state of mind into which our perplexed affairs often throw me.

I have the honor to be with very great esteem, Sir, your most humble and most obedient servant,

THO. HUTCHINSON.

READING AND DISCUSSION QUESTIONS

1. What does Hutchinson emphasize in his assessment of the political turmoil disrupting Boston?

2. How might Hutchinson have responded to Bland's argument (Document 5-1) about the natural rights of colonists?

5-6 | Thomas Paine Attacks the Monarchy

THOMAS PAINE, *Common Sense* (1776)

Much of the political argumentation in the Revolutionary period focused on whether Parliament had the authority to legislate for the colonies. Patriots rallied behind the slogan "no taxation without representation," and once they became convinced that Parliament was not their legislature, it was only their connection as subjects of the king that tethered them to the empire. Published in 1776, months before the signing of the Declaration of Independence, Thomas Paine's *Common Sense* focused on that relationship and called into disrepute the very idea of monarchy. *Common Sense* was significant for how it helped reluctant colonists sever their connection to what Paine implied was an irrational institution.

Of Monarchy and Hereditary Succession

Mankind being originally equals in the order of creation, the equality could only be destroyed by some subsequent circumstance; the distinctions of rich, and

Life and Writings of Thomas Paine, ed. Daniel Edwin Wheeler (New York: Vincent Parke and Company, 1908), 12–13, 19–20, 24, 26–32, 35–37.

poor, may in a great measure be accounted for, and that without having recourse to the harsh ill sounding names of oppression and avarice. Oppression is often the consequence, but seldom or never the means of riches; and though avarice will preserve a man from being necessitously poor, it generally makes him too timorous to be wealthy.

But there is another and greater distinction for which no truly natural or religious reason can be assigned, and that is, the distinction of men into KINGS and SUBJECTS. Male and female are the distinctions of nature, good and bad the distinctions of heaven; but how a race of men came into the world so exalted above the rest, and distinguished like some new species, is worth enquiring into, and whether they are the means of happiness or of misery to mankind.

In the early ages of the world, according to the scripture chronology, there were no kings; the consequence of which was there were no wars; it is the pride of kings which throw mankind into confusion. Holland without a king hath enjoyed more peace for this last century than any of the monarchical governments in Europe. Antiquity favors the same remark; for the quiet and rural lives of the first patriarchs hath a happy something in them, which vanishes away when we come to the history of Jewish royalty.

Government by kings was first introduced into the world by the Heathens, from whom the children of Israel copied the custom. It was the most prosperous invention the Devil ever set on foot for the promotion of idolatry. The Heathens paid divine honors to their deceased kings, and the Christian world hath improved on the plan by doing the same to their living ones. How impious is the title of sacred majesty applied to a worm, who in the midst of his splendor is crumbling into dust! . . .

To the evil of monarchy we have added that of hereditary succession; and as the first is a degradation and lessening of ourselves, so the second, claimed as a matter of right, is an insult and an imposition on posterity. For all men being originally equals, no one by birth could have a right to set up his own family in perpetual preference to all others for ever, and though himself might deserve some decent degree of honors of his contemporaries, yet his descendants might be far too unworthy to inherit them. One of the strongest natural proofs of the folly of hereditary right in kings, is, that nature disapproves it, otherwise, she would not so frequently turn it into ridicule by giving mankind an ass for a lion.

Secondly, as no man at first could possess any other public honors than were bestowed upon him, so the givers of those honors could have no power to give away the right of posterity, and though they might say "We choose you for our head," they could not, without manifest injustice to their children, say "that your children and your children's children shall reign over ours for ever." Because such an unwise, unjust, unnatural compact might (perhaps) in the next succession put them under the government of a rogue or a fool. Most wise men, in their private sentiments, have ever treated hereditary right with contempt; yet it is one of those evils, which when once established is not easily removed; many submit from fear, others from superstition, and the more powerful part shares with the king the plunder of the rest. . . .

But it is not so much the absurdity as the evil of hereditary succession which concerns mankind. Did it ensure a race of good and wise men it would have the seal of divine authority, but as it opens a door to the foolish, the wicked, and the improper, it hath in it the nature of oppression. Men who look upon themselves born to reign, and others to obey, soon grow insolent; selected from the rest of mankind their minds are early poisoned by importance; and the world they act in differs so materially from the world at large, that they have but little opportunity of knowing its true interests, and when they succeed to the government are frequently the most ignorant and unfit of any throughout the dominions. . . .

If we inquire into the business of a king, we shall find that in some countries they have none; and after sauntering away their lives without pleasure to themselves or advantage to the nation, withdraw from the scene, and leave their successors to tread the same idle round. In absolute monarchies the whole weight of business, civil and military, lies on the king; the children of Israel in their request for a king, urged this plea "that he may judge us, and go out before us and fight our battles." But in countries where he is neither a judge nor a general, as in England, a man would be puzzled to know what is his business.

The nearer any government approaches to a republic the less business there is for a king. It is somewhat difficult to find a proper name for the government of England. Sir William Meredith calls it a republic; but in its present state it is unworthy of the name, because the corrupt influence of the crown, by having all the places in its disposal, hath so effectually swallowed up the power, and eaten out the virtue of the house of commons (the republican part in the constitution) that the government of England is nearly as monarchical as that of France or Spain. . . .

[I]t is the republican and not the monarchical part of the constitution of England which Englishmen glory in, viz. the liberty of choosing an house of commons from out of their own body—and it is easy to see that when republican virtue fails, slavery ensues. Why is the constitution of England sickly, but because monarchy hath poisoned the republic, the crown hath engrossed the commons?

In England a king hath little more to do than to make war and give away places; which in plain terms, is to impoverish the nation and set it together by the ears. . . . Of more worth is one honest man to society and in the sight of God, than all the crowned ruffians that ever lived.

Thoughts on the Present State of American Affairs

In the following pages I offer nothing more than simple facts, plain arguments, and common sense; and have no other preliminaries to settle with the reader, than that he will divest himself of prejudice and prepossession, and suffer his reason and his feelings to determine for themselves; that he will put on, or rather that he will not put off, the true character of a man, and generously enlarge his views beyond the present day.

Volumes have been written on the subject of the struggle between England and America. Men of all ranks have embarked in the controversy, from different motives, and with various designs; but all have been ineffectual, and the period of debate is closed. Arms, as the last resource, decide the contest; the appeal was the choice of the king, and the continent hath accepted the challenge.

It hath been reported of the late Mr Pelham (who tho' an able minister was not without his faults) that on his being attacked in the house of commons, on the score, that his measures were only of a temporary kind, replied, "They will last my time." Should a thought so fatal and unmanly possess the colonies in the present contest, the name of ancestors will be remembered by future generations with detestation.

The sun never shined on a cause of greater worth. 'Tis not the affair of a city, a country, a province, or a kingdom, but of a continent—of at least one eighth part of the habitable globe. 'Tis not the concern of a day, a year, or an age; posterity are virtually involved in the contest, and will be more or less affected, even to the end of time, by the proceedings now. Now is the seed time of continental union, faith and honor. The least fracture now will be like a name engraved with the point of a pin on the tender rind of a young oak; The wound will enlarge with the tree, and posterity read it in full grown characters.

By referring the matter from argument to arms, a new era for politics is struck; a new method of thinking hath arisen. All plans, proposals, &c. prior to the nineteenth of April, i.e. to the commencement of hostilities, are like the almanacks of the last year; which, though proper then, are superceded and useless now. Whatever was advanced by the advocates on either side of the question then, terminated in one and the same point, viz. a union with Great Britain; the only difference between the parties was the method of effecting it; the one proposing force, the other friendship; but it hath so far happened that the first hath failed, and the second hath withdrawn her influence. . . .

I have heard it asserted by some, that as America hath flourished under her former connexion with Great Britain, that the same connexion is necessary towards her future happiness, and will always have the same effect. Nothing can be more fallacious than this kind of argument. We may as well assert that because a child has thrived upon milk, that it is never to have meat, or that the first twenty years of our lives is to become a precedent for the next twenty. But even this is admitting more than is true, for I answer roundly, that America would have flourished as much, and probably much more, had no European power had anything to do with her. The commerce, by which she hath enriched herself are the necessaries of life, and will always have a market while eating is the custom of Europe. . . .

Much hath been said of the united strength of Britain and the colonies, that in conjunction they might bid defiance to the world. But this is mere presumption; the fate of war is uncertain, neither do the expressions mean anything; for this continent would never suffer itself to be drained of inhabitants, to support the British arms in either Asia, Africa, or Europe.

Besides, what have we to do with setting the world at defiance? Our plan is commerce, and that, well attended to, will secure us the peace and friendship of all Europe; because, it is the interest of all Europe to have America a free port. Her trade will always be a protection, and her barrenness of gold and silver secure her from invaders.

I challenge the warmest advocate for reconciliation, to shew, a single advantage that this continent can reap, by being connected with Great Britain. I repeat the challenge, not a single advantage is derived. Our corn will fetch its price in any market in Europe, and our imported goods must be paid for buy them where we will.

But the injuries and disadvantages we sustain by that connection, are without number; and our duty to mankind at large, as well as to ourselves, instruct us to renounce the alliance: Because, any submission to, or dependance on Great Britain, tends directly to involve this continent in European wars and quarrels; and sets us at variance with nations, who would otherwise seek our friendship, and against whom, we have neither anger nor complaint. As Europe is our market for trade, we ought to form no partial connection with any part of it. It is the true interest of America to steer clear of European contentions, which she never can do, while by her dependance on Britain, she is made the make-weight in the scale on British politics.

Europe is too thickly planted with kingdoms to be long at peace, and whenever a war breaks out between England and any foreign power, the trade of America goes to ruin, because of her connection with England. The next war may not turn out like the last, and should it not, the advocates for reconciliation now will be wishing for separation then, because, neutrality in that case, would be a safer convoy than a man of war. Every thing that is right or natural pleads for separation. The blood of the slain, the weeping voice of nature cries, 'tis time to part.

READING AND DISCUSSION QUESTIONS

1. Paine describes monarchy as dependent on artificial distinctions. What does he mean, and how were those distinctions created?

2. Paine invokes "the nineteenth of April"; what is the significance of that date? How did what happened on that date change the relationship between king and colonists?

3. What about Paine's text might account for its widespread and immediate popularity?

■ COMPARATIVE QUESTIONS ■

1. From what you have read in this chapter, do you think colonists who objected to Parliament's legislative actions saw themselves as revolutionaries or as conservatives?

2. Three of the sources here (Bland's essay, the declaration of the Stamp Act Congress, and Paine's *Common Sense*) all represent the Patriot cause. How do their arguments and tone compare? What differences do you see, and what might account for those differences?

3. What seem to be the major issues dividing Patriots and Loyalists? What might these sources reveal as factors determining which side a person chose during the revolutionary struggle?

4. To what extent did audience shape the tone, style, and substance of these documents?

Making War and Republican Governments

1776–1789

In March 1775, a month before fighting broke out at Lexington and Concord, Edmund Burke, a member of Parliament, advocated conciliation before the House of Commons. Having witnessed the colonists' deep-rooted devotion to liberty, he thought it better to make peace than to postpone the inevitability of independence. Parliament passed the Massachusetts Government Act in 1774 in response to the Tea Party, revoking its charter, but the colonists were undaunted and protests persisted. Many in Parliament and even many Loyalists in the colonies assumed a strong hand would force colonists back into the fold, but Burke knew better.

The sources in this chapter tell the story of a revolutionary people awakening to the meaning of their rights. A "democratical" spirit touched not only those who had long enjoyed political power, like the male citizens of Mecklenburg County, North Carolina, but also women and enslaved people, many of whom began to draw on a revolutionary rhetoric. Even after the Revolution, this spirit framed arguments about citizenship and equity. Shays's Rebellion, defended in one of the sources included here, used the language of revolution to aid poor farmers facing economic collapse in the 1780s. The new Constitution, drafted in 1787, responded to these crises and, as James Madison stated, balanced conflicting interests, preserving liberties yet ensuring a stable political order.

6-1 | Democratic Spirit Empowers the People

Instructions to the Delegates from Mecklenburg to the Provincial Congress at Halifax in November (1776)

Just months following the Declaration of Independence, the citizens of Mecklenburg County, North Carolina, drew up instructions to guide those chosen to represent them at the Provincial Congress of the newly declared state of North Carolina. The Provincial Congress had become the governing authority in the state once the colony's royal governor fled the previous year. Delegates to this congress ratified the state's new constitution. The instructions to delegates reproduced below reveal citizens' anxieties in this turbulent period of revolution. They also indicate priorities that emerged as ideas of proper government began to take shape.

At a general Conference of the inhabitants of Mecklenburg assembled at the Court-house on the first of November, 1776, for the express purpose of drawing up instructions for the present Representatives in Congress the following were agreed to by the assent of the people present and ordered to be signed by John M. Alexander, Chairman chosen to preside for the day in said Conference.

To Waightstill Avery, Hezekiah Alexander, John Phifer, Robert Erwin and Zacheus Wilson, Esquires:

GENTLEMEN: You are chosen by the inhabitants of this county to serve them in Congress or General Assembly for one year and they have agreed to the following Instructions which you are to observe with the strictest regard viz.: You are instructed:

1. That you shall consent to and approve the Declaration of the Continental Congress declaring the thirteen United Colonies free and independent States.
2. That you shall endeavor to establish a free government under the authority of the people of the State of North Carolina and that the Government be a simple Democracy or as near it as possible.
3. That in fixing the fundamental principles of Government you shall oppose everything that leans to aristocracy or power in the hands of the rich and chief men exercised to the oppression of the poor.
4. That you shall endeavor that the form of Government shall set forth a bill of rights containing the rights of the people and of individuals which shall never be infringed in any future time by the law-making power or other derived powers in the State.
5. That you shall endeavour that the following maxims be substantially acknowledged in the Bills of Rights (viz.):
    > 1st. Political power is of two kinds, one principal and superior, the other derived and inferior.

The Colonial Records of North Carolina, vol. 10, ed. William L. Saunders (Raleigh, NC: Josephus Daniels, 1890), 870a–870f.

2d. The principal supreme power is possessed by the people at large, the derived and inferior power by the servants which they employ.

3d. Whatever persons are delegated, chosen, employed and intrusted by the people are their servants and can possess only derived inferior power.

4th. Whatever is constituted and ordained by the principal supreme power can not be altered, suspended or abrogated by any other power, but the same power that ordained may alter, suspend and abrogate its own ordinances.

5th. The rules whereby the inferior power is to be exercised are to be constituted by the principal supreme power, and can be altered, suspended and abrogated by the same and no other.

6th. No authority can exist or be exercised but what shall appear to be ordained and created by the principal supreme power or by derived inferior power which the principal supreme power hath authorized to create such authority.

7th. That the derived inferior power can by no construction or pretence assume or exercise a power to subvert the principal supreme power.

6. That you shall endeavour that the Government shall be so formed that the derived inferior power shall be divided into three branches distinct from each other, viz.:

    The power of making laws

    The power of executing laws and

    The power of Judging.

7. That the law making power shall have full and ample authority for the good of the people to provide legal remedies for all evils and abuses that may arise in the State, the executive power shall have authority to apply the legal remedies when the judging power shall have ascertained where and upon what individuals the remedies ought to be applied.

8. You shall endeavour that in the original Constitution of the Government now to be formed the authority of officers possessing any branch of derived power shall be restrained; for example,

9. The law making power shall be restrained in all future time from making any alteration in the form of Government.

10. You shall endeavour that the persons in whose hands the law making power shall be lodged, shall be formed into two Houses or Assemblies independent of each other, but both dependent upon the people, viz.:

    A COUNCIL AND GENERAL ASSEMBLY.

11. You shall endeavour that the good people of this State shall be justly and equally represented in the two Houses; that the Council shall consist of at least thirteen persons, twelve of whom shall be annually chosen by the people in the several districts, and that every person who has a right to vote for members of the General Assembly shall also have a right to vote for member of Council, and that the Council and General Assembly shall every year at their first meeting form one body for the purpose of electing a

Governor who shall then be chosen by ballot and that the Governor by virtue of his office shall be a member of Council but shall never vote in Council on the subject of making laws unless when the Council are divided, in which case the Governor shall have the casting vote.

12. That the law making power shall be lodged in the hands of one General Assembly composed of Representatives annually chosen by the people freely and equally in every part of the State according to ——.

13. N. B. Considering the long time that would be taken up and consequent delay of business the choice of a Council by the people would at this time occasion, it is thought best for the dispatch of public business, and this county do assent that after the form of Government shall be agreed to by the people, the present delegates in Congress shall resolve themselves into a General Assembly for one year and that they choose 12 persons, inhabitants residing in the several districts, to form a Council and the persons so chosen shall be possessed of all the powers of a Council for one year as fully as if chosen by the people.

14. You shall endeavour that no officer of the regular troops or collector of public money shall be eligible as a member of General Assembly or if being elected he shall afterwards accept of such office or collectorship he shall thereby vacate his seat. And in general that no persons in arrears for public money shall have a seat in General Assembly.

15. You shall endeavour that the delegates to represent this State in any future Continental Senate shall never be appointed for longer time than one year and shall not be capable to serve more than three years successively and that the Council and General Assembly shall have power to appoint the said delegates for one year and give them instructions and power to bind this State in matters relating to peace and War and making treaties for that purpose with Foreign Powers and also for the purposes of General Trade and Commerce of the United States.

16. You shall endeavour that all Treasurers and Secretaries for this State shall be appointed by the General Assembly.

17. You shall endeavour that all Judges of the Court of Equity, Judges of the Court of Appeals and Writs of Error and all Judges of the Superior Courts shall be appointed by the General Assembly and hold their office during one year.

18. You shall endeavour that Trials by Jury shall be forever had and used in their utmost purity.

19. You shall endeavour that any person who shall hereafter profess himself to be an Atheist or deny the Being of God or shall deny or blaspheme any of the persons of the Holy Trinity or shall deny the divine authority of the Old and New Testament or shall be of the Roman Catholic religion shall not sustain hold or enjoy any office of trust or profit in the State of North Carolina.

20. That in all times hereafter no professing christian of any denomination whatever shall be compelled to pay any tax or duty towards the support of the clergy or worship of any other denomination.

21. That all professing christians shall enjoy the free and undisturbed exercise of religion and may worship God according to their consciences without restraint except idolatrous worshipers.

22. You shall endeavour that the form of Government when made out and agreed to by the Congress shall be transmitted to the several counties of this State to be considered by the people at large for their approbation and consent if they should choose to give it to the end that it may derive its force from the principal supreme power.

And after the Constitution and form of Government shall be agreed upon and established [and] the General Assembly formed you shall endeavour that they may exercise the law making power on the following subjects of legislation (viz):

1. You shall endeavour to have all vestry [church] laws and marriage acts heretofore in force totally and forever abolished.

2. You shall endeavour to obtain an attachment law providing for creditors a full and ample remedy against debtors who run away to avoid payment.

3. You shall endeavour to obtain an appraisement law for the relief of the poor when their goods are sold by execution.

4. You shall endeavour to obtain a law to establish a college in this county and procure a handsome endowment for the same.

5. You shall endeavour to diminish the fees of Clerks in the Superior and Inferior Courts and make the Fee Bill more perspicuous and clear it of all ambiguities.

6. You shall endeavour to obtain a law that Overseers may be elected annually in every county, with power to provide for the poor.

7. You shall endeavour to obtain a law to prevent clandestine marriages, and that Gospel ministers regularly ordained, whether by Bishops, by Presbyteries or by Association of regular ministers, shall have legal authority to marry after due publication of banns where the parties live.

8. You shall endeavour that all Judges and Justices may be impowered and required by law to administer oaths with uplifted hand when the party to be sworn shall desire that the same may be done without the book.

9. You shall endeavour to pass laws for establishing and immediately opening superior and inferior Courts.

10. You shall endeavour to pass a law for establishing a Court of Equity.

11. You shall endeavour to obtain a law for paying the Justices of the County Court.

12. You shall endeavour by law to inforce the attendance of the Judges of the Superior Court, and in case of due attendance to make them —— allowance.

13. You shall endeavour that so much of the Habeas Corpus Act and the Common and Statute law heretofore in force and use and favorable to the liberties of the people shall be continued in force in this State, excluding every idea of the kingly office and power.

14. That persons be chosen annually in every county to collect taxes.

15. That a General and equal land tax be laid throughout the State.
16. That people shall be taxed according to their estates.
17. That sheriff, clerk and register shall be chosen by the freeholders in every county, the register to continue in office during good behaviour, the sheriff to be elected every year. The same person to be capable to be elected every year if all moneys due by virtue of his office shall be faithfully paid up.
18. That men shall be quieted in their titles and possessions and that provision shall be made to secure men from being disturbed by old and foreign claims against their landed possessions.

READING AND DISCUSSION QUESTIONS

1. How would you summarize the type of government that the delegates were instructed to support? Why do you think the citizens of Mecklenburg County wanted the kind of government they described?

2. Did any of the instructions to delegates surprise you? How might you explain, for instance, the instructions related to questions of religion?

6-2 | A Call to "Remember the Ladies"
ABIGAIL AND JOHN ADAMS, *Correspondence* (1776)

Just as the citizens of Mecklenburg County instructed their delegates on which rights to demand, Abigail Adams sent similar instructions to her husband, John, then serving at the Second Continental Congress meeting in Philadelphia. John was pivotal in moving the delegates to declare independence, and the couple's wonderfully rich letters provide a window into the buildup to that historic moment. In addition to the personal hardships they endured during the Revolutionary period, the letters reveal the lively discussions John and Abigail shared over the place of women in the emerging republic. Abigail did not miss the opportunity to lobby for her sex, and in one letter, reproduced here, she famously instructs her husband to "remember the ladies" as he and his fellow delegates contemplate laws for the newly independent states.

Abigail Adams to John Adams

Braintree, 31 March, 1776.

I wish you would ever write me a letter half as long as I write you; and tell me if you may where your fleet are gone? What sort of defense Virginia can make against our common enemy; whether it is so situated as to make an able defense. Are not the gentry lords and the common people vassals, are they not like the uncivilized vassals Britain represents us to be? I hope their riflemen, who have shown themselves very savage and even blood-thirsty, are not a specimen of the

Charles Francis Adams, *Familiar Letters of John Adams and His Wife Abigail Adams, During the Revolution* (Cambridge, MA: The Riverside Press, 1875), 148–155, 158–159.

generality of the people. I am willing to allow the colony great merit for having produced a Washington; but they have been shamefully duped by a Dunmore.

I have sometimes been ready to think that the passion for liberty cannot be equally strong in the breasts of those who have been accustomed to deprive their fellow-creatures of theirs. Of this I am certain, that it is not founded upon that generous and Christian principal of doing to others as we would that others should do unto us.

Do not you want to see Boston; I am fearful of the small-pox, or I should have been in before this time. I got Mr. Crane to go to our House and see what state it was in. I find it has been occupied by one of the doctors of a regiment, very dirty, but no other damage has been done to it. The few things which were left in it are all gone. I look upon it a new acquisition of property, a property which one month ago I did not value at a single shilling, and could with pleasure have seen it in flames.

The town in general is left in a better state than we expected, more owing to a precipitate flight than any regard to the inhabitants, though some individuals discovered a sense of honor and justice and have left the rent of the Houses in which they were, for the owners and the furniture unhurt, or, if damaged, sufficient to make it good. Others have committed abominable ravages. The mansion-house of your President is safe and the furniture unhurt whilst both the House and Furniture of the Solicitor General have fallen a prey to their own merciless party. Surely the very fiends feel a reverential awe for virtue and patriotism, whilst they detest the parricide and traitor.

I feel very differently at the approach of spring to what I did a month ago. We knew not then whether we could plant or sow with safety, whether when we had tilled we could reap the fruits of our own industry, whether we could rest in our own cottages, or whether we should not be driven from the sea coasts to seek shelter in the wilderness; but now we feel a temporary peace, and the poor fugitives are returning to their deserted habitations.

Though we felicitate ourselves, we sympathize with those who are trembling lest the lot of Boston should be theirs. But they cannot be in similar circumstances unless pusillanimity and cowardice should take possession of them. They have time and warning given them to see the evil and shun it.

I long to hear that you have declared an independency. And, by the way, in the new code of laws which I suppose it will be necessary for you to make, I desire you would remember the ladies, and be more generous and favorable to them than your ancestors. Do not put such unlimited power into the hands of the husbands. Remember all men would be tyrants if they could. If particular care and attention is not paid to the ladies, we are determined to foment a rebellion, and will not hold ourselves bound by any laws in which we have no voice or representation.

That your sex are naturally tyrannical is a truth so thoroughly established as to admit of no dispute; but such of you as wish to be happy willingly give up the harsh title of master for the more tender and endearing one of friend. Why, then, not put it out of the power of the vicious and the lawless to use us with cruelty and indignity with impunity? Men of sense in all ages abhor those customs which treat us only as the vassals of your sex; regard us then as beings placed by Providence under your protection, and in imitation of the Supreme Being make use of that power only for our happiness.

11 April.

I take my pen and write just as I can get time; my letters will be a strange mixture. I really am "cumbered about many things," and scarcely know which way to turn myself. I miss my partner, and find myself unequal to the cares which fall upon me. I find it necessary to be the directress of our husbandry. I hope in time to have the reputation of being as a good a *farmeress* as my partner has of being a good statesman. To ask you anything about your return would, I suppose, be asking a question which you cannot answer.

Retirement, rural quiet domestic pleasures, all, all must give place to the weighty cares of state. It would be —

"Meanly poor in solitude to hide
An honest zeal, unwarped by party rage."

"Though certain pains attend the cares of state,
A good man owes his country to be great,
Should act abroad the high distinguished part,
And show, at least, the purpose of his heart."

I hope your Prussian General[1] will answer the high character which is given of him. But we, who have been bred in a land of liberty, scarcely know how to give credit to so unjust and arbitrary a mandate of a despot. To cast off a faithful servant, only for being the unhappy bearer of ill news, degrades the man and dishonors the prince. The Congress, by employing him, have shown a liberality of sentiment not confined to colonies or continents, but, to use the words of "Common Sense," have "carried their friendship on a larger scale, by claiming brotherhood with every European Christian, and may justly triumph in the generosity of the sentiment."

Yesterday, was taken and carried into Cohasset, by three whaleboats, which went from the shore on purpose, a snow from the Grenadas, laden with three hundred and fifty-four puncheons of West India rum, forty-three barrels of sugar, twelve thousand and five hundred-weight of coffee; a valuable prize. A number of Eastern sloops have brought wood into town since the fleet sailed. We have a rumor of Admiral Hopkins being engaged with a number of ships and tenders off Rhode Island, and are anxious to know the event.

Be so good as to send me a list of the vessels which sail with Hopkins, their names, weight of metal, and number of men; all the news you know, etc.

---

[1]**your Prussian General**: Baron de Woedtke, appointed by Congress a brigadier-general and ordered to Canada. He died soon afterward at Lake George.

I hear our jurors refuse to serve, because the writs are issued in the King's name. Surely they are for independence.

Write me how you do this winter. I want to say many things I must omit. It is not fit "to wake the soul by tender strokes of art," or to ruminate upon happiness we might enjoy, lest absence become intolerable. Adieu.

Yours.

I wish you would burn all my letters.

John Adams to Abigail Adams

12 April, 1776.

I inclose a few sheets of paper,[2] and will send more as fast as opportunities present. . . . You will see by the papers the news, the speculations, and the political plans of the day. The ports are opened wide enough at last, and privateers are allowed to prey upon British trade. This is not independency, you know. What is? Why, government in every colony, a confederation among them all, and treaties with foreign nations to acknowledge us a sovereign state, and all that. When these things will be done, or any of them, time must discover. Perhaps the time is near, perhaps a great way off.

14 April.

You justly complain of my short letters, but the critical state of things and the multiplicity of avocations must plead my excuse. You ask where the fleet is? The inclosed papers will inform you. You ask what sort of defense Virginia can make? I believe they will make an able defense. Their militia and minute-men have been some time employed in training themselves, and they have nine battalions of regulars, as they call them, maintained among them, under good officers, at the Continental expense. They have set up a number of manufactories of firearms, which are busily employed. They are tolerably supplied with powder, and are successful and assiduous in making saltpetre. Their neighboring sister, or rather daughter colony of North Carolina, which is a warlike colony, and has several battalions at the Continental expense, as well as a pretty good militia, are ready to assist them, and they are in very good spirits and seem determined to make a brave resistance. The gentry are very rich, and the common people very poor. This inequality of property gives an aristocratical turn to all their proceedings, and occasions a strong aversion in their patricians to "Common Sense." But the spirit of these Barons is coming down, and it must submit. It is very true, as you observe, they have been duped by Dunmore. But this is a common case. All the colonies are duped, more or less, at one time and another. A more egregious bubble was never blown up than the story of Commissioners coming to treat with the Congress, yet it has gained credit like a charm, not only with, but against the clearest evidence. I never shall forget the delusion which seized our best and most sagacious friends, the dear inhabitants of Boston, the winter before last.

---

[2]Writing paper was scarce during the occupation of Boston.

Credulity and the want of foresight are imperfections in the human character, that no politician can sufficiently guard against.

You give me some pleasure by your account of a certain house in Queen Street. I had burned it long ago in imagination. It rises now to my view like a phoenix. What shall I say of the Solicitor General? I pity his pretty children. I pity his father and his sisters. I wish I could be clear that it is no moral evil to pity him and his lady. Upon repentance, they will certainly have a large share in the compassions of many. But let us take warning, and give it to our children. Whenever vanity and gayety, a love of pomp and dress, furniture, equipage, buildings, great company, expensive diversions, and elegant entertainments get the better of the principles and judgments of men or women, there is no knowing where they will stop, nor into what evils, natural, moral, or political, they will lead us.

Your description of your own *gaieté de cœur* charms me. Thanks be to God, you have just cause to rejoice, and may the bright prospect be obscured by no cloud. As to declarations of independency, be patient. Read our privateering laws and our commercial laws. What signifies a word?

As to your extraordinary code of laws, I cannot but laugh. We have been told that our struggle has loosened the bonds of government everywhere; that children and apprentices were disobedient; that schools and colleges were grown turbulent; that Indians slighted their guardians, and negroes grew insolent to their masters. But your letter was the first intimation that another tribe, more numerous and powerful than all the rest, were grown discontented. This is rather too coarse a compliment, but you are so saucy, I won't blot it out. Depend upon it, we know better than to repeal our masculine systems. Although they are in full force, you know they are little more than theory. We dare not exert our power in its full latitude. We are obliged to go fair and softly, and, in practice, you know we are the subjects. We have only the name of masters, and rather than give up this, which would completely subject us to the despotism of the petticoat, I hope General Washington and all our brave heroes would fight; I am sure every good politician would plot, as long as he would against despotism, empire, monarchy, aristocracy, oligarchy, or ochlocracy. A fine story, indeed! I begin to think the ministry as deep as they are wicked. After stirring up Tories, land-jobbers, trimmers, bigots, Canadians, Indians, negroes, Hanoverians, Hessians, Russians, Irish Roman Catholics, Scotch renegadoes, at last they have stimulated the —— to demand new privileges and threaten to rebel. . . .

15 April.

I send you every newspaper that comes out, and I send you, now and then, a few sheets of paper, but this article is as scarce here as with you. I would send a quire, if I could get a conveyance.

I write you now and then a line, as often as I can, but I can tell you no news but what I send in the public papers.

We are waiting, it is said, for Commissioners; a messiah that will never come. This story of Commissioners is as arrant an illusion as ever was hatched in the brain of an enthusiast, a politician, or a maniac. I have laughed at it, scolded at it, grieved at it, and I don't know but I may, at an unguarded moment, have rip'd at it. But it is vain to reason against such delusions. I was very sorry to see, in a letter from the General, that he had been bubbled with it; and still more, to see, in a letter from my sagacious friend W.,[3] at Plymouth, that he was taken in too.

My opinion is that the Commissioners and the commission have been here (I mean in America), these two months. The Governors, Mandamus Councillors, Collectors and Comptrollers, and Commanders of the army and navy, I conjecture, compose the list, and their power is to receive submissions. But we are not in a very submissive mood. They will get no advantage of us. We shall go on to perfection, I believe. I have been very busy for some time; have written about ten sheets of paper, with my own hand, about some trifling affairs, which I may mention some time or other — not now, for fear of accidents.

What will come of this labor, time will discover. I shall get nothing by it, I believe, because I never get anything by anything that I do. I am sure the public or posterity ought to get something. I believe my children will think I might as well have thought and labored a little, night and day, for their benefit. But I will not bear the reproaches of my children. I will tell them that I studied and labored to procure a free constitution of government for them to solace themselves under, and if they do not prefer this to ample fortune, to ease and elegance, they are not my children, and I care not what becomes of them. They shall live upon thin diet, wear mean clothes, and work hard with cheerful hearts and free spirits, or they may be the children of the earth, or of no one, for me.

John has genius, and so has Charles. Take care that they don't go astray. Cultivate their minds, inspire their little hearts, raise their wishes. Fix their attention upon great and glorious objects. Root out every little thing. Weed out every meanness. Make them great and manly. Teach them to scorn injustice, ingratitude, cowardice, and falsehood. Let them revere nothing but religion, morality, and liberty.

Abby and Tommy are not forgotten by me, although I did not mention them before. The first, by reason of her sex, requires a different education from the two I have mentioned. Of this, you are the only judge. I want to send each of my little pretty flock some present or other. I have walked over this city twenty times, and gaped at every shop, like a countryman, to find something, but could not. Ask every one of them what they would choose to have, and write it to me in your next letter. From this I shall judge of their taste and fancy and discretion.

READING AND DISCUSSION QUESTIONS

1. How did the war affect the lives of ordinary Americans? What challenges did they face, as glimpsed through the letters Abigail writes to John?

2. Abigail's admonition to "remember the ladies" has become one of the most famous lines from this period. But what do you think she meant? In a period

---

[3]**W.**: James Warren.

when women had no formal political power, what do you think she wanted? How does John respond?

3. To what extent does John suggest that class played a role in shaping the revolutionary struggle within the colonies?

6-3 | Enslaved Blacks Adopt the Cause of Liberty

PRINCE HALL, *Petition for Freedom to the Massachusetts Council and the House of Representatives* (1777)

John Adams observed that the Revolution had "loosened the bonds of government everywhere." A clear case of this expanding democratic spirit came from his home state, where enslaved Africans petitioned first the colonial government in 1773 and then the state legislature in January 1777 asking for their freedom. Not until 1783, by a judicial ruling, did enslaved persons in Massachusetts win their freedom when the State Supreme Judicial Court interpreted the 1780 state constitution as guaranteeing all men the right to enjoy their life and liberty. Prince Hall (1735–1807), born a slave but freed by 1770, drafted the petition at the behest of "A Great Number of Blackes."

To The Honorable Counsel & House of [Representa]tives for the State of Massachusitte [Massachusetts] Bay in General Court assembled, Jan. 13, 1777.

The petition of A Great Number of Blackes detained in a State of slavery in the Bowels of a free & Christian Country Humbly shuwith [showeth] that your Petitioners apprehend that thay [they] have in Common with all other men a Natural and Unaliable [inalienable] Right to that freedom which the Grat Parent of the Unavers hath Bestowed equalley on all menkind and which they have Never forfuted by any Compact or agreement whatever—but thay wher Unjustly Dragged by the hand of cruel Power from their Derest friends and sum of them Even torn from the Embraces of their tender Parents—from A popolous Pleasant and plentiful contry and in violation of Laws of Nature and off Nations and in defiance of all the tender feelings of humanity Brough hear Either to Be sold Like Beast of Burthen & Like them Condemnd to Slavery for Life—Among A People Profesing the mild Religion of Jesus A people Not Insensible of the Secrets of Rational Being Nor without spirit to Resent the unjust endeavours of others to Reduce them to a state of Bondage and Subjection your honouer Need not to be informed that A Life of Slavery Like that of your petioners Deprived of Every social privilege of Every thing Requisit to Render Life Tolable is far worse then Nonexistence.

[In Imitat]ion of the Lawdable Example of the Good People of these States your petitionoers have Long and Patiently waited the Evnt of petition after petition By them presented to the Legislative Body of this state and cannot but with Grief Reflect that their Success hath ben but too similar they Cannot but express their Astonishment that It has Never Bin Consirdered that Every Principle form which Amarica has Acted in the Cours of their unhappy Dificultes with Great Briton Pleads Stronger than A thousand arguments in favowrs of your petioners they therfor humble Beseech your honours to give this petion [petition] its due weight & consideration & cause an act of the Legislatur to be past Wherby they may be Restored to the Enjoyments of that which is the Naturel Right of all men—and their Children who wher Born in this Land of Liberty may not be heald as Slaves after they arrive at the age of twenty one years so may the Inhabitance of this Stats No longer chargeable with the inconsistancey of acting themselves the part which they condem and oppose in others Be prospered in their present Glorious struggle for Liberty and have those Blessing to them, &c.

READING AND DISCUSSION QUESTIONS

1. How did the enslaved petitioners frame their request for freedom?

2. To what extent were these enslaved petitioners familiar with the revolutionary rhetoric used by the Patriots? How did they coopt revolutionary ideas to make their argument?

6-4 | A Republican Hero Emerges

JAMES PEALE, *General George Washington at Yorktown* (c. 1782)

Charles Willson Peale's full-length George Washington portrait helped the general become the icon of the American Revolution. Charles and his brother, James, created several versions depicting Washington in different landscapes. In this version by James, Washington has just defeated the British at the decisive battle at Yorktown (1781), which led swiftly to the British general Charles Cornwallis's surrender and the war's end. The French and American flags behind Washington acknowledge the 1773 Treaty of Alliance. The Yorktown battlefield can be seen in the background.

READING AND DISCUSSION QUESTIONS

1. What do the details Peale included in the painting tell you about his point of view toward Washington and the Battle of Yorktown?

2. What significance can you infer from Peale's decision to depict Washington leaning against the cannon with his legs crossed? How does this pose compare to more formal portraits you may have seen?

3. What conclusion about Washington's popularity can you draw from the Peale brothers' decision to produce multiple versions of the general's portrait?

6-5 | A Shaysite Defends the "Risings of the People"

DANIEL GRAY, *Address to the People of Several Towns* (1786)

The victory over the British and the establishment of the Articles of Confederation hardly settled all the challenges facing the newly independent states. The class conflict John Adams
noted during the Revolutionary era (Document 6-2) persisted into the 1780s. A financial crisis
following the war dealt poor debtors a difficult challenge: they could not repay debts because
there was so little circulating currency, credit was tight, courts enforced judgments against
them, and the state legislature increased taxes on already strapped farmers. Resentment
boiled over, and men like Daniel Shays and others attempted to shut down the courts to prevent them from foreclosing on farmers' land. These rebellions were ultimately crushed, but
the insurgencies shocked many who went on to urge constitutional reforms. This process
ultimately resulted in the ratification of the Constitution of the United States. In this speech at
the height of the insurgency in western Massachusetts, Daniel Gray (1728–1803), chairman of
the committee supporting the protests, outlines the insurgents' cause.

Worcester Dec[ember] 7th 1786

An address to the People of the Several towns in the County of Hampshire from
the body now at Arms

Gentlemen, we have thought Proper to inform you of some of the principle
Causes of the late Risings of the People, and also of their present Movement
(viz)[:]

1st The Present expencive mode of Collecting Debts, which by reason of the
Great Scarcity of Cash will of Necessity fill our Gaols with unhappy Debtors, and
there by Hinder a respectable body of People incapable of being Serviceable
Either to them selves or Community.

2dly The moneys raised by impost and Excise being appropriated to
Discharge the Interest of Government Securities; (and the forreign Debt) when
those Securities are in no wise subject to taxation.

3dly A Suspension of the writ of Habeas Corpes; by which those Persons
who have steped forth to ascert and maintain the rights of the People are liable to
be taken and Conveyed even to the most Distant Parts of the Commonwealth
and there by Subject to an unjust Punishment.

4thly The unlimited Power granted to Justices of the Peice, thereof Deputy
Sherifs, and Constables by the riot act indemnefying them in the Prosecution
thereof, when Perhaps situated wholly by a principle of revenge Hatred and
invy. Futhermore be it asured that this body Dispise the Idea of being instigated
by british Emisaries which is so streniously Propigated by the Emimies of our

---

Daniel Gray, "Address to the People of Several Towns." December 7, 1786.

Liberties, we also wish the most Proper and speedy measures may be taken to Discharge both of our foreign and Domistick Debt.

Per Order Daniel Gray {Chairman of a
{committee for
{the above Purpose

READING AND DISCUSSION QUESTIONS

1. To what extent were these insurgent farmers drawing on their Revolutionary War experiences to make the case against the policies of the state of Massachusetts?

2. How do these insurgents present themselves to their fellow citizens?

3. What does this document suggest about the economic challenges faced by the newly formed states? How did these challenges affect the daily lives of the citizens?

6-6 | Madison Defends the Constitution

JAMES MADISON, *Federalist No. 10* and *Federalist No. 51* (1787)

Events like Shays's Rebellion convinced many that the weaknesses of the Articles of Confederation were fatal. In 1787, delegates who had originally been called to a convention to propose reforms were instead pushed to draft a document that would provide an entirely new framework for government. The resulting Constitution of the United States then faced ratification battles in the state conventions. James Madison and Alexander Hamilton, both delegates to the Constitutional Convention, joined John Jay in drafting a series of eighty-five articles, published in New York newspapers, urging the citizens to ratify the new constitution. In two of these articles, *Federalist No. 10* and *No. 51*, Madison addresses key criticisms leveled against the Constitution.

Federalist No. 10

AMONG the numerous advantages promised by a well-constructed Union, none deserves to be more accurately developed than its tendency to break and control the violence of faction. The friend of popular governments never finds himself so much alarmed for their character and fate, as when he contemplates their propensity to this dangerous vice. He will not fail, therefore, to set a due value on any plan which, without violating the principles to which he is attached,

Federalist No. 10: James Madison, "The Same Subject Continued: The Union as a Safeguard Against Domestic Faction and Insurrection," *The New York Packet*, November 23, 1787.

Federalist No. 51: James Madison, "The Structure of the Government Must Furnish the Proper Checks and Balances Between the Different Departments," *The New York Packet*, February 8, 1788.

provides a proper cure for it. The instability, injustice, and confusion introduced into the public councils, have, in truth, been the mortal diseases under which popular governments have everywhere perished; as they continue to be the favorite and fruitful topics from which the adversaries to liberty derive their most specious declamations. The valuable improvements made by the American constitutions on the popular models, both ancient and modern, cannot certainly be too much admired; but it would be an unwarrantable partiality, to contend that they have as effectually obviated the danger on this side, as was wished and expected. Complaints are everywhere heard from our most considerate and virtuous citizens, equally the friends of public and private faith, and of public and personal liberty, that our governments are too unstable, that the public good is disregarded in the conflicts of rival parties, and that measures are too often decided, not according to the rules of justice and the rights of the minor party, but by the superior force of an interested and overbearing majority. However anxiously we may wish that these complaints had no foundation, the evidence, of known facts will not permit us to deny that they are in some degree true. It will be found, indeed, on a candid review of our situation, that some of the distresses under which we labor have been erroneously charged on the operation of our governments; but it will be found, at the same time, that other causes will not alone account for many of our heaviest misfortunes; and, particularly, for that prevailing and increasing distrust of public engagements, and alarm for private rights, which are echoed from one end of the continent to the other. These must be chiefly, if not wholly, effects of the unsteadiness and injustice with which a factious spirit has tainted our public administrations.

By a faction, I understand a number of citizens, whether amounting to a majority or a minority of the whole, who are united and actuated by some common impulse of passion, or of interest, adversed to the rights of other citizens, or to the permanent and aggregate interests of the community.

There are two methods of curing the mischiefs of faction: the one, by removing its causes; the other, by controlling its effects.

There are again two methods of removing the causes of faction: the one, by destroying the liberty which is essential to its existence; the other, by giving to every citizen the same opinions, the same passions, and the same interests.

It could never be more truly said than of the first remedy, that it was worse than the disease. Liberty is to faction what air is to fire, an aliment without which it instantly expires. But it could not be less folly to abolish liberty, which is essential to political life, because it nourishes faction, than it would be to wish the annihilation of air, which is essential to animal life, because it imparts to fire its destructive agency.

The second expedient is as impracticable as the first would be unwise. As long as the reason of man continues fallible, and he is at liberty to exercise it, different opinions will be formed. As long as the connection subsists between his reason and his self-love, his opinions and his passions will have a reciprocal influence on each other; and the former will be objects to which the latter will attach themselves. The diversity in the faculties of men, from which the rights of property originate, is not less an insuperable obstacle to a uniformity of interests. The protection of these faculties is the first object of government. From the protection of different and unequal faculties of acquiring property, the possession of different degrees and kinds of property immediately results; and from the influence of these on the sentiments and views of the respective proprietors, ensues a division of the society into different interests and parties.

The latent causes of faction are thus sown in the nature of man; and we see them everywhere brought into different degrees of activity, according to the different circumstances of civil society. A zeal for different opinions concerning religion, concerning government, and many other points, as well of speculation as of practice; an attachment to different leaders ambitiously contending for preeminence and power; or to persons of other descriptions whose fortunes have been interesting to the human passions, have, in turn, divided mankind into parties, inflamed them with mutual animosity, and rendered them much more disposed to vex and oppress each other than to co-operate for their common good. So strong is this propensity of mankind to fall into mutual animosities, that where no substantial occasion presents itself, the most frivolous and fanciful distinctions have been sufficient to kindle their unfriendly passions and excite their most violent conflicts. But the most common and durable source of factions has been the various and unequal distribution of property. Those who hold and those who are without property have ever formed distinct interests in society. Those who are creditors, and those who are debtors, fall under a like discrimination. A landed interest, a manufacturing interest, a mercantile interest, a moneyed interest, with many lesser interests, grow up of necessity in civilized nations, and divide them into different classes, actuated by different sentiments and views. The regulation of these various and interfering interests forms the principal task of modern legislation, and involves the spirit of party and faction in the necessary and ordinary operations of the government. . . .

It is in vain to say that enlightened statesmen will be able to adjust these clashing interests, and render them all subservient to the public good. Enlightened statesmen will not always be at the helm. Nor, in many cases, can such an adjustment be made at all without taking into view indirect and remote considerations, which will rarely prevail over the immediate interest which one party may find in disregarding the rights of another or the good of the whole.

The inference to which we are brought is, that the CAUSES of faction cannot be removed, and that relief is only to be sought in the means of controlling its EFFECTS.

If a faction consists of less than a majority, relief is supplied by the republican principle, which enables the majority to defeat its sinister views by regular vote. It may clog the administration, it may convulse the society; but it will be unable to execute and mask its violence under the forms of the Constitution. When a majority is included in a faction, the form of popular government, on the other hand, enables it to sacrifice to its ruling passion or interest both the public good and the rights of other citizens. To secure the public good and private rights against the danger of such a faction, and at the same time to preserve the spirit and the form of popular government, is then the great object to which our inquiries are directed. . . .

It may be concluded that a pure democracy, by which I mean a society consisting of a small number of citizens, who assemble and administer the government in person, can admit of no cure for the mischiefs of faction. A common passion or interest will, in almost every case, be felt by a majority of the whole; a communication and concert result from the form of government itself; and there is nothing to check the inducements to sacrifice the weaker party or an obnoxious individual. Hence it is that such democracies have ever been spectacles of turbulence and contention; have ever been found incompatible with personal security or the rights of property; and have in general been as short in their lives as they have been violent in their deaths. Theoretic politicians, who have patronized this species of government, have erroneously supposed that by reducing mankind to a perfect equality in their political rights, they would, at the same time, be perfectly equalized and assimilated in their possessions, their opinions, and their passions.

A republic, by which I mean a government in which the scheme of representation takes place, opens a different prospect, and promises the cure for which we are seeking. Let us examine the points in which it varies from pure democracy, and we shall comprehend both the nature of the cure and the efficacy which it must derive from the Union.

The two great points of difference between a democracy and a republic are: first, the delegation of the government, in the latter, to a small number of citizens elected by the rest; secondly, the greater number of citizens, and greater sphere of country, over which the latter may be extended.

The effect of the first difference is, on the one hand, to refine and enlarge the public views, by passing them through the medium of a chosen body of citizens, whose wisdom may best discern the true interest of their country, and whose patriotism and love of justice will be least likely to sacrifice it to temporary or partial considerations. Under such a regulation, it may well happen that the public voice, pronounced by the representatives of the people, will be more consonant to the public good than if pronounced by the people themselves, convened for the purpose. On the other hand, the effect may be inverted. Men of factious tempers, of local prejudices, or of sinister designs, may, by intrigue, by corruption, or by other means, first obtain the suffrages, and then betray the interests, of the people. The question resulting is, whether small or extensive republics are more favorable to the election of proper guardians of the public weal; and it is clearly decided in favor of the latter by two obvious considerations:

In the first place, it is to be remarked that, however small the republic may be, the representatives must be raised to a certain number, in order to guard against the cabals[1] of a few; and that, however large it may be, they must be limited to a certain number, in order to guard against the confusion of a multitude. Hence, the number of representatives in the two cases not being in proportion to

---

[1]**cabals**: Secret schemes or plots against the government.

that of the two constituents, and being proportionally greater in the small republic, it follows that, if the proportion of fit characters be not less in the large than in the small republic, the former will present a greater option, and consequently a greater probability of a fit choice.

In the next place, as each representative will be chosen by a greater number of citizens in the large than in the small republic, it will be more difficult for unworthy candidates to practice with success the vicious arts by which elections are too often carried; and the suffrages of the people being more free, will be more likely to centre in men who possess the most attractive merit and the most diffusive and established characters.

It must be confessed that in this, as in most other cases, there is a mean, on both sides of which inconveniences will be found to lie. By enlarging too much the number of electors, you render the representatives too little acquainted with all their local circumstances and lesser interests; as by reducing it too much, you render him unduly attached to these, and too little fit to comprehend and pursue great and national objects. The federal Constitution forms a happy combination in this respect; the great and aggregate interests being referred to the national, the local and particular to the State legislatures.

The other point of difference is, the greater number of citizens and extent of territory which may be brought within the compass of republican than of democratic government; and it is this circumstance principally which renders factious combinations less to be dreaded in the former than in the latter. The smaller the society, the fewer probably will be the distinct parties and interests composing it; the fewer the distinct parties and interests, the more frequently will a majority be found of the same party; and the smaller the number of individuals composing a majority, and the smaller the compass within which they are placed, the more easily will they concert and execute their plans of oppression. Extend the sphere, and you take in a greater variety of parties and interests; you make it less probable that a majority of the whole will have a common motive to invade the rights of other citizens; or if such a common motive exists, it will be more difficult for all who feel it to discover their own strength, and to act in unison with each other. Besides other impediments, it may be remarked that, where there is a consciousness of unjust or dishonorable purposes, communication is always checked by distrust in proportion to the number whose concurrence is necessary. . . .

In the extent and proper structure of the Union, therefore, we behold a republican remedy for the diseases most incident to republican government. And according to the degree of pleasure and pride we feel in being republicans, ought to be our zeal in cherishing the spirit and supporting the character of Federalists.

Federalist No. 51

TO WHAT expedient, then, shall we finally resort, for maintaining in practice the necessary partition of power among the several departments, as laid down in the Constitution? The only answer that can be given is, that as all these exterior provisions are found to be inadequate, the defect must be supplied, by so contriving the interior structure of the government as that its several constituent parts may, by their mutual relations, be the means of keeping each other in their proper places. Without presuming to undertake a full development of this important idea, I will hazard a few general observations, which may perhaps place it in a clearer light, and enable us to form a more correct judgment of the principles and structure of the government planned by the convention. In order to lay a due foundation for that separate and distinct exercise of the different powers of government, which to a certain extent is admitted on all hands to be essential to the preservation of liberty, it is evident that each department should have a will of its own; and consequently should be so constituted that the members of each should have as little agency as possible in the appointment of the members of the others. Were this principle rigorously adhered to, it would require that all the appointments for the supreme executive, legislative, and judiciary magistracies should be drawn from the same fountain of authority, the people, through channels having no communication whatever with one another. Perhaps such a plan of constructing the several departments would be less difficult in practice than it may in contemplation appear. Some difficulties, however, and some additional expense would attend the execution of it. Some deviations, therefore, from the principle must be admitted. In the constitution of the judiciary department in particular, it might be inexpedient to insist rigorously on the principle: first, because peculiar qualifications being essential in the members, the primary consideration ought to be to select that mode of choice which best secures these qualifications; secondly, because the permanent tenure by which the appointments are held in that department, must soon destroy all sense of dependence on the authority conferring them. It is equally evident, that the members of each department should be as little dependent as possible on those of the others, for the emoluments annexed to their offices. Were the executive magistrate, or the judges, not independent of the legislature in this particular, their independence in every other would be merely nominal. But the great security against a gradual concentration of the several powers in the same department, consists in giving to those who administer each department the necessary constitutional means and personal motives to resist encroachments of the others. The provision for defense must in this, as in all other cases, be made commensurate to the danger of attack. Ambition must be made to counteract ambition. The interest of the man must be connected with the constitutional rights of the place. It may be a reflection on human nature, that such devices should be necessary to control the abuses of government. But what is government itself, but the greatest of all reflections on human nature? If men were angels, no government would be necessary. If angels were to govern men, neither external nor internal controls on government would be necessary. In framing a government which is to be administered by men over men, the great difficulty lies in this: you must first enable the government to control the governed; and in the next place oblige it to control itself. A dependence on the people is, no doubt, the primary control on the government; but experience has taught mankind the necessity of auxiliary precautions. This policy of supplying, by opposite and rival interests, the defect of better motives, might be traced through the whole system of human affairs, private as well as public. We see it particularly displayed in all the subordinate distributions of power, where the constant aim is to divide and arrange the several offices in such a manner as that each may be a check on the other — that the private interest of every individual may be a sentinel over the public rights. These inventions of prudence cannot be less requisite in the distribution of the supreme powers of the State. But it is not possible to give to each department an equal power of self-defense. In republican government, the legislative authority necessarily predominates. The remedy for this inconveniency is to divide the legislature into different branches; and to render them, by different modes of election and different principles of action, as little connected with each other as the nature of their common functions and their common dependence on the society will admit. It may even be necessary to guard against dangerous encroachments by still further precautions. As the weight of the legislative authority requires that it should be thus divided, the weakness of the executive may require, on the other hand, that it should be fortified. An absolute negative on the legislature appears, at first view, to be the natural defense with which the executive magistrate should be armed. But perhaps it would be neither altogether safe nor alone sufficient. On ordinary occasions it might not be exerted with the requisite firmness, and on extraordinary occasions it might be perfidiously abused. May not this defect of an absolute negative be supplied by some qualified connection between this weaker department and the weaker branch of the stronger department, by which the latter may be led to support the constitutional rights of the former, without being too much detached from the rights of its own department? If the principles on which these observations are founded be just, as I persuade myself they are, and they be applied as a criterion to the several State constitutions, and to the federal Constitution it will be found that if the latter does not perfectly correspond with them, the former are infinitely less able to bear such a test. There are, moreover, two considerations particularly applicable to the federal system of America, which place that system in a very interesting point of view. First. In a single republic, all the power surrendered by the people is submitted to the administration of a single government; and the usurpations are guarded against by a division of the government into distinct and separate departments. In the compound republic of America, the power surrendered by the people is first divided between two distinct governments, and then the portion allotted to each subdivided among distinct and separate departments. Hence a double security arises to the rights of the people. The different governments will control each other, at the same time that each will be controlled by itself. Second. It is of great importance in a republic not only to guard the society against the oppression of its rulers, but to guard one part of the society against the injustice of the other part. Different interests necessarily exist in different classes of citizens. If a majority be united by a common interest, the rights of the minority will be insecure. There are but two methods of providing against this evil: the one by creating a will in the community independent of the majority — that is, of the society itself; the other, by comprehending in the society so many separate descriptions of citizens as will render an unjust combination of a majority of the whole very improbable, if not impracticable. The first method prevails in all governments possessing an hereditary or self-appointed authority. This, at best, is but a precarious security; because a power independent of the society may as well espouse the unjust views of the major, as the rightful interests of the minor party, and may possibly be turned against both parties. The second method will be exemplified in the federal republic of the United States. Whilst all authority in it will be derived from and dependent on the society, the society itself will be broken into so many parts, interests, and classes of citizens, that the rights of individuals, or of the minority, will be in little danger from interested combinations of the majority. In a free government the security for civil rights must be the same as that for religious rights. It consists in the one case in the multiplicity of interests, and in the other in the multiplicity of sects. The degree of security in both cases will depend on the number of interests and sects; and this may be presumed to depend on the extent of country and number of people comprehended under the same government. This view of the subject must particularly recommend a proper federal system to all the sincere and considerate friends of republican government, since it shows that in exact proportion as the territory of the Union may be formed into more circumscribed Confederacies, or States oppressive combinations of a majority will be facilitated: the best security, under the republican forms, for the rights of every class of citizens, will be diminished: and consequently the stability and independence of some member of the government, the only other security, must be proportionately increased. Justice is the end of government. It is the end of civil society. It ever has been and ever will be pursued until it be obtained, or until liberty be lost in the pursuit. In a society under the forms of which the stronger faction can readily unite and oppress the weaker, anarchy may as truly be said to reign as in a state of nature, where the weaker individual is not secured against the violence of the stronger; and as, in the latter state, even the stronger individuals are prompted, by the uncertainty of their condition, to submit to a government which may protect the weak as well as themselves; so, in the former state, will the more powerful factions or parties be gradually induced, by a like motive, to wish for a government which will protect all parties, the weaker as well as the more powerful. It can be little doubted that if the State of Rhode Island was separated from the Confederacy and left to itself, the insecurity of rights under the popular form of government within such narrow limits would be displayed by such reiterated oppressions of factious majorities that some power altogether independent of the people would soon be called for by the voice of the very factions whose misrule had proved the necessity of it. In the extended republic of the United States, and among the great variety of interests, parties, and sects which it embraces, a coalition of a majority of the whole society could seldom take place on any other principles than those of justice and the general good; whilst there being thus less danger to a minor from the will of a major party, there must be less pretext, also, to provide for the security of the former, by introducing into the government a will not dependent on the latter, or, in other words, a will independent of the society itself. It is no less certain than it is important, notwithstanding the contrary opinions which have been entertained, that the larger the society, provided it lie within a practical sphere, the more duly capable it will be of self-government. And happily for the REPUBLICAN CAUSE, the practicable sphere may be carried to a very great extent, by a judicious modification and mixture of the FEDERAL PRINCIPLE.

READING AND DISCUSSION QUESTIONS

1. Many at the time feared the divisive impact of factions, and some critics suggested these self-interested political groups would be fatal to a republic as large as the one proposed by the Constitution. How does Madison address the concerns about factions? What unorthodox remedy does he propose?

2. In *Federalist No. 51*, Madison addresses another concern: the danger of a concentration of power in the national government. How does Madison explain the Constitution's solution to this problem?

3. In the same article, Madison argues, "if men were angels, no government would be necessary." Clearly, Madison recognized man's fallibility. How did this view of human nature shape the way the founders constructed the new form of government under the Constitution?

▪ COMPARATIVE QUESTIONS ▪

1. To what extent did the language of rights and liberties prevalent during this period touch various groups within the colonies? How did they use that language for their own purposes?

2. How did ideas about government change as a result of the Revolutionary War experience?

3. How might the Constitution have read had Abigail Adams, Daniel Gray, and the enslaved Africans in Massachusetts been delegates to the Philadelphia convention?

4. Do you see the Revolutionary era more as a radical social movement (the people demanding liberty and equality) or a conservative political movement (colonists demanding respect for their traditional rights)? Explain.

7

Hammering Out a Federal Republic

1787–1820

The new republic, formed with the ratification of the Constitution, wrestled with the meaning of the Revolution. What did it mean to be a citizen when Americans were no longer subjects of a distant monarch? How should they behave? What might republican politics look like? For some, fine clothes and elaborate titles for officeholders bespoke dangerous aristocratic pretensions. For others, like Federalist Fisher Ames, egalitarianism threatened to plunge the new nation into "the mire of a democracy, which pollutes the morals of citizens before it swallows up their liberties." In many ways, the first decade under the Constitution was about coming to terms with conflicting interpretations of the Revolution's legacy.

The sources in this chapter highlight the conflicts that Americans faced as they struggled to understand the new political order they had created. The first two documents illustrate some of the varying political visions that emerged, while the third highlights one of the flashpoints of the 1790s: France's alleged influence over American politics. The remaining sources address the young republic's geographical expansion and the other major foreign policy crisis of this early period: the War of 1812. As we see here, this conflict also drove domestic politics, ultimately crushing New England Federalists and ushering in an era of submerged political drama.

7-1 | Hamilton Diverges from Jefferson on the Economy
ALEXANDER HAMILTON, *Letter to Edward Carrington* (1792)

The political crisis of the 1790s was fueled by more than personality. However, two strong individuals dominated the era, and their difficult relationship helps to clarify the issues up for debate. In this selection and the next, Alexander Hamilton and Thomas Jefferson reveal some of the political disagreements that drove the early national era, mostly centered on divergent views of the economy. Hamilton's important reports on manufactures, public credit, and the national bank outlined a Federalist political-economic agenda, which Jefferson and James Madison opposed. While Hamilton's letter highlights these policy disputes, it also reveals the personal dimension of the political conflicts in an era before the trappings of political party became institutionalized.

It was not till the last session that I became unequivocally convinced of the following truth: *"that Mr. Madison, cooperating with Mr. Jefferson, is at the head of a faction decidedly hostile to me and my administration; and actuated by views, in my judgment, subversive of the principles of good government and dangerous to the Union, peace, and happiness of the country."*

These are strong expressions, they may pain your friendship for one or both of the gentlemen whom I have named. I have not lightly resolved to hazard them. They are the result of a *serious alarm* in my mind for the public welfare, and of a full conviction that what I have alleged is a truth, and a truth which ought to be told, and well attended to by all the friends of the Union and efficient national government. The suggestion will, I hope, at least, awaken attention free from the bias of former prepossessions.

This conviction, in my mind, is the result of a long train of circumstances, many of them minute. To attempt to detail them all would fill a volume. I shall therefore confine myself to the mention of a few.

First.—As to the point of opposition to me and my administration.

Mr. Jefferson, with very little reserve, manifests his dislike of the funding system generally, calling in question the expediency of funding a debt at all. Some expressions, which he has dropped in my presence (sometimes without sufficient attention to delicacy), will not permit me to doubt on this point representations which I have had from various respectable quarters. I do not mean that he advocates directly the undoing of what has been done, but he censures the whole, on principles which, if they should become general, could not but end in the subversion of the system.

In various conversations, with *foreigners* as well as citizens, he has thrown censure on my *principles* of government and on my measures of administration. He has predicted that the people would not long tolerate my proceedings, and that I should not long maintain my ground. Some of those whom he *immediately*

The Works of Alexander Hamilton, ed. Henry Cabot Lodge (New York: G. P. Putnam's Sons, 1903), 517–535.

and *notoriously* moves have *even* whispered suspicions of the rectitude of my motives and conduct. In the question concerning the bank he not only delivered an opinion in writing against its constitutionality and expediency, but he did it *in a style and manner* which I felt as partaking of asperity [harshness] and ill humor toward me. As one of the trustees of the sinking fund, I have experienced in almost every leading question opposition from him. When any turn of things in the community has threatened either odium or embarrassment to me, he has not been able to suppress the satisfaction which it gave him. . . .

With regard to Mr. Madison, the matter stands thus: I have not heard, but in the one instance to which I have alluded, of his having held language unfriendly to me in private conversation, but in his public conduct there has been a more uniform and persevering opposition than I have been able to resolve into a sincere difference of opinion. I cannot persuade myself that Mr. Madison and I, whose politics had formerly so much the *same point of departure*, should now diverge so widely in our opinions of the measures which are proper to be pursued. The opinion I once entertained of the candor and simplicity and fairness of Mr. Madison's character, has, I acknowledge, given way to a decided opinion that *it is one of a peculiarly artificial and complicated kind.* . . .

Mr. Jefferson is an avowed enemy to a funded debt. Mr. Madison disavows, in public, any intention to *undo* what has been done, but, in private conversation with Mr. Charles Carroll, Senator . . . he favored the sentiment in Mr. Mercer's speech, that a Legislature had no right to *fund* the debt by mortgaging permanently the public revenues, because they had no right to bind posterity. The inference is that what has been unlawfully done may be undone.

The discourse of partisans in the Legislature, and the publication in the party newspapers, direct their main battery against the *principle* of a funded debt, and represent it in the most odious light as a perfect *Pandora's box.* . . .

Whatever were the original merits of the funding system, after having been so solemnly adopted, and after so great a transfer of property under it, what would become of the government should it be reversed? What of the national reputation? Upon what system of morality can so atrocious a doctrine be maintained? In me, I confess it excited *indignation and horror*!

What are we to think of those maxims of government by which the power of a Legislature is denied to bind the nation, by a *contract* in the affair of *property* for twenty-four years? For this is precisely the case of the debt. What are to become of all the legal rights of property, of all charters to corporations, nay, of all grants to a man, his heirs and assigns, for ever, if this doctrine be true? What is the term for which a government is in capacity to *contract*? Questions might be multiplied without end, to demonstrate the perniciousness and absurdity of such a doctrine.

In almost all the questions, great and small, which have arisen since the first session of Congress, Mr. Jefferson and Mr. Madison have been found among those who are disposed to narrow the federal authority. The question of a national bank is one example. The question of bounties to the fisheries is another. Mr. Madison resisted it on the ground of constitutionality, till it was evident, by the intermediate questions taken, that the bill would pass; and he then, under the wretched subterfuge of a change of a single word, "bounty" for "allowance," went over to the majority, and voted for the bill. On the militia bill, and in a variety of minor cases, he has leaned to abridging the exercise of federal authority, and leaving as much as possible to the States; and he lost no opportunity of *sounding the alarm*, with great affected solemnity, at encroachments, meditated on the rights of the States, and of holding up the bugbear of a faction in the government having designs unfriendly to liberty.

This kind of conduct has appeared to me the more extraordinary on the part of Mr. Madison, as I know for a certainty, it was a primary article in his creed, that the real danger in our system was the subversion of the national authority by the preponderancy of the State governments. All his measures have proceeded on an opposite supposition. . . .

In respect to foreign politics, the views of these gentlemen are, in my judgment, equally unsound and dangerous. *They have a womanish attachment to France and a womanish resentment against Great Britain.* They would draw us into the closest embrace of the former, and involve us in all the consequences of her politics; and they would risk the peace of the country in their endeavors to keep us at the greatest possible distance from the latter. This disposition goes to a length, particularly in Mr. Jefferson, of which, till lately, I had no adequate idea. Various circumstances prove to me that if these gentlemen were left to pursue their own course, there would be, in less than six months, *an open war between the United States and Great Britain.*

I trust I have a due sense of the conduct of France towards this country in the late revolution; and that I shall always be among the foremost in making her every suitable return; but there is a wide difference between this and implicating ourselves in all her politics; between bearing good-will to her and hating and wrangling with all those whom she hates. The neutral and the pacific policy appears to me to mark the true path to the United States. . . .

Mr. Jefferson, it is known, did not in the first instance cordially acquiesce in the new Constitution for the United States; he had many doubts and reserves. He left this country before we had experienced the imbecilities of the former.

In France, he saw government only on the side of its abuses. He drank freely of the French philosophy, in religion, in science, in politics. He came from France in the moment of a fermentation, which he had a share in exciting, and in the passions and feelings of which he shared both from temperament and situation.

He came here probably with a too partial idea of his own powers; and with the expectation of a greater share in the direction of our councils than he has in reality enjoyed. I am not sure that he had not peculiarly marked out for himself the department of the finances.

He came, electrified *plus* with attachment to France, and with the project of knitting together the two countries in the closest political bands.

Mr. Madison had always entertained an exalted opinion of the talents, knowledge, and virtues of Mr. Jefferson. The sentiment was probably reciprocal. A close correspondence subsisted between them during the time of Mr. Jefferson's absence from the country. A close intimacy arose upon his return.

Whether any peculiar opinions of Mr. Jefferson's concerning the public debt wrought a change in the sentiments of Mr. Madison (for it is certain that the former is more radically wrong than the latter), or whether Mr. Madison, seduced by the expectation of popularity, and possibly by the calculation of advantage to the State of Virginia, was led to change his own opinion, certain it is that a very material *change* took place, and that the two gentlemen were united in the new ideas. . . .

Attempts were made by these gentlemen, in different ways, to produce a commercial warfare with Great Britain. In this, too, they were disappointed. And, as they had the liveliest wishes on the subject, their dissatisfaction has been proportionally great; and, as I had not favored the project, I was comprehended in their displeasure.

These causes, and perhaps some others, created, much sooner than I was aware of it, a systematic opposition to me, on the part of these gentlemen. My subversion, I am now satisfied, has been long an object with them. . . .

Under the influence of all these circumstances the attachment to the government of the United States, originally weak in Mr. Jefferson's mind, has given way to something very like dislike in Mr. Madison's. It is so counteracted by personal feelings as to be more an affair of the head than of the heart; more the result of a conviction of the necessity of Union than of cordiality to the thing itself. I hope it does not stand worse than this with him.

In such a state of mind both these gentlemen are prepared to hazard a great deal to effect a change. Most of the important measures of every government are connected with the treasury. To subvert the present head of it, they deem it expedient to risk rendering the government itself odious; perhaps foolishly thinking that they can easily recover the lost affections and confidence of the people, and not appreciating, as they ought to do, the natural resistance to government, which in every community results from the human passions, the degree to which this is strengthened by the *organized rivalry* [sic] of State governments, and the infinite danger that the national government, once rendered odious, will be kept so by these powerful and indefatigable enemies. . . .

In giving you this picture of political parties, my design is, I confess, to awaken your attention, if it has not yet been awakened, to the conduct of the gentlemen in question. If my opinion of them is founded, it is certainly of great moment to the public weal that they should be understood. I rely on the strength of your mind to appreciate men as they merit, when you have a clue to their real views.

A word on another point. I am told that serious apprehensions are disseminated in your State as to the existence of a monarchical party meditating the destruction of State and republican government. If it is possible that so absurd an idea can gain ground, it is necessary that it should be combated. I assure you, on *my private faith* and *honor* as a man, that there is not, in my judgment, a shadow of foundation for it. A very small number of men indeed may entertain theories less republican than Mr. Jefferson and Mr. Madison, but I am persuaded there is not a man among them who would not regard as both *criminal* and *visionary* any attempt to subvert the republican system of the country. Most of these men rather fear that it may not justify itself by its fruits, than feel a predilection for a different form; and their fears are not diminished by the factious and fanatical politics which they find prevailing among a certain set of gentlemen and threatening to disturb the tranquillity and order of the government.

As to the destruction of State governments, the *great* and *real* anxiety is to be able to preserve the national from the too potent and counteracting influence of those governments. As to my own political creed, I give it to you with the utmost sincerity. I am *affectionately* attached to the republican theory. I desire *above all things* to see the *equality* of political rights, exclusive of all *hereditary* distinction, firmly established by a practical demonstration of its being consistent with the order and happiness of society. . . .

I said that I was *affectionately* attached to the republican theory. This is the real language of my heart, which I open to you in the sincerity of friendship; and I add that I have strong hopes of the success of that theory; but, in candor, I ought also to add that I am far from being without doubts. I consider its success as yet a problem.

It is yet to be determined by experience whether it be consistent with that *stability* and *order* in government which are essential to public strength and private security and happiness. On the whole, the only enemy which Republicanism has to fear in this country is in the spirit of faction and anarchy. If this will not permit the ends of government to be attained under it, if it engenders disorders in the community, all regular and orderly minds will wish for a change, and the demagogues who have produced the disorder will make it for their own aggrandizement. This is the old story.

If I were disposed to promote monarchy and overthrow State governments, I would mount the hobby-horse of popularity; I would cry out "usurpation," "danger to liberty," etc., etc.; I would endeavor to prostrate the national government, raise a ferment, and then "ride in the whirlwind, and direct the storm." That there are men acting with Jefferson and Madison who have this in view, I verily believe; I could lay my finger on some of them. That Madison does *not* mean it, I also verily believe; and I rather believe the same of Jefferson, but I read him upon the whole thus: "A man of profound ambition and violent passions."

READING AND DISCUSSION QUESTIONS

1. What do Hamilton's views on the economy suggest about his larger political philosophy?

2. What is the nature of this dispute with Jefferson and Madison? How does Hamilton explain their relationship?

3. What insight about the conduct of early national politics does Hamilton's letter reveal? What does it suggest about the emergence of political parties and the role they played in national politics?

7-2 | Jefferson's Agrarian Vision for the New Republic

THOMAS JEFFERSON, *Notes on the State of Virginia* (1781)

Thomas Jefferson had a distinguished political career even before assuming the presidency in 1801. Son of a prominent Virginia family, Jefferson took his position at the front of colonial politics, serving in the Second Continental Congress, as governor of Virginia, minister to France, secretary of state, and vice president. While serving as secretary of state under Washington, he sparred with Hamilton over the direction of the young republic, especially with regard to the economy and whether it should be centered on agriculture or manufacturing. During the 1780s, Jefferson wrote and published his major work, *Notes on the State of Virginia*, in which he offers his own vision of America's economic future, one clearly at odds with Hamilton's views.

The Present State of Manufactures, Commerce, Interior and Exterior Trade

We never had an interior trade of any importance. Our exterior commerce has suffered very much from the beginning of the present contest. During this time we have manufactured within our families the most necessary articles of cloathing. Those of cotton will bear some comparison with the same kinds of manufacture in Europe; but those of wool, flax and hemp are very coarse, unsightly, and unpleasant: and such is our attachment to agriculture, and such our preference for foreign manufactures, that be it wise or unwise, our people will certainly return as soon as they can, to the raising [of] raw materials, and exchanging them for finer manufactures than they are able to execute themselves.

The political economists of Europe have established it as a principle that every state should endeavour to manufacture for itself: and this principle, like many others, we transfer to America, without calculating the difference of circumstance which should often produce a difference of result. In Europe the lands are either cultivated, or locked up against the cultivator. Manufacture must therefore be resorted to of necessity not of choice, to support the surplus of their people. But we have an immensity of land courting the industry of the husbandman. Is it best then that all our citizens should be employed in its improvement, or that one half should be called off from that to exercise manufactures and handicraft arts for the other? Those who labour in the earth are the chosen people of God, if ever he had a chosen people, whose breasts he has made his peculiar deposit for substantial and genuine virtue. It is the focus in which he keeps alive that sacred fire, which otherwise might escape from the face of the earth. Corruption of morals in the mass of cultivators is a phenomenon of which no age nor nation has furnished an example. It is the mark set on those, who not looking up to heaven, to their own soil and industry, as does the husbandman,

Thomas Jefferson, *Notes on the State of Virginia* (London: John Stockdale, 1787), 273–275, 289–291, 293.

for their subsistance, depend for it on the casualties and caprice of customers. Dependance begets subservience and venality, suffocates the germ of virtue, and prepares fit tools for the designs of ambition. This, the natural progress and consequence of the arts, has sometimes perhaps been retarded by accidental circumstances: but, generally speaking, the proportion which the aggregate of the other classes of citizens bears in any state to that of its husbandmen, is the proportion of its unsound to its healthy parts, and is a good-enough barometer whereby to measure its degree of corruption. While we have land to labour then, let us never wish to see our citizens occupied at a work-bench, or twirling a distaff. Carpenters, masons, smiths, are wanting in husbandry: but, for the general operations of manufacture, let our work-shops remain in Europe. It is better to carry provisions and materials to workmen there, than bring them to the provisions and materials, and with them their manners and principles. The loss by the transportation of commodities across the Atlantic will be made up in happiness and permanence of government. The mobs of great cities add just so much to the support of pure government, as sores do to the strength of the human body. It is the manners and spirit of a people which preserve a republic in vigour. A degeneracy in these is a canker which soon eats to the heart of its laws and constitution. . . .

It should be our endeavour to cultivate the peace and friendship of every nation, even of that which has injured us most, when we shall have carried our point against her. Our interest will be to throw open the doors of commerce, and to knock off all its shackles, giving perfect freedom to all persons for the vent of whatever they may chuse to bring into our ports, and asking the same in theirs. Never was so much false arithmetic employed on any subject, as that which has been employed to persuade nations that it is their interest to go to war. Were the money which it has cost to gain, at the close of a long war, a little town, or a little territory, the right to cut wood here, or to catch fish there, expended in improving what they already possess, in making roads, opening rivers, building ports, improving the arts, and finding employment for their idle poor, it would render them much stronger, much wealthier and happier. This I hope will be our wisdom. And, perhaps, to remove as much as possible the occasions of making war, it might be better for us to abandon the ocean altogether, that being the element whereon we shall be principally exposed to jostle with other nations: to leave to others to bring what we shall want, and to carry what we can spare. This would make us invulnerable to Europe, by offering none of our property to their prize, and would turn all our citizens to the cultivation of the earth; and, I repeat it again, cultivators of the earth are the most virtuous and independent citizens. It might be time enough to seek employment for them at sea, when the land no longer offers it. But the actual habits of our countrymen attach them to commerce. They will exercise it for themselves. Wars then must sometimes be our lot; and all the wise can do, will be to avoid that half of them which would be produced by our own follies, and our own acts of injustice; and to make for the other half the best preparations we can. Of what nature should these be? A land army would be useless for offence, and not the best nor safest instrument of defence. For either of these purposes, the sea is the field on which we should meet an European enemy. On that element it is necessary we should possess some power. To aim at such a navy as the greater nations of Europe possess, would be a foolish and wicked waste of the energies of our countrymen. It would be to pull on our own heads that load of military expence, which makes the European labourer go supperless to bed, and moistens his bread with the sweat of his brows. It will be enough if we enable ourselves to prevent insults from those nations of Europe which are weak on the sea, because circumstances exist, which render even the stronger ones weak as to us. Providence has placed their richest and most defenceless possessions at our door; has obliged their most precious commerce to pass as it were in review before us. . . .

The value of our lands and slaves, taken conjunctly, doubles in about twenty years. This arises from the multiplication of our slaves, from the extension of culture, and increased demand for lands. The amount of what may be raised will of course rise in the same proportion.

READING AND DISCUSSION QUESTIONS

1. In one of the most famous lines in *Notes*, Jefferson writes that "those who labor in the earth are the chosen people of God." He meant white farmers, not African slaves, but why do you think he accorded them such respect?

2. How does this source help you to understand Jefferson's opposition to Hamilton's economic policies?

7-3 | A Federalist Warns Against French Influence on American Politics

FISHER AMES, *Foreign Politics* (c. 1801–1805)

While economics was one source of division in the new republic, foreign affairs was another. During the 1790s, as the French Revolution broke out, leading to the execution of the absolutist King Louis XVI and the triumph of *"liberté, égalité, fraternité,"* Federalists and Republicans (as Jefferson's supporters were called) took sides, interpreting the French Revolution in light of their own. Jeffersonian Republicans supported the French revolutionaries, who seemed to embrace the same republican ideals that had fueled the American Revolution. Federalists like Fisher Ames, whose essay on "Foreign Politics" is excerpted here, were horrified, especially after the French Revolution darkened into a "Reign of Terror." For Federalists, the excesses of the French Revolution bespoke the dangers of too much liberty. Here, Ames despairs of a Jeffersonian infatuation with France.

European events have long had such a monopoly of the attention of Americans, that we scarcely find leisure or disposition to backbite and persecute each other,

---

Works of Fisher Ames (Boston: T. B. Wait & Co., 1809), 209–212.

as much as the rage of party spirit requires. Our pride is often offended, that our country makes a figure in the world so little conspicuous, that others overlook it; and we almost forget ourselves, while we suffer our sympathy and reflections to be exclusively engrossed by the events of the foreign War.

Yet the champions of party ought to be consoled, for the diversion of any party of our patriotick energies from the domestick scene of controversy, by their own success in rendering foreign politicks subservient to their design. France, though nerve all over, does not feel the dread nor the shame of her defeats, nor the insolent joy of her victories, with more emotion than our jacobins.[1] They can allege, in excuse for the deep concern they take in all the confusion and all the injustice of France, that they are not mere speculatists, nor subject to impulses that are blind and without object; but that their *pure love for the people* never ceases to animate them enough to imitate what they admire, and to introduce what they so long have studied, and so well understand.

The men of sense and virtue have excuses too for their anxious solicitude about European affairs: there, they may say, faction culls her poisons; and in that bloody field, at length, we can perceive the antidote is sprouting. Already the Aurora tells us, it is nonsense to talk of liberty under Buonaparte. Nevertheless, if France should be superiour in the war, and should dictate the terms of peace, our inbred faction, her faithful ally, would be superiour here. The civilized world can enjoy neither safety nor repose, if the most restless and ambitious nation in it, obtains what it has struggled for, a more than Roman sway, and a resistless power to render the interests of all other states as subservient to its own, as those of her Cisalpine allies.[2] The forest that harbours one wild cat, should breed many squirrels. Ambition like that of France, requires, for its daily sustenance, tameness like that of Spain or Holland: if all her neighbours were like Britain, where could this royal tigress find prey?

So far, indeed, is the attention paid by Americans to the affairs of Europe from being a subject of reproach, that, on the contrary, no period of history will be deemed more worthy of study by our statesmen, as well as our youth, than that of the last twelve years.

In France, we behold the effects of trying by the test of experience the most plausible metaphysical principles, in appearance the most pure, yet the most surprisingly in contrast with the corruption of the national manners. Theories, fit for angels, have been adopted for the use of a multitude, who have been found, when left to what is called their self-government, unfit to be called men; as if the misrule of chaos or of pandemonium would yield to a little instruction in singing psalms and divine songs; as if the passions inherent in man, and a constituent

---

[1]**Jacobin**: Radical faction supporting the overthrow of the monarchy during the French Revolution.

[2]**Cisalpine allies**: Ames refers here to a client state created by Napoleon in 1797 on the Italian side of the Alps.

part of his nature, were so many devils that even unbelievers could cast out, without a miracle, and without fasting and prayer. By stamping the rights of man on pocket handkerchiefs, it was supposed they were understood by those who understand nothing; and by voting them through the convention, it would cost a man his life and estate to say, that they were not established.

On grounds *so solid* Condorcet could proclaim to the enlightened, the fish women, and the mob of the suburbs of St. Antoine, all disciples of "the new school of philosophy," Mr. Jefferson could assure Thomas Paine; and even the circumspect Madison could pronounce in congress, that France had improved on all known plans of government, and that her liberty was immortal.

Experience has shewn, and it ought to be of all teaching the most profitable, that any government by mere popular impulses, any plan that *excites*, instead of restraining, the passions of the multitude, is a despotism: it is not, even in its beginning, much less in its progress, nor in its issue and effects, *liberty*. As well might we suppose, that the assassin's dagger conveys a restorative balsam to the heart, when it stabs it; or that the rottenness and dry bones of the grave will spring up again, in this life, endued with imperishable vigour and the perfection of angels. To cure expectations, at once so foolish and so sanguine, what can be more rational than to inspect sometimes the sepulchre of French liberty? The body is not deposited there, for indeed it never existed; but much instruction is to be gained by carefully considering the lying vanity of its epitaph.

The great contest between England and France, also, shews the stability and the resources of free governments, and the precariousness and wide-spreading ruin of the resort to revolutionary means. We shall not, therefore, hesitate to present, from time to time, the most correct and extensive views we can take of events in Europe.

We have made these observations, and we address them with the more deliberation to the good sense of the citizens, because it has been a part of the common place of democratick foppery to say, what have we to do with Europe? We are a world by ourselves. This they have said a thousand times, while they told us the cause of France was the cause of liberty, and inseparably our cause. Every body knows, that the mad zeal for France was wrought up with the intent to influence American politicks; and it did influence, and yet influences them. A trading nation, whose concerns extend over the commercial world, and whose interests are affected by their wars and revolutions, cannot expect to be a merely disinterested, though by good fortune it may be a neutral, spectator. Unless, therefore, we survey Europe, as well as America, we do not "take a view of the whole ground." And if we must survey it, and our interests are concerned in the course of foreign events, it is obviously important that we should understand what we observe, and separate, as much as possible, errour from the wisdom that is to be gleaned by experience.

We invite our able patrons and correspondents to assist us in our labours; and to exercise their candour, if, at any time, we should present an imperfect or mistaken view of European affairs: we shall not wilfully misrepresent.

READING AND DISCUSSION QUESTIONS

1. Why is Ames so worried about the French Revolution and its effects on American politics?

2. Pay attention to the language used. How does Ames describe the French and their politics? To what extent is he attempting to discredit American defenders of France?

7-4 | Anxiety Over Western Expansion

THE PANOPLIST AND MISSIONARY HERALD, *Retrograde Movement of National Character* (1818)

Land policy was another arena of political debate. Federalists supported the sale of large tracts of the western territories to ensure an orderly settlement. By contrast, once Jeffersonian Republicans took office, they worked to reduce the federal minimum on land purchases from 640 acres (which excluded everyone but wealthy speculators) to 320 acres in 1800, and to even smaller amounts in subsequent years. By 1832, the minimum plot available for sale had been reduced to 40 acres, opening the territories to yeomen farmers, the same men whom Jefferson praised as God's chosen. Not everyone agreed that the westward movement that territorial expansion invited was a good thing. In this selection, an article from a Christian monthly magazine published in 1818, the author describes his anxiety.

The manner in which the population is spreading over this continent has no parallel in history. The first settlers of every other country have been barbarians, whose habits and institutions were suited to a wild and wandering life. As their numbers multiplied, they have gradually become civilized and refined. The progress has been from ignorance to knowledge, from the rudeness, of savage life to the refinements of polished society. But in the settlement of North America the case is reversed. The tendency is from civilization to barbarism.

Every one knows the manner in which our new settlements are formed. Single families, sometimes single individuals, proceed from this cultivated country, and, leaving behind them the religion and institutions of their fathers, they penetrate the western forest. It is usually several years before they are able to erect a comfortable dwelling-house, and many more before they can enjoy some of the most common privileges of older settlements. During this whole period, they are from necessity without schools, without ministers, without any of that influence, or those institutions which form the sober, steady, sterling character of older parts of the country. By the time that they are able to support these institutions, long habit has made them easy without them. With many the expense is an objection; and, not unfrequently a new generation have sprung up, who are unacquainted with their value, and unwilling to make any sacrifices for their support. In such a soil we should naturally suppose that infidelity and error of every species would take root and flourish. And such is the fact. The accounts which we hear represent the state of these settlements as deplorable for ignorance and irreligion.

The tendency of the American character is then to degenerate, and to degenerate rapidly; and that not from any peculiar vice in the American people, but from the very nature of a spreading population. The population of the country is out-growing its institutions.

But would we have a more convincing evidence of this degeneracy, let us go back to the days of our fathers. It is but a few years; our aged men can almost reach the time, when they first landed on these shores. They were good men, men of prayer, upright, and perfect in their generations, men who walked with God. Go now to our western borders — and who are these without Bibles, without Sabbaths — to whom the news of a Savior was never preached — who blaspheme God day and night? Are these the sons of the pilgrims? — these the children of their prayers — these the offspring for whom they endured persecution — the perils of the sea, and the perils of the wilderness — for whom they toiled and bled to procure the blessings of the Gospel? You search history in vain for degeneracy like this. Yet this is the beginning of sorrows. Could we draw aside the veil from the future, we might see these degraded men giving birth to settlements still more remote; we might see whole nations sprung from their loins — yes, we might see these men, at whose degeneracy we are now shocked, regarded as venerable, as holy, by their still more degenerate offspring. We talk of India — of Juggernaut — of the bloody rites of Pagan worship — but who can tell, how soon our own Missouri will be a Ganges, and our own children pass through the fire to Moloch.

M. N.

READING AND DISCUSSION QUESTIONS

1. What does the author suggest will be the consequences of the rapid movement of people from the East into the western territories?

2. How do his views align with the political philosophies of the Federalists and Republicans?

7-5 | A Shawnee Chief Calls for Native American Unity

TECUMSEH, *"Sleep Not Longer, O' Choctaws and Chickasaws"* (1811)

The movement west cheered some and worried others, but it angered many Native Americans. Tecumseh (1768–1813), a Shawnee chief, focused Native American attention on the encroachments of whites onto native lands. In this speech to the Choctaws and the

Horatio Bardwell Cushman, *History of the Choctaw, Chickasaw and Natchez Indians* (Greenville, TX: Headlight Printing House, 1899), 310–314.

Chickasaws, he describes the threat that Americans pose and urges a united front to turn back white intrusions. Here Tecumseh announces his alliance with the British, who once again found themselves at war with the Americans in 1812. Western "war hawks," Americans who lived on the frontier and hoped to eliminate the native peoples who blocked their expansion west, urged war against the British, who had supported Tecumseh's people. Tecumseh, in this speech, rallies his allies to join the British in attacking the common American enemy.

In view of questions of vast importance, have we met together in solemn council to-night. Nor should we here debate whether we have been wronged and injured, but by what measures we should avenge ourselves; for our merciless oppressors, having long since planned out their proceedings, are not about to make, but have and are still making attacks upon those of our race who have as yet come to no resolution. Nor are we ignorant by what steps, and by what gradual advances, the whites break in upon our neighbors. Imagining themselves to be still undiscovered, they show themselves the less audacious because you are insensible. The whites are already nearly a match for us all united, and too strong for any one tribe alone to resist; so that unless we support one another with our collective and united forces; unless every tribe unanimously combines to give a check to the ambition and avarice of the whites, they will soon conquer us apart and disunited, and we will be driven away from our native country and scattered as autumnal leaves before the wind.

But have we not courage enough remaining to defend our country and maintain our ancient independence? Will we calmly suffer the white intruders and tyrants to enslave us? Shall it be said of our race that we knew not how to extricate ourselves from the three most to be dreaded calamities—folly, inactivity and cowardice? But what need is there to speak of the past? It speaks for itself and asks, "Where to-day is the Pequod? Where the Narragansetts, the Mohawks, Pocanokets, and many other once powerful tribes of our race? They have vanished before the avarice and oppression of the white men, as snow before a summer sun. In the vain hope of alone defending their ancient possessions, they have fallen in the wars with the white men. Look abroad over their once beautiful country, and what see you now? Naught but the ravages of the pale-face destroyers meet your eyes. So it will be with you Choctaws and Chickasaws! Soon your mighty forest trees, under the shade of whose wide spreading branches you have played in infancy, sported in boyhood, and now rest your wearied limbs after the fatigue of the chase, will be cut down to fence in the land which the white intruders dare to call their own. Soon their broad roads will pass over the grave of your fathers, and the place of their rest will be blotted out forever. The annihilation of our race is at hand unless we unite in one common cause against the common foe. Think not, brave Choctaws and Chickasaws, that you can remain passive and indifferent to the common danger, and thus escape the common fate. Your people too will soon be as falling leaves and scattering clouds before their blighting breath. You too will be driven away from your native land and ancient domains as leaves are driven before the wintry storms. . . ."

Sleep not longer, O Choctaws and Chickasaws . . . in false security and delusive hopes. Our broad domains are fast escaping from our grasp. Every year our white intruders become more greedy, exacting, oppressive and overbearing. Every year contentions spring up between them and our people and when blood is shed we have to make atonement whether right or wrong, at the cost of the lives of our greatest chiefs, and the yielding up of large tracts of our lands. Before the palefaces came among us, we enjoyed the happiness of unbounded freedom, and were acquainted with neither riches, wants, nor oppression. How is it now? Wants and oppressions are our lot; for are we not controlled in everything, and dare we move without asking, by your leave? Are we not being stripped day by day of the little that remains of our ancient liberty? Do they not even now kick and strike us as they do their black-faces? How long will it be before they will tie us to a post and whip us, and make us work for them in their corn fields as they do them? Shall we wait for that moment or shall we die fighting before submitting to such ignominy?[. . .]

Have we not for years had before our eyes a sample of their designs, and are they not sufficient harbingers of their future determinations? Will we not soon be driven from our respective countries and the graves of our ancestors? Will not the bones of our dead be plowed up, and their graves be turned into fields? Shall we calmly wait until they become so numerous that we will no longer be able to resist oppression? Will we wait to be destroyed in our turn, without making an effort worthy of our race? Shall we give up our homes, our country, bequeathed to us by the Great Spirit, the graves of our dead, and everything that is dear and sacred to us, without a struggle? I know you will cry with me, Never! Never! Then let us by unity of action destroy them all, which we now can do, or drive them back whence they came. War or extermination is now our only choice. You choose? I know your answer. Therefore, I now call on you, brave Choctaws and Chickasaws, to assist in the just cause of liberating our race from the grasp of our faithless invaders and heartless oppressors. The white usurpation in our common country must be stopped, or we, its rightful owners, be forever destroyed and wiped out as a race of people. I am now at the head of many warriors backed by the strong arm of English soldiers. Choctaws and Chickasaws, you have too long borne with grievous usurpation inflicted by the arrogant Americans. Be no longer their dupes. If there be one here to-night who believes that his rights will not sooner or later, be taken from him by the avaricious American pale-faces, his ignorance ought to excite pity, for he knows little of the character of our common foe. And if there be one among you mad enough to undervalue the growing power of the white race among us, let him tremble in considering the fearful woes he will bring down upon our entire race, if by his criminal indifference he assists the designs of our common enemy against our common country. Then listen to the voice of duty, of honor, of nature and of your endangered country. Let us form one body, one heart, and defend to the last warrior our country, our homes, our liberty, and the graves of our fathers.

Choctaws and Chickasaws, you are among the few of our race who sit indolently at ease. You have indeed enjoyed the reputation of being brave, but will you be indebted for it more from report than fact? Will you let the whites encroach upon your domains even to your very door before you will assert your rights in resistance? Let no one in this council imagine that I speak more from malice against the pale-face Americans than just grounds of complaint. Complaint is just toward friends who have failed in their duty; accusation is against enemies guilty of injustice. And surely, if any people ever had, we have good and just reasons to believe we have ample grounds to accuse the Americans of injustice; especially when such great acts of injustice have been committed by them upon our race, of which they seem to have no manner of regard, or even to reflect. They are a people fond of innovations, quick to contrive and quick to put their schemes into effectual execution, no matter how great the wrong and injury to us; while we are content to preserve what we already have. Their designs are to enlarge their possessions by taking yours in turn; and will you, can you longer dally, O Choctaws and Chickasaws? Do you imagine that that people will not continue longest in the enjoyment of peace who timely prepare to vindicate themselves, and manifest a determined resolution to do themselves right whenever they are wronged? Far otherwise. Then haste to the relief of our common cause, as by consanguinity of blood you are bound; lest the day be not far distant when you will be left single-handed and alone to the cruel mercy of our most inveterate foe.

READING AND DISCUSSION QUESTIONS

1. What parallels do you see in the way Tecumseh describes Americans and the way Americans described the British during the Revolution?

2. What arguments does Tecumseh use to rally Choctaws and Chickasaws?

3. What can we learn from Tecumseh's speech about the consequences of American land policy in the early years of the republic?

7-6 | New England Federalists Oppose the War of 1812
Report of the Hartford Convention (1815)

The War of 1812 revived the Federalists, who used it to mount a vicious attack on Jefferson and Madison. Jefferson's 1807 Embargo Act outraged New England Federalists, whose shipping interests suffered as a result, but his critics also ridiculed him for grasping enormous power, contrary to his own political philosophy. Madison fared no better. He was excoriated for stumbling into a war the nation was ill prepared to fight. Federalists met in Hartford to cohere their protests into a series of resolutions they intended to present to Congress. The resolutions included here were more moderate than others proposed, including some that

Theodore Dwight, *History of the Hartford Convention: With a Review of the Policy of the United States Government, Which Led to the War of 1812* (New York: N. & J. White; Boston: Russell, Odiorne, & Co., 1833), 352–356, 375–379.

called on the New England states to secede from the Union. The convention's timing, however, worked against their interests. Soon after the convention ended, news of General Andrew Jackson's astounding victory over the British at the Battle of New Orleans, followed by news of the peace signed at Ghent, rendered the Federalists' attack moot and unpatriotic. The party quickly dissolved.

The delegates from the legislatures of the states of Massachusetts, Connecticut, and Rhode-Island, and from the counties of Grafton and Cheshire in the state of New-Hampshire and the county of Windham in the state of Vermont, assembled in convention, beg leave to report the following result of their conference.

The convention is deeply impressed with a sense of the arduous nature of the commission which they were appointed to execute, of devising the means of defence against dangers, and of relief from oppressions proceeding from the acts of their own government, without violating constitutional principles, or disappointing the hopes of a suffering and injured people. To prescribe patience and firmness to those who are already exhausted by distress, is sometimes to drive them to despair, and the progress towards reform by the regular road, is irksome to those whose imaginations discern, and whose feelings prompt, to a shorter course. But when abuses, reduced to a system, and accumulated through a course of years, have pervaded every department of government, and spread corruption through every region of the state; when these are clothed with the forms of law, and enforced by an executive whose will is their source, no summary means of relief can be applied without recourse to direct and open resistance. This experiment, even when justifiable, cannot fail to be painful to the good citizen; and the success of the effort will be no security against the danger of the example. Precedents of resistance to the worst administration, are eagerly seized by those who are naturally hostile to the best. Necessity alone can sanction a resort to this measure; and it should never be extended in duration or degree beyond the exigency, until the people, not merely in the fervour of sudden excitement, but after full deliberation, are determined to change the constitution. . . .

If the Union be destined to dissolution, by reason of the multiplied abuses of bad administrations, it should, if possible, be the work of peaceable times, and deliberate consent. Some new form of confederacy should be substituted among those states which shall intend to maintain a federal relation to each other. Events may prove that the causes of our calamities are deep and permanent. They may be found to proceed, not merely from the blindness of prejudice, pride of opinion, violence of party spirit, or the confusion of the times; but they may be traced to implacable combinations of individuals, or of states, to monopolize power and office, and to trample without remorse upon the rights and interests of commercial sections of the Union. Whenever it shall appear that these causes are radical and permanent, a separation, by equitable arrangement, will be preferable to an alliance by constraint, among nominal friends, but real enemies, inflamed by mutual hatred and jealousy, and inviting, by intestine divisions, contempt and aggression from abroad. But a severance of the Union by one or more states, against the will of the rest, and especially in a time of war, can be justified only by absolute necessity. These are among the principal objections against precipitate measures tending to disunite the states, and when examined in connection with the farewell address of the Father of his country, they must, it is believed, be deemed conclusive. . . .

Negotiations for peace are at this hour supposed to be pending, the issue of which must be deeply interesting to all. No measures should be adopted which might unfavourably affect that issue; none which should embarrass the administration, if their professed desire for peace is sincere; and none which on supposition of their insincerity, should afford them pretexts for prolonging the war, or relieving themselves from the responsibility of a dishonourable peace. It is also devoutly to be wished, that an occasion may be afforded to all friends of the country, of all parties, and in all places, to pause and consider the awful state to which pernicious counsels and blind passions have brought this people. The number of those who perceive, and who are ready to retrace errors, must, it is believed be yet sufficient to redeem the nation. It is necessary to rally and unite them by the assurance that no hostility to the constitution is meditated, and to obtain their aid in placing it under guardians who alone can save it from destruction. Should this fortunate change be effected the hope of happiness and honour may once more dispel the surrounding gloom. Our nation may yet be great, our union durable. But should this prospect be utterly hopeless, the time will not have been lost which shall have ripened a general sentiment of the necessity of more mighty efforts to rescue from ruin, at least some portion of our beloved country.

THEREFORE RESOLVED,

That it be and hereby is recommended to the legislatures of the several states represented in this Convention, to adopt all such measures as may be necessary effectually to protect the citizens of said states from the operation and effects of all acts which have been or may be passed by the Congress of the United States, which shall contain provisions, subjecting the militia or other citizens to forcible drafts, conscriptions, or impressments, not authorised by the constitution of the United States.

Resolved, That it be and hereby is recommended to the said Legislatures, to authorize an immediate and earnest application to be made to the government of the United States, requesting their consent to some arrangement, whereby the said states may, separately or in concert, be empowered to assume upon themselves the defence of their territory against the enemy; and a reasonable portion of the taxes, collected within said States, may be paid into the respective treasuries thereof, and appropriated to the payment of the balance due said states, and to the future defence of the same. The amount so paid into the said treasuries to be credited, and the disbursements made as aforesaid to be charged to the United States.

Resolved, That it be, and hereby is, recommended to the legislatures of the aforesaid states, to pass laws (where it has not already been done) authorizing the governors or commanders-in-chief of their militia to make detachments from the same, or to form voluntary corps, as shall be most convenient and conformable to their constitutions, and to cause the same to be well armed, equipped, and disciplined, and held in readiness for service; and upon the request of the governor of either of the other states to employ the whole of such detachment or corps, as well as the regular forces of the state, or such part thereof as may be required and can be spared consistently with the safety of the state, in assisting the state, making such request to repel any invasion thereof which shall be made or attempted by the public enemy.

Resolved, That the following amendments of the constitution of the United States be recommended to the states represented as aforesaid, to be proposed by them for adoption by the state legislatures, and in such cases as may be deemed expedient by a convention chosen by the people of each state.

And it is further recommended, that the said states shall persevere in their efforts to obtain such amendments, until the same shall be effected.

First. Representatives and direct taxes shall be apportioned among the several states which may be included within this Union, according to their respective numbers of free persons, including those bound to serve for a term of years, and excluding Indians not taxed, and all other persons.

Second. No new state shall be admitted into the Union by Congress, in virtue of the power granted by the constitution, without the concurrence of two thirds of both houses.

Third. Congress shall not have power to lay any embargo on the ships or vessels of the citizens of the United States, in the ports or harbours thereof, for more than sixty days.

Fourth. Congress shall not have power, without the concurrence of two thirds of both houses, to interdict the commercial intercourse between the United States and any foreign nation, or the dependencies thereof.

Fifth. Congress shall not make or declare war, or authorize acts of hostility against any foreign nation, without the concurrence of two thirds of both houses, except such acts of hostility be in defence of the territories of the United States when actually invaded.

Sixth. No person who shall hereafter be naturalized, shall be eligible as a member of the senate or house of representatives of the United States, nor capable of holding any civil office under the authority of the United States.

Seventh. The same person shall not be elected president of the United States a second time; nor shall the president be elected from the same state two terms in succession.

Resolved, That if the application of these states to the government of the United States, recommended in a foregoing resolution, should be unsuccessful, and peace should not be concluded, and the defence of these states should be neglected, as it has been since the commencement of the war, it will, in the opinion of this convention, be expedient for the legislatures of the several states to appoint delegates to another convention, to meet at Boston in the state of Massachusetts, on the third Thursday of June next, with such powers and instructions as the exigency of a crisis so momentous may require.

Resolved, That the Hon. George Cabot, the Hon. Chauncey Goodrich, and the Hon. Daniel Lyman, or any two of them, be authorized to call another meeting of this convention, to be holden in Boston, at any time before new delegates shall be chosen, as recommended in the above resolution, if in their judgment the situation of the country shall urgently require it.

READING AND DISCUSSION QUESTIONS

1. What do you think gave the Federalists confidence that their resolutions would be sympathetically received in Congress?
2. How would the Federalists' proposed constitutional amendments have addressed the problems they identified?
3. What does the Hartford Convention tell us about early national politics?

■ COMPARATIVE QUESTIONS ■

1. What might account for the difference in American responses to the French Revolution? What impact might those differences have had on American politics?
2. Compare and contrast the political program of the Federalists and Republicans based on the sources included in this chapter. How did the emergence of these early political parties affect American society during this time?
3. What did the two major political parties see as the source of strength for the American republic? Did they have the same or different answers?
4. To what extent were the disputes between Federalists and Republicans fueled by policy or personality?
5. How would you interpret the War of 1812? Is it the end of one era or the start of another? Did the War of 1812 introduce new issues or settle old ones?

8

Creating a Republican Culture
1790–1820

In 1818, John Adams reflected that "the real American Revolution" was the "radical change in the principles, opinions, sentiments, and affections of the people." Adams was hinting at the profound transformation that Americans experienced, moving from subject to citizen, and creating a republican government and society. While many wondered about the fate of the new republic, the young nation quickly embraced the dynamics of change, and a new republican culture was born.

America's developing market economy shaped many aspects of that culture, and manufacturing became part of an American identity, especially after the War of 1812 weaned Americans off foreign goods. On the home front, the democratic ideals of republicanism weakened hierarchical social relationships, enabling women and others once considered "dependents" to imagine lives in a more equal society. Republican values also affected religion, where the Second Great Awakening's democratic appeal invested men and women with belief in their own power to choose their eternal fate. Enslaved men and women, by contrast, were excluded from this republican idealism, though they were very much a part of the nation's economic life. Slavery coexisted uneasily with celebrations of American liberty, and even Thomas Jefferson, himself a slave owner, warned of slavery's gathering clouds.

8-1 | Building the Economy

J. HILL, *Junction of Erie and Northern Canal* (c. 1830–1832)

Hamilton's commercial vision for the new republic flourished in the years after the War of 1812, aided by private and public investments in canals, roads, and bridges. In this scene from the early 1830s, a developing market economy is clearly under way. Canal traffic brought the manufacturing revolution to inland regions, opening markets, and encouraging trade and consumption on a scale previously unknown. These "artificial rivers" literally changed the landscape, transforming Jefferson's agrarian world into the mill and factory economy Hamilton hoped for.

READING AND DISCUSSION QUESTIONS

1. What point of view about the market economy does this lithograph express? Was the artist celebrating or lamenting the changes brought by the canal economy?

2. How would you use the evidence from this illustration to discuss specific changes to daily life those living along the canals might have experienced?

Junction of Erie and Northern Canal, engraved by J. Hill, c. 1830–1832 (color litho), American School (19th century) / © Collection of the New-York Historical Society, USA / The Bridgeman Art Library.

8-2 | In Praise of Domestic Manufacturing
THE WEEKLY REGISTER, *Home Influence* (1813)

The War of 1812 had economic origins and consequences. Here, in an article from the January 23, 1813, *Weekly Register*, published in the commercial city of Baltimore, Maryland, the author describes one effect of the war with Britain: an encouragement of domestic manufacturing. With trade curtailed because of the war, Americans were forced to "wean" themselves from foreign goods and rely on American manufactures. This necessity transformed into a virtue, as it became another element of republican self-reliance, industry, and pride.

The belief of years has resolved into moral certainty. It was an old opinion that the United States could never become a *really* independent, distinct and Separate nation, while so many of our necessaries, conveniences and luxuries were received from abroad. Our ablest politicians, knowing the *influence* generated by these considerations, always predicted what the declaration of war against *England* has realized; for now it is evident matter of fact, that our people on the sea board must be weaned from their late great commercial intercourse with that country, before they can possess one genuine and generous *American* feeling. To the shreds of the *old predilection* in favor of *Great Britain*, handed down from father to son, and imbibed through a multitude of mediums, such as books, business and all the circumstances of social life, is superadded the more powerful dispositions of *pecuniary interest*. In the scale of affections, the love of self preponderates; and the many thousands who grow rich by dealing in *foreign* goods must needs be under *foreign* influence. "*Where the treasure is the heart will lie also*" and it is too much the case with the *trading* world that money is the god they worship. It is not to be expected that these narrow personal feelings can be eradicated; but time and perseverance may divert them to better objects *at home*.

It is cause of rejoicing that many, very many millions of dollars have latterly been invested in *domestic manufacturing establishments*, and to observe the current of wealth still urging the erection of new and magnificent works. This mighty and increasing capital begets a new feeling; for the "treasure" is *at home*. The influence of money is wonderful; and the mind changes as the means of acquiring it are presented. Hence a powerful *home influence* is spreading itself through society, and the people are becoming more abstracted from *foreign* considerations. In the city of *Baltimore* are now sold various kinds of goods to the value of at least half million of dollars *per annum*, all of which species, five years ago, were received from *abroad*: and the pith and marrow of the matter is this, that the supply is immensely increasing, because all who deal in them find their *profit* in doing so—

"Men follow money
As bees follow honey"

The Weekly Register: Documents, Essays, and Facts, vol. 3, ed. H. Niles (Baltimore: The Franklin Press, 1813), 328–329.

And many very valuable establishments for the chief sale of *domestic goods* have sprung up in different parts of the city; while every day brings to market some *new commodity*.

It is true that the manufactures of the United States are not yet adequate to the consumption of the country; but hundreds of thousands are clothed entirely with *home-made* apparel; while many of our most important branches of mechanical industry are completely supplied with all their tools and apparatus from other work-shops among us. Our bountiful country pours forth its resources; and genius applies its productions to the wants and conveniences of life. Our progress in improvement has no parallel; nor is the increase of our population more surprising than the proceeds of our manufactures, rising in all their varied form in every direction, and pursued *with an eye to profit* in almost every farm house in the *United States*. The *merino breed* of sheep is spreading with astonishing rapidity—they are already numerous, and much attention is paid to improving the common species. The manufacture of all the coarser kinds of *cotton goods*, with some of the most delicate fabrics, may be considered as *fully established*. The western states will supply us with an abundance of *hemp* and *hempen manufactures*. The chief part of the *heavy metallic articles* are now made amongst us, while many of the lighter kinds are extensively and profitably furnished. The *woolen manufacture* keeps pace with the rest, and great investitures are made in its various departments. Ancient prejudices have yielded to the impulses of patriotism or the dictates of prudence, and it has become *fashionable* to use *home manufactures*. This is a most important point gained, for we are creatures of prejudice; and, "like blind horses in a mill," pursue the beaten track without a why or wherefore. Six years ago our whole export of *flour, beef, pork* and *provisions*, generally, did no more than pay for the *foreign* liquors we consumed: the case is materially altered—the long despised *whiskey*, rectified, and improved, has driven from the side-board *English* rum and *French* brandy, or suffers them to remain as mere monuments of former favor. Our most dashing bucks are proud to boast a *homespun coat*; and the prudent house-wife delighted exhibits her newly made table linen, sheeting, carpets, etc. This is that pride that destroys a *foreign* influence—it is an honest pride, and should be encouraged, and so indeed it is—for no man is ashamed for his apparel, though it be coarse, if it is clean and decent, and HOME-SPUN.

Seeing the importance of *domestic manufactures* in lessening our connection with the old world, corrupted and corrupting, the patriot heart leaps with joy at the speedy prospect of "reversing the tables" upon it, in making it the *necessity* of *foreign* nations to *depend* on us for those raw materials and articles of food which it was *our* object to exchange for *their* productions—*but which they must have*, not possessing within themselves the means to furnish them.—*Then* will our country stand on high ground; and wealth flow gradually in from all quarters, without subjecting us to *foreign* partialities or the *gamblings* of commerce. The trade of the country will increase; but the anxiety of the merchant will be not to receive from *Europe* the chief articles of his adventure, but to obtain of his neighbors, responsible men vouching for their good qualities and on whose faith he can recommend them abroad, all that he wants.—This time is not far distant—the *political mellenium* in America is fast approaching, and will come; though like the croaking raven, a FOREIGN INFLUENCE predicts all calamity. The righteous war for our *seamen* and our *rights*, grossly violated, is one of the grand means by which a good Providence will bring about a blessed union of the people, in directing them to look AT HOME for all they desire. Let the real *American* be of good cheer—we shall triumph by land as well as by sea; but more than all in establishing a HOME INFLUENCE that will guard and defend happy *Columbia* amidst the "throes and convulsions of the old world," when "infuriated man, th[r]ough blood and slaughter, shall seek his liberty," with horrors unprecedented.

This state of things is clearly manifested to the view of *England*. With unspeakable hatred and bitterness of spirit, like *Babylon* of old, she sees the time "when no man [in America] shall buy her merchandize any more"—and herein is the *true cause* of that rancour of party which is excited in the United States by her turbulent advocates. We should bear with that patiently, well assured that *her influence* here is at its last gasp. It will not expire without great screamings and noise; but they shall not divert us from our course. *Home manufactures*, with steady perseverance, will destroy the hydra; and when, hereafter, we shall calmly view his deformity, great will be our wonder that we bore with it so long.

READING AND DISCUSSION QUESTIONS

1. What evidence of an emerging market economy does this source provide for the early national period?

2. Besides providing goods for Americans to consume, what other benefit does the author claim will come from a strong and vibrant domestic manufacturing economy?

8-3 | Warren Discusses Women's Roles

MERCY OTIS WARREN, *Letter to a Young Friend* (1790) and *Letter to Catharine Sawbridge Macaulay Graham* (1791)

Mercy Otis Warren (1728–1814) was an extraordinary woman in extraordinary times. Though constrained by the gender discrimination pervasive in her day, she pushed against those boundaries, demonstrating in her books and essays that women were capable of political participation in the young republic. She was an astute observer, and her family connections to Massachusetts's political elite enabled her to see and experience firsthand the major conflicts

Alice Brown, *Mercy Warren* (New York: Charles Scribner's Sons, 1896), 241–242.

Mercy Otis Warren Selected Letters, ed. Jeffrey H. Richards and Sharon M. Harris (Athens: The University of Georgia Press, 2009), 230–232.

of her day. Her letters, including two excerpted here, reveal her engagement with the political debates of the 1790s and her interest in pushing women's rights.

Letter to a Young Friend

You seem hurt by the general aspersions so often thrown on the Understanding of ours by the Illiberal Part of the other Sex.—I think I feel no partiality on the Female Side but what arises from a love to Justice, & freely acknowledge we too often give occasion (by an Eager Pursuit of Trifles) for Reflections of this Nature.—Yet a discerning & generous Mind should look to the origin of the Error, and when that is done, I believe it will be found that the Deficiency lies not so much in the Inferior Contexture of Female Intellects as in the different Education bestow'd on the Sexes, for when the Cultivation of the Mind is neglected in Either, we see Ignorance, Stupidity, & Ferocity of Manners equally Conspicuous in both.

It is my Opinion that that Part of the human Species who think Nature (as well as the infinitely wise & Supreme Author thereof) has given them the Superiority over the other, mistake their own Happiness when they neglect the Culture of Reason in their Daughters while they take all possible Methods of improving it in their sons.

The Pride you feel on hearing Reflections indiscriminately Cast on the Sex, is laudable if any is so.—I take it, it is a kind of Conscious Dignity that ought rather to be cherish'd, for while we own the Appointed Subordination (perhaps for the sake of Order in Families) let us by no Means Acknowledge such an Inferiority as would Check the Ardour of our Endeavours to equal in all Accomplishments the most masculine Heights, that when these temporary Distinctions subside we may be equally qualified to taste the full Draughts of Knowledge & Happiness prepared for the Upright of every Nation & Sex; when Virtue alone will be the Test of Rank, & the grand Economy for an Eternal Duration will be properly Adjusted.

Letter to Catharine Sawbridge Macaulay Graham

Plymouth May 31st 1791

I have my dear madam been particularly obliged by two of your favours since I have taken up my pen to write to my friend. Were I fully to express my sentiments with regard to your letters on education and on your learned and metaphysical disquisitions, you might think they savoured of flattery. This is a fault not less despised by myself than it is detested by a lady whose talents, set her very much above it.

I will therefore only say, I was entertained and delighted with the volume and pleased that you had taken up your pen on subjects so important: nor was I less gratified with the manner of executing the design. I have since been obliged by your ingenious and just observations on Mr. Burke's strictures on the national assembly of France. What an inconsistent creature is man!

I am sorry for the sake of the human character, that a gentleman whose oratorical powers have been so often so honourably employed and exerted in favour of the rights of society, should so far deviate from the principles he has supported, as to vilify the advocates for freedom, and to abuse characters that have discovered more firmness and consistency than himself, yet his celebrated pamphlet may be productive of good, both to Europe and to America. It appears to me that it will lead to the discussion of questions that have for some time lain dormant, and to the revival and vindication of opinions that have of late been too unfashionable to avow.

Even some Americans who have fought for their country and been instrumental in her emancipation from a foreign yoke, seem to be at war with every Democratic principle:—and some men of genius, professed republicans, who formerly shared the confidence of the people, are now become the advocates for Monarchy and all the trappings of Royalty. *The British constitution* is the idol of their warmest devotion and they daily sigh for *Patrician rank*, hereditary titles, stars, garters, and nobility, with all the insignia of arbitrary sway.

Thus from age to age, are the people coaxed, cheated, or bullied until the hood-winked multitude set their own seal to a renunciation of their priviledges, and with their own hand rivet the chains of servitude on their posterity.

This is a painful reflection to the patriot in retirement and the philosopher in his closet: but when we consider it is the usual course of human conduct, one is almost led to assent to the Federal creed lately established in America. First that mankind are incapable of the enjoyment of liberty; second that the mass of the people have not the capacity nor the right to choose their own master; therefore the game of deception must be played over and over to mislead their judgment and work on their enthusiasm until by the assent, *hereditary crowns* and distinctions are fixed, when their posterity may load the authors thereof with as many curses, as now daily fall on the first *Federal head* who it is said conveyed an hereditary taint to all succeeding generations.

Yet it is my opinion commotions in France will check the designs of certain characters, about the *American Court*: and for a time keep them within some bounds of moderation and perhaps awake the vigilance of others, so far as to keep in awe those who are buzzing for a crown for their President and hereditary title, lordships, and revenues for his ministers and favourites. . . .

I hope you have received a small packet from *Dilly*; if the amusements of some leisure hours should meet your approbation, I should be highly gratified. The volume I know will be read by you Madam with candour, if not partiality. What the critics may say I know not—but sensible many a hapless reputation has been wrecked on the ocean of public opinion, I have endeavoured to arm myself with fortitude either to ride out the storm or to see my little shallop[1] stranded on the quicksands of neglect.

I am my dear madam with unalterable esteem your very sincere friend,

M WARREN

---

[1] **shallop**: A small, shallow-water boat.

READING AND DISCUSSION QUESTIONS

1. How does Warren account for the unflattering views her correspondent claims men entertain about women's "Understanding," by which she means their intellectual abilities?

2. This letter hints at Warren's efforts to navigate a world of limited expectations for women and her desire to push against those limits. What advice does she give to help her young friend do the same?

3. To what extent was Warren affected by the rhetoric of republicanism? How did it shape her view of women's role in the republic?

8-4 | An Argument for the Education of Republican Women

BENJAMIN RUSH, *Thoughts Upon Female Education* (1787)

Like Warren, Benjamin Rush was on center stage during the American Revolution. A signer of the Declaration of Independence, Rush embraced the republican values of the era. He was a champion of reform in areas of medicine, prisons, antislavery, and education. In this selection, taken from his essay "Thoughts Upon Female Education" published in 1787, Rush outlines the various subjects he considers necessary to women's education. In a consistently male-dominated time, Rush's defense of female education is surprising.

GENTLEMEN,

I have yielded with diffidence to the solicitations of the Principal of the Academy, in undertaking to express my regard for the prosperity of this seminary of learning, by submitting to your candor, a few Thoughts upon Female Education.

The first remark that I shall make upon this subject, is, that female education should be accommodated to the state of society, manners, and government of the country, in which it is conducted.

This remark leads me at once to add, that the education of young ladies, in this country, should be conducted upon principles very different from what it is in Great Britain, and in some respects, different from what it was when we were part of a monarchical empire.

There are several circumstances in the situation, employments, and duties of women in America, which require a peculiar mode of education.

I. The early marriages of our women, by contracting the time allowed for education, renders it necessary to contract its plan, and to confine it chiefly to the more useful branches of literature.

II. The state of property in America, renders it necessary for the greatest part of our citizens to employ themselves, in different occupations, for the

---

Benjamin Rush, *Essays, Literary, Moral and Philosophical* (Philadelphia: Thomas and William Bradford, 1806), 75–85, 87–88, 90–92.

advancement of their fortunes. This cannot be done without the assistance of the female members of the community. They must be the stewards, and guardians of their husbands' property. That education, therefore, will be most proper for our women, which teaches them to discharge the duties of those offices with the most success and reputation.

III. From the numerous avocations from their families, to which professional life exposes gentlemen in America, a principal share of the instruction of children naturally devolves upon the women. It becomes us therefore to prepare them by a suitable education, for the discharge of this most important duty of mothers.

IV. The equal share that every citizen has in the liberty, and the possible share he may have in the government of our country, make it necessary that our ladies should be qualified to a certain degree by a peculiar and suitable education, to concur in instructing their sons in the principles of liberty and government.

V. In Great Britain the business of servants is a regular occupation; but in America this humble station is the usual retreat of unexpected indigence; hence the servants in this country possess less knowledge and subordination than are required from them; and hence, our ladies are obliged to attend more to the private affairs of their families, than ladies generally do, of the same rank in Great Britain. "They are good servants," said an American lady of distinguished merit, in a letter to a favorite daughter, "who will do well with good looking after." This circumstance should have great influence upon the nature and extent of female education in America.

The branches of literature most essential for a young lady in this country, appear to be,

I. A knowledge of the English language. She should not only read, but speak and spell it correctly. And to enable her to do this, she should be taught the English grammar, and be frequently examined in applying its rules in common conversation.

II. Pleasure and interest conspire to make the writing of a fair and legible hand, a necessary branch of a lady's education. For this purpose she should be taught not only to shape every letter properly, but to pay the strictest regard to points and capitals. . . .

III. Some knowledge of figures and book-keeping is absolutely necessary to qualify a young lady for the duties which await her in this country. There are certain occupations in which she may assist her husband with this knowledge; and should she survive him, and agreeably to the custom of our country be the executrix of his will, she cannot fail of deriving immense advantages from it.

IV. An acquaintance with geography and some instruction in chronology will enable a young lady to read history, biography, and travels, with advantage; and thereby qualify her not only for a general intercourse with the world, but to be an agreeable companion for a sensible man. To these branches of knowledge may be added, in some instances, a general acquaintance with the first principles of astronomy[,] natural philosophy and chemistry, particularly, with such parts of them as are calculated to prevent superstition, by explaining the causes, or obviating the effects of natural evil, and such as are capable of being applied to domestic, and culinary purposes.

V. Vocal music should never be neglected, in the education of a young lady, in this country. Besides preparing her to join in that part of public worship which consists in psalmody, it will enable her to soothe the cares of domestic life. The distress and vexation of a husband—the noise of a nursery, and, even, the sorrows that will sometimes intrude into her own bosom, may all be relieved by a song, where sound and sentiment unite to act upon mind. . . .

VI. Dancing is by no means an improper branch of education for an American lady. It promotes health, and renders the figure and motions of the body easy and agreeable. . . .

VII. The attention of our young ladies should be directed, as soon as they are prepared for it, to the reading of history—travels—poetry—and moral essays. These studies are accommodated, in a peculiar manner, to the present state of society in America, and when a relish is excited for them, in early life, they subdue that passion for reading novels, which so generally prevails among the fair sex. . . .

VIII. It will be necessary to connect all these branches of education with regular instruction in the Christian religion. For this purpose the principles of the different sects of christians should be taught and explained, and our pupils should early be furnished with some of the most simple arguments in favour of the truth of christianity. A portion of the bible (of late improperly banished from our schools) should be read by them every day, and such questions should be asked, after reading it as are calculated to imprint upon their minds the interesting stories contained in it. . . .

There are certain simple propositions in the christian religion, which are suited in a peculiar manner, to the infant state of reason and moral sensibility. A clergyman of long experience in the instruction of youth informed me, that he always found children acquired religious knowledge more easily than knowledge upon other subjects; and that young girls acquired this kind of knowledge more readily than boys. The female breast is the natural soil of Christianity; and while our women are taught to believe its doctrines, and obey its precepts, the wit of Voltaire, and the stile of Bolingbroke, will never be able to destroy its influence upon our citizens. . . .

I have said nothing in favour of instrumental music as a branch of female education, because I conceive it is by no means accommodated to the present state of society and manners in America. The price of musical instruments, and the extravagant fees demanded by the teachers of instrumental music, form but a small part of my objections to it.

To perform well, upon a musical instrument, requires much time and long practice. From two to four hours in a day, for three or four years appropriated to music, are an immense deduction from that short period of time which is allowed by the peculiar circumstances of our country for the acquisition of the useful branches of literature that have been mentioned. How many useful ideas might be picked up in these hours from history, philosophy, poetry, and the numerous moral essays with which our language abounds, and how much more would the knowledge acquired upon these subjects add to the consequence of a lady, with her husband and with society, than the best performed pieces of music upon a harpsichord or a guittar! Of the many ladies whom we have known, who have spent the most important years of their lives, in learning to play upon instruments of music, how few of them do we see amuse themselves or their friends with them, after they become mistresses of families! Their harpsichords serve only as side-boards for their parlours, and prove by their silence, that necessity and circumstances, will always prevail over fashion, and false maxims of education. . . .

It should not surprise us that British customs, with respect to female education, have been transplanted into our American schools and families. We see marks of the same incongruity, of time and place, in many other things. We behold our houses accomodated to the climate of Great Britain, by eastern and western directions. We behold our ladies panting in a heat of ninety degrees, under a hat and cushion, which were calculated for the temperature of a British summer. We behold our citizens condemned and punished by a criminal law, which was copied from a country, where maturity in corruption renders public executions a part of the amusements of the nation. It is high time to awake from this servility—to study our own character—to examine the age of our country—and to adopt manners in every thing, that shall be accomodated to our state of society, and to the forms of our government. In particular it is incumbent upon us to make ornamental accomplishments yield to principles and knowledge, in the education of our women.

A philosopher once said "let me make all the ballads of a country and I care not who makes its laws." He might with more propriety have said, let the ladies of a country be educated properly, and they will not only make and administer its laws, but form its manners and character. It would require a lively imagination to describe, or even to comprehend the happiness of a country, where knowledge and virtue, were generally diffused among the female sex. Our young men would then be restrained from vice by the terror of being banished from their company. The loud laugh, and the malignant smile, at the expence of innocence, or of personal infirmities—the feats of successful mimickry—and the low priced wit, which is borrowed from a misapplication of scripture phrases, would no more be considered as recommendations to the society of the ladies. A double entendre in their presence, would then exclude a gentleman forever from the company of both sexes, and probably oblige him to seek an asylum from contempt, in a foreign country. The influence of female education would be still more extensive and useful in domestic life. The obligations of gentlemen to qualify themselves by knowledge and industry to discharge the duties of benevolence, would be encreased by marriage; and the patriot—the hero—and the legislator, would find the sweetest reward of their toils, in the approbation and applause of their wives. Children would discover the marks of maternal prudence and wisdom in every station of life; for it has been remarked that there have been few great or good men who have not been blessed with wise and prudent mothers. . . .

I cannot dismiss the subject of female education without remarking, that the city of Philadelphia first saw a number of gentlemen associated for the purpose of directing the education of young ladies. By means of this plan, the power of teachers is regulated and restrained, and the objects of education are extended. By the separation of the sexes in the unformed state of their manners, female delicacy is cherished and preserved. Here the young ladies may enjoy all the literary advantages of a boarding school, and at the same time live under the protection of their parents. Here emulation may be excited without jealousy,—ambition without envy,—and competition without strife. The attempt to establish this new mode of education for young ladies, was an experiment, and the success of it hath answered our expectations. Too much praise cannot be given to our principal and his assistants, for the abilities and fidelity with which they have carried the plan into execution. The proficiency which the young ladies have discovered in reading—writing—spelling—arithmetic—grammar—geography—music—and their different catechisms, since the last, examination, is a less equivocal mark of the merit of our teachers, than any thing I am able to express in their favour.

But the reputation of the academy must be suspended, till the public are convinced, by the future conduct and character of our pupils, of the advantages of the institution. To you, therefore, YOUNG LADIES, an important problem is committed for solution; and that is, whether our present plan of education be a wise one, and whether it be calculated to prepare you for the duties of social and domestic life. I know that the elevation of the female mind, by means of moral, physical and religious truth, is considered by some men as unfriendly to the domestic character of a woman. But this is the prejudice of little minds, and springs from the same spirit which opposes the general diffusion of knowledge among the citizens of our republics. If men believe that ignorance is favourable to the government of the female sex, they are certainly deceived; for a weak and ignorant woman will always be governed with the greatest difficulty. I have sometimes been led to ascribe the invention of ridiculous and expensive fashions in female dress, entirely to the gentlemen, in order to divert the ladies from improving their minds, and thereby to secure a more arbitrary and unlimited authority over them. It will be in your power, Ladies, to correct the mistakes and practice of our sex upon these subjects, by demonstrating, that the female temper can only be governed by reason, and that the cultivation of reason in women, is alike friendly to the order of nature, and to private as well as public happiness.

READING AND DISCUSSION QUESTIONS

1. Upon what grounds does Rush argue that women ought to receive the benefits of a thorough education in the wide curriculum of subjects he proposes?

2. How does Rush integrate republican ideals into his argument in support of female education? To what extent does he suggest that education for women would support republican values?

3. To what extent was Rush's argument a product of the times? Could you imagine a similar essay being written one hundred years earlier?

8-5 | Jefferson Warns Against Slavery's Expansion
THOMAS JEFFERSON, *Letter to John Holmes* (1820)

The values of republicanism, which prized the virtuous and independent citizen's dedication to the common good, existed in tension with the reality of America's slave-based economy. Though slavery existed in America well before the Revolution, that war's rhetoric of rights made visible the paradox of slavery in a land of liberty. The Missouri Compromise, which Thomas Jefferson mentions in his 1820 letter to John Holmes, divided the Louisiana Territory into free and slave regions. As Jefferson noted, the compromise delayed but did not settle the fundamental crisis: what to do with slavery?

Monticello April 22, 1820.

I thank you, Dear Sir, for the copy you have been so kind as to send me of the letter to your constituents on the Missouri question. It is a perfect justification to them. I had for a long time ceased to read the newspapers or pay any attention to public affairs, confident they were in good hands, and content to be a passenger in our bark to the shore from which I am not distant. But this momentous question, like a fire bell in the night, awakened and filled me with terror. I considered it at once as the knell of the Union. It is hushed indeed for the moment. But this is a reprieve only, not a final sentence. A geographical line, coinciding with a marked principle, moral and political, once conceived and held up to the angry passions of men, will never be obliterated; and every new irritation will mark it deeper and deeper. I can say with conscious truth that there is not a man on earth who would sacrifice more than I would to relieve us from this heavy reproach, in any practicable way. The cession of that kind of property, for so it is misnamed, is a bagatelle which would not cost me a second thought, if, in that way, a general emancipation and expatriation could be effected: and, gradually, and with due sacrifices, I think it might be. But, as it is, we have the wolf by the ears, and we can neither hold him, nor safely let him go. Justice is in one scale, and self-preservation in the other. Of one thing I am certain, that as the passage of slaves from one state to another would not make a slave of a single human being who would not be so without it, so their diffusion over a greater surface would make them individually happier and proportionally facilitate the accomplishment of their emancipation, by dividing the burthen on a greater number of coadjutors. An abstinence too from this act of power would remove the jealousy excited by the undertaking of Congress, to regulate the condition of the different descriptions of men composing a state. This certainly is the exclusive right of every state,

Thomas Jefferson, letter to John Holmes, April 22, 1820. The Thomas Jefferson Papers, Series 1. General Correspondence, 1651–1827. Library of Congress. http://hdl.loc.gov/loc.mss /mtjbib023795.

which nothing in the constitution has taken from them and given to the general government. Could congress, for example, say that the Non-freemen of Connecticut, shall be freemen, or that they shall not emigrate into any other state?

I regret that I am now to die in the belief that the useless sacrifice of themselves, by the generation of 1776, to acquire self-government and happiness to their country, is to be thrown away by the unwise and unworthy passions of their sons, and that my only consolation is to be that I live not to weep over it. If they would but dispassionately weigh the blessings they will throw away against an abstract principle more likely to be effected by union than by scission, they would pause before they would perpetrate this act of suicide on themselves and of treason against the hopes of the world.

To yourself as the faithful advocate of union I tender the offering of my high esteem and respect. Th. Jefferson

READING AND DISCUSSION QUESTIONS

1. How does Jefferson use the metaphor of holding a "wolf by the ears" to explain the nation's dilemma over slavery?

2. What solution to the slavery problem does Jefferson suggest?

8-6 | An Egalitarian View of Religion

LORENZO DOW, *Analects Upon the Rights of Man* (1816)

The Second Great Awakening, an outpouring of religious enthusiasm that began in the early national era, drew on the common set of ideals that, since the Revolution, had emboldened Americans to act with self-possession and independence. The message of the awakening urged Americans to actively choose salvation over sin, an act of self-creation that mirrored the republican culture of the early national period. Here Lorenzo Dow, a charismatic preacher of the time, adapts the political rhetoric about the rights of man for religious purposes.

"Personal Rights" are by virtue of *existence*. "Social Rights," by virtue of being a *member* of society. "Moral Rights" by virtue of Moral obligation to the Moral governor. *Equality* and *independence* being the "Law of Nature," from them government should spring by delegation and Representation. But from *assumption* sprang tyrannical governments. And "religious establishments by Law," founded on ignorance and false "Moral obligation," was *imposed* on the world, to answer the purposes of ambitious *usurpers*. Hence arose the "*Papal Power*," as man was *not* suffered to think, and judge, and practice for *himself*; but the *nonsense* of others must be believed before his own *senses*; which produced the "*seas of blood*,"

Lorenzo Dow, *Four Volumes of Lorenzo's Journal Concentrated into One* (New York: John C. Totten, 1814), 215–221.

which flowed by the intolerant hand of persecution! At length "Light" broke in! "Common sense" waked up, and embraced a new theory of "*Philosophy*," both in "*Nature*" and "*Divinity*"! The Old World being chained, did not admit of a general and thorough reform; hence *America* was the only place, both in the *Political* and *Natural World*, that opened a fair prospect for a beginning. And such as began to think, and to judge, and to act for themselves, and felt the spirit of "*independence* and *equality* of man, which is the *law of nature*," arose from their depressed state, and felt the spirit of enterprize.—They *flew to* the *wilderness* of *America*, pregnant with the *spirit* of freedom in *embryo*, in their emigration, which then laid the foundation, and still marks the outlines of our national character. Moral virtue came, by *revelation*, and is enjoyed by *inspiration* in the heart, called "*restraining grace*." Hence the necessity of a "*moral social compact*." *Abraham* and his *successors* formed the beginning of the true Church of God; through whose succession the promised *Messiah* came.—The *Jews* are a standing monument of the just dispensations of Divine Providence. *Justice*, when administered in the removal of societies corrupted through "*moral evil*," who are *incorrigible*, and unworthy of a political existence, proves a mercy to rising generations. And such revolutions will continue, until it appears whose right is to reign, and his kingdom come, and reign over all! The *sword* of the Lord is drawn out; and the *five* scourges of the Almighty are abroad in the earth; and O! that the people would "learn Righteousness!!!" [. . .]

By what *right* or authority may one person, or a body of men, raise a *persecution* against another? It is not authorised in the records of Christ, either by his "*commands*" or his "*example*." And of course, such a right or power was never *delegated* or sanctioned by him. Man could not bestow the right, because he does not possess the *authority* to do it; unless it be "*assumed*," which is an *unjust* TYRANNY.

Persecution, for differences of *opinion* and *modes*, &c. in religion, is an "ANTI-CHRISTIAN SPIRIT"; and is contrary to every "*rule of right*," and repugnant to every "*moral obligation*; and of course it is a violation of the LAW OF NATURE," as well as of the "MORAL LAW," and of the "RULE OF PRACTICE." Of course, NATURAL AND MORAL JUSTICE must *condemn* it.

Those people who *usurp* the *liberty* to attach the *absent* CHARACTER of others, in an *unjust* manner, to *weaken* their *influence*, by *destroying* their good *reputation*, and sinking them into CONTEMPT in public estimation; rejoicing at their *misfortune* and *calamity*, as if a very great victory was gained, do not know what *spirit* they are of! It would be well for such persons to study the "*law of nature*," with the "*Moral Law*," and reconsider them by comparing them with the "*Rule of Practice*," examining their own SPIRIT and conduct, and *then* see how they agree and comport together, according to LOVE and UNION, which is enjoined by the gospel of Jesus Christ. For if the PRACTICE flows from an unjust and an unhallowed spirit of *jealousy*, from ambition, pride, and self-will, the SOUL is surely destitute of that *heavenly principle*, that *noble mind*, which was in CHRIST; and which was designed to reign in the HEART and PRACTICE of His Followers;

to be made manifest in their spirit and tempers; and shine forth in their example continually. And hence they are to be called *"the light of the world,"* and as a *city* set on a hill which cannot be hid. . . .

Therefore "let all those who name the name of Christ, be careful to depart from *iniquity*," and never take the *devil's tools*, with which to do the *Almighty's work*. . . .

Consequently, that the cause of Christ be not hindered, but that his gospel take an universal spread, instead of being actuated by a short-sighted, mean, sinister, low, contentious party spirit, we should have a heart full of love to God and man, to expand the mind with that "Charity which never faileth, and thinketh no evil, but suffereth long and is kind, is gentle, and easy to be intreated" And look at the universal or most extensive GOOD; and encourage such *means* and institutions, as are most likely to accomplish the most noble ends and purposes to mankind. And hence, not like the *Jews*, who long looked with expectation for the Messiah, and when he came, rejected him. Or, as some others, who pray God to revive his work, and send forth more labourers into the harvest; then oppose both the work and the *means*, which the wisdom of God is pleased to make use of to accomplish it. — God doth work and accomplish great and important ends, by simple means, which are noble and worthy of himself, to exhibit his "finger, hand, or arm," of *Power* and *Wisdom* to mankind; whilst his mercy and goodness is magnified, and his Justice displayed to the most ordinary understanding. And thus, out of the mouth of BABES and sucklings, God will perfect praise! [. . .]

Therefore forbid not those whom God hath sent to preach the Gospel of HIS *dear* SON, lest you be found fighting against God, and it cause you tears of sorrow and repentance when it is too late. For the cause is the LORD's, and the Eternity of mankind is connected therewith, and hangs upon it. . . .

"Natural Evil" is the effect or consequence of *"Moral Evil."* And ignorance, superstition and tyranny, with impositions and wicked laws, have been, and still are the chains by which "social privileges" are curtailed. They are the means also, which have brought what is called "Natural Evil," as the necessary consequence of "Moral Evil," upon society, in the different ages and nations of the world, which hath been and still is such a *curse* to the world of mankind!

General *information*, and the spread of *"Moral Virtue"* are a necessary antidote to such obnoxious PRINCIPLES; that the *"moral faculty"* may be repaired, and *peace* and *righteousness* reign in every clime.

While inventions are increasing, and the arts and sciences are improving, it may not be amiss for all the well-wishers of Zion, to watch the openings of *Providence*, for the furtherance of truth, and the spread of knowledge valuable to society among mankind. And provided some suitable point should someday be taken on the *Isthmus*, which connects the NORTH and SOUTH of the "NEW WORLD," now probably held in reversion, as a mercy to rising generations, to be a *Theatre* for great things to be displayed, worthy of its AUTHOR, and there should be the proper arrangements made for the spread of the true knowledge through the whole world. How long a space could be required to circumnavigate, and circumfuse such knowledge of the *Causeless Causator*, as would inspire all nations with sensations of gratitude to the Redeemer of Mankind; whose commandment we have for our encouragement; "Go ye into all the world, and preach the Gospel, and lo I am with you!!"

READING AND DISCUSSION QUESTIONS

1. To what extent are Dow's religious views affected by his understanding of America's democratic culture?

2. Who do you suspect might have been the audience Dow had in mind when writing? What do you think he was hoping to accomplish?

▪ COMPARATIVE QUESTIONS ▪

1. How important was America's republican culture to the nation's economic, cultural, and religious experiences?

2. To what extent did Warren and Rush view women's rights and education through the same republican lens?

3. What do these sources tell you about the adaptability of the republican ideal? In what way was this ideal an intellectual resource for reformers?

4. How did slavery contradict or clarify America's republican ideals?

The Emergence of Democratic Ideals and a New National Identity

1763–1820

Upon his election as president in 1788, George Washington described his feelings as "not unlike those of a culprit who is going to the place of his execution." The period of revolution and republic-building that began with Washington's election was challenging not only for the new president, but for the newly independent nation as a whole. The American people, once freed from British rule, were challenged to create and enact a republican government and a national identity in a period when elites continued to liken ordinary folk to the "common herd." This traditional distrust of "the people" came up against the democratic ideals that energized non-elites, who increasingly regarded liberty as a birthright. Competing conceptions of national identity gave rise to tension, and yet an emergent idealism trumped the difficulties Washington anticipated, creating a political culture pregnant with the optimism of the age. The emerging democratic ideals shaped values, sparked reform efforts, and created an enduring republican culture out of a complex diversity of people.

P3-1 | Rallying Americans to the Cause of Freedom
JOHN DICKINSON, *The Liberty Song* (1768)

Many British colonists were reluctant revolutionaries. Good subjects of the king had to be persuaded to see what the Patriot minority saw: a threat to their liberties in the shape of king and Parliament. Though John Dickinson (1732–1808) refused to sign the Declaration of Independence, hoping for a nonviolent reconciliation, he was an early defender of American rights against Parliament's encroachments. His 1768 "The Liberty Song" became a popular cry for colonial unity, pulling fence sitters into the struggle for freedom and unwittingly crafting a national identity along democratic ideals.

COME join Hand in Hand, brave AMERICANS all,
And rouse your bold Hearts at fair LIBERTY'S Call;
No *tyrannous Acts* shall suppress your *just Claim*,
Or stain with *Dishonor* AMERICA'S name —
In FREEDOM we're BORN, and in FREEDOM we'll LIVE,
Our purses are ready,
Steady, Friends, Steady,
Not as SLAVES, but as FREEMEN our Money we'll give.

Our worthy *Forefathers* — let's give them a Cheer —
To *Climates unknown* did courageously steer;
Thro' *Oceans* to *Deserts* for *Freedom* they came,
And dying, bequeath'd us their *Freedom* and *Fame*. —
In FREEDOM we're BORN, etc.

Their generous Bosoms all Dangers despis'd
So *highly*, so *wisely*, their BIRTH-RIGHTS they priz'd,
We'll keep what they gave, we will piously keep,
Nor frustrate their Toils on the Land and the Deep.
In FREEDOM we're BORN, etc.

The TREE their own Hands had to LIBERTY rear'd,
They liv'd to behold growing strong and rever'd;
With Transport they cry'd, "Now our Wishes we gain,
For our Children shall gather the Fruits of our Pain."
In Freedom we're BORN, etc.

How sweet are the labors that Freemen endure,
That *they* shall enjoy all the Profit, secure —
No more such sweet Labors AMERICANS know
If Britons shall *reap* what Americans sow.

The Writings of John Dickinson, vol. I, Political Writings 1764–1774, ed. Paul Leicester Ford (Philadelphia: The Historical Society of Pennsylvania, 1895), 431–432.

Swarms of PLACEMEN and PENSIONERS soon will appear
Like Locusts deforming the Charms of the Year;
Suns vainly will rise, Showers vainly descend,
If *we* are to *drudge for* what *others* shall *spend*.
In FREEDOM we're BORN, etc.

Then join Hand in Hand brave AMERICANS all,
By *uniting* We stand, by *dividing* We fall;
IN SO RIGHTEOUS A CAUSE let us hope to succeed,
For Heaven approves of each generous Deed—
In FREEDOM we're BORN, etc.

All Ages shall speak with *Amaze* and *Applause,*
Of the *Courage* we'll show IN SUPPORT OF OUR LAWS;
To DIE we can *bear,*—but, to SERVE we *distain*—
For SHAME is to *Freemen* more dreadful than PAIN—
In FREEDOM we're BORN, etc.

This Bumper I crown for our SOVEREIGN's Health.
And this for BRITTANNIA's Glory and Wealth;
That Wealth and that Glory immortal may be,
If *She* is but *just*—and if *We* are but *Free*—
In FREEDOM we're BORN, etc.

READING AND DISCUSSION QUESTIONS

1. To what extent does Dickinson's song reveal competing American and British conceptions of national identity? How important were those differences to Dickinson's understanding of the causes of the political dispute with Great Britain?

2. How does Dickinson interpret colonial American history? Why do you think he mentions "Our worthy forefathers"? What associations do you think Dickinson was hoping his audience would make?

3. What does this source reveal about the emergence of democratic ideals during this period?

P3-2 | Defining the American Character

J. HECTOR ST. JOHN DE CRÈVECOEUR, *Letters from an American Farmer* (1782)

In 1782, the same year de Crèvecoeur (1735–1813) published his famous *Letters from an American Farmer*, the Continental Congress adopted the Great Seal for the United States, including the Latin motto *E pluribus unum*, "out of many, one." But "one" what? Congress of course intended it to mean one nation, comprising the thirteen newly independent states. For de Crèvecoeur, the French-born emigrant to New York who became an American citizen, the question was more philosophical. In one of his essays, excerpted below, he attempts an answer to his most famous question: "What then is the American, this new man?"

I wish I could be acquainted with the feelings and thoughts which must agitate the heart and present themselves to the mind of an enlightened Englishman, when he first lands on this continent . . . a modern society offers itself to his contemplation, different from what he had hitherto seen. It is not composed, as in Europe, of great lords who possess everything, and of a herd of people who have nothing. Here are no aristocratical families, no courts, no kings, no bishops, no ecclesiastical dominion, no invisible power giving to a few a very visible one, no great manufacturers employing thousands, no great refinements of luxury. The rich and the poor are not so far removed from each other as they are in Europe. Some few towns excepted, we are all tillers of the earth, from Nova Scotia to West Florida. We are a people of cultivators, scattered over an immense territory, communicating with each other by means of good roads and navigable rivers, united by the silken bands of mild government, all respecting the laws, without dreading their power, because they are equitable. We are all animated with the spirit of an industry which is unfettered and unrestrained, because each person works for himself. If he travels through our rural districts he views not the hostile castle, and the haughty mansion, contrasted with the clay-built hut and miserable cabin, where cattle and men help to keep each other warm, and dwell in meanness, smoke, and indigence. A pleasing uniformity of decent competence appears throughout our habitations. . . . We have no princes, for whom we toil, starve, and bleed: we are the most perfect society now existing in the world. Here man is free as he ought to be; nor is this pleasing equality so transitory as many others are. . . .

In this great American asylum, the poor of Europe have by some means met together, and in consequence of various causes; to what purpose should they ask one another what countrymen they are? Alas, two thirds of them had no country. Can a wretch who wanders about, who works and starves, whose life is a continual scene of sore affliction or pinching penury; can that man call England or any other kingdom his country? A country that had no bread for him, whose

Hector St. John Crèvecoeur, *Letters from an American Farmer* (New York: Fox, Duffield & Company, 1904), 48–50, 52–56.

fields procured him no harvest, who met with nothing but the frowns of the rich, the severity of the laws, with jails and punishments; who owned not a single foot of the extensive surface of this planet? No! urged by a variety of motives, here they came. Every thing has tended to regenerate them; new laws, a new mode of living, a new social system; here they are become men: in Europe they were as so many useless plants, wanting vegetative mould, and refreshing showers; they withered, and were mowed down by want, hunger, and war; but now by the power of transplantation, like all other plants they have taken root and flourished! Formerly they were not numbered in any civil lists of their country, except in those of the poor; here they rank as citizens. By what invisible power has this surprising metamorphosis been performed? By that of the laws and that of their industry. The laws, the indulgent laws, protect them as they arrive, stamping on them the symbol of adoption; they receive ample rewards for their labours; these accumulated rewards procure them lands; those lands confer on them the title of freemen, and to that title every benefit is affixed which men can possibly require. . . .

What attachment can a poor European emigrant have for a country where he had nothing? The knowledge of the language, the love a few kindred as poor as himself, were the only cords that tied him: his country is now that which gives him land, bread, protection, and consequence: *Ubi panis ibi patria*,[1] is the motto of all emigrants. What then is the American, this new man? He is either an European, or the descendant of an European, hence that strange mixture of blood, which you will find in no other country. I could point out to you a family whose grandfather was an Englishman, whose wife was Dutch, whose son married a French woman, and whose present four sons have now four wives of different nations. *He* is an American, who, leaving behind him all his ancient prejudices and manners, receives new ones from the new mode of life he has embraced, the new government he obeys, and the new rank he holds. He becomes an American by being received in the broad lap of our great *Alma Mater*. Here individuals of all nations are melted into a new race of men, whose labours and posterity will one day cause great changes in the world. Americans are the western pilgrims, who are carrying along with them that great mass of arts, sciences, vigour, and industry which began long since in the east; they will finish the great circle. The Americans were once scattered all over Europe; here they are incorporated into one of the finest systems of population which has ever appeared, and which will hereafter become distinct by the power of the different climates they inhabit. The American ought therefore to love this country much better than that wherein either he or his forefathers were born. Here the rewards of his industry follow with equal steps the progress of his labour; his labour is founded on the basis of nature, *self-interest*; can it want a stronger allurement? Wives and children, who before in vain demanded of him a morsel of bread, now, fat and frolicsome, gladly help their father to clear those fields whence exuberant crops are to

---

[1] "Where there is bread, there is my country."

arise to feed and to clothe them all; without any part being claimed, either by a despotic prince, a rich abbot, or a mighty lord. Here religion demands but little of him; a small voluntary salary to the minister and gratitude to God; can he refuse these? The American is a new man, who acts upon new principles; he must therefore entertain new ideas, and form new opinions. From involuntary idleness, service dependence, penury, and useless labour, he has passed to toils of a very different nature, reward by ample subsistence. — This is an American.

READING AND DISCUSSION QUESTIONS

1. De Crèvecoeur's essays were first published in London for a European audience. How did he explain to them what made Americans a distinctive people? Which themes did he emphasize?

2. How would you summarize de Crèvecoeur's understanding of American citizenship? He himself was born in France but "became an American." Assuming he meant more than completing a legal process of naturalization, what did he understand "becoming an American" to involve?

3. To what extent is de Crèvecoeur's construction of American identity relevant to contemporary Americans? Compare his views with your own.

P3-3 | Women's Right to Education in the New Republic
JUDITH SARGENT MURRAY, *On the Equality of the Sexes* (1790)

The Revolution's legacy on reformers was both immediate and enduring. The growing emphasis on democratic ideals helped to shape cultural values, as did Jefferson's claim of inalienable rights to "life, liberty, and the pursuit of happiness." Growing demands for a strong and democratic nation inspired reform efforts to eradicate slavery, promote religious revival and temperance campaigns, and expand women's rights. Judith Sargent Murray's essay, written in 1779 but published in 1790, decried gender inequalities and called for equal educational opportunities for women. This was a radical statement for the time and inspired later feminist efforts to advance women's rights.

Is it upon mature consideration we adopt the idea, that nature is thus partial in her distributions? Is it indeed a fact, that she hath yielded to one half of the human species so unquestionable a mental superiority? I know that to both sexes elevated understandings, and the reverse, are common. But, suffer me to ask, in what the minds of females are so notoriously deficient, or unequal. May not the intellectual powers be ranged under these four heads — imagination, reason, memory and judgment. The province of imagination hath long since been surrendered to us, and we have been crowned and undoubted sovereigns of the regions of fancy. Invention is perhaps the most arduous effort of the mind; this branch of imagination hath been particularly ceded to us, and we have been time out of mind invested with that creative faculty. Observe the variety of fashions (here I bar the contemptuous smile) which distinguish and adorn the female world: how continually are they changing, insomuch that they almost render the wise man's assertion problematical, and we are ready to say, *there is something new under the sun.* . . .

Another instance of our creative powers, is our talent for slander; how ingenious are we at inventive scandal? what a formidable story can we in a moment fabricate merely from the force of a prolifick imagination? how many reputations, in the fertile brain of a female, have been utterly despoiled? [. . .] Perhaps it will be asked if I furnish these facts as instances of excellency in our sex. Certainly not; but as proofs of a creative faculty, of a lively imagination. Assuredly great activity of mind is thereby discovered, and was this activity properly directed, what beneficial effects would follow. Is the needle and kitchen sufficient to employ the operations of a soul thus organized? I should conceive not. . . . Are we deficient in reason? we can only reason from what we know, and if an opportunity of acquiring knowledge hath been denied us, the inferiority of our sex cannot fairly be deduced from thence. Memory, I believe, will be allowed us in common, since everyone's experience must testify, that a loquacious old woman is as frequently met with, as a communicative man. . . .

"But our judgment is not so strong—we do not distinguish so well."—Yet it may be questioned, from what doth this superiority, in this determining faculty of the soul, proceed. May we not trace its source in the difference of education, and continued advantages? Will it be said that the judgment of a male of two years old, is more sage than that of a female's of the same age? I believe the reverse is generally observed to be true. But from that period what partiality! how is the one exalted, and the other depressed, by the contrary modes of education which are adopted! the one is taught to aspire, and the other is early confined and limited. As their years increase, the sister must be wholly domesticated, while the brother is led by the hand through all the flowery paths of science. Grant that their minds are by nature equal, yet who shall wonder at the *apparent* superiority, if indeed custom becomes *second nature.* . . . At length arrived at womanhood, the uncultivated fair one feels a void, which the employments allotted her are by no means capable of filling. What can she do? to books she may not apply; or if she doth, *to those only of the novel kind*, lest she merit the appellation of a *learned lady*; and what ideas have been affixed to this term, the observation of many can testify. Fashion, scandal, and sometimes what is still more reprehensible, are then called in to her relief; and who can say to what lengths the liberties she takes may proceed. Meantimes she herself is most unhappy; she feels the want of a cultivated mind. . . . Now, was she permitted the same instructors as her brother, (with an eye however to their particular departments) for the employment of a rational mind an ample field would be opened. . . . A mind, thus filled, would have little room for the trifles with which our sex are, with too much justice, accused of amusing themselves, and they would thus be rendered fit companions for those, who should one day wear them as their crown. . . . Females would become discreet, their judgments would be invigorated, and their partners for life being circumspectly chosen, an unhappy Hymen would then be as rare, as is now the reverse.

Will it be urged that those acquirements would supersede our domestick duties. I answer that every requisite in female economy is easily attained; and, with truth I can add, that when once attained, they require no further *mental attention*. Nay, while we are pursuing the needle, or the superintendency of the family, I repeat, that our minds are at full liberty for reflection; that imagination may exert itself in full vigor; and that if a just foundation is early laid, our ideas will then be worthy of rational beings. . . . Should it still be vociferated, "Your domestick employments are sufficient"—I would calmly ask, is it reasonable, that a candidate for immortality, for the joys of heaven, an intelligent being, who is to spend an eternity in contemplating the works of the Deity, should at present be so degraded, as to be allowed no other ideas, than those which are suggested by the mechanism of a pudding, or the sewing the seams of a garment?...

Yes, ye lordly, ye haughty sex, our souls are by nature *equal* to yours; the same breath of God animates, enlivens, and invigorates us; and that we are not fallen lower than yourselves, let those witness who have greatly towered above the various discouragements by which they have been so heavily oppressed; and though I am unacquainted with the list of celebrated characters on either side, yet from the observations I have made in the contracted circle in which I have moved, I dare confidently believe, that from the commencement of time to the present day, there hath been as many females, as males, who, by the *mere force of natural powers*, have merited the crown of applause; who, *thus unassisted*, have seized the wreath of fame. . . .

The exquisite delicacy of the female mind proclaimeth the exactness of its texture, while its nice sense of honour announceth its innate, its native grandeur. And indeed, in one respect, the preeminence seems to be tacitly allowed us; for after an education which limits and confines, and employments and recreations which naturally tend to enervate the body, and debilitate the mind; after we have from early youth been adorned with ribbons, and other gewgaws, dressed out like the ancient victims previous to a sacrifice, being taught by the care of our parents in collecting the most showy materials that the ornamenting our exteriour ought to be the principal object of our attention; after, I say, fifteen years thus spent, we are introduced into the world, amid the united adulation of every beholder. . . . It is expected that with the other sex we should commence immediate war, and that we should triumph over the machinations of the most artful. We must be constantly upon our guard; prudence and discretion must be our characteristiks; and we must rise superiour to, and obtain a complete victory over those who have been long adding to the native strength of their minds, by an unremitted study of men and books, and who have, moreover, conceived from the loose characters which they have seen portrayed in the extensive variety of their reading, a most contemptible opinion of the sex. . . . If we are allowed an equality of acquirements, let serious studies equally employ our minds, and we will bid our souls arise to equal strengths. We will meet upon even ground, the despot man; we will rush with alacrity to the combat, and, crowned by success, we shall then answer the exalted expectations, which are formed. Though sensibility, soft compassion, and gentle commiseration, are inmates in the female bosom. . . . If we meet an equal, a sensible friend, we will reward him with the hand of amity, and through life we will be assiduous to promote his happiness; but from every deep laid scheme, for our ruin, retiring into ourselves, amid the flowery paths of science, we will indulge in all the refined and sentimental pleasures of contemplation: And should it still be urged, that the studies thus insisted upon would interfere with our more peculiar department, I must further reply, that *early hours*, and close application, will do wonders; and to her who is from the first dawn of reason taught to fill up time rationally, both the requisites will be easy. I grant that niggard [stingy or selfish] fortune is too generally unfriendly to the mind; and that much of that valuable treasure, time, is necessarily expended upon the wants of the body; but it should be remembered; that in embarrassed circumstances our companions have as little leisure for literary improvements, as is afforded to us; for most certainly their provident care is at least as requisite as our exertions. . . . In high life, or, in other words, where the parties are in possession of affluence, the objection respecting time is wholly obviated, and of course falls to the ground. . . . But in one respect, O ye arbiters of our fate! we confess that the superiority is indubitably yours; you are by nature formed for our protectors; we pretend not to vie with you in bodily strength; upon this point we will never contend for victory. Shield us then, we beseech you, from external evils, and in return we will transact *your* domestick affairs. Yes, *your*, for are you not equally interested in those matters with ourselves? Is not the elegancy of neatness as agreeable to your sight as to ours; is not the well favoured viand equally delightful to your taste; and doth not your sense of hearing suffer as much, from the discordant sounds prevalent in an ill regulated family, produced by the voices of children and many *et ceteras*?

CONSTANTIA.

READING AND DISCUSSION QUESTIONS

1. How important were the democratic ideals of the period to shaping Murray's argument about the inequality of the sexes, which she experienced? What does her argument suggest about her vision for the new nation?

2. Who do you think Murray's audience is for this essay? What effect do you think she expected to have on the cultural values of her day?

3. Assess the historical significance of Murray's essay as an artifact of the late-eighteenth-century debate over democratic ideals and national identity.

P3-4 | A Warning for the Young Republic
George Washington's Farewell Address (1796)

In everyone's estimation, Washington was the new nation's indispensable man. His two terms as president established the working structure of the national government and created a national identity around republican ideals. Washington's neutral course in foreign affairs aimed to ensure America's separate destiny from the war-wracked fate of Europe. By embracing Hamilton's economic policies, Washington supported a national bank and established public credit, thereby creating the political institutions affirming federal power. As his term closed, he cautioned his fellow Americans in a farewell address published in 1796.

Friends and Fellow Citizens:

In looking forward to the moment which is intended to terminate the career of my public life, my feelings do not permit me to suspend the deep acknowledgment of that debt of gratitude which I owe to my beloved country for the many honors it has conferred upon me; still more for the steadfast confidence with which it has supported me; and for the opportunities I have thence enjoyed of manifesting my inviolable attachment, by services faithful and persevering, though in usefulness unequal to my zeal. If benefits have resulted to our country from these services, let it always be remembered to your praise, and as an instructive example in our annals, that under circumstances in which the passions, agitated in every direction, were liable to mislead, amidst appearances sometimes dubious, vicissitudes of fortune often discouraging, in situations in which not unfrequently want of success has countenanced the spirit of criticism, the constancy of your support was the essential prop of the efforts, and a guarantee of the plans by which they were effected. . . .

Here, perhaps, I ought to stop. But a solicitude for your welfare, which cannot end but with my life, and the apprehension of danger, natural to that solicitude, urge me, on an occasion like the present, to offer to your solemn contemplation, and to recommend to your frequent review, some sentiments which are the result of much reflection, of no inconsiderable observation, and which appear to me all-important to the permanency of your felicity as a people. . . .

Interwoven as is the love of liberty with every ligament of your hearts, no recommendation of mine is necessary to fortify or confirm the attachment.

The unity of government which constitutes you one people is also now dear to you. It is justly so, for it is a main pillar in the edifice of your real independence, the support of your tranquility at home, your peace abroad; of your safety; of your prosperity; of that very liberty which you so highly prize. But as it is easy to foresee that, from different causes and from different quarters, much pains will be taken, many artifices employed to weaken in your minds the conviction of this truth; as this is the point in your political fortress against which the batteries of internal and external enemies will be most constantly and actively (though often covertly and insidiously) directed, it is of infinite moment that you should properly estimate the immense value of your national union to your collective and individual happiness; that you should cherish a cordial, habitual, and immovable attachment to it; accustoming yourselves to think and speak of it as of the palladium of your political safety and prosperity; watching for its preservation with jealous anxiety; discountenancing whatever may suggest even a suspicion that it can in any event be abandoned; and indignantly frowning upon the first dawning of every attempt to alienate any portion of our country from the rest, or to enfeeble the sacred ties which now link together the various parts. . . .

The name of American, which belongs to you in your national capacity, must always exalt the just pride of patriotism more than any appellation derived from local discriminations. With slight shades of difference, you have the same religion, manners, habits, and political principles. You have in a common cause fought and triumphed together; the independence and liberty you possess are the work of joint counsels, and joint efforts of common dangers, sufferings, and successes.

But these considerations, however powerfully they address themselves to your sensibility, are greatly outweighed by those which apply more immediately to your interest. Here every portion of our country finds the most commanding motives for carefully guarding and preserving the Union of the whole. . . .

These considerations speak a persuasive language to every reflecting and virtuous mind, and exhibit the continuance of the Union as a primary object of patriotic desire. Is there a doubt whether a common government can embrace so large a sphere? Let experience solve it. To listen to mere speculation in such a case were criminal. We are authorized to hope that a proper organization of the whole with the auxiliary agency of governments for the respective subdivisions, will afford a happy issue to the experiment. It is well worth a fair and full experiment. With such powerful and obvious motives to union, affecting all parts of our country, while experience shall not have demonstrated its impracticability, there will always be reason to distrust the patriotism of those who in any quarter may endeavor to weaken its bands.

In contemplating the causes which may disturb our Union, it occurs as matter of serious concern that any ground should have been furnished for characterizing parties by geographical discriminations, *Northern* and *Southern*, *Atlantic* and *Western*; whence designing men may endeavor to excite a belief that there is a real difference of local interests and views. One of the expedients of party to acquire influence within particular districts is to misrepresent the opinions and aims of other districts. You cannot shield yourselves too much against the jealousies and heartburnings which spring from these misrepresentations; they tend to render alien to each other those who ought to be bound together by fraternal affection. . . .

To the efficacy and permanency of your Union, a government for the whole is indispensable. . . . Sensible of this momentous truth, you have improved upon your first essay, by the adoption of a constitution of government better calculated than your former for an intimate union, and for the efficacious management of your common concerns. This government, the offspring of our own choice,

uninfluenced and unawed, adopted upon full investigation and mature deliberation, completely free in its principles, in the distribution of its powers, uniting
security with energy, and containing within itself a provision for its own amendment, has a just claim to your confidence and your support. Respect for its
authority, compliance with its laws, acquiescence in its measures, are duties
enjoined by the fundamental maxims of true liberty. The basis of our political
systems is the right of the people to make and to alter their constitutions of government. But the Constitution which at any time exists, till changed by an explicit
and authentic act of the whole people, is sacredly obligatory upon all. The very
idea of the power and the right of the people to establish government presupposes the duty of every individual to obey the established government.

All obstructions to the execution of the laws, all combinations and associations, under whatever plausible character, with the real design to direct, control,
counteract, or awe the regular deliberation and action of the constituted authorities, are destructive of this fundamental principle, and of fatal tendency. They
serve to organize faction, to give it an artificial and extraordinary force; to put, in
the place of the delegated will of the nation the will of a party, often a small but
artful and enterprising minority of the community. . . .

However combinations or associations of the above description may now
and then answer popular ends, they are likely, in the course of time and things,
to become potent engines, by which cunning, ambitious, and unprincipled men
will be enabled to subvert the power of the people and to usurp for themselves
the reins of government, destroying afterwards the very engines which have
lifted them to unjust dominion.

Towards the preservation of your government, and the permanency of your
present happy state, it is requisite, not only that you steadily discountenance
irregular oppositions to its acknowledged authority, but also that you resist with
care the spirit of innovation upon its principles, however specious the pretexts. . . .

I have already intimated to you the danger of parties in the State, with particular reference to the founding of them on geographical discriminations. Let
me now take a more comprehensive view, and warn you in the most solemn
manner against the baneful effects of the spirit of party generally.

This spirit, unfortunately, is inseparable from our nature, having its root in
the strongest passions of the human mind. It exists under different shapes in all
governments, more or less stifled, controlled, or repressed; but, in those of the
popular form, it is seen in its greatest rankness, and is truly their worst enemy.

The alternate domination of one faction over another, sharpened by the
spirit of revenge, natural to party dissension, which in different ages and countries has perpetrated the most horrid enormities, is itself a frightful despotism.
But this leads at length to a more formal and permanent despotism. The disorders and miseries which result gradually incline the minds of men to seek security and repose in the absolute power of an individual; and sooner or later the
chief of some prevailing faction, more able or more fortunate than his competitors, turns this disposition to the purposes of his own elevation, on the ruins of
public liberty. . . .

It is important, likewise, that the habits of thinking in a free country should inspire caution in those entrusted with its administration, to confine themselves within their respective constitutional spheres, avoiding in the exercise of the powers of one department to encroach upon another. . . . The necessity of reciprocal checks in the exercise of political power, by dividing and distributing it into different depositaries, and constituting each the guardian of the public weal against invasions by the others, has been evinced by experiments ancient and modern; some of them in our country and under our own eyes. To preserve them must be as necessary as to institute them. If, in the opinion of the people, the distribution or modification of the constitutional powers be in any particular wrong, let it be corrected by an amendment in the way which the Constitution designates. But let there be no change by usurpation; for though this, in one instance, may be the instrument of good, it is the customary weapon by which free governments are destroyed. The precedent must always greatly overbalance in permanent evil any partial or transient benefit, which the use can at any time yield.

Of all the dispositions and habits which lead to political prosperity, religion and morality are indispensable supports. In vain would that man claim the tribute of patriotism, who should labor to subvert these great pillars of human happiness, these firmest props of the duties of men and citizens. The mere politician, equally with the pious man, ought to respect and to cherish them. A volume could not trace all their connections with private and public felicity. Let it simply be asked: Where is the security for property, for reputation, for life, if the sense of religious obligation desert the oaths which are the instruments of investigation in courts of justice? And let us with caution indulge the supposition that morality can be maintained without religion. Whatever may be conceded to the influence of refined education on minds of peculiar structure, reason and experience both forbid us to expect that national morality can prevail in exclusion of religious principle. . . .

Observe good faith and justice towards all nations; cultivate peace and harmony with all. Religion and morality enjoin this conduct; and can it be, that good policy does not equally enjoin it?

In the execution of such a plan, nothing is more essential than that permanent, inveterate antipathies against particular nations, and passionate attachments for others, should be excluded; and that, in place of them, just and amicable feelings towards all should be cultivated. The nation which indulges towards another a habitual hatred or a habitual fondness is in some degree a slave. It is a slave to its animosity or to its affection, either of which is sufficient to lead it astray from its duty and its interest. . . .

The great rule of conduct for us in regard to foreign nations is in extending our commercial relations, to have with them as little *political* connection as possible. So far as we have already formed engagements, let them be fulfilled with perfect good faith. Here let us stop.

Europe has a set of primary interests which to us have none; or a very remote relation. Hence she must be engaged in frequent controversies, the causes of which are essentially foreign to our concerns. Hence, therefore, it must be unwise in us to implicate ourselves by artificial ties in the ordinary vicissitudes of her politics, or the ordinary combinations and collisions of her friendships or enmities.

Our detached and distant situation invites and enables us to pursue a different course. . . . It is our true policy to steer clear of permanent alliances with any portion of the foreign world. . . .

In offering to you, my countrymen, these counsels of an old and affectionate friend, I . . . may even flatter myself that they may be productive of some partial benefit, some occasional good; that they may now and then recur to moderate the fury of party spirit, to warn against the mischiefs of foreign intrigue, to guard against the impostures of pretended patriotism. . . .

Relying on its kindness in this as in other things, and actuated by that fervent love towards it, which is so natural to a man who views in it the native soil of himself and his progenitors for several generations, I anticipate with pleasing expectation that retreat in which I promise myself to realize, without alloy, the sweet enjoyment of partaking, in the midst of my fellow-citizens, the benign influence of good laws under a free government, the ever-favorite object of my heart, and the happy reward, as I trust, of our mutual cares, labors, and dangers.

United States
19th September, 1796
Geo. Washington

READING AND DISCUSSION QUESTIONS

1. Which challenges does Washington think are most threatening to the new nation? What clues in the text led to your conclusions?

2. How would you characterize Washington's point of view? Was he generally optimistic or pessimistic in his assessment of America's future?

3. Washington witnessed the development of new political institutions, like political parties, which he described as dangerous. Why does he see them as incompatible with America's national identity? What in Washington's critique is still valuable today?

P3-5 | A Woman's Perspective on Backcountry America

MARGARET VAN HORN DWIGHT, *A Journey to Ohio* (1810)

The democratic America that de Crèvecoeur celebrated (Document P3-2) was the same one Margaret Van Horn Dwight barely endured while traveling from Connecticut through southern Pennsylvania to join her family in Warren, Ohio. Margaret was twenty when she left her

Margaret Van Horn Dwight, *A Journey to Ohio in 1810*, ed. Max Farrand, Intr. Jay Gitlin (Lincoln and London: University of Nebraska Press, 1991), 16–20, 22–24, 28–29, 48–51.

well-heeled Connecticut family (both her uncle and a cousin were presidents of Yale), and her observations of the young republic, with its multiethnic and economically diverse population, betray her gendered and class-bound conception of American society, one in competition with other perspectives she encountered.

Sunday Eve—Sundown—

I can wait no longer to write you, for I have a great deal to say—I should not have thought it possible to pass a Sabbath in our country among such a dissolute vicious set of wretches as we are now among—I believe at least 50 dutchmen have been here to day to smoke, drink, swear, pitch cents, almost dance, laugh & talk dutch & stare at us. They come in, in droves young & old—black & white—women & children. It is dreadful to see so many people that you cannot speak to or understand—They are all high dutch, but I hope not a true specimen of the Pennsylvanians generally—Just as we set down to tea, in came a dozen or two of women, each with a child in her arms, & stood round the room—I did not know but they had come in a body to claim me as one of their kin, for they all resemble me—but as they said nothing to me, I concluded they came to see us Yankees, as they would a learned pig—The women dress in striped linsey wool-sey petticoats & short gowns not 6 inches in length—they look very strangely—The men dress much better—they put on their best cloaths on sunday, which I suppose is their only holiday, & "keep it up" as they call it—A stage came on from Bethlehem & stopt here, with 2 girls & a well dress'd fellow who sat between them an arm round each—They were probably going to the next town to a dance or a frolic of some kind—for the driver, who was very familiar with them, said he felt just right for a frolic—I suspect more liquor has been sold to day than all the week besides—The children have been calling us Yankees (which is the only english word they can speak) all day long—Whether it was meant as a term of derision or not, I neither know nor care—of this I am sure, they cannot feel more contempt for me than I do for them;—tho' I most sincerely pity their ignorance & folly—There seems to be no hope of their improvement as they will not attend to any means—After saying so much about the people, I will describe our yesterday's ride—but first I will describe our last nights lodging—Susan & me ask'd to go to bed—& Mrs W spoke to Mr Riker the landlord—(for no woman was visible)—So he took up a candle to light us & we ask'd Mrs W to go up with us, for we did not dare go alone—when we got into a room he went to the bed & open'd it for us, while we were almost dying with laughter, & then stood waiting with the candle for us to get into bed—but Mrs W—as soon as she could speak, told him she would wait & bring down the candle & he then left us. . . . I did not undress at all, for I expected dutchmen in every moment & you may suppose slept very comfortably in that expectation——Mr & Mrs W, & another woman slept in the same room . . . in the middle of the night, I was awaken'd by the entrance of three dutchmen, who were in search of a bed—I was almost frightened to death—but Mr W at length heard & stopt them before they had quite reach'd our bed. . . . I think wild Indians will be less terrible to me, than these creatures—Nothing vexes me more than to see them set & look at us & talk in dutch and laugh. . . .

From Easton, we came to Bethlehem, which is 12 miles distant from it— Mr W. went a mile out of his way, that we might see the town—It contains almost entirely dutch people—The houses there are nearly all stone—but like Easton it contains some pretty brick houses—It has not half as many stores as Easton——The meeting house is a curious building-it looks like a castle—I suppose it is stone,—the outside is plaister'd—We left our waggon to view the town—we did not know whether the building was a church or the moravian school, so we enquir'd of 2 or 3 men who only answer'd in dutch—Mr & Mrs W were purchasing bread, & Susan & I walk'd on to enquire—we next saw a little boy on horseback, & he could only say "me cannot english" but he I believe, spoke to another, for a very pretty boy came near us & bow'd & expecting us to speak, which we soon did; & he pointed out the school & explained the different buildings to us as well as he was able; but we found it difficult to understand him, for he could but just "english"—We felt very much oblig'd to him, though we neglected to tell him so—He is the only polite dutchman small or great, we have yet seen; & I am unwilling to suppose him a *Dutchman*. . . .

Wednesday October 31st Highdlegurg—Penn—

We pass'd through Reading yesterday which is one of the largest & prettiest towns I have seen. . . . Almost every one could talk english—but I believe the greatest part of them were dutch people—As soon as we left Reading, we cross'd the Schuylkill—It was not deeper than the Lehi, & we rode thro' it in our wagon. . . . We put up for the night at Leonard Shaver's tavern—He is a dutchman, but has one of the most agreeable women for his wife I have seen in this State—I was extremely tir'd when we stopt, & went immediately to bed after tea—& for the first time for a long while, undress'd me & had a comfortable nights rest—We are oblig'd to sleep every & any way—at most of the inns now——My companions were all disturb'd by the waggoners who put up here & were all night in the room below us, eating, drinking, talking, laughing & swearing—Poor Mr W—was so disturb'd that he is not well this morning, & what is more unpleasant to us, is not good natur'd. . . . If I were going to be married I would give my intended, a gentle emetic, or some such thing to see how he would bear being sick a little—for I could not coax a husband as I would a child, only because he was a little sick & a great deal cross—I trust I shall never have the trial—I am sure I should never bear it with temper & patience. . . .

Harrisburg—P—Thursday—Eve—November—1st 1810—

We put up for the Sabbath at a tavern where none but the servants deign to look at us—When I am with such people, my proud spirit rises & I feel superior to them all—I believe no regard is paid to the sabbath any where in this State—It is only made a holiday of—So much swearing as I have heard amongst the Pensylvanians both men & women I have never heard before during my whole life—I feel afraid I shall become so accustom'd to hearing it, as to feel no uneasiness at it. Harrisburgh is a most dissipated place I am sure—& the small towns seem to partake of the vice & dissipation of the great ones—I believe Mrs Jackson has cast her eyes on Susan or me for a daughter in law—for my part, though I feel very well disposed toward the young man, I had not thought of making a bargain with him, but I have jolted off most of my high notions, & perhaps I may be willing to descend from a judge to a blacksmith—I shall not absolutely determine with respect to him till I get to Warren & have time to look about me & compare him with the judges Dobson & Stephenson—It is clever to have two or three strings to ones bow—But in spite of my prejudices, they are very clever. . . .

Saturday Eve—2 Miles from Laurel Hill—Penn—

We came but 9 or 10 miles to day, & are now near the 6th Mountain—in a tavern fill'd with half drunken noisy waggoners—One of them lies singing directly before the fire; proposing just now to call for a song from the young ladies——I can neither think nor write he makes so much noise with his love songs; I am every moment expecting something dreadful & dare not lay down my pen lest they should think me listening to them—They are the very worst wretches that ever liv'd, I do believe,—I am out of all patience with them—The whole world nor any thing in it, would tempt me to stay in this State three months—I dislike everything belonging to it—I am not so foolish as to suppose there are no better people in it than those we have seen; but let them be ever so good, I never desire to see any of them——We overtook an old waggoner whose waggon had got set in the mud, & I never heard a creature swear so—& whipt his horses till I thought they would die—I could not but wonder at the patience and forbearance of the Almighty, whose awful name was so blasphem'd—We also overtook a young Doctor-who is going with his father to Mad river in the state of Ohio——He has been studying physic in New Jersey,—but appears to be an uneducated man from the language he makes use of——I believe both himself & his father are very clever—I heard them reproving a swearer—He dresses smart, & was so polite as to assist us in getting over the mud—Susan & I walk'd on before the waggon as usual, & he overtook us and invited us into the house & call'd for some brandy sling—we did not drink, which he appear'd not to like very well, & has scarcely spoken to us since. . . .

Sunday Eve—Nov-19th—Foot of Laurel Hill—Penn—

I wish my dear Elizabeth, you could be here for half an hour, & hear the strangest man talk, that you or I ever saw in this world—He is either mad or a fool—I don't know which, but he looking over me & telling me I can make a writer—He is the most rating, ranting fellow—I wish you could hear him——I begin to think him mad—His name is Smith—He & his wife are journeying either to New Orleans or the Ohio——I never was more diverted than to hear him (he is certainly crazy—repeating a prayer & a sermon & forty other things in a breath) talk about the Dutchmen in Pennsylvania—He & his wife came amongst them one evening & stopt at several houses to get entertainment, but was sent on by each one to the tavern — He began by stating his religious tenets, & at length after every body & thing was created, he says the under Gods (of whom he supposes there were a great number) took some of the skum & stir'd it up, & those fellows came out — or rather Hell boil'd over & they were form'd of the skum —— I believe he has been studying all his life for hard words & pompous speeches, & he rattled them off at a strange rate — His language is very ungrammatical — but the Jacksons are all in raptures with him — They cannot understand his language (nor indeed could any one else) & therefore concluded he must be very learned — Their observations are almost as diverting as his conversation — I could make them believe in ten minutes, that I was a girl of great larnin — if I were to say over Kermogenious — Heterogenious & a few such words without any connection — no matter if I do but bring them in some how.

READING AND DISCUSSION QUESTIONS

1. What inferences can you draw from Dwight's diary that help you understand the cultural values she embraced?

2. How might the historian use Dwight's diary to illustrate divergent conceptions of America's national identity as revealed, for example, by her interactions with the Pennsylvania Dutch?

3. To what extent does Dwight's diary provide evidence for a social history of the early American republic? What themes does her travel account touch? What are some of the limitations of her work that the historian must consider before using it?

P3-6 | Democratic Enthusiasm Shapes Religion
JAMES FLINT, *Letters from America* (1820)

James Flint was born in Scotland and traveled to the United States, arriving in New York in May 1818 and embarking on a two-year tour of America. Like other Europeans who made similar trips, Flint published his observations to acquaint his European readers with American society. What piqued his interest most were not the urban centers on the East Coast, but the trans-Allegheny west, where Flint saw America's democratic values on display. Flint's outsider's observation of a Methodist camp meeting, or religious revival, along Indiana's Ohio River, reveals that those egalitarian values touched not merely the young republic's political institutions but also Americans' experience of religion.

I lately returned from visiting the camp meeting of Wesleyan methodists, where I remained about twenty four hours. On approaching the scene of action . . . I

James Flint, *Letters from America: Containing Observations on the Climate and Agriculture of the Western States, the Manners of the People, the Prospects of Emigrants, &c., &c.* (Cleveland: The Arthur H. Clark Company, 1904), 257–264.

was struck with surprise, my feet were for a moment involuntarily arrested, while I gazed on a preacher vociferating from a high rostrum, raised between two trees, and an agitated crowd immediately before him, that were making a loud noise, and the most singular gesticulations which can be imagined. On advancing a few paces, I discovered that the turmoil was chiefly confined within a small inclosure of about thirty feet square, in front of the orator, and that the ground occupied by the congregation was laid with felled trees for seats. A rail fence divided it into two parts, one for females, and the other for males. . . . The inclosure already mentioned was for the reception of those who undergo religious awakenings, and was filled by both sexes, who were exercising violently. Shouting, screaming, clapping of hands, leaping, jerking, falling, and swooning. The preacher could not be distinctly heard, great as his exertions were; certainly had it not been for his elevated position, his voice would have been entirely blended with the clamours below. I took my stand close by the fence, for the purpose of noting down exclamations uttered by the exercised, but found myself unable to pick up any thing like a distinct paragraph. . . . I had to content myself with such vociferations as *glory, glory, power, Jesus Christ,*—with "groans and woes unutterable."

After dinner another orator took his place. The inclosure was again filled with the penitent, or with others wishing to become so, and a vast congregation arranged themselves on their seats in the rear. A most pathetic prayer was poured forth, and a profound silence reigned over all the camp, except the fenced inclosure, from whence a low hollow murmuring sound issued. Now and then, Amen was articulated in a pitiful and indistinct tone of voice. You have seen a menagerie of wild animals on a journey, and have perhaps heard the king of beasts, and other powerful quadrupeds, excited to grumbling by the jolting of the waggon. Probably you will call this a rude simile; but it is the most accurate that I can think of. Sermon commenced. The preacher announced his determination of discontinuing his labours in this part of the world, and leaving his dear brethren for ever. He addressed the old men present, telling them that they and he must soon be removed from this mortal state of existence, and that the melancholy reflection arose in his mind,—"*What will become of the church when we are dead and gone?*"—A loud response of groaning and howling was sounded by the aged in the inclosure, and throughout the congregation. He next noticed that he saw a multitude of young men before him, and, addressing himself to them, said, "I trust in *God*, that many of you will be *now* converted, and will become the *preachers* and the pious Christians of after days."—The clamour now thickened, for young and old shouted together. Turning his eyes toward the female side of the fence, he continued, "And you, my dear sisters."—What he had farther to say to the future "nursing mothers of the church," could not be heard, for the burst of acclamation, on their part, completely prevented his voice from being heard, on which account he withdrew; and a tune was struck up and sung with grand enthusiasm. The worship now proceeded with a new energy; the prompter in the pulpit had succeeded in giving it an impulse, and the music was sufficient to preserve emotion. The inclosure was so much crowded that its inmates had not the liberty of lateral motion, but were literally hobbling *en masse*. My attention was particularly directed to a girl of about twelve years of age, who while standing could not be seen over her taller neighbours; but at every leap she was conspicuous above them. The velocity of every plunge made her long loose hair flirt up as if a handkerchief were held by one of its corners and twitched violently. Another female, who had arrived at womanhood, was so much overcome that she was held up to the breeze by two persons who went to her relief. I never before saw such exhaustion. The vertebral column was completely pliant, her body, her neck, and her extended arms, bent in every direction successively. It would be impossible to describe the diversity of cases; they were not now confined within the fence, but were numerous among the people without. Only a small proportion of them could fall within the observation of any one bystander. The scene was to me equally novel and curious.

About dusk I retired several hundred yards into the woods to enjoy the distant effect of the meeting. Female voices were mournfully predominant, and my imagination figured to me a multitude of mothers, widows, and sisters, giving the first vent to their grief, in bewailing the loss of a male population, by war, shipwreck, or some other great catastrophe.

It had been thought proper to place sentinels without the camp. Females were not allowed to pass out into the woods after dark. Spirituous liquors were not permitted to be sold in the neighbourhood.

Large fires of timber were kindled, which cast a new lustre on every object. The white tents gleamed in the glare. Over them the dusky woods formed a most romantic gloom, only the tall trunks of the front rank were distinctly visible, and these seemed so many members of a lofty colonnade. The illuminated camp lay on a declivity, and exposed a scene that suggested to my mind the moonlight gambols of beings known to us only through the fictions of credulous ages. The greatest turmoil prevailed within the fence, where the inmates were leaping and hobbling together with upward looks and extended arms. Around this busy mass, the crowd formed a thicker ring than the famous Macedonian phalanx; and among them, a mixture of the exercised were interspersed. Most faces were turned inward to gaze on the grand exhibition, the rear ranks on tip-toe, to see over those in front of them, and not a few mounted on the log-seats, to have a more commanding view of the show. People were constantly passing out and into the ring in brisk motion, so that the white drapery of females, and the darker apparel of the men were alternately vanishing and reappearing in the most elegant confusion. The sublimity of the music served to give an enchanting effect to the whole. My mind involuntarily reverted to the leading feature of the tale of Alloway Kirk:

Warlocks and witches in a dance;

Where Tam O'Shanter

  . . . Stood like ane bewitch'd,
And thought his very een enrich'd.

At nine [the next morning] the meeting adjourned to breakfast. A multitude of small fires being previously struck up, an extensive cooking process commenced, and the smell of bacon tainted the air. I took this opportunity of reconnoitring the evacuated field. The little inclosure, so often mentioned, is by the religious called *Altar*, and some scoffers are wicked enough to call it *Pen*, from its similarity to the structures in which hogs are confined. Its area was covered over with straw, in some parts more wetted than the litter of a stable. If it could be ascertained that all this moisture was from the tears of the penitent, the fact would be a surprising one. Waving all inquiry into this phenomenon, however, the incident now recorded may be held forth as a very suitable counterpart to a wonderful story recorded by the Methodistic oracle Lorenzo Dow, of a heavy shower drenching a neighbourhood, while a small speck including a camp meeting was passed over and left entirely dry. In Lorenzo's case, the rain fell all round the camp, but in that noticed by me, the moisture was in the very centre.

You can form no adequate idea of a camp meeting from any description which can be given of it. Any one who would have a complete view of enthusiasm can only obtain it by visiting such a meeting and seeing it himself. I should be sorry to abuse the Methodist sect by the illiberal application of such terms as fanaticism, superstition, or illusion. I have known many of them who are valuable members of society, and several who have rendered important services to their country, but have not seen any one prostrated, or even visibly affected, at the camp meeting or elsewhere, whom I knew to be men of strong minds or of much intelligence. Females seem to be more susceptible of the impressions than men are. A quality perhaps that is to be imputed to the greater sensibility of their feelings.

READING AND DISCUSSION QUESTIONS

1. From Flint's description of the Methodist camp meeting, what can you infer about his own religious beliefs and practices? What point of view concerning revivals does he express?

2. What argument is Flint making about the intersection between Americans' democratic values and religion as a cultural movement?

3. What American cultural values do you think Flint most wants his British readers to understand? Is he sympathetic to what he believes to be America's national identity?

■ COMPARATIVE QUESTIONS ■

1. How did Federalists such as Washington, Alexander Hamilton (Document 7-1), and Fisher Ames (Document 7-3) conceive of America's national identity in ways different from Republicans such as Thomas Jefferson (Document 7-2)?

2. Do these sources present an optimistic or a pessimistic view of early American national identity? What factors account for the different attitudes toward America's new prospects?

3. What legacy of the Revolution's democratic values appears in the language and ideas of the sources included here?

4. Imagine how Flint and Lorenzo Dow (Document 8-6) would have assessed the relationship between America's democratic culture and the practice of Christianity in the early republic. Do they have similar or contrasting views?

5. Compare Murray's argument (Document P3-3) to those of Abigail Adams (Document 6-2), Mercy Otis Warren (Document 8-3), and Benjamin Rush (Document 8-4), all of whom advocated for expanded rights for women. What do these sources, considered together, suggest about the role of women and the question of gender roles in the formation of the new American identity?

9

Transforming the Economy
1800–1860

The British writer Harriet Martineau visited Chicago during a "rage for speculation" as frenzied investors bought title to unimproved land along a proposed canal route. "Storekeepers hailed them from their doors," she said, "with offers of farms, and all manner of land-lots, advising them to speculate before the price of land rose higher." More sober than most Chicagoans, Martineau predicted "a bursting of the bubble" and feared the worst: "Many a high-spirited, but inexperienced, young man; many a simple settler, will be ruined for the advantage of knaves." She wasn't wrong. The 1837 depression hit just as her book was published.

The "delusion" she described was the effect of the Market Revolution, an economic expansion accelerating in the years following the War of 1812. Brought on by improvements in transportation, such as canals and roads, and manufacturing, more Americans entered the market for goods, purchasing items they desired rather than making those goods they needed. The market empowered the individual as an agent of his or her own destiny, but it also strained social relations, creating, for instance, the need for a temperance movement. Religious revivals were both a product of and a reaction to the Market Revolution, emphasizing the necessity of the individual to choose to do God's work.

9-1 | A Factory Girl Remembers Mill Work

LUCY LARCOM, *Among Lowell Mill-Girls: A Reminiscence* (1881)

One effect of the Market Revolution was to shift work from the home to the factory. In Lowell, Massachusetts, young Lucy Larcom (1824–1893) experienced this shift at age eleven, when family circumstances pushed her to paid employment in the textile mill. Like many of her contemporaries, Larcom was forced to sacrifice her childhood to provide much-needed income to her family. Larcom was unusual in that she developed a literary talent, publishing poetry and songs and a memoir of her childhood, an excerpt from which appears below.

During my father's life, a few years before my birth, his thoughts had been turned towards the new manufacturing town growing up on the banks of the Merrimack. He had once taken a journey there, with the possibility in his mind of making the place his home, his limited income furnishing no adequate promise of a maintenance for his large family of daughters. From the beginning, Lowell had a high reputation for good order, morality, piety, and all that was dear to the old-fashioned New Englander's heart.

After his death, my mother's thoughts naturally followed the direction his had taken; and seeing no other opening for herself, she sold her small estate, and moved to Lowell, with the intention of taking a corporation-house for mill-girl boarders. Some of the family objected, for the Old World traditions about factory life were anything but attractive; and they were current in New England until the experiment at Lowell had shown that independent and intelligent workers invariably give their own character to their occupation. My mother had visited Lowell, and she was willing and glad, knowing all about the place, to make it our home. . . .

Our house was quickly filled with a large feminine family. As a child, the gulf between little girlhood and young womanhood had always looked to me very wide. I supposed we should get across it by some sudden jump, by and by. But among these new companions of all ages, from fifteen to thirty years, we slipped into womanhood without knowing when or how.

Most of my mother's boarders were from New Hampshire and Vermont, and there was a fresh, breezy sociability about them which made them seem almost like a different race of beings from any we children had hitherto known.

We helped a little about the housework, before and after school, making beds, trimming lamps, and washing dishes. The heaviest work was done by a strong Irish girl, my mother always attending to the cooking herself. She was, however, a better caterer than the circumstances required or permitted. She liked to make nice things for the table, and, having been accustomed to an abundant supply, could never learn to economize. At a dollar and a quarter a week for board (the price allowed for mill-girls by the corporations), great care in expenditure was necessary. It was not in my mother's nature closely to calculate costs,

Lucy Larcom, *A New England Girlhood* (Boston: Houghton Mifflin, 1889), 145–146, 152–156.

and in this way there came to be a continually increasing leak in the family purse. The older members of the family did everything they could, but it was not enough. I heard it said one day, in a distressed tone, "The children will have to leave school and go into the mill."

There were many pros and cons between my mother and sisters before this was positively decided. The mill-agent did not want to take us two little girls, but consented on condition we should be sure to attend school the full number of months prescribed each year. I, the younger one, was then between eleven and twelve years old.

I listened to all that was said about it, very much fearing that I should not be permitted to do the coveted work. For the feeling had already frequently come to me, that I was the one too many in the overcrowded family nest. Once, before we left our old home, I had heard a neighbor condoling with my mother because there were so many of us, and her emphatic reply had been a great relief to my mind: —

"There isn't one more than I want. I could not spare a single one of my children."

But her difficulties were increasing, and I thought it would be a pleasure to feel that I was not a trouble or burden or expense to anybody. So I went to my first day's work in the mill with a light heart. The novelty of it made it seem easy, and it really was not hard, just to change the bobbins on the spinning-frames every three quarters of an hour or so, with half a dozen other little girls who were doing the same thing. When I came back at night, the family began to pity me for my long, tiresome day's work, but I laughed and said, —

"Why, it is nothing but fun. It is just like play."

And for a little while it was only a new amusement; I liked it better than going to school and "making believe" I was learning when I was not. And there was a great deal of play mixed with it. We were not occupied more than half the time. The intervals were spent frolicking around among the spinning-frames, teasing and talking to the older girls, or entertaining ourselves with games and stories in a corner, or exploring, with the overseer's permission, the mysteries of the carding-room, the dressing-room, and the weaving-room.

I never cared much for machinery. The buzzing and hissing and whizzing of pulleys and rollers and spindles and flyers around me often grew tiresome. I could not see into their complications, or feel interested in them. But in a room below us we were sometimes allowed to peer in through a sort of blind door at the great waterwheel that carried the works of the whole mill. It was so huge that we could only watch a few of its spokes at a time, and part of its dripping rim, moving with a slow, measured strength through the darkness that shut it in. It impressed me with something of the awe which comes to us in thinking of the great Power which keeps the mechanism of the universe in motion. . . .

There were compensations for being shut in to daily toil so early. The mill itself had its lessons for us. But it was not, and could not be, the right sort of life for a child, and we were happy in the knowledge that, at the longest, our employment was only to be temporary.

When I took my next three months at the grammar school, everything there was changed, and I too was changed. The teachers were kind, and thorough in their instruction; and my mind seemed to have been ploughed up during that year of work, so that knowledge took root in it easily. It was a great delight to me to study, and at the end of the three months the master told me that I was prepared for the high school.

But alas! I could not go. The little money I could earn—one dollar a week, besides the price of my board—was needed in the family, and I must return to the mill. It was a severe disappointment to me, though I did not say so at home.

READING AND DISCUSSION QUESTIONS

1. How does Larcom's memoir help us to understand some of the effects of the Market Revolution on the lives of ordinary Americans?

2. What does Larcom see as the advantages and disadvantages of work in the factory?

3. How might Larcom's initial impression of the mill have been different if she had started as a machine worker?

9-2 | Making the Case for Internal Improvements

HON. P. B. PORTER, *Speech on Internal Improvements* (1810)

Internal improvements (roads, canals, bridges) became a topic of debate in the early national period. Advocates linked economic development to public support of these projects. Opponents questioned the propriety of using public funds for improvements, which they saw as primarily local or regional. Congressman Peter B. Porter (1773–1844), from western New York State, championed construction of the Erie Canal, serving on the commission tasked with surveying a canal route linking the Hudson River to the Great Lakes. In this speech, delivered to the U.S. House of Representatives in 1810, Porter makes the case for internal improvements.

And permit me, in the first place, to say, sir, that some great system of internal navigation, such as is contemplated in the bill introduced into the Senate, is not only an object of the first consequence to the future prosperity of this country, considered as a measure of political economy, but as a measure of state policy, it is indispensable to the preservation of the integrity of this government.

The United States have for twenty years past been favoured in their external commerce, in a manner unequalled perhaps in the history of the world. Our citizens have not only grown rich, but they have gone almost mad in pursuit of this commerce. Such have been its temptations, as to engage in it almost the whole of

---

David Hosack, *Memoir of De Witt Clinton* (New York: J. Seymour, 1829), 360–362, 365–366.

the floating capital of the country, and a great part of its enterprise; and every other occupation has been considered as secondary and subordinate. This extraordinary success of commerce has been owing partly to our local situation, partly to the native enterprise of our citizens, but primarily to the unparalleled succession of events in Europe. The course of these events, before so propitious to our interests, has of late very materially changed, and with it has changed the tide of our commercial prosperity. I am far, however, from believing that this sudden reverse may not eventually prove fortunate for the true interests of the United States. The embarrassments which the belligerents have thrown in the way of our external commerce, have turned the attention of the people of this country to their own internal resources. And in viewing these resources, we perceive with pride, that there is no country on earth, which in the fertility of its soil, the extent and variety of its climate and productions, affords the means of national wealth and greatness in the measure they are enjoyed by the people of the United States. If these means are properly fostered and encouraged by a liberal and enlightened policy, we shall soon be able not only to defend our independence at home (which, however, I confidently trust, we have now both the ability and the disposition to do, notwithstanding the fears that are attempted to be excited on this subject), but we shall be able to protect our foreign commerce against the united power of the world. One great object of the system I am about to propose, is to unlock these internal resources, to enable the citizen of one part of the United States to exchange his products for those of another, and to open a great internal commerce, which is acknowledged by all who profess any skill in the science of political economy, to be much more profitable and advantageous than the most favoured external commerce which we could enjoy. The system, however, has another object in view not less important.

The people of the United States are divided by a geographical line into two great and distinct sections—the people who live along the Atlantic on the east side of the Alleghany mountains, and who compose the three great classes of merchants, manufacturers, and agriculturists; and those who occupy the west side of these mountains, who are exclusively agriculturists. This diversity and supposed contrariety of interest and pursuit between the people of these two great divisions of country, and the difference of character to which these occupations give rise, it has been confidently asserted, and is still believed by many, will lead to the separation of the United States at no very distant day. In my humble opinion, sir, this very diversity of interest will, if skilfully managed, be the means of producing a closer and more intimate union of the states. It will be obviously for the interests of the interior states, to exchange the great surplus products of their lands, and the raw materials of manufactures, for the merchandize and manufactured articles of the eastern states; and on the other hand, the interests of the merchants and manufacturers of the Atlantic will be equally promoted by this internal commerce; and it is by promoting this commerce, by encouraging and facilitating this intercourse—it is by producing a mutual dependence of interests between these two great sections, and by these means only, that the United States can ever be kept together.

The great evil, and it is a serious one indeed, sir, under which the inhabitants of the western country labour, arises from the want of a market. There is no place where the great staple articles for the use of civilized life can be produced in greater abundance or with greater ease; and yet as respects most of the luxuries and many of the conveniences of life, the people are poor. They have no vent for their produce at home; because, being all agriculturists, they produce alike the same articles with the same facility; and such is the present difficulty and expense of transporting their produce to an Atlantic port, that little benefits are realized from that quarter. The single circumstance, of the want of a market, is already beginning to produce the most disastrous effects, not only on the industry, but upon the morals of the inhabitants. Such is the fertility of their lands, that one half of their time spent in labour, is sufficient to produce every article which their farms are capable of yielding, in sufficient quantities for their own consumption, and there is nothing to incite them to produce more. They are, therefore, naturally led to spend the other part of their time in idleness and dissipation. Their increase in numbers, and the ease with which children are brought up and fed, far from encouraging them to become manufacturers for themselves, puts at a great distance the time, when, quitting the freedom and independence of masters of the soil, they will submit to the labour and confinement of manufacturers. This, sir, is the true situation of the western agriculturist. It becomes then an object of national importance, far outweighing almost every other that can occupy the attention of this house, to inquire whether the evils incident to this state of things, may not be removed by opening a great navigable canal from the Atlantic to the western states; and thus promoting the natural connexion and intercourse between the farmer and the merchant, so highly conducive to the interests of both. . . .

How many hundred millions of dollars such an operation would add to the solid wealth of the western country, I will not venture to conjecture. But, sir, I may well say, that there is no work in the power of man, which would give such life, such vigour, such enterprise, and such riches to the citizens of that country, as the execution of this canal. The inhabitants near the lakes would have a direct communication to and from New-York, by means of the canal, and the effect of it would be to double the price of their produce, and to add three or four hundred per cent, to the value of their lands. The people of the Ohio and the Mississippi would descend with their produce to New-Orleans, and to any port on the Atlantic, from whence they might return with the articles received in exchange by way of the Hudson and the lakes, to their own homes. The idea of benefitting the people of the Ohio and Mississippi to any great extent by this northern navigation, may perhaps, at first, appear visionary; but I can state it as a fact, that even at this time, under all the disadvantages of that route, goods may be transported from the city of New-York, by the way of the Hudson and the lakes, to any part of the Ohio, and to all those parts of the Mississippi above its confluence with the Ohio, at as cheap a rate as they can be transported from any port on the Atlantic, by any other route. The effect of opening this navigation, would then be to reduce the price of transportation to those parts of the country, at least fifty, and probably seventy-five per cent. Another important advantage, independent of the general commerce of the lakes, would be felt in the reduction of at least fifty per cent, in the price of salt. The salt springs in the state of New-York, are within a few miles of the proposed line of circumnavigation, and are connected with it by a navigable river. This article may be manufactured at those springs in sufficient quantities for the whole of the population of the United States, and it is now sold there for twenty-five and thirty cents a bushel; but such is the present expense of transportation, that it sells in the Pittsburg market for two dollars a bushel. If the effect of opening a canal navigation were only to reduce the price at Pittsburg to one dollar, it would make a saving on the quantity now sent to that market, of one hundred thousand dollars a year. But, sir, aside from all the pecuniary benefits I have mentioned, the great political effect of this work would be, by opening extensive communications, encouraging intercourse, and promoting connexions between the various ports of the Atlantic and western states, to subdue local jealousies, and to bind the union together by the indissoluble ties of interest and friendship.

READING AND DISCUSSION QUESTIONS

1. How does Porter overcome skeptics' reluctance to support internal improvements?

2. Is it significant that Porter gave this speech in 1810 while representing western New York? What might have been motivating him to push for the bill authorizing internal improvements?

3. How does Porter "nationalize" the argument in support of canal building? In other words, how does he try to convince members of the national legislature that a canal in upstate New York is in the national interest?

9-3 | A View of the Factory System

Repeating Fire-Arms. A Day at the Armory of Colt's Patent Fire-Arms Manufacturing Company (1857)

The extent of Americans' fascination with the technological innovations that fueled the manufacturing revolution can be glimpsed in this enthusiastic report of a visit to Samuel Colt's armory. In this article published in the *United States Magazine* in 1857, the author describes in detail the armory's design and Colt's innovative process of manufacturing revolvers using interchangeable parts.

The new armory . . . is located about one hundred yards south of the mouth of Little River, immediately inside of the dyke, and fronting on the west side of the Connecticut River. It was finished and operations commenced in it in the Fall of

The United States Magazine, vol. 4 (New York: J. M. Emerson & Co., 1857), 233–235.

1855. . . . . It is a massive structure of brown sand-stone, of the variety usually designated "Portland freestone." The front parallel is 500 feet long, 60 wide, and three stories high; at the center, for about sixty feet of the front, there is a projection of eighteen feet wide, surmounted by a pediment. This forms ample space for hall and stairways to give access to the several stories. On top is the cupalo, with a canopy of blue, emblazoned with gilt stars, the whole surmounted by a large gilt ball, on which stands a colt, rampant. The rear parallel is 500 feet long by 40 wide; the center building is 150 feet long by 60 wide, and three stories high. At each end, between the extremities of the parallels, are two small two-story dwellings, both of which are occupied by the watchmen; from these erections to the main buildings are heavy walls, with massive gates; thus the space inclosed by the stone walls is just 500 by 250 feet square. Nearly adjoining on the north, and connected to the main building by a light latticework bridge, is a brick building, three stories high, 60 by 75 feet square, and surmounted by a turret and clock. This is occupied by the officers, and as a wareroom.

The motive power is located about in the center of the main building. It consists of a beam engine—cylinder, 36 inches in diameter, 7 feet stroke, fly-wheel 30 feet in diameter, weighing 7 tuns. This engine, which is rated at 250 horse-power, is supplied with the well-known "Sickel's Cut-off," which the superintendent and engineer speak of as the most useful and important addition to the steam-engine since the days of Watt. The steam is furnished from two cylindrical boilers, each 22 feet long and 7 feet in diameter. The power is carried to the attic by a belt working on the fly-wheel; this belt is 118 feet long by 22 inches wide, and travels at the rate of 2,500 feet per minute.

Fully appreciating the great interest manifested by our readers in descriptions of this kind, we will now proceed to conduct them through the interior of this immense industrial pile, and on the way we will endeavor to explain, as understandingly as possible, the various processes of the manufacture, from the raw metal and wood, to the complete and effective arms familiarly known as Colt's Revolvers. . . .

At this point it is well to inform the reader that almost the entire manual labor of the establishment is performed by contract. The contractors are furnished room, power, tools, material, heat, light, in fact all but muscle and brains; themselves, however, and their subordinates are all subject to the immediate government, as prescribed by the code of rules, laid down by the Company. The contractors number some scores—some particular manipulators requiring only their individual exertions, while others employ from one to forty assistants. Many of them are men of more than ordinary ability, and some have rendered themselves pecuniarily comfortable by their exertions.

We now pass into the forge shop, an apartment 40 by 200 feet square, comprising the whole of one arm of the parallel. Along each side range stacks of double-covered forges—the blasts for which, entering and discharging through flues in the walls, carry off the smoke and gases. Here, for the first time in our life, we were in a blacksmith shop in full operation, yet free from smoke and cinders, and with a pure atmosphere. Several kinds of hammers are used—those most in use, however, being "drops" of a novel construction and peculiar to the establishment; they are raised on the endless screw principle, and tripped by a trigger at the will of the operator. All the parts of the fire-arm composed of iron or steel are forged in swedges, in which, although they may have ever so many preliminary operations, the shape is finally completed at a single blow. That some idea may be formed of the amount of work on a single rifle or pistol, we have determined to state the number of separate operations of each portion, and in each department. We adopt the navy or belt pistol, the weight of which is thirty-eight ounces, as the example. In forging, the number of separate heats are enumerated: lockframe, 2; barrel, 3; lever, 2; rammer, 1; hammer, 2; hand, 2; trigger, 2; bolt, 2; main spring, 2; key, 2; nipples, two each, 12; thus we find that no less than *thirty-two* separate and distinct operations, some of which contain in themselves several sub-divisions, are required in the forging for a single pistol. . . .

We now follow them to the armory proper, which, in the first place, is the second story of the front parallel. This is probably not only the most spacious, but the best arranged and fitted workshop extant. We fully understand this to be a broad and sweeping assertion, yet we have an abundance of competent authority to back the opinion. On first entering this immense room, from the office, the *tout ensemble* is really grand and imposing, and the beholder is readily impressed with an exalted opinion of the vast mechanical resources of the corporation. The room is 500 feet long by 60 feet wide, and 16 feet high. It is lighted, on all sides, by 112 windows that reach nearly from floor to ceiling; it is warmed by steam from the boilers—the pipes being under the benches, running completely around the sides and ends; there are also perfect arrangements for ventilation, and sufficient gasburners to illuminate the whole for night-work. Running through the center is a row of cast-iron columns, sixty in number, to which is attached the shafting—which here is arranged as a continuous pulley—for driving the machines, as close together as possible, only allowing sufficient space to get around and work them. The whole of this immense floor space is covered with machine tools. Each portion of the fire-arm has its particular section. As we enter the door the first group of machines appears to be exclusively employed in chambering cylinders; the next is turning and shaping them; here another is boring barrels; another group is milling the lockframes; still another is drilling them; beyond are a score of machines boring and screw-cutting the nipples, and next them a number of others are making screws; here are the rifling machines, and there the machines for boring rifle-barrels; now we come to the jigging machines that mortice out the lock-frames; and thus it goes on all over this great hive of physical and mental exertion.

This machinery, though at first sight like that employed in the manufacture of cotton and silk, apparently intricate, is in reality mostly composed of simple and well-known elements, ingeniously and specially applied to effect the mechanical actions required; no better evidence of its perfection can be adduced than the fact that the various parts of the arms produced are so perfectly identical that, in assembling a pistol, the several pieces, taken promiscuously from the heaps, unite almost without manual labor. The limited space of this paper prevents a detailed description of the various machines, nearly 400 of which are in use in the several departments; however, it would be well for some other establishments that we have in our time visited if a portion of the mechanical advantages which they insure were more universally adopted for all general purposes.

READING AND DISCUSSION QUESTIONS

1. Why does the author provide so many specific details about the size of the armory, the speed of the flywheel, and the number of operations involved in manufacturing a revolver?

2. What "lesson" does the author believe other manufacturers might learn from Colt's armory? To what extent does the author suggest Colt's armory is a model for America's continued manufacturing revolution?

3. How was the Colt factory similar to or different from a textile mill? How were the manufacturing processes similar or different? How might the experiences of the workers have been different in the Colt factory? What accounts for these differences?

9-4 | Contrasting Images of Urban Life
Frontispiece from *Sunshine and Shadow in New York* (1868)

The economic transformation of the early nineteenth century left a complex legacy as is suggested by this image, which appeared on the title page of Matthew Hale Smith's midcentury book, *Sunshine and Shadow in New York*. Smith's book profiled the city's famous residents and described its distinct cultures. He emphasized the contrasts New York presented: Broadway and Five Points, Wall Street and the Bowery, swindlers and the clergy. It was a city of extremes, shaped by the rapidly expanding market, immigration, and urbanization.

Matthew Hale Smith, *Sunshine and Shadow in New York* (Hartford, CT: J. B. Burr and Company, 1868).

READING AND DISCUSSION QUESTIONS

1. Describe the contrasts Smith sees in New York City. What details are highlighted in these contrasting images of the city?

2. To what extent do you think Smith is suggesting these contrasts are a product of the economic transformations of the first half of the nineteenth century?

3. Why might these contrasts be more evident in urban areas? In other words, how did the economic transformations impact cities?

9-5 | Taking the Temperance Pledge

Preface to *The Temperance Manual of the American Temperance Society for the Young Men of the United States* (1836)

The "shadows" of Matthew Hale Smith's New York were home to all sorts of disorders that reformers organized to address. Leading the list was alcohol abuse, an increasing problem that middle-class shopkeepers and business owners targeted in the hopes of sobering their workers. The American Temperance Society, founded in 1826, mobilized to encourage young men especially to take their pledge to abstain from alcohol and quickly developed several thousand local chapters, mostly in the northern states. The *Temperance Manual*, excerpted here, itemizes the Society's arguments against intoxicating liquors.

TO EACH YOUNG MAN
IN THE UNITED STATES

RESPECTED FRIEND:

We are engaged in a great and good work; and to accomplish it we need your aid. It is the work of extending the principle of abstinence from the use of intoxicating liquor, as a beverage, throughout our country, and throughout the world. By means of the press, and of living agents, a strong impression has already been made, and a great change effected with regard to this subject. More than two millions of persons in the United States have ceased to use ardent spirit, and several hundred thousand of them have ceased to use any intoxicating drink. More than three thousand distilleries have been stopped; more than eight thousand merchants have ceased to traffic in ardent spirit, and more than ten thousand drunkards have ceased to use intoxicating drink. More than 100,000 persons, as appears from numerous facts, have been saved from becoming drunkards, who, had it not been for the change of sentiment and practice in the community, had, before now, been involved in all the horrors of that loathsome and fatal vice. The quantity of intoxicating liquor used, over extensive districts of country, has been greatly diminished; and pauperism, crime, sickness, insanity,

---

The Temperance Manual of the American Temperance Society for the Young Men of the United States (Boston: Seth Bliss, 1836), 3, 7–12.

and premature deaths have been diminished in proportion. Sobriety, industry, and economy have been greatly revived; and it is estimated by those who are acquainted with the subject, and have the best means of judging, that, in the state of New York alone, there have been saved in a year by the change with regard to the use of strong drink more than $3,000,000. The chief means of effecting this change, has been the formation, throughout the state, of Temperance Societies. Should such Societies be formed throughout our country, all persons join them, and the use of intoxicating liquor be done away, it would save annually more than $100,000,000; and more than 30,000 valuable lives. It would remove one of the greatest obstructions to all means for human improvement; one of the principal dangers to our social, civil, and religious institutions; and one of the chief causes, throughout our land, of human wretchedness and wo[e].

And what we ask of you, and of each young man in the United States, is, that you will not only abstain from the use of intoxicating liquor, but, for the sake of doing good to others, will unite with a Temperance Society; and for this purpose, that you will give your name, and the influence which is attached to it, to a pledge like the one which is annexed to this paper. And we do this for the following reasons, viz.

1. Intoxicating liquor, as a beverage is not *needful* or *useful*. . . .

2. Alcohol, which is the intoxicating principle in liquor, is a *poison*. When taken unmixed, in no very large quantity, it destroys life; and when taken even moderately, it induces disease, and forms an artificial, an unnatural, and a very dangerous appetite. . . .

3. The use of intoxicating liquor impairs, and in many cases destroys[,] reason. Of 781 maniacs in different insane hospitals, 392, according to the testimony of their own friends, were rendered maniacs by strong drink; and the physicians gave it as their opinion, that this was also the case with many others. . . .

4. It weakens the power of motives to do right. It is thus shown decisively to be in its tendency *immoral*; and no man can, consistently with his duty, either use it, or be accessory to the use of it by others. . . .

5. It strengthens the power of motives to do wrong. Temptation to crime, which men will withstand when they have not been drinking, will lead them when they have, in numerous cases, to go and commit it. Of 39 prisoners in the jail of Litchfield county, Connecticut, 35 were intemperate men. In the jail of Ogdensburg, New York, 7-8ths of the criminals were addicted to strong drink; of 647 in the state prison at Auburn, N.Y. 467 were intemperate. . . .

And did it destroy merely property, health, reason, and life, we could bear it. Though it should destroy more than $100,000,000 a year and bring down more than 30,000 persons annually to an untimely grave; though it should continue to make wives widows, and children orphans, and scatter on every side firebrands, arrows and death; yet, if it illuminated and purified the soul, and prepared that undying part of man, for glory and honor, immortality and eternal life, we could endure it; and for the continuance of its inexpressible and overwhelming evils, there might be a reason. But,

6. *It destroys the soul.* It makes sinners more sinful, and tends to prevent them from experiencing God's illuminating and purifying power. It tends directly and strongly to make men feel, as Jesus Christ hates—rich spiritually, increased in goods, and in need of nothing; and for ever to prevent them from feeling as men must feel in order to be interested in the blessings of his salvation. The Holy Spirit will not visit, much less will he dwell with him who is under the polluting, debasing effects of intoxicating drink. . . .

And yet these evils, great as they are, rising up to heaven, and overwhelming, as, if continued, they certainly will be, may, nevertheless, with certainty, all be done away. Let each individual cease to use intoxicating drink, and intemperance and all its abominations will vanish; and temperance, with all its blessings to body and soul, will universally prevail. . . .

We, therefore, cannot but confidently anticipate that you will cheerfully, for the sake of doing good, add to the pledge which is annexed, the influence of your name. But some may say, Why sign a pledge? Why is it not as well, and even better, for each one to abstain, take care of himself, and let all others do the same?—What is the benefit of visible, organized union? [. . .]

What was the benefit of that combination? That visible agreement? That universal pledge? *Strength, action,* SUCCESS. . . .

But says another, I should be ashamed if I could not abstain from intoxicating liquor without binding myself, and signing a paper. And suppose that one had said, when the declaration of independence was handed to him to sign, I should be ashamed if I could not be a patriot without binding myself, and signing a pledge. The object of signing that paper was not to make men patriots; but it was to lead all patriots to unite and free their country. The great object of temperance societies is not to lead their members, by signing a paper, to abstain from the use of liquor, and make them temperate; but it is to unite, in a visible, organized union, all that do abstain, and are temperate; in order to show, by example, the most powerful of teachers, that men of all ages and conditions, and in all kinds of business, are, in all respects, better without it. And when this is shown, as by visible, united example, it may be, no one, enlightened on this subject, can avoid the conviction, *that it is morally wrong to use it, or to furnish it for the use of others,* because of the evils which are inseparately connected with the use of it. . . .

But why, it is asked, should women belong to temperance societies? Because under the light of the gospel, which raises women in excellence of character and ability to do good, to an equality with men, every association, composed of both, will more than double its influence over the public mind, especially over the minds of youth and children. And the grand object of efforts for the promotion of temperance, is the salvation of the young. And to accomplish it, we need, and must have, the influence of mothers as well as fathers; sisters, as well as brothers.

There is another reason why all women should unite with temperance societies. More than a hundred thousand of the lovely daughters of the last generation were doomed to the tremendous curse of having drunken husbands, and rearing their little ones under the blasting, withering influence of drunken fathers. But there is no need of it. Let the fathers and mothers, the brothers and sisters of this generation, *all* cease to use intoxicating drink, and unite their influence in temperance societies, and the daughters of the next generation, and of all future generations, practising on the same plan, shall be for ever free. . . .

We, therefore, renewedly, and earnestly request you, and all the youth of the United States, to sign the annexed pledge, and let your names be enrolled as members of the temperance society.

And we earnestly entreat all, by the diffusion of information, the exertion of kind moral influence, and by consistent and united example, to do all in their power to cause the use of intoxicating liquor, as a beverage, universally to cease. And could we exhibit to the world the noble and sublime spectacle, of fifteen millions of people rising in their strength, and voluntarily renouncing the tyranny of pernicious custom, and resolving henceforward not to be in bondage, even to *themselves*, but to be *doubly* free, we should be indeed the people which the Lord hath blessed. And it would do more than all which has ever yet been done, to render our free institutions *permanent*; and by the manifestation of their blessings, to spread their causes and their attendants, knowledge, virtue, and blessedness, throughout the world.

PLEDGE.

We, whose names are hereunto annexed, believing that the use of intoxicating liquor, as a beverage, is not only needless, but hurtful to the social, civil, and religious interests of men; that it tends to form intemperate appetites and habits, and that while it is continued, the evils of intemperance can never be done away;—do therefore agree, that we will not use it, or traffic in it; that we will not provide it as an article of entertainment, or for persons in our employment; and that, in all suitable ways, we will discountenance the use of it throughout the community.

READING AND DISCUSSION QUESTIONS

1. How would you characterize the reasons why temperance advocates thought alcohol posed dangers to the individual and to society?

2. Why do you think the temperance movement gained steam in the 1820s and 1830s?

3. While the *Temperance Manual* was aimed specifically at young men in the United States, to whom do you think the temperance reform movement appealed? Why?

9-6 | Finney Discussing the Revival of Religion

CHARLES GRANDISON FINNEY, *Lectures on Revivals of Religion* (1835)

Charles Grandison Finney (1792–1875) was the most popular revivalist of the antebellum era. He led a series of revivals in upstate New York in the 1820s and 1830s, the period of rapid economic development spurred by the building of the Erie Canal. Departing from strict Calvinism, which had emphasized man's depravity and predestination, Finney highlighted the individual's effort in accepting God's gift of salvation. In his *Lectures on Revivals of Religion*, excerpted below, Finney challenges the orthodox view of revivals as miracles brought on by God.

Religion is the work of man. It is something for man to do. It consists in obeying God. It is man's duty. It is true, God induces him to do it. He influences him by his Spirit, because of his great wickedness and reluctance to obey. If it were not necessary for God to influence men—if men were disposed to obey God, there would be no occasion to pray, "O Lord, revive thy work." The ground of necessity for such a prayer is, that men are wholly indisposed to obey; and unless God interpose the influence of his Spirit, not a man on earth will ever obey the commands of God.

A "Revival of Religion" presupposes a declension. Almost all the religion in the world has been produced by revivals. God has found it necessary to take advantage of the excitability there is in mankind, to produce powerful excitements among them, before he can lead them to obey. Men are so sluggish, there are so many things to lead their minds off from religion, and to oppose the influence of the gospel, that it is necessary to raise an excitement among them, till the tide rises so high as to sweep away the opposing obstacles. They must be so excited that they will break over these counteracting influences, before they will obey God. . . .

There is so little *principle* in the church, so little firmness and stability of purpose, that unless they are greatly excited, they will not obey God. They have so little knowledge, and their principles are so weak, that unless they are excited, they will go back from the path of duty, and do nothing to promote the glory of God. The state of the world is still such, and probably will be till the millenium is fully come, that religion must be mainly promoted by these excitements. How long and how often has the experiment been tried, to bring the church to act steadily for God, without these periodical excitements! Many good men have supposed, and still suppose, that the best way to promote religion, is to go along *uniformly*, and gather in the ungodly gradually, and without excitement. But however such reasoning may appear in the abstract, *facts* demonstrate its futility. If the church were far enough advanced in knowledge, and had stability of

Charles G. Finney, *Lectures on Revivals of Religion* (New York: Leavitt, Lord & Co., 1835), 9–10, 13, 18–19, 181, 183.

principle enough to *keep awake*, such a course would do; but the church is so little enlightened, and there are so many counteracting causes, that the church will not go steadily to work without a special excitement. . . .

I wish this idea to be impressed on all your minds, for there has long been an idea prevalent that promoting religion has something very peculiar in it, not to be judged of by the ordinary rules of cause and effect; in short, that there is no connection of the means with the result, and no tendency in the means to produce the effect. No doctrine is more dangerous than this to the prosperity of the church, and nothing more absurd.

Suppose a man were to go and preach this doctrine among farmers, about their sowing grain. Let him tell them that God is a sovereign, and will give them a crop only when it pleases him, and that for them to plow and plant and labor as if they expected to raise a crop is very wrong, and taking the work out of the hands of God, that it interferes with his sovereignty, and is going on in their own strength; and that there is no connection between the means and the result on which they can depend. And now, suppose the farmers should believe such doctrine. Why, they would starve the world to death.

Just such results will follow from the church's being pursuaded that promoting religion is somehow so mysteriously a subject of Divine sovereignty, that there is no natural connection between the means and the end. What *are* the results? Why, generation after generation have gone down to hell. No doubt more than five thousand millions have gone down to hell, while the church has been dreaming, and waiting for God to save them without the use of means. It has been the devil's most successful means of destroying souls. The connection is as clear in religion as it is when the farmer sows his grain. . . .

Many people have supposed God's sovereignty to be something very different from what it is. They have supposed it to be such an arbitrary disposal of events, and particularly of the gift of his Spirit, as precluded a rational employment of means for promoting a revival of religion. But there is no evidence from the Bible, that God exercises any such sovereignty as that. There are no facts to prove it. But every thing goes to show, that God has connected means with the end through all the departments of his government—in nature and in grace. There is no *natural* event in which his own agency is not concerned. He has not built the creation like a vast machine, that will go on alone without his further care. He has not retired from the universe, to let it work for itself. This is mere atheism. He exercises a universal superintendence and control. And yet every event in nature has been brought about by means. He neither administers providence nor grace with that sort of sovereignty, that dispenses with the use of means. There is no more sovereignty in one than in the other.

And yet some people are terribly alarmed at all direct efforts to promote a revival, and they cry out, "You are trying to get up a revival in your own strength. Take care, you are interfering with the sovereignty of God. Better keep along in the usual course, and let God give a revival when he thinks it is best. God is a sovereign, and it is very wrong for you to attempt to get up a revival, just because *you think* a revival is needed." This is just such preaching as the devil wants. And men cannot do the devil's work more effectually, than by preaching up the sovereignty of God, as a reason why we should not put forth efforts to produce a revival. . . .

The Scriptures ascribe the conversion of a sinner to four different agencies— to *men*, to *God*, to the *truth*, and to the *sinner himself*. The passages which ascribe it to the truth are the largest class. That men should ever have overlooked this distinction, and should have regarded conversion as a work performed exclusively by God, is surprising. Or that any difficulty should ever have been felt on the subject, or that people should ever have professed themselves unable to reconcile these several classes of passages.

Why, the Bible speaks on this subject, precisely as we speak on common subjects. There is a man who has been very sick. How natural it is for him to say of his physician, "That man saved my life." Does he mean to say that the physician saved his life without reference to God? Certainly not, unless he is an infidel. God made the physician, and he made the medicine too. And it never can be shown but that the agency of God is just as truly concerned in making the medicine take effect to save life, as it is in making the truth take effect to save a soul. To affirm the contrary is downright atheism. It is true then, that the physician saved him, and it is also true that God saved him. It is equally true that the medicine saved his life, and that he saved his own life by taking the medicine; for the medicine would have done no good if he had not voluntarily taken it, or yielded his body to its power.

In the conversion of a sinner, it is true that God gives the truth efficiency to turn the sinner to God. He is an active, voluntary, powerful agent in changing the mind. But he is not the only agent. The one who brings the truth to his notice is also an agent. We are apt to speak of ministers and other men as only *instruments* in converting sinners. This is not exactly correct. Man is something more than an instrument. Truth is the mere unconscious instrument. But man is more, he is a voluntary, responsible agent in the business. . . .

The Spirit of God, by the truth, influences the sinner to change, and in this sense is the efficient cause of the change. But the sinner actually changes, and is therefore himself, in the most proper sense, the author of the change. . . .

And let me tell you, sinner, if you do not do it you will go to hell, and to all eternity you will feel that you deserved to be sent there for not having done it.

READING AND DISCUSSION QUESTIONS

1. Explain Finney's argument about man's role in bringing on revivals for his own salvation. Why might this have been controversial?

2. Some of Finney's greatest revival successes occurred in the Burned-over District of upstate New York, those "overnight" towns and cities along the newly created Erie Canal. Why do you think his message resonated there?

3. Some historians have described the era of the Second Great Awakening as the "democratization of American Christianity." To what extent was Finney's revival message "democratic"?

▪ COMPARATIVE QUESTIONS ▪

1. How would you characterize the consequences of the rapid economic transformations that occurred in the United States during the first half of the nineteenth century? Were there clear beneficiaries of the economic development in this period? If so, who were they?

2. To what extent did the Market Revolution create the problems reformers mobilized to fix?

3. Did the economic changes that occurred during this period encourage a more or less optimistic view of American society? Consider the tone of the authors/creators of the documents in this chapter.

4. Do you think Matthew Hale Smith would have agreed with Congressman Porter's argument in favor of building the Erie Canal? Why or why not?

5. Where do you see the influence of Finney and other revivalists in the agenda of the American Temperance Society?

10

A Democratic Revolution
1800–1844

Andrew Jackson's 1829 inauguration inspired a wide variety of responses. At the White House reception that followed Jackson's swearing-in, many of his political opponents recoiled at the mob scene that developed. Those who witnessed Jackson's supporters mud-stomping silk upholstered chairs and toppling china dishes predicted the Republic's collapse at the hand of mob rule. "The Majesty of the People had disappeared," said one weary observer. Jacksonians, on the other hand, heralded the inauguration as the fulfillment of the Revolutionary promise of equality and freedom. Jackson's election, they argued, was a triumph of democracy.

The contradictory reactions that Jackson's election evoked highlight the lines of political battle that would define the era. The Democrats and the Whigs, the two predominant political parties of the period, sparred over fundamental questions about the role of government, the distribution of federal and state power, and economic development. Both sides came to accept the implications of the Democratic Revolution: that the parties must court the people. The documents in this chapter highlight the political drama that divided the major parties. They also reveal the extent to which Americans embraced the language of equal rights to fuel democracy's expansion.

10-1 | A Professional Politician on the Necessity of Political Parties

MARTIN VAN BUREN, *The Autobiography of Martin Van Buren* (1854)

Martin Van Buren (1782–1862), who would be elected the eighth president of the United States in 1836, rose quickly within New York political circles, serving as the state's attorney general, senator, and governor before becoming secretary of state, then vice president under Andrew Jackson. Though short of stature, he loomed large as one of the predominant figures within the Democratic Party. His political savvy earned him the nickname "Little Magician," but he championed political parties as a moderating influence on the sectionalism then emerging over the issue of slavery. In this selection from his autobiography, written in 1854, Van Buren defends political parties, presenting a view at odds with those of the founding generation who decried party spirit as factionalism.

The Administrations of Jefferson and Madison, embracing a period of sixteen years, were, from first to last, opposed by the federal party with a degree of violence unsurpassed in modern times. From this statement one of two conclusions must result. Either the conduct of these two parties which had been kept on foot so long, been sustained with such determined zeal and under such patriotic professions and had created distinctions that became the badges of families—transmitted from father to son—was a series of shameless impostures, covering mere struggles for power and patronage; or there were differences of opinion and principle between them of the greatest character, to which their respective devotion and active service could not be relaxed with safety or abandoned without dishonor. We should, I think, be doing great injustice to our predecessors if we doubted for a moment the sincerity of those differences, or the honesty with which they were entertained at least by the masses on both sides. The majority of the People, the sovereign power in our Government, had again and again, and on every occasion since those differences of opinion had been distinctly disclosed, decided them in favor of the Republican creed. That creed required only that unity among its friends should be preserved to make it the ark of their political safety. The Country had been prosperous and happy under its sway, and has been so through our whole history excepting only the period when it was convulsed and confounded by the criminal intrigues and commercial disturbances of the Bank of the United States. To maintain that unity became the obligation of him whom its supporters had elevated to the highest place among its guardians. Jefferson and Madison so interpreted their duty. On the other hand, Mr. Monroe, at the commencement of his second term, took the ground openly, and maintained it against all remonstrances, that no difference should be made by the

Annual Report of the American Historical Association for the Year 1918, vol. II, *The Autobiography of Martin Van Buren*, ed. John C. Fitzpatrick (Washington, DC: Government Printing Office, 1920), 123–125.

Government in the distribution of its patronage and confidence on account of the political opinions and course of applicants. The question was distinctly brought before him for decision by the Republican representatives from the states of Pennsylvania and New York, in cases that had deeply excited the feelings of their constituents and in which those constituents had very formally and decidedly expressed their opinions.

If the movement grew out of a belief that an actual dissolution of the federal party was likely to take place or could be produced by the course that was adopted, it showed little acquaintance with the nature of Parties to suppose that a political association that had existed so long, that had so many traditions to appeal to its pride, and so many grievances, real and fancied, to cry out for redress, could be disbanded by means of personal favors from the Executive or by the connivance of any of its leaders. Such has not been the fate of long established political parties in any country. Their course may be qualified and their pretentions abated for a season by ill success, but the cohesive influences and innate qualities which originally united them remain with the mass and spring up in their former vigour with the return of propitious skies. Of this truth we need no more striking illustrations than are furnished by our own experience. Without going into the details of events familiar to all, I need only say that during the very "Era of good feelings," the federal party, under the names of federal republicans and whigs, elected their President over those old republicans William H. Crawford, Andrew Jackson and John C. Calhoun—have, since his time, twice elected old school federalists—have possessed the most effective portions of the power of the Federal Government during their respective terms, with the exception, (if it was one) of the politically episodical administration of Vice President Tyler— and are at this time in power in the government of almost every free state. We shall find as a general rule that among the native inhabitants of each State, the politics of families who were federalists during the War of 1812, are the same now—holding, for the most part, under the name of Whigs, to the political opinions and governed by the feelings of their ancestors.

I have been led to take a more extended notice of this subject by my repugnance to a species of cant against Parties in which too many are apt to indulge when their own side is out of power and to forget when they come in. I have not, I think, been considered even by opponents as particularly rancorous in my party prejudices, and might not perhaps have anything to apprehend from a comparison, in this respect, with my contemporaries. But knowing, as all men of sense know, that political parties are inseparable from free governments, and that in many and material respects they are highly useful to the country, I never could bring myself for party purposes to deprecate their existence. Doubtless excesses frequently attend them and produce many evils, but not so many as are prevented by the maintenance of their organization and vigilance. The disposition to abuse power, so deeply planted in the human heart, can by no other means be more effectually checked; and it has always therefore struck me as more honorable and manly and more in harmony with the character of our People and of our Institutions to deal with the subject of Political Parties in a sincerer and wiser spirit—to recognize their necessity, to give them the credit they deserve, and to devote ourselves to improve and to elevate the principles and objects of our own and to support it ingenuously and faithfully.

READING AND DISCUSSION QUESTIONS

1. What does Van Buren mean when he says "political parties are inseparable from free governments"?

2. Why might Van Buren have felt the need to defend parties? What arguments does he use to do so?

10-2 | Insurgent Democrats Flex Political Power

FITZWILLIAM BYRDSALL, *The History of the Loco-Foco or Equal Rights Party* (1842)

The curiously named Loco-Foco faction within the Democratic Party is an example of the extent to which the Revolutionary-era ideals of liberty affected popular politics in this period. Increasingly, party leaders discovered how difficult it was to control rank-and-file members. In the scene described here, the Loco-Focos (or the Equal Rights Party), a working men's splinter group of Democrats led by Joel Curtis, crashes a party meeting managed by Tammany Hall, the name of the traditional party leadership. Disgruntled, the party bosses leave the hall and turn off the gaslights. The insurgents light "loco-focos," a kind of match, to keep the meeting going. The passage ends with a list of resolutions adopted at the meeting. These resolutions illustrate the radicalism of this group. Their opposition to the Second Bank, however, was a standard part of the Jacksonian political program.

Everything being arranged, the sovereign people are again called upon to approve or disapprove the acts of their nominating (appointing) committee. At the hour named, the doors of the great room are opened from the inside, to the congregated hundreds on the outside;—when lo! the actors by some secret passage are already on the stage and perfect in their parts. Order being partially obtained, the tickets are read, the vote is taken and declared in the affirmative; the farce is over, the meeting is adjourned, and the "regular ticket" is announced next day to those who always submit to the majority, and never vote any other.

The clock has just struck seven, and the doors of Tammany Hall are opening for the democracy. What a mass of human beings rush forward into the room! Yet they are late, for George D. Strong,[1] who came up the back stairs, has already

F. Byrdsall, *The History of the Loco-Foco or Equal Rights Party, Its Movements, Conventions and Proceedings, with Short Characteristic Sketches of Its Prominent Men* (New York: Clement & Packard, 1842), 24–27.

[1]**George D. Strong**: President of Commercial Bank.

nominated Isaac L. Varian,[2] who also ascended by the same way, for the chair, and the latter is hastening towards it before the question is heard by a fifth part of the crowd. Joel Curtis is nominated as the room is filling up, and the loud "aye" of the Equal Rights Democracy calls him to the chair. The honest workingman approaches it, and now begins the contest between monopoly and its opponents. There is a struggle of gladiators on the platform around the chair;—the loudest vociferations are heard, and Tammany trembles with intestine war. The contest at length becomes more furious; men are struggling with each other as if for empire, while the multitude in the body of the room are like the waves of a tempestuous sea. But who is he, that man of slender form and youthful appearance, the foremost in the struggle? Equal Rights men, your chief should be a man of stalwart frame; but there is hope, for your cause is good, and the indomitable spirit of equality is in that slender man. "Cheers for Ming!"—What! is that the office-holder? He who is always up with every rising of the people? *He* openly dares the majesty of monopoly, even in its temple;—*he* disregards the tenure of his office, for the elevating principle of Equality of Rights—the honest war-cry of "opposition to all monopolies" have aroused the democratic enthusiasm of his heart, and he counts not the cost. It is so!—he is unconsciously, for the occasion, and the time being, the natural hero of humanity, striving with all his energy of character to place Joel Curtis in the chair, as the representative of the masses. Unquestionably it is a contest for empire between man and monopoly.

Behold! a broad banner is spread before the eyes of the vast assemblage, and all can read its inscription: *"Joel Curtis, the Anti-Monopolist chairman."*

The efforts of Isaac L. Varian and the monopoly democracy are futile to obtain order, or to read their ticket of nominations so as to be heard, or any decision had thereon. They are struck with amazement at the sight of another banner with the inscription *"Anti-Monopolist Democrats are opposed to Gideon Lee,[3] Ringgold, West, and Conner[4]"*; and another with *"We go all gold but Ringgold."* What a desecration of the usages! [. . .]

But behold—there is the broadest banner of all, and it is greeted with cheers. It is the whole of the antimonopoly ticket for Congress and the Legislature, so that all can see and read where none can distinctly hear. The shouts of the Equal Rights' Democracy are still more deafening. But heartfelt cheers are given to that banner which declares for Leggett: *"The Times must change ere we desert our Post."*

The struggle is drawing towards a close. Isaac L. Varian believes the evidence presented to his senses, and in attempting to leave the chair, to which he is forcibly held down by George D. Strong and a member of the Common Council since dead, he exclaims, "Let me get out, gentlemen, we are in the minority here!" They held him fast;—but there! the chair is upset, and Isaac L. Varian is thrown from it. Instantly Joel Curtis, the true-hearted workingman is in it, both by right

---

[2]**Isaac A. Varian**: A bank director.

[3]**Gideon Lee**: President of Leather Manufacturers' Bank.

[4]**Ringgold, West, and Conner**: Bank partisans.

and fact, while two banners speak to the democracy, "Don't adjourn"—"Sustain the chair." There is clapping of hands and triumphant cheers. What can the discomfited do?

They have done it. When they got down stairs they turned off the gas. It is half-past seven, and the darkness of midnight is in Tammany Hall. Nothing but the demon spirit of monopoly, in its war upon humanity, could have been wicked enough to involve such an excited throng in total darkness.

"*Let there be light, and there is light!*" A host of fire-fly lights are in the room—loco-foco matches are ignited, candles are lit, and they are held up by living and breathing chandeliers. It is a glorious illumination! There are loud and long plaudits and huzzas, such as Tammany never before echoed from its foundations.

Reader, if this were not a victory over Monopoly, a blow, at least, was struck upon the hydra-headed monster, from which it never recovered.

The anti-monopoly ticket was enthusiastically adopted by the apparently undiminished multitude. Resolutions of the same character were passed, from which we select the following:

"*Resolved*—That, in a free state, all distinctions but those of merit are odious and oppressive, and ought to be discouraged by a people jealous of their liberties.

"*Resolved*—That all laws which directly or indirectly infringe the free exercise and enjoyment of equal rights and privileges by the great body of the people, are odious, unjust, and unconstitutional in their nature and effect, and ought to be abolished.

"*Resolved*—For all amounts of money, gold and silver are the only legitimate, substantial, and proper, circulating medium of our country.

"*Resolved*—That perpetuities and monopolies are offensive to freedom, contrary to the genius and spirit of a free state and the principles of commerce, and ought not to be allowed.

"*Resolved*—That we are in favor of a strict construction of the Constitution of the United States, and we are therefore opposed to the United States Bank, as being unconstitutional and opposed to the genius and spirit of our democratic institutions, and subversive of the great and fundamental principles of equal rights and privileges, asserted in the charter of our liberties.

"*Resolved*—That we are opposed to all bank charters granted by individual states, because we believe them founded on, and as giving an impulse to principles of speculation and gambling, at war with good morals and just and equal government, and calculated to build up and strengthen in our country the odious distribution of wealth and power against merit and equal rights; and every good citizen is bound to war against them as he values the blessings of free government.

"*Resolved*—That we receive the Evening Post with open arms to the bosom of the Democratic family, and that the efforts of its talented editors must and shall receive our uncompromising support."

READING AND DISCUSSION QUESTIONS

1. The Loco-Focos were Democrats, yet they stormed a Democratic Party meeting and took over its leadership positions under the banner of "anti-monopoly." What criticism of traditional party leadership were they making?

2. How would you summarize the political program the Equal Rights Party championed?

3. In the last resolution, the Loco-Focos praise the *Evening Post*. What value do you think they believed the newspaper played in party politics?

10-3 | President Defeats Monopoly Threat

ANDREW JACKSON, *Veto Message Regarding the Bank of the United States* (1832)

Andrew Jackson's famous attack on the Second Bank of the United States symbolized one of the key policy differences between Democrats and Whigs. Led by Henry Clay, the Whigs' American System supported building canals, roads, bridges, and banks to encourage economic development. Many Democrats opposed using government funds to support these projects. Like the Loco-Foco faction within his own party, Jackson thundered against the "monster bank's" monopoly power, which profited private investors who earned interest on federal revenue deposited in the bank. When Clay tried to make the bank's recharter an issue in the 1832 presidential election, Jackson called his bluff. In the document excerpted below, Jackson explains to Congress the reasons for his veto.

WASHINGTON, July 10, 1832.

To the Senate:

The bill "to modify and continue" the act entitled "An act to incorporate the subscribers to the Bank of the United States" was presented to me on the 4th July instant. Having considered it with that solemn regard to the principles of the Constitution which the day was calculated to inspire, and come to the conclusion that it ought not to become a law, I herewith return it to the Senate, in which it originated, with my objections.

A bank of the United States is in many respects convenient for the Government and useful to the people. Entertaining this opinion, and deeply impressed with the belief that some of the powers and privileges possessed by the existing bank are unauthorized by the Constitution, subversive of the rights of the States, and dangerous to the liberties of the people, I felt it my duty at an early period of my Administration to call the attention of Congress to the practicability of organizing an institution combining all its advantages and obviating these objections. I sincerely regret that in the act before me I can perceive none of those

A Compilation of the Messages and Papers of the Presidents Prepared under the direction of the Joint Committee on Printing, of the House and Senate Pursuant to an Act of the Fifty-Second Congress of the United States (New York: Bureau of National Literature, 1897), 1139–1141, 1144–1146, 1152–1154.

modifications of the bank charter which are necessary, in my opinion, to make it compatible with justice, with sound policy, or with the Constitution of our country.

The present corporate body, denominated the president, directors, and company of the Bank of the United States, will have existed at the time this act is intended to take effect twenty years. It enjoys an exclusive privilege of banking under the authority of the General Government, a monopoly of its favor and support, and, as a necessary consequence, almost a monopoly of the foreign and domestic exchange. The powers, privileges, and favors bestowed upon it in the original charter, by increasing the value of the stock far above its par value, operated as a gratuity of many millions to the stockholders.

An apology may be found for the failure to guard against this result in the consideration that the effect of the original act of incorporation could not be certainly foreseen at the time of its passage. The act before me proposes another gratuity to the holders of the same stock, and in many cases to the same men, of at least seven millions more. This donation finds no apology in any uncertainty as to the effect of the act. On all hands it is conceded that its passage will increase at least 20 or 30 per cent more the market price of the stock, subject to the payment of the annuity of $200,000 per year secured by the act, thus adding in a moment one-fourth to its par value. It is not our own citizens only who are to receive the bounty of our Government. More than eight millions of the stock of this bank are held by foreigners. By this act the American Republic proposes virtually to make them a present of some millions of dollars. For these gratuities to foreigners and to some of our own opulent citizens the act secures no equivalent whatever. They are the certain gains of the present stockholders under the operation of this act, after making full allowance for the payment of the bonus.

Every monopoly and all exclusive privileges are granted at the expense of the public, which ought to receive a fair equivalent. The many millions which this act proposes to bestow on the stockholders of the existing bank must come directly or indirectly out of the earnings of the American people. It is due to them, therefore, if their Government sell monopolies and exclusive privileges, that they should at least exact for them as much as they are worth in open market. The value of the monopoly in this case may be correctly ascertained. The twenty-eight millions of stock would probably be at an advance of 50 per cent, and command in market at least $42,000,000, subject to the payment of the present bonus. The present value of the monopoly, therefore, is $17,000,000, and this the act proposes to sell for three millions, payable in fifteen annual installments of $200,000 each.

It is not conceivable how the present stockholders can have any claim to the special favor of the Government. The present corporation has enjoyed its monopoly during the period stipulated in the original contract. If we must have such a corporation, why should not the Government sell out the whole stock and thus secure to the people the full market value of the privileges granted? Why should not Congress create and sell twenty-eight millions of stock, incorporating the purchasers with all the powers and privileges secured in this act and putting the premium upon the sales into the Treasury? . . .

The modifications of the existing charter proposed by this act are not such, in my view, as make it consistent with the rights of the States or the liberties of the people. The qualification of the right of the bank to hold real estate, the limitation of its power to establish branches, and the power reserved to Congress to forbid the circulation of small notes are restrictions comparatively of little value or importance. All the objectionable principles of the existing corporation, and most of its odious features, are retained without alleviation. . . .

Is there no danger to our liberty and independence in a bank that in its nature has so little to bind it to our country? The president of the bank has told us that most of the State banks exist by its forbearance. Should its influence become concentered, as it may under the operation of such an act as this, in the hands of a self-elected directory whose interests are identified with those of the foreign stockholders, will there not be cause to tremble for the purity of our elections in peace and for the independence of our country in war? Their power would be great whenever they might choose to exert it; but if this monopoly were regularly renewed every fifteen or twenty years on terms proposed by themselves, they might seldom in peace put forth their strength to influence elections or control the affairs of the nation. But if any private citizen or public functionary should interpose to curtail its powers or prevent a renewal of its privileges, it can not be doubted that he would be made to feel its influence. . . .

If we must have a bank with private stockholders, every consideration of sound policy and every impulse of American feeling admonishes that it should be purely American. Its stockholders should be composed exclusively of our own citizens, who at least ought to be friendly to our Government and willing to support it in times of difficulty and danger. So abundant is domestic capital that competition in subscribing for the stock of local banks has recently led almost to riots. To a bank exclusively of American stockholders, possessing the powers and privileges granted by this act, subscriptions for $200,000,000 could be readily obtained. . . .

It is maintained by the advocates of the bank that its constitutionality in all its features ought to be considered as settled by precedent and by the decision of the Supreme Court. To this conclusion I can not assent. Mere precedent is a dangerous source of authority, and should not be regarded as deciding questions of constitutional power except where the acquiescence of the people and the States can be considered as well settled. So far from this being the case on this subject, an argument against the bank might be based on precedent. One Congress, in 1791, decided in favor of a bank; another, in 1811, decided against it. One Congress, in 1815, decided against a bank; another, in 1816, decided in its favor. Prior to the present Congress, therefore, the precedents drawn from that source were equal. If we resort to the States, the expressions of legislative, judicial, and executive opinions against the bank have been probably to those in its favor as 4 to 1. There is nothing in precedent, therefore, which, if its authority were admitted, ought to weigh in favor of the act before me.

If the opinion of the Supreme Court covered the whole ground of this act, it ought not to control the coordinate authorities of this Government. The Congress, the Executive, and the Court must each for itself be guided by its own opinion of the Constitution. Each public officer who takes an oath to support the Constitution swears that he will support it as he understands it, and not as it is understood by others. It is as much the duty of the House of Representatives, of the Senate, and of the President to decide upon the constitutionality of any bill or resolution which may be presented to them for passage or approval as it is of the supreme judges when it may be brought before them for judicial decision. The opinion of the judges has no more authority over Congress than the opinion of Congress has over the judges, and on that point the President is independent of both. The authority of the Supreme Court must not, therefore, be permitted to control the Congress or the Executive when acting in their legislative capacities, but to have only such influence as the force of their reasoning may deserve.

But in the case relied upon the Supreme Court have not decided that all the features of this corporation are compatible with the Constitution. It is true that the court have said that the law incorporating the bank is a constitutional exercise of power by Congress; but taking into view the whole opinion of the court and the reasoning by which they have come to that conclusion, I understand them to have decided that inasmuch as a bank is an appropriate means for carrying into effect the enumerated powers of the General Government, therefore the law incorporating it is in accordance with that provision of the Constitution which declares that Congress shall have power "to make all laws which shall be necessary and proper for carrying those powers into execution." Having satisfied themselves that the word "necessary" in the Constitution means "needful," "requisite," "essential," "conducive to," and that "a bank" is a convenient, a useful, and essential instrument in the prosecution of the Government's "fiscal operations," they conclude that to "use one must be within the discretion of Congress" and that "the act to incorporate the Bank of the United States is a law made in pursuance of the Constitution"; "but," say they, "where the law is not prohibited and is really calculated to effect any of the objects intrusted to the Government, to undertake here to inquire into the degree of its necessity would be to pass the line which circumscribes the judicial department and to tread on legislative ground."

The principle here affirmed is that the "degree of its necessity," involving all the details of a banking institution, is a question exclusively for legislative consideration. A bank is constitutional, but it is the province of the Legislature to determine whether this or that particular power, privilege, or exemption is "necessary and proper" to enable the bank to discharge its duties to the Government, and from their decision there is no appeal to the courts of justice. Under the decision of the Supreme Court, therefore, it is the exclusive province of Congress and the President to decide whether the particular features of this act are necessary and proper in order to enable the bank to perform conveniently and efficiently the public duties assigned to it as a fiscal agent, and therefore constitutional, or unnecessary and improper, and therefore unconstitutional.

Without commenting on the general principle affirmed by the Supreme Court, let us examine the details of this act in accordance with the rule of legislative action which they have laid down. It will be found that many of the powers and privileges conferred on it can not be supposed necessary for the purpose for which it is proposed to be created, and are not, therefore, means necessary to attain the end in view, and consequently not justified by the Constitution. . . .

Under such circumstances the bank comes forward and asks a renewal of its charter for a term of fifteen years upon conditions which not only operate as a gratuity to the stockholders of many millions of dollars, but will sanction any abuses and legalize any encroachments.

Suspicions are entertained and charges are made of gross abuse and violation of its charter. An investigation unwillingly conceded and so restricted in time as necessarily to make it incomplete and unsatisfactory discloses enough to excite suspicion and alarm. In the practices of the principal bank partially unveiled, in the absence of important witnesses, and in numerous charges confidently made and as yet wholly uninvestigated there was enough to induce a majority of the committee of investigation—a committee which was selected from the most able and honorable members of the House of Representatives—to recommend a suspension of further action upon the bill and a prosecution of the inquiry. As the charter had yet four years to run, and as a renewal now was not necessary to the successful prosecution of its business, it was to have been expected that the bank itself, conscious of its purity and proud of its character, would have withdrawn its application for the present, and demanded the severest scrutiny into all its transactions. In their declining to do so there seems to be an additional reason why the functionaries of the Government should proceed with less haste and more caution in the renewal of their monopoly.

The bank is professedly established as an agent of the executive branch of the Government, and its constitutionality is maintained on that ground. Neither upon the propriety of present action nor upon the provisions of this act was the Executive consulted. It has had no opportunity to say that it neither needs nor wants an agent clothed with such powers and favored by such exemptions. There is nothing in its legitimate functions which makes it necessary or proper. Whatever interest or influence, whether public or private, has given birth to this act, it can not be found either in the wishes or necessities of the executive department, by which present action is deemed premature, and the powers conferred upon its agent not only unnecessary, but dangerous to the Government and country.

It is to be regretted that the rich and powerful too often bend the acts of government to their selfish purposes. Distinctions in society will always exist under every just government. Equality of talents, of education, or of wealth can not be produced by human institutions. In the full enjoyment of the gifts of Heaven and the fruits of superior industry, economy, and virtue, every man is equally entitled to protection by law; but when the laws undertake to add to these natural and just advantages artificial distinctions, to grant titles, gratuities, and exclusive privileges, to make the rich richer and the potent more powerful, the humble members of society—the farmers, mechanics, and laborers—who have neither the time nor the means of securing like favors to themselves, have a right to complain of the injustice of their Government. There are no necessary evils in government. Its evils exist only in its abuses. If it would confine itself to equal protection, and, as Heaven does its rains, shower its favors alike on the high and the low, the rich and the poor, it would be an unqualified blessing. In the act before me there seems to be a wide and unnecessary departure from these just principles.

Nor is our Government to be maintained or our Union preserved by invasions of the rights and powers of the several States. In thus attempting to make our General Government strong we make it weak. Its true strength consists in leaving individuals and States as much as possible to themselves—in making itself felt, not in its power, but in its beneficence; not in its control, but in its protection; not in binding the States more closely to the center, but leaving each to move unobstructed in its proper orbit.

Experience should teach us wisdom. Most of the difficulties our Government now encounters and most of the dangers which impend over our Union have sprung from an abandonment of the legitimate objects of Government by our national legislation, and the adoption of such principles as are embodied in this act. Many of our rich men have not been content with equal protection and equal benefits, but have besought us to make them richer by act of Congress. By attempting to gratify their desires we have in the results of our legislation arrayed section against section, interest against interest, and man against man, in a fearful commotion which threatens to shake the foundations of our Union. It is time to pause in our career to review our principles, and if possible revive that devoted patriotism and spirit of compromise which distinguished the sages of the Revolution and the fathers of our Union. If we can not at once, in justice to interests vested under improvident legislation, make our Government what it ought to be, we can at least take a stand against all new grants of monopolies and exclusive privileges, against any prostitution of our Government to the advancement of the few at the expense of the many, and in favor of compromise and gradual reform in our code of laws and system of political economy.

I have now done my duty to my country. If sustained by my fellow citizens, I shall be grateful and happy; if not, I shall find in the motives which impel me ample grounds for contentment and peace. In the difficulties which surround us and the dangers which threaten our institutions there is cause for neither dismay nor alarm. For relief and deliverance let us firmly rely on that kind Providence which I am sure watches with peculiar care over the destinies of our Republic, and on the intelligence and wisdom of our countrymen. Through His abundant goodness and their patriotic devotion our liberty and Union will be preserved.

ANDREW JACKSON.

READING AND DISCUSSION QUESTIONS

1. What arguments against the bank does Jackson think the American people will find persuasive?

2. Why does Jackson see the bank as a threat to "our liberty and independence"? Do you think he believed a threat existed, or do you think he was playing politics?

3. What does Jackson see as the role of the Supreme Court in relationship to the other branches of government?

10-4 | Whig Partisan Describes Party's Political Economy
HENRY CAREY, *The Harmony of Interests* (1851)

Henry C. Carey (1793–1879) was a leading Whig intellectual and political economist. It was largely through his efforts that the Whigs transformed from merely an anti-Jackson party into a party with a coherent political philosophy. Carey's 1851 book, *The Harmony of Interests*, conveys the Whig view of government as a legitimate and necessary spur to economic development. Whereas Jackson saw such efforts as enriching the wealthy at the expense of the poor, Carey argued that the interests of rich and poor harmonized in a robust economy. In this section, Carey defends protectionism by countering the arguments from "free trade" Democrats.

If protection be a "war upon labour and capital," it must tend to prevent the growth of wealth, and thus to deteriorate the political condition of man.

The farmer who exchanges his food with the man who produces iron by means of horses, wagons, canal-boats, merchants, ships, and sailors, gives much food for little iron. The iron man, who exchanges his products for food through the instrumentality of the same machinery, gives much iron for little food. The chief part of the product is swallowed up by the men who stand between, and grow rich while the producers remain poor. The growth of wealth is thus prevented, and inequality of political condition is maintained.

The farmer who exchanges directly with the producer of iron gives labour for labour. Both thus grow rich, because the class that desires to stand between has no opportunity of enriching themselves at their expense. Equality of condition is thus promoted.

The object of protection is that of bringing the consumer of food to take his place by the side of the producer of food, and thus promoting the growth of wealth and the improvement of political condition. That it does produce that effect, is obvious from the fact that, in periods of protection, such vast numbers seek our shores, and that immigration becomes stationary, or diminishes, with every approach towards that system which is usually denominated free trade.

The colonial system is based upon cheap labour. Protection seeks to increase the reward of labour. The one fills factories with children of tender years, and expels men to Canada and Australia; the other unites the men and sends the children to school.

Henry C. Carey, *The Harmony of Interests, Agricultural, Manufacturing, and Commercial* (Philadelphia: J. S. Skinner, 1851), 214–215.

The Irishman at home is a slave. He prays for permission to remain and pay in pounds sterling for quarters of acres, and his request is refused. Transfer him here and he becomes a freeman, choosing his employer and fixing the price of his labour. The Highlander is a slave that would gladly remain at home; but he is expelled to make room for sheep. One-ninth of the population of England are slaves to the parish beadle, eating the bread of enforced charity, and a large portion of the remaining eight-ninths are slaves to the policy which produces a constant recurrence of chills and fevers—overwork at small wages at one time, and no work at any wages at another. Transfer them here and they become freemen, selecting their employers and fixing the hours and the reward of labour. The Hindoo is a slave. His landlord's officers fix the quantity of land that he must cultivate, and the rent he must pay. He is not allowed, on payment even of the high survey assessment fixed on each field, to cultivate only those fields to which he gives the preference; his task is assigned to him, and he is constrained to occupy all such fields as are allotted to him by the revenue officers, and whether he cultivates them or not, he is saddled with the rent of all. If driven by these oppressions to fly and seek a subsistence elsewhere, he is followed wherever he goes and oppressed at discretion, or deprived of the advantages he might expect from a change of residence. If he work for wages, he is paid in money when grain is high, and in grain when it is low. He, therefore, has no power to determine the price of his labour. Could he be transferred here, he would be found an efficient labourer, and would consume more cotton in a week than he now does in a year, and by the change his political condition would be greatly improved.

Protection looks to the improvement of the political condition of the human race. To accomplish that object, it is needed that the value of man be raised, and that men should everywhere be placed in a condition to sell their labour to the highest bidder—to the man who will give in return the largest quantity of food, clothing, shelter, and other of the comforts of life. To enable the Hindoo to sell his labour and to fix its price, it is necessary to raise the price of his chief product, cotton. That is to be done by increasing the consumption, and that object is to be attained by diminishing the waste of labour attendant upon its transit between the producer and the consumer. Fill this country with furnaces and mills, and railroads will be made in every direction, and the consumption of cotton will speedily rise to twenty pounds per head, while millions of European labourers, mechanics, farmers, and capitalists will cross the Atlantic, and every million will be a customer for one-fourth as much as was consumed by the people of Great Britain and Ireland in 1847. The harmony of the interests of the cotton-growers throughout the world is perfect, and all the discord comes from the power of the exchangers to produce apparent discord.

It is asserted, however, that protection tends to build up a body of capitalists at the expense of the consumer, and thus produce inequality of condition. That such is the effect of *inadequate* protection is not to be doubted. So long as we continue under a *necessity* for seeking in England a market for our surplus products, her markets will fix the price for the world, and so long as we shall continue to be under a *necessity* for seeking there a small supply of cloth or iron, so long will the prices in her markets fix the price of all, and the domestic producer of cloth and iron will profit by the difference of freight both out and home. With this profit he takes the risk of ruin, which is of perpetual occurrence among the men of small capitals. Those who are already wealthy have but to stop their furnaces or mills until prices rise, and then they have the markets to themselves, for their poorer competitors have been ruined. Such is the history of many of the large fortunes accumulated by the manufacture of cloth and iron in this country, and such the almost universal history of every effort to establish manufactures south and west of New England.

Inadequate and uncertain protection benefits the farmer and planter little, while the uncertainty attending it tends to make the rich richer and the poor poorer, thus producing social and political inequality.

Adequate and certain protection, on the contrary, tends to the production of equality—first, because by its aid the *necessity* for depending on foreign markets for the sale of our products, or the supply of our wants, will be brought to an end, and thenceforth the prices, being fixed at home, will be steady, and then the smaller capitalist will be enabled to maintain competition with the larger one, with great advantage to the consumers—farmers, planters, and labourers; and, second, because its benefits will be, as they always have been, felt chiefly by the many with whom the price of labour constitutes the sole fund out of which they are to be maintained.

READING AND DISCUSSION QUESTIONS

1. What advantages does Carey say laborers will see under a policy of protectionism?

2. Why does he focus on these workers? In addition to the economic argument he makes, do you think Carey had political motives in talking about labor?

10-5 | Decrying Jackson's Use of Presidential Power
King Andrew the First (c. 1833)

With the revolutions in printing technology, cartoons became an effective weapon in the divisive political campaigns of the antebellum period. Both the Democrats and Whigs employed cheaply produced newspapers and other campaign materials to rally voters with images of their party's standard-bearers and opponents. Members of the Whig Party, who had supported renewing the charter of the Second Bank of the United States, were enraged by Jackson's veto of the bank bill. In this image, produced by supporters of the Whig Party, Jackson is depicted as King Andrew the First, holding a scepter in his right hand and his veto of the bill in his left.

King Andrew the First, c. 1833 (litho), American School (19th century) / American Antiquarian Society, Worcester, Massachusetts, USA / The Bridgeman Art Library.

READING AND DISCUSSION QUESTIONS

1. Analyze the elements of this cartoon. What do you infer about the artist's political perspective? Who was the intended audience? What effect do you think the artist expected the image to have?

2. How might a historian use cartoons like this one to understand popular politics during the 1830s? What does the image suggest about how political parties used the press to spread their ideas?

10-6 | Native American Women Urge Resistance to Removal Policy

CHEROKEE WOMEN, *Petition* (1821 [1831?])

Andrew Jackson saw himself as the protector of the people, but his treatment of Native Americans reveals the limits of his vision. Jackson justified his policy of Indian removal, which resulted in the infamous Trail of Tears, as necessary to "protect" Indians from white encroachment by removing them from eastern lands and resettling them in the interior. Native Americans saw the move differently. In this petition, published in 1831 in *The Cherokee Phoenix*, a tribal newspaper, Cherokee women denounced the Indian removal policy.

October 17, 1821 [1831?]

To the Committee and Council,

We the females, residing in Salequoree and Pine Log, believing that the present difficulties and embarrassments under which this nation is placed demands a full expression of the mind of every individual, on the subject of emigrating to Arkansas, would take upon ourselves to address you. Although it is not common for our sex to take part in public measures, we nevertheless feel justified in expressing our sentiment on any subject where our interest is as much at stake as any other part of the community.

We believe the present plan of the General Government to effect our removal West of the Mississippi, and thus obtain our lands for the use of the State of Georgia, to be highly oppressive, cruel and unjust. And we sincerely hope there is no consideration which can induce our citizens to forsake the land of our fathers of which they have been in possession from time immemorial, and thus compel us, against our will, to undergo the toils and difficulties of removing with our helpless families hundreds of miles to unhealthy and unproductive country. We hope therefore the Committee and Council will take into deep consideration our deplorable situation, and do everything in their power to avert such a state of things. And we trust by a prudent course their transactions with the General Government will enlist in our behalf the sympathies of the good people of the United States.

The Cherokee Removal: A Brief History with Documents, ed. Theda Perdue and Michael D. Green (Boston: Bedford/St. Martin's, 2005), 134.

READING AND DISCUSSION QUESTIONS

1. How do these Cherokee women craft their petition against the federal government's policy of removal?

2. What conclusions about the extent and limits of women's political power in this period can you draw from this source? How significant do you think it is that the Cherokee women issued a petition?

▪ COMPARATIVE QUESTIONS ▪

1. What conclusions can you draw from the sources in this chapter about the extent of "democratization" during the Jacksonian era? To what degree did different groups of people during these years benefit from this egalitarian ethos?

2. Contrast the competing political philosophies spurring the Whig and Democratic parties during the 1830s and 1840s. How did these policy disputes manifest themselves in policy differences?

3. Compare Van Buren's attitude toward parties with those views expressed by James Madison in *Federalist No. 10* (Document 6-6) and George Washington in his *Farewell Address* (Document P3-4). How might you explain the differences you see?

4. What can you infer about the argument historians make when they label the years 1800 to 1844 a Democratic Revolution? What comparison do you see between these years and those years of the American Revolution during the 1770s?

11

Religion and Reform
1800–1860

"The Americans combine the notions of religion and liberty so intimately in their minds," noted Alexis de Tocqueville in the 1830s, "that it is impossible to make them conceive of one without the other." The antebellum religious revivals stressed a person's freedom to choose God's gift of salvation. Life everlasting became a matter of choice and not, as the Calvinists had proclaimed, the prerogative of God alone. Religious enthusiasm also inspired new religious sects, denominations, and utopian communities, like Joseph Smith's Mormonism. The spiritual excitement of the era combined with Jefferson's "inalienable right" to pursue one's happiness to produce a powerful devotion to individualism that had widespread repercussions.

This theme of individualism also influenced culture, politics, and reform. The transcendentalists used this ideal in creative ways, inspiring utopian communities and the campaign for women's rights. The political dimension of individualism, as glimpsed in the Jacksonian era, also liberated urban culture from the constraints of upper-class "respectability." Some, particularly advocates of women's and African American rights, used the language of individualism to strike blows against gender and racial discrimination and slavery. Others quickly saw the limits, even dangers, of excessive individualism: political turmoil, sectionalism, and social discord.

11-1 | A Transcendentalist View of Women's Rights

MARGARET FULLER, *Woman in the Nineteenth Century* (1845)

Margaret Fuller (1810–1850) was nurtured among the New England literary and philosophical circle known as the transcendentalists, and along with Ralph Waldo Emerson and others she became one of its leading interpreters. In this selection, from her 1845 book, *Woman in the Nineteenth Century*, Fuller reveals the extent of her philosophical commitment to transcendentalism and to gender equality, a stand in line with, but more radical than, calls for women's suffrage.

Of all its banners, none has been more steadily upheld, and under none have more valor and willingness for real sacrifices been shown, than that of the champions of the enslaved African. And this band it is, which, partly from a natural following out of principles, partly because many women have been prominent in that cause, makes, just now, the warmest appeal in behalf of Woman.

Though there has been a growing liberality on this subject, yet society at large is not so prepared for the demands of this party, but that its members are, and will be for some time, coldly regarded as the Jacobins of their day.

"Is it not enough," cries the irritated trader, "that you have done all you could to break up the national union, and thus destroy the prosperity of our country but now you must be trying to break up family union, to take my wife away from the cradle and the kitchen-hearth to vote at polls, and preach from a pulpit? Of course, if she does such things, she cannot attend to those of her own sphere. She is happy enough as she is. She has more leisure than I have,—every means of improvement, every indulgence."

"Have you asked her whether she was satisfied with these *indulgences*?"

"'No, but I know she is. She is too amiable to desire what would make me unhappy, and too judicious to wish to step beyond the sphere of her sex. I will never consent to have our peace disturbed by any such discussions."

"Consent—you? it is not consent from you that is in question—it is assent from your wife."

"Am not I the head of my house?"

"You are not the head of your wife. God has given her a mind of her own."

"I am the head, and she the heart."

"God grant you play true to one another, then! I suppose I am to be grateful that you did not say she was only the hand. If the head represses no natural pulse of the heart, there can be no question as to your giving your consent. Both will be of one accord, and there needs but to present any question to get a full and true answer. There is no need of precaution, of indulgence, nor consent. But our doubt

Margaret Fuller Ossoli, *Woman in the Nineteenth Century and Kindred Papers Relating to the Sphere, Condition, and Duties of Woman* (Boston: Brown, Taggard and Chase, 1860), 28–30, 115–116, 174–176.

is whether the heart does consent with the head, or only obeys its decrees with a passiveness that precludes the exercise of its natural powers, or a repugnance that turns sweet qualities to bitter, or a doubt that lays waste the fair occasions of life. It is to ascertain the truth that we propose some liberating measures."

Thus vaguely are these questions proposed and discussed at present. But their being proposed at all implies much thought, and suggests more. Many women are considering within themselves what they need that they have not, and what they can have if they find they need it. Many men are considering whether women are capable of being and having more than they are and have, and whether, if so, it will be best to consent to improvement in their condition. . . .

The especial genius of Woman I believe to be electrical in movement, intuitive in function, spiritual in tendency. She excels not so easily in classification, or recreation, as in an instinctive seizure of causes, and a simple breathing out of what she receives, that has the singleness of life, rather than the selecting and energizing of art.

More native is it to her to be the living model of the artist than to set apart from herself any one form in objective reality; more native to inspire and receive the poem, than to create it. In so far as soul is in her completely developed, all soul is the same; but in so far as it is modified in her as Woman, it flows, it breathes, it sings, rather than deposits soil, or finishes work; and that which is especially feminine flushes, in blossom, the face of earth, and pervades, like air and water, all this seeming solid globe, daily renewing and purifying its life. Such may be the especially feminine element spoken of as Femality. But it is no more the order of nature that it should be incarnated pure in any form, than that the masculine energy should exist unmingled with it in any form.

Male and female represent the two sides of the great radical dualism. But, in fact, they are perpetually passing into one another. Fluid hardens to solid, solid rushes to fluid. There is no wholly masculine man, no purely feminine woman. . . .

But if you ask me what offices they [women] may fill, I reply—any. I do not care what case you put; let them be sea-captains, if you will. I do not doubt there are women well fitted for such an office, and, if so, I should be as glad to see them in it, as to welcome the maid of Saragossa, or the maid of Missolonghi, or the Suliote heroine, or Emily Plater.[1]

I think women need, especially at this juncture, a much greater range of occupation than they have, to rouse their latent powers. A party of travellers lately visited a lonely hut on a mountain. There they found an old woman, who told them she and her husband had lived there forty years. "Why," they said, "did you choose so barren a spot?" She "did not know; *it was the man's notion.*"

And, during forty years, she had been content to act, without knowing why, upon "the man's notion." I would not have it so.

---

[1]**Saragossa . . . Plater**: Fuller draws from early-nineteenth-century European history, including the Spanish and Greek wars for independence and the 1830 Polish uprising, to identify these examples of female valor.

In families that I know, some little girls like to saw wood, others to use carpenters' tools. Where these tastes are indulged, cheerfulness and good-humor are promoted. Where they are forbidden, because "such things are not proper for girls," they grow sullen and mischievous.

Fourier[2] had observed these wants of women, as no one can fail to do who watches the desires of little girls, or knows the ennui that haunts grown women, except where they make to themselves a serene little world by art of some kind. He, therefore, in proposing a great variety of employments, in manufactures or the care of plants and animals, allows for one third of women as likely to have a taste for masculine pursuits, one third of men for feminine.

Who does not observe the immediate glow and serenity that is diffused over the life of women, before restless or fretful, by engaging in gardening, building, or the lowest department of art? Here is something that is not routine, something that draws forth life towards the infinite.

I have no doubt, however, that a large proportion of women would give themselves to the same employments as now, because there are circumstances that must lead them. Mothers will delight to make the nest soft and warm. Nature would take care of that; no need to clip the wings of any bird that wants to soar and sing, or finds in itself the strength of pinion for a migratory flight unusual to its kind. The difference would be that all need not be constrained to employments for which some are unfit.

I have urged upon the sex self-subsistence in its two forms of self-reliance and self-impulse, because I believe them to be the needed means of the present juncture.

I have urged on Woman independence of Man, not that I do not think the sexes mutually needed by one another, but because in Woman this fact has led to an excessive devotion, which has cooled love, degraded marriage, and prevented either sex from being what it should be to itself or the other.

I wish Woman to live, first for God's sake. Then she will not make an imperfect man her god, and thus sink to idolatry. Then she will not take what is not fit for her from a sense of weakness and poverty. Then, if she finds what she needs in Man embodied, she will know how to love, and be worthy of being loved.

By being more a soul, she will not be less Woman, for nature is perfected through spirit.

READING AND DISCUSSION QUESTIONS

1. To what extent did Fuller's claim that there is "no wholly masculine man, no purely feminine woman" challenge prevailing ideas of men and women's roles in nineteenth-century society?

---

[2]**Fourier**: Charles Fourier, French philosopher and reformer, advocated for women's rights and inspired the development of several utopian communities in America, including Brook Farm in West Roxbury, Massachusetts.

2. Paying attention to the language Fuller uses in making her argument, what evidence of transcendentalism's influence can you identify? Are there particular words or phrases that help you see her writing as having been influenced by transcendentalist ideas?

11-2 | Mormon Leader's Vision of Religious Community

JOSEPH SMITH, *History of Joseph Smith, the Prophet* (c. 1830s)

The competing claims of religious truth that emerged from the proliferating denominations of the era liberated some from the constraints of the church, but alienated others, including Joseph Smith (1805–1844). Reared in western New York during the revivals of the 1820s, Smith was unsatisfied with the churches he knew. Spiritually driven, Smith experienced visions foretelling the arrival of a new gospel of God, which under his personal leadership bloomed into the church of Mormonism.

Some time in the second year after our removal to Manchester, there was in the place where we lived an unusual excitement on the subject of religion. It commenced with the Methodists, but soon became general among all the sects in that region of country. Indeed, the whole district of country seemed affected by it, and great multitudes united themselves to the different religious parties, which created no small stir and division amongst the people, some crying, "Lo, here!" and others, "Lo, there!" Some were contending for the Methodist faith, some for the Presbyterian, and some for the Baptist. For notwithstanding the great love which the converts to these different faiths expressed at the time of their conversion, and the great zeal manifested by the respective clergy, who were active in getting up and promoting this extraordinary scene of religious feeling, in order to have everybody converted, as they were pleased to call it, let them join what sect they pleased — yet when the converts began to file off, some to one party and some to another, it was seen that the seemingly good feelings of both the priests and the converts were more pretended than real; for a scene of great confusion and bad feeling ensued; priest contending against priest, and convert against convert; so that all their good feelings one for another, if they ever had any, were entirely lost in a strife of words and a contest about opinions.

I was at this time in my fifteenth year. My father's family was proselyted to the Presbyterian faith, and four of them joined that church, namely, my mother, Lucy; my brothers Hyrum and Samuel Harrison; and my sister Sophronia. During this time of great excitement my mind was called up to serious reflection and great uneasiness; but though my feelings were deep and often poignant, still

---

Joseph Smith, *History of the Church of Jesus Christ of Latter-Day Saints, Period I. History of Joseph Smith, the Prophet,* Intr. B. H. Roberts (Salt Lake City: Church of Jesus Christ of Latter-Day Saints, 1902), 2–13.

I kept myself aloof from all these parties, though I attended their several meetings as often as occasion would permit. In process of time my mind became somewhat partial to the Methodist sect, and I felt some desire to be united with them; but so great were the confusion and strife among the different denominations, that it was impossible for a person young as I was, and so unacquainted with men and things, to come to any certain conclusion who was right and who was wrong. My mind at times was greatly excited, the cry and tumult were so great and incessant. The Presbyterians were most decided against the Baptists and Methodists, and used all the powers of both reason and sophistry to prove their errors, or, at least, to make the people think they were in error. On the other hand, the Baptists and Methodists in their turn were equally zealous in endeavoring to establish their own tenets and disprove all others.

In the midst of this war of words and tumult of opinions, I often said to myself, What is to be done? Who of all these parties are right; or, are they all wrong together? If any one of them be right, which is it, and how shall I know it? While I was laboring under the extreme difficulties caused by the contests of these parties of religionists, I was one day reading the Epistle of James, first chapter and fifth verse, which reads:

> If any of you lack wisdom, let him ask of God, that giveth to all men liberally, and upbraideth not; and it shall be given him.

Never did any passage of Scripture come with more power to the heart of man than this did at this time to mine. It seemed to enter with great force into every feeling of my heart. I reflected on it again and again, knowing that if any person needed wisdom from God, I did; for how to act I did not know, and unless I could get more wisdom than I then had, I would never know; for the teachers of religion of the different sects understood the same passages of Scripture so differently as to destroy all confidence in settling the question by an appeal to the Bible. At length I came to the conclusion that I must either remain in darkness and confusion, or else I must do as James directs, that is, ask of God. I at length came to the determination to "ask of God," concluding that if he gave wisdom to them that lacked wisdom, and would give liberally, and not upbraid, I might venture. So, in accordance with this, my determination to ask of God, I retired to the woods to make the attempt. It was on the morning of a beautiful, clear day, early in the spring of eighteen hundred and twenty. It was the first time in my life that I had made such an attempt, for amidst all my anxieties I had never as yet made the attempt to pray vocally.

After I had retired to the place where I had previously designed to go, having looked around me, and finding myself alone, I kneeled down and began to offer up the desires of my heart to God. I had scarcely done so, when immediately I was seized upon by some power which entirely overcame me, and had such an astonishing influence over me as to bind my tongue so that I could not speak. Thick darkness gathered around me, and it seemed to me for a time as if I were doomed to sudden destruction. But, exerting all my powers to call upon God to deliver me out of the power of this enemy which had seized upon me, and at the very moment when I was ready to sink into despair and abandon myself to destruction—not to an imaginary ruin, but to the power of some actual being from the unseen world, who had such marvelous power as I had never before felt in any being—just at this moment of great alarm, I saw a pillar of light exactly over my head, above the brightness of the sun, which descended gradually until it fell upon me.

It no sooner appeared than I found myself delivered from the enemy which held me bound. When the light rested upon me I saw two Personages, whose brightness and glory defy all description, standing above me in the air. One of them spake unto me, calling me by name and said, pointing to the other—

THIS IS MY BELOVED SON. HEAR HIM!

My object in going to inquire of the Lord was to know which of all the sects was right, that I might know which to join. No sooner, therefore, did I get possession of myself, so as to be able to speak, than I asked the Personages who stood above me in the light, which of all the sects was right (for at this time it had never entered into my heart that all were wrong)—and which I should join. I was answered that I must join none of them, for they were all wrong; and the Personage who addressed me said that all their creeds were an abomination in His sight: that those professors were all corrupt; that "they draw near to me with their lips, but their hearts are far from me; they teach for doctrines the commandments of men: having a form of godliness, but they deny the power thereof." He again forbade me to join with any of them: and many other things did he say unto me, which I cannot write at this time. When I came to myself again, I found myself lying on my back, looking up into heaven. When the light had departed, I had no strength; but soon recovering in some degree, I went home. And as I leaned up to the fireplace, mother inquired what the matter was. I replied, "Never mind, all is well—I am well enough off." I then said to my mother, "I have learned for myself that Presbyterianism is not true."

It seems as though the adversary was aware, at a very early period of my life, that I was destined to prove a disturber and an annoyer of his kingdom; else why should the powers of darkness combine against me? Why the opposition and persecution that arose against me, almost in my infancy? Some few days after I had this vision, I happened to be in company with one of the Methodist preachers, who was very active in the before-mentioned religious excitement; and, conversing with him on the subject of religion, I took occasion to give him an account of the vision which I had had. I was greatly surprised at his behavior; he treated my communication not only lightly, but with great contempt, saying it was all of the devil, that there were no such things as visions or revelations in these days; that all such things had ceased with the apostles, and that there would never be any more of them. I soon found, however, that my telling the story had excited a great deal of prejudice against me among professors of religion, and was the cause of great persecution, which continued to increase; and though I was an obscure boy, only between fourteen and fifteen years of age, and my circumstances in life such as to make a boy of no consequence in the world, yet men of high standing would take notice sufficient to excite the public mind against me, and create a bitter persecution; and this was common among all the sects—all united to persecute me.

It caused me serious reflection then, and often has since, how very strange it was that an obscure boy, of a little over fourteen years of age, and one, too, who was doomed to the necessity of obtaining a scanty maintenance by his daily labor, should be thought a character of sufficient importance to attract the attention of the great ones of the most popular sects of the day, and in a manner to create in them a spirit of the most bitter persecution and reviling. But strange or not, so it was, and it was often the cause of great sorrow to myself. However, it was nevertheless a fact that I had beheld a vision. I have thought since, that I felt much like Paul, when he made his defense before King Agrippa, and related the account of the vision he had when he saw a light, and heard a voice; but still there were but few who believed him; some said he was dishonest, others said he was mad; and he was ridiculed and reviled. But all this did not destroy the reality of his vision. He had seen a vision, he knew he had, and all the persecution under heaven could not make it otherwise; and though they should persecute him unto death, yet he knew, and would know to his latest breath, that he had both seen a light and heard a voice speaking unto him, and all the world could not make him think or believe otherwise. So it was with me. I had actually seen a light, and in the midst of that light I saw two personages, and they did in reality speak to me; and though I was hated and persecuted for saying that I had seen a vision, yet it was true; and while they were persecuting me, reviling me, and speaking all manner of evil against me falsely for so saying, I was led to say in my heart, Why persecute me for telling the truth! I have actually seen a vision, and who am I that I can withstand God, or why does the world think to make me deny what I have actually seen? For I had seen a vision; I knew it, and I knew that God knew it, and I could not deny it, neither dared I do it, at least I knew that by so doing I would offend God, and come under condemnation.

I had now got my mind satisfied so far as the sectarian world was concerned; that it was not my duty to join with any of them, but to continue as I was until further directed. I had found the testimony of James to be true, that a man who lacked wisdom might ask of God, and obtain, and not be upbraided.

Chapter II: The Visitation of Moroni— Existence of the Book of Mormon Made Known

I continued to pursue my common vocations in life until the twenty-first of September, one thousand eight hundred and twenty-three, all the time suffering severe persecution at the hands of all classes of men, both religious and irreligious, because I continued to affirm that I had seen a vision.

During the space of time which intervened between the time I had the vision and the year eighteen hundred and twenty-three—having been forbidden to join any of the religious sects of the day, and being of very tender years, and persecuted by those who ought to have been my friends and to have treated me kindly, and if they supposed me to be deluded to have endeavored in a proper and affectionate manner to have reclaimed me—I was left to all kinds of temptations; and, mingling with all kinds of society, I frequently fell into many foolish errors, and displayed the weakness of youth, and the foibles of human nature; which, I am sorry to say, led me into divers temptations, offensive in the sight of God. In making this confession, no one need suppose me guilty of any great or malignant sins. A disposition to commit such was never in my nature. But I was guilty of levity, and sometimes associated with jovial company, etc., not consistent with that character which ought to be maintained by one who was called of God as I had been. But this will not seem very strange to any one who recollects my youth, and is acquainted with my native cheery temperament.

In consequence of these things, I often felt condemned for my weakness and imperfections; when, on the evening of the above-mentioned twenty-first of September, after I had retired to my bed for the night, I betook myself to prayer and supplication to Almighty God for forgiveness of all my sins and follies, and also for a manifestation to me, that I might know of my state and standing before him; for I had full confidence in obtaining a divine manifestation, as I previously had one. While I was thus in the act of calling upon God, I discovered a light appearing in my room, which continued to increase until the room was lighter than at noonday, when immediately a personage appeared at my bedside, standing in the air, for his feet did not touch the floor. He had on a loose robe of most exquisite whiteness. It was a whiteness beyond anything earthly I had ever seen; nor do I believe that any earthly thing could be made to appear so exceedingly white and brilliant. His hands were naked, and his arms also, a little above the wrist; so, also, were his feet naked, as were his legs, a little above the ankles. His head and neck were also bare. I could discover that he had no other clothing on but this robe, as it was open, so that I could see into his bosom. Not only was his robe exceedingly white, but his whole person was glorious beyond description, and his countenance truly like lightning. The room was exceedingly light, but not so very bright as immediately around his person.

When I first looked upon him, I was afraid; but the fear soon left me. He called me by name, and said unto me that he was a messenger sent from the presence of God to me, and that his name was Moroni; that God had a work for me to do; and that my name should be had for good and evil among all nations, kindreds, and tongues, or that it should be both good and evil spoken of among all people. He said there was a book deposited, written upon gold plates, giving an account of the former inhabitants of this continent, and the source from whence they sprang. He also said that the fullness of the everlasting Gospel was contained in it, as delivered by the Savior to the ancient inhabitants; also, that there were two stones in silver bows—and these stones, fastened to a breastplate, constituted what is called the Urim and Thummim—deposited with the plates; and the possession and use of these stones were what constituted "Seers" in ancient or former times; and that God had prepared them for the purpose of translating the book. . . .

Again, he told me, that when I got those plates of which he had spoken — for the time that they should be obtained was not yet fulfilled — I should not show them to any person; neither the breastplate with the Urim and Thummim; only to those to whom I should be commanded to show them; if I did I should be destroyed. While he was conversing with me about the plates, the vision was opened to my mind that I could see the place where the plates were deposited, and that so clearly and distinctly that I knew the place again when I visited it.

After this communication, I saw the light in the room begin to gather immediately around the person of him who had been speaking to me, and it continued to do so until the room was again left dark, except just around him; when, instantly I saw, as it were, a conduit open right up into heaven, and he ascended till he entirely disappeared, and the room was left as it had been before this heavenly light had made its appearance.

READING AND DISCUSSION QUESTIONS

1. What does Smith's account suggest about the historical context of religion during the 1820s and 1830s? How would you characterize Smith's perspective on the existing religious denominations of his day?

2. How might you account for the timing of Smith's visions, the first of which occurred in 1820 when Smith was only fourteen? What details from his biography, as he shares them here, shed light on his life and his early visions?

3. How might a historian explain the success of Smith's ministry during the 1820s and 1830s?

11-3 | Remembering Bowery Culture

ABRAM C. DAYTON, *Last Days of Knickerbocker Life in New York* (1882)

The transcendentalist world — airy, abstract, intellectual — contrasts sharply with the view Abram C. Dayton (1818–1877) offered of New York's urban culture during the 1840s. Dayton was one of the city's elites, and his memoir captures the spirit of a city in transition. In the selection excerpted here, Dayton describes the "Bowery Boys," whose distinctive style of dress and working-class culture snubbed the expectations of upper- and middle-class respectability. These young, independent, unmarried men, freed from parental restraint, indulged in leisure pursuits they defined and controlled.

A considerable element in the [fire] department was composed of a class known as "Bowery boys," peculiar in dress, gait, manner, tone; an inimitable species of the race, attempted for some time to be copied on the stage, but the portraiture

Abram C. Dayton, *Last Days of Knickerbocker Life in New York* (New York: George W. Harlan, 1882), 164–167.

was either so weak or so grossly exaggerated as scarcely to be recognized. These "B'hoys" had fashions of their own, which they adhered to with all the tenacity of a reigning belle; they were the most consummate dandies of the day, though they affected to look upon a Broadway swell with most decided contempt. The hair of the b'hoy or fire laddie was one of his chief cares, and from appearance the engrossing object of his solicitude. At the back of the head it was cropped as close as scissors could cut, while the front locks permitted to grow to considerable length were matted by a lavish application of *bears grease*, the ends tucked under so as to form a roll, and brushed until they shone like glass bottles. His broad, massive face, was closely shaven, as beards in any shape were deemed effeminate, and so forbidden by their creed; a black, straight, broad-brimmed hat, polished as highly as a hot iron could effect, was worn with a pitch forward, with a slight inclination to one side, intended to impart a rakish air; a large shirt collar turned down and loosely fastened, school boy fashion, so as to expose the full proportions of a thick, brawny neck; a black frock coat with skirts extending below the knee; a flashy satin or velvet vest, cut so low as to display the entire bosom of a shirt, often embroidered; pantaloons tight to the knee, thence gradually swelling in size to the bottom, so as nearly to conceal a foot usually of most ample dimensions. This stunning make-up was heightened by a profusion of jewelry as varied and costly as the b'hoy could procure. His rolling swaggering gait on the promenade on the Bowery; his position, at rest, reclining against a lamp or awning post; the precise angle of the ever-present cigar; the tone of voice, something between a falsetto and a growl; the unwritten slang which constituted his vocabulary cannot be described; even the talented Chanfrau,[1] after devoted study of the role, failed to come up to the full reality in his popular and much admired delineation of *Mose*.

The b'hoys female friend, whether wife, sister or sweetheart, was as odd and eccentric as her curious protector. Her style of attire was a cheap but always greatly exaggerated copy of the prevailing Broadway mode; her skirt was shorter and fuller; her bodice longer and lower; her hat more flaring and more gaudily trimmed; her handkerchief more ample and more flauntingly carried; her cork-screw curls thinner, longer and stiffer, but her gait and swing were studied imitations of her lord and master, and she tripped by the side of her beau ideal with an air which plainly said "I know no fear and ask no favor."

Running with his favorite machine or sauntering on the Bowery the fire-laddie was a most interesting study to the naturalist, but on the ball-room floor at Tammany he was "seen, felt and understood," unapproachable, "alone in his glory." The b'hoy danced; to dance he required space. "No pent up Utica, etc.," for his every movement was widespread as the swoop of the American eagle, which, by-the-bye, was his favorite bird; the symbol of his patriotism; its effigy was the crowning glory of his darling engine. Each cotillion was opened by a

---

[1]**Chanfrau:** Frank Chanfrau (1824–1884), mid-nineteenth-century American actor who popularized the Bowery stage character Mose in *A Glance at New York.*

bow to his partner and another to the lady on the right. This bow, composed of a twitch, a jerk and a profound salaam, was an affair so grand, so complicated, that to witness it amply repaid a somewhat dangerous visit to one of their festive gatherings. It behooved, however, the outside visitor to be very cautious and undemonstrative while gratifying his curiosity, for the laddies were proud, jealous of intruders; they would not brook the slightest approach to a sneer or unseemly stare; but, above all, the Broadway exquisite who ventured "within the pale" was compelled to be very guarded in his advances towards any fair one whose peculiar style he might chance for the moment to admire. These gaily caparisoned ladies were closely watched by their muscular admirers, and any approach to familiarity either by word or look was certain to be visited by instant punishment of a positive nature.

The pistol and knife now used by the modern cowardly bravado were not then in vogue, but these formidable *braves* carried fists backed by muscle, which were powerful weapons for aggressive purposes.

READING AND DISCUSSION QUESTIONS

1. What was the attitude of Bowery Boys to the girls they associated with? Did they think about women's role in society in the same way Fuller did?

2. What role does violence seem to play in working-class urban culture as Dayton describes it?

11-4 | Attacking the Legal Disabilities of Women

SARAH GRIMKÉ, *Letters on the Equality of the Sexes and the Condition of Woman* (1837)

Like Margaret Fuller, Sarah Grimké (1792–1873) also championed women's rights by fighting an uphill battle against the prejudices of her day. In her famous series of essays written as letters to her sister, Grimké attacked conventional religious doctrines that had subordinated women. Born into a slave-owning family in South Carolina, she embraced abolitionism and the Quaker faith. In this essay, Grimké targets the legal prescriptions against women, the same ones that prevented women's education and her dream of becoming a lawyer.

Concord, 9th Mo., 6th, 1837

My Dear Sister,—There are few things which present greater obstacles to the improvement and elevation of woman to her appropriate sphere of usefulness and duty, than the laws which have been enacted to destroy her independence, and crush her individuality; laws which, although they are framed for her government, she has had no voice in establishing, and which rob her of some of her *essential*

Sarah M. Grimké, *Letters on the Equality of the Sexes, and the Condition of Woman* (Boston: Isaac Knapp, 1838), 74–83.

rights. Woman has no political existence. With the single exception of presenting a petition to the legislative body, she is a cipher in the nation; or, if not actually so in representative governments, she is only counted, like the slaves of the South, to swell the numbers of law-makers who form decrees for her government, with little reference to her benefit, except so far as her good may promote their own. I am not sufficiently acquainted with the laws respecting women on the continent of Europe, to say anything about them. But Prof. Follen, in his essay on "The Cause of Freedom in our Country," says, "Woman, though fully possessed of that rational and moral nature which is the foundation of all rights, enjoys amongst us fewer legal rights than under the civil law of continental Europe." I shall confine myself to the laws of our country. These laws bear with peculiar rigor on married women. Blackstone, in the chapter entitled "Of husband and wife," says:—

> By marriage, the husband and wife are one person in law; that is, *the very being, or legal existence of the woman* is suspended during the marriage, or at least is incorporated and consolidated into that of the husband under whose wing, protection and cover she performs everything. For this reason, a man cannot grant anything to his wife, or enter into covenant with her; for the grant would be to suppose her separate existence, and to covenant with her would be to covenant with himself; and therefore it is also generally true, that all compacts made between husband and wife when single, are voided by the intermarriage. A woman indeed may be attorney for her husband, but that implies no separation from, but is rather a representation of, her love.

Here now, the very being of a woman, like that of a slave, is absorbed in her master. All contracts made with her, like those made with slaves by their owners, are a mere nullity. Our kind defenders have legislated away almost all our legal rights, and in the true spirit of such injustice and oppressions, have kept us in ignorance of those very laws by which we are governed. They have persuaded us, that we have no rights to investigate the laws, and that, if we did, we could not comprehend them; they alone are capable of understanding the mysteries of Blackstone, &c. But they are not backward to make us feel the practical operation of their power over our actions.

> The husband is bound to provide his wife with necessaries by law, as much as himself; and if she contracts debts for them, he is obligated to pay for them; but for anything besides necessaries, he is not chargeable.

Yet a man may spend the property he has acquired by marriage at the ale-house, the gambling table, or in any other way that he pleases. Many instances of this kind have come to my knowledge; and women, who have brought their husbands handsome fortunes, have been left, in consequence of the wasteful and dissolute habits of their husbands, in straitened circumstances, and compelled to toil for the support of their families.

> If the wife be indebted before marriage, the husband is bound afterwards to pay the debt; for he has adopted her and her circumstances together.

The wife's property is, I believe, equally liable for her husband's debts contracted before marriage.

If the wife be injured in her person or property, she can bring no action for redress without her husband's concurrence, and his name as well as her own: neither can she be sued, without making her husband a defendant.

This law that "a wife can bring no action," &c., is similar to the law respecting slaves. "A slave cannot bring a suit against his master, or any other person, for an injury—his master, must bring it." So if any damages are recovered for an injury committed on a wife, the husband pockets it; in the case of the slave, the master does the same.

> In criminal prosecutions, the wife may be indicted and punished separately, unless there be evidence of coercion from the fact that the offense was committed in the presence, or by the command of her husband. A wife is excused from punishment for theft committed in the presence, or by the command of her husband.

It would be difficult to frame a law better calculated to destroy the responsibility of woman as a moral being, or a free agent. Her husband is supposed to possess unlimited control over her; and if she can offer the flimsy excuse that he bade her steal, she may break the eighth commandment with impunity, as far as human laws are concerned.

> Our law, in general, considers man and wife as one person; yet there are some instances in which she is separately considered, as inferior to him and acting by his compulsion. Therefore, all deeds executed, and are done by her during her coverture (i.e., marriage) are void, except it be a fine, or like matter of record, in which case she must be solely and secretly examined, to learn if her act be voluntary.

Such a law speaks volumes of the abuse of that power which men have vested in their own hands. Still the private examination of a wife, to know whether she accedes to the disposition of property made by her husband is, in most cases, a mere form; a wife dares not do what will be disagreeable to one who is, in his own estimation, her superior, and who makes her feel, in the privacy of domestic life, that she has thwarted him. With respect to the nullity of deeds or acts done by a wife, I will mention one circumstance. A respectable woman borrowed of a female friend a sum of money to relieve her son from some distressing pecuniary embarrassment. Her husband was [away] from home, and she assured the lender, that as soon as he returned, he would gratefully discharge the debt. She gave her note, and the lender, entirely ignorant of the law that a man is not obliged to discharge such a debt, actually borrowed the money, and lent it to the distressed and weeping mother. The father returned home, refused to pay the debt, and the person who had loaned the money was obligated to pay both principal and interest to the friend who lent it to her. Women should certainly know the laws by which they are governed, and from which they frequently suffer; yet they are kept in ignorance, nearly as profound, of their legal rights, and of the legislative enactments which are to regulate their actions, as slaves.

> The husband, by the old law, might give his wife moderate correction, as he is to answer for her misbehavior. The law thought it reasonable to entrust

him with this power of restraining her by domestic chastisement. The courts of law will still permit a husband to restrain a wife of her liberty, in case of any gross misbehavior.

What a mortifying proof this law affords, of the estimation in which woman is held! She is placed completely in the hands of a being subject like herself to the outbursts of passion, and therefore unworthy to be trusted with power. Perhaps I may be told respecting this law, that it is a dead letter, as I am sometimes told about the slave laws; but this is not true in either case. The slaveholder does kill his slave by moderate correction, as the law allows; and many a husband, among the poor, exercises the right given him by the law, of degrading women by personal chastisement. And among the higher ranks, if actual imprisonment is not resorted to, women are not unfrequently restrained of the liberty of going to places of worship by irreligious husbands, and of doing many other things about which, as moral and responsible beings, they should be the sole judges. Such laws remind me of the reply of some little girls at a children's meeting held recently at Ipswich. The lecturer told them that god had created four orders of beings with which he had made us acquainted through the Bible. The first was angels, the second was man, the third beasts; and now, children, what is the fourth? After a pause, several girls replied, "WOMEN."

> A woman's personal property by marriage becomes absolutely her husband's, which, at his death, he may leave entirely away from her.

And farther, all the avails of her labor are absolutely in the power of her husband. All that she acquires by her industry is his; so that she cannot, with her own honest earnings, become the legal purchaser of any property. If she expends her money for articles of furniture, to contribute to the comfort of her family, they are liable to be seized for her husband's debts: and I know an instance of a woman, who by labor and economy had scraped together a little maintenance for herself and a do-little husband, who was left, at his death, by virtue of his last will and testament, to be supported by charity. I knew another woman, who by great industry had acquired a little money which she deposited in a bank for safe keeping. She had saved this pittance whilst able to work, in hopes that when age or sickness disqualified her for exertion, she might have something to render life comfortable, without being a burden to her friends. Her husband, a worthless, idle man, discovered this hid treasure, drew her little stock from the bank, and expended it all in extravagance and vicious indulgence. I know of another woman, who married without the least idea that she was surrendering her rights to all her personal property. Accordingly, she went to the bank as usual to draw her dividends, and the person who paid her the money, and to whom she was personally known as the owner of the shares in that bank, remarking the change in her signature, withdrew the money, informing her that if she were married, she had no longer a right to draw her dividends without an order from her husband. It appeared that she intended having a little fund for private use, and had not even told her husband that she owned this stock, and she was not a little chagrined, when she found that it was not at her disposal. I think she was wrong to conceal the circumstances. The relation of husband and wife is too near and sacred to admit of secrecy about money matters, unless positive necessity demands it; and I can see no excuse for any woman entering into a marriage engagement with a design to keep her husband ignorant that she was possessed of property. If she was unwilling to give up her property to his disposal, she had infinitely better have remained single.

The laws above cited are not very unlike the slave laws of Louisiana.

> All that a slave possesses belongs to his master; he possesses nothing of his own, except what his master chooses he should possess.

By the marriage, the husband is absolutely master of the profits of the wife's land during the coverture, and if he has had a living child, and survives the wife, he retains the whole of those lands, if they are estates of inheritance, during his life; but the wife is entitled only to one third if she survives, out of the husband's estates on inheritance. But this she has, whether she has had a child or not. With regard to the property of women, there is taxation without representation; for they pay taxes without having the liberty of voting for representatives.

And this taxation, without representation, be it remembered, was the cause of our Revolutionary war, a grievance so heavy, that it was thought necessary to purchase exemption from it at an immense expense of blood and treasure, yet the daughters of New England, as well as of all the other States of this free Republic, are suffering a similar injustice—but for one, I had rather we should suffer any injustice or oppression, than that my sex should have any voice in the political affairs of the nation.

The laws I have quoted, are, I believe, the laws of Massachusetts, and, with few exceptions, of all the States in the Union. "In Louisiana and Missouri, and possibly, in some other southern States, a woman not only has half her husband's property by right at his death, but may always be considered as possessed of half his gains during his life; having at all times power to bequeath that amount." That the laws which have generally been adopted in the United States, for the government of women, have been framed almost entirely for the exclusive bene-fit of men, and with a design to oppress women, by depriving them of all control over their property, is too manifest to be denied. Some liberal and enlightened men, I know, regret the existence of these laws; and I quote with pleasure an extract from Harriet Martineau's Society in America as proof of the assertion. "A liberal minded lawyer of Boston, told me that his advice to testators always is to leave the largest possible amount to the widow, subject to the condition of her leaving it to the children; but that it is with shame that he reflects that any woman should owe that to his professional advice, which the law should have secured to her as a right." I have known a few instances where men have left their whole property to their wives, when they have died, leaving only minor children; but I have known of more instances of "the friend and helper of many years, being portioned off like a salaried domestic," instead of having a comfortable indepen-dence secured to her, while the children were amply provided for.

As these abuses do exist, and women suffer intensely from them, our brethren are called upon in this enlightened age, by every sentiment to honor, religion and justice, to repeal these unjust and unequal laws, and restore to woman those rights which they have wrested from her. Such laws approximated too nearly to the laws enacted by slaveholders for the government of their slaves, and must tend to debase and depress the mind of that being, whom God created as a help meet for man, or "helper like unto himself," and designed to be his equal and his companion. Until such laws are annulled, woman never can occupy that exalted station for which she was intended by her Maker. And just in proportion as they are practically disregarded, which is the case to some extent, just so far is woman assuming that independence and nobility of character which she ought to exhibit.

The various laws which I have transcribed leave women very little more liberty, or power, in some respects, than the slave. "A slave," says the civil code of Louisiana, "is one who is in the power of a master, to whom he belongs. He can possess nothing, nor acquire anything, but what must belong to his master." I do not wish by any means to intimate that the condition of free women can be compared to that of slaves in suffering, or in degradation; still, I believe the laws which deprive married women of their rights and privileges, have a tendency to lessen them in their own estimation as moral and responsible beings, and that their being made by civil law inferior to their husbands, has a debasing and mischievous effect upon them, teaching them practically the fatal lesson to look unto man for protection and indulgence.

Ecclesiastical bodies, I believe, without exception, follow the example of legislative assemblies, in excluding women from any participation in forming the discipline by which she is governed. The men frame the laws, and, with few exceptions, claim to execute them on both sexes. In ecclesiastical, as well as civil courts, woman is tried and condemned, not by a jury of her peers, but by beings, who regard themselves as her superiors in the scale of creation. Although looked upon as an inferior, when considered as an intellectual being, woman is punished with the same severity as man, when she is guilty of moral offenses. Her condition resembles, in some measure, that of the slave, who, while he is denied the advantages of his more enlightened master, is treated with even greater rigor of the law. Hoping that in the various reformations of the day, women may be relieved from some of their legal disabilities, I remain,

Thine in the bonds of womanhood,

SARAH M. GRIMKÉ

READING AND DISCUSSION QUESTIONS

1. What comparisons does Grimké see in the condition of women and slaves in antebellum America? How does she describe both in relation to the law?

2. Compare Grimké's attitude toward religion with the spiritual or transcendentalist perspective of Margaret Fuller. Do they see religion in the same way, as a help or hindrance to women?

11-5 | Abolitionist Decries Slavery's Dehumanizing Power

DAVID WALKER, Preamble to *Walker's Appeal in Four Articles* (1830)

David Walker's powerful *Appeal to the Coloured Citizens of the World* offered a scorching attack of American slavery. Born free in North Carolina, Walker moved north, spending most of his short life in Boston, where he quickly became a leading abolitionist, deriding popular colonization plans embraced by many whites that aimed to send blacks "back" to Africa, a continent few African Americans, free or slave, had ever seen. Walker's preamble, excerpted here, is directed to a black audience who he argues must awaken to the cruelties of slavery and the hypocrisy of America and lead the charge for freedom.

My dearly beloved Brethren and Fellow Citizens.

Having travelled over a considerable portion of these United States, and having, in the course of my travels, taken the most accurate observations of things as they exist—the result of my observations has warranted the full and unshaken conviction, that we, (coloured people of these United States,) are the most degraded, wretched, and abject set of beings that ever lived since the world began; and I pray God that none like us ever may live again until time shall be no more. They tell us of the Israelites in Egypt, the Helots in Sparta, and of the Roman Slaves, which last were made up from almost every nation under heaven, whose sufferings under those ancient and heathen nations, were, in comparison with ours, under this enlightened and Christian nation, no more than a cypher— or, in other words, those heathen nations of antiquity, had but little more among them than the name and form of slavery; while wretchedness and endless miseries were reserved, apparently in a phial, to be poured out upon our fathers, ourselves and our children, by *Christian* Americans!

These positions I shall endeavour, by the help of the Lord, to demonstrate in the course of this *Appeal*, to the satisfaction of the most incredulous mind—and may God Almighty, who is the Father of our Lord Jesus Christ, open your hearts to understand and believe the truth.

The *causes,* my brethren, which produce our wretchedness and miseries, are so very numerous and aggravating, that I believe the pen only of a Josephus or a Plutarch, can well enumerate and explain them. Upon subjects, then, of such incomprehensible magnitude, so impenetrable, and so notorious, I shall be obliged to omit a large class of, and content myself with giving you an exposition of a few of those, which do indeed rage to such an alarming pitch, that they cannot but be a perpetual source of terror and dismay to every reflecting mind.

I am fully aware, in making this appeal to my much afflicted and suffering brethren, that I shall not only be assailed by those whose greatest earthly desires are, to keep us in abject ignorance and wretchedness, and who are of the firm conviction that Heaven has designed us and our children to be slaves and *beasts*

David Walker, *Walker's Appeal in Four Articles* (Boston: Revised and Published by David Walker, 1830), 3–5.

of burden to them and their children. I say, I do not only expect to be held up to the public as an ignorant, impudent and restless disturber of the public peace, by such avaricious creatures, as well as a mover of insubordination—and perhaps put in prison or to death, for giving a superficial exposition of our miseries, and exposing tyrants. But I am persuaded, that many of my brethren, particularly those who are ignorantly in league with slaveholders or tyrants, who acquire their daily bread by the blood and sweat of their more ignorant brethren—and not a few of those too, who are too ignorant to see an inch beyond their noses, will rise up and call me cursed—Yea, the jealous ones among us will perhaps use more abject subtlety, by affirming that this work is not worth perusing, that we are well situated, and there is no use in trying to better our condition, for we cannot. I will ask one question here.—Can our condition be any worse?—Can it be more mean and abject? If there are any changes, will they not be for the better though they may appear for the worst at first? Can they get us any lower? Where can they get us? They are afraid to treat us worse, for they know well, the day they do it they are gone. But against all accusations which may or can be preferred against me, I appeal to Heaven for my motive in writing—who knows that my object is, if possible, to awaken in the breasts of my afflicted, degraded and slumbering brethren, a spirit of inquiry and investigation respecting our miseries and wretchedness in this Republican Land of Liberty!!!!!!

READING AND DISCUSSION QUESTIONS

1. Upon what basis does Walker seek to challenge American slavery? Why do you think he believes his argument has persuasive power?

2. What obstacles does he acknowledge facing in launching his attack? Were you surprised by some of them, and if so, why?

11-6 | Antiabolitionist Attacks Reformers' Efforts
CALVIN COLTON, *Abolition a Sedition* (1839)

Calvin Colton (1789–1857) was a minister active in Whig political circles. He spent the early part of his career in New York, then Kentucky, where he wrote a biography of leading Whig politician Henry Clay. In his 1839 book *Abolition a Sedition*, which he published anonymously, Colton attacked those he described as antislavery radicals for using religion as a political weapon and for engaging in violent actions. He feared that abolitionists were playing on Americans' Christian sympathies to gain control of the political machinery, which could only antagonize southerners and lead them to the breaking point. In the selection excerpted here, Colton frames the threat abolitionists pose as a political attack on America's republican system.

Calvin Colton, *Abolition a Sedition, By a Northern Man* (Philadelphia: Geo. W. Donohue, 1839), 180–182.

So long as the American Anti-slavery Society is permitted to exist, and to carry on its operations under its present form, it is not the reason of their cause that prevails, but the power of their machinery in its action on the public mind. All opposing influences, so long as the Government is inactive, are like the scattering, random, and over-shoulder shot of a routed and retreating host that is flying in the field before the well-formed, steady, and disciplined march of a triumphant army—triumphant, because there is no corresponding agency to oppose them, not because they have the right. Such, precisely, is the effect of all the newspaper squibs that are fired off on the Abolitionists, and such the effect of the unorganized remonstrances of the public. The Abolitionists are in the field with a disciplined army, officered, paid, with a full staff, and an adequate Commissariat. In other words, they are a regularly organized and permanent political body, acting under a complete State machinery in all that their exigences require, adding to it at pleasure, with ever active and industrious agents, with money at command and the power of the press, and as independent of the Government of this country as the throne of the Sultan at Constantinople—and yet doing the business of the country!

There are most obvious reasons, why such a power, once recognized as suitable and proper, will carry all before it, till it shall have dissolved the Government of this country. The Abolitionists have all the native and long cherished feeling of the North on their side, as being opposed to slavery in principle; they have all the advantage of the sympathies of our nature, when we consider the *manner* in which they represent the case; they have the common and prevailing popular ignorance of the nature of our political fabric to aid them—for it is not to be supposed, that the people generally will have clear and uniform views on a question upon which Statesmen differ; and to the effect of all these natural and social auxiliaries, they superadd the power of their immense, combined, and variously ramified machinery, which steals every where upon the public, catching every man, woman, and child, whose benevolent sympathies are naturally open to their appeals, and when once they are indoctrinated after the manner and in the school of the Abolitionists, and become possessed of their spirit, there is little chance for the sway of those principles on which our political society is based. It is not the fair argument of the cause, but the power of this political combination, that bears such sway. There is no chance for a candid hearing before the public, and for the due influence of all the considerations which appertain to this momentous and complicated question, because the constitutional balance of power, designed for such exigences, has been prostrated by an usurpation, and every thing is made to give way to isolated and abstract opinions, and to the dictations of political quackery. Fanaticism rules, and not reason; and the natural and inevitable consequence will be, that the gradual accumulation of this moral power, thus acquired, will swell to a magnitude, and urge on a momentum, before the pressure of which the Union will be compelled to yield and break down. The people of the South will be annoyed and vexed, till they can be annoyed and vexed no longer. Then will be the beginning of the end.

Are we understood? Is it not clear, that it is this political usurpation of an unlawful power, that puts the country in peril? Let this irregularity, this transcending of law, be reduced again to the Constitutional basis, and all this excitement, alarm, and danger, will die away, because the healthful Constitutional balance of influence would be restored. Opinion would then encounter opinion on common ground, with no undue advantage of one party over another.

READING AND DISCUSSION QUESTIONS

1. What audience do you think Colton had in mind when he wrote his denunciation of abolitionists?

2. What clues to his thinking about the proper functioning of the republic does he provide when he says, of the abolitionist threat, "fanaticism rules, and not reason"? In other words, what kind of government does he imagine America to have?

▪ COMPARATIVE QUESTIONS ▪

1. What ideal of American society emerges when you compare the various reformers highlighted in this chapter?

2. What were the limits or obstacles reformers encountered in the antebellum period?

3. How important was religion in shaping antebellum reform efforts?

4. Which do you think was the stronger appeal during this period: the idea of American individualism or the idea of community? Explain.

12

The South Expands: Slavery and Society

1800–1860

There was no unified South; the region was a complex patchwork of distinctive populations. Yet the South was united by the existence of slavery, which marked its politics, economics, and social relations. Over the period from 1800 to the eve of the Civil War, southerners became increasingly tethered to the economics of slavery. Planters moved in search of arable land to maximize their investment in human property. They enforced a discipline upon enslaved African Americans to control their lives, but fancied themselves to be good masters overseeing a servile race, otherwise destined for barbarism. Of course, African Americans experienced slavery from the other end of the whip. The brutalities they faced were not limited to the punishing physical violence many bore, but included the emotional and psychological toll mothers faced when their children and husbands were sold away from them. Still, African Americans drew on remarkable reserves to endure and survive. The South that careened toward war was the product of these diverse populations, acting and reacting within a context of slavery.

12-1 | Reporting on the South's Peculiar Institution
ETHAN ANDREWS, *Slavery and the Domestic Slave-Trade* (1836)

While the Constitution ended the importation of slaves beginning in 1808, a thriving internal (or domestic) trade in slaves continued. Treated as property, enslaved African Americans became a tradable commodity and source of wealth for southern planters. As moveable property, slaves were useful to planters who left exhausted farms in search of more fertile fields in the Gulf coast states. As a professor of ancient languages at the University of North Carolina, Ethan Andrews (1787–1858) observed first-hand the effects of slavery and the slave trade. At the behest of the American Union for the Relief and Improvement of the Colored Race, he published in 1836 a series of letters recounting his observations.

Fredericksburg, July 26, 1835.

A gentleman in this city has a female slave whom he purchased from a trader, for the purpose of preventing her separation from her husband. Her former mistress had taken some offence at her, and had sold her to the trader, with the intention of having her carried out of the state. The husband and wife were both greatly distressed, and from compassion to them this gentleman purchased her. After this trouble was over, a year or two passed quietly away, when suddenly the husband, who had belonged to the minor heirs of an estate, was seized, just as a drove of negroes were setting off for the south, and immediately hand-cuffed to prevent his escape. He had been sold some little time previously, but had not been informed of his fate, until the hour of departure arrived. The gentleman who had purchased the wife, learning the circumstances, attempted again to prevent the separation of the husband and wife, by offering to sell the latter to the trader, provided he would guarantee that they should not be separated, when sold at the south. The trader was willing to purchase her, but said he could give no such guaranty, as he always sold his slaves to those who would pay the highest price, and he supposed it possible, that for this purpose he should have to separate them. Under these circumstances, the husband, who was much attached to his wife, begged her not to leave her present situation, and thus they were finally separated.

A friend, to whom and to whose family I am indebted for many attentions, considers the final extinction of slavery as decisively indicated by the treatment which slaves now receive in the south, and particularly in Virginia, when compared with that which was common twenty or thirty years since. Even the advertisements for runaway slaves would serve to indicate a change in public sentiment, and in fact, as the same gentleman observes, are collectively a good index of the state of feeling, not only at the same place at different periods, but in

E. A. Andrews, *Slavery and the Domestic Slave-Trade in the United States. In a Series of Letters Addressed to the Executive Committee of the American Union for the Relief and Improvement of the Colored Race* (Boston: Light & Stearns, 1836), 167–174, 193–196.

different places at the same time. A Virginia advertisement usually contains a clause, stating, or implying, that the slave has run away, notwithstanding he has always been treated with the greatest indulgence; while advertisements from the extreme south are solely occupied, like those for stray oxen and horses, in describing their natural and artificial marks, their ages and habits.

He thinks, also, that in this state, slaves would have no value whatever as field-hands, were it not for the southern market. The labor performed by them is not sufficient to meet the current expenses of the plantations, at least of the more ordinary ones, and the only profit of the planter is derived from the negroes whom he raises for market.

It remains still to be determined whether, if wages were paid to the slaves in place of their present regular supplies, and in proportion to the amount of services rendered, a different result would not be obtained. That this experiment will soon be made, I have great confidence, and am inclined to believe that, if judiciously made, it will succeed.

Richmond, July 28, 1835.

In my journey yesterday from Fredericksburg to this place, I travelled with a planter, who had emigrated from North Carolina to Louisiana, where he has resided for several years, but is now about to remove from his plantation to a more healthy one in a different part of the same state. His present journey was undertaken partly for the purpose of increasing the number of his slaves; and he had just completed the purchase of one hundred and fifty-five, the entire stock of a plantation near Fredericksburg. For these he had given seventy-five thousand dollars, or about five hundred dollars, on an average, for each. They included mechanics of every kind necessary upon a great plantation. The purchaser was still young, and exhibited, in a striking degree, that promptitude and decision of character, so often observable in those accustomed early to direct their own conduct and that of others. Visions, perhaps I ought rather to say sober calculations, of boundless wealth, to be acquired by the labor of his slaves, were alluring him forward, and though naturally humane in his feelings, his kindness to the slaves will probably go no farther than to provide for their animal wants, regardless of their high destinies as moral and intelligent beings. He was not wholly without apprehension that his hopes of soon acquiring a vast fortune might be frustrated by a fall in the price of his staple production, cotton. He remarked that he should soon pay for his slaves, if the present price of cotton continued; and that he should ultimately succeed, if it did not fall below twelve and a half, or even ten cents, but that he could not afford to go below that price.

He represents the cares of the master upon an extensive plantation as very great. These are much increased in case of sickness among the slaves, as they cannot in general be depended upon to nurse one another, and the whole care of them while sick often devolves upon the master. He says "their weekly rations in Louisiana consist of eight or ten quarts of corn meal and four pounds of northern pork; for the latter of which, in the winter, bacon is commonly given to them, and molasses also is frequently substituted for the whole or a part of the pork, at the rate of a pint of the former for a pound of the latter. Some make use of salt fish instead of pork; but this is generally thought objectionable, on account of its tendency to create violent thirst. The negroes commonly choose to receive their corn-meal, rather than its equivalent in bread, that they may cook it for themselves. Rations of spirits are never given to them, except upon peculiar and rare occasions, as at *corn shucking*, and the like. It is therefore extremely rare that a negro is seen intoxicated, and still more so that he acquires a habit of intemperance."

To the inquiry, how do the slaves in Louisiana usually spend the Sabbath? he replied: "generally in complete idleness; lolling in the shade, or basking in the sun. Some of them are disposed to go to preaching, when there is an opportunity; but the greater part consider it a hardship to be compelled to attend meeting. They are universally attached to the Baptist, rather than to any other church, and seem to consider 'going into the water,' as a most essential part of religion. 'This,' he observes, 'may perhaps be attributed in part to its involving an act of self-denial, as they are doggedly averse to bathing or washing, for the purposes of cleanliness.' This indisposition to practise ablutions for the promotion of health and cleanliness, is nearly universal, and they can scarcely be more offended by anything, than by a compulsory system of bathing or of washing their clothes. If not compelled to do it, they would never wash a garment from the time when it is put on new, until it is worn out. Even house servants must be watched like children, or most of them would neglect attention to cleanliness.

"Whatever indulgences, in regard to dress or other things, custom has established, as the right of the slave, he is very particular to require; and if any-thing is withheld, he remembers it as his due, and asks for it, when he has an opportunity.

"The slave-traders have exacted such a profit upon their slaves, that the planters, when intending to make a considerable purchase, either come to the north for the purpose, or employ a factor to whom they allow a stipulated commission on the purchase money. By such means only, can they prevent the combinations among the traders, to keep up the prices, as the infamy of the traffic operates to prevent great competition."

A gentleman from Halifax N.C. represents the slaves as rapidly diminishing in that part of the state, by their removal to Alabama, and other southern states. In most cases, the masters emigrate with their slaves. . . .

Baltimore, July 30, 1835.

To a stranger, one of the most revolting features in American slavery is, the domestic slave-trade; and hence the inquiry is so frequently made, whether this evil at least may not be abolished. Various plans have been proposed for the purpose, but none which appear feasible; and it may well be doubted, whether this feature can ever be obliterated while the general system remains. All which it appears possible to do, is to regulate the sales in such a manner, that husbands and wives, parents and young children, shall never be separated. This, no one can deny, ought to be done; and if the system cannot exist with this innovation, it ought not to be tolerated for a single hour. The domestic relations are at the foundation of all the virtue, and consequently of all the happiness of society, and everything inconsistent with the perpetuity of these relations ought at once, everywhere, and forever, to cease. But whether even this is practicable, is a question which I confess my inability to answer. I cannot see how these separations are to be prevented, while the husband is the property of one master, and the wife and children of another, each master being wholly independent, and his slaves being considered as in the most absolute sense his property. The mode of accomplishing this change belongs to southern moralists to determine; but it is not a subject which they are at liberty to neglect, and least of all, can the christian, who acts in view of his Master's command not to separate those whom God has joined in the marriage relation, consent that such separations should be legalized by the laws of a state of which he is an active and responsible member.

When these relations are not violated, the character of the domestic slave-trade, considered as a part of the general system of slavery, depends upon the circumstances under which the transfer is made. If the condition of the slave is improved in everything essential, and especially if, with a full understanding of the nature of the transaction, he really desires the transfer, no additional wrong appears to be done by the new relation in which the parties are placed. This case, so far from being uncommon, is one which frequently occurs.

A literary friend who is a native of North Carolina, remarked to me to-day, that he could tolerate every thing else about slavery better than the shocking separations, which he saw continually caused by the removal of slaves to the south and west. When I told him that the evil seemed inseparable from slavery in such a country as this, he reluctantly assented to the position, after a moment's hesitation, in a manner that seemed to me little short of ludicrous. My meaning had been, that a system, to which such evils were necessary incidents, was intolerable; his conclusion evidently was, that if it cannot be made better, it must be submitted to with all its inconveniences.

READING AND DISCUSSION QUESTIONS

1. What evidence does Andrews's report provide for understanding both the domestic trade in slaves and the geographical movement of southern planters?

2. How does knowing that an advocacy group organized for the "relief and improvement of the colored race" commissioned Andrews's work impact how a historian might interpret the evidence it contains?

12-2 | Witness to the Punishment of a Runaway Slave
LEVI COFFIN, *Reminiscences of Levi Coffin* (1876)

Enslaved African Americans coped with the brutalities of their bonded lives in myriad ways, which sometimes included running away. Countless thousands escaped their masters' reach by heading north and seeking aid on the Underground Railroad. Others were captured and punished. Levi Coffin (1798–1877), a Quaker abolitionist, devoted his energies to helping runaway slaves by hiding them and providing material support as they made their escape. Here he recounts the tragic fate of one fugitive whom he could not help.

Sometimes I witnessed scenes of cruelty and injustice and had to stand passively by. The following is an instance of that kind: I had been sent one day on an errand to a place in the neighborhood, called Clemen's Store, and was returning home along the Salem road, when I met a party of movers, with wagons, teams, slaves and household goods, on their way to another State. After passing them I came to a blacksmith's shop, in front of which were several men, talking and smoking, in idle chat, and proceeding on my way I met a negro man trudging along slowly on foot, carrying a bundle. He inquired of me regarding the party of movers; asked how far they were ahead, etc. I told him "About half a mile," and as he passed on, the thought occurred to me that this man was probably a runaway slave who was following the party of movers. I had heard of instances when families were separated — the wife and children being taken by their owners to another part of the country — of the husband and father following the party of emigrants, keeping a short distance behind the train of wagons during the day, and creeping up to the camp at night, close enough for his wife to see him and bring him food. A few days afterward I learned that this man had been stopped and questioned by the party of men at the blacksmith's shop, that he had produced a pass, but they being satisfied that it was a forgery had lodged him in jail at Greensboro, and sent word to his master concerning him. A week or two afterward I was sent to a blacksmith's shop, at Greensboro, to get some work done. The slave's master had, that very day, arrived and taken possession of him, and brought him to the blacksmith's shop to get some irons put on him before starting back to his home. While a chain was being riveted around the negro's neck, and handcuffs fastened on his wrists, his master upbraided him for having run away. He asked:

"Wer'n't you well treated?"

"Yes, massa."

"Then what made you run away?"

"My wife and children were taken away from me, massa, and I think as much of them as you do of yours, or any white man does of his. Their massa tried

Levi Coffin, *Reminiscences of Levi Coffin, The Reputed President of the Underground Railroad; Being a Brief History of the Labors of a Lifetime in Behalf of the Slave, with the Stories of Numerous Fugitives, Who Gained Their Freedom Through His Instrumentality, and Many Other Incidents*, Second Edition — With Appendix (Cincinnati: Robert Clarke & Co., 1880), 17–20.

to buy me too, but you would not sell me, so when I saw them go away, I followed." The mere recital of his words can convey little idea of the pitiful and pathetic manner in which they were uttered; his whole frame trembled, and the glance of piteous, despairing appeal he turned upon his master would have melted any heart less hard than stone.

The master said, "I've always treated you well, trusting you with my keys, and treating you more like a confidential servant than a slave, but now you shall know what slavery is. Just wait till I get you back home!" He then tried to make the negro tell where he had got his pass, who wrote it for him, etc., but he refused to betray the person who had befriended him. The master threatened him with the severest punishment, but he persisted in his refusal. Then torture was tried, in order to force the name from him. Laying the slave's fettered hand on the blacksmith's anvil, the master struck it with a hammer until the blood settled under the finger nails. The negro winced under each cruel blow, but said not a word. As I stood by and watched this scene, my heart swelled with indignation, and I longed to rescue the slave and punish the master. I was not converted to peace principles then, and I felt like fighting for the slave. One end of the chain, riveted to the negro's neck, was made fast to the axle of his master's buggy, then the master sprang in and drove off at a sweeping trot, compelling the slave to run at full speed or fall and be dragged by his neck. I watched them till they disappeared in the distance, and as long as I could see them, the slave was running.

READING AND DISCUSSION QUESTIONS

1. Though Coffin's memoirs were published more than a decade after the abolition of slavery, what impact might anecdotes such as the one he recounts have had on the antislavery movement?

2. Compare and evaluate the treatment of slaves from the late seventeenth century to the mid-nineteenth century by identifying similarities and differences in Coffin's account of the punishment of the escaped slave and the Virginia codes concerning outlying slaves (Document 3-3).

3. What can you infer from Coffin's story about the efforts of enslaved African Americans to mitigate the brutalities of the slave system?

12-3 | A Southern City Affirms the Morality of the Slave Trade
Proceedings of the Charleston City Council (1856)

The coastal city of Charleston, South Carolina, became a thriving commercial center during the first half of the nineteenth century, buoyed by its flourishing trade in cotton and slaves. The domestic trade in slaves was a lucrative source of city income. Those bringing slaves into the city for sale were subject to a head tax of $10 per slave. Benjamin Mordecai, a Jewish merchant from Charleston who became a leading financial supporter of the Confederate cause, petitioned the city council for exemption. His petition was rejected, but the city's aldermen, as reported in the January 10, 1856, *Charleston Daily Courier*, took the opportunity to affirm the propriety of the tax and the trade in slaves.

Alderman Gourdin, from the Committee of Ways and Means, made the following report, which was adopted:

The Committee of Ways and Means, to whom was referred the memorial of Benjamin Mordecai, Esq., asking relief in the matter of an ordinance of the City Council requiring a tax of ten dollars on each slave brought into the city for sale from beyond the limits of the State, beg leave to report:

The ordinance for raising supplies for the years 1851, 1852 and 1853, provides that every slave brought into the city for sale, from beyond the limits of the State, shall be subjected to a tax of $3. Those for the same objects for the years 1854 and 1855 placed this tax at $10. The memorialist recites two points of objection to this provision of the ordinance of 1855 — the first founded upon the operation of the law upon him individually; the second upon the impolicy of the law, alleging that it operates as a commercial restraint.

On the first point, the memorialist alleges that the actual enforcement of this ordinance has been waived; that all others in the same business with himself have been charged to this time according to such rates as were in existence prior to its passage; that it seems to be only against him that the enforcement was directed, to his individual hardship and suffering; that all others having escaped this tax, he prays in his behalf a similar exemption; and he further asks an opportunity that he may show that all others in the same business with himself have been exempted.

The ordinance provides "that it shall be the duty of the City Assessor to ascertain the number of all such slaves and to assess the said tax on the owners, or persons in possession of such slaves, for the purpose of sale, &c."

The Committee have communicated with the memorialist and with the City Assessor on the subject, and from the statements of the former, are induced to believe that the tax of $10 on each slave brought into the city for sale from beyond the limits of the State, has not been uniformly paid by others in the same business with himself. The Assessor on the other hand, alleges the difficulty of

---

"Proceedings of the Charleston City Council Committee of Ways and Means," *The Charleston Daily Courier*, January 10, 1856.

discovering the particular negros on sale in the city brought from beyond the limits of the State, and his dependence upon Brokers and others to make the return required by the Ordinance; that if this tax has not been uniformly levied, it is because of his failure to detect the particular cases of such negros being on sale, and because of the neglect or avoidance of parties in such instances to comply with the law. The Assessor further alleges that in no case or cases known to him has the party been exempted from the payment of this tax, and that when levied, subsequent to the passage of the Ordinance of 1854, he has acted under the provisions of this Ordinance, and not according to those previously in force. The Committee are of opinion that the failure or neglect of an officer, to compel parties (in previous cases) to comply with the law, and that the failure by others, through ignorance, or from any other cause, to comply with the law, constitute no valid grounds for suspending its operation in ascertained cases, to which it is strictly applicable. They therefore recommend that the prayer of the memorialist be not granted, and that the City Assessor be instructed to assess this tax on such parties as are now known to him, or may become known to him, as having sold slaves in the city from beyond the limits of the State without having paid the same. The Committee might here conclude their report without adverting to the second point of objection; the policy of the law, leaving this to be discussed when their bill for raising supplies shall be under consideration; but this topic having been introduced to public attention by the memorialist, they propose to give it a cursory and a brief review.

The Committee apprehend that this community entertains no morbid or fanatical sentiment on the subject of slavery. The discussions of the last twenty years have lead it to clear and decided opinions as to its complete consistency with moral principle, and with the highest order of civilization. It regards the removal of slaves from place to place, and their transfer from master to master, by gift, purchase or otherwise, as incidents necessarily connected with the institution. The law has refrained (and wisely, perhaps,) from defining the manner in which these rights of ownership may be exercised, leaving the usages in reference to them to the dictation and control of an intelligent and humane public sentiment. To apply these remarks. The statute law of Georgia makes it a penal offence to import into that State slaves for sale or speculation. The offender is guilty of a high misdemeanor, and the conviction, therefore, shall be punished by a fine not exceeding $500, for each and every slave so brought into that State, and by imprisonment and labor in the Penitentiary for any time not less than one year, nor longer than four years; and persons knowingly purchasing or recovering slaves so brought into Georgia, are also guilty of a high misdemeanor, and shall be fined in a sum not exceeding $500, for each slave so illegally imported. The effect of this stringent law, in force in a neighboring and a border State, was to make Charleston a mart for the sale of slaves, drawn from the slave States lying to the north of us. This community has not forgotten, that previous to the passage of the ordinance of 1854, imposing this tax of $10, it was thought a common spectacle to see troups of slaves, of all ages, and of both sexes, uniformly dressed, paraded for air, exercise and exhibition, through our streets and thoroughfares.

This spectacle of a large number of slaves, for the most part single, brought together from all quarters, without regard to family ties, for purposes purely of speculation and of cupidity, entailed upon this community by strangers, citizens of other States, was repugnant to the moral tone and sense of our people, and lead, doubtless, to the municipal regulation now complained of. The tax of $10 was, it is believed, intended to operate as a check upon the growing annoyance and evil, and the Committee think that they represent the feeling and the sentiment of this community, when they express the conviction that it will be far better that a few individual interests should suffer, and that something should be lost to the general interests of agriculture, rather than such exhibitions shall again be intruded upon it.

But it is an assumption to allege that the interest of agriculture must suffer should this tax exclude slaves, from other States, from sale in Charleston. The communications from other States of the Union, by rail roads and steamers are daily, rapid, certain and economical, and capital which seeks investment in slaves for Agricultural purposes within the State need not be defeated in its object—slaves may be brought beyond the limits of the State, and placed upon the soil, as readily as though they were brought first to Charleston, then sold and removed to the plantation. If an argument may be inferred, from a fact well known to the brokers and to others in this community, namely that the sales of slaves, the property of estates in neighboring States, Georgia and Florida for instance, have not unfrequently been transferred to Charleston, it would be that the interest of agriculture will be the better subserved by the former course, by purchases made in other States; for the expenses and risks incidental to removal would not be incurred was not a larger price than could be obtained abroad, the inducement for seeking Charleston as a market.

ROBEET [*sic*] N. GOURDIN.
WM. McBURNEY.
E. W. EDGERTON.
W. PORCHER MILES,
Mayor

READING AND DISCUSSION QUESTIONS

1. From the Council's defense of slavery, what can you infer about the historical context that shaped their response?

2. How would you characterize the tone of the Council's statement about slavery? Whom do you think the councilmen were trying to convince?

12-4 | Religious Life of Enslaved African Americans
Slave Songs of the United States (1867)

Enslaved African Americans left few written records like diaries or letters, so the attempt by historians to re-create their spiritual and intellectual world is fraught with difficulties. Spirituals, however, provide tantalizing clues to their interior lives, and historians can analyze these songs for evidence of their worldview. Masters sometimes encouraged Christian conversion among slaves, underscoring passages defending slavery as the punishment for sin, but slaves adapted Protestant Christianity to their own purposes. They rejected the interpretation to obey one's master, which whites emphasized, for a gospel of deliverance and communal salvation as seen in this spiritual, "Michael Row the Boat Ashore." Michael likely referred to the Archangel Michael, who, in the New Testament, leads God's people to victory over Satan.

Michael Row the Boat Ashore

Michael row de boat ashore, Hallelujah!
Michael boat a gospel boat, Hallelujah!
I wonder where my mudder deh [there].
See my mudder on de rock gwine home.
On de rock gwine home in Jesus' name.
Michael boat a music boat.
Gabriel blow de trumpet horn.
O you mind your boastin' talk.
Boastin' talk will sink your soul.
Brudder, lend a helpin' hand.
Sister, help for trim dat boat.
Jordan stream is wide and deep.
Jesus stand on t'oder side.
I wonder if my maussa deh.
My fader gone to unknown land.
O de Lord he plant his garden deh.
He raise de fruit for you to eat.
He dat eat shall neber die.
When de riber overflow.
O poor sinner, how you land?
Riber run and darkness comin'.
Sinner row to save your soul.

READING AND DISCUSSION QUESTIONS

1. What challenges and opportunities do historians face in using spirituals as historical evidence? How are these songs, as sources, different from diaries or letters?

William Francis Allen, Charles Pickard Ware, and Lucy McKim Garrison, *Slave Songs of the United States* (New York: A. Simpson & Co., 1867), 23–24.

2. What historical argument about the lives of slaves can you make by analyzing and interpreting the lyrics of slave songs?

3. What kinds of imagery do the song lyrics evoke? What kinds of messages do the lyrics convey?

12-5 | Southern Hospitality on Display

SUSAN DABNEY SMEDES, *Memorials of a Southern Planter* (1887)

The planter class in the Old South cultivated a self-image as benevolent stewards whose sense of *noblesse oblige* led naturally to their open hospitality and gentle nurturing of their "servants," a common euphemism for slaves. The reality was frequently at odds with the romance they created. The image was part of their broader appreciation of the differences they drew between themselves and northerners, whom they frequently viewed as less genteel, cold-fisted capitalists intruding into their affairs. Susan Smedes's memoir of her father, Thomas Smith Gregory Dabney, is a classic example of the genre: a flattering portrait of a "good master" who treated his slaves as family, and whose love and affection was returned by the grateful servants. Here, Smedes remembers holiday celebrations on her father's Burleigh plantation in Lebanon, Mississippi, where he had moved his family in the early 1830s, part of the migration of planters in search of more productive soil.

A Southern Planter

Perhaps no life was more independent than that of a Southern planter before the late war. One of the Mississippi neighbors said that he would rather be Colonel Dabney on his plantation than the President of the United States.

Managing a plantation was something like managing a kingdom. The ruler had need of a great store, not only of wisdom, but of tact and patience as well.

When there was trouble in the house the real kindness and sympathy of the servants came out. They seemed to anticipate every wish. In a thousand touching little ways they showed their desire to give all the comfort and help that lay in their power. They seemed to claim a right to share in the sorrow that was their master's, and to make it their own. It was small wonder that the master and mistress were forbearing and patient when the same servants who sorrowed with them in their affliction should, at times, be perverse in their days of prosperity. Many persons said that the Burleigh servants were treated with overindulgence. It is true that at times some of them acted like spoiled children, seeming not to know what they would have. Nothing went quite to their taste at these times. The white family would say among themselves, "What is the matter now? Why

---

Susan Dabney Smedes, *Memorials of a Southern Planter* (Baltimore: Cushings & Bailey, 1887), 115–117, 160–163.

these martyr-like looks?" Mammy Maria usually threw light on these occasions. She was disgusted with her race for posing as martyrs when there was no grievance. A striking illustration of this difficulty in making things run smoothly occurred one summer, when the family was preparing to go to the Pass. The mistress made out her list of the servants whom she wished to accompany her. She let them know that they were to be allowed extra time to get their houses and clothes in order for the three months' absence from home. Some of them answered with tears. It would be cruel to be torn from home and friends, perhaps husband and children, and not to see them for all that time. Sophia regretfully made out a new list, leaving out the most clamorous ones. There were no tears shed nor mournful looks given by the newly elected, for dear to the colored heart was the thought of change and travel. It was a secret imparted by Mammy Maria to her mistress that great was the disappointment of those who had overacted their part, thereby cutting themselves off from a much-coveted pleasure. . . .

Holiday Times on the Plantation

A life of Thomas Dabney could not be written without some reference to the Christmas at Burleigh. It was as looked forward to not only by the family and by friends in the neighborhood and at a distance, but by the house and plantation servants. The house was crowded with guests, young people and older ones too. During the holiday season Thomas and his guests were ready to accept invitations to parties in other houses, but no one in the neighborhood invited company for Christmas-Day, as, for years, everybody was expected at Burleigh on that day. On one of the nights during the holidays it was his custom to invite his former overseer and other plain neighbors to an eggnog-party. In the concoction of this beverage he took a hand himself, and the freedom and ease of the company, as they saw the master of the house beating his half of the eggs in the great china bowl, made it a pleasant scene for those who cared nothing for the eggnog.

During the holidays there were refreshments, in the old Virginia style, of more sorts than one. The oysters were roasted on the coals on the dining-room hearth, under the eyes of the guests.

Great bunches of holly and magnolia, of pine and mistletoe, were suspended from the ceiling of hall and dining-room and drawing-room.

Sometimes, not often, there was a Christmas-tree,—on one occasion one for the colored Sunday-school. One Christmas everybody hung up a sock or stocking; a long line, on the hall staircase. There were twenty-two of them, white silk stockings, black silk stockings, thread and cotton and woollen socks and stockings. And at the end of the line was, side by side with the old-fashioned homespun and home-knit sock of the head of the house, the dainty pink sock of the three-weeks-old baby.

Who of that company does not remember the morning scramble over the stockings and the notes in prose and poetry that tumbled out!

The children's nurses modestly hung their stockings up by the nursery fireplace.

Music and dancing and cards and games of all sorts filled up a large share of the days and half the nights. The plantation was as gay as the house. The negroes in their holiday clothes were enjoying themselves in their own houses and in the "great house" too. A visit of a day to one of the neighboring towns was considered by them necessary to the complete enjoyments of the holidays.

They had their music and dancing too. The sound of the fiddles and banjos, and the steady rhythm of their dancing feet, floated on the air by day and night to the Burleigh house. But a time came when this was to cease. The whole plantation joined the Baptist church. Henceforth not a musical note nor the joyful motion of a negro's foot was ever again heard on the plantation. "I done buss' my fiddle an' my banjo, an' done fling 'em 'way," the most music-loving fellow on the place said to the preacher, when asked for his religious experience. It was surely the greatest sacrifice of feeling that such a race could make. Although it was a sin to have music and dancing of their own, it was none to enjoy that at the "great house." They filled the porches and doors, and in serried ranks stood men, women, and children, gazing as long as the music and dancing went on. Frequently they stood there till the night was more than half gone. In the crowd of faces could be recognized the venerable ones of the aged preachers, surrounded by their flocks.

Christmas was incomplete until the master of the house had sung his songs. He was full of action and gesture. His family used to say that although he was in character and general bearing an Englishman, his French blood asserted itself in his manner. In his motions he was quick, and at times, when he chose to make them so, very amusing, yet too full of grace to be undignified. He was fond of dancing, and put fresh interest in it, as he did in everything that he joined in.

On Christmas mornings the servants delighted in catching the family with "Christmas giff!" "Christmas giff!" betimes in the morning. They would spring out of unexpected corners and from behind doors on the young masters and mistresses. At such times there was an affectionate throwing off of the reserve and decorum of every-day life.

"Hi! ain't dis Chris'mus?" one of the quietest and most low-voiced of the maid-servants asked, in a voice as loud as a sea-captain's. One of the ladies of the house had heard an unfamiliar and astonishingly loud laugh under her window, and had ventured to put an inquiring head out.

In times of sorrow, when no Christmas or other festivities gladdened the Mississippi home, the negroes felt it sensibly. "It 'pears so lonesome; it mak' me feel bad not to see no comp'ny comin'," our faithful Aunt Abby said on one of these occasions. Her post as the head maid rendered her duties onerous when the house was full of guests. We had thought that she would be glad to have a quiet Christmas, which she could spend by her own fireside, instead of attending to the wants of a houseful of young people.

In the presence of the guests, unless they were old friends, the dignity of the family required that no light behavior should be indulged in, even though it were Christmas. In no hands was the dignity of the family so safe as with negro slaves. A negro was as proud of the "blood" of his master and mistress as if it had been his own. Indeed, they greatly magnified the importance of their owners, and were readily affronted if aspersion of any sort were cast on their master's family. It was very humiliating to them, for they are all aristocrats by nature, to belong to what they call "poor white trash."

Our steady Lewis was often sent to take us to evening entertainments, on account of his being so quiet and nice in his ways. On one of these occasions he became so incensed that he refused to set his foot on that plantation again. Mammy Maria informed us of the cause of Lewis's anger. One of the maids in the house in which we were spending the evening had insulted him by saying that her mistress wore more trimming on her clothes than his young ladies did!

READING AND DISCUSSION QUESTIONS

1. Analyze and evaluate Smedes's description of the family's relationship with the slaves living and working at the Burleigh plantation. What point of view about the slaves' feelings toward the family does she emphasize?

2. From the portrait Smedes offers of her father, what do you imagine his reaction would have been had one of his slaves escaped, like the slave in Coffin's anecdote?

3. Analyze the role hospitality played in shaping a southern planter's perception of his roles and responsibilities on the plantation and within the broader community. To what extent did his welcoming generosity have political implications? What role did slaves play in the hospitality of the plantation?

12-6 | Free Blacks Push for Elevation of the Race
Proceedings of the Colored National Convention (1848)

Frederick Douglass (1818–1895) was busy in 1848. In July, he attended the women's rights convention at Seneca Falls, New York, speaking eloquently on behalf of women's right to vote. In September, Douglass was in Cleveland, Ohio, presiding over the Colored National Convention of free African Americans. This convention, attended only by African American men, was part of the era's "convention movement," an organizational approach to reform that emphasized collective action. This meeting endorsed a series of resolutions addressed to the "mutual improvement and social elevation" of free blacks.

2. Resolved, That whatever is necessary for the elevation of one class is necessary for the elevation of another; the respectable industrial occupations, as mechanical trades, farming or agriculture, mercantile and professional

Report of the Proceedings of the Colored National Convention, Held at Cleveland, Ohio, on Wednesday, September 6, 1848 (Rochester, NY: Printed by John Dick, at the North Star Office, 1848), 13–17.

business, wealth and education, being necessary for the elevation of the whites; therefore those attainments are necessary for the elevation of us. Adopted.

3. Resolved, That we impressively recommend to our brethren throughout the country, the necessity of obtaining a knowledge of mechanical trade, farming, mercantile business, the learned professions, as well as the accumulation of wealth, — as the essential means of elevating us as a class. — Adopted.

4. Resolved, That the occupation of domestics and servants among our people is degrading to us as a class, and we deem it our bounden duty to discountenance such pursuits, except where necessity compels the person to resort thereto as a means of livelihood.

5. Resolved, That as Education is necessary in all departments, we recommend to our people, as far as in their power lies, to give their children especially, a business Education.

6. Resolved, That the better to unite and concentrate our efforts as a people, we recommend the formation of an association, to be known as the ———. [Referred to a Committee, and subsequently the whole Resolution referred to the next Convention.]

7. Resolved, That while our efforts shall be entirely moral in their tendency, it is no less the duty of this Convention to take Cognizance of the Political action of our brethren, and recommend to them that course which shall best promote the cause of Liberty and Humanity.

8. Resolved, That we recommend to our brethren throughout the several states, to support no person or party, let the name or pretensions be what they may, that shall not have for their object the establishment of equal rights and privileges, without distinction of color, clime or condition.

9. Resolved, That holding Liberty paramount to all earthly considerations, we pledge ourselves, to resist properly, every attempt to infringe upon our rights.

10. Resolved, That Slavery is the greatest curse ever inflicted on man, being of hellish origin, the legitimate offspring of the Devil, and we therefore pledge ourselves, individually, to use all justifiable means for its speedy and immediate over-throw.

11. Whereas a knowledge of the real moral, social, and political condition of our people is not only desirable but absolutely essential to the intelligent prosecution of measures for our elevation and improvement, and whereas our present isolated condition makes the attainment of such knowledge exceedingly difficult, Therefore Resolved, That this National Convention does hereby request the colored ministers and others [*sic*] persons throughout the Northern States, to collect, or cause to be collected accurate statistics of the condition of our people, during the coming year, in the various stations and circuits in which they may find themselves located, and that they be, and hereby are requested to prepare lists, stating —
1st. The number of colored persons in the localities where they may be stationed; their general moral and social condition; and especially how many

are farmers and mechanics, how many are merchants or storekeepers, how many are teachers, lawyers, doctors, ministers, and editors; how many are known to take and pay for newspapers; how many literary, debating, and other societies, for moral, mental, and social improvement; and that said ministers be, and hereby are, respectfully requested to forward all such information to a Committee of one, who shall be appointed for this purpose, and that the said Committee of one be requested to make out a synopsis of such information and to report the same to the next colored National Convention.

12. Resolved, That Temperance is another great lever for Elevation, which we would urge upon our people and all others to use, and earnestly recommend the formation of societies for its promotion.

13. Resolved, That while we heartily engage in recommending to our people the Free Soil movement, and the support of the Buffalo Convention, nevertheless we claim and are determined to maintain the higher standard and more liberal views which have heretofore characterized us as abolitionists.

14. Resolved, That as Liberty is a right inherent in man, and cannot be arrested without the most flagrant outrage, we recommend to our brethren in bonds, to embrace every favorable opportunity of effecting their escape.

15. Resolved, that we pledge ourselves individually, to use all justifiable means in aiding our enslaved brethren in escaping from the Southern Prison House of Bondage.

16. Resolved, that we recommend to the colored people every where, to use every just effort in getting their children into schools, in common with others in their several locations.

17. Whereas, American Slavery is politically and morally an evil of which this country stands guilty, and cannot be abolished alone through the instrumentality of moral suasion and whereas the two great political parties of the Union have by their acts and nominations betrayed the sacred cause of human freedom, and

    Whereas, a Convention recently assembled in the city of Buffalo having for its object the establishment of a party in support of free soil for a free people, and Whereas said Convention adopted for its platform the following noble expression, viz; "Free Soil, Free Speech, Free Labor and Free Men," and believing these expressions well calculated to increase the interest now felt in behalf of the down-trodden and oppressed of this land; therefore,

    Resolved, That we recommend to all colored persons in possession of the right of the elective Franchise, the nominees of that body for their suffrages, and earnestly request all good citizens to use their united efforts to secure their election to the chief offices in the gift of the people.

    Resolved, that the great Free Soil Party of the United States, is bound together by a common sentiment expressing the wish of a large portion of the people of this Union, and that we hail with delight this great movement as the dawn of a bright and more auspicious day. [The Resolutions were rejected, but the Preamble prefixed to the 13th Resolution.]

18. Resolved, That Love to God and man, and Fidelity to ourselves ought to be the great motto which we will urge upon our people. . . .

23. Resolved, That among the means instrumental in the elevation of a people there is none more effectual than a well-conducted and efficient newspaper; and believing the North Star, published and edited by Frederick Douglass and M. R. Delany at Rochester, fully to answer all the ends and purposes of a national press, we therefore recommend its support to the colored people throughout North America.

24. Resolved, That the Convention recommend to the colored citizens of the several Free States, to assemble in Mass State Conventions annually, and petition the Legislatures thereof to repeal the Black Laws, or all laws militating against the interests of colored people.

25. Whereas, we firmly believe with the Fathers of '76, that "taxation and representation ought to go together"; therefore,
    Resolved, That we are very much in doubt as to the propriety of our paying any tax upon which representation is based, until we are permitted to be represented.

26. Resolved, That, as a body, the professed Christian American Churches generally, by their support, defence, and participation in the damning sin of American Slavery, as well as cruel prejudice and proscription of the nominally free colored people, have forfeited every claim of confidence on our part, and therefore merit our severest reprobation.

27. Resolved, That Conventions of a similar character to this are well calculated to enhance the interests of suffering humanity, and the colored people generally, and that we recommend such assemblages to the favorable consideration of our people.

28. Resolved, That the next National Convention of Colored Freemen shall be held in Detroit, Michigan, or at Pittsburgh, Pa., some time in the year 1850.

29. Resolved, That among the many oppressive schemes against the colored people in the United States, we view the American Colonization Society as the most deceptive and hypocritical—"clothed with the livery of heaven to serve the devil in," with President Roberts, of Liberia, a colored man, for its leader.

30. Resolved, That we tender to the citizens of Cleveland our unfeigned thanks for the noble resolution passed by them in approval of the doings of this Convention.

31. Resolved, That the prejudice against color, so called, is vulgar, unnatural, and wicked in the sight of God, and wholly unknown in any country where slavery does not exist. . . .

33. Whereas, we fully believe in the equality of the sexes, therefore,
    Resolved, That we hereby invite females hereafter to take part in our deliberations.

34. Whereas, a portion of those of our colored citizens called barbers, by refusing to treat colored men on equality with the whites, do encourage prejudice among the whites of the several States; therefore,

Resolved, That we recommend to this class of men a change in their course of action relative to us; and if this change is not immediately made, we consider them base serviles, worthy only of the condemnation, censure, and defamation of all lovers of liberty, equality, and right.

READING AND DISCUSSION QUESTIONS

1. Summarize the goals and means of achieving them as adopted by the delegates to the Colored National Convention. What can you infer about their approach to reform from the resolutions they passed?

2. How do the resolutions passed by the convention reflect the historical context of reform and politics during the antebellum period?

▪ COMPARATIVE QUESTIONS ▪

1. Explain and evaluate the multiple perspectives on southern slavery to identify similarities and differences in the way the institution was perceived during the period. To what extent do the points of view of these sources impact the interpretation of slavery they present?

2. How can you interpret the historical evidence in this chapter to construct an argument about the lives of enslaved African Americans? What evidence might point to ways slaves exercised some degree of power and autonomy within a system of white dominance?

3. How do your insights about the historical context of antebellum slavery help you understand the broader history of American race relations?

4. In addition to slave songs, what types of primary source evidence would help historians understand slavery from the perspective of the slaves themselves, most of whom left no written records?

5. What historical patterns of continuity or change concerning the politics of slavery can you observe, comparing 1850s Charleston with Luis Brandaon's 1610 letter (Document 1-6), Virginia's slave codes (Document 3-3), and the free blacks' 1777 petition (Document 6-3)?

DOCUMENT SET

Environment and Identity in an Age of Revolutions
1800–1860

The profound political, economic, and social transformations we associate with the period from the early republic to the Civil War took place within a physical context shaped by North America's environment, geography, and climate. America was largely an agricultural nation, and its climate and geography drove economic and political decisions and forged distinctive regional identities. The rocky soil and short growing season of the Northeast, for example, discouraged the adoption of the plantation system, which took root instead on the arable soils of the more temperate southern states.

The physical environment and conditions Americans faced evoked different responses manifested in the ways they chose to interpret, preserve, manage, or exploit the natural world. Most often, nature presented challenges to overcome, as was the case for farmers who had to clear the land of trees before sowing seeds or canal workers who had to dig ditches to enable waterborne commerce. Nature also provided riches in the form of agricultural bounty and deposits of minerals and precious metals, which Americans commoditized to fuel their growing economy. The landscape could also inspire with its transcendent beauty. Americans' complex interaction with nature both constrained and shaped the lives they led and the world they created.

P4-1 | Commerce Overcomes Nature's Obstacles
Canal Commissioners of Ohio Contract (c. 1820s)

The 1820s was a "canal era" in America's economic development. The Erie Canal was completed in 1825, connecting New York's Hudson River to the Great Lakes. Its success inspired other efforts, including Ohio's canal network. These internal improvements had obvious economic benefits, but they were also marvels of engineering and labor. As the canal commissioners who superintended the planning and construction of these canals well understood, the projects pitted man's ingenuity and effort against the obstacles of geography imposed by nature. The commissioners' articles of agreement with contractors reveal their confidence in man's ability to triumph over nature.

ARTICLES OF AN AGREEMENT, made and concluded this——day of——in the year——between——of the one part, and the canal commissioners of the State of Ohio, for and on behalf of the said State, of the other part, whereby it is covenanted and agreed as follows, to-wit: the said part——of the first part contract and agree to construct, in a good, substantial, and workmanlike manner, all that part of the line of the Ohio canal, which is included in section——reference being herein had to the location and map of the said line made by——engineer agreeably to the following plan, that is to say: First, in all places where the natural surface of the earth is above the bottom of the canal and where the line requires excavation, all the trees, saplings, bushes, stumps, and roots shall be grubbed and dug up at least sixty feet wide; that is, thirty-three on the towing path side of the center, and twenty-seven feet on the opposite side of the centre of the canal, and together with all logs, brush, and wood of every description, shall be removed at least fifteen feet beyond the outward line of the said grubbing on each side; and on said space of fifteen feet on each side of said grubbing, all trees, saplings, bushes, and stumps shall be cut down close to the ground, so that no part of any of them shall be left more than one foot in height above the natural surface of the earth, and shall also, together with all logs, brush, and wood of every kind, be removed entirely from said space. And the trees, saplings, and bushes shall also be cut down twenty feet wide on each side of said space, so as to be cleared, and also all trees which in falling would be liable to break or injure the banks of the canal. And no part of the trees, saplings, brush, stumps, wood or rubbish of any kind shall be felled, laid, or deposited on either of the sections adjoining this contract. Second: The canal and banks shall be so constructed and formed, by excavation or embankment, as either or both may be necessary, in order to bring the same to the proper level, as designated by the engineers or either of them in the employ of said commissioners, so that the water may in all places be at least forty feet wide in the canal at the surface, twenty-six feet wide at the bottom, and four feet deep; each of the banks shall be at least two feet,

---

Concerning the Ohio Canals, Which Are to Connect Lake Erie with the Ohio River, Comprising a Complete Official History of These Great Works of Internal Improvement (Columbus, OH: John Kilbourn, 1828), 212–216.

perpendicular measurement, above the top water line; and such a slope shall be preserved on the inner side of the banks, both above and below the top water line, that every foot perpendicular rise in said banks shall give a horizontal base of one foot nine inches; the towing path, which shall be made on such side of the canal as said commissioners or either of them, or any engineer in their employ may direct, shall be at least ten feet wide at its surface, and not more than five feet in any place above the top water line. . . . All loose and porous materials, and those which are perishable or permeable to water shall occupy the outer extremities of the bank, and for the distance of at least ten feet, measured outwardly from extremity of the top water line on each side, the banks shall be composed, both above and below the top water line, of the most pure, solid, compact and water tight earth which the adjoining excavation can supply: and no vegetable mould, leaves, roots, grass, weeds, herbage, logs, sticks, brush, or any other substance of a porous or perishable nature, shall be left, laid or in any way admitted into the said space of ten feet last described. Third: In all cases of embankment, and where the bottom line of canal is above the natural surface of the earth, all the trees, bushes, saplings and stumps, on the space to be occupied by the canal and its banks, shall be cut close to the ground, and together with all logs, brush and wood of every description, shall be removed from a space of at least forty-five feet wide on each side of the centre of the canal. . . .

The lock shall be so constructed that the chamber will be 90 feet in length and 15 in breadth in the clear. The walls of the lock shall be of solid masonry laid in water cement, and well grouted with water cement as frequently as once in every two feet, as the walls progress in height from the bottom. The walls shall be five feet in thickness at the bottom of the lock, and four feet at the top water line of the upper canal, with buttresses firmly united and connected with the main wall, and rising from the bottom of the lock to the top water line, four feet in length each and extending back from the main wall four feet. These buttresses shall be 12 feet apart (measuring from centre to centre). Buttresses shall be so built that 20 feet in length of the walls opposite the upper gates, and 17 feet in length opposite the lower lock gates shall be 9 feet thick at bottom and 8 feet at the top water line. The face of the walls shall be laid in courses; the stone forming each course to be of uniform thickness throughout the course, well bedded and the joints well cut so as to make tight joints at least six inches back from the face of the wall. The face of the stones shall be rough cut or hammer dressed, except at the hollow quoins, which shall be cut smooth and true, agreeably to a pattern to be furnished by the engineer. When the face stone are of coarse sandstone or free-stone, each course shall be at least one foot in thickness, and in all other cases not less than 10 inches. No face stone shall have in any place less than one foot bed, and in no case less bed than face. Binders or headers shall be placed in each course, extending from the face back through the main wall, so as not to leave more than ten feet in any one place between headers. The headers in each successive course shall be placed over the space between the headers in the next course beneath; and the face stones shall not be more than half an inch thinner on the back than on the face; culverts, to be formed with stone cut to the proper pattern, shall be constructed in the walls to pass the water from the upper canal into the chamber of the lock, with proper gates, all to be of such form and dimensions as the engineer having charge of the work may direct. The walls shall be covered with a copeing of firm, solid stone, of not less than three feet in width, well cut, jointed and bedded, and those next the gates securely cramped together with iron cramps. . . . The foundation of the lock unless a smooth and firm rock foundation can be obtained, shall be composed of solid white oak timber, hewed square, and one foot in thickness, to be laid horizontally across the foundation, level and even as near together as such engineer may direct, and well puddled between the timbers and covered with three inch white oak or pine plank free from knots, rots or shakes, well jointed and firmly tunneled or spiked to the timber beneath; a flooring composed of two inch white oak pine plank, free from rots, knots or shakes, well jointed and securely spiked with spikes ten inches in length, shall be laid throughout the whole chamber of the lock. . . .

And the said part——of the first part further covenant and agree to erect and build, in a good, substantial and workmanlike manner, a culvert or culverts in such place or places, and of such form, dimensions and plan, as the Commissioners or either of them, the Resident Engineer, or any other engineer in the employ of said Commissioners, may direct, which shall in all cases be built of good substantial stone, laid in water cement, and made true and smooth, on the outer as well as in the inner side. And the said part——of the first part further agree to construct a mole or pier of such breadth and height as said Commissioners or the engineer having superintendence of the work under them may direct, along the wash or slate banks on said section. Said mole shall be formed of good, solid, durable timber, of which that forming the sides of the mole shall be well hewed, and shall be at least twelve inches square and at least 25 feet in length; the sides shall be laid perpendicularly and securely connected together with ties not less than 10 inches in diameter, clear of bark, which shall be let into the side timbers with a dove tail and square shoulder at each end well fitted to said timbers so as to prevent their moving or sliding upon each other. Each tie shall be let into the timbers, on which it rests, half the thickness of the dove tail at the end, and the other half shall be let into the side timber next above, so that the side timbers will meet and form a tight joint, and the ends of the ties shall be cut off smooth and even with the outside of the mole. The cribs so formed shall be filled with slate, soap stone, or other stone or gravel, and a bank shall be formed on the inner side, next the canal, of the usual slope, of good solid earth as in other cases. The moles so formed shall at each end be securely united with the bank of the canal. All of which shall be done agreeably to the directions of the engineer having charge of the work. . . .

And it is further agreed, that whenever this contract, in the opinion of the inspector aforesaid, shall have been completely performed, in every respect, on the part of the said part—— of the first part, the said inspector shall certify the same in writing under his hand, together with his estimate of the amount of the various kinds of work herein specified . . . for the grubbing——for clearing and removing the vegetable substances, agreeably to the terms of this contract,——, for earth excavation, estimated all earth necessarily excavated between and under the banks, including loose pieces of rock, or stones, of less than one-fourth of a cubic yard each, (which are to be estimated as earth excavation,)——cents per cubic yard: for the excavation of all solid rock which may occur in this contract,——cents per cubic yard: for excavation of loose or detached pieces of rock or stones, (those only to be estimated under this item which are over one-fourth of a cubic yard each,) at the rate of——cents per cubic yard: for each cubic yard of embankment necessarily made, (to be measured in the bank)——cents: provided, that where any embankment is or can be formed in whole or in part from earth necessarily excavated in the construction of the adjoining parts of the canal, nothing shall be allowed for such embankment, or such part thereof as is, or can be, so formed, unless the earth to form the same shall be necessarily removed over one hundred feet: for each perch of mason work (of 16½ cubic feet) laid into the lock, agreeably to the plan furnished, or the direction of the Commissioners or either of them, the Resident Engineer, or other engineer in the employ of said Commissioners, to be measured in the wall, the sum of——which price is understood to include the expense of the foundation, lock gates, timber and iron work connected with the lock, sheet piling, puddling and securing the head, sides, and foundation of the lock, from the passage of the water around or under the lock. . . .

It is further understood that all payments made by the commissioners, under this contract, are to be by draft or check on——or other bank or agent of the Commissioners of the canal fund, where, or with whom, deposits of money may from time to time be made for the construction of the canal.

READING AND DISCUSSION QUESTIONS

1. What evidence does this contract provide for understanding the relationship between America's commercial development and the natural world?

2. To what extent does the confidence of canal builders as evidenced in this article of agreement reflect the historical context of the 1820s Market Revolution?

P4-2 | Cultivating the "Garden of Graves"

JOSEPH STORY, *Address Delivered on the Dedication of the Cemetery at Mount Auburn* (1831)

The rural cemetery movement in America began in the early 1830s when Jacob Bigelow's idea of domesticating a landscape into a parklike setting for the final repose of the deceased won approval and resulted in the opening outside Boston of the Mount Auburn Cemetery. This idealization of nature ran counter to earlier landscape manipulations of the eighteenth century, which had emphasized formal, symmetrical plans. At Mount Auburn and similar sites that followed, the living were intended to enjoy the cemetery as a place of recreation and leisure in a cultivated setting "improved" by man's design and management. Massachusetts native Joseph Story, associate justice of the Supreme Court, participated in the dedication ceremonies opening Mount Auburn, where he was interred when he died in 1845.

A rural Cemetery seems to combine in itself all the advantages, which can be proposed to gratify human feelings, or tranquillize human fears; to secure the best religious influences, and to cherish all those associations, which cast a cheerful light over the darkness of the grave.

And what spot can be more appropriate than this for such a purpose? Nature seems to point it out with significant energy, as the favourite retirement for the dead. There are around us all the varied features of her beauty and grandeur—the forest-crowned height; the abrupt acclivity; the sheltered valley; the deep glen; the grassy glade, and the silent grove. Here are the lofty oak, the beech, that "wreathes its old fantastick roots so high," the rustling pine, and the drooping willow;—the tree, that sheds its pale leaves with every autumn, a fit emblem of our own transitory bloom; and the evergreen, with its perennial shoots, instructing us, that "the wintry blast of death kills not the buds of virtue." Here is the thick shrubbery, to protect and conceal the new-made grave; and there is the wild-flower creeping along the narrow path, and planting its seeds in the upturned earth. All around us there breathes a solemn calm, as if we were in the bosom of a wilderness, broken only by the breeze as it murmurs through the tops of the forest, or by the notes of the warbler pouring forth his matin or his evening song.

Ascend but a few steps, and what a change of scenery to surprise and delight us. We seem, as it were, in an instant, to pass from the confines of death to the bright and balmy regions of life. Below us flows the winding Charles, with its rippling current, like the stream of time hastening to the ocean of eternity. In the distance, the City,—at once the object of our admiration and our love,—rears its proud eminences, its glittering spires, its lofty towers, its graceful mansions, its curling smoke, its crowded haunts of business and pleasure, which speak to the eye, and yet leave a noiseless loneliness on the ear. Again we turn, and the walls of our venerable University rise before us, with many a recollection of happy

Joseph Story, *An Address Delivered on the Dedication of the Cemetery at Mount Auburn, September 24, 1831* (Boston: Joseph T. & Edwin Buckingham, 1831), 16–22.

days passed there in the interchange of study and friendship, and many a grateful thought of the affluence of its learning, which has adorned and nourished the literature of our country. Again we turn, and the cultivated farm, the neat cottage, the village church, the sparkling lake, the rich valley, and the distant hills, are before us through opening vistas; and we breathe amidst the fresh and varied labours of man.

There is, therefore, within our reach, every variety of natural and artificial scenery, which is fitted to awaken emotions of the highest and most affecting character. We stand, as it were, upon the borders of two worlds; and as the mood of our minds may be, we may gather lessons of profound wisdom by contrasting the one with the other, or indulge in the dreams of hope and ambition, or solace our hearts by melancholy meditations.

Who is there that in the contemplation of such a scene, is not ready to exclaim, with the enthusiasm of the Poet,

Mine be the breezy hill, that skirts the down,
Where a green, grassy turf is all I crave,
With here and there a violet bestrown,
Fast by a brook, or fountain's murmuring wave,
And many an evening sun shine sweetly on my grave.

And we are met here to consecrate this spot, by these solemn ceremonies, to such a purpose. The Legislature of this Commonwealth, with a parental foresight, has clothed the Horticultural Society with authority (if I may use its own language) to make a perpetual dedication of it, as a Rural Cemetery or Burying-Ground, and to plant and embellish it with shrubbery, and flowers, and trees, and walks, and other rural ornaments. And I stand here, by the order and in behalf of this Society, to declare that, by these services, it is to be deemed henceforth and for ever so dedicated. Mount Auburn, in the noblest sense, belongs no longer to the living, but to the dead. It is a sacred, it is an eternal trust. It is consecrated ground. May it remain forever inviolate!

What a multitude of thoughts crowd upon the mind in the contemplation of such a scene. How much of the future, even in its far distant reaches, rises before us with all its persuasive realities. Take but one little narrow space of time, and how affecting are its associations! Within the flight of one half century, how many of the great, the good, and the wise will be gathered here! How many in the loveliness of infancy, the beauty of youth, the vigour of manhood, and the maturity of age, will lie down here, and dwell in the bosom of their mother earth! The rich and the poor, the gay and the wretched, the favourites of thousands, and the forsaken of the world, the stranger in his solitary grave, and the patriarch surrounded by the kindred of a long lineage! How many will here bury their brightest hopes, or blasted expectations! How many bitter tears will here be shed! How many agonizing sighs will here be heaved! How many trembling feet will cross the pathways, and returning, leave behind them the dearest objects of their reverence or their love!

And if this were all, sad indeed, and funereal would be our thoughts; gloomy, indeed, would be these shades, and desolate these prospects.

But—thanks be to God—the evils, which he permits, have their attendant mercies, and are blessings in disguise. The bruised reed will not be laid utterly prostrate. The wounded heart will not always bleed. The voice of consolation will spring up in the midst of the silence of these regions of death. The mourner will revisit these shades with a secret, though melancholy pleasure. The hand of friendship will delight to cherish the flowers, and the shrubs, that fringe the lowly grave, or the sculptured monument. The earliest beams of the morning will play upon these summits with a refreshing cheerfulness; and the lingering tints of evening hover on them with a tranquilizing glow. Spring will invite thither the footsteps of the young by its opening foliage; and Autumn detain the contemplative by its latest bloom. The votary of learning and science will here learn to elevate his genius by the holiest studies. The devout will here offer up the silent tribute of pity, or the prayer of gratitude. The rivalries of the world will here drop from the heart; the spirit of forgiveness will gather new impulses; the selfishness of avarice will be checked; the restlessness of ambition will be rebuked; vanity will let fall its plumes; and pride, as it sees "what shadows we are, and what shadows we pursue," will acknowledge the value of virtue as far, immeasurably far, beyond that of fame. . . .

Let us banish then, the thought, that this is to be the abode of a gloom, which will haunt the imagination by its terrors, or chill the heart by its solitude. Let us cultivate feelings and sentiments more worthy of ourselves, and more worthy of Christianity. Here let us erect the memorials of our love, and our gratitude, and our glory. Here let the brave repose, who have died in the cause of their country. Here let the statesman rest, who has achieved the victories of peace, not less renowned than war. Here let genius find a home, that has sung immortal strains, or has instructed with still diviner eloquence. Here let learning and science, the votaries of inventive art, and the teacher of the philosophy of nature come. Here let youth and beauty, blighted by premature decay, drop, like tender blossoms, into the virgin earth; and here let age retire, ripened for the harvest. Above all, here let the benefactors of mankind, the good, the merciful, the meek, the pure in heart, be congregated; for to them belongs an undying praise. And let us take comfort, nay, let us rejoice, that in future ages, long after we are gathered to the generations of other days, thousands of kindling hearts will here repeat the sublime declaration, "Blessed are the dead, that die in the Lord, for they rest from their labors; and their works do follow them."

READING AND DISCUSSION QUESTIONS

1. From Story's dedication, what can you infer about emerging American attitudes toward nature in the 1830s? What values does Story ascribe to the landscape?

2. How does Story summarize the benefits of this cultivated cemetery for both the living and the dead? What interaction with the landscape does Story anticipate his audience will experience?

P4-3 | A Woman's Perspective on the Overland Journey West
EMMELINE B. WELLS, *Diary* (1846)

The bucolic setting Joseph Story described contrasts with the unforgiving landscape through which Emmeline Wells journeyed in the mid-1840s, part of a Mormon exodus leaving Nauvoo, Illinois. The Mormons, or Latter-day Saints, a Christian denomination founded by Joseph Smith in 1830, were persecuted for their beliefs and practices. At Nauvoo in 1844 and 1845, a political crisis precipitated the Mormon flight westward to Utah. Wells fled with her family, keeping a diary that describes some of the trials they endured and highlights the environmental factors that constrained and shaped her experiences heading west.

Sun. March 1, 1846

In the morning I awakened out of a sound sleep and saw Mary was preparing breakfast and the word was be ready to go at twelve o'clock we took breakfast; picked up and packed off as soon as possible, I rode with Orson in his wagon, about one o'clock we took up a line of march and left Sugar Creek, travelled over a very bad muddy road, reached the encampment about four o'clock, formed a line with the wagons, pitched their tents, made their fires and soon had a place fitted and prepared to pass the night. We are all happy and contented as yet and determined to go ahead.

Mon. March 2, 1846

This morning was warm and sunny the most pleasant day we have had since we left the city we stared behind the principal part of the teams. the first hill we came to a balking horse they had in the family wagon began to show his obstinacy and hindered us considerably we went on about seven miles and camped in a hollow with Br. Kimball's company Joseph's teams had gone on with the company ahead of us. and he was obliged to tent with his father. Sarah and I had a bed in the wagon and slept first-rate.

Tues. March 3, 1846

This morning [we] arose early and Sarah Ann taking her mother in her carriage and Joseph on horse back beside them went on to overtake their teams. After breakfast Loenza Maria and I took a walk in the woods just behind the tent we found stems of strawberry leaves green and fresh I intend to keep them as a memorial of the time when we returned we found they were about starting Ann and I came up the hill which was very long on foot seated our selves on a prostrate log and here I am at the present time scribbling. We reached the place of encampment about noon having travelled 3 miles finding almost all of the teams had gone we proceeded on our journey together with Joseph he having waited

Diaries of Emmeline B. Wells, Library of Congress (http://memory.loc.gov/cgi-in/query /r?ammem/upbover:@field(DOCID+@lit(dia55744).

for our coming. About ___ miles ride brought us to Farmington a very pritty Western town. Here we saw thirty or more loafers loitering around the Groceries &c. Porter Rockwell on his mule rode up among them all armed and equipped which seemed to excite some of them considerably there being those there who knew him and they were overheard talking by themselves in a low tone of shooting &c. saying there would never be a better chance however nothing occurred of consequence. From the village we had a very bad road it was so dreadful muddy and crooked. Some of us walked along on the bank of the. Des moine considerable distance the roads being so exceedingly bad the horses could scarcly draw their loads. It was after dark when we came in sight of the camp and a dismal looking [place] it is the tents are all huddled in together and the [horses and] wagons are interspersed some are singing and laughing some are praying children crying &c. every sound may be heard from one tent to another; it is late and I must retire.

Wednesday March 4, 1846

We have stopped all day in order to recruit the teams they being nearly tired out after dragging through the mud. We have washed mended visited &c. It has been a very pleasant day.

Thursday March 5, 1846

This morn we started at ten o' clock. I walked perhaps a mile and a half along the shore of the Desmoine river when Porter came riding on his mule and said that [one of] Mr Whitney wagons had broke down I then went back to the wagons they were not yet up the first hill they took the load from the broken wagon and put it on another and hitched on the horses. We travelled about three miles and came to the village of Bonaparte a very pretty Western town here we forded the river; it was very bad travelling and continued to grow worse; we went about a mile farther and camped on the bank of the river where we have an excellent view of Bona. The rest of the company have gone on about two miles farther there are only the two families camped here.

Friday March 6, 1846

This morning at ten o clock we were again on the road which we found very muddy and bad until we came to the prairie there it was better. We arrived at the camp about three in the P.M. having travelled about eight miles the teams were very tired and so were some of the folks, we found they were on very damp ground by the side of a little muddy brook. After the tents were pitched Mr Whitney and Orson made a rustic bedstead of poles for Sarah.

Saturday March 7, 1846

This morning about the time we were ready to start a man by the name of Cochrun came and laid claim to a yoke of oxen belonging to Mr W. said they strayed or were stolen from him three years before to avoid trouble Mr. M paid him his price which was thirty dollars in gold. This day we have had rather better roads we travelled about nine miles and camped in a pleasant valley by a small stream of water about three miles from the principal encampment.

Sunday March 8, 1846

Today we have been detained in consequence of Sarah's being sick she has a fine boy her father has named this place the Valley of David in honor of the child it is situated in Iowa [2½ miles East of Richardson's] Point Chequest township Van Buren Co. At evening Brigham & Heber came down from the camp with Mary Ann Young & Vilate Kimball their wives, and, took supper and blessed the child; it has been a lovely day, warm and beautiful.

Monday March 9, 1846

About noon William Kimball came with an easy carriage, to convey S__ to the camp; she started about two o'clock Horace and I rode in the buggy behind them, the teams followed after, all arrived in safety about four o'clock. Pitched their tents on the side hill, next to Dr. Kimball, the tents here in rows like [a] city; it is really a houseless village. Just at dusk the band commenced playing and some of the young people collected and amused themselves by dancing.

Tuesday March 10, 1846

This is a stormy day, a part of the camp intended to have moved on but it impossible; it is very muddy without yet the tents seem to be quite dry. Tuesday night at twelve o'clock the tent hooks on one side gave way and the tent pole leaned but from being on guard saved it from falling. The rain is pouring down in torrents here and there it sprinkles through the tent yet we keep a good fire and are quite comfortable.

Wednesday March 11, 1846

Today I slept till one o'clock after being up all night the rain had beat through the tent and wet my pillow and the quilts but I did not take cold Mrs W. has been quite [unwell] all day Sarah gets along finely. Horace has gone to Keosaugua to a concert I am sitting up again tonight.

Thursday March 12, 1846

It has been an unpleasant day at times a slow drizzly rain and then thick clouds gloomy and dismal they are all asleep around me Sarah is not quite so well to night.

March 19, 1846

We continued in this place being prevented by the mud until Thursday the 19. we then proceeded on our journey Sarah had an ox wagon fixed to ride in we left about eleven o'clock we had not gone far before S__ began to grow sick from the easy rocking of the wagon and she was no better until we arrived at the stopping place

Friday March 20, 1846

This day has been cold and chilly we had a stove fixed in the wagon and a bed for Sarah; her mother, and I rode there with her we had pretty good road all day travelled about fouteen miles stopped in a mean damp place Sarah stayed in in her wagon and had a fire all night.

Saturday March 21, 1846

This morning we started at ten o'clock had a pretty decent road most of the way travelled eleven miles and camped in a pleasant place almost at the outside of the camp it has been a dark gloomy day.

Sunday March 22, 1846

This morning about nine o'clock we left the camp went about a mile and came to the bottoms they were not so bad as we had anticipated after we got across the bottom we went into the wood came in sight of the camp crossed the Chariton river here the scene was indescribable some in a boat teams wading through and men dragging them up the hill with a long rope the banks were very steep and muddy and the road very bad for a mile beyond one very long steep hill where they had to double team just at the top of the hill was the camp we came on beyond all the rest so we might be a little more retired. it is quite a pleasant situation here we all rejoice that we came over the river today for it rains very hard we have had some thunder and lightning this evening we have only travelled about five miles. This is Sarah's birthday.

Monday March 23, 1846

This has been a stormy day we were obliged to tarry on account of the weather about two in the afternoon we had some hail they fell as large or larger than buckshot it continued to rain through the night.

Tuesday March 24, 1846

Today as yesterday is rainy and unpleas[ant] very exceedingly muddy at evening Sarah thought it being so very wet and damp it would be more comfortable in her wagon so they prepared it and about four in the afternoon she left the tent.

Wednesday March 25, 1846

Last night considerable snow fell this morning was quite cold some snow has fallen during the day very muddy Mrs. Whitney has taken up her abode in the family wagon two or three doors from Sarah this evening Horace has been playing on his flute sounded very melodious at a little distance.

READING AND DISCUSSION QUESTIONS

1. Evaluate the historical context of Wells's westward migration in the 1840s. What evidence can you find of the environmental factors impacting the overland journey of men and women during this period?

2. To what extent do you think Wells's interaction with the environment, geography, and climate of the territory she traversed contributed to her Mormon identity as part of a distinct people? What role might environmental factors play in shaping identity?

P4-4 | Depicting America's Transcendent Landscape

ASHER BROWN DURAND, *Kindred Spirits* (1849)

The group of writers, artists, poets, and philosophers associated with the transcendentalist movement conceived of nature in ways quite different from those felling trees and digging ditches to build the nation's economic interests. Entrepreneurs saw nature as an obstacle to overcome. Transcendentalists, by contrast, emphasized humans' intimate connections to nature. The sublime beauty of the American landscape provided inspiration, transporting individuals to a communion with beauty and truth. The most famous expression of this view of nature came from the brush of Asher B. Durand in *Kindred Spirits*, a painting that depicts two friends, artist Thomas Cole and poet William Cullen Bryant, standing on a precipice in the Catskills in New York State.

READING AND DISCUSSION QUESTIONS

1. What point of view toward humans and their relationship to nature does Durand express in *Kindred Spirits*?

2. Compare Durand's views of nature to those expressed by Joseph Story in his dedicatory address at Mount Auburn. What similarities and differences do you see in their attitudes toward nature?

P4-5 | Assessing Climate's Effect on Americans

FREDERICK LAW OLMSTED, *A Journey Through Texas* (1854)

Few Americans are as closely associated with the idea of a cultivated landscape as Frederick Law Olmsted. As a landscape architect, he designed Central Park in New York City to provide visitors with a calming and contemplative space apart from the urban world just beyond its borders. In the 1850s, Olmsted undertook a research tour of the South and published the results in several volumes, including *A Journey Through Texas*. Here, Olmsted describes the role of environment, geography, and climate as factors shaping the west Texas region he visited.

That part of Western Texas lying near the Rio Grande, has a character of its own. It is a region so sterile and valueless, as to be commonly reputed a desert, and, being incapable of settlement, serves as a barrier—separating the nationalities, and protecting from encroachment, at least temporarily, the retreating race.

The extreme Texan settlements have reached the verge of this waste region. A line drawn from the head of the San Saba southward, to the upper waters of the Guadalupe, thence westward, along the mountain-range bordering the sterile plains, to the head of the Leona at Fort Inge, thence along the course of the Leona, the Frio, and the Nueces to the coast, will mark the limits of valuable land, of probable agricultural occupation.

Along the coast lies a sandy tract, with salt lagoons and small, brackish streams. This is the desert country, which became familiar to our army on its way from Corpus to Point Isabel, at the outbreak of the Mexican war in 1846. It merges into the level coast prairies which, forty to sixty miles inland, become undulating and covered with a growth of prickly shrubs, upon a dry, barren, gravelly soil. The same character, with trifling variations, belongs to the whole region as far north as the Pecos, where the sterility becomes so great, that even the dwarfed shrubs disappear as the country rises into the great plains.

The coast prairies have large districts of fertile soil, and, if supplied with water, might be available as pastures for rough cattle and sheep; but water is only to be found in gullies and holes, where it is not only muddy and of bad

Frederick Law Olmsted, *A Journey Through Texas; or, A Saddle-Trip on the Southwestern Frontier* (New York: Dix, Edwards & Co., 1857), 441–447.

quality, but liable to disappear entirely during the heats of summer, when even the grass withers and dries up. . . .

The valley of the Nueces contains much rich land, but low-lying and malarious. The river is navigable for small steamboats for about forty miles. The bar of Corpus has about six feet of water.

The grassed region below the chaparral wilderness, extending to the coast, is the resort of immense herds of wild horses, as well as of numbers of deer, antelope, and hares. The mustangs are the degenerated progeny of Spanish estrays, now as wild and fully naturalized as the deer themselves. They associate in incredible numbers, like the buffaloes, a single herd sometimes covering a large tract, and, if frightened, rushing to and fro in sweeping lines, with the irresistible force of an army. From their numbers are recruited additions to the stocks of Texan and Mexican herdsmen, and the business of entrapping them has given rise to a class of men called "mustangers," composed of runaway vagabonds, and outlaws of all nations, the legitimate border-ruffians of Texas. While their ostensible employment is this of catching wild horses, they often add the practice of highway robbery, and are, in fact, simply prairie pirates, seizing any Property that comes in their way, murdering travelers, and making descents upon trains and border villages. Their operations of this sort are carried on under the guise of savages, and, at the scene of a murder, some "Indian sign," as an arrow-head or a moccasin, is left to mislead justice.

The wild horses are easily collected, by means of long fences, called "wings," diverging on either side from the mouth of a "pen." Having been driven within this, the mares of a herd are caught with the lasso, and the stallions, which do not repay breaking, turned loose or wantonly shot. Here and there a "ranch" is established, forming a temporary home and retreat for the "mustangers." The herds probably suffer extremely in the dry season, and have been much injured during generations of exposure and hardship. They are narrow-chested, weak in haunches, and of bad disposition, and are worth about one tenth the price of improved stock, a herd tamed to be driven, selling, delivered at the settlements, at $8 to $15 per head. Many stories are told of the incurable viciousness of tamed mustangs. An old animal which you have ridden daily for twenty years, will, when his opportunity comes at last, suddenly jump upon you, and stamp you in pieces, his vengeance all the hotter for delay.

No part of the immense remaining territory towards the North, seems to possess the slightest value. It is a dry gravelly desert, supporting only worthless shrubs. Such was distinctly its character at the point where we crossed it, and from all the definite description we could obtain from officers who had led trains, or scouting parties, here and there over it, or Texans who had traversed the various routes into Mexico, it nowhere offers more attractive features. Should it become desirable to plant settlements within it, for reasons other than economical, probably a few spots might be selected, where a sufficiently good soil, with wood and water, exists for such a purpose, and it is also true, that our acquaintance with it is but limited and somewhat vague; for what one calls desert, another calls prairie, and what to one is pure sand or clay, to another is a light or heavy soil the impression depending much upon the soil the traveler has been accustomed to cultivate, as well as especially upon the season in which his observation is made.

The climate, which, throughout West Texas, begins to approach that of Mexico, has here become absolutely Mexican, and is marked by an extreme dryness — rain so seldom falling during the summer, that ordinary vegetation perishes for lack of moisture, leaving the soil to the occupation of such Bedouin tribes of vegetation as have the necessary powers of endurance. . . .

We saw this country in April, probably to the best advantage. Our road lay across a series of elevations, between the beds of insignificant brooks, tributaries of the Nueces. Several of these, dry in later months, contained now running water, and in their valleys, here and there, the gravelly soil was black, and grass was abundant beneath the shrubs, while upon the barren surface of the ridges, even the chaparral growth almost disappeared. The "bottoms" of two or three of these creeks were marked by a thin belt of wood, as hack-berry and elm, and those of the Nueces and of Turkey creek, its principal branch on our route, were well shaded by timber. But even at this season, pasturage was the only use that suggested itself for these lands, and this would be impracticable, where sheep would lose their whole fleece in the labyrinths of thorns, and cattle stray instantly out of sight, and beyond possible control.

There is, however, one circumstance which may ultimately lead to important modifications in the fate of this region. It is the fact that a change has recently been gradually manifesting itself in its meteorological conditions toward a steadily increasing amount of moisture. By common Mexican report the commencement of this change is coincident with American occupation. It is certainly, if well attested, a remarkable scientific phenomenon. In the settled districts of Western Texas, the evidence seems to have been so palpable as to have become a matter of common allusion. New springs were repeatedly pointed out to us; upon our route into the hills north of San Antonio, at least three or four such were met with, and we were told of a neighboring farm which, when purchased, had its only water from the river, while since, first one, and, subsequently, four perennial springs had broken out upon it, whose flow was steadily increasing. Around the city, irrigation, which, ten years before, had been indispensable, was almost entirely disused, the canals being suffered to fall out of repair, and all the farmers who have settled the vicinity trust their crops to the skies alone, as in the East. Our guide to the Rio Grande attested the fact, and observed that he had never before this trip found running water in the bed of one of the creeks (I think the Chican) which we crossed.

The volume of water in all the Texan rivers has been observed to be increasing, and a number of streams, whose flow, at intervals, has been subterranean, are said to fill their superficial beds. These facts connect themselves with an increased growth of trees and grass upon the plains. Julius Froebel reports having seen, near the Pecos, an abundant young growth of mesquit trees, beneath millions of old trunks which still stand, though they have been dead no one knows how long, while no intermediate growth exists, and among the present chaparral large stumps are not unfrequently to be found, indicating a former forest. We ourselves noticed a similar young growth of mesquit trees upon open prairies.

These phenomena are thought to be explained by the comparative rarity of fires since Americans entered the country. Hundreds of miles, formerly burned over each year by Indians, now escape, and the young seedlings, then destroyed, have had time, where this has occurred, to become strong enough to resist prairie flame. This growth retards evaporation as well as the instant flowing off of rain water, so that freshets are fewer and streams more steady, while the retained water furnishes vapor to the summer atmosphere, for precipitation, upon slighter causes. The theory connects itself with those upon the original formation of prairies, and must be left to the discussion of experts.

READING AND DISCUSSION QUESTIONS

1. From Olmsted's description of west Texas, what conclusions can you draw about the role of climate in shaping the settlement patterns, demographics, and economy of a particular region?

2. What inference can you make about Olmsted's understanding of the influence of environmental factors on the shaping of the institutions and values of various groups? What argument about environment does he seem to make about the "mustangers" of west Texas?

■ COMPARATIVE QUESTIONS ■

1. Compare the multiple perspectives of the sources in this chapter to identify similarities and differences in attitudes toward nature. What positive and negative associations with the environment emerge from these sources?

2. To what extent did environmental factors such as geography and climate constrain and shape Americans' actions?

3. Analyze and evaluate Olmsted's depiction of west Texas by comparing it to John Barnard's view of Marblehead, Massachusetts (Document 3-5). How does each evoke a sense of place? What similarities and differences in point of view toward the environment does each express?

4. What effect might the consideration of environmental factors have on a historian's interpretation of America's past? How, for instance, might the political or economic interpretation of the period from 1800 to 1860 compare to an interpretation from an environmental perspective?

13

Expansion, War, and Sectional Crisis

1844–1860

Catching the spirit of the times, a young Walt Whitman asked in 1846: "What has miserable, inefficient Mexico—with her superstition, her burlesque upon freedom, her actual tyranny by the few over the many—what has she to do with the great mission of peopling the new world with a noble race? Be it ours, to achieve that mission!" America's poet of democracy spoke the language of Manifest Destiny, the ideology of expansion that caused the Mexican War, fueled the subsequent sectional crisis, and led ultimately to the Civil War. America's territorial ambitions, only partially satisfied with the Mexican land cession following the war, forced a debate over the fate of slavery: Should the territories be free or slave? This central question focused the political crisis of the 1850s and led partisans North and South to attribute to each other tyrannical motives, either to spread a Slave Power conspiracy (if you were a northerner) or to crush constitutional rights to property (if you were a southerner). By the time Abraham Lincoln was elected president in 1860, southern leaders had convinced themselves that only secession from the Union would save their cherished rights.

13-1 | The Lure of the West

LANSFORD HASTINGS, *The Emigrant's Guide to Oregon and California* (1845)

Americans' desire to move west was encouraged by books like Lansford Hastings's *The Emigrant's Guide*. An example of "booster" literature, the guide provided practical advice about routes to follow, items to bring, and destinations to settle. Sometimes, these guides were embroidered with exaggeration. In this case, Hastings, who had made an overland trek to Oregon in 1842, hoped to entice emigrants to California, then still a province of Mexico. His hopes for an independent republic of California ended when Mexico ceded California to the United States as part of the 1848 Treaty of Guadalupe Hidalgo that ended the Mexican War.

The settlements and improvements, which are disconnected with the forts and missions, are chiefly at the Wallammette valley, the Fualitine plains, and the Wallammette falls. The settlement at the Wallammette valley, is at present, the most extensive settlement in the country. It contains about one hundred families, who have extensive farms, and who are otherwise comfortably situated. Each of the farmers in this valley, generally have, from one hundred to five hundred acres of land under fence, and in a good state of cultivation, upon which, they grow annually, from five hundred to a thousand bushels of wheat for exportation, besides beans, peas and potatoes, turnips and various other vegetables, which they grow in great abundance. They also usually rear cattle, horses, sheep and hogs, in large numbers; each farmer generally having, from fifty to five hundred head of cattle, from ten to one hundred head of horses, and as many sheep and hogs; for all of which, the continued, annual emigration, affords an ample market. . . . In the winter of 1843, a town was laid off, near the falls, which has since improved, with unparalleled rapidity. . . . In the autumn of 1843, there were fifty three buildings in this town, among which, were four stores, four mills, two of which were flouring mills, one public-house, one black smith's shop and various other mechanic's shops; a church was also in contemplation, and in fact, commenced. Many of the lots, which were obtained gratuitously, only the spring previous, were then worth at least, one thousand dollars each, and their value was daily increasing, with the improvements of the town. Such were the improvements of Oregon City, in the autumn of 1843, but about eight months, after its emergent appearance. Oregon City is situated upon a very favorable site for a town, and it is, beyond a doubt, destined to become a place of very considerable manufacturing and commercial importance. . . . For the present, and until other towns spring up, emigrants will, in a great measure, concentrate at this place, especially merchants, mechanics and those of the learned professions. But

Lansford W. Hastings, *The Emigrants' Guide, to Oregon and California, Containing Scenes and Incidents of a Party of Oregon Emigrants* (Cincinnati: George Conclin, 1845; rept., Bedford, MA: Applewood Books, n.d.), 55–59.

other towns are already, springing into existence, as additional evidences of the unbounded energy and enterprise of American citizens. . . .

The buildings in Oregon City, are, with a few exceptions, framed and well-finished. Including saw and flouring mills, there are now fourteen in Oregon, many of which, are doing a very extensive and profitable business; and there are innumerable sites for mills and other machinery, which are destined, soon to be occupied. There are perhaps, very few countries which afford more numerous, or more advantageous sites for the most extensive water power than Oregon. The people of this territory, in their anxiety to provide for their individual necessities, and to promote their individual interests, have paid but very little attention to the making of roads, and other public improvements. Traveling and transportation, are, as yet, chiefly on horseback, and by water, but from the nature of the soil however, there can be no difficulty, in making good roads, and thereby, rendering intercommunication easy, and transportation cheap, throughout all portions of the country. The foregoing facts, in reference to the improvements of Oregon, afford a few evidences of the very enterprising character of the Oregon emigrants; but a further evidence is found in the fact of their having recently sent to New York for a printing-press and a steam-engine, which will be received sometime during the next summer or autumn; when the same energy and enterprise that procured them, will soon put them into extensive and successful operation. . . .

In every thing that tends to the advancement of the interests of the country, there appears to be a hearty co-operation, between the gentlemen of the Hudson Bay Company, and the American citizens. As one instance of extraordinary, and entire devotion to the best interest of the country, the whole community, with one unanimous voice, determined to abandon the use of all alcoholic or inebriating liquors; and to prevent their introduction or sale, under any state of circumstances. In this measure, the gentlemen of the company perform a very efficient part, and although their own store-houses are full of intoxicating liquors, they sell none to any person. . . . This certainly speaks volumes, for the morality and intelligence of the citizens of Oregon, and it is, no doubt, the chief cause of all that order and quiet, which so universally prevail, throughout all the different settlements.

A kindness and hospitality exist, among those pioneers of the west, which is almost unparalleled. Upon the arrival of emigrants, in the country, immediate arrangements are made by the former settlers, to provide them with houses and provisions, and every aid is rendered them in making their selections of lands, and procuring houses for themselves. . . .

There are several powerful and warlike tribes of Indians, occupying each of the different sections. The principal tribes inhabiting the Eastern section, are the Shoshonies, or Snakes, the Black-feet, and the Bonarks. The Nezpercies also frequent this section, but their country is properly in the Middle section, where they are principally found. The Indians of this section are much less advanced in civilization, than those of the other sections. They are all said to be friendly, excepting the Black-feet, who have always been hostile. Emigrants, however, very seldom meet with them, in traveling to Oregon, by the way of Fort Hall, as their country lies far to the north of that route. They are not to be dreaded, however, when met by a large party of whites; even forty or fifty armed men, are ample to deter them from any hostile movements. They should always be considered, and treated as enemies, whatever may be their pretensions of friendship. . . . Petit larceny is the most common offence committed at these places, while grand larceny, and robbery are constantly being committed by them elsewhere; but as they are "friendly," murder is an offence which they seldom commit.

READING AND DISCUSSION QUESTIONS

1. What can you infer about Hastings's audience from the details he chose to share about migrating to the Oregon and California territories?

2. What conclusions can you draw from this source about the experience of traveling in the mid-nineteenth century?

3. Compare Hastings's book with contemporary travel guides (or Web sites) you may have seen or used. How do you interpret the differences you see?

13-2 | Two Views of the War with Mexico

JOHN D. SLOAT, *To the Inhabitants of California* (1846) and GENERAL FRANCISCO MEJIA, *A Proclamation at Matamoros* (1846)

In 1846, General Francisco Mejia was the commander of Mexico's military forces at Matamoros, a city on the southern bank of the Rio Grande, opposite the U.S. troops that President James K. Polk had ordered forward to provoke a war with Mexico. The United States and Mexico disputed the southern border of Texas, recently annexed by the United States as its twenty-eighth state. Once hostilities broke out, Commodore John D. Sloat of the U.S. Navy stationed off California, then a province of Mexico, landed at Monterey and claimed California as a territory of the United States. These sources present conflicting perspectives on the cause of the U.S. war with Mexico.

To the Inhabitants of California

The central government of Mexico having commenced hostilities against the United States of America, by invading its territory and attacking the troops of the United States stationed on the north side of the Rio Grande, and with a force of seven thousand men, under the command of General Arista, which army was totally destroyed and all their artillery, baggage, &c., captured on the 8th and 9th

---

A Documentary History of the Mexican War, ed. Steven R. Butler (Richardson, TX: Descendants of Mexican War Veterans, 1995), 146 (Sloat), 25 (Mejia).

of May last, by a force of two thousand three hundred men, under the command of General Taylor, and the city of Matamoras taken and occupied by the forces of the United States; and the two nations being actually at war by this transaction, I shall hoist the standard of the United States at Monterey immediately, and shall carry it throughout California.

I declare to the inhabitants of California, that although I come in arms with a powerful force, I do not come among them as an enemy to California; on the contrary, I come as their best friend as henceforward California will be a portion of the United States, and its peaceable inhabitants will enjoy the same rights and privileges they now enjoy; together with the privileges of choosing their own magistrates and other officers for the administration of justice among themselves, and the same protection will be extended to them as to any other State in the Union. They will also enjoy a permanent government under which life, property and the constitutional right and lawful security to worship the Creator in the way most congenial to each one's sense of duty will be secured, which unfortunately the central government of Mexico cannot afford them, destroyed as her resources are by internal factions and corrupt officers, who create constant revolutions to promote their own interests and to oppress the people. Under the flag of the United States California will be free from all such troubles and expense, consequently the country will rapidly advance and improve both in agriculture and commerce; as of course the revenue laws will be the same in California as in all other parts of the United States, affording them all manufactures and produce of the United States, free of any duty, and all foreign goods at one quarter of the duty they now pay, a great increase in the value of real estate and the products of California may also be anticipated.

With the great interest and kind feelings I know the government and people of the United States possess towards the citizens of California, the country cannot but improve more rapidly than any other on the continent of America. Such of the inhabitants of California, whether natives or foreigners, as may not be disposed to accept the high privileges of citizenship, and to live peaceably under the government of the United States, will be allowed time to dispose of their property and to remove out of the country, if they choose, without any restriction, or remain in it, observing strict neutrality.

With full confidence in the honor and integrity of the inhabitants of the country, I invite the judges, alcaldes,[1] and other civil officers, to retain their offices and to execute their functions as heretofore, that the public tranquility may not be disturbed; at least, until the government of the territory can be more definitely arranged.

All persons holding titles to real estate, or in quiet possession of lands under a color of right, shall have those titles and rights guarantied to them.

All churches, and the property they contain, in possession of the clergy of California, shall continue in the same rights and possessions they now enjoy.

---

[1]**alcalde**: A local judicial and administrative officer.

All provisions and supplies of every kind, furnished by the inhabitants for the use of United States ships and soldiers, will be paid for at fair rates, and no private property will be taken for public use without just compensation at the moment.

JOHN D. SLOAT,

Commander-in-chief of the United States naval forces in the Pacific ocean.
United States Flag-ship Savannah, Harbor of Monterey, July 7, 1846.

A Proclamation by the General-in-Chief of the Forces Assembled Against the Enemy, to the Inhabitants of This Department and the Troops Under His Command

FELLOW-CITIZENS: The annexation of the department of Texas to the United States, projected and consummated by the tortuous policy of the cabinet of the Union, does not yet satisfy the ambitious desires of the degenerate sons of Washington. The civilized world has already recognized in that act all the marks of injustice, iniquity, and the most scandalous violation of the rights of nations. Indelible is the stain which will for ever darken the character for virtue falsely attributed to the people of the United States; and posterity will regard with horror their perfidious conduct, and the immorality of the means employed by them to carry into effect that most degrading depredation. The right of conquest has always been a crime against humanity; but nations jealous of their dignity and reputation have endeavoured at least to cover it by the splendour of arms and the prestige of victory. To the United States, it has been reserved to put in practice dissimulation, fraud, and the basest treachery, in order to obtain possession, in the midst of peace, of the territory of a friendly nation, which generously relied upon the faith of promises and the solemnity of treaties.

The cabinet of the United States does not, however, stop in its career of usurpation. Not only does it aspire to the possession of the department of Texas, but it covets also the regions on the left bank of the Rio Bravo. Its army, hitherto for some time stationed at Corpus Christi, is now advancing to take possession of a large part of Tamaulipas; and its vanguard has arrived at the Arroya Colorado, distant eighteen leagues from this place. What expectations, therefore, can the Mexican government have of treating with an enemy, who, whilst endeavouring to lull us into security, by opening diplomatic negotiations, proceeds to occupy a territory which never could have been the object of the pending discussion? The limits of Texas are certain and recognized; never have they extended beyond the river Nueces; notwithstanding which, the American army has crossed the line separating Tamaulipas from that department. Even though Mexico could forget that the United States urged and aided the rebellion of the former colonists, and that the principle, giving to an independent people the right to annex itself to another nation, is not applicable to the case, in which the latter has been the protector of the independence of the former, with the object of admitting it into its own bosom; even though it could be accepted as an axiom of international law, that the violation of every rule of morality and justice might serve as a legitimate title for acquisition; nevertheless, the territory of Tamaulipas would still remain beyond the law of annexation, sanctioned by the American Congress; because that law comprises independent Texas, the ground occupied by the rebellious colony, and in no wise includes other departments, in which the Mexican government has uninterruptedly exercised its legitimate authority.

Fellow-countrymen: With an enemy which respects not its own laws, which shamelessly derides the very principles invoked by it previously, in order to excuse its ambitious views, we have no other resource than arms. We are fortunately always prepared to take them up with glory, in defence of our country; little do we regard the blood in our veins, when we are called on to shed it in vindication of our honour, to assure our nationality and independence. If to the torrent of devastation which threatens us it be necessary to oppose a dike of steel, our swords will form it; and on their sharp points will the enemy receive the fruits of his anticipated conquest. If the banks of the Panuco have been immortalized by the defeat of an enemy, respectable and worthy of the valour of Mexico, those of the Bravo shall witness the ignominy of the proud sons of the north, and its deep waters shall serve as the sepulchre for those who dare to approach it. The flames of patriotism which burns in our hearts will receive new fuel from the odious presence of the conquerors; and the cry of Dolores and Iguala[2] shall be re-echoed with harmony to our ears, when we take up our march to oppose our naked breasts to the rifles of the hunters of the Mississippi.

FRANCISCO MEJIA.
Matamoros, March 18, 1846.

READING AND DISCUSSION QUESTIONS

1. Compare how each of these sources describes the conflict between the United States and Mexico. What is the cause of the conflict each identifies?

2. To what extent does each author tailor his message to the specific audience he was addressing? What can you infer about the audience from the language of each source?

13-3 | A Southern Perspective on the Political Crisis
JOHN C. CALHOUN, *Speech on the Slavery Question* (1850)

A former nationalist, during the last phase of his public career, John C. Calhoun became the South's leading defender. In 1849, he wrote *Disquisition on Government*, a work of political theory, advancing the idea of the "concurrent majority" to prevent the South's political eclipse by the numerically superior North. In his last major address before his death, delivered in the

The Works of John C. Calhoun, Vol. IV (New York: D. Appleton and Company, 1854), 542–544, 551–553, 555–556, 559, 571–573.

[2]**cry of Dolores and Iguala**: Two Mexican cities traditionally associated with the beginning and the end of the Mexican War for Independence.

Senate on March 4, 1850, Calhoun diagnosed the political crisis threatening disunion, laying the blame at the feet of northern antislavery agitators.

As . . . the North has the absolute control over the Government, it is manifest, that on all questions between it and the South, where there is a diversity of interests, the interest of the latter will be sacrificed to the former, however oppressive the effects may be; as the South possesses no means by which it can resist, through the action of the Government. But if there was no question of vital importance to the South . . . this state of things might be endured . . . [b]ut such is not the fact. There is a question of vital importance to the Southern section. . . . I refer to the relation between the two races in the Southern section, which constitutes a vital portion of her social organization. Every portion of the North entertains views and feelings more or less hostile to it. Those most opposed and hostile, regard it as a sin, and consider themselves under the most sacred obligation to use every effort to destroy it. Indeed, to the extent that they conceive they have power, they regard themselves as implicated in the sin, and responsible for not suppressing it by the use of all and every means. Those less opposed and hostile, regard it as a crime—an offence against humanity, as they call it; and, although not so fanatical, feel themselves bound to use all efforts to effect the same object; while those who are least opposed and hostile, regard it as a blot and a stain on the character of what they call the Nation, and feel themselves accordingly bound to give it no countenance or support. On the contrary, the Southern section regards the relation as one which cannot be destroyed without subjecting the two races to the greatest calamity, and the section to poverty, desolation, and wretchedness; and accordingly they feel bound, by every consideration of interest and safety, to defend it.

This hostile feeling on the part of the North towards the social organization of the South long lay dormant, but it only required some cause to act on those who felt most intensely that they were responsible for its continuance, to call it into action. The increasing power of this Government, and of the control of the Northern section over all its departments, furnished the cause. It was this which made an impression on the minds of many, that there was little or no restraint to prevent the Government from doing whatever it might choose to do. This was sufficient of itself to put the most fanatical portion of the North in action, for the purpose of destroying the existing relation between the two races in the South.

The first organized movement towards it commenced in 1835. Then, for the first time, societies were organized, presses established, lecturers sent forth to excite the people of the North, and incendiary publications scattered over the whole South, through the mail. The South was thoroughly aroused. Meetings were held every where, and resolutions adopted, calling upon the North to apply a remedy to arrest the threatened evil, and pledging themselves to adopt measures for their own protection, if it was not arrested. At the meeting of Congress, petitions poured in from the North, calling upon Congress to abolish slavery in the District of Columbia, and to prohibit, what they called, the internal slave trade between the States—announcing at the same time, that their ultimate object was to abolish slavery, not only in the District, but in the States and throughout the Union. At this period, the number engaged in the agitation was small, and possessed little or no personal influence. . . .

What has since followed are but natural consequences. With the success of their first movement, this small fanatical party began to acquire strength; and with that, to become an object of courtship to both the great parties. . . . In a short time after the commencement of their first movement, they . . . induce[d] the legislatures of most of the Northern States to pass acts, which in effect abrogated the clause of the constitution that provides for the delivery up of fugitive slaves. Not long after, petitions followed to abolish slavery in forts, magazines, and dockyards, and all other places where Congress had exclusive power of legislation. This was followed by petitions and resolutions of legislatures of the Northern States, and popular meetings, to exclude the Southern States from all territories acquired, or to be acquired, and to prevent the admission of any State hereafter into the Union, which, by its constitution, does not prohibit slavery. . . . That has been avowed to be the ultimate object from the beginning of the agitation until the present time; and yet the great body of both parties of the North, with the full knowledge of the fact, although disavowing the abolitionists, have co-operated with them in almost all their measures. . . .

Now I ask, Senators, what is there to prevent its further progress, until it fulfills the ultimate end proposed, unless some decisive measure should be adopted to prevent it? Has any one of the causes, which has added to its increase from its original small and contemptible beginning until it has attained its present magnitude, diminished in force? Is the original cause of the movement—that slavery is a sin, and ought to be suppressed—weaker now than at the commencement? Or is the abolition party less numerous or influential, or have they less influence with, or control over the two great parties of the North in elections? Or has the South greater means of influencing or controlling the movements of this Government now, than it had when the agitation commenced? To all these questions but one answer can be given: No—no—no. The very reverse is true. Instead of being weaker, all the elements in favor of agitation are stronger now than they were in 1835, when it first commenced, while all the elements of influence on the part of the South are weaker. Unless something decisive is done, I again ask, what is to stop this agitation, before the great and final object at which it aims—the abolition of slavery in the States—is consummated? Is it, then, not certain, that if something is not done to arrest it, the South will be forced to choose between abolition and secession? . . .

How can the Union be saved? To this I answer, there is but one way by which it can be—and that is—by adopting such measures as will satisfy the States belonging to the Southern section, that they can remain in the Union consistently with their honor and their safety. . . . The South asks for justice, simple justice, and less she ought not to take. She has no compromise to offer, but the constitution; and no concession or surrender to make. She has already surrendered so much that she has little left to surrender. Such a settlement would go to the root of the evil, and remove all cause of discontent, by satisfying the South, she could remain honorably and safely in the Union, and thereby restore the harmony and fraternal feelings between the sections, which existed anterior to the Missouri agitation. Nothing else can, with any certainty, finally and for ever settle the questions at issue, terminate agitation, and save the Union.

But can this be done? Yes, easily; not by the weaker party, for it can of itself do nothing — not even protect itself — but by the stronger. The North has only to will it to accomplish it — to do justice by conceding to the South an equal right in the acquired territory, and to do her duty by causing the stipulations relative to fugitive slaves to be faithfully fulfilled — to cease the agitation of the slave question, and to provide for the insertion of a provision in the constitution, by an amendment, which will restore to the South, in substance, the power she possessed of protecting herself, before the equilibrium between the sections was destroyed by the action of this Government.

READING AND DISCUSSION QUESTIONS

1. How does Calhoun define the causes of the sectional conflict between the northern and southern states?

2. Calhoun died four weeks after delivering this speech. What did he hope to accomplish with his final act on the public stage?

13-4 | Attacking the Slave Power Conspiracy

CHARLES SUMNER, *The Crime of Kansas* (1856)

Northern antislavery activists like Massachusetts senator Charles Sumner railed against fellow senator Stephen Douglas's "solution" to the slavery extension issue, which called for popular sovereignty, or allowing the people to decide. Though democratic, the plan opened the possibility of slavery extending into regions where it had never before gone. The rush of both abolitionists and proslavery men into the territories to claim a majority resulted in bloody conflict, a violent prelude to the 1861 Civil War. When the proslavery Kansas constitution was recognized as the legitimate government, Sumner described the outcome as a "crime against humanity."

[B]efore entering upon the argument, I must say something of a general character, particularly in response to what has fallen from senators who have raised themselves to eminence on this floor in championship of human wrongs; I mean the Senator from South Carolina [Mr. Butler], and the Senator from Illinois [Mr. Douglas], who, though unlike as Don Quixote and Sancho Panza, yet, like this couple, sally forth together in the same adventure. I regret much to miss the elder Senator from his seat; but the cause, against which he has run a tilt, with such

---

Speech of Hon. Charles Sumner, in the Senate of the United States, 19th and 20th May, 1856 (Boston: John P. Jewett & Company, 1856), 9–10, 12–14.

activity of animosity, demands that the opportunity of exposing him should not be lost; and it is for the cause that I speak. The Senator from South Carolina has read many books of chivalry, and believes himself a chivalrous knight, with sentiments of honor and courage. Of course he has chosen a mistress to whom he has made his vows, and who, though ugly to others, is always lovely to him; though polluted in the sight of the world, is chaste in his sight;—I mean the harlot, Slavery. For her his tongue is always profuse with words. Let her be impeached in character, or any proposition made to shut her out from the extension of her wantonness, and no extravagance of manner or hardihood of assertion is then too great for this Senator. The frenzy of Don Quixote in behalf of his wench Dulcinea del Toboso is all surpassed. The asserted rights of Slavery, which shock equality of all kinds, are cloaked by a fantastic claim of equality. If the slave States cannot enjoy what, in mockery of the great fathers of the Republic, he misnames equality under the constitution,—in other words, the full power in the National Territories to compel fellow-men to unpaid toil, to separate husband and wife, and to sell little children at the auction block,—then, sir, the chivalric Senator will conduct the State of South Carolina out of the Union! Heroic knight! Exalted Senator! A second Moses come for a second exodus!

But, not content with this poor menace, which we have been twice told was "measured," the senator, in the unrestrained chivalry of his nature, has undertaken to apply opprobrious words to those who differ from him on this floor. He calls them "sectional and fanatical"; and opposition to the usurpation in Kansas he denounces as "an uncalculating fanaticism." To be sure these charges lack all grace of originality, and all sentiment of truth; but the adventurous Senator does not hesitate. He is the uncompromising, unblushing representative on this floor of a flagrant *sectionalism*, which now domineers over the Republic; and yet with a ludicrous ignorance of his own position,—unable to see himself as others see him,—or with an effrontery which even his white head ought not to protect from rebuke, he applies to those here who resist his sectionalism the very epithet which designates himself. The men who strive to bring back the government to its original policy, when Freedom and not Slavery was national, while Slavery and not freedom was sectional, he arraigns as *sectional*. This will not do. It involves too great a perversion of terms. I tell that Senator that it is to himself, and to the "organization" of which he is the "committed advocate," that this epithet belongs. I now fasten it upon them. For myself, I care little for names; but, since the question has been raised here, I affirm that the Republican party of the Union is in no just sense *sectional*, but, more than any other party, *national*; and that it now goes forth to dislodge from the high places of the government the tyrannical sectionalism of which the senator from South Carolina is one of the maddest zealots.

But I have not done with the senator. There is another matter, regarded by him of such consequence, that he interpolated it into the speech of the senator from New Hampshire [Mr. Hale] and also announced that he had prepared himself with it, to take in his pocket all the way to Boston, when he expected to address the people of that community. On this account, and for the sake of truth,

I stop for one moment, and tread it to the earth. The North, according to the senator, was engaged in the slave trade, and helped to introduce slaves into the Southern States; and this undeniable fact he proposed to establish by statistics, in stating which, his errors surpassed his sentences in number. But I let these pass for the present, that I may deal with his argument. Pray, sir, is the acknowledged turpitude of a departed generation to become an example for us? And yet the suggestion of the senator, if entitled to any consideration in this discussion, must have this extent. I join my friend from New Hampshire in thanking the senator from South Carolina for adducing this instance; for it gives me an opportunity to say, that the northern merchants, with homes in Boston, Bristol, Newport, New York, and Philadelphia, who catered for Slavery during the years of the slave trade, are the lineal progenitors of the northern men, with homes in these places, who lend themselves to Slavery in our day; and especially that all, whether north or south, who take part, directly or indirectly, in the conspiracy against Kansas, do but continue the work of the slave-traders, which you condemn. It is true—too true, alas!—that our fathers were engaged in this traffic; but that is no apology for it. And, in repelling the authority of this example, I repel also the trite argument founded on the earlier example of England. It is true that our mother country, at the peace of Utrecht, extorted from Spain the Assiento Contract, securing the monopoly of the slave-trade with the Spanish Colonies, as the whole price of all the blood of great victories; that she higgled at Aix-la Chapelle for another lease of this exclusive traffic; and again, at the treaty of Madrid, clung to the wretched piracy. It is true, that in this spirit the power of the mother country was prostituted to the same base ends in her American colonies, against indignant protests from our fathers. All these things now rise up in judgment against her. Let us not follow the senator from South Carolina to do this very evil to-day, which in another generation we condemn.

As the senator from South Carolina is the Don Quixote, the senator from Illinois [Mr. Douglas] is the squire of slavery, its very Sancho Panza, ready to do all its humiliating offices. This senator, in his labored address, vindicating his labored report—piling one mass of elaborate error upon another mass—constrained himself, as you will remember, to unfamiliar, decencies of speech. Of that address I have nothing to say at this moment, though before I sit down I shall show something of its fallacies. But I go back now to an earlier occasion, when, true to his native impulses, he threw into this discussion, "for a charm of powerful trouble," personalities most discreditable to this body. I will not stop to repel the imputations which he cast upon myself; but I mention them to remind you of the "sweltered venom sleeping got," which, with other poisoned ingredients, he cast into the cauldron of this debate. Of other things I speak. Standing on this floor, the senator issued his rescript, requiring submission to the usurped power of Kansas; and this was accompanied by a manner—all his own—such as befits the tyrannical threat. Very well. Let the senator try. I tell him now that he cannot enforce any such submission. The senator, with the slave power at his back, is strong; but he is not strong enough for this purpose. He is bold. He shrinks from nothing. Like Danton, he may cry, *"l'audace, l'audace, toujours l'audace!*"[1] but even his audacity cannot compass this work. The senator copies the British officer, who, with boastful swagger, said that with the hilt of his sword he would cram the "stamps" down the throats of the American people; and he will meet a similar failure. He may convulse this country with civil feud. Like the ancient madman, he may set fire to this temple of Constitutional Liberty, grander than Ephesian dome;[2] but he cannot enforce obedience to that tyrannical usurpation.

The senator dreams that he can subdue the North. He disclaims the open threat, but his conduct still implies it. How little that senator knows himself, or the strength of the cause which he persecutes! He is but a mortal man; against him is an immortal principle. With finite power he wrestles with the infinite, and he must fall. Against him are stronger battalions than any marshaled by mortal man—the inborn, ineradicable, invincible sentiments of the human heart; against him is nature in all her subtle forces; against him is God. Let him try to subdue these.

READING AND DISCUSSION QUESTIONS

1. Would you define the issues Sumner raised in his speech as short- or long-term causes of the Civil War? Explain your answer.

2. Compare Sumner's argument with the argument of Calhoun. How do they differ in the ways they understood the political conflict of the 1850s?

3. After delivering this speech, Sumner was savagely beaten on the floor of the U.S. Senate, sustaining injuries that incapacitated him for years. How did Sumner's speech and the response to it reflect the broader historical context of the 1850s?

13-5 | Supreme Court Rules Against Antislavery Cause
Dred Scott v. Sandford (1857)

Few Supreme Court cases have been as divisive as *Dred Scott v. Sandford*, which ruled against Dred Scott, an enslaved African American who sued his master for his freedom after he had been taken into territories where slavery was banned. Chief Justice Roger B. Taney not only ruled that slaves were property, not people, but also invalidated the Missouri Compromise of 1820, which barred slavery in much of the Louisiana Purchase. This legal triumph for slaveholders enflamed abolitionists, who feared slavery's spread throughout the nation.

Library of Congress (www.ourdocuments.gov).

[1]French Revolutionary Georges-Jacques Danton reputedly uttered this line, misquoted by Sumner, meaning, "We need audacity, yet more audacity, and always audacity."

[2]**Ephesian dome**: An elaborate and grand sixth-century temple built in Ephesus (modern-day Turkey), burned to the ground two hundred years later by an arsonist, who hoped his act of destruction would secure his lasting fame.

Dred Scott, Plaintiff In Error, v. John F. A. Sandford.[1]

The question is simply this: Can a negro whose ancestors were imported into this country, and sold as slaves, become a member of the political community formed and brought into existence by the Constitution of the United States, and as such become entitled to all the rights and privileges and immunities guaranteed to the citizen? One of which rights is the privilege of suing in a court of the United States in the cases specified in the Constitution.

It will be observed, that the plea applies to that class of persons only whose ancestors were negroes of the African race, and imported into this country, and sold and held as slaves. The only matter in issue before the court, therefore, is, whether the descendants of such slaves, when they shall be emancipated, or who are born of parents who had become free before their birth, are citizens of a State, in the sense in which the word citizen is used in the Constitution of the United States. And this being the only matter in dispute on the pleadings, the court must be understood as speaking in this opinion of that class only, that is, of those persons who are the descendants of Africans who were imported into this country, and sold as slaves. . . .

The words "people of the United States" and "citizens" are synonymous terms, and mean the same thing. They both describe the political body who, according to our republican institutions, form the sovereignty, and who hold the power and conduct the Government through their representatives. They are what we familiarly call the "sovereign people," and every citizen is one of this people and a constituent member of this sovereignty. The question before us is, whether the class of persons described in the plea in abatement compose a portion of this people, and are constituent members of this sovereignty? We think they are not, and that they are not included, and were not intended to be included, under the word "citizens" in the Constitution, and can therefore claim none of the rights and privileges which that instrument provides for and secures to citizens of the United States. On the contrary, they were at that time considered as a subordinate and inferior class of beings, who had been subjugated by the dominant race, and, whether emancipated or not, yet remained subject to their authority, and had no rights or privileges but such as those who held the power and the government might choose to grant them. . . .

The question then arises, whether the provisions of the Constitution, in relation to the personal rights and privileges to which the citizen of a State should be entitled, embraced the negro African race, at that time in this country, or who might afterwards be imported, who had then or should afterwards be made free in any State; and to put it in the power of a single State to make him a citizen of the United States, and endue him with the tall rights of citizenship in every other State without their consent? Does the Constitution of the United States act upon him whenever he shall be made free under the laws of a State, and raised there to

---

[1]The Supreme Court misspelled John F. A. Sanford's name in its decision.

the rank of a citizen, and immediately clothe him with all the privileges of a citizen in every other State, and in its own courts?

The court think the affirmative of these propositions cannot be maintained. And if it cannot, the plaintiff in error could not be a citizen of the State of Missouri, within the meaning of the Constitution of the United States, and, consequently, was not entitled to sue in its courts. . . .

In the opinion of the court, the legislation and histories of the times, and the language used in the Declaration of Independence, show, that neither the class of persons who had been imported as slaves, nor their descendants, whether they had become free or not, were then acknowledged as a part of the people, nor intended to be included in the general words used in that memorable instrument. . . .

They had for more than a century before been regarded as beings of an inferior order, and altogether unfit to associate with the white race, either in social or political relations; and so far inferior, that they had no rights which the white man was bound to respect; and that the negro might justly and lawfully be reduced to slavery for his benefit. He was bought and sold, and treated as an ordinary article of merchandise and traffic, whenever a profit could be made by it. This opinion was at that time fixed and universal in the civilized portion of the white race. It was regarded as an axiom in morals as well as in politics, which no one thought of disputing, or supposed to be open to dispute; and men in every grade and position in society daily and habitually acted upon it in their private pursuits, as well as in matters of public concern; without doubting for a moment the correctness of this opinion. . . .

[U]pon a full and careful consideration of the subject, the court is of opinion, that, upon the facts stated in the plea in abatement, Dred Scott was not a citizen of Missouri within the meaning of the Constitution of the United States, and not entitled as such to sue in its courts; and, consequently, that the Circuit Court had no jurisdiction of the case, and that the judgment on the plea in abatement is erroneous. . . .

Now, if the removal of which he speaks did not give them their freedom, then by his own admission he is still a slave; and whatever opinions may be entertained in favor of the citizenship of a free person of the African race, no one supposes that a slave is a citizen of the State or of the United States. If, therefore, the acts done by his owner did not make them free persons, he is still a slave, and certainly incapable of suing in the character of a citizen. . . .

We proceed, therefore, to inquire whether the facts relied on by the plaintiff entitled him to his freedom. . . .

The act of Congress, upon which the plaintiff relies [the Missouri Compromise], declares that slavery and involuntary servitude, except as a punishment for crime, shall be forever prohibited in all that part of the territory ceded by France, under the name of Louisiana, which lies north of thirty-six degrees thirty minutes north latitude, and not included within the limits of Missouri. And the difficulty which meets us at the threshold of this part of the inquiry is, whether Congress was authorised to pass this law under any of the powers granted to it by the Constitution; for if the authority is not given by that instrument, it is the duty of this court to declare it void and inoperative, and incapable of conferring freedom upon any one who is held as a slave under the laws of any one of the States. . . .

An act of Congress which deprives a citizen of the United States of his liberty or property, merely because he came himself or brought his property into a particular Territory of the United States, and who had committed no offence against the laws, could hardly be dignified with the name of due process of law. . . .

The powers over person and property of which we speak are not only not granted to Congress, but are in express terms denied, and they are forbidden to exercise them. And this prohibition is not confined to the States, but the words are general, and extend to the whole territory over which the Constitution gives it power to legislate, including those portions of it remaining under Territorial Government, as well as that covered by States. It is a total absence of power everywhere within the dominion of the United States, and places the citizens of a Territory, so far as these rights are concerned, on the same footing with citizens of the States, and, guards them as firmly and plainly against any inroads which the General Government might attempt, under the plea of implied or incidental powers. And if Congress itself cannot do this—if it is beyond the powers conferred on the Federal Government—it will be admitted, we presume, that it could not authorise a Territorial Government to exercise them. It could confer no power on any local Government, established by its authority, to violate the provisions of the Constitution. . . .

Upon these considerations, it is the opinion of the court that the act of Congress which prohibited a citizen from holding and owning property of this kind in the territory of the United States north of the line therein mentioned, is not warranted by the Constitution, and is therefore void; and that neither Dred Scott himself, nor any of his family, were made free by being carried into this territory; even if they had been carried there by the owner, with the intention of becoming a permanent resident. . . .

Upon the whole, therefore, it is the judgment of this court, that it appears by the record before us that the plaintiff in error is not a citizen of Missouri, in the sense in which that word is used in the Constitution; and that the Circuit Court of the United States, for that reason, had no jurisdiction in the case, and could give no judgment in it. Its judgment for the defendant must, consequently, be reversed, and a mandate issued, directing the suit to be dismissed for want of jurisdiction.

READING AND DISCUSSION QUESTIONS

1. How does this court case connect to both the antislavery movement and the political crisis of the 1850s?

2. What do you think were the differing reactions to the *Dred Scott* decision? How might a northern abolitionist's reaction compare to the perspective of a southern plantation owner?

13-6 | A Southern Woman Reacts to Lincoln's Election

KEZIAH GOODWIN HOPKINS BREVARD, *Diary* (1860–1861)

Born and raised in South Carolina, Keziah Brevard was an educated and determined woman. Widowed in 1842, she managed and expanded her late husband's estate, becoming one of the region's leading planters, cultivating more than 2,600 acres with the labor of 209 enslaved African Americans. In her diary from late 1860 and early 1861, she notes the election of President Abraham Lincoln, a Republican from Illinois. Like many southerners, her anxiety about Republican intentions toward the issue of slavery colored her reaction to Lincoln's election and pushed her toward secession.

[*September*] *15th Saturday* . . . This night, if reports are true, had been set apart to cut us off—Oh God, because we own slaves—Lord thou knowest our hearts—save us for a calmer end & let us never cease to think & to bless thee for thy loving kindness—Lord, save this our good country & make us *all* & *every one*, bond & free, to love thee & do thy will as good servants—*we* are *all* thy servants—all in thy hands—Oh save us.

18 . . . Oh my God I have so many little things to unnerve me—I wish I was prepared to die & could go to my God. I wish to be kind to my negroes—but I receive little but impudence from Rosanna & Sylvia—it is a truth if I am compelled to speak harshly to them—after bearing every thing from them I get impudence—Oh my God give me fortitude to do what is right to these then give me firmness to go no farther—At my death it is my solemn desire that Tama—Sylvia—Mack—Maria & Rosanna be sold—I cannot think of imposing such servants on any one of my heirs.

[*October*] *13th Saturday* . . . —it is time for us to shew the rabble of the North we are not to be murdered in cold blood because we own slaves—there are no doubts but thousands would have prefered being born in this beautiful country without the encumbrance—but they have been transmitted down to us & what can we do with them?—free such a multitude of half barbarians in our midst—no— no—we must sooner give up our lives than submit to such a degradation—From the time I could reason with myself I wished there was a way to get rid of them—but not free them in our midst yet. They are not prepared for freedom, many of them set no higher value on themselves than the beasts of the field do—I know a family in five miles of me where there are six women who have & have had children for thirty years back & not one of them but have [been] bastards & only one ever had a husband. . . . That wretch John Brown—if he had come as one of christ's Apostles & preached down sin he might have been the instrument of good—but he come to cut our throats because we held property we could not do otherwise with—was preposterous—Did God set the children

Glenn M. Linden, *Voices from the Gathering Storm: The Coming of the American Civil War* (Wilmington, DE: Scholarly Resources, Inc., 2001), 222–227.

of Israel to cutting their masters' throats to flee [free] them from bondage—no—no—he brought them out of Egypt in his own peculiar way & he can send Africa's sons & daughters back when he knows they are ready for their exode. I own many slaves & many of the females are of the lowest cast—making miserable their own fellow servants by medling with the husbands of others— . . . This is a dirty subject—& had I not thought of those cruel abolitionists who wish to free such people in our midst I would not have spoken this truth here.

[9th November] Oh My God!!! This morning heard that Lincoln was elected—I had prayed that God would thwart his election in some way & I prayed for my *Country*—Lord we know not what is to be the result of this—but I do pray if there is to be a crisis—that we all lay down our lives sooner than free our slaves in our midst—no soul on this earth is more willing for justice than I am, but the idea of being mixed up with free blacks is *horrid*!! I must trust in God that he will not forget us as unworthy as we are—Lord save us—*I would give my life to save my Country*. I have never been opposed to giveing up slavery if we could send them out of our Country— . . . but the die is cast—"Caesar has past the Rubicon."[1] We now have to act, God be with us is my prayer & let us all be willing to die rather than free our slaves in their present uncivilized state.

[*December*] *Monday 10th* . . . I hope & trust in God as soon as Secession is carried out—we of the South begin to find a way to get all the Negroes sent back to Africa & let the generations to come after us live in more peace than we do—I can't see how we are ever to be safe with them in our midst—I wish every soul of them were in Africa contented in their own homes—let us begin on corn bread & live in peace & security—as long as they are here & number so many more than the whites there is no safety any way—Men of the South—I fear our end is near & the Yankeys will glory over their work. I do hate a Northern Abolitionist—Lord forgive me—but who can love those whose highest ambition is to cut our throats.

28 Friday Mrs. James H. Adams with Janie, Laura, Carry, Ellen & Jim spent the day with Goodwyn & myself—Randy's little Jane with them. They brought this morning's paper with them, the "Guardian," from it we read that Ft. Moultrie[2] had been evacuated on the 27th & the Ft. was on fire at 5 O'clock thursday evening. God alone knows the design of it—we are all in the dark as to the future—Oh that this strife could be ended for the good of the whole country—I know not what to think, certainly awful troubles seem hanging over us—

[*January*] *Thursday 10* . . . Last night we received the news of the Star of the West—from Charleston—O God put it into the hearts of the Northern people to do right & let us once more shew to the world we can yield to all that is right in thy sight—We have never invaded Northern rights—all we want is *right* in its plainest sense.

---

[1]**"Caesar has past the Rubicon"**: Reference to Julius Caesar, first century BC Roman general who crossed the Rubicon River with his troops to seize Rome. When one crosses the Rubicon, it means he or she has passed the point of no return.

[2]**Ft. Moultrie**: By the time Brevard is writing, federal troops had been sent from Fort Moultrie on Sullivan's Island in Charleston harbor to nearby Fort Sumter.

Wednesday 30 Oh my God I see nothing ahead but trouble—Our country will pass from bad to worse—the South never would be united or it might have sent Douglass [Stephen Douglas] instead of Lincoln—if she could have been united 'twould have been far better for her—I do hope if we have Civil war—that God will take me before the first drop of blood is shed—O God canst thou, wilt thou not spare us—I do not say we deserve it—no—no—slavery ever will make trouble I care not where found—I wish I had been born without them with a sufficiency to keep me from want in as good a country as this with our liberal religion—

February 28th . . . Now what of my country?—a few short days & we shall hear from Lincoln's lips what we may expect—if he makes war on us the whole body of men No. & So. should rise against him & make a blow at the man himself who would dare to bring such trouble on this land won by the blood of our fore fathers from British encroachments. If the N. should be let loose on us, the fanatics will run mad with joy & tongues cannot tell where the scene will end—if ever, until a dark age sinks the nation into brutes— . . . I thank the Heavenly Father I have never had a son to mix my blood with *negro blood*—Oh such a sin would [be] & is disheartening to Christian Mothers—

Monday [March] 4th . . . I pray that Lincoln's administration may disappoint his friends & his opposers—his friends are black republicans, our enemies—they must have dreadful hearts to wish to cut our throats because we are sinners—as if they were pure & undefiled—no surer sign of what deceivers they are than to see how self conceited they are—God can punish every sinner & will do it—perhaps many of them may yet have their eyes opened to the enormity of *their own* sins—if not in this world [then] in the next. Blessed be the Lord God Almighty who will make each answer for their own sins—& this will be like millstones to many deceivers. Thankful I am that I have a just God to go before & not Northern fanatics nor black Republicans—Lord let me have right feelings towards them because it [is] thy will, we should forgive our enemies. 'Tis hard for us to feel right towards those who sent John Brown (that Devil) to cut our throats—

April 2nd . . . O Lord let me not murmur—I am sorry our once strong country is now severed & I believe forever—for I see no disposition in the stubborn North to yield any thing from advantage—& the South thought she would make the North succumb to her—*I* never thought it—& have ever thought we have began troubles for ourselves & cannot see how we are to be one tittle better off than we were—if all the South had gone united we might have maintained ourselves—but six states only—we are doomed I fear to be the division of the Old United States. O my God *help us*—*help us*—Let me not live to see these six states disagree & I fear it very much.

April 3rd Wednesday . . . I still fear So. Ca. cannot be pleased—I do not love her disposition to cavil at every move—My heart has never been in this breaking up of the Union—but if we could be united lovingly & firmly, I will cling to my dear native land—for I love my country—but I hate contention:—too many are waiting for the loaves & fishes, South as well as North—

[April 11] How thankful I am—my Country is still spared—Lord save us & make us better—I pray that all things will be ordered for peace. How changeable

my feelings are—sometimes buoyed with a hope of good times (this is momentary), then I can see & hear nothing to hang my hopes on—Why are they stubborn about the forts if they have any thought of reconciliation?

[13th April] Spent Sunday at home—had two little negroes sick—sent for Dr Taylor—he came in the afternoon & gave me the news from Charleston—Said Ft. Sumpter had been taken—Col. Anderson surrendered—he lost 9 or ten men—So. Ca. not one—Oh my God I thank thee for spareing blood here—Lord 'twas hard the citizens of Charleston should be rendered so miserable by that Fort—I am thankful it is no longer there a terror, but Oh my God we may still tremble for we have enemies in our midst—Oh God send them away to a land they love better than ours & Oh devise a way for our peace & safety & let the praise be thine—for who can doubt but thou didst so order it. A few months ago & 'twas said man could not take Ft. Sumpter unless walking over five or ten thousand dead—it has been taken—& not *one* life lost of those who aided in taking it—My God the work is thine & if we serve the[e] truthfully thou wilt save us—Oh save us & make us still a united contented people—we wish no ill to the North—all we ask is that they leave us to ourselves or gra[n]t us privileges & laws that will protect us—My God be with all thy dear Children—Oh how desolate many are now—Husbands & sons gone to the scenes of war—to save their [country].

READING AND DISCUSSION QUESTIONS

1. Based on your analysis and evaluation of Brevard's diary, what inferences and conclusions can you draw about southern reactions to Lincoln's election in 1860? How do you explain her particular reaction?

2. What point of view does Brevard's diary express? What are the advantages and limitations to using diaries as historical evidence?

■ COMPARATIVE QUESTIONS ■

1. Compare multiple perspectives over time on the issue of slavery's expansion by identifying similarities and differences in the views of Calhoun, Sumner, and Thomas Jefferson (Document 8-5).

2. Evaluate and synthesize the evidence in this chapter to construct a persuasive historical argument explaining why the Civil War broke out in 1861.

3. To what extent does the concept of Manifest Destiny (or territorial expansionism) provide an appropriate historical context for understanding the political events during the period from 1844 to 1860?

4. What are the advantages and limitations of identifying 1844 to 1860 as a coherent period in United States history? What argument do historians make about American history by emphasizing this periodization?

14

Two Societies at War
1861–1865

In the fading months of war, during his second inaugural address, Abraham Lincoln expressed the hope that the war would end "with malice toward none; with charity for all." It was an audacious wish given the carnage of the four bloody years of war and a hope dimmed by his martyrdom at the hands of an assassin just six weeks later. The peace he hoped for would have to overcome the strains of war. The economy of the South suffered miserable setbacks, reversing fortunes and exacerbating the impoverished lives of those already on the margins. The war overturned the political and social structure of southern communities and polarized opinions between the sections. Northerners squabbled with northerners and southerners with other southerners, heightening the challenge of finding common ground to build the just and lasting peace Lincoln wanted. Slavery, as Lincoln said, was "the cause of the war," and its destruction was the war's crowning achievement. The struggle to achieve freedom, initially won with Lincoln's Emancipation Proclamation then generally by the Thirteenth Amendment, changed the lives of former slaves. At the same time, it transformed the two societies at war, leaving no one untouched.

14-1 | A Southern Woman Opposes Secession

MARY BERKELEY MINOR BLACKFORD, *Letter to John Minor* (1861)

A month before the Virginia secession convention met in Richmond, Mary Blackford wrote to her cousin John Minor to express her anguish at the thought of a divided Union. Like many, she lived with the contradictions of a slave society. A vocal champion of colonization, she raised funds to send free blacks and emancipated slaves to Liberia, yet her family also owned a few slaves, whom her husband deemed essential to helping his physically debilitated wife. In this letter, she expresses her views on the secession crisis.

Lynchburg, Jany 18th 1861.

My dear friend & Cousin

I suffer at times such anguish of mind about the ruin of our great Country, and the prospect of Civil war, that I feel impelled to write to you, just to pour out my heart—not that I think it can do any good, No, No one can help us now but God, all our hope and trust must be in Him.

Oh! for the faith that can look at the threatened ruin and see God in all, and believe He can and will, make "the wrath of man to praise Him." To feel with the Prophet, "That though the fig tree shall not blossom, neither shall fruit be in the vines. The labor of the olive shall fail, and the fields shall yield no meat, the flock shall be cut off from the fold, and there shall be no herd in the stalls. Yet, I will rejoice in the Lord, I will joy in the God of my salvation."

But such faith is hard to have for though I know His power, and believe and trust—still it seems that the working of His will inflicts a sorrow that I sink under. I know we deserve His chastisements, for we have been most ungrateful and committed great wrongs but it falls on me with a weight that I feel sometimes will sink me into my grave.

When my Lucy died, though, she was the charm of our life, I felt so sure she had gone into everlasting happiness that it was a sort of holy sorrow, it seemed to stimulate me to try to meet her. It deepens as I grow older and feel more and more how good a child I lost—but Oh how different from this—To see my sons arrayed against one part of their Country, and our own "Star spangled banner," and *in such a cause*, is a sorrow that makes me feel that the grave is the only place for me. You did not know my dear John the pains I took to train my five sons in sentiments of patriotism and other noble thoughts.

But the world is too much for me—My voice is drowned, And I have nothing left but to die.

In the war of 1812 I used to hear from my Father sentiments that sunk into my heart, when he little thought of the impression he was making—they were like those of the revolution, Oh, how unlike what are held now.

Mary Berkeley Minor Blackford to John Barbee Minor, January 18, 1861 (Minor and Wilson Family Papers, Special Collections, University of Virginia).

But why talk any more of my own feelings, but bear with me, it is a relief. There are *very* few I can talk to. Pray don't shew my letter you know it is treason in the eyes of many, to hold these sentiments I do—And I do not want to injure my husband and children.

I suppose my Mary is with you now. I was glad to have her pay you a visit—How she used to enjoy her visits at your house, and what kind and judicious friends you were to her. May my Mary retain your friendship as *She* did to the last, and have your counsels, and Nannie as to her conduct—and as regards her immortal interests.

Give my best love to all of them, but perhaps it would be best not speak of getting this letter.

Your affectionate Cousin

M B. BLACKFORD

READING AND DISCUSSION QUESTIONS

1. How does Blackford's letter provide historians with evidence of multiple and differing perspectives on secession in the short period following Abraham Lincoln's election as president? What perspective on secession does she have? What are the differing perspectives she alludes to?

2. What is the historical context she is reacting to that prompted the letter's last line: "but perhaps it would be best not [to] speak of getting this letter"?

14-2 | War's Impact on Southern Economy
STAUNTON SPECTATOR, *The Uses of Economy* (1862)

The war's impact on the home front was felt especially hard in the South, where most of the fighting took place. In this newspaper article from the November 1862 *Staunton Spectator*, Virginians are urged to practice economy at home. The article alludes to the Union blockade of Virginia's James River and coast, part of Lincoln's strategy announced in 1861 to encircle the Confederacy and starve it of resources. A year and a half into the war, the effect of the blockade and the "presence of the enemy" were clearly felt.

There is every reason to believe, from present appearances, says the Lynchburg Virginian, that we shall be short of supplies for one army and people next year. The short crop of wheat and corn for the past year, the fatality that has attended the hog crop; the waste superinduced by large standing armies; the drought which has retarded the Fall operations of farmers in getting their wheat sown, and the embarrassments that the agricultural portion of our citizens have

"The Uses of Economy," *Staunton Spectator*, November 4, 1862 (Valley of the Shadow project, University of Virginia Library), http://vshadow.vcdh.virginia.edu.

suffered, in consequence of the presence of the enemy, and the demand made upon them by our Governments, State and Confederate, will we fear, be manifest in a short supply of bread and meat next year. It behooves us therefore to observe the greatest frugality and economy in the use of what we have. It matters not that we have a plethora of money, or that there be an abundance elsewhere to supply our lack, when we are excluded from the markets of the world, and are compelled to rely upon what we have within ourselves. Money cannot produce one grain of corn, or increase by one pound, our quantity of meat. Our supply will be limited by the circumstances that surround us, and to that, whether much or little, we must contine [*sic*] ourselves. We cannot increase it by the ordinary means of commercial intercourse. Under these circumstances, we are called upon to husband our resources of bread and meat, by the diminution, so far as practicable, of consumption. We should stint ourselves, and those who have spread a bounteous board heretofore, should, no matter what their means may be, endeavor to do with less. Thousands of our gallant soldiers who were nursed in the lap of plenty, and brought up in the midst of affluence, have known what it was to go for days together without a meal:—and cannot we, to increase the stores that may be necessary for their sustenance in the field, endure some little of their patient self-denial? We can do with much less than we consume, and instead of priding ourselves upon spreading an ample board, groaning with every luxury, we should feel a sense of reproach for indulging in such improprieties. This is no time for feasting and high carnival, but for earnest self-denial, and abounding patriotism and charity. Our suffering countrymen, and the dependent families they have committed to our care whilst they are fighting our battles, demand that we appropriate less to ourselves, and more to those who would be glad to gather the crumbs that fall from many of our tables. The season, the condition of the country, the wants of those to whom we have referred, and the prospect before us, all call upon us, trumpet-tongued, to forego every species of luxury during the existence of this war.

READING AND DISCUSSION QUESTIONS

1. In addition to the blockade and the presence of the Union army in the South, the article mentions other factors impacting the southern economy. How would you analyze and evaluate the interaction of these multiple causes and effects on the outcome of the war?

2. Based on your analysis and evaluation of this piece of historical evidence, what inferences can you draw about the prospects for a Confederate victory at the end of 1862? What point of view does the article express about the South's ability to win?

14-3 | A Battlefield View of the Cost of War

CORNELIA HANCOCK, *Letters of a Civil War Nurse* (1863)

While the economic costs of the war were visible in the unplowed fields, unsold cotton bales, and bread riots, the emotional sacrifices were borne by the families who experienced the brutalities of war and the loss of life. Cornelia Hancock witnessed the effects of that brutality while nursing soldiers back to health or toward as peaceful a death as possible. In her letters home, she recounts her experiences in the field hospitals following the major battle at Gettysburg, Pennsylvania, in July 1863, one of the "turning point" battles of the war.

Gettysburg, Pa. July 7th, 1863.

My dear cousin

I am very tired tonight; have been on the field all day—went to the 3rd Division 2nd Army Corps. I suppose there are about five hundred wounded belonging to it. They have one patch of woods devoted to each army corps for a hospital. I being interested in the 2nd, because Will [her brother] had been in it, got into one of its ambulances, and went out at eight this morning and came back at six this evening. There are no words in the English language to express the sufferings I witnessed today. The men lie on the ground; their clothes have been cut off them to dress their wounds; they are half naked, have nothing but hard-tack to eat only as Sanitary Commissions, Christian Associations, and so forth give them. I was the first woman who reached the 2nd Corps after the three days fight at Gettysburg. I was in that Corps all day, not another woman within a half mile. Mrs. Harris was in first division of 2nd Corps. I was introduced to the surgeon of the post, went anywhere through the Corps, and received nothing but the greatest politeness from even the lowest private. You can tell Aunt that there is every opportunity for "secesh" sympathizers to do a good work among the butternuts;[1] we have lots of them here suffering fearfully. To give you some idea of the extent and numbers of the wounds, four surgeons, none of whom were idle fifteen minutes at a time, were busy all day amputating legs and arms. I gave to every man that had a leg or arm off a gill of wine, to every wounded in Third Division, one glass of lemonade, some bread and preserves and tobacco—as much as I am opposed to the latter, for they need it very much, they are so exhausted.

I feel very thankful that this was a successful battle; the spirit of the men is so high that many of the poor fellows said today, "What is an arm or leg to whipping Lee out of Penn." I would get on first rate if they would not ask me to write to their wives; that I cannot do without crying, which is not pleasant to either party. I do not mind the sight of blood, have seen limbs taken off and was not sick at all.

South After Gettysburg: Letters of Cornelia Hancock from the Army of the Potomac, 1863–1865, ed. Henrietta Stratton Jaquette (Philadelphia: University of Pennsylvania Press, 1937), 7–20.

[1]**butternuts**: An extreme faction of the Peace Democrats.

It is a very beautiful, rolling country here; under favorable circumstances I should think healthy, but now for five miles around, there is an awful smell of putrefaction. Women are needed here very badly, anyone who is willing to go to field hospitals, but nothing short of an order from Secretary Stanton or General Halleck will let you through the lines. Major General Schenk's order for us was not regarded as anything; if we had not met Miss Dix at Baltimore Depot, we should not have gotten through. It seems a strange taste but I am glad we did. We stay at Doctor Horner's house at night—direct letters care of Dr. Horner, Gettysburg, Pa. If you could mail me a newspaper, it would be a great satisfaction, as we do not get the news here and the soldiers are so anxious to hear; things will be different here in a short time.

CORNELIA

Gettysburg—July 8th, 1863.

My dear sister

We have been two days on the field; go out about eight and come in about six—go in ambulances or army buggies. The surgeons of the Second Corps had one put at our disposal. I feel assured I shall never feel horrified at anything that may happen to me hereafter. There is a great want of surgeons here; there are hundreds of brave fellows, who have not had their wounds dressed since the battle. Brave is not the word; more, more Christian fortitude never was witnessed than they exhibit, always say—"Help my neighbor first he is worse." The Second Corps did the heaviest fighting, and, of course, all who were badly wounded, were in the thickest of the fight, and, therefore, we deal with the very best class of the men—that is the bravest. My name is particularly grateful to them because it is Hancock. General Hancock is very popular with his men. The reason why they suffer more in this battle is because our army is victorious and marching on after Lee, leaving the wounded for citizens and a very few surgeons. The citizens are stripped of everything they have, so you must see the exhausting state of affairs. The Second Army Corps alone had two thousand men wounded, this I had from the Surgeon's head quarters. I cannot write more. There is no mail that comes in, we send letters out: I believe the Government has possession of the road. I hope you will write. It would be very pleasant to have letters to read in the evening, for I am so tired I cannot write them. Get the Penn Relief to send clothing here; there are many men without anything but a shirt lying in poor shelter tents, calling on God to take them from this world of suffering; in fact the air is rent with petitions to deliver them from their sufferings.

C. HANCOCK

Direct boxes—E. W. Farnham, care of Dr. Homer, Gettysburg, Penna. for Second Corps Hospital. Do not neglect this; clothing is shockingly needed. We fare pretty well for delicacies sent up by men from Baltimore.

If you direct your letters Miss Hancock, Second Corps, Third Division Hospital, do not scruple to put the Miss to it, and leave out Cornelia, as I am known only by that cognomen. I do not know when I shall go home—it will be according to how long this hospital stays here and whether another battle comes soon. I can go right in an ambulance without being any expense to myself. The Christian Committee support us and when they get tired the Sanitary is on hand. Uncle Sam is very rich, but very slow, and if it was not for the Sanitary, much suffering would ensue. We give the men toast and eggs for breakfast, beef tea at ten o'clock, ham and bread for dinner, and jelly and bread for supper. Dried rusk[2] would be nice if they were only here. Old sheets we would give much for. Bandages are plenty but sheets very scarce. We have plenty of woolen blankets now, in fact the hospital is well supplied, but for about five days after the battle, the men had no blankets nor scarce any shelter.

It took nearly five days for some three hundred surgeons to perform the amputations that occurred here, during which time the rebels lay in a dying condition without their wounds being dressed or scarcely any food. If the rebels did not get severely punished for this battle, then I am no judge. We have but one rebel in our camp now; he says he never fired his gun if he could help it, and, therefore, we treat him first rate. One man died this morning. I fixed him up as nicely as the place will allow; he will be buried this afternoon. We are becoming somewhat civilized here now and the men are cared for well.

On reading the news of the copperhead[3] performance, in a tent where eight men lay with nothing but stumps (they call a leg cut off above the knee a "stump") they said if they held on a little longer they would form a stump brigade and go and fight them. We have some plucky boys in the hospital, but they suffer awfully. One had his leg cut off yesterday, and some of the ladies, newcomers, were up to see him. I told them if they had seen as many as I had they would not go far to see the sight again. I could stand by and see a man's head taken off I believe—you get so used to it here. I should be perfectly contented if I could receive my letters. I have the cooking all on my mind pretty much. I have torn almost all my clothes off of me, and Uncle Sam has given me a new suit. William says I am very popular here as I am such a contrast to some of the office-seeking women who swarm around hospitals. I am black as an Indian and dirty as a pig and as well as I ever was in my life—have a nice bunk and tent about twelve feet square. I have a bed that is made of four crotch sticks and some sticks laid across and pine boughs laid on that with blankets on top. It is equal to any mattress ever made. The tent is open at night and sometimes I have laid in the damp all night long, and got up all right in the morning.

The suffering we get used to and the nurses and doctors, stewards, etc., are very jolly and sometimes we have a good time. It is very pleasant weather now. There is all in getting to do what you want to do and I am doing that. . . .

Pads are terribly needed here. Bandages and lint are plenty. I would like to see seven barrels of dried rusk here. I do not know the day of the week or

---

[2]**Dried rusk**: A dried biscuit.
[3]**copperhead**: A term of derision used to refer to antiwar northern Democrats.

anything else. Business is slackening a little though—order is beginning to reign in the hospital and soon things will be right. One poor fellow is hollowing fearfully now while his wounds are being dressed.

There is no more impropriety in a young person being here provided they are sensible than a sexagenarian. Most polite and obliging are all the soldiers to me.

It is a very good place to meet celebrities; they come here from all parts of the United States to see their wounded. Senator Wilson, Mr. Washburn, and one of the Minnesota Senators have been here. I get beef tenderloin for dinner.—Ladies who work are favored but the dress-up palaverers are passed by on the other side. I tell you I have lost my memory almost entirely, but it is gradually returning. Dr. Child has done very good service here. All is well with me; we do not know much war news, but I know I am doing all I can, so I do not concern further. Kill the copperheads. Write everything, however trifling, it is all interest here.

From thy affectionate
C. HANCOCK

3rd Division—2nd Army Corps Hospital
Gettysburg, Pa. July 26th—Sunday.

My dear mother

Today is Sunday but there is no semblance of it here. It is now about five o'clock in the morning. Our hospital has been moved and our stores have given out. There is nothing to cook with, hence I have nothing to do, and, therefore, have time to write. Such days will come here that we have to see our wounded men fed with dry bread and poor coffee; and I can tell you it is hard to witness some cursing for food, some praying for it. It seems to be no one's fault but will happen. All the luxuries that the men get come through the Christian Commission, Sanitary, Ladies Aid, etc. I would give anything to have a barrel of butter, and some dried rusk that I have seen in our parlor. I wish you would get up something of the kind and have Mrs. Jones requested to forward to me. I should think it would be as satisfactory for me to have them as for them to be sown broadcast on the land. I could make a report of everything I received and write to the Society.

I received a silver medal from the soldiers which cost twenty dollars. I know what thee will say—that the money could have been better laid out. It was very complimentary though. One of the soldiers has a sword that he found on the battlefield, which he is going to give to me before I come home. If they were only where they could buy I should be so loaded with baggage, I should never be able to get home. I shall not come home, unless I get sick, while this hospital lasts. I have two men detailed to wait on me, which suits of course. They are now fixing up nice little tables and all such things all around the tent. I have eight wall tents full of amputated men. The tents of the wounded I look right out on—it is a melancholy sight, but you have no idea how soon one gets used to it. Their screams of agony do not make as much impression on me now as the reading of this letter will on you. The most painful task we have to perform here, is entertaining the friends who come from home and see their friends all mangled up. I do hate to see them. Soldiers take everything as it comes, but citizens are not inured. You will think it is a short time for me to get used to things, but it seems to me as if all my past life was a myth, and as if I had been away from home seventeen years. What I do here one would think would kill at home, but I am well and comfortable. When we get up early in the morning, our clothes are so wet that we could wring them. On they go, and by noon they are dry.

From thy affectionate daughter —
C. HANCOCK

General Hospital Gettysburg, Pa.
Aug. 6th, 1863.

My dear sister

We have all our men moved now to General Hospital. I am there, too, but the order in regard to women nurses has not yet been issued, and I do not know what my fate will be; I only know that the boys want me to stay very much, and I have been assigned to ward E. It is a great deal nicer here except that I have but fourteen of my old boys which is very trying — it is just like parting with part of one's family. I go to see the boys and some of them cry that I cannot stay. I have the first four tents abreast of the cook house, the handiest tents in the whole hospital. I have Steward Olmstead for my headquarter influence, and we have an elderly doctor for our ward. I have a large hospital tent and sleep with three other ladies, so unless I struggle very hard to find it my friends need fear no harm for me. I am better than I am at home. I feel so good when I wake up in the morning. I received a letter announcing Sallie S's death. It does not appear to me as if one death is anything to me now. I do want my watch very much indeed; if you can get any show of a safe way of sending it do so; I want my own gold one. I expect I shall be able to draw twelve dollars from the government now, but if thee can draw any money for hospital purposes or for me, send it along, for it is a poor place to be without money. If there should be an opportunity to send my purple dress, best bonnet and mantilla, I should like to have them; this hospital will not stay here more than three weeks and nobody knows what I may want to do by that time. I may come home if there is no other battle. Dr. Dwinelle gave me a splendid recommendation to Dr. Chamberlain, Surgeon in charge here. I am good friends with Sanitary, Christian, and all here, if it only lasts. One of the boys died yesterday, and one had his leg amputated fresh. Cadet Brown I sent to your house to tell you I was well. Col. Colville is getting some better; he expects Dr. Child here.

No citizens are allowed in Camp without a pass only after four o'clock. The militia go around after dark and pick up stragglers to take them out of camp. The other night they asked me if I was a detailed nurse. As it was before I was sworn in, I had to say "No." They said their orders were peremptory, so I would have to go, but Steward Olmstead appeared and told them that I was all right, so they went away. I expect I shall be in the guard house! — but that is only a part of soldiering if I am. I do not meddle or make up with any one here but the ward master, doctor of our ward and Steward Olmstead. We have twenty women here about, some of them are excellent, but a more willful, determined set you never saw. Send this letter to mother for I hate to take the time to write often.

C. HANCOCK

General Hospital — Aug. 8th, 1863.

My dear Sallie[4]

It is well that thee is persevering enough to write to me without an answer for it is almost impossible for me to find time to write. In the morning before breakfast, before the men wake up, is the time we write, for as soon as the men are awake, they want something and continue in that state until late at night. Our hospital is on rising ground, divided off into six avenues, and eighteen tents holding twelve men each on each avenue. We call four tents a ward and name them by a letter; mine is ward E. The water is excellent and there is order about everything. I like it a great deal better than the battlefield, but the battlefield is where one does most good. I shall go to the front if there comes another battle, if not we shall stay in this hospital until fall. If thee was here thee would be very useful to run errands. I make friends with every one on the ground and get on first rate. Sallie S. I hear has passed away. But as surely as I live it does not seem to me as if I should ever make any account of death again. I have seen it disposed of in such a summary manner out here.

It is now about nine o'clock, every tent has a light in it, and a lot of groaning sick men. Our cook-house alone is a sight; they have meals cooked for thirteen hundred men, so you may know that they have to have the pots middling size. If you ever saw anything done on a large scale, it is done so here. There are many sights here, but the most melancholy one is to see the wounded come in in a long train of ambulances after night fall. I must be hardhearted though, for I do not feel these things as strangers do. What is the war news? I do not know the news at all. I never read the papers now, which is a slight change for me. I look at it in this way that I am doing all a woman can do to help the war along, and, therefore, I feel no responsibility. If people take an interest in me because I am a heroine, it is a great mistake for I feel like anything but a heroine.

Miss Dix was in camp today and stuck her head in the tents, but she does not work at all, and her nurses are being superseded very fast. I think we have some excellent nurses; we must have at least thirty women in the whole hospital. I have one tent of Johnnies in my ward, but I am not obliged to give them anything but whiskey.

I have no doubt that most people think I came into the army to get a husband. It is a capital place for that, as there are very many nice men here, and all men are required to give great respect to women. There are many good-looking women here who galavant around in the evening, and have a good time. I do not

---

[4]**Sallie:** Her niece.

trouble myself much with the common herd. There is one man who is my right-hand man; he is about nineteen years old—is a hospital steward and will do anything to accommodate.

I want you to direct your boxes General Hospital, Ward E—Gettysburg. Things ought to be sent to Gettysburg, as here is the place where there are the most wounded, whether my name is on them or not. Things are all put into Mrs. Duncan's hands in this hospital; I should not have control as I had at Corps Hospital. I am going to town soon to look after the boxes that have been sent to me.

THY AUNT, CORNELIA

Camp Letterman Hospital—Gettysburg,
Aug. 14th, 1863.

My dear mother

I received thy letter this morning and was glad to get it; letters are the desideratum in this part of the world. I am regularly installed in the General Hospital now, and like it better even than the Corps Hospital. The main reason for my staying, aside from duty, is that I am so well, if it only lasts. I feel like a new person, eat onions, potatoes, cucumbers, anything that comes up and walk as straight as a soldier, feel life and vigor which you well know I never felt at home. The place here is very healthy. I cannot explain it, but I feel so erect, and can go steadily from one thing to another from half past six o'clock in the morning until ten o'clock at night, and feel more like work at ten than when I got up at home.

My Twelve dollars per month from the government, if it should come, would pay my washing, and that is all the expense I am at, at present. I got a barrel of pads and dried fruit, and handkerchiefs to-day from express office. I have not received the box from the Salem ladies yet but I expect I shall.

From thy affectionate daughter—
C. HANCOCK

Camp Letterman, General Hospital,
Aug. 17, 1863.

Dear mother

I always spend my evenings in the post office. I am alive and well, doing duty still in the general hospital. I do think military matters are enough to aggravate a saint. We no sooner get a good physician than an order comes to remove, promote, demote or something. Everything seems to be done to aggravate the wounded. They do not get any butter; there is certainly a want of generalship somewhere for there is surely enough butter in the United States to feed these brave wounded. There are many hardships that soldiers have to endure that cannot be explained unless experienced. I have nothing to do in the hospital after dark which is well for me—all the skin is off my toes, marching so much. I am not tired of being here, feel so much interest in the men under my charge. The friends of men who have died seem so grateful to me for the little that it was in my power to do for them. I saw a man die in half a minute from the effects of chloroform; there is nothing that has affected me so much since I have been here; it seems almost like deliberate murder. His friends arrived to-day but he had to be buried before they came. Every kind of distress comes upon the friends of soldiers.

We have a nice table, meals regularly, and the nicest roast beef every day, cornbread too.

To think there is not one of the men under my care that can get up yet! How patient they are though, never complain and lay still from day to day—how different from sick men at home. I am published on the walls of the tent as the "Lady-nurse." All kinds of conversation go on here every day. . . . Tell father that I have my shoes greased and do everything in army style.

From thy daughter,
C. HANCOCK

READING AND DISCUSSION QUESTIONS

1. Analyze Hancock's letters as a historical source. Consider her audience and what you think was her purpose in writing. What argument about women's experiences during wartime can you make based on the evidence contained in her letters?

2. What conclusions can you draw, based on Hancock's letters, about the effect of war on the lives of soldiers and their families?

14-4 | Political Divisions over Freeing the Slaves

ABRAHAM LINCOLN, *Emancipation Proclamation* (1863) and JEFFERSON DAVIS, *President's Message* (1863)

Abraham Lincoln's Emancipation Proclamation, which he announced in September 1862, became official on January 1, 1863. It declared free all those enslaved persons within states then in rebellion against the United States. Jefferson Davis, president of the Confederate States of America, responded to Lincoln's measure with a message condemning emancipation, which he sent to the Confederacy's Senate and House of Representatives.

Emancipation Proclamation

Whereas, on the twenty-second day of September, in the year of our Lord one thousand eight hundred and sixty-two, a proclamation was issued by the President of the United States, containing, among other things, the following, to wit:

"That on the first day of January, in the year of our Lord one thousand eight hundred and sixty-three, all persons held as slaves within any State or desig-

---

Abraham Lincoln, *Emancipation Proclamation*, The Avalon Project (avalon.law.yale.edu).

nated part of a State, the people whereof shall then be in rebellion against the United States, shall be then, thenceforward, and forever free; and the Executive Government of the United States, including the military and naval authority thereof, will recognize and maintain the freedom of such persons, and will do no act or acts to repress such persons, or any of them, in any efforts they may make for their actual freedom.

"That the Executive will, on the first day of January aforesaid, by proclamation, designate the States and parts of States, if any, in which the people thereof, respectively, shall then be in rebellion against the United States; and the fact that any State, or the people thereof, shall on that day be, in good faith, represented in the Congress of the United States by members chosen thereto at elections wherein a majority of the qualified voters of such State shall have participated, shall, in the absence of strong countervailing testimony, be deemed conclusive evidence that such State, and the people thereof, are not then in rebellion against the United States."

Now, therefore I, Abraham Lincoln, President of the United States, by virtue of the power in me vested as Commander-in-Chief, of the Army and Navy of the United States in time of actual armed rebellion against the authority and government of the United States, and as a fit and necessary war measure for suppressing said rebellion, do, on this first day of January, in the year of our Lord one thousand eight hundred and sixty-three, and in accordance with my purpose so to do publicly proclaimed for the full period of one hundred days, from the day first above mentioned, order and designate as the States and parts of States wherein the people thereof respectively, are this day in rebellion against the United States, the following, to wit:

Arkansas, Texas, Louisiana, (except the Parishes of St. Bernard, Plaquemines, Jefferson, St. John, St. Charles, St. James Ascension, Assumption, Terrebonne, Lafourche, St. Mary, St. Martin, and Orleans, including the City of New Orleans) Mississippi, Alabama, Florida, Georgia, South Carolina, North Carolina, and Virginia, (except the forty-eight counties designated as West Virginia, and also the counties of Berkley, Accomac, Northampton, Elizabeth City, York, Princess Ann, and Norfolk, including the cities of Norfolk and Portsmouth[)], and which excepted parts, are for the present, left precisely as if this proclamation were not issued.

And by virtue of the power, and for the purpose aforesaid, I do order and declare that all persons held as slaves within said designated States, and parts of States, are, and henceforward shall be free; and that the Executive government of the United States, including the military and naval authorities thereof, will recognize and maintain the freedom of said persons.

And I hereby enjoin upon the people so declared to be free to abstain from all violence, unless in necessary self-defence; and I recommend to them that, in all cases when allowed, they labor faithfully for reasonable wages.

And I further declare and make known, that such persons of suitable condition, will be received into the armed service of the United States to garrison forts, positions, stations, and other places, and to man vessels of all sorts in said service.

And upon this act, sincerely believed to be an act of justice, warranted by the Constitution, upon military necessity, I invoke the considerate judgment of mankind, and the gracious favor of Almighty God.

In witness whereof, I have hereunto set my hand and caused the seal of the United States to be affixed.

Done at the City of Washington, this first day of January, in the year of our Lord one thousand eight hundred and sixty three, and of the Independence of the United States of America the eighty-seventh.

> By the President: Abraham Lincoln
> William H. Seward, Secretary of State.

Message from Jefferson Davis to the Confederate Congress

The public journals of the North have been received containing a proclamation dated on the first day of the present month signed by the President of the United States in which he orders and declares all slaves within ten States of the Confederacy to be free, except such as are found in certain districts now occupied in part by the armed forces of the enemy.

We may well leave it to the instincts of that common humanity which a beneficent Creator has implanted in the breasts of our fellowmen of all countries to pass judgment on a measure by which several millions of human beings of an inferior race, peaceful and contented laborers in their sphere, are doomed to extermination, while at the same time they are encouraged to a general assassination of their masters by the insidious recommendation "to abstain from violence unless in necessary self-defense." Our own detestation of those who have attempted the most execrable measure recorded in the history of guilty man is tempered by profound contempt for the impotent rage which it discloses. So far as regards the action of this Government on such criminals as may attempt its execution I confine myself to informing you that I shall unless in your wisdom you deem some other course more expedient deliver to the several State authorities all commissioned officers of the United States that may hereafter be captured by our forces in any of the States embraced in the proclamation that they may be dealt with in accordance with the laws of those States providing for the punishment of criminals engaged in exciting servile insurrection. The enlisted soldiers I shall continue to treat as unwilling instruments in the commission of these crimes and shall direct their discharge and return to their homes on the proper and usual parole.

JEFF'N DAVIS.

The War of the Rebellion: A Compilation of the Official Records of the Union and Confederate Armies, Series 2, Vol. 5, Part 1 (Washington, DC: Government Printing Office, 1898–1899), 807–808.

READING AND DISCUSSION QUESTIONS

1. Compare the views toward emancipation revealed in Lincoln's proclamation and Davis's response. How do their views reflect the historical context of race relations in the mid-nineteenth century?

2. Summarize Lincoln's policy toward enslaved African Americans and the states in rebellion against the Union. Upon what ground did he justify his emancipation policy? How radical do you consider Lincoln's policy at the time?

3. What does Davis's message reveal about his strategy for dealing with Lincoln's Emancipation Proclamation? What is the veiled threat Davis makes regarding the Confederacy's policy respecting Union efforts to enforce emancipation?

14-5 | Hearing the News of Emancipation

HARRY SMITH, *Fifty Years of Slavery* (1891)

Born a slave in 1815, Harry Smith witnessed the violence of slavery firsthand. In his memoir, published in 1891, he remembered a vicious attack against a free African American by rogue Confederates retaliating against Lincoln's Emancipation Proclamation. The horror of that scene contrasts with his recollection of the day Master Charles Hays reluctantly told his slaves, Harry included, that they were free. Harry was lucky. Many masters hid the news from their slaves until the presence of Union troops forced their hand.

Twelve negro men and women were caught in giving information where a lot of guerrellas were secreted. The men were taken down to salt river, a hole cut in the ice and they were singled out, shot and pushed under the ice.

Nearly one mile from this toll-gate fifty slaves were overtaken, who were on their way to join the Union army, and shot by their friends. Smith assisted in burying all of them.

Smith was a witness to the following inhuman treatment: several negroes were overtaken, on the pike to join the Yankees, by the Southern men, and their ears cut off, they then rode up to a saloon where a Yankee was selling liquor, and after drinking, threw the ears in the saloon-keeper's face, saying to him, "there you Yankee, is some scrip for you, take that." And then they passed on to hunt for some one else to practice their beastly treatment on.

Before proceeding further in this work, least it might be neglected, we will relate a horrible and beastly crime which took place under Smith's observation. An old man who had been free for some time, had no use of his feet being born a cripple, and being a great religious man, he was often found praying. He was taken by the Rebels, holes cut through his thighs large enough to receive his crippled feet, and crossing them, they forced them through the holes and left him to die, which he very soon did. The poor negro praying all the time. They left him

Harry Smith, *Fifty Years of Slavery in the United States of America* (Grand Rapids, MI: West Michigan Printing Co., 1891), 119–126.

in this dying condition with curses on their lips, exclaiming at the same time, "now die you d--d negro, and pray for yourself instead of us."

It would be impossible to give the reader even a faint idea of all the scenes and circumstances enacted by our Union men, with these notorious guerrillas.

There was great excitement and amusing scenes occured when the slaves on Hay's plantation heard the news of Lincoln's emancipation proclamation.

Some days had elapsed after the freedom of the slaves, when a number of Union men were passing, enquired of the slaves if their master had set them free. Massa Hays began to be alarmed for fear of being arrested, in case he did not inform them of their freedom. One morning as the slaves were eating, Massa Hays came in an walked around the table very uneasy, and bracing himself up in the best manner possible, spoke to them in this manner, "Men and women hear me, I am about to tell you something I never expected to be obliged to tell you in my life, it is this: it becomes my duty to inform you, one and all, [women], men and children, belonging to me, you are free to go where you please." At the same time cursing Lincoln and exclaiming, if he was here, I would kill him for taking all you negroes away from me.

After old Massa had cooled off from this painful duty, he told them to go to the grocery where he had whiskey barreled up and help themselves and get what they wanted. Then commenced a great jubilee among, not only the slaves, but old Massa, and all on the plantation seemed to join in the festivities. Old Massa got drunk and repaired to his room. His daughter, a fine young lady never known to drink, was much the worse for drinking. All were cheering Abraham Lincoln, while old Massa was too drunk to notice much. Old Aunt Bess an old colored woman, and very religious, who looked after the children, as well as the rest, used too much wine and to show her mode of rejoicing, sang old time songs, which added very much to the celebration. Preparations were made and at night dancing was began in earnest, and kept up until morning. Old Massa giving all liberty to help themselves to everything. Some of the slaves did not fully comprehend what it all meant, while others, more intelligent, enjoyed it to the full extent. Never was such a scene witnessed on the plantation before.

The writer cannot picture it to the reader, the rejoicing on this plantation and other places in the vicinity, on the announcement of the freedom of the slaves. Old Aunt Bess exclaimed, "bress de Lord, Im glad de Lord has spared me to see dis great day, my children are all free," she singing and shouting all the time.

Knowing what a great day this was to the enslaved negro, it is truly no wonder to the intelligent reader that they rejoiced and still keep in memory the emancipation day and will for all future time to come. History will repeat itself, and in ages to come, President Lincoln and many of the brave men will be immortalized.

One month after the announcement of the freedom of the slaves, there was a day appointed in Louisville to celebrate this great event. Senator Palmer and several other noted speakers, both white and black, made appropriate speeches and shout after shout rent the air. Old men and women praised God that they were free. Old plantation songs rent the air. Louisville was alive with people, negroes coming from all over the country. The speeches made by the colored people at this great day would make the sadest heart laugh, while many wept for joy. Music and dancing was indulged in. Every preparation was made to make this day memorable in the annals of history. A number went back and lived with their masters for years, choosing to live in the Sunny South where their joys and sorrows had mingled together so many years.

Massa Hays would explain, after the Yankees were away out of danger, how he would like to serve them, but when he discovered any Yanks he would be sure to keep out of their way. Sometimes he would be asked by the Yankees, "Who lives in that house?" His reply would be Mr. Hays. Telling him that they would like to find the old rebel, Hays would be much pleased when they left him. Then he would blow about the Yankees again, and inform his slaves if he could see a Yankee he would kill him on the spot, always being careful that none of the Yanks were near when he had one of his courageous freaks.

READING AND DISCUSSION QUESTIONS

1. How might the thirty-year interval between the publication of his memoir and the events it purports to describe have shaped Smith's memory of his emancipation? How might the historian corroborate Smith's testimony to form an accurate history of the end of slavery?

2. What is Smith's view of his master? What image of the master's character do you think he attempted to convey with the anecdote about Hays's "courageous freaks"?

3. To what extent does Smith's memoir provide evidence of the multitude of opinions about Lincoln's Emancipation Proclamation and its impact on various groups of Americans?

14-6 | Redistributing the Land to Black Refugees

WILLIAM T. SHERMAN, *Special Field Order No. 15* (1865)

Union major general William T. Sherman was instrumental in forcing the defeat of the Confederacy. His notorious "march to the sea" across Georgia destroyed the Confederacy's resources and liberated tens of thousands of enslaved Africans who trailed Sherman's troops. His Special Field Order No. 15, issued in January 1865, aimed to deal with the challenge of displaced former slaves. Once President Andrew Johnson assumed the presidency upon Lincoln's death, he reversed Sherman's policy.

In the Field, Savannah, Ga., January 16th, 1865.

I. The islands from Charleston, south, the abandoned rice fields along the rivers for thirty miles back from the sea, and the country bordering the St. Johns river, Florida, are reserved and set apart for the settlement of the negroes now

William T. Sherman, Special Order Number 15, in *War of the Rebellion: Official Records of the Union and Confederate Armies,* ed. United States War Department (Washington, DC: Government Printing Office, 1880), 60–62.

made free by the acts of war and the proclamation of the President of the United States.

II. At Beaufort, Hilton Head, Savannah, Fernandina, St. Augustine and Jacksonville, the blacks may remain in their chosen or accustomed vocations—but on the islands, and in the settlements hereafter to be established, no white person whatever, unless military officers and soldiers detailed for duty, will be permitted to reside; and the sole and exclusive management of affairs will be left to the freed people themselves, subject only to the United States military authority and the acts of Congress. By the laws of war, and orders of the President of the United States, the negro is free and must be dealt with as such. He cannot be subjected to conscription or forced military service, save by the written orders of the highest military authority of the Department, under such regulations as the President or Congress may prescribe. Domestic servants, blacksmiths, carpenters and other mechanics, will be free to select their own work and residence, but the young and able-bodied negroes must be encouraged to enlist as soldiers in the service of the United States, to contribute their share towards maintaining their own freedom, and securing their rights as citizens of the United States.

Negroes so enlisted will be organized into companies, battalions and regiments, under the orders of the United States military authorities, and will be paid, fed and clothed according to law. The bounties paid on enlistment may, with the consent of the recruit, go to assist his family and settlement in procuring agricultural implements, seed, tools, boots, clothing, and other articles necessary for their livelihood.

III. Whenever three respectable negroes, heads of families, shall desire to settle on land, and shall have selected for that purpose an island or a locality clearly defined, within the limits above designated, the Inspector of Settlements and Plantations will himself, or by such subordinate officer as he may appoint, give them a license to settle such island or district, and afford them such assistance as he can to enable them to establish a peaceable agricultural settlement. The three parties named will subdivide the land, under the supervision of the Inspector, among themselves and such others as may choose to settle near them, so that each family shall have a plot of not more than (40) forty acres of tillable ground, and when it borders on some water channel, with not more than 800 feet water front, in the possession of which land the military authorities will afford them protection, until such time as they can protect themselves, or until Congress shall regulate their title. The Quartermaster may, on the requisition of the Inspector of Settlements and Plantations, place at the disposal of the Inspector, one or more of the captured steamers, to ply between the settlements and one or more of the commercial points heretofore named in orders, to afford the settlers the opportunity to supply their necessary wants, and to sell the products of their land and labor.

IV. Whenever a negro has enlisted in the military service of the United States, he may locate his family in any one of the settlements at pleasure, and acquire a homestead, and all other rights and privileges of a settler, as though present in person. In like manner, negroes may settle their families and engage on board the gunboats, or in fishing, or in the navigation of the inland waters, without losing any claim to land or other advantages derived from this system. But no one, unless an actual settler as above defined, or unless absent on Government service, will be entitled to claim any right to land or property in any settlement by virtue of these orders.

V. In order to carry out this system of settlement, a general officer will be detailed as Inspector of Settlements and Plantations, whose duty it shall be to visit the settlements, to regulate their police and general management, and who will furnish personally to each head of a family, subject to the approval of the President of the United States, a possessory title in writing, giving as near as possible the description of boundaries; and who shall adjust all claims or conflicts that may arise under the same, subject to the like approval, treating such titles altogether as possessory. The same general officer will also be charged with the enlistment and organization of the negro recruits, and protecting their interests while absent from their settlements; and will be governed by the rules and regulations prescribed by the War Department for such purposes.

VI. Brigadier General R. SAXTON is hereby appointed Inspector of Settlements and Plantations, and will at once enter on the performance of his duties. No change is intended or desired in the settlement now on Beaufort [Port Royal] Island, nor will any rights to property heretofore acquired be affected thereby.

By Order of Major General W. T. Sherman

READING AND DISCUSSION QUESTIONS

1. Summarize the policy regarding freed slaves that Sherman announced in January 1865. What need did he identify as pressing for those newly liberated former slaves?

2. To what extent do you see Sherman's order as part of the civil rights history of the United States? Do you see Sherman's order as a radical innovation or as limited in its scope? Explain.

▪ COMPARATIVE QUESTIONS ▪

1. Analyze and evaluate Sherman's policy regarding land redistribution. How does it compare to other sources related to land as a meaningful part of citizenship? Consider, for instance, Thomas Jefferson's comments about land (Document 7-2) and Lansford Hastings's encouragement to migrants (Document 13-1).

2. Analyze the diverse evidence from the primary sources collected in this chapter to determine the cost of war on American society. Were there any positive outcomes from the war experience? If so, what were they?

3. What can you infer from the evidence here concerning the impact of war on the lives of women? How might you account for differences in women's experiences and attitudes toward the war?

4. To what extent did midcentury ideas about race and slavery inform the various perspectives on wartime society contained in these sources?

15

Reconstruction
1865–1877

The Civil War sparked more questions than it settled. While the Thirteenth Amendment to the Constitution unambiguously decided the question of slavery, practical issues concerning freedmen's rights persisted. In the face of white southern resistance and northern fatigue, the national government created federal agencies to help freedmen transition from slavery to freedom, a journey that was burdened by persistent racism. Opposition came from those who continued to believe African Americans were either incapable of self-government—much less governing the state—or were susceptible to the political manipulation of northern opportunists. Policymakers faced other perplexing questions regarding the relationship of the former Confederate states to the Union and the social, economic, and political challenges facing a defeated South. Though this political turmoil led to a presidential impeachment, exacerbated strained relationships between the North and South, and gave birth to white-hooded violence, one undeniable truth stood out: African Americans were free.

15-1 | President Focuses on Work of Reconstruction
ABRAHAM LINCOLN, *Last Public Address* (1865)

On the night of April 11, 1865, Abraham Lincoln spoke to a joy-filled crowd gathered at the White House to celebrate the surrender of Robert E. Lee's Confederate army, a sign of the war's imminent end. Lincoln took the occasion to address the work ahead. In this speech, Lincoln discussed Louisiana's recent legislative efforts and, by doing so, signaled his approach to Reconstruction. John Wilkes Booth was in the audience that night and heard Lincoln speak. Three days later, at Ford's Theatre, he aimed a pistol at the back of Lincoln's head and pulled the trigger.

We meet this evening, not in sorrow, but in gladness of heart. The evacuation of Petersburg and Richmond, and the surrender of the principal insurgent army, give hope of a righteous and speedy peace whose joyous expression can not be restrained. In the midst of this, however, He from whom all blessings flow, must not be forgotten. A call for a national thanksgiving is being prepared, and will be duly promulgated. Nor must those whose harder part gives us the cause of rejoicing, be overlooked. Their honors must not be parcelled out with others. I myself was near the front, and had the high pleasure of transmitting much of the good news to you; but no part of the honor, for plan or execution, is mine. To Gen. Grant, his skilful officers, and brave men, all belongs. The gallant Navy stood ready, but was not in reach to take active part.

By these recent successes the re-inauguration of the national authority—reconstruction—which has had a large share of thought from the first, is pressed much more closely upon our attention. It is fraught with great difficulty. Unlike a case of a war between independent nations, there is no authorized organ for us to treat with. No one man has authority to give up the rebellion for any other man. We simply must begin with, and mould from, disorganized and discordant elements. Nor is it a small additional embarrassment that we, the loyal people, differ among ourselves as to the mode, manner, and means of reconstruction.

As a general rule, I abstain from reading the reports of attacks upon myself, wishing not to be provoked by that to which I can not properly offer an answer. In spite of this precaution, however, it comes to my knowledge that I am much censured for some supposed agency in setting up, and seeking to sustain, the new State government of Louisiana. In this I have done just so much as, and no more than, the public knows. In the Annual Message of Dec. 1863 and accompanying Proclamation, I presented a plan of re-construction (as the phrase goes) which, I promised, if adopted by any State, should be acceptable to, and sustained by, the Executive government of the nation. I distinctly stated that this was not the only plan which might possibly be acceptable; and I also distinctly protested that the Executive claimed no right to say when, or whether members should be admitted to seats in Congress from such States. This plan was, in

www.abrahamlincolnonline.org/lincoln/speeches/last.htm.

advance, submitted to the then Cabinet, and distinctly approved by every member of it. One of them suggested that I should then, and in that connection, apply the Emancipation Proclamation to the theretofore excepted parts of Virginia and Louisiana; that I should drop the suggestion about apprenticeship for freed-people, and that I should omit the protest against my own power, in regard to the admission of members to Congress; but even he approved every part and parcel of the plan which has since been employed or touched by the action of Louisiana. The new constitution of Louisiana, declaring emancipation for the whole State, practically applies the Proclamation to the part previously excepted. It does not adopt apprenticeship for freed-people; and it is silent, as it could not well be otherwise, about the admission of members to Congress. So that, as it applies to Louisiana, every member of the Cabinet fully approved the plan. The message went to Congress, and I received many commendations of the plan, written and verbal; and not a single objection to it, from any professed emancipationist, came to my knowledge, until after the news reached Washington that the people of Louisiana had begun to move in accordance with it. From about July 1862, I had corresponded with different persons, supposed to be interested, seeking a reconstruction of a State government for Louisiana. When the message of 1863, with the plan before mentioned, reached New-Orleans, Gen. Banks wrote me that he was confident the people, with his military co-operation, would reconstruct, substantially on that plan. I wrote him, and some of them to try it; they tried it, and the result is known. Such only has been my agency in getting up the Louisiana government. As to sustaining it, my promise is out, as before stated. But, as bad promises are better broken than kept, I shall treat this as a bad promise, and break it, whenever I shall be convinced that keeping it is adverse to the public interest. But I have not yet been so convinced.

I have been shown a letter on this subject, supposed to be an able one, in which the writer expresses regret that my mind has not seemed to be definitely fixed on the question whether the seceding States, so called, are in the Union or out of it. It would perhaps, add astonishment to his regret, were he to learn that since I have found professed Union men endeavoring to make that question, I have purposely forborne any public expression upon it. As appears to me that question has not been, nor yet is, a practically material one, and that any discussion of it, while it thus remains practically immaterial, could have no effect other than the mischievous one of dividing our friends. As yet, whatever it may hereafter become, that question is bad, as the basis of a controversy, and good for nothing at all—a merely pernicious abstraction.

We all agree that the seceded States, so called, are out of their proper relation with the Union; and that the sole object of the government, civil and military, in regard to those States is to again get them into that proper practical relation. I believe it is not only possible, but in fact, easier to do this, without deciding, or even considering, whether these States have ever been out of the Union, than with it. Finding themselves safely at home, it would be utterly immaterial whether they had ever been abroad. Let us all join in doing the acts necessary to restoring the proper practical relations between these States and the Union; and each forever after, innocently indulge his own opinion whether, in doing the acts, he brought the States from without, into the Union, or only gave them proper assistance, they never having been out of it.

The amount of constituency, so to speak, on which the new Louisiana government rests, would be more satisfactory to all, if it contained fifty, thirty, or even twenty thousand, instead of only about twelve thousand, as it does. It is also unsatisfactory to some that the elective franchise is not given to the colored man. I would myself prefer that it were now conferred on the very intelligent, and on those who serve our cause as soldiers. Still the question is not whether the Louisiana government, as it stands, is quite all that is desirable. The question is, "Will it be wiser to take it as it is, and help to improve it; or to reject, and disperse it?" "Can Louisiana be brought into proper practical relation with the Union sooner by sustaining, or by discarding her new State government?"

Some twelve thousand voters in the heretofore slave-state of Louisiana have sworn allegiance to the Union, assumed to be the rightful political power of the State, held elections, organized a State government, adopted a free-state constitution, giving the benefit of public schools equally to black and white, and empowering the Legislature to confer the elective franchise upon the colored man. Their Legislature has already voted to ratify the constitutional amendment recently passed by Congress, abolishing slavery throughout the nation. These twelve thousand persons are thus fully committed to the Union, and to perpetual freedom in the state—committed to the very things, and nearly all the things the nation wants—and they ask the nation[']s recognition and it's [sic] assistance to make good their committal. Now, if we reject, and spurn them, we do our utmost to disorganize and disperse them. We in effect say to the white men "You are worthless, or worse—we will neither help you, nor be helped by you." To the blacks we say "This cup of liberty which these, your old masters, hold to your lips, we will dash from you, and leave you to the chances of gathering the spilled and scattered contents in some vague and undefined when, where, and how." If this course, discouraging and paralyzing both white and black, has any tendency to bring Louisiana into proper practical relations with the Union, I have, so far, been unable to perceive it. If, on the contrary, we recognize, and sustain the new government of Louisiana the converse of all this is made true. We encourage the hearts, and nerve the arms of the twelve thousand to adhere to their work, and argue for it, and proselyte for it, and fight for it, and feed it, and grow it, and ripen it to a complete success. The colored man too, in seeing all united for him, is inspired with vigilance, and energy, and daring, to the same end. Grant that he desires the elective franchise, will he not attain it sooner by saving the already advanced steps toward it, than by running backward over them? Concede that the new government of Louisiana is only to what it should be as the egg is to the fowl, we shall sooner have the fowl by hatching the egg than by smashing it? Again, if we reject Louisiana, we also reject one vote in favor of the proposed amendment to the national Constitution. To meet this proposition, it has been argued that no more than three fourths of those States which have not attempted secession are necessary to validly ratify the amendment. I do not commit myself against this, further than to say that such a ratification would be questionable, and sure to be persistently questioned; while a ratification by three-fourths of all the States would be unquestioned and unquestionable.

I repeat the question, "Can Louisiana be brought into proper practical relation with the Union *sooner* by *sustaining* or by *discarding* her new State Government?"

What has been said of Louisiana will apply generally to other States. And yet so great peculiarities pertain to each state, and such important and sudden changes occur in the same state; and withal, so new and unprecedented is the whole case, that no exclusive, and inflexible plan can be safely prescribed as to details and colatterals [*sic*]. Such exclusive, and inflexible plan, would surely become a new entanglement. Important principles may, and must, be inflexible.

In the present *"situation"* as the phrase goes, it may be my duty to make some new announcement to the people of the South. I am considering, and shall not fail to act, when satisfied that action will be proper.

READING AND DISCUSSION QUESTIONS

1. How would you characterize Lincoln's policy toward Reconstruction? Does Lincoln come across as an idealist, like Radical Republicans, or a pragmatist who accepted compromise for the sake of progress?

2. What can you infer about Louisiana's recent experience that angered some, encouraged others, and led to Lincoln's support and approval?

3. What about his speech do you think provoked John Wilkes Booth, a southerner and Confederate sympathizer, to murder Lincoln?

15-2 | A Freed Family's Dream of Landownership

BETTY POWERS, *Federal Writers' Project Interview* (c. 1936)

Betty Powers was eight or nine years old when the Civil War ended. She was born a slave on a Texas plantation and shared in her family's jubilation when slavery ended. Seventy years later, she was interviewed by the New Deal's Federal Writers' Project, which conducted oral histories with former slaves. Despite her "head mis'ry," which she claimed impaired her memory, she recalled poignant details of her family's life in slavery and their transition to freedom with a farm of their own.

What for you wants dis old nigger's story 'bout de old slavery days? 'Tain't worth anythin'. I's jus' a hard workin' person all my life and raised de family and done right by 'em as best I knowed. To tell de truf 'bout my age, I don't know

Library of Congress, *Born in Slavery: Slave Narratives from the Federal Writers' Project, 1936–1938,* Texas Narratives, vol. XVI, Part 3, 190–192.

'zactly. I 'members de war time and de surrender time. O's old 'nough to fan flies off de white folks and de tables when surrender come. If you come 'bout five year ago, I could telt you lots more, but I's had de head mis'ry.

I's born in Harrison County, 'bout twenty-five miles from Marshall. Mass's name am Dr. Howard Perry and next he house am a li'l buildin' for he office. De plantation an awful big one, and miles long, and more'n two hundred slaves was dere. Each cabin have one family and dere am three rows of cabins 'bout half a mile long.

Mammy and pappy and us twelve chillen live in one cabin, so mammy has to cook for fourteen people, 'sides her field work. She am up way befo' daylight fixin' breakfast and supper after dark, with de pine knot torch to make de light. She cook on de fireplace in winter and in de yard in summer. All de rations measure out Sunday mornin' and it have to do for de week. It am not 'nough for heavy eaters and we has to be real careful or we goes hungry. We has meat and cornmeal and 'lasses and 'taters and peas and beans and milk. Dem short rations causes plenty trouble, 'cause de niggers has to steal food and it am de whippin' if dey gets cotched. Dey am in a fix if dey can't work for bein' hungry, 'cause it am de whippin' den, sho', so dey has to steal, and most of 'em did and takes de whippin'. Dey has de full stomach, anyway.

De babies has plenty food, so dey grow up into strong, portly men and women. Dey stays in de nursery whilst dey mammies works in de fields, and has plenty milk with cornbread crumble up in it, and potlicker, too, and honey and 'lasses on bread.

De massa and he wife am fine, but de overseer am tough, and he wife, too. Dat woman have no mercy. You see dem long ears I has? Dat's from de pullin' dey gits from her. De field hands works early and late and often all night. Pappy makes de shoes and mammy weaves, and you could hear de bump, bump of dat loom at night, when she done work in de field all day.

Missy know everything what go on, 'cause she have de spies 'mongst de slaves. She purty good, though. Sometimes de overseer tie de nigger to a log and lash him with de whip. If de lash cut de skin, dey puts salt on it. We ain't 'low to go to church and has 'bout two parties a year, so dere ain't much fun. Lawd, Lawd, most dem slaves too tired to have fun noway. When all dat work am finish, dey's glad to git in de bed and sleep.

Did we'uns have weddin's? White man, you knows better'n dat. Dem times, cullud folks am jus' put together. De massa say, "Jim and Nancy, you go live together," and when dat order give, it better be done. Dey thinks nothin' on de plantation 'bout de feelin's of de women and dere ain't no 'spect for dem. De overseer and white mens took 'vantage of de women like dey wants to. De woman better not make no fuss 'bout sich. If she do, it am de whippin' for her. I sho' thanks the Lawd surrender done come befo' I's old 'nough to have to stand for sich. Yes, sar, surrender saves dis nigger from sich.

When de war am over, thousands of sojers passes our place. Some camps nearby, and massa doctors dem. When massa call us to say we's free, dere am a yardful of niggers. He give every nigger de age statement and say dey could work on halves or for wages. He 'vises dem to stay till dey git de foothold and larn how to do. Lots stays and lots goes. My folks stays 'bout four years and works on shares. Den pappy buys de piece of land 'bout five miles from dere.

De land ain't clear, so we'uns al pitches in and clears it and builds de cabin. Was we'uns proud? There 'twas, our place to do as we pleases, after bein' slaves. Dat sho' am de good feelin'. We works live beavers puttin' de crop in, and my folks stays dere till dey dies. I leaves to git married de next year and I's only thirteen years old, and marries Boss Powers.

We'uns lives on rent land nearby for six years and has three chillen and den he dies. After two years I marries Henry Ruffins and has three more chillen, and he dies in 1911. I's livin' with two of dem now. I never took de name of Ruffins, 'cause I's dearly love Powers and can't stand to give up he name. Powers done make de will and wrote on de paper, "To my beloved wife, I gives all I has." Wasn't dat sweet of him?

I comes to Fort Worth after Ruffin dies and does housework till I's too old. Now I gits de $12.00 pension every month and dat help me git by.

READING AND DISCUSSION QUESTIONS

1. How does Powers's account help historians understand the period of Reconstruction from the perspective of social history, or the history of ordinary people?

2. Analyze and evaluate the details Powers recalls about her fellow slaves' experiences to understand the contrast she draws with her life in the era after slavery. How do those details help you understand the meaning of freedom as former slaves experienced it?

3. How does the context of this historical source, an oral history recorded decades after the events it describes, impact your assessment of its utility as evidence for the Civil War and Reconstruction eras?

15-3 | A Former Slave Owner Complains of "Negro Problem"
FRANCES BUTLER LEIGH, *Letter to a Friend in England* (1867)

While Betty Powers experienced the era of Reconstruction with the optimism of the newly freed, Frances Butler Leigh wrote defiant and discouraging letters from her father's Sea Island plantation on St. Simon's Island, Georgia. She and her father, divorced years earlier from Leigh's mother, the British actress and antislavery advocate Frances Kemble, moved from Philadelphia to the plantation just after the war ended in a failed effort to keep the family's estate afloat. Within a few years, she sold the plantation and moved to England, where she wrote *Ten Years on a Georgia Plantation Since the War* in 1883, a memoir defending the Old South.

Frances Butler Leigh, *Ten Years on a Georgia Plantation Since the War* (London: Richard Bentley & Son, Publishers in Ordinary to her Majesty the Queen, 1883), 66–71.

S. Simon's Island: June 23, 1867

Dearest S——, We are, I am afraid, going to have terrible trouble by-and-by with the Negroes, and I see nothing but gloomy prospects for us ahead. The unlimited power that the war has put into the hands of the present government at Washington seems to have turned the heads of the party now in office, and they don't know where to stop. The whole South is settled and quiet, and the people too ruined and crushed to do anything against the government, even if they felt so inclined, and all are returning to their former pursuits, trying to rebuild their fortunes and thinking of nothing else. Yet the treatment we receive from the government becomes more and more severe every day, the last act being to divide the whole South into five military districts, putting each under the command of a United States general, doing away with all civil courts and law. Even D——who you know is a Northern republican, says it is most unjustifiable, not being in any way authorised by the existing state of things, which he confesses he finds very different from what he expected before he came. If they would frankly say they intend to keep us down, it would be fairer than making a pretence of readmitting us to equal rights, and then trumping up stories of violence to give a show of justice to treating us as the conquered foes of the most despotic Government on earth, and by exciting the negroes to every kind of insolent lawlessness, to goad the people into acts of rebellion and resistance.

The other day in Charleston, which is under the command of that respectable creature General S——, they had a firemen's parade, and took the occasion to hoist a United States flag, to which this modern Gesler[1] insisted on everyone raising his cap as he passed underneath. And by a hundred other such petty tyrannies are the people, bruised and sore, being roused to desperation; and had this been done directly after the war it would have been bad enough, but it was done the other day, three years after the close of the war.

The true reason is the desire and intention of the Government to control the elections of the South, which under the constitution of the country they could not legally do. So they have determined to make an excuse for setting aside the laws, and in order to accomplish this more fully, each commander in his separate district has issued an order declaring that unless a man can take an oath that he had not voluntarily borne arms against the United States Government, nor in any way aided or abetted the rebellion, he cannot vote. This simply disqualifies every white man at the South from voting, disfranchising the whole white population, while the negroes are allowed to vote *en masse*.

This is particularly unjust, as the question of negro voting was introduced and passed in Congress as an amendment to the constitution, but in order to become a law a majority of two-thirds of the State Legislatures must ratify it, and so to them it was submitted, and rejected by all the Northern States with two exceptions, where the number of negro voters would be so small as to be

---

[1]Gesler, or Gessler, was the tyrant in the folktale *William Tell* who abused the people and forced the title character to shoot an arrow through an apple resting atop the head of Tell's son.

harmless. Our Legislatures are not allowed to meet, but this law, which the North has rejected, is to be forced upon us, whose very heart it pierces and prosperity it kills. Meanwhile, in order to prepare the negroes to vote properly, stump speakers from the North are going all through the South, holding political meetings for the negroes, saying things like this to them: "My friends, you will have your rights, won't you?" ("Yes," from the negroes.) "Shall I not go back to Massachusetts and tell your brothers there that you are going to ride in the street cars with white ladies if you please?" ("Yes, yes," from the crowd.) "That if you pay your money to go to the theatre you will sit where you please, in the best boxes if you like?" ("Yes," and applause.) This I copy verbatim from a speech made at Richmond the other day, since which there have been two serious negro riots there, and the General commanding had to call out the military to suppress them.

These men are making a tour through the South, speaking in the same way to the negroes everywhere. Do you wonder we are frightened? I have been so forcibly struck lately while reading Baker's "Travels in Africa," and some of Du Chaillu's lectures,[2] at finding how exactly the same characteristics show themselves among the negroes there, in their own native country, where no outside influences have ever affected them, as with ours here. Forced to work, they improve and are useful; left to themselves they become idle and useless, and never improve. Hard ethnological facts for the abolitionists to swallow, but facts nevertheless.

It seems foolish to fill my letter to you with such matters, but all this comes home to us with such vital force that it is hard to write, or speak, or think of anything else, and the one subject that Southerners discuss whenever they meet is, "What is to become of us?"

Affectionately yours,
F——

READING AND DISCUSSION QUESTIONS

1. Compare Leigh's point of view concerning slaves and slavery with the perspective of Susan Dabney Smedes (Document 12-5). How might you account for the differences you see in their assessments of the Old South? What factors might have shaped each viewpoint?

2. From Leigh's letter, what conclusions can you draw regarding the challenges facing the national government in mending the political divisions between northern and southern states and between the federal and state or local governments in the South?

---

[2]Leigh may be referring to Samuel White Baker's 1855 book *Eight Years' Wandering in Ceylon* and to Paul du Chaillu's 1861 *Explorations and Adventures in Equatorial Africa.*

15-4 | A Liberal Republican Opposes Universal Suffrage

CHARLES FRANCIS ADAMS JR., *The Protection of the Ballot in National Elections* (1869)

Southerners like Frances Leigh were not the only ones who doubted the wisdom of granting former slaves the right to vote. Charles Francis Adams Jr., the grandson and great-grandson of presidents, penned an article in the 1869 issue of the *Journal of Social Science* advocating restrictions on voting rights, a timely issue as the Fifteenth Amendment was wending its way toward ratification in February 1870. Adams was sympathetic to the Republican Party's liberal wing, a faction opposed to the continued federal presence in the South and to President Grant's administration for its apparent corruption. Their ideal was government by the "best men," which they hoped to achieve through civil service reforms and a more scientific approach to government administration. Restricting the vote to those with the education to understand its meaning, Adams assumed, ensured enlightened government.

If the study of social problems teaches any one lesson more distinctly than another, it is that political virtue and political corruption are never the peculiar property of any particular party in the State. Only the partisan believes that all virtue is to be found in one organization, and all vice in another. The observer soon discovers that an almost imperceptible line separates, in these respects, contemporary political organizations, and that the charges made against one faction existing in the State, with slight changes of form and detail, may, with equal justice, be made against every other. Fraud in one party begets fraud in another, and corruption begets corruption, if only under the plausible argument that the devil must be fought with the weapons of darkness. . . .

Government, through representation and suffrage, as at present developed into a system, is but one way, and a very imperfect and unsatisfactory one, of arriving at a given result. The object of every political system is to bring the loftiest development of moral and intellectual education which any given community affords to the direction of its affairs. Just at present it is the fashion to consider an extension of the suffrage,—a more elaborate and careful enumeration of noses as it were,—as the grand and effectual panacea for all political evils. This idea will certainly last out the present, and probably several succeeding generations. Without at all conceding that this system is the best that can, or, in process of time, will be devised, it is yet the system under which we and our children have perforce got to live, and the student of Social Science can devote himself to no better task than to the purifying and protecting of the system, however crude and unsatisfactory it at best may appear to him. . . .

An exciting and important national election has just been passed through, and the usual good fortune of the American people has presided over the result, in that it has not proved to be in result a disputed election. The popular verdict has been sufficiently decisive to cover any margin of fraud, on the one side or the other, and all parties concede that the new occupant will not be cheated into the Presidential Chair. This may not always be the case. The election was preceded by loud charges of wholesale fraud, made indiscriminately by each of the parties which divided the country, against the other,—the election day was marked by many scandalous incidents which well might have vitiated the results in important localities, and, finally, it has been succeeded by a general desire that something should be done, resulting in the usual unlimited suggestions of crude legislation. Two things seem likely to result from the agitation now dying away,—first, an extension of the suffrage, and, secondly, a renewed discussion of the long vexed question of the naturalization laws.

Both are important questions; in fact, without exaggeration, they might be spoken of as vital questions; and both are deserving of a calmer and more philosophical discussion, and of a decision more exempt from party exigencies, than they seem likely to receive. Yet it may possibly be that the immediate evil which presses upon the country does not lie in either of these directions; it may well be found more on the surface, a mere matter of detail or of defective organic law. The first question necessarily is,—what is the difficulty? That found, the remedy may not be far to seek. What is it that the popular instinct has been apprehensive of? What dangerous elements have developed, themselves,—what weak points in our system, which create this manifest uneasiness for the future, and the desire for change? It probably would be generally conceded that the real trouble has been that the mass of the people of all parties has been apprehensive that the purity of the ballot was not sufficiently protected; that somehow the election both could and would be carried by fraud; that the will of the people was to be corruptly set aside through some perversion of the forms of law. If this brief statement of the case is accepted as correct, it only remains to consider the manner in which, and the machinery through which the election was held, and the result arrived at, and then to suggest, if possible, some remedy for the evil experienced. . . .

Under the existing system . . . a premium is placed upon fraud. The violation of the ballot-box by one party, makes its violation by the other what is called, in the parlance of the day, a political necessity. This, indeed, is the saddest and most alarming feature of the whole system. The community not only becomes accustomed to political fraud, but it learns to excuse it as in some way a necessity. We are losing the moral sense, and censure failure alone. While the moral perceptions thus become blunted, the opportunity for fraud is more and more, in each successive election, localized and designated. The least astute politician knows just where votes are necessary and just where they are useless. The more astute know also just how many are wanted and how they are to be had, as well as where they are wanted. Fraud,—energetic, well-directed fraud, will probably soon decide every closely contested Presidential election, unless the system of Electoral Colleges is reformed out of existence. . . .

Hitherto the discussion has looked solely to the removal from our system of the great fictitious incentive to fraud at the polls,—that which unconsciously makes the whole community approach this question with an instinctive sense of its importance. It now remains to say a few words of the fraud itself, as we see and feel it, and to consider if anything can be done to insure to the ballot exemption from it. . . .

As society develops itself, and wealth, population and ignorance increase,— as the struggle for existence becomes more and more severe, the inherent difficulties of a broadly extended suffrage will make themselves felt. Starving men and women care very little for abstract questions of the general good. Political power becomes one means simply of private subsistence. In any case there are, however, but two ways of perverting the expression of the popular will,—one by the corruption of the individual voter, the other by the falsification of votes. The first of these methods is easily disposed of. It is useless and almost silly to try to prevent bribery and corruption by law. There is, in fact, no sound distinction between the citizen who sells his vote for cash, and the citizen who makes his political course subserve his personal ambition, or lends himself to some demagogue who bribes by an agrarian law. . . . No real protection to the ballot lies in that direction.

Though the law, however, cannot well prevent a man from selling his own single vote, and no penalty can reach him who does, the law can prevent a man from multiplying ballots at his own will, and selling himself for a day's steady voting, from early dawn to dewy eve, unlimited by any eight-hour law, and for every recurring election. Men cannot by law be made to respect their own rights, but they can be made not to violate those of other people. In this point of view again, the suffrage question is a national one. Under the present system, a single fraudulent vote in New York or Philadelphia is of infinitely greater public interest than a score of such votes in Boston or Chicago. Yet the control of the citizen over this question, upon which more than upon any other, his rights as a citizen depend, is limited to his own immediate neighborhood, and just beyond that, neighborhood, within his sight almost, he is conscious that he is defrauded to an unlimited extent, and yet has no power for reform. Such a condition of affairs is not a healthy one. It is one thing as regards local and State, and another as regards National elections. If certain local communities are willing to live under a lax and unregulated system of suffrage, if they do not object to seeing the franchise rendered valueless by fraud within their own limits, of course they have a right to gratify their inclinations; but they have not a right to extend that system beyond their own limits to the grave prejudice of their neighbors.

The only real protection of the purity of the ballot, under an extended system of suffrage, must, of necessity, be found in some arrangement for the careful registration of voters. . . . In view of our vastly, increasing emigration, and of the direct bearing of the naturalization laws upon every National election, it may become a serious question whether the United States will not ultimately be obliged to take the whole management of National elections into the hands of National officers. One uniform law and day for such elections, once in two years, conducted by officers of the United States for the time being, under a well digested system of registration, and with an effective law for the detection and punishment of fraud, would, while in itself open to grave objections, yet strike at the root of many of the most crying evils of the present system. . . .

For the first time in the history of mankind, America seems now approaching a practical trial of universal suffrage. It is not manhood suffrage, as at present; nor white suffrage, as formerly; nor impartial suffrage, as sometimes proposed; nor educational suffrage;—but universal suffrage in the largest sense of the term. All signs point that way. One day we hear of a Womans Rights Convention, and some Legislature barely fails to concede the principle of female suffrage; the next day some Senator proposes the total repeal of the naturalization laws, while the adopted citizen demands that he shall no longer be legally excluded from the chair of Washington. It is then proposed to extend the ballot to children, as it has already been given to freedmen. Presently impartial suffrage is suggested, and party organs at once declare it to be a dogma of American faith, that the ballot is the *inherent* right of all *white* men, "be they rich or poor, learned or unlearned." Finally the Senate of the United States, that body to which all the political wisdom of the country is supposed to gravitate, has recently, after long discussion, proposed to submit to the Legislatures an amendment to the Constitution, prohibiting all discrimination for the future among the citizens of the United States, in the right to hold office or in the exercise of the elective franchise, because "of race, color, nativity, property, education or creed." Had the single word "sex" but been included in this amendment, the bars would have been wholly thrown down, and the experiment of universal suffrage, incorporated into the organic law, would have been tried in its full simplicity.

It may well be questioned whether the American people fully appreciate the logical conclusions of the present tendency to make the suffrage a free gift to all comers. The new experiment will indeed eradicate the last vestige of caste from our institutions, and in so far is consistent with reason and experience. The future has nothing to fear from that quarter. In avoiding one danger, however, there is no absolute necessity of running into another. Caste will have been eradicated at a fearful price, if the elements leading directly to a proletariat are introduced in its place. Now universal suffrage necessarily introduces three new and untried influences into the action of the body politic. Of these the female is the first; for, though in order of time she must be enfranchised after the African and the alien, yet only those who believe in that strange political science which is evolved from party exigencies, can bow to a logic, which, while pretending to eradicate caste, refuses to grant to the Anglo-Saxon female what has been thrust on the African male. Opinions differ more as to the expediency of female suffrage than as to its logic. Experience has seemed to indicate that a certain vigorous, masculine, common-sense and self-control,—a faculty of restraint under excitement—a certain persistence and belief in the wisdom of biding his time, which characteristics have hitherto more especially developed themselves in the Anglo-Saxon race, have everywhere proved the only real safe-guards of popular liberty. Excitable natures rarely strengthen free institutions. How far a large infusion of the more voluble, demonstrative and impulsive female element into the arena of politics will tend to affect what little of calmness and reason is still found therein, remains to be seen. The white female, however, is at least of the same blood and education as the white male. This cannot be said of the African, the second of the untried influences now to be introduced. Whatever may be his latent faculty of development, however high he now should or ultimately may stand in the scale of created beings, it is safe to say that the sudden and indiscriminate elevation of his whole race to the ballot is a portentous experiment. The Anglo-Saxon was not educated to his efforts at self-government, at best but partially successful, by two centuries of Slavery superimposed on unnumbered centuries of barbarism.

The third influence about to be infused by wholesale into our system, is that of the aliens. Of the workings and tendency of this influence we have already enjoyed some experience. We now appreciate to a degree how much the purity and the significance of the suffrage have deteriorated with us through the irruption of those swarms of foreigners, who have within forty years landed on our shores. While the experience of the past throws some light on the future in this respect, it, in all probability, very inadequately foreshadows it. We have as yet witnessed only the day of small things in the way of emigration. Take the Irish exodus as an example. It has been no easy thing for us to deplete the Celtic race from one small island, and to absorb it into our body politic: still it has been done, and has resulted only in deterioration, not in catastrophe. But how is it for the future, as regards China and the East? . . .

Working upon such a mass as must result from the blending of all these incongruous elements, Universal Suffrage can only mean in plain English the government of ignorance and vice: — it means a European, and especially Celtic, proletariat on the Atlantic coast; an African proletariat on the shores of the Gulf, and a Chinese proletariat on the Pacific. One only of these has developed itself as yet and acquired firm political power, — the Celtic proletariat has possessed itself of the New York City Government and will soon be in control of that of the State; — those who wish to study the early development of the system will find ample food for reflection in the daily columns of the New York press. Those who choose may then strive to extend it.

If then the proletariat, — the organization of ignorance and vice to obtain political control, — is destructive both to the purity and significance of the ballot; — if Universal Suffrage inevitably tends with an advancing civilization to bring about such a vicious combination, then no one who believes in a Social Science as applied to the study of permanence in free institutions, can place any faith in that form of suffrage. The tendency of the day is clearly in a wrong direction. . . .

Education then only remains. A knowledge of the language of our laws and the faculty of informing oneself without aid of their provisions, would in itself constitute a test, if rigorously enforced, incompatible with the existence of a proletariat. Our efforts should be devoted to the practical development of these two principles of intelligence and impartiality in the suffrage, and of the kindred theory of the just representation of minorities. In the ideal Government, founded on the popular consent, every voice will be audible through a system of perfect representation. No barrier to a purified suffrage will be recognized which cannot be surmounted by the moderate efforts of average humanity, and the highest privilege of the citizen, at once a right and a reward, will be given or refused on the principles of even justice and stern regard for the common good.

CHARLES FRANCIS ADAMS JR.

READING AND DISCUSSION QUESTIONS

1. Analyze and evaluate Adams's argument for evidence of a historical pattern of continuity or change in America's commitment to expanded democratic rights. Are there truths within his claims?

2. How does the historical context of the Reconstruction era help you to understand the point of view held by Adams?

15-5 | Nast Lampoons Freedmen's Government

THOMAS NAST, *Colored Rule in a Reconstructed State* (1874)

Political cartoons developed sophistication in the years after the Civil War largely through the talents of the influential artist Thomas Nast, whose compositions effectively captured a frustrated electorate's disgust. In this image, Nast plays on then-common stereotypes and foregrounds the pervasive assumption northern and southern whites held about black political incompetence and corruption. Many white South Carolinians popularized these beliefs in their effort to redeem state government from the African American majority that controlled the legislature.

COLORED RULE IN A RECONSTRUCTED (?) STATE.—(SEE PAGE 242.)

(THE MEMBERS CALL EACH OTHER THIEVES, LIARS, RASCALS, AND COWARDS.)

COLUMBIA. "You are Aping the lowest Whites. If you disgrace your Race in this way you had better take Back Seats."

READING AND DISCUSSION QUESTIONS

1. Analyze and evaluate Nast's image to identify the racial stereotypes it conveys. Whose view of black political abilities does it express?

2. What is the significance of the Columbia figure standing at the speaker's platform, and what is she trying to accomplish?

3. To what extent do the stereotypes Nast employed reflect the historical context of race relations during the Reconstruction period?

15-6 | African American Congressman Urges Support of Civil Rights Bill

ROBERT BROWNE ELLIOTT, *Speech to Congress* (1874)

While planters and their former slaves negotiated a new relationship in the wake of slavery's abolition, Congress was abuzz with legislative activity to secure the rights of citizenship freedmen had so recently won. The Civil Rights Act of 1875, which the African American member of Congress Robert Elliott supported in a speech to Congress, guaranteed to African Americans equal treatment in public accommodations. In 1873, the U.S. Supreme Court decided in the *Slaughterhouse Cases* to construe the Fourteenth Amendment protections narrowly, arguing that states properly retained the exercise of power over domestic and civil rights. Here Elliott is attempting to counter anti–civil rights efforts to use these cases to frustrate federal legislative action on behalf of freedmen.

Mr. Speaker: While I am sincerely grateful for this high mark of courtesy that has been accorded to me by this House, it is a matter of regret to me that it is necessary at this day that I should rise in the presence of an American Congress to advocate a bill which simply asserts equal rights and equal public privileges for all classes of American citizens. I regret, sir, that the dark hue of my skin may lend a color to the imputation that I am controlled by motives personal to myself in my advocacy of this great measure of national justice. Sir, the motive that impels me is restricted by no such narrow boundary, but is as broad as your Constitution. I advocate it, sir, because it is right. The bill, however, not only appeals to your justice, but it demands a response from your gratitude. . . .

[S]ir, we are told by the distinguished gentleman from Georgia (Mr. Stephens) that Congress has no power under the Constitution to pass such a law, and that the passage of such an act is in direct contravention of the rights of the states. I cannot assent to any such proposition. The Constitution of a free government ought always to be construed in favor of human rights. Indeed, the thirteenth, fourteenth, and fifteenth amendments, in positive words, invest Congress with the power to protect the citizen in his civil and political rights. Now, sir, what are

Lift Every Voice: African American Oratory, 1787–1900, ed. Philip S. Foner and Robert James Branham (Tuscaloosa and London: The University of Alabama Press, 1998), 521–525, 527–528, 532–536.

civil rights? Rights natural, modified by civil society. Mr. Lieber says: "By civil liberty is meant, not only the absence of individual restraint, but liberty within the social system and political organism—a combination of principles and laws which acknowledge, protect and favor the dignity of man . . . civil liberty is the result of man's twofold character as an individual and social being, so soon as both are equally respected." . . .

Are we then, sir, with the amendments to our Constitution staring us in the face; with these grand truths of history before our eyes; with innumerable wrongs daily inflicted upon five million citizens demanding redress, to commit this question to the diversity of legislation? In the words of Hamilton, "Is it the interest of the government to sacrifice individual rights to the preservation of the rights of an artificial being called the states? There can be no truer principle than this, that every individual of the community at large has an equal right to the protection of government. Can this be a free government if partial distinctions are tolerated or maintained?"

The rights contended for in this bill are among "the sacred rights of mankind, which are not to be rummaged for among old parchments or musty records; they are written as with a sunbeam in the whole volume of human nature, by the hand of the divinity itself, and can never be erased or obscured by mortal power."

But the Slaughterhouse cases! — The Slaughterhouse cases!

The honorable gentleman from Kentucky, always swift to sustain the failing and dishonored cause of proscription, rushes forward and flaunts in our faces the decision of the Supreme Court of the United States in the Slaughterhouse cases, and in that act he has been willingly aided by the gentleman from Georgia. Hitherto, in the contests which have marked the progress of the cause of equal civil rights, our opponents have appealed sometimes to custom, sometimes to prejudice, more often to pride of race, but they have never sought to shield themselves behind the Supreme Court. But now, for the first time, we are told that we are barred by a decision of that court, from which there is no appeal. If this be true we must stay our hands. The cause of equal civil rights must pause at the command of a power whose edicts must be obeyed till the fundamental law of our country is changed.

Has the honorable gentleman from Kentucky considered well the claim he now advances? If it were not disrespectful I would ask, has he ever read the decision which he now tells us is an insuperable barrier to the adoption of this great measure of justice?

In the consideration of this subject, has not the judgment of the gentleman from Georgia been warped by the ghost of the dead doctrines of states' rights? Has he been altogether free from prejudices engendered by long training in that school of politics that well-nigh destroyed this government?

Mr. Speaker, I venture to say here in the presence of the gentleman from Kentucky and the gentleman from Georgia, and in the presence of the whole country, that there is not a line or word, not a thought or dictum even, in the decision of the Supreme Court in the great Slaughterhouse cases, which casts a shadow of doubt on the right of Congress to pass the pending bill, or to adopt such other legislation as it may judge proper and necessary to secure perfect equality before the law to every citizen of the Republic. Sir, I protest against the dishonor now cast upon our Supreme Court by both the gentleman from Kentucky and the gentleman from Georgia. In other days, when the whole country was bowing beneath the yoke of slavery, when press, pulpit, platform, Congress and courts felt the fatal power of the slave oligarchy, I remember a decision of that court which no American now reads without shame and humiliation. But those days are past; the Supreme Court of today is a tribunal as true to freedom as any department of this government, and I am honored with the opportunity of repelling a deep disgrace which the gentleman from Kentucky, backed and sustained as he is by the gentleman from Georgia, seeks to put upon it. . . .

Before we proceed to examine more critically the provisions of this amendment, on which the plaintiffs in error rely, let us complete and discuss the history of the recent amendments, as that history related to the general purpose which pervades them all. A few years' experience satisfied the thoughtful men who had been the authors of the other two amendments that, notwithstanding the restraints of those articles on the States and the laws passed under the additional powers granted to Congress, these were inadequate for the protection of life, liberty, and property, without which freedom to the slave was no boon. They were in all those States denied the right of suffrage. The laws were administered by the white man alone. It was urged that a race of men distinctively marked as was the negro, living in the midst of another and dominant race, could never be fully secured in their person and their property without the right of suffrage.

Hence the fifteenth amendment, which declares that "the right of a citizen of the United States to vote shall not be denied or abridged by any State on account of race, color, or previous condition of servitude." The negro having, by the fourteenth amendment, been declared to be a citizen of the United States, is thus made a voter in every State of the Union.

We repeat, then, in the light of this recapitulation of events almost too recent to be called history, but which are familiar to us all, and on the most casual examination of the language of these amendments, no one can fail to be impressed with the one pervading purpose found in them all, lying at the foundation of each, and without which none of them would have been even suggested: we mean, the freedom of the slave race, the security and firm establishment of that freedom, and the protection of the newly made freeman and citizen from the oppressions of those who had formerly exercised unlimited dominion over him. It is true that only the fifteenth amendment in terms mentions the negro by speaking of his color and his slavery. But it is just as true that each of the other articles was addressed to the grievances of that race, and designed to remedy them, as the fifteenth.

These amendments, one and all, are thus declared to have as their all-pervading design and ends the security of the recently enslaved race, not only their nominal freedom, but their complete protection from those who had formerly exercised unlimited dominion over them. It is in this broad light that all these amendments must be read, the purpose to secure the perfect equality before the law of all citizens of the United States. What you give to one class you must give to all, what you deny to one class you shall deny to all, unless in the exercise of the common and universal police power of the state, you find it needful to confer exclusive privileges on certain citizens, to be held and exercised still for the common good of all. . . .

Now, sir, recurring to the venerable and distinguished gentleman from Georgia (Mr. Stephens) who has added his remonstrance against the passage of this bill, permit me to say that I share in the feeling of high personal regard for that gentleman which pervades this House. His years, his ability, and his long experience in public affairs entitle him to the measure of consideration which has been accorded to him on this floor. But in this discussion I cannot and will not forget that the welfare and rights of my whole race in this country are involved. When, therefore, the honorable gentleman from Georgia lends his voice and influence to defeat this measure, I do not shrink from saying that it is not from him that the American House of Representatives should take lessons in matters touching human rights or the joint relations of the state and national governments. While the honorable gentleman contented himself with harmless speculations in his study, or in the columns of a newspaper, we might well smile at the impotence of his efforts to turn back the advancing tide of opinion and progress, but, when he comes again upon this national arena, and throws himself with all his power and influence across the path which leads to the full enfranchisement of my race, I meet him only as an adversary; nor shall age or any other consideration restrain me from saying that he now offers this government, which he has done his utmost to destroy, a very poor return for its magnanimous treatment, to come here and seek to continue, by the assertion of doctrines obnoxious to the true principles of our government, the burdens and oppressions which rest upon five millions of his countrymen who never failed to lift their earnest prayers for the success of this government when the gentleman was seeking to break up the union of these states and to blot the American Republic from the galaxy of nations. [Loud applause.]

Sir, it is scarcely twelve years since that gentleman shocked the civilized world by announcing the birth of a government which rested on human slavery as its cornerstone. The progress of events has swept away that pseudo government which rested on greed, pride and tyranny, and the race whom he then ruthlessly spurned and trampled on is here to meet him in debate, and to demand that the rights which are enjoyed by its former oppressors—who vainly sought to overthrow a government which they could not prostitute to the base uses of slavery—shall be accorded to those who even in the darkness of slavery kept their allegiance true to freedom and the Union. Sir, the gentleman from Georgia has learned much since 1861, but he is still a laggard. Let him put away entirely the false and fatal theories which have so greatly marred an otherwise enviable record. Let him accept, in its fullness and beneficence, the great doctrine that American citizenship carries with it every civil and political right which manhood can confer. Let him lend his influence with all his masterly ability, to complete the proud structure of legislation which makes this nation worthy of the great declaration which heralded its birth, and he will have done that which will most nearly redeem his reputation in the eyes of the world and best vindicate the wisdom of that policy which has permitted him to regain his seat upon this floor. . . .

Sir, equality before the law is now the broad, universal, glorious rule and mandate of the Republic. No state can violate that. Kentucky and Georgia may crowd their statute books with retrograde and barbarous legislation; they may rejoice in the odious eminence of their consistent hostility to all the great steps of human progress which have marked our national history since slavery tore down the Stars and Stripes on Fort Sumter; but, if Congress shall do its duty, if Congress shall enforce the great guarantees which the Supreme Court has declared to be the one pervading purpose of all the recent amendments, then their unwise and unenlightened conduct will fall with the same weight upon the gentlemen from those states who now lend their influence to defeat this bill, as upon the poorest slave who once had no rights which the honorable gentlemen were bound to respect. . . .

Sir, I have replied to the extent of my ability to the arguments which have been presented by the opponents of this measure. I have replied also to some of the legal propositions advanced by gentlemen on the other side; and now that I am about to conclude, I am deeply sensible of the imperfect manner in which I have performed the task. Technically, this bill is to decide upon the civil status of the colored American citizen; a point disputed at the very formation of our present form of government, when by a short-sighted policy repugnant to true republican government, one Negro counted as three fifths of a man. The logical result of this mistake of the framers of the Constitution strengthened the cancer of slavery, which finally spread its poisonous tentacles over the Southern portion of the body politic. To arrest its growth and save the nation we have passed through the harrowing operation of intestine war, dreaded at all times, resorted to at the last extremity, like the surgeon's knife, but absolutely necessary to extirpate the disease which threatened with the life of the nation the overthrow of civil and political liberty on this continent. In that dire extremity the members of the race which I have the honor in part to represent — the race which pleads for justice at your hands to-day — forgetful of their inhuman and brutalizing servitude at the South, their degradation and ostracism at the North, flew willingly and gallantly to the support of the national government. Their sufferings, assistance, privations and trials in the swamps and in the rice fields, their valor on the land and on the sea, form a part of the ever-glorious record which makes up the history of a nation preserved, and might, should I urge the claim, incline you to respect and guarantee their rights and privileges as citizens of our common Republic. But I remember that valor, devotion and loyalty are not always rewarded according to their just deserts, and that after the battle some who have borne the brunt of the fray may, through neglect or contempt, be assigned to a subordinate place, while the enemies in war may be preferred to the sufferers.

The results of the war, as seen in reconstruction, have settled forever the political status of my race. The passage of this bill will determine the civil status, not only of the Negro, but of any other class of citizens who may feel themselves discriminated against. It will form the capstone of that temple of liberty, begun on this continent under discouraging circumstances, carried on in spite of the sneers of monarchists and the cavils of pretended friends of freedom, until at last it stands, in all its beautiful symmetry and proportions, a building the grandest which the world has ever seen, realizing the most sanguine expectations and the highest hopes of those who, in the name of equal, impartial and universal liberty, laid the foundation stone.

The Holy Scriptures tell us of an humble handmaiden who long, faithfully and patiently gleaned in the rich fields of her wealthy kinsman, and we are told further that at last, in spite of her humble antecedents she found favor in his sight. For over two centuries our race has "reaped down your fields," the cries and woes which we have uttered have "entered into the ears of the Lord of Sabaoth" and we are at last politically free. The last vestiture only is needed—civil rights. Having gained this, we may, with hearts overflowing with gratitude and thankful that our prayer has been answered, repeat the prayer of Ruth: "Entreat me not to leave thee, or to return from following after thee, for whither thou goest, I will go; and where thou lodgest, I will lodge; thy people shall be my people, and thy God my God; where thou diest I will die, and there will I be buried; the Lord do so to me, and more also, if ought but death part thee and me." [Great applause.]

READING AND DISCUSSION QUESTIONS

1. Summarize and evaluate the argument Elliott makes in support of the civil rights bill. What can you infer about the opposition from his argument?

2. What does it suggest to you about the nature of politics in the Reconstruction-era South that an African American member of Congress from South Carolina was able to speak in support of a civil rights bill on the floor of the House of Representatives in 1874? How does this document help you to understand the historical context of the period?

■ COMPARATIVE QUESTIONS ■

1. Explain whether you see the era of Reconstruction as the end or the beginning of a distinctive period in American history. What evidence from the documents in this chapter can you provide to prove your thesis?

2. Compare Reconstruction and the early national period as historical moments when issues of federal-state power and citizenship were debated. What similarities and differences do you note in the eligibility requirements for citizenship as referenced by Adams?

3. To what extent was the Jeffersonian regard for land as a source of one's independence an enduring ideal in the era of Reconstruction?

4. Historians have debated whether Reconstruction was a success, a failure, or an incomplete fulfillment of the American promise. How do the multiple perspectives represented by these sources help you develop your own argument about the historical significance of Reconstruction?

16

Conquering a Continent
1854–1890

The Civil War is a pivot point in American history, but the focused attention it receives sometimes obscures significant continuities. Such is the case with Americans' drive to expand the bounds of their country. The earlier period of Manifest Destiny in the 1840s led to the Mexican War and the political crises over the extension of slavery that precipitated the Civil War. In the postwar years, however, the itch to move was no less powerful a motive than it had been decades earlier. This continuing historical pattern of expansion shaped the latter decades of the nineteenth century. Railroads became the means of realizing continental dreams. The political muscle required to push them west both reflected the economic goals of the Republican Party and jeopardized the lives of Native Americans whose territorial claims became obstacles to industrialists' expansionist efforts. Western boosters convinced others that the cost to American Indians served the broader aims of integrating the West into the national economy, tapping the vast mineral, timber, and animal resources the continent offered. The costs were indeed high, and not only to Native Americans. Chinese laborers were hired to lay the tracks for railroads that hauled away the West's natural resources and changed its geography forever.

16-1 | Promoting the Transcontinental Railroad
The Pacific Railway Act (1862)

A year into the Civil War, President Lincoln signed the Pacific Railway Act, a bill that harvested old Whig Party ideas supporting internal improvements, to encourage the building of a transcontinental railway. This bill and the 1862 Homestead Act, which granted title to parcels of

Pacific Railway Act, July 1, 1862; Enrolled Acts and Resolutions of Congress, 1789–1996; Record Group 11; General Records of the United States Government; National Archives.

federal territory to adult citizens who resided on and improved the land for five years, were part of Republicans' efforts to encourage national economic development. The Union Pacific Railroad Company received grants of federal land to survey and build a line connecting the Missouri River and the Pacific Ocean. It raised funds by selling land along rail lines, a pull factor for those seeking new opportunities.

Be it enacted by the Senate and House of Representatives of the United States of America in Congress assembled, That [the commissioners] together with commissioners to be appointed by the Secretary of the Interior, and all persons who shall or may be associated with them, and their successors, are hereby created and erected into a body corporate and politic in deed and in law, by the name, style, and title of "The Union Pacific Railroad Company"; and by that name shall have perpetual succession, and shall be able to sue and to be sued, plead and be impleaded, defend and be defended, in all courts of law and equity within the United States, and may make and have a common seal; and the said corporation is hereby authorized and empowered to layout, locate, construct, furnish, maintain, and enjoy a continuous railroad and telegraph, with the appurtenances, from a point on the one hundredth meridian of longitude west from Greenwich, between the south margin of the valley of the Republican River and the north margin of the valley of the Platte River, in the Territory of Nebraska, to the western boundary of Nevada Territory, upon the route and terms hereinafter provided, and is hereby vested with all the powers, privileges, and immunities necessary to carry into effect the purposes of this act as herein set forth. The capital stock of said company shall consist of one hundred thousand shares of one thousand dollars each, which shall be subscribed for and held in not more than two hundred shares by anyone person, and shall be transferable in such manner as the by-laws of said corporation shall provide.

SEC. 2. And be it further enacted, That the right of way through the public lands be, and the same is hereby, granted to said company for the construction of said railroad and telegraph line; and the right, power, and authority is hereby given to said company to take from the public lands adjacent to the line of said road, earth, stone, timber, and other materials for the construction thereof; said right of way is granted to said railroad to the extent of two hundred feet in width on each side of said railroad where it may pass over the public lands, including all necessary grounds for stations, buildings, workshops, and depots, machine shops, switches, side tracks, turntables, and, water stations. The United States shall extinguish as rapidly as may be the Indian titles to all lands falling under the operation of this act and required for the said right of way and; grants hereinafter made.

SEC 3. And be it further enacted, That there be, and is hereby, granted to the said company, for the purpose of aiding in the construction, of said railroad and telegraph line, and to secure the safe and speedy transportation of the mails, troops, munitions of war, and public stores thereon, every alternate section of public land, designated by odd numbers, to the amount of five alternate sections per mile on each side of said railroad, on the line thereof, and within the limits of ten miles on each side of said road, not sold, reserved, or otherwise disposed of by the United States, and to which a preemption or homestead claim may not have attached, at the time the line of said road is definitely fixed: Provided, That all mineral lands shall be excepted from the operation of this act; but where the same shall contain timber, the timber thereon is hereby granted to said company. And all such lands, so granted by this section, which shall not be sold or disposed of by said company within three years after the entire road shall have been completed, shall be subject to settlement and preemption, like other lands, at a price not exceeding one dollar and twenty-five cents per acre, to be paid to said company.

SEC. 4. And be it further enacted, That whenever said company shall have completed forty consecutive miles of any portion of said railroad and telegraph line, ready for the service contemplated by this act, and supplied with all necessary . . . appurtenances of a first class railroad . . . the President of the United States shall appoint three commissioners to examine the same and report to him in relation thereto; and if it shall appear to him that forty consecutive miles of said railroad and telegraph line have been completed and equipped in all respects as required by this act, then, upon certificate of said commissioners to that effect, patents shall issue conveying the right and title to said lands to said company, on each side of the road as far as the same is completed, to the amount aforesaid; and patents shall in like manner issue as each forty miles of said railroad and telegraph line are completed, upon certificate of said commissioners.

SEC. 5. And be it further enacted, That for the purposes herein mentioned the Secretary of the Treasury shall, upon the certificate in writing of said commissioners of the completion and equipment of forty consecutive miles of said railroad and telegraph, in accordance with the provisions of this act, issue to said company bonds of the United States of one thousand dollars each, payable in thirty years after date, bearing six per centum per annum interest (said interest payable semi-annually), which interest may be paid in United States treasury notes or any other money or currency which the United States have or shall declare lawful money and a legal tender, to the amount of sixteen of said bonds per mile for such section of forty miles. . . .

SEC. 7. And be it further enacted, That said company shall file their assent to this act, under the seal of said company, in the Department of the Interior, within one year after the passage of this act, and shall complete said railroad and telegraph from the point of beginning, as herein provided, to the western boundary of Nevada Territory before the first day of July, one thousand eight hundred and seventy-four: Provided, That within two years after the passage of this act said company shall designate the general route of said road, as near as may be, and shall file a map of the same in the Department of the Interior, whereupon the Secretary of the Interior shall cause the lands within fifteen miles of said designated route or routes to be withdrawn from preemption, private entry, and sale; and when any portion of said route shall be finally located, the Secretary of the Interior shall cause the said lands herein before granted to be surveyed and set off as fast as may be necessary for the purposes herein named: Provided, That in fixing the point of connection of the main trunk with the eastern connections, it shall be fixed at the most practicable point for the construction of the Iowa and Missouri branches, as hereinafter provided.

SEC. 8. And be it further enacted, That the line of said railroad and telegraph shall commence at a point on the one hundredth meridian of a longitude west from Greenwich, between the south margin of the valley of the Republican River and the north margin of the valley of the Platte River, in the Territory of Nebraska, at a point to be fixed by the President of the United States, after actual surveys; thence running westerly upon the most direct, central, and practicable route, through the territories of the United States, the western boundary of the Territory of Nevada, there to meet and connect with the line of the Central Pacific Railroad Company of California. . . .

SEC. 11. And be it further enacted, That for three hundred miles of said road most mountainous and difficult of construction, to wit: one hundred and fifty miles westwardly from the eastern base of the Rocky Mountains, and one hundred and fifty miles eastwardly from the western base of the Sierra Nevada mountains, said points to be fixed by the President of the United States, the bonds to be issued to aid in the construction thereof shall be treble the number per mile hereinbefore provided, and the same shall be issued, and the lands herein granted be set apart, upon the construction of every twenty miles thereof, upon the certificate of the commissioners as aforesaid that twenty consecutive miles of the same are completed, and between the sections last named of one hundred and fifty miles each, the bonds to be issued to aid in the construction thereof shall be double the number per mile first mentioned, and the same shall be issued, and the lands herein granted be set apart, upon the construction of every twenty miles thereof, upon the certificate of the commissioners as aforesaid that twenty consecutive miles of the same are completed: Provided, That no more than fifty thousand of said bonds shall be issued under this act to aid in constructing the main line of said railroad and telegraph.

SEC. 12. And be it further enacted, That whenever the route of said railroad shall cross the boundary of any State or Territory, or said meridian of longitude, the two companies meeting or uniting there shall agree upon its location at that point, with reference to the most direct and practicable through route, and in case of difference between them as to said location the President of the United States shall determine the said location; the companies named in each State and Territory to locate the road across the same between the points so agreed upon, except as herein provided. The track upon the entire line of railroad and branches shall be of uniform width, to be determined by the President of the United States, so that, when completed, cars can be run from the Missouri River to the Pacific coast; the grades and curves shall not exceed the maximum grades and curves of the Baltimore and Ohio railroad; the whole line of said railroad and branches and telegraph shall be operated and used for all purposes of communication, travel, and transportation, so far as the public and government are concerned, as one connected, continuous line; and the companies herein named in Missouri, Kansas, and California, filing their assent to the provisions of this act, shall receive and transport . . . all materials required for constructing and furnishing said first-mentioned line between the aforesaid point, on the one hundredth meridian of longitude and western boundary of Nevada Territory, whenever the same is required by said first-named company, at cost, over that portion of the roads of said companies constructed under the provisions of this act.

SEC. 15. And be it further enacted, That any other railroad company now incorporated, or hereafter to be incorporated, shall have the right to connect their road with the road and branches provided for by this act, at such places and upon such just and equitable terms as the President of the United States may prescribe. Wherever the word company is used in this act it shall be construed to embrace the words their associates, successors, and assigns, the same as if the words had been properly added thereto.

SEC. 16. And be it further enacted, That at any time after the passage of this act all of the railroad companies named herein, and assenting hereto, or any two or more of them, are authorized to form themselves into one consolidated company; notice of such consolidation, in writing, shall be filed in the Department of the Interior, and such consolidated company shall thereafter proceed to construct said railroad and branches and telegraph line upon the terms and conditions provided in this act.

SEC. 17. And be it further enacted, That in case said company or companies shall fail to comply with the terms and conditions of this act, by not completing said road and telegraph and branches within a reasonable time, or by not keeping the same in repair and use, but shall permit the same, for an unreasonable time, to remain unfinished, or out of repair, and unfit for use, Congress may pass any act to insure the speedy completion of said road and branches, or put the same in repair and use, and may direct the income of said railroad and telegraph line to be thereafter devoted to the use of the United States, to repay all such expenditures caused by the default and neglect of such company or companies: Provided, That if said roads are not completed, so as to form a continuous line of railroad, ready for use, from the Missouri River to the navigable waters of the Sacramento River, in California, by the first day of July, eighteen hundred and seventy-six, the whole of all of said railroads before mentioned and to be constructed under the provisions of this act, and property of every kind and character, shall be forfeited to and be taken possession of by the United States.

SEC. 18. And be it further enacted, That whenever it appears that the net earnings of the entire road and telegraph, including the amount allowed for services rendered for the United States, after deducting all, expenditures, including repairs, and the furnishing, running, and managing of said road, shall exceed ten per centum upon its cost, exclusive of the five per centum to be paid to the United States, Congress may reduce the rates of fare thereon, if unreasonable in amount, and may fix and establish the same by law. And the better to accomplish the object of this act, namely, to promote the public interest and welfare by the construction of said railroad and telegraph line, and keeping the same in working order, and to secure to the government at all times (but particularly in time of war) the use and benefits of the same for postal, military and other purposes,

Congress may, at any time, having due regard for the rights of said companies named herein, add to, alter, amend, or repeal this act.

SEC. 19. And be it further enacted, That the several railroad companies herein named are authorized to enter into an arrangement with the Pacific Telegraph Company, the Overland Telegraph Company, and the California State Telegraph Company, so that the present line of telegraph between the Missouri River and San Francisco may be moved upon or along the line of said railroad and branches as fast as said roads and branches are built; and if said arrangement be entered into and the transfer of said telegraph line be made in accordance therewith to the line of said railroad and branches, such transfer shall, for all purposes of this act, be held and considered a fulfillment on the part of said railroad companies of the provisions of this act in regard to the construction of said line of telegraph. And, in case of disagreement, said telegraph companies are authorized to remove their line of telegraph along and upon the line of railroad herein contemplated without prejudice to the rights of said railroad companies named herein.

SEC. 20. And be it further enacted, That the corporation hereby created and the roads connected therewith, under the provisions of this act, shall make to the Secretary of the Treasury an annual report wherein shall be set forth—

First. The names of the stockholders and their places of residence, so far as the same can be ascertained;

Second. The names and residences of the directors, and all other officers of the company;

Third. The amount of stock subscribed, and the amount thereof actually paid in;

Fourth. A description of the lines of road surveyed, of the lines thereof fixed upon for the construction of the road, and the cost of such surveys;

Fifth. The amount received from passengers on the road;

Sixth. The amount received for freight thereon;

Seventh. A statement of the expense of said road and its fixtures;

Eighth. A statement of the indebtedness of said company, setting forth the various kinds thereof. Which report shall be sworn to by the president of the said company, and shall be presented to the Secretary of the Treasury on or before the first day of July in each year.

APPROVED, July 1, 1862.

READING AND DISCUSSION QUESTIONS

1. The latter half of the nineteenth century is often depicted as a laissez-faire era when the federal government embraced a "hands-off" approach to the national economy. What evidence can you find in the Pacific Railway Act that supports or challenges this traditional interpretation?

2. What can you infer from the act regarding its sponsors' expectations of the railroad's importance to the nation's economic, political, and social growth and development?

3. Considering this source from multiple perspectives, which aspects of the legislation would have encouraged supporters and angered opponents?

16-2 | Railroad Transforms the Nation

CURRIER & IVES, *Across the Continent* (1868)

For better or worse, the railroad altered the geography of America and ushered in economic, social, and political changes that touched the lives of nearly all Americans. Like the canal era before it, the period of rapid railroad development promised market revolutions as goods and resources crossed the continent and local economies integrated with national and global trade networks. Once-isolated communities found themselves connected to consumer and communication webs hardly imagined in the horse and wagon days. The Currier & Ives print "Across the Continent, Westward the Course of Empire Takes Its Way" captures the revolution at its beginning, with the anticipation and foreboding it inspired.

Across the Continent, Westward the Course of Empire Takes Its Way, 1868 (litho), Currier, N. (1813–1888), and Ives, J. M. (1824–1895) / Private Collection / The Bridgeman Art Library.

READING AND DISCUSSION QUESTIONS

1. Analyze and evaluate the elements of this print for evidence of the artist's point of view with respect to the railroad and western development. What does the artist suggest about the effect the railroad had on Americans and their communities?

2. How might you explain the popularity of this Currier & Ives print? Why do you think this image resonated with those who purchased it to decorate their homes?

16-3 | Harvesting the Bison Herds

J. WRIGHT MOOAR, *Buffalo Days* (1933)

Railroads helped integrate the West into the national and global economy. The Great Plains, in particular, developed as a key region for America's economic growth, a development that would have surprised an earlier generation accustomed to thinking of the vast interior as a worthless desert. Commercialized buffalo hunting drove the economic transformation while also working to eliminate American Indians as obstacles to westward expansion. J. Wright Mooar, whose stories of his buffalo-hunting days were first published in 1933, claimed to have killed twenty thousand buffalo, selling meat to feed the proliferating numbers of railroad workers and the hides to East Coast tanneries. The destruction of the herds opened the plains to cattle ranching and sealed the fate of Plains Indians whose lives were organized around the buffalo.

Curing Buffalo Meat

It was in October, 1877, while I was killing buffalo on Deep Creek, that John returned from a trip to Fort Griffin after the mail, and reported that a large herd of cattle was coming into the country, and that the John Hum outfit was then only twenty miles east of our hunting grounds.

It was immediately determined to move camp seventy miles north, to Double Lake in Lynn County. Here headquarters were maintained and the meat was hauled to the old Deep Creek camp, where the smokehouse for curing the meat was located.

As soon as the hide was stripped from the fallen bison, the meat was cut from the hams in four large pieces, the bone being cut out. When from one thousand to twelve hundred pounds of meat was thus collected, it was piled in a vat constructed by driving four stakes into the ground in a square four by four feet, the stakes standing four feet high. To these four corner stakes, a hide, hair side out, was tied by its corners, and let sag in the middle to form a sack or sort of vat. Into this the meat was thrown, and salted as it was thrown in. A brine was then

J. Wright Mooar, "The Killing of the White Buffalo," *Buffalo Days: Stories from J. Wright Mooar as Told to James Winford Hunt*, ed. Robert F. Pace (Abilene, TX: State House Press, McMurry University, 2005), 76–81.

poured over this until the meat was covered. A hide was stretched over the whole for a lid, thus keeping out sun and dirt. Four days later, sugar and saltpeter were added in precise measure to the brine. This was left for two weeks. The thoroughly medicated meat was then taken out and placed in the smokehouse for final seasoning.

The smokehouse was constructed by stretching buffalo hides over a framework of hackberry poles, put together with eightpenny nails, one hundred pounds of which had been hauled from Fort Worth. The house thus constructed was one hundred and ten feet long and twenty feet wide. Along the center of the floor space were ten square pits for the fire. For wood, hackberry and chinaberry logs were used, and the smoking process required ten or twelve days. This prepared meat was hauled to Fort Griffin and sold.

During this winter of '77, we took three thousand seven hundred hides, which were hauled to Fort Worth, and twenty-five thousand pounds of meat, which were sold locally.

Cattle were now being driven into the country very rapidly, and the Mooar Brothers bought the John Goff cattle in Fisher County and changed the brand from XTS to SXT. This brand was kept up in Fisher County for ten years, and then moved to the old buffalo camp on Deep Creek, where my ranch is today.

Passing of the Buffalo

By the arrival of 1879, the hunters were leaving for the mining states, or seeking other lines of business, as they realized the great hunting days were over. Mooar Brothers, however, continued pursuit of the dwindling herds to the great plains country, and during the year of 1878 secured two thousand eight hundred hides and twenty thousand pounds of meat. The last of the buffalo, save a few scattered bands of young animals too young for the hunters to bother with, fell to my big guns in March, 1879. Loading seven thousand pounds of cured meat on two wagons drawn by six good mules, and accompanied by a seventeen-year-old boy, [we] headed west on a fifty-two day trip to Prescott and Phoenix, Arizona, where the meat was sold to the miners. I did not return to Texas until October, 1880.

In the meantime, John had moved the Deep Creek camp to the Fisher County cattle camp. The last of the buffalo hides were sold to Charley Rath, who had bought all interest in the Reynolds store in Stonewall County. As the buffalo days ended, he moved the goods remaining in this store to Camp Supply, in Indian Territory. John did the hauling for Rath on this move, making the long journey with his ox teams. From Camp Supply, he made one trip for Rath to Dodge City, and returned to Texas in December, 1879, loaded with corn from the Red River Country. This he sold to the Texas Ranger camp at Big Spring, Texas. R.C. Ware was in charge of the Ranger camp. He became a noted citizen of the changing Southwest.

Thus ended eight full years of continuous and eventful hunting of the great American bison.

The Indians realized very keenly that the work of the buffalo hunters was the real menace to the wild, free life they wished to lead, and never lost an opportunity to wreak vengeance. This made the life of the hunter one of constant peril. He was always under observation, wild eyes from some covert watching his every move. It is past comprehension to people of today how, under such circumstances, a lone hunter could wander at will and escape ambush or sudden assault in overwhelming numbers. Two things alone protected him: his rifle and his marksmanship. Perhaps one might also add that, while seemingly wandering at will, be was as alert as an Indian and seldom caught off his guard.

The Half-Inch Rifle

His rifle was one made at the request of his guild at the very outset, and was manufactured by the Sharps Rifle Manufacturing Company to meet the requirements for the biggest game on the North American continent — the buffalo. The weapon was a gun weighing from twelve to sixteen pounds, and the caliber was .50-110. One hundred and ten grains of powder, in a long brass shell, hurled from the beautifully rifled muzzle of the great gun a heavy leaden missle that in its impact and its tearing, shattering qualities would instantly bring down the biggest bison, if properly aimed, and that reached out to incredible distances for rifles of that period.

In the account of our trek to Deep Creek, a strip of country like the plains country is mentioned. This plain was evidently once a part of the great Central Plain, but this was at some distant period cut off to itself by upheavals in the general level. In extent it is thirty or forty miles long and from five to fifteen miles wide. Deep Creek marks its western boundary.

Riding eastward across this level, open stretch, and with a wagon and mule team following, I came one afternoon to the broken country east of the tableland. A sunken country rolled away to the east, and the terrain was marked by deep draws, mesquite flats, and small knolls and mesas called the Sugar Loaf Hills. The country looked to be a good place for hunting, with plenty of wood and water at hand, but somewhat dangerous because furnishing plenty of covert for Indian ambuscades. No Indians had been seen in that part, however, and I was about to select a place for a camp and indicate it to my wagoner, when a slight movement at the head of a brushy draw caught my attention. Watching closely I was rewarded in a moment by seeing an Indian rush his pony down into the draw, and in a few moments another stealthily followed him. I had been just alert enough to see the last two Indians of what turned out to be a large band.

Concealing myself, I became the eyewitness of Indian travel tactics. When the band reappeared it had reached the mouth of the draw, and dashed one at a time across to the mouth of another draw breaking down from the plain. They traveled back up this, concealed from all observers, until they would be forced to rush across to the head of another draw and so down it, approaching in this stealthy and devious manner the objective sought.

We drove quickly back to the camp on Deep Creek, content to hunt in more open country.

READING AND DISCUSSION QUESTIONS

1. What evidence do Mooar's stories provide for understanding the historical patterns of change transforming the Great Plains into a commercialized region of economic activity?

2. What can you infer about the historical interpretation, or meaning, Mooar gave to his 1870s Great Plains adventures? Do you think he saw himself participating in a historically significant moment?

16-4 | Addressing the Indian Question

FRANCIS A. WALKER, *Annual Report of the Commissioner of Indian Affairs* (1872)

Another war raged during the 1860s, but unlike the Civil War, the war with the Plains Indians persisted for decades. Following policies established by Andrew Jackson in the 1830s, the federal government in the 1860s and 1870s attempted to open western settlement by corralling American Indians onto reservations. Native resistance to these efforts inevitably resulted in a military response from the federal government, leading to notorious conflicts at such places as Sand Creek, Colorado; Fort Phil Kearny, Wyoming; Little Big Horn in the Montana Territory; and Wounded Knee, South Dakota. These clashes stirred debate about the long-term effectiveness of U.S. policy, which Francis Walker, commissioner of Indian affairs in the early 1870s, attempts to describe and justify.

The Indian policy, so called, of the Government, is a policy, and it is not a policy, or rather it consists of two policies, entirely distinct, seeming, indeed, to be mutually inconsistent and to reflect each upon the other: the one regulating the treatment of the tribes which are potentially hostile, that is, whose hostility is only repressed just so long as, and so far as, they are supported in idleness by the Government; the other regulating the treatment of those tribes which, from traditional friendship, from numerical weakness, or by the force of their location, are either indisposed toward, or incapable of, resistance to the demands of the Government. . . . This want of completeness and consistency in the treatment of the Indian tribes by the Government has been made the occasion of much ridicule and partisan abuse; and it is indeed calculated to provoke criticism and to afford scope for satire; but it is none the less compatible with the highest expediency of the situation. . . . And yet, for all this, the Government is right and its

---

Francis A. Walker, *Annual Report of the Commissioner of Indian Affairs*, November 1, 1872. *Documents of United States Indian Policy*, 3rd ed., ed. Francis Paul Prucha (Lincoln: University of Nebraska Press, 2000), 135–140.

392 PART 5 / Chapter 16 Conquering a Continent, 1854–1890

critics wrong; and the "Indian policy" is sound, sensible, and beneficent, because it reduces to the minimum the loss of life and property upon our frontier, and allows the freest development of our settlements and railways possible under the circumstances. . . .

The Use of the Military Arm

The system now pursued in dealing with the roving tribes dangerous to our frontier population and obstructing our industrial progress, is entirely consistent with, and, indeed, requires the occasional use of the military arm, in restraining or chastising refractory individuals and bands. Such a use of the military constitutes no abandonment of the "peace policy," and involves no disparagement of it. It was not to be expected — it was not in the nature of things — that the entire body of wild Indians should submit to be restrained in their Ishmaelitish proclivities without a struggle on the part of the more audacious to maintain their traditional freedom. In the first announcement made of the reservation system, it was expressly declared that the Indians should be made as comfortable on, and as uncomfortable off, their reservations as it was in the power of the Government to make them; that such of them as went right should be protected and fed, and such as went wrong should be harassed and scourged without intermission. It was not anticipated that the first proclamation of this policy to the tribes concerned would effect the entire cessation of existing evils; but it was believed that persistence in the course marked out would steadily reduce the number of the refractory, both by the losses sustained in actual conflict and by the desertion of individuals as they should become weary of a profitless and hopeless struggle, until, in the near result, the system adopted should apply without exception to all the then roving and hostile tribes. Such a use of the strong arm of the Government is not war, but discipline. . . .

The Forbearance of the Government

It is unquestionably true that the Government has seemed somewhat tardy in proceeding under the second half of the reservation policy, and in applying the scourge to individuals and bands leaving their prescribed limits without authority, or for hostile purposes. This has been partly from a legitimate deference to the conviction of the great body of citizens that the Indians have been in the past unjustly and cruelly treated, and that great patience and long forbearance ought to be exercised in bringing them around to submission to the present reasonable requirements of the Government, and partly from the knowledge on the part of the officers of the Government charged with administering Indian affairs, that, from the natural jealously [sic] of these people, their sense of wrongs suffered in the past, and their suspiciousness arising from repeated acts of treachery on the part of the whites; from the great distance of many bands and individuals from points of personal communication with the agents of the Government, and the absence of all means of written communication with them; from the efforts of abandoned and degraded whites, living among the Indians and exerting much influence over them, to misrepresent the policy of the Government, and to keep alive the hostility and suspicion of the savages; and, lastly, from the extreme untrustworthiness of many of the interpreters on whom the Government is obliged to rely for bringing its intentions to the knowledge of the Indians: that by the joint effect of all these obstacles, many tribes and bands could come very slowly to hear, comprehend, and trust the professions and promises of the Government. . . .

The patience and forbearance exercised have been fully justified in their fruits. The main body of the roving Indians have, with good grace or with ill grace, submitted to the reservation system. Of those who still remain away from the assigned limits, by far the greater part are careful to do so with as little offense as possible; and when their range is such as for the present not to bring them into annoying or dangerous contact with the whites, this Office, has, from the motive of economy, generally been disposed to allow them to pick up their own living still by hunting and fishing, in preference to tying them up at agencies where they would require to be fed mainly or wholly at the expense of the Government. . . .

The Beginning of the End

It belongs not to a sanguine, but to a sober view of the situation, that three years will see the alternative of war eliminated from the Indian question, and the most powerful and hostile bands of to-day thrown in entire helplessness on the mercy of the Government. Indeed, the progress of two years more, if not of another summer, on the Northern Pacific Railroad will of itself completely solve the great Sioux problem, and leave the ninety thousand Indians ranging between the two trans-continental lines as incapable of resisting the Government as are the Indians of New York or Massachusetts. Columns moving north from the Union Pacific, and south from the Northern Pacific, would crush the Sioux and their confederates as between the upper and the nether millstone; while the rapid movement of troops along the northern line would prevent the escape of the savages, when hard pressed, into the British Possessions, which have heretofore afforded a convenient refuge on the approach of a military expedition.

Toward the south the day of deliverance from the fear of Indian hostility is more distant, yet it is not too much to expect that three summers of peaceful progress will forever put it out of the power of the tribes and bands which at present disturb Colorado, Utah, Arizona, and New Mexico to claim consideration of the country in any other attitude than as pensioners upon the national bounty. The railroads now under construction, or projected with a reasonable assurance of early completion, will multiply fourfold the striking force of the Army in that section; the little rifts of mining settlement, now found all through the mountains of the southern Territories will have become self-protecting communities; the feeble, wavering line of agricultural occupation, now sensitive to the faintest breath of Indian hostility, will then have grown to be the powerful "reserve" to lines still more closely advanced upon the last range of the intractable tribes.

Submission the Only Hope of the Indians

No one certainly will rejoice more heartily than the present Commissioner when the Indians of this county cease to be in a position to dictate, in any form or degree, to the Government; when, in fact, the last hostile tribe becomes reduced to the condition of suppliants for charity. This is, indeed, the only hope of salvation for the aborigines of the continent. If they stand up against the progress of civilization and industry, they must be relentlessly crushed. The westward course of population is neither to be denied nor delayed for the sake of all the Indians that ever called this country their home. They must yield or perish; and there is something that savors of providential mercy in the rapidity with which their fate advances upon them, leaving them scarcely the chance to resist before they shall be surrounded and disarmed. It is not feebly and futilely to attempt to stay this tide, whose depth and strength can hardly be measured, but to snatch the remnants of the Indian race from destruction from before it, that the friends of humanity should exert themselves in this juncture, and lose no time. And it is because the present system allows the freest extension of settlement and industry possible under the circumstances, while affording space and time for humane endeavors to rescue the Indian tribes from a position altogether barbarous and incompatible with civilization and social progress, that this system must be approved by all enlightened citizens. . . .

The Claims of the Indian

The people of the United States can never without dishonor refuse to respect these two considerations: 1st. That this continent was originally owned and occupied by the Indians, who have on this account a claim somewhat larger than the privilege of one hundred and sixty acres of land, and "find himself" in tools and stock, which is granted as a matter of course to any newly-arrived foreigner who declares his intention to become a citizen; that something in the nature of an endowment, either capitalized or in the form of annual expenditures for a series of years for the benefit of the Indians, though at the discretion of the Government as to the specific objects, should be provided for every tribe or band which is deprived of its roaming privilege and confined to a diminished reservation: such an endowment being not in the nature of a gratuity, but in common honesty the right of the Indian on account of his original interest in the soil. 2d. That inasmuch as the progress of our industrial enterprise has cut these people off from modes of livelihood entirely sufficient for their wants, and for which they were qualified, in a degree which has been the wonder of more civilized races, by inherited aptitudes and by long pursuit, and has left them utterly without resource, they have a claim on this account again to temporary support and to such assistance as may be necessary to place them in a position to obtain a livelihood by means which shall be compatible with civilization.

Had the settlements of the United States not been extended beyond the frontier of 1867, all the Indians of the continent would to the end of time have found upon the plains an inexhaustible supply of food and clothing. Were the westward course of population to be stayed at the barriers of to-day, notwithstanding the tremendous inroads made upon their hunting-grounds since 1867, the Indians would still have hope of life. But another such five years will see the Indians of Dakota and Montana as poor as the Indians of Nevada and Southern California; that is, reduced to an habitual condition of suffering from want of food.

The freedom of expansion which is working these results is to us of incalculable value. To the Indian it is of incalculable cost. Every year's advance of our frontier takes in a territory as large as some of the kingdoms of Europe. We are richer by hundreds of millions; the Indian is poorer by a large part of the little that he has. This growth is bringing imperial greatness to the nation; to the Indian it brings wretchedness, destitution, beggary. Surely there is obligation found in considerations like these, requiring us in some way, and in the best way, to make good to these original owners of the soil the loss by which we so greatly gain.

Can any principle of national morality be clearer than that, when the expansion and development of a civilized race involve the rapid destruction of the only means of subsistence possessed by the members of a less fortunate race, the higher is bound as a simple right to provide for the lower some substitute for the means of subsistence which it has destroyed? That substitute is, of course, best realized, not by systematic gratuities of food and clothing continued beyond a present emergency, but by directing these people to new pursuits which shall be consistent with the progress of civilization upon the continent; helping them over the first rough places on "the white man's road," and, meanwhile, supplying such subsistence as is absolutely necessary during the period of initiation and experiment. . . .

READING AND DISCUSSION QUESTIONS

1. Analyze and evaluate the policy recommendations Walker endorses with respect to Native American tribes facing the expansion of white commerce and settlement. To what extent is he sympathetic to their plight?

2. What does Walker see as the ultimate fate of American Indians?

3. What conclusions about the political culture of the 1870s can you draw from Walker's annual report as commissioner of Indian affairs?

16-5 | Remembering Indian Boarding School Days

MOURNING DOVE, *A Salishan Autobiography* (1990)

Okanogan Indian Christine Quintasket, or Mourning Dove, experienced the effects of America's Native American policies in the late nineteenth century, a period she writes about in her autobiography, published half a century after her death. By the time of her birth in the mid-1880s, those policies rejected earlier efforts to concentrate Native Americans onto

Mourning Dove, *Mourning Dove: A Salishan Autobiography*, ed. Jay Miller (Lincoln: University of Nebraska Press, 1990), 24–31.

reservations. With the passage of the Dawes Severalty Act in 1887, the federal government's new aim was to eradicate "the Indian" within Native Americans. By discouraging reservations, where tribes had been able to maintain native languages and customs, the new policy hoped to "Americanize" them. Part of that effort led to an Indian boarding school movement where Native Americans were taught English, forced to adopt non-native clothes and customs, and made to live apart from their extended families.

Although Mother continued persistently to give me my ancient education with the help of my native teacher, she was also a fanatically religious Catholic. We never missed mass or church unless it was absolutely necessary. If church was not scheduled at the little mission below our cabin, then we "pilgrimed" to Goodwin Mission to attend church. Winter and summer, she never failed to make her confession and communion on the first Friday of every month. To her mind, and that of many of the early converts, the word of the priest was law. She strictly observed anything that the pioneer Father De Rouge so much as hinted at. On the other hand, my father was considered a "slacker" or a black sheep of the flock. He attended church only occasionally and without the devotion of my mother. . . .

During one of our monthly trips to Goodwin for the first Friday service, we met Father De Rouge on the big steps of the church, where he had come outside to mingle with his beloved Indian congregation.

The good [Jesuit] priest came forward and shook hands with Mother, spying me behind her wide skirts. He looked right at me and asked if I had made my first communion. He had a way of jumbling up words from several Indian languages he had learned so that his words sounded childish, but I dared not chuckle at his comment. Instead, I shook my head in answer to his question. He looked at mother reproachfully and, shaking his head, said, "Tut, Tut, Lucy. You must let your child go to school with the good sisters to learn her religion so that she can make her first communion like other children of her age." Mother tried to make a protest, saying she needed me at home to care for the babies. But Father De Rouge could seldom be enticed to change his mind. He always had a very strict, ruling hand with the Indians. His word was much respected by the natives of the Colville Reservation.

He shook his finger at Mother and said, "Tut, Tut, Lucy. I command you." Then, pointing at the cross atop the bell tower of the church, he continued, "Your church commands that your child must go to school to learn her religion and the laws of the church." In obedience, Mother promised to send me to the mission for the fall term of 1898.

I had known Father De Rouge all my life. He had been a stationary superior at the Goodwin Mission until the arrival of Father Carnia [Caruana], whom the Indians called T-quit-na-wiss (Large Stomach), since the new priest had plenty of abdominal carriage. After that De Rouge became a traveling priest, covering all the territory of the Colville Reservation and beyond. He taught the Indians their prayers and erected the first little cabins that served as chapels until they were later remodeled into larger frame churches. These early church locations included Ellisford, St. Mary's Mission on Omak Creek, Nespelem, Keller, and Inchelium. These last four compose the modern districts of the Colville Reservation. Earlier these districts all had their share of the faithful work of the self-sacrificing Father Etienne (Stephen) De Rouge.

He was the descendant of a rich and influential French count, but he rejected his claim to this title to fulfill his mission among his beloved Colville. Many times he would stop by our cabin home at Pia to visit with the family. He traveled astride his cayuse leading a pack animal loaded with the sacred belongings needed to say mass. This gave him the convenience of holding services in any Indian tipi or cabin where night would overtake him. He was never too busy to answer a call for help, rushing in the night to visit the sick or administer the last sacraments to poor, dying natives. His life was thoroughly wrapped up in his chosen work. He spent every penny he could get from his rich family and from small Indian contributions to aid the needy.

It was through his influence and encouragement that the Indians gradually discontinued their ancient customs and were more willing to send their children to school at Goodwin. He later erected a fine and roomy school at St. Mary's Mission, after he had permanently established other churches that were maintained either by traveling priests or by one permanently settled in the location to teach the Indians and provide an example. This boarding school, built with his own money and contributions from Catholic whites in the East, remains a successful monument to his life's work. . . .

When my father told me I had better start at school, I was scared. It took much coaxing, and buying me candy and nuts along with other luxuries at the log store at Marcus, before I consented to go.

Father was holding my hand when we went through the big white gates into the clean yard of the school. A high whitewashed fence enclosed all the huge buildings, which looked so uninviting. I hated to stay but promised Father I would not get lonesome. I walked at his side as he briskly entered a building to meet a woman in a long black skirt, with a roll of stiff white, oval cloth around her pale face. I looked away from her lovely, tapered fingers. I loved my mother's careworn hands better.

Since I could not understand English, I could not comprehend the conversation between Father and the kind woman in black. Later I learned she was the superior at the school. When my father was ready to leave, I screamed, kicked, and clung to him, begging to go home. This had always worked before, but now his eyes grew dim and he gently handed me to the sister and shamelessly ran out the door. When the sister tried to calm me, I screamed all the louder and kicked her. She picked me up off the floor and marched me into a dark closet under the long stairway to scream as loud as I could. She left me to sob myself to sleep. This cured my temper.

I was too young to understand. I did not know English, and the other girls were forbidden to speak any native language. I was very much alone. Most of the time I played with wooden blocks and the youngest girls. I did not attend much school.

Each morning the children got up and dressed to attend church before breakfast. We walked in a double row along the path that climbed the slope to the large church, where my parents came for feast days. We entered the church from the west side door as the boys entered from the east one. The few adults came through the front double doors. There was also a small school chapel that we used when the weather was too bad to march outside.

Our dormitory had three rows of single iron beds, covered every day with white spreads and stiff-starched pillow shams that we folded each night and laid on a small stand beside the bed. Every Sunday night we were issued spotlessly clean nighties. This was the first nightgown I ever wore. Previously, I had slept in all my clothes.

Our dining hall, called the refectory, looked big to me, perhaps because I was used to eating in a cramped space. I was afraid of falling off the chair and always waited for others to sit first. The tables were lined up close to the walls, and the sister in charge had her table in the center, where she served our food on white enamel plates. We brought them up to her empty and carried them back full. Then we all waited until she rang the bell to begin eating.

The school ran strictly. We never talked during meals without permission, given only on Sunday or special holidays. Otherwise there was silence—a terrible silent silence. I was used to the freedom of the forest, and it was hard to learn this strict discipline. I was punished many times before I learned.

I stayed at the mission for less than a year because I took ill and father had to come and take me to the family camp at Kettle Falls. People were catching late salmon and eel. I returned to the mission again until my mother died in 1902 and I went home to care for my siblings. . . .

My second stay at the school was less traumatic. I was anxious to learn more English and read. The school had been enlarged, with much larger buildings adjoining the old ones. The old chicken yard was moved farther away from the hospital windows. There was a fine white modern building, with a full veranda along the front, for the white students who paid fifteen dollars a month to board there. Although they were next door, we never met them; it was as if we lived in different worlds. They had their own playroom, refectory, classrooms, and dormitory. We only saw them in church, when they filed in ahead of us and sat in front of the guardian sisters. Our own teachers sat on long benches behind our rows. The only white girls we got to know were the charity orphans who boarded with us.

The paying boarders got school tuition, books, meals, and free music lessons for their money. This price was so low that many white families around Marcus, Meyers Falls, Colville, and Chewelah sent their children to Goodwin. Native children only went as far as the lower grades, but some had the privilege of attending more academic grades in the classroom of the white girls. Only two girls ever did this, and they were both white charity cases. Some Indian children studied music free, learning piano and organ. We all learned to sing church hymns. Eva, the chunky little daughter of Bridgett Lemere, became a fine organist and choir leader at the Pia Mission. She had a beautiful voice, and her fingers flew over the keys so lightly that the sacred music would ring through the building. Her sister Annie was a few years older than I and became my chum. I stayed away from the girls my own age because my whole life was spent around older people, except for my sisters. . . .

I was very interested in my work. With the knowledge Jimmy Ryan[1] had taught me from his yellowback novels, I passed first grade during the first semester. After my promotion the sisters had no second reader, so I had to study out of the third-year one. My marks were so good in all classes but grammar, which I never could understand, that I graduated at third level. I worked hard on catechism, which Mother had taught me in the native language. When I passed, I made my first communion in the big church, with many younger girls, including Eva and Annie Lemere. Our white dresses and shoes were supplied by the sisters. We wore flowing veils with flowered wreaths to hold them in place. It was Easter morning of 1899. We filed back to the convent, and the sisters gave us a big banquet with many goodies. It was a memorable day, and I thoroughly believed in the Catholic creed. I honored it as much as my native tutor had taught me to revere the ancient traditions of my forebears. I saw no difference between them and never questioned the priest.

I was so enthusiastic that I promised the sisters and girls I would come back in the fall. We were dismissed in June on the feast of Corpus Christi, always a big event in our year.

I never got back to Goodwin, however. Mother had a son, christened Johnny, whom I had to take care of because the duties of the ranch took much of her time. I began secretly to read Jimmy's books. My parents scolded and rebuked me many times because they thought reading was an excuse for being idle. There was much work to be done around the cabin and in the fields.

One day I heard about the Tonasket Indian School, where the Pierre children went to school. I begged Mother to go, but she replied in agitated tones, "Do you want to know too much, and be like the other schoolgirls around here? They come home from school and have no shame for their good character. That is all girls learn in government schools — running around and exposing their bodies." I ran outside into the rosebushes and cried in bitter humiliation. I wanted to go to school and learn the Mysteries of books. My meager education was just enough to make out the simplest words. Jimmy Ryan was only a little better, but he could speak English well.

READING AND DISCUSSION QUESTIONS

1. Describe Mourning Dove's experiences at school. What can you infer about the school's educational goals, practices, and policies with respect to Native American children?

2. What conclusions can you draw about Mourning Dove's attitude toward the education she received at the boarding school? To what extent did her native traditions exist alongside the culture of whites she was expected to embrace?

---

[1]**Jimmy Ryan**: A young Irish boy adopted by Mourning Dove's parents. He shared his collection of cheap dime novels, from which she learned to read.

■ COMPARATIVE QUESTIONS ■

1. How do the decades following the Civil War compare to the 1840s as two periods of expansionism? Were the motivations similar or different?

2. Compare the history of white–American Indian relations during the 1870s to the point of view expressed by Thomas Hariot (Document 1-1) and the Reverend Father Louis Cellot (Document 2-6). How do these documents show continuity or change in attitudes toward Native Americans?

3. To what extent do the multiple perspectives in this chapter support or challenge the argument that railroads and western expansion represented positive developments in the history of the United States?

4. Compare the image of "the west" that emerges from these sources with earlier sources such as *The Panoplist and Missionary Herald* (Document 7-4) and Lansford Hastings's *Emigrant's Guide* (Document 13-1). Explain how these documents reveal a diversity of perspective about the region as a land of opportunity, a hazard to life and limb, or a bit of both depending on one's experience.

5. Compare the artist's perspective in *Across the Continent* with the point of view expressed by the artist depicting the Erie Canal (Document 8-1). What historical patterns of continuity and change are suggested by these two images?

DOCUMENT SET

Americans Debate the Meaning of the Constitution
1844–1877

The Civil War era was driven by themes of politics and power. The political crisis over slavery and territorial expansion that surfaced in the wake of the war with Mexico engaged reformers, politicians, and ordinary Americans in heated debates over the true meaning of the Constitution, the relationship between federal and state government, and the definition of citizenship. The outbreak of war in 1861 was evidence of the failure of those debates to reach agreement. While many no doubt harbored a hope that the Union victory had settled accounts, fundamental disagreements persisted into the Reconstruction era and linger even today. Different political and social groups during these years competed for influence, shaping political institutions and values, and contested the meaning of citizenship. The status of enslaved African Americans was, of course, central to these debates, but so too were the rights of women and Native Americans and the participation of immigrant groups who diversified the nation's growing population. In the boisterous democracy of the mid-nineteenth century, all those who called America home were caught up in the deafening argument over the values shaping the political system and the part they were to play in strengthening the political process.

P5-1 | Women Reformers Demand Citizenship Rights

ELIZABETH CADY STANTON, *Declaration of Rights and Sentiments* (1848)

In 1848, the basic rights of citizenship guaranteed in the Constitution were denied to half of the population on account of their sex. Women could not exercise the right to vote, and they enjoyed limited legal rights to property. They were excluded by custom and barred by law from certain professions and suffered discrimination in wages. Elizabeth Cady Stanton and other reformers convened a meeting in Seneca Falls, New York, in 1848 to organize a protest of society's narrow interpretation of female citizenship under the Constitution. Using the model of Jefferson's Declaration of Independence, Stanton and ninety-nine others signed the Declaration of Rights and Sentiments, thereby focusing the debate on the meaning of citizenship for women.

When, in the course of human events, it becomes necessary for one portion of the family of man to assume among the people of the earth a position different from that which they have hitherto occupied, but one to which the laws of nature and of nature's God entitle them, a decent respect to the opinions of mankind requires that they should declare the causes that impel them to such a course.

We hold these truths to be self-evident: that all men and women are created equal; that they are endowed by their Creator with certain inalienable rights; that among these are life, liberty, and the pursuit of happiness; that to secure these rights governments are instituted, deriving their just powers from the consent of the governed. Whenever any form of government becomes destructive of these ends, it is the right of those who suffer from it to refuse allegiance to it, and to insist upon the institution of a new government, laying its foundation on such principles, and organizing its powers in such form, as to them shall seem most likely to effect their safety and happiness. Prudence, indeed, will dictate that governments long established should not be changed for light and transient causes; and accordingly all experience hath shown that mankind are more disposed to suffer while evils are sufferable, than to right themselves by abolishing the forms to which they are accustomed. But when a long train of abuses and usurpations, pursuing invariably the same object, evinces a design to reduce them under absolute despotism, it is their duty to throw off such government, and to provide new guards for their future security. Such has been the patient sufferance of the women under this government, and such is now the necessity which constrains them to demand the equal station to which they are entitled. The history of mankind is a history of repeated injuries and usurpations on the part of man toward woman, having in direct object the establishment of an absolute tyranny over her. To prove this, let facts be submitted to a candid world.

He has never permitted her to exercise her inalienable right to the elective franchise.

Elizabeth Cady Stanton, *A History of Woman Suffrage*, vol. 1 (Rochester, NY: Fowler and Wells, 1889), 70–71.

He has compelled her to submit to laws, in the formation of which she had no voice.

He has withheld from her rights which are given to the most ignorant and degraded men—both natives and foreigners.

Having deprived her of this first right of a citizen, the elective franchise, thereby leaving her without representation in the halls of legislation, he has oppressed her on all sides.

He has made her, if married, in the eye of the law, civilly dead.

He has taken from her all right in property, even to the wages she earns.

He has made her, morally, an irresponsible being, as she can commit many crimes with impunity, provided they be done in the presence of her husband. In the covenant of marriage, she is compelled to promise obedience to her husband, he becoming, to all intents and purposes, her master—the law giving him power to deprive her of her liberty, and to administer chastisement.

He has so framed the laws of divorce, as to what shall be the proper causes of divorce; in case of separation, to whom the guardianship of the children shall be given; as to be wholly regardless of the happiness of women—the law, in all cases, going upon a false supposition of the supremacy of man, and giving all power into his hands.

After depriving her of all rights as a married woman, if single, and the owner of property, he has taxed her to support a government which recognizes her only when her property can be made profitable to it.

He has monopolized nearly all the profitable employments, and from those she is permitted to follow, she receives but a scanty remuneration.

He closes against her all the avenues to wealth and distinction which he considers most honorable to himself. As a teacher of theology, medicine, or law, she is not known.

He has denied her the facilities for obtaining a thorough education—all colleges being closed against her.

He allows her in Church, as well as State, but a subordinate position, claiming Apostolic authority for her exclusion from the ministry, and, with some exceptions, from any public participation in the affairs of the Church.

He has created a false public sentiment, by giving to the world a different code of morals for men and women, by which moral delinquencies which exclude women from society, are not only tolerated, but deemed of little account in man.

He has usurped the prerogative of Jehovah himself, claiming it as his right to assign for her a sphere of action, when that belongs to her conscience and to her God.

He has endeavored, in every way that he could, to destroy her confidence in her own powers, to lessen her self-respect, and to make her willing to lead a dependent and abject life.

Now, in view of this entire disfranchisement of one-half the people of this country, their social and religious degradation,—in view of the unjust laws above mentioned, and because women do feel themselves aggrieved, oppressed, and fraudulently deprived of their most sacred rights, we insist that they have immediate admission to all the rights and privileges which belong to them as citizens of the United States.

In entering upon the great work before us, we anticipate no small amount of misconception, misrepresentation, and ridicule; but we shall use every instrumentality within our power to effect our object. We shall employ agents, circulate tracts, petition the state and national legislatures, and endeavor to enlist the pulpit and the press in our behalf. We hope this Convention will be followed by a series of Conventions, embracing every part of the country. . . .

Resolutions

Whereas the great precept of nature is conceded to be, "that man shall pursue his own true and substantial happiness." Blackstone,[1] in his Commentaries, remarks, that this law of Nature being coeval with mankind, and dictated by God himself, is of course superior in obligation to any other. It is binding over all the globe, in all countries, and at all times; no human laws are of any validity if contrary to this, and such of them as are valid, derive all their force, and all their validity, and all their authority, mediately and immediately, from this original; therefore,

Resolved, That such laws as conflict, in any way, with the true and substantial happiness of woman, are contrary to the great precept of nature, and of no validity; for this is "superior in obligation to any other."

Resolved, That all laws which prevent woman from occupying such a station in society as her conscience shall dictate, or which place her in a position inferior to that of man, are contrary to the great precept of nature, and therefore of no force or authority.

Resolved, That woman is man's equal—was intended to be so by the Creator—and the highest good of the race demands that she should be recognized as such.

Resolved, That the women of this country ought to be enlightened in regard to the laws under which they live, that they may no longer publish their degradation, by declaring themselves satisfied with their present position, nor their ignorance, by asserting that they have all the rights they want.

Resolved, That inasmuch as man, while claiming for himself intellectual superiority, does accord to woman moral superiority, it is pre-eminently his duty to encourage her to speak, and teach, as she has an opportunity, in all religious assemblies.

Resolved, That the same amount of virtue, delicacy, and refinement of behavior, that is required of woman in the social state, should also be required of man, and the same transgressions should be visited with equal severity on both man and woman.

---

[1]Sir William Blackstone, English jurist, published volume 1 of his *Commentaries on the Laws of England* in 1766, which became the most authoritative scholarly overview of English common law, influencing American legal thinkers through the nineteenth century.

Resolved, That the objection of indelicacy and impropriety, which is so often brought against woman when she addresses a public audience, comes with a very ill-grace from those who encourage, by their attendance, her appearance on the stage, in the concert, or in the feats of the circus.

Resolved, That woman has too long rested satisfied in the circumscribed limits which corrupt customs and a perverted application of the Scriptures have marked out for her, and that it is time she should move in the enlarged sphere which her great Creator has assigned her.

Resolved, That it is the duty of the women of this country to secure to themselves their sacred right to the elective franchise.

Resolved, That the equality of human rights results necessarily from the fact of the identity of the race in capabilities and responsibilities.

Resolved, therefore, That, being invested by the Creator with the same capabilities, and the same consciousness of responsibility for their exercise, it is demonstrably the right and duty of woman, equally with man, to promote every righteous cause, by every righteous means; and especially in regard to the great subjects of morals and religion, it is self-evidently her right to participate with her brother in teaching them, both in private and in public, by writing and by speaking, by any instrumentalities proper to be used, and in any assemblies proper to be held; and this being a self-evident truth, growing out of the divinely implanted principles of human nature, any custom or authority adverse to it, whether modern or wearing the hoary sanction of antiquity, is to be regarded as self-evident falsehood, and at war with the interests of mankind.

READING AND DISCUSSION QUESTIONS

1. Analyze the efforts of the Seneca Falls delegates to define and gain access to individual rights and citizenship for women. What definition of citizenship did they embrace for women?

2. What impact on the interpretation of constitutional rights do you think these women expected their reforms to provoke?

P5-2 | Defining Native American Rights and Limits

STATUTES OF CALIFORNIA, *An Act for the Government and Protection of Indians* (1850)

California entered the Union on September 9, 1850, having ratified its state constitution the year before forbidding slavery and declaring that "all men are by nature free and independent." Thus it embraced the rhetoric of the U.S. Constitution. However, on April 22, 1850,

Compiled Laws of the State of California: Containing all the Acts of the Legislature of a Public and General Nature, Now in Force, Passed at the Sessions of 1850–51–52–53, comp. S. Garfielde and F. A. Snyder (Boston: Press of the Franklin Printing House, 1853), 822–825.

more than four months before officially entering the Union, the state Senate and Assembly passed legislation ostensibly for the protection of Native Americans that in reality restricted them, evidence of the state's narrow and exclusive interpretation of Bill of Rights protections.

The People of the State of California, represented in Senate and Assembly, do enact as follows:

SECTION 1. Justices of the Peace shall have jurisdiction in all cases of complaints by, for or against Indians, in their respective townships in this State.

SEC. 2. Persons and proprietors of land on which Indians are residing, shall permit such Indians peaceably to reside on such lands, unmolested in the pursuit of their usual avocations for the maintenance of themselves and families: Provided; the white person or proprietor in possession of lands may apply to a justice of the peace in the township where the Indians reside, to set off to such Indians a certain amount of land, and, on such application, the justice shall set off a sufficient amount of land for the necessary wants of such Indians, including the site of their village or residence, if they so prefer it; and in no case shall such selection be made to the prejudice of such Indians, nor shall they be forced to abandon their homes or villages where they have resided for a number of years; and either party feeling themselves aggrieved, can appeal to the county court from the decision of the justice: and then divided, a record shall be made of the lands so set off in the court so dividing them, and the Indians shall be permitted to remain thereon until otherwise provided for.

SEC. 3. Any person having or hereafter obtaining a minor Indian, male or female, from the parents or relations of such Indian minor, and wishing to keep it, such person shall go before a justice of the peace in his township, with the parents or friends of the child, and if the justice of the peace becomes satisfied that no compulsory means have been used to obtain the child from its parents or friends, shall enter on record, in a book kept for that purpose, the sex and probable age of the child, and shall give to such person a certificate, authorizing him or her to have the care, custody, control, and earnings of such minor, until he or she attain the age of majority. Every male Indian shall be deemed to have attained his majority at eighteen, and the female at fifteen years.

SEC. 4. Any person having a minor Indian in his care, as described in the foregoing section of this act, who shall neglect to clothe and suitably feed such minor Indian, or shall inhumanely treat him or her, on conviction thereof shall be subject to a fine not less than ten dollars, at the discretion of a court or jury; and the justice of the peace, in his own discretion, may place the minor Indian in the care of some other person, giving him the same rights and liabilities that the former master of said minor was entitled and subject to.

SEC. 5. Any person wishing to hire an Indian, shall go before a justice of the peace with the Indian, and make such contract as the justice may approve, and the justice shall file such contract in writing in his office, and all contracts so made shall be binding between the parties; but no contract between a white man and an Indian, for labor shall otherwise be obligatory on the part of the Indian.

Sec. 6. Complaints may be made before a justice of the peace, by white persons or Indians; but in no case shall a white man be convicted on any offence upon the testimony of an Indian, or Indians. And in all cases it shall be discretionary with the court or jury after hearing the complaint of an Indian.

Sec. 7. If any person forcibly conveys any Indian from his home, or compels him to work, or perform any service against his will, in this state, except as provided in this act, he or they shall, on conviction, be fined in any sum not less than fifty dollars, at the discretion of the court or jury.

Sec. 8. It shall be the duty of the justices of the peace, once in six months in every year, to make a full and correct statement to the court of sessions of their county, of all moneys received for fines imposed on Indians . . . and the treasurer shall keep a correct statement of all money so received, which shall be termed the "Indian fund" of the county. The treasurer shall pay out any money of said funds in his hands . . . for fees and expenditures incurred in carrying out the provisions of this law.

Sec. 9. It shall be the duty of the justices of the peace, in their respective townships, as well as all other peace officers in this state, to instruct the Indians in their neighborhood in the laws which relate to them, giving them such advice as they may deem necessary and proper; and if any tribe or village of Indians refuse or neglect to obey the laws, the justice of the peace may punish the guilty chiefs or principal men by reprimand or fine, or otherwise reasonably chastise them.

Sec. 10. If any person or persons shall set the prairie on fire, or refuse to use proper exertions to extinguish the fire when the prairies are burning, such persons shall be subject to fine or punishment, as court may adjudge proper.

Sec. 11. If any Indian shall commit an unlawful offence against a white person, such person shall not inflict punishment for such offence, but may, without process, take the Indian before a justice of the peace, and, on conviction, the Indian shall be punished according to the provisions of this act.

Sec. 12. In all cases of trial between a white man and an Indian, either party may require a jury.

Sec. 13. Justices may require the chiefs and influential men of any village to apprehend and bring before them or him any Indian charged or suspected of an offence.

Sec. 14. When an Indian is convicted of an offence before a justice of the peace punishable by fine, any white person may, by consent of the justice, give bond for said Indian, conditioned for the payment of said fine and costs, and in such case the Indian shall be compelled to work for the person so bailing, until he has discharged or cancelled the fine assessed against him: Provided; the person bailing shall treat the Indian humanely, and feed and clothe him properly; the allowance given for such labor shall be fixed by the Court, when the bond is taken.

Sec. 15. If any person in this State shall sell, give, or furnish to any Indian, male or female, any intoxicating liquors (except when administered for sickness), for good cause shown, he, she, or they so offending shall, on conviction thereof, be fined not less than twenty dollars for each offence, or be imprisoned not less than five days, or fined and imprisoned as the court may determine.

SEC. 16. An Indian convicted of stealing horses, mules, cattle, or any valuable thing, shall be subject to receive any number of lashes not exceeding twenty-five, or shall be subject to a fine not exceeding two hundred dollars, at the discretion of the court or jury.

SEC. 17. When an Indian is sentenced to be whipped, the justice may appoint a white man, or an Indian at his discretion, to execute the sentence in his presence, and shall not permit unnecessary cruelty in the execution of the sentence.

SEC. 18. All fines, forfeitures, penalties recovered under or by this act, shall be paid into the treasury of the county, to the credit of the Indian fund as provided in section eight.

SEC. 19. All white persons making application to a justice of the peace, for confirmation of a contract with or in relation to an Indian, shall pay the fee, which shall not exceed two dollars for each contract determined and filed as provided in this act, and for all other services, such fees are allowed for similar services under other laws of this state: Provided, the application fee for hiring Indians, or keeping minors, and fees and expenses for setting off lands to Indians, shall be paid by the white person applying.

SEC. 20. Any Indian able to work and support himself in some honest calling, not having wherewithal to maintain himself, who shall be found loitering and strolling about, or frequenting public places where liquors are sold, begging, or leading an immoral or profligate course of life, shall be liable to be arrested on the complaint of any resident citizen of the county, and brought before the justice of the peace of the proper county, mayor or recorder of any incorporated town or city, who shall examine said accused Indian, and hear the testimony in relation thereto, and if said justice, mayor, or recorder shall be satisfied that he is a vagrant . . . he shall make out a warrant under his hand and seal, authorizing and requiring the officer having him in charge or custody, to hire out such vagrant within twenty-four hours to the highest bidder.

READING AND DISCUSSION QUESTIONS

1. What can you infer about the values that guided the political system in 1850s California with respect to citizenship rights for whites and Native Americans?

2. What do these provisions directed to Native Americans tell you about the conflicting interpretation and application of rights guaranteed by the U.S. Constitution? How did California legislators interpret those Bill of Rights protections as applied to American Indians in California?

P5-3 | The Catholic Threat to American Politics

SAMUEL F. B. MORSE, *Foreign Conspiracy Against the Liberties of the United States* (1855)

European immigration was on the rise in the 1830s, when Samuel Morse published in book form his editorials first serialized in the *New York Observer*. By the time the seventh edition was published in the mid-1850s, immigration had increased even more, spurred on by the revolutions in Europe in 1848. Morse, who is better known for the telegraphic code he invented, was a nativist who justified his opposition to Catholic immigration as a defense of constitutional liberties and republican government against papal conspiracies directed from Rome. His understanding of the Constitution powered such antebellum political movements as the Nativist or Know-Nothing Party of the 1840s and 1850s.

[S]ome of my readers . . . may be inclined to ask in what manner can the despots of Europe effect, by means of Popish emissaries, any thing in this country to counteract the influence of our liberal institutions? In what way can they operate here?

With the *necessity existing of doing something, from the instinct of self-preservation*, to check the influence of our free institutions on Europe, with the *funds* provided, and *agents* on the spot interested in their plans, one would think it needed but little sagacity to find modes and opportunities of operating; especially, too, when such *vulnerable points* as I have exposed (and there are many more which I have not brought forward) invite attack.

To any such inquirers, let me say there are many ways in which a body organized as are the Catholics, and moving in concert, might *disturb* (to use the mildest term) the good order of the republic, and thus compel us to present to observing Europe the spectacle of republican anarchy. Who is not aware that a great portion of that stuff which composes a mob, ripe for riot or excess of any kind, and of which we have every week or two a fresh example in some part of the country, is a Catholic population? And what makes it turbulent? Ignorance — an ignorance which it is for the interest of its leaders not to enlighten; for, enlighten a man, and he will think for himself, and have some self-respect; he will understand the laws, and know his interest in obeying them. Keep him in ignorance, and he is the slave of the man who will flatter his passions and appetites, or awe him by superstitious fears. Against the outbreakings of such men, society, as it is constituted on our free system, can protect itself only in one of two ways: it must either bring these men under the influence and control of a sound republican and religious education, or it must call in the aid of *the priests* who govern them, and who may *permit* and *direct*, or *restrain* their turbulence, in accordance with what they may judge at any particular time to be the *interest of the church*. Yes, be it well remarked, the same hands that can, whenever it suits

Samuel F. B. Morse, *Foreign Conspiracy Against the Liberties of the United States* (New York: American and Foreign Christian Union, 1855), 89–96, 98–99.

their interest, *restrain*, can also, at the proper time, *"let slip the dogs of war."* In this mode of restraint by a *police of priests*, by substituting the *ecclesiastical* for the *civil* power, the *priest-led* mobs of Portugal and Spain, and South America, are instructive examples. And start not, American reader, *this kind of police is already established in our country!* We have had mobs again and again, which neither the civil nor military power have availed any thing to quell, until the magic *"peace, be still,"* of the *Catholic priest* has hushed the winds, and calmed the waves of popular tumult. . . .

And what now prevents the interference of Catholics, as a sect, directly in the *political elections* of the country? They are organized under their priests: is there any thing in their religious principles to restrain them? Do not Catholics of the present day use the bonds of religious union to effect political objects in other countries? . . .

It is not true that Popery meddles not with the politics of the country. The cloven foot has already shown itself. *Popery is organized at the elections!* For example: in Michigan, the Bishop Richard, a Jesuit (since deceased), was several times chosen delegate to Congress from the territory, the majority of the people being Catholics. As Protestants became more numerous, the contest between the bishop and his Protestant rival was more and more close, until at length, by the increase of Protestant emigration, the latter triumphed. The bishop, in order to detect any delinquency in his flock at the polls, *had his ticket printed on colored paper!* . . . Does it not show that Popery, with all its speciousness, is the same here as elsewhere? It manifests, when it has the opportunity, its genuine disposition to use *spiritual* power for the promotion of its *temporal* ambition. It uses its ecclesiastical weapons to control an election. . . .

It is unnecessary to multiply facts of this nature. . . . Surely American Protestants . . . will see that Popery is now, what it has ever been, a system of the darkest *political* intrigue and despotism, cloaking itself, to avoid attack, under the sacred name of religion. They will be deeply impressed with the truth, that Popery is a political as well as a religious system; that in this respect it differs totally from all other sects, from all other forms of religion in the country. *Popery imbodies in itself* THE CLOSEST UNION OF CHURCH AND STATE. . . .

Can we not discern the *political* character of Popery? Shall the name of *Religion*, artfully connected with it, still blind our eyes? Let us suppose a body of men to combine together, and claim as their right, that *all public and private property, of whatever kind, is held at their disposal; that they alone are to judge of their own right to dispose of it; that they alone are authorized to think or speak on the subject; that they who speak or write in opposition to them are traitors, and must be put to death; that all temporal power is secondary to theirs, and amenable to their superior and infallible judgment*; and the better to hide the presumption of these tyrannical claims, suppose that these men should pretend to *divine right*, and call their system *Religion*, and so claim the protection of our laws, and pleading *conscience*, demand to be tolerated. Would the name of *Religion* be a cloak sufficiently thick to hide such absurdity, and shield it from public indignation? Take, then, from *Popery* its name of *Religion*; strip its *officers* of their pompous titles of *sacredness*, and its *decrees* of the nauseous cant of piety, and what have you remaining? Is it not a *naked, odious Despotism*, depending for its strength on the observance of the strictest military discipline in its ranks, from the Pope, through his Cardinals, Archbishops, Bishops, &c. down to the lowest priest of his dominions? And is not this despotism acting *politically* in this country? . . .

What is the difference between the *real* claims, and efforts, and condition of Popery at this moment in these United States, and the *supposed* claims, and efforts, and condition of the Russian despotism? The one comes disguised under the name of *Religion*, the other, more honest and more harmless, would come in its real *political* name. Give the latter the name of *Religion*, call the *Emperor, Pope*, and his *Viceroys, Bishops*, interlard the *imperial decrees* with *pious cant*, and you have the case of pretension, and intrigue, and success, too, which has actually passed in these United States! Yes, the King of Rome, acting by the promptings of the Austrian Cabinet, and in the plentitude of his usurpation, has already extended his sceptre over our land; he has divided us up into provinces, and appointed his Viceroys, who claim their *jurisdiction* from a higher power than exists in this country, even from his majesty himself, who appoints them, who removes them at will, to whom they owe allegiance; for the extension of whose temporal kingdom they are exerting themselves, and whose success, let it be indelibly impressed on your minds, is the *certain destruction of the free institutions of our country.*

READING AND DISCUSSION QUESTIONS

1. How does Morse's argument about the Catholic threat to America provide evidence for the impact of anti-immigrant ideas on the political system? What social effect might his efforts to limit participation by Catholics have had on antebellum American politics?

2. Why do you think his ideas about the Constitution's vulnerabilities toward Catholic influence found a receptive audience?

P5-4 | Debating the Meaning of the Constitution

ABRAHAM LINCOLN, *Cooper Union Address* (1860)

In 1860, the clear point of contention between Republicans and Democrats was the authority of Congress to regulate slavery within the territories. Illinois senator Stephen Douglas, whom Lincoln had famously debated in 1858, promoted the idea of "popular sovereignty" whereby voters would decide the fate of slavery in a territory, claiming the founding fathers had endorsed such a policy in the Constitution. Lincoln's meticulous rejoinder in his Cooper Union address in New York City argued instead that the founders had acknowledged Congress's duty to regulate slavery in the territories. A minor political figure before the speech, Lincoln's New

www.abrahamlincolnonline.org/lincoln/speeches/cooper.htm.

York triumph propelled him to the front ranks of Republican Party politics, leading later that year to his nomination for president.

The facts with which I shall deal this evening are mainly old and familiar; nor is there anything new in the general use I shall make of them. If there shall be any novelty, it will be in the mode of presenting the facts, and the inferences and observations following that presentation.

In his speech last autumn, at Columbus, Ohio, as reported in "The New-York Times," Senator Douglas said:

"Our fathers, when they framed the Government under which we live, understood this question just as well, and even better, than we do now."

I fully indorse this, and I adopt it as a text for this discourse. I so adopt it because it furnishes a precise and an agreed starting point for a discussion between Republicans and that wing of the Democracy headed by Senator Douglas. It simply leaves the inquiry: "What was the understanding those fathers had of the question mentioned?"

What is the frame of government under which we live?

The answer must be: "The Constitution of the United States." That Constitution consists of the original, framed in 1787 (and under which the present government first went into operation), and twelve subsequently framed amendments, the first ten of which were framed in 1789.

Who were our fathers that framed the Constitution? I suppose the "thirty-nine" who signed the original instrument may be fairly called our fathers who framed that part of the present Government. It is almost exactly true to say they framed it, and it is altogether true to say they fairly represented the opinion and sentiment of the whole nation at that time. Their names, being familiar to nearly all, and accessible to quite all, need not now be repeated.

I take these "thirty-nine," for the present, as being "our fathers who framed the Government under which we live."

What is the question which, according to the text, those fathers understood "just as well, and even better than we do now"?

It is this: Does the proper division of local from federal authority, or anything in the Constitution, forbid our *Federal Government* to control as to slavery in *our Federal Territories*?

Upon this, Senator Douglas holds the affirmative, and Republicans the negative. This affirmation and denial form an issue; and this issue — this question — is precisely what the text declares our fathers understood "better than we."

Let us now inquire whether the "thirty-nine," or any of them, ever acted upon this question; and if they did, how they acted upon it — how they expressed that better understanding?

In 1784, three years before the Constitution — the United States then owning the Northwestern Territory, and no other, the Congress of the Confederation had before them the question of prohibiting slavery in that Territory; and four of the "thirty-nine" who afterward framed the Constitution, were in that Congress, and voted on that question. Of these, Roger Sherman, Thomas Mifflin, and Hugh

Williamson voted for the prohibition, thus showing that, in their understanding, no line dividing local from federal authority, nor anything else, properly forbade the Federal Government to control as to slavery in federal territory. . . .

In 1787, still before the Constitution . . . the same question of prohibiting slavery in the territory again came before the Congress of the Confederation; and two more of the "thirty-nine" who afterward signed the Constitution . . . both voted for the prohibition—thus showing that, in their understanding, no line dividing local from federal authority, nor anything else, properly forbids the Federal Government to control as to slavery in Federal territory. . . .

In 1789, by the first Congress which sat under the Constitution, an act was passed to enforce the Ordinance of '87, including the prohibition of slavery in the Northwestern Territory. The bill . . . passed both branches without yeas and nays, which is equivalent to a unanimous passage. In this Congress there were sixteen of the thirty-nine fathers who framed the original Constitution. . . .

This shows that, in their understanding, no line dividing local from federal authority, nor anything in the Constitution, properly forbade Congress to prohibit slavery in the federal territory; else both their fidelity to correct principle, and their oath to support the Constitution, would have constrained them to oppose the prohibition.

Again, George Washington, another of the "thirty-nine," was then President of the United States, and, as such approved and signed the bill; thus completing its validity as a law, and thus showing that, in his understanding, no line dividing local from federal authority, nor anything in the Constitution, forbade the Federal Government, to control as to slavery in federal territory. . . .

In 1803, the Federal Government purchased the Louisiana country. . . . Congress did not, in the Territorial Act, prohibit slavery; but they did interfere with it—take control of it—in a more marked and extensive way than they did in the case of Mississippi. The substance of the provision therein made, in relation to slaves, was:

First. That no slave should be imported into the territory from foreign parts.

Second. That no slave should be carried into it who had been imported into the United States since the first day of May, 1798.

Third. That no slave should be carried into it, except by the owner, and for his own use as a settler; the penalty in all the cases being a fine upon the violator of the law, and freedom to the slave. . . .

In the Congress which passed it, there were two of the "thirty-nine." . . . They would not have allowed it to pass without recording their opposition to it, if, in their understanding, it violated either the line properly dividing local from federal authority, or any provision of the Constitution. . . .

The cases I have mentioned are the only acts of the "thirty-nine," or of any of them, upon the direct issue, which I have been able to discover. . . .

The sum of the whole is, that of our thirty-nine fathers who framed the original Constitution, twenty-one—a clear majority of the whole—certainly understood that no proper division of local from federal authority, nor any part of the Constitution, forbade the Federal Government to control slavery in the federal territories; while all the rest probably had the same understanding. Such, unquestionably, was the understanding of our fathers who framed the original Constitution; and the text affirms that they understood the question "better than we." . . .

But enough! *Let all who believe that "our fathers, who framed the Government under which we live, understood this question just as well, and even better, than we do now," speak as they spoke, and act as they acted upon it. This is all Republicans ask—all Republicans desire—in relation to slavery. As those fathers marked it, so let it be again marked, as an evil not to be extended, but to be tolerated and protected only because of and so far as its actual presence among us makes that toleration and protection a necessity. Let all the guarantees those fathers gave it, be, not grudgingly, but fully and fairly, maintained.* For this Republicans contend, and with this, so far as I know or believe, they will be content.

And now, if they would listen—as I suppose they will not—I would address a few words to the Southern people. . . .

You say we are sectional. We deny it. That makes an issue; and the burden of proof is upon you. You produce your proof; and what is it? Why, that our party has no existence in your section—gets no votes in your section. The fact is substantially true; but does it prove the issue? . . . The fact that we get no votes in your section, is a fact of your making, and not of ours. And if there be fault in that fact, that fault is primarily yours, and remains until you show that we repel you by some wrong principle or practice. . . . Do you accept the challenge? No! Then you really believe that the principle which "our fathers who framed the Government under which we live" thought so clearly right as to adopt it, and indorse it again and again, upon their official oaths, is in fact so clearly wrong as to demand your condemnation without a moment's consideration.

Some of you delight to flaunt in our faces the warning against sectional parties given by Washington in his Farewell Address. Less than eight years before Washington gave that warning, he had, as President of the United States, approved and signed an act of Congress, enforcing the prohibition of slavery in the Northwestern Territory, which act embodied the policy of the Government upon that subject up to and at the very moment he penned that warning; and about one year after he penned it, he wrote LaFayette[1] that he considered that prohibition a wise measure, expressing in the same connection his hope that we should at some time have a confederacy of free States. . . .

Again, you say we have made the slavery question more prominent than it formerly was. We deny it. We admit that it is more prominent, but we deny that we made it so. It was not we, but you, who discarded the old policy of the fathers. We resisted, and still resist, your innovation; and thence comes the greater prominence of the question. Would you have that question reduced to its former proportions? Go back to that old policy. What has been will be again, under the same

---

[1]**LaFayette**: Marquis de Lafayette was a French aristocrat who served with Washington as a major general in the Continental army during the American Revolution.

conditions. If you would have the peace of the old times, readopt the precepts and policy of the old times.

You charge that we stir up insurrections among your slaves. We deny it; and what is your proof? Harper's Ferry! John Brown!! John Brown was no Republican; and you have failed to implicate a single Republican in his Harper's Ferry enterprise. . . .

Under all these circumstances, do you really feel yourselves justified to break up this Government unless such a court decision as yours is, shall be at once submitted to as a conclusive and final rule of political action? But you will not abide the election of a Republican president! In that supposed event, you say, you will destroy the Union; and then, you say, the great crime of having destroyed it will be upon us! That is cool. A highwayman holds a pistol to my ear, and mutters through his teeth, "Stand and deliver, or I shall kill you, and then you will be a murderer!" . . .

A few words now to Republicans. . . .

Wrong as we think slavery is, we can yet afford to let it alone where it is, because that much is due to the necessity arising from its actual presence in the nation; but can we, while our votes will prevent it, allow it to spread into the National Territories, and to overrun us here in these Free States? If our sense of duty forbids this, then let us stand by our duty, fearlessly and effectively. Let us be diverted by none of those sophistical contrivances wherewith we are so industriously plied and belabored—contrivances such as groping for some middle ground between the right and the wrong, vain as the search for a man who should be neither a living man nor a dead man—such as a policy of "don't care" on a question about which all true men do care—such as Union appeals beseeching true Union men to yield to Disunionists, reversing the divine rule, and calling, not the sinners, but the righteous to repentance—such as invocations to Washington, imploring men to unsay what Washington said, and undo what Washington did.

Neither let us be slandered from our duty by false accusations against us, nor frightened from it by menaces of destruction to the Government nor of dungeons to ourselves. LET US HAVE FAITH THAT RIGHT MAKES MIGHT, AND IN THAT FAITH, LET US, TO THE END, DARE TO DO OUR DUTY AS WE UNDERSTAND IT.

READING AND DISCUSSION QUESTIONS

1. Summarize Lincoln's interpretation of the Constitution with respect to the issue of slavery's expansion within federal territories. What impact do you think his views had on southerners in the historical context of the 1850s and 1860s?

2. What argument does Lincoln make about the role of the federal government and its potential as an agent of political change in the context of the slavery issue?

P5-5 | Southern Leader Contrasts Union and Confederate Constitutions

ALEXANDER STEPHENS, *"Cornerstone" Speech* (1861)

The federal and Confederate constitutions that Alexander Stephens described during the secession crisis in March 1861 were a study in contrasts. Whereas Lincoln at Cooper Union had claimed that the Constitution granted Congress the authority to regulate slavery in the territories, Stephens emphasized instead its guarantee of slavery. Regardless, Stephens declared that the federal Constitution rested on flawed assumptions concerning the equality of the races. He therefore championed the new Confederate Constitution for its attachment to what he called "this great physical, philosophical, and moral truth." This truth, which he labeled the cornerstone of the Confederacy, was the inflexible belief in "the Negro's" inferiority.

This new constitution, or form of government, constitutes the subject to which your attention will be partly invited. In reference to it, I make this first general remark. It amply secures all our ancient rights, franchises, and liberties. All the great principles of Magna Charta are retained in it. No citizen is deprived of life, liberty, or property, but by the judgment of his peers under the laws of the land. The great principle of religious liberty, which was the honor and pride of the old constitution, is still maintained and secured. All the essentials of the old constitution, which have endeared it to the hearts of the American people, have been preserved and perpetuated. [Applause.] Some changes have been made. Of these I shall speak presently. Some of these I should have preferred not to have seen made; but these, perhaps, meet the cordial approbation of a majority of this audience, if not an overwhelming majority of the people of the Confederacy. Of them, therefore, I will not speak. But other important changes do meet my cordial approbation. They form great improvements upon the old constitution. So, taking the whole new constitution, I have no hesitancy in giving it as my judgment that it is decidedly better than the old. [Applause.]

Allow me briefly to allude to some of these improvements. The question of building up class interests, or fostering one branch of industry to the prejudice of another under the exercise of the revenue power, which gave us so much trouble under the old constitution, is put at rest forever under the new. We allow the imposition of no duty with a view of giving advantage to one class of persons, in any trade or business, over those of another. All, under our system, stand upon the same broad principles of perfect equality. Honest labor and enterprise are left free and unrestricted in whatever pursuit they may be engaged. . . .

Again, the subject of internal improvements, under the power of Congress regulate commerce, is put at rest under our system. The power claimed by c struction under the old constitution, was at least a doubtful one—it rested s' upon construction. We of the South, generally apart from consideratic

---

Alexander H. Stephens, in Public and Private. With Letters and Speeches, Before, During, ar War, ed. Henry Cleveland (Philadelphia: National Publishing Company, 1866), 718–'

constitutional principles, opposed its exercise upon grounds of its inexpediency and injustice. Notwithstanding this opposition, millions of money, from the common treasury had been drawn for such purposes. Our opposition sprang from no hostility to commerce, or all necessary aids for facilitating it. With us it was simply a question, upon whom the burden should fall. . . .

The true principle is to subject the commerce of every locality, to whatever burdens may be necessary to facilitate it. If Charleston harbor needs improvement, let the commerce of Charleston bear the burden. If the mouth of the Savannah river has to be cleared out, let the sea-going navigation which is benefitted by it, bear the burden. . . . Just as the products of the interior, our cotton, wheat, corn, and other articles, have to bear the necessary rates of freight over our railroads to reach the seas. This is again the broad principle of perfect equality and justice. [Applause.] And it is especially set forth and established in our new constitution. . . .

But not to be tedious in enumerating the numerous changes for the better, allow me to allude to one other — though last, not least. The new constitution has put at rest, *forever,* all the agitating questions relating to our peculiar institution — African slavery as it exists amongst us — the proper *status* of the negro in our form of civilization. This was the immediate cause of the late rupture and present revolution. Jefferson in his forecast, had anticipated this, as the "rock upon which the old Union would split." He was right. What was conjecture with him, is now a realized fact. But whether he fully comprehended the great truth upon which that rock *stood* and *stands,* may be doubted. The prevailing ideas entertained by him and most of the leading statesmen at the time of the formation of the old constitution, were that the enslavement of the African was in violation of the laws of nature; that it was wrong in *principle,* socially, morally, and politically. It was an evil they knew not well how to deal with, but the general opinion of the men of that day was that, somehow or other in the order of Providence, the institution would be evanescent and pass away. This idea, though not incorporated in the constitution, was the prevailing idea at that time. The constitution, it is true, secured every essential guarantee to the institution while it should last, and hence no argument can be justly urged against the constitutional guarantees thus secured, because of the common sentiment of the day. Those ideas, however, were fundamentally wrong. They rested upon the assumption of the equality of races. This was an error. It was a sandy foundation, and the government built upon it fell when the "storm came and the wind blew."

Our new government is founded upon exactly the opposite idea; its foundations are laid, its corner-stone rests upon the great truth, that the negro is not equal to the white man; that slavery — subordination to the superior race — is his natural and normal condition. [Applause.]

This, our new government, is the first, in the history of the world, based upon this great physical, philosophical, and moral truth. This truth has been slow in the process of its development, like all other truths in the various departments of science. It has been so even amongst us. Many who hear me, perhaps, can recollect well, that this truth was not generally admitted, even within their day. The errors of the past generation still clung to many as late as twenty years ago. Those at the North, who still cling to these errors, with a zeal above knowledge, we justly denominate fanatics. All fanaticism springs from an aberration of the mind—from a defect in reasoning. It is a species of insanity. One of the most striking characteristics of insanity, in many instances, is forming correct conclusions from fancied or erroneous premises; so with the anti-slavery fanatics; their conclusions are right if their premises were. They assume that the negro is equal, and hence conclude that he is entitled to equal privileges and rights with the white man. If their premises were correct, their conclusions would be logical and just—but their premise being wrong, their whole argument fails. . . .

May we not, therefore, look with confidence to the ultimate universal acknowledgment of the truths upon which our system rests? It is the first government ever instituted upon the principles in strict conformity to nature, and the ordination of Providence, in furnishing the materials of human society. Many governments have been founded upon the principle of the subordination and serfdom of certain classes of the same race; such were and are in violation of the laws of nature. Our system commits no such violation of nature's laws. With us, all of the white race, however high or low, rich or poor, are equal in the eye of the law. Not so with the negro. Subordination is his place. He, by nature, or by the curse against Canaan, is fitted for that condition which he occupies in our system. The architect, in the construction of buildings, lays the foundation with the proper material—the granite; then comes the brick or the marble. The substratum of our society is made of the material fitted by nature for it, and by experience we know that it is best, not only for the superior, but for the inferior race, that it should be so. It is, indeed, in conformity with the ordinance of the Creator. It is not for us to inquire into the wisdom of his ordinances, or to question them. For his own purposes, he has made one race to differ from another, as he has made "one star to differ from another star in glory."

The great objects of humanity are best attained when there is conformity to his laws and decrees, in the formation of governments as well as in all things else. Our confederacy is founded upon principles in strict conformity with these laws. This stone which was rejected by the first builders "is become the chief of the corner"—the real "corner-stone"—in our new edifice. [Applause.]

READING AND DISCUSSION QUESTIONS

1. Summarize the differences in interpretation that separated Lincoln and Stephens on the question of the federal Constitution's position on slavery and the slavery extension issue. How did these arguments over the meaning of the Constitution affect American politics in the 1850s and 1860s?

2. To what extent do these interpretive differences represent short- or long-term causes of the Civil War?

3. How did the Confederate interpretation of constitutional values, as reflected in Stephens's speech, help southern politicians distinguish their Constitution from the federal Constitution they rejected?

P5-6 | Freedman Claiming the Rights of Citizenship

REV. HENRY MCNEAL TURNER, *Speech Before the Georgia State Legislature* (1868)

Despite the ratification of the Fourteenth and Fifteenth Amendments to the Constitution in 1868 and 1870 respectively, core questions of citizenship remained in dispute for African Americans, who suffered the withering and persistent racism of the era. Some African American men, like the Reverend Henry Turner, won election to state office in the postwar years, but their triumph dimmed under the ridicule and deceit they faced. In his case, the white majority in the Georgia legislature, in a blatant obstruction of the democratic process, expelled Turner from his elected office. Their vote prompted Turner's impassioned speech where he claimed his rights under the Constitution as he read it.

MR. SPEAKER: Before proceeding to argue this question upon its intrinsic merits, I wish the members of this House to understand the position that I take. I hold that I am a member of this body. Therefore, sir, I shall neither fawn nor cringe before any party, nor stoop to beg them for my rights. Some of my colored fellow members, in the course of their remarks, took occasion to appeal to the sympathies of members on the opposite side, and to eulogize their character for magnanimity. It reminds me very much, sir, of slaves begging under the lash. I am here to demand my rights and to hurl thunderbolts at the men who would dare to cross the threshold of my manhood. There is an old aphorism which says, "fight the devil with fire," and if I should observe the rule in this instance, I wish gentlemen to understand that it is but fighting them with their own weapon.

The scene presented in this House, today, is one unparalleled in the history of the world. From this day, back to the day when God breathed the breath of life into Adam, no analogy for it can be found. Never, in the history of the world, has a man been arraigned before a body clothed with legislative, judicial or executive functions, charged with the offense of being a darker hue than his fellow men. I know that questions have been before the courts of this country, and of other countries, involving topics not altogether dissimilar to that which is being discussed here today. But, sir, never in the history of the great nations of this world never before has a man been arraigned, charged with an offense committed by the God of Heaven Himself. Cases may be found where men have been deprived of their rights for crimes and misdemeanors; but it has remained for the state of Georgia, in the very heart of the nineteenth century, to call a man before the bar, and there charge him with an act for which he is no more responsible than for the head which he carries upon his shoulders. The Anglo-Saxon race, sir, is a most surprising one. No man has ever been more deceived in that race than I have been for the last three weeks. I was not aware that there was in the character of that race so much cowardice or so much pusillanimity. The treachery which has

Lift Every Voice: African American Oratory, 1787–1900 (Tuscaloosa and London: The University of Alabama Press, 1998), 476–483.

been exhibited in it by gentlemen belonging to that race has shaken my confidence in it more than anything that has come under my observation from the day of my birth. . . .

Whose legislature is this? Is it a white man's legislature, or is it a black man's legislature? Who voted for a constitutional convention, in obedience to the mandate of the Congress of the United States? Who first rallied around the standard of Reconstruction? Who set the ball of loyalty rolling in the state of Georgia? And whose voice was heard on the hills and in the valleys of this state? It was the voice of the brawny armed Negro, with the few humanitarian hearted white men who came to our assistance. I claim the honor, sir, of having been the instrument of convincing hundreds—yea, thousands—of white men, that to reconstruct under the measures of the United States Congress was the safest and the best course for the interest of the state. . . .

The great question, sir, is this: Am I a man? If I am such, I claim the rights of a man. Am I not a man because I happen to be of a darker hue than honorable gentlemen around me? Let me see whether I am or not. I want to convince the House today that I am entitled to my seat here. A certain gentleman has argued that the Negro was a mere development similar to the orangoutang or chimpanzee, but it so happens that, when a Negro is examined, physiologically, phrenologically and anatomically, and I may say, physiognomically, he is found to be the same as persons of different color. I would like to ask any gentleman on this floor, where is the analogy? Do you find me a quadruped, or do you find me a man? Do you find three bones less in my back than in that of the white man? Do you find fewer organs in the brain? If you know nothing of this, I do; for I have helped to dissect fifty men, black and white, and I assert that by the time you take off the mucous pigment—the color of the skin—you cannot, to save your life, distinguish between the black man and the white. Am I a man? Have I a soul to save, as you have? Am I susceptible of eternal development, as you are? Can I learn all the arts and sciences that you can? Has it ever been demonstrated in the history of the world? Have black men ever exhibited bravery as white men have done? Have they ever been in the professions? Have they not as good articulative organs as you? . . . God has weaved and tissued variety and versatility throughout the boundless space of His creation. Because God saw fit to make some red, and some white, and some black, and some brown, are we to sit here in judgment upon what God has seen fit to do? As well might one play with the thunderbolts of heaven as with that creature that bears God's image—God's photograph. . . .

It is said that Congress never gave us the right to hold office. I want to know, sir, if the Reconstruction measures did not base their action on the ground that no distinction should be made on account of race, color or previous condition? Was not that the grand fulcrum on which they rested? And did not every reconstructed state have to reconstruct on the idea that no discrimination, in any sense of the term, should be made? There is not a man here who will dare say No. . . .

We are a persecuted people. Luther was persecuted; Galileo was persecuted; good men in all nations have been persecuted; but the persecutors have been handed down to posterity with shame and ignominy. If you pass this bill, you will never get Congress to pardon or enfranchise another rebel in your lives. You are going to fix an everlasting disfranchisement upon Mr. Toombs and the other leading men of Georgia. You may think you are doing yourselves honor by expelling us from this House; but when we go, we will do as Wickliffe and as Latimer did. We will light a torch of truth that will never be extinguished — the impression that will run through the country, as people picture in their mind's eye these poor black men, in all parts of this Southern country, pleading for their rights. When you expel us, you make us forever your political foes, and you will never find a black man to vote a Democratic ticket again; for, so help me God, I will go through all the length and breadth of the land, where a man of my race is to be found, and advise him to beware of the Democratic party. Justice is the great doctrine taught in the Bible. God's Eternal justice is founded upon Truth, and the man who steps from justice steps from Truth, and cannot make his principles to prevail. . . .

I hope that our poor, downtrodden race may act well and wisely through this period of trial, and that they will exercise patience and discretion under all circumstances.

You may expel us, gentlemen, by your votes, today; but, while you do it, remember that there is a just God in Heaven, whose All-Seeing Eye beholds alike the acts of the oppressor and the oppressed, and who, despite the machinations of the wicked, never fails to vindicate the cause of Justice, and the sanctity of His own handiwork.

READING AND DISCUSSION QUESTIONS

1. What can you infer about Turner's interpretation of the Constitution and the contrary meaning his white legislative colleagues drew from the same source?

2. What changes to state institutions and society did African American activists like Turner cause by their rhetoric and actions?

3. What conclusions about the values Turner believed should guide America's political system can you draw from the speech he delivered before the Georgia legislature?

▪ COMPARATIVE QUESTIONS ▪

1. How would you examine and evaluate the multiple perspectives on American politics for evidence of the values guiding the political system during the Civil War era?

2. How did arguments over the meaning and interpretation of the nation's founding documents, such as the Declaration of Independence and the Constitution, affect American politics in the period from the Mexican War through Reconstruction?

3. What do you discover when you compare the interpretation of federal power as defined by Lincoln and Stephens with earlier appraisals from Alexander Hamilton (Document 7-1), Andrew Jackson (Document 10-3), and John C. Calhoun (Document 13-3)?

4. How would you assess the long-term legacy of the constitutional debates from the mid-nineteenth century? Are the underlying issues they struggled to define relevant to contemporary political discussion?

Acknowledgments *(continued from p. ii)*

Chapter 1

1-5 "Letter to King of Spain" (1560). From *Beyond the Codices*, translated and edited by Arthur J. O. Anderson, Frances Berdan, and James Lockhart, pp. 179, 181, 183, 185 187, 189. Copyright © 1976 by The Regents of the University of California. Used by permission of the University of California Press.

Chapter 2

2-1 "Testimony of Acoma Indians" (1599). From *Don Juan de Oñate: Colonizer of New Mexico, 1595–1628*, edited by George Hammond and Agapito Rey, Volume 5, pp. 464–468. Copyright © 1953 University of New Mexico Press, 1953. Used by permission of the University of New Mexico Press, 1953.

2-2 "A Model of Christian Charity" (1630). From *A Modell of Christian Charity*, by John Winthrop. Collections of the Massachusetts Historical Society, 1838. Courtesy of Hanover Historical Texts Collection, History Department, Hanover College.

2-5 "Letter to Joseph Morton" (1687). From *The South Carolina Historical and Genealogical Magazine*, Vol. XXX, January 1929. Used by permission of the South Carolina Historical Society.

Part 4

P4-3 "Diary" (1846) From *Diaries of Emmeline B. Wells*, vol. 1 (Vault MSS 510), Special Collections, Perry Lee Library, Brigham Young University, Provo, Utah. Used by permission.

Chapter 13

13-2 "To the Inhabitants of California" (1846) and General Francisco Mejia, "A Proclamation at Matamoros" (1846). From *A Documentary History of the Mexican War*, edited by Steven R. Butler, pp. 25 and 146. Descendants of Mexican War Veterans, 1995. Used by permission of the Descendants of Mexican War Veterans.

Chapter 14

14-1 "Letter to John Minor" (1861). From *Mary Berkeley Minor Blackford to John Barbee Minor, January 18, 1861*. Minor and Wilson Family Papers, Special Collections, University of Virginia (www.virginiamemory.com/docs/blackford_1861_01_18.pdf). Transcription courtesy of the Library of Virginia. Original documents property of the University of Virginia.

Chapter 16

16-3 "Buffalo Days" (1933). From J. Wright Mooar, "The Killing of the White Buffalo." In *Buffalo Days: Stories from J. Wright Mooar As Told to James Winford Hunt*, edited by Robert F. Pace, pp. 76–81. Copyright © 2005 by State House Press. *Buffalo Days* provided by State House Press.

16-5 "A Salishan Autobiography" (1990). Reprinted from *Mourning Dove: A Salishan Autobiography* edited by Jay Miller by permission of the University of Nebraska Press. Copyright 1990 by the University of Nebraska Press.